Latin America and international investment law

Manchester University Press

MELLAND SCHILL PERSPECTIVES ON INTERNATIONAL LAW

General editors
Jean d'Aspremont
Iain Scobbie
Sufyan Droubi

MELLAND SCHILL
Studies in
INTERNATIONAL LAW

Building on the history of Melland Schill Classics and Melland Schill Studies at Manchester University Press, Melland Schill Perspectives on International Law was established to reflect the diversity of international legal scholarship worldwide. This inclusive, accessible series aims to offer a platform for scholars from different regions who adopt innovative approaches to new and old topics.

Melland Schill Perspectives on International Law is founded on the idea that every international legal issue should be debated from various and, at times, incommensurable perspectives. Though there is a great deal of diversity in international legal debates and practice, this diversity is often obfuscated by prevailing Euro-centric and positivist narratives, which not only creates difficulties for non-Western scholars to be heard but hinders the development of different approaches.

Previously published

African perspectives in international investment law   Edited by
Yenkong Ngangjoh Hodu and Makane Moïse Mbengue

International organisations, non-state actors and the formation of customary international law   Edited by Sufyan Droubi and
Jean d'Aspremont

Latin America and international investment law

A mosaic of resistance

Edited by

Sufyan Droubi and Cecilia Juliana
Flores Elizondo

MANCHESTER UNIVERSITY PRESS

Published by Manchester University Press
Oxford Road, Manchester M13 9PL

www.manchesteruniversitypress.co.uk

British Library Cataloguing-in-Publication Data
A catalogue record for this book is available from the British
Library

ISBN 978 1 5261 5507 8 hardback
ISBN 978 1 5261 9555 5 paperback

First published 2024
Paperback published 2026

EU authorised representative for GPSR:
Easy Access System Europe – Mustamäe tee 50,
10621 Tallinn, Estonia
gpsr.requests@easproject.com

Typeset by Newgen Publishing UK

Contents

Part III: The mosaic of narratives

Figures

Tables

Contributors

Magdalena Bas is Postdoctoral Researcher at the Institute for Human Rights and Business, University of Monterrey, Mexico and member of the National Researchers System, Uruguay. She holds a PhD in International Relations from the National University of La Plata, Argentina. Her current research focused on investor–state dispute settlement, Mercosur, regionalism, multilateralism, international economic law, and didactics of international relations.

Ilan Brun-Vargas is an international arbitration practitioner based in London where he covers disputes involving international corporations and sovereign states. He applies his litigation experience in a pro bono capacity on environmental and human rights issues. He has previously contributed to advocacy missions in Africa and Latin-America, and collaborated with the Cornell Human Rights Clinic. He is a graduate of the University Paris-1 Panthéon-Sorbonne, Columbia Law School and SciencesPo alliance degree in International Economic Law and Governance.

Philip Burton is Teaching Associate in Law, University of Bristol Law School. He holds a PhD (University of Manchester), an LLM (University of Amsterdam) and an LLB (University of Glasgow). Philip's research interests largely lie in international history focusing on inter-war institutions and the play between municipal and international legal orders.

Fabian Cardenas is Professor of International Law at Pontificia Universidad Javeriana; currently associated with the Economic Law Department, he teaches and carries out research on international environmental law, international legal theory as well as law and sustainability. He is founder and board member of the Colombian Academy of International Law, and member of the Ad Hoc Group of International Responsibility and Environment of the Latin American Society of International Law.

Felipe Ferreira Catalán is a legal adviser specializing in intellectual property, international trade law, and investment. He currently serves as a trade negotiator in Chile's Ministry of Foreign Affairs. Felipe holds a law degree from Universidad de Chile and a Master of Advanced Studies (MAS) in International Law and Economics (MILE) from the World Trade Institute, University of Bern.

Henrique Choer Moraes is a PhD candidate at the Centre for Global Governance Studies, KU Leuven (Belgium). He is also a Diplomat at the Ministry of Foreign Affairs in Brazil. He has authored both academic and policy work in the areas of international economic law and global economic governance, which mostly reflects his experience with economic diplomacy and strategic planning.

Jean d'Aspremont is Professor of Public International Law at the University of Manchester. He also is Professor of International Law at Sciences Po Law School. He is General Editor of *the Cambridge Studies in International and Comparative Law* and Director of Oxford International Organizations (OXIO). He writes on questions of international law and international legal theory.

Patrick Devine is a litigator and international arbitration practitioner based in London. He advises on investor–state disputes, cross-border commercial litigation and multi-jurisdictional investigations. He has a particular interest in business and human rights and has lectured and published on the subject. As part of his pro bono practice, Patrick has also advised on claims under the European Convention of Human Rights. He holds undergraduate and postgraduate degrees from the University of Cambridge and also studied at the École Normale Supérieure de Lyon.

Sufyan Droubi is Lecturer in Law within the School of Social Sciences, University of Dundee. Previously, Sufyan was a Postdoctoral Research Fellow at the University of São Paulo and at the University of Manchester, sponsored by a FAPESP Postdoctoral Fellowship. He holds a PhD in Law from the University of Essex. A fully qualified lawyer in Brazil since 1996, he spent twelve years in practice in business law before turning to academia. He is one of the editors of the *Melland Shill Perspectives to International Law*; a coordinator of the Interest Group on International Organisations of the European Society of International Law; co-director of the International Investments in Latin America Network, and co-director of the Just Transition Hub, University of Dundee.

Leonardo V. P. de Oliveira qualified as a lawyer in Brazil in 2002. Having graduated and passed the Brazilian Bar exam, he worked as a legal assistant at the Rio de Janeiro State Control System Secretariat in the sphere of the Rio de Janeiro State Government. After the public sector, Leonardo worked for five years in two different law firms where he practiced in matters related to tort law, contract law, labor law and tax law. In 2008, Leonardo stopped practicing to pursue an LLM in International Trade Law which was followed by a PhD in law, both at the University of Essex. Before joining Royal Holloway, University of London, Leonardo worked as a Lecturer at the Law School at Anglia Ruskin University and as a supervisor for paper 9 in the Department of Land Economy at University of Cambridge.

Javier Echaide Doctor en Derecho por la Universidad de Buenos Aires (UBA). Abogado (UBA) especializado en Derecho Internacional. Posgrado en Mecanismos de Solución de Controversias en Comercio Internacional e Inversión (Facultad de Derecho, UBA). Investigador Adjunto del CONICET (Consejo Nacional de Investigaciones Científicas y Técnicas) de Argentina. Investigador Formado del Instituto de Investigaciones Jurídicas y Sociales "Ambrosio L. Gioja" (Facultad de Derecho, UBA). Consultor Externo Experto para el Alto Comisionado de Naciones Unidas para los Derechos Humanos (2019) y para la UNCTAD (2017). Ex Editor en español de la Revista Investment Treaty News del International Institute for Sustainable Developement (IISD), Canadá y EE.UU. (2015). Ex Vicepresidente de la CAITISA (Comisión de Auditoría Integral ciudadana de los Tratados de Inversión y del Sistema de Arbitraje) de la Rep. De Ecuador (2013–2014). Ex Miembro de la Comisión de Juristas para el Digesto Jurídico Argentino (Ministerio de Justicia y Derechos Humanos, Presidencia de la Nación, 2010–2011). Miembro de la red International Investment in Latin America Network (IILANet), University of Dundee, Escocia, Reino Unido. Miembro de la red de investigadores WATERLAT, University of Newcastle, Reino Unido. Miembro del Grupo de Trabajo "Lex Mercatoria, derechos humanos y democracia," del Centro Latinoamericano de Ciencias Sociales (CLACSO). Profesor de la Facultad de Derecho de la Universidad de Buenos Aires (UBA), y de la Facultad de Derecho de la Universidad Nacional de Lomas de Zamora (UNLZ). Autor de seis libros y múltiples artículos académicos sobre el derecho humano al agua, comercio internacional e inversiones.

Farouk El-Hosseny is an international arbitration practitioner based in London. He advises on arbitrations governed by the ICC, ICSID, and UNCITRAL rules, with a focus on complex commercial and investor–state disputes. In addition, Farouk has acted as arbitrator under the ICC and DIAC rules. He has an active pro bono practice, having recently assisted REDRESS in a landmark case before the African Commission on Human and Peoples' Rights (ACHPR). Farouk holds a PhD degree in public international law from Leiden University and was a visiting scholar at the Lauterpacht Centre for International Law at the University of Cambridge. He obtained a bachelor's degree in civil law from the University of Ottawa and an LLM from the University of Montreal. Farouk regularly publishes on subjects of international law and international arbitration. His book *Civil Society in Investment Treaty Arbitration: Status and Prospects* (Brill Njihoff, 2018) is regularly quoted on the interplay between international investment law and human rights.

Cecilia Juliana Flores Elizondo is Lecturer in Law at Manchester Metropolitan University. Previously, she held Research Associate positions at the University of Manchester in three funded research projects. She has taught at the University of Manchester, the China-EU School of Law and the Universidad Autónoma de Tamaulipas. She holds a PhD in Law and an LLM in International Business Law from the University of Manchester and an LLB from the Universidad Autónoma de Tamaulipas. Having qualified as a lawyer in Mexico, she practiced in various law firms before entering into academia. Cecilia is co-director of the International Investments in Latin America Network and contributes as trade development editor for the *Manchester Journal of International Economic Law*.

Luciana Ghiotto is a researcher at National Research Council (CONICET) in Argentina. She teaches International Political Economy in the Politics and Government School at Universidad Nacional de San Martín (EPyG/ UNSAM). She is an Associate Researcher at Transnational Institute (TNI).

Adoración Guamán is Professor of Law at the University of Valencia. PhD in Law from Paris Nanterre and Valencia Universities. She is Visiting Professor and Associate Researcher at the University of Nanterre, the Homa – International Human Rights and Business center, the Libre University in Colombia and the Joaquín Herrera Flores Human Rights Institute. Coordinator of the CLACSO Working Group "Lex Mercatoria, Human Rights and Democracy." She actively collaborates with different socials movements and trade unions in the field of human rights and transnational corporations.

Raphael Heffron is Dean of the Faculty of Law at the University of the West Indies, St. Augustine and also Professor in Global Energy Law & Sustainability. He is also a Jean Monnet Professor in the Just Transition to a Low-Carbon Economy awarded by the European Commission (2019–2022). In 2020, he was also appointed as Senior Counsel at Janson law firm in Brussels (Belgium). Professor Heffron is a qualified Barrister-at-Law, and a graduate of both Oxford (MSc) and Cambridge (MPhil & PhD). His work all has a principal focus on achieving a just transition to a low-carbon economy and combines a mix of energy law, policy, and economics. He has published over 150 publications of different types and is the most cited scholar in his field worldwide (1680+Scopus) with translated work in multiple languages including Chinese. Professor Heffron has given just over 160 keynote or guest lectures in 51 countries worldwide.

Facundo Pérez Aznar is Senior Researcher at the Geneva Center for International Dispute Settlement (CIDS) and adjoint Professor of International Economic Law in the Masters in International Relations at the University of Buenos Aires.

Rodrigo Polanco Lazo is a senior lecturer, researcher, and academic coordinator of Advanced Master Programmes at the World Trade Institute (WTI), University of Bern; a Legal Adviser for Spanish and Portuguese-speaking jurisdictions at the Swiss Institute of Comparative Law. He is also a visiting professor at the University of Chile and a lecturer at the University of Luzern. Rodrigo holds a Bachelor and a Master of Laws from Universidad de Chile, an LLM in International Legal Studies from New York University and a PhD in Law from the University of Bern. He has published extensively as an author and editor in leading international academic publishers and international journals on investment, trade, tax and environmental law. He is co-founder of the Electronic Database of Investment Treaties (EDIT). At the WTI, Rodrigo coordinated the WTI/SECO Project, which supported regional competence centers for trade law and policy in Peru, South Africa, Vietnam, Indonesia and Chile. He also coordinated the SNIS Project "Diffusion of International Law: A Textual Analysis of International Investment Agreements." Rodrigo was also a post-doctoral researcher at the University of Luzern ("The Governance of Big Data in Trade Agreements: Design, Diffusion and Implications – NFP 75") and served as an assistant professor and director of international affairs at the University of Chile's Faculty of Law. He has been visiting professor at Universidad Externado of Colombia and the Pontifical Catholic University of Peru. He is also a co-founder and member of the board of Fiscalía del Medio Ambiente (FIMA), a Chilean non-profit environmental organization, where he also serves as a member of the editorial committee of their environmental law journal (Justicia Ambiental).

María Angélica Prada-Uribe is a lecturer at the Faculty of Jurisprudence, Universidad del Rosario, Bogota, Colombia. María Angélica is a lawyer, and she holds a Masters in International Law and a Masters in Anthropology both from Universidad de los Andes. She has been a researcher in different projects and consultancies from the Centre of Socio-juridical Research and coordinator of the Global Administrative Law Network – Improving Inter-Institutional Connections to Promote Inclusive Growth: Inter-Institutional Relations in Global and National Regulatory Governance. Her research interests are in areas of international development, international law and law and anthropology.

Sebastián Preller-Bórquez, LLM, PhD (Universitat Pompeu Fabra), is Lecturer of International and European Law at Universitat Pompeu Fabra, Visiting Professor at Universitat Autònoma de Barcelona. Research fellow at the Centre for Sustainability and the Global Law Initiatives for Sustainable Development. He has joined the Manchester International Law Centre and the International Tribunal for the Law of the Sea as visiting research fellow. He obtained his Degree in Law in Chile. His fields of interest include international policy and law on sustainable development, and international economic law.

Marcus Spangenberger is Senior Associate at Deloitte Legal in Hamburg, Germany. He is a member of the restructuring, corporate and M&A practice group and advises national and international clients on all aspects of insolvency as well as corporate law. Before joining Deloitte, Marcus worked in the restructuring department of an international law firm in Düsseldorf, Germany. He gained international experience in London and Zurich. Parallel to his practice, Marcus pursued a M.B.L. in European and international business law at the University of St. Gallen. This is currently followed by PhD studies at the Royal Holloway, University of London.

René Urueña is Associate Professor in International Law at the Faculty of Law of the Universidad de Los Andes in Bogota, Colombia. He received his LLM (laudatur) and his Doctor of Law (eximia cum laude) from the University of Helsinki in Finland. He has been a Fellow at New York University and the Max Planck Institute for Comparative Public Law and International Law; a *docent* at the Institute for Global Law and Policy at the University of Harvard and guest lecture at Universities in Tel-Aviv, Utah and Helsinki. René has been several times an expert witness before the Inter-American Court of Human Rights, and served as an adviser of the Selection Committee of the Special Jurisdiction for Peace (Colombia).

Claus von Wobeser is a founding partner of Von Wobeser y Sierra and has more than forty years of experience in dispute resolution. He has acted in more than two hundred international arbitration and conciliation proceeding, either as arbitrator or counsel, in diverse fora. Claus is currently the President of the Latin American Arbitration Association and of the Mexican chapter of the ICC. He has been Vice President of the International Court of Arbitration (ICA) of the ICC, Co-President of the Arbitration Committee of the International Bar Association (IBA) and President of the Arbitration Commission of the Mexican chapter of the ICC. He has been a leading voice in Latin America in pro bono work for the last thirty years, and together with four other lawyers drafted the Pro bono Standards for the American Continent, which served as a basis for the Mexican Probono Network and later were adopted by the IBA globally. In 2017, Claus won the Lifetime Achievement Award from Chambers and Partners for his contribution to the legal profession.

Table of cases

International arbitration

WTO Cases

International Court of Justice

Inter-American Court of Human Rights

European Court of Human Rights

European Union Courts

Domestic Courts

Introduction: A mosaic of resistance and accommodation

Sufyan Droubi and Cecilia Juliana Flores Elizondo

International law, and in particular international investment law, has been shaped by the struggles of resistance between the diversity of material realities and worldviews within and beyond regions. Rather than a threat to the universality of international investment law, the diverse – sometimes clashing – approaches to, and interpretations of, international investment law, both from states and non-state actors, as well as scholars, has greatly contributed to the development of the field.[1] In this regard, the Latin America and the Caribbean region has been a complex laboratory for the development of international investment law. On the one hand, some actors, such as non-governmental organizations, indigenous peoples, local communities, and of course governments, have remained true to the region's tradition of resistance towards the international investment law regime that *derives* from investment treaties that follow the models that originate in the Europe–North America region. On the other hand, new actors such as corporations, international investment lawyers, and again governments, sought to accommodate said regime in the region. Consequently, a profusion of theories and doctrines – which, notably, come embedded in different, often clashing narratives – has emerged. This mosaic of clashing actors and narratives – too complex to be fully apprehended in this introduction and, alas, in this volume – has been resisting and accommodating the international investment law regime, as defined above, and has been Latin America's major contribution to international investment law.

In this introduction, we offer some initial thoughts about this mosaic, and about the forces of resistance and accommodation that emerge in it, to frame a debate that the following chapters will carry out. A note on the methodology employed becomes important. This is a volume that

---

1 For an account of comparative international law, please see Anthea Roberts, Paul B Stephen, Pierre-Hugues Verdier, and Mila Versteeg, "Comparative International Law: Framing the Field" (2015) 109 (3) *American Journal of International Law* 467, 474.

contributes *critiques* of the law from the perspective of the main actors involved with international investment law in Latin America. For the most part, these critiques are historically and socially oriented. The authors are not only lawyers but also political scientists, not only academics but also practitioners. The editors presented the authors of the following chapters with two interrelated arguments – that many different Latin Americas exist and that these Latin Americas have been resisting and accommodating the mainstream perspectives, namely, the North American and European perspectives, on international investment law. The authors were left enough room to contribute their own ideas – and come up with their own ontologies, epistemologies and methodologies. Authors were not asked to address the arguments exhaustively, as the volume *does not* intend to read as a monograph – but only to write their contributions as a *reflection* on either or both arguments. A dialogue ensued between all contributors, a rich and fruitful dialogue, which begun when the editors started working on this project in 2017, in the Manchester International Law Centre, at the University of Manchester, and which developed to involve two international seminars – the first held at the University of Dundee, Scotland (2018), and the second, at Universidad Nacional de San Martin in Argentina (2019).

The contributions confirm the thesis initially presented – there are different Latin Americas – or, to borrow from Magdalena Bas,[2] we can distinguish a true Latin American *mosaic* – a mosaic of states, as the chapters by Bas and Henrique Choer Moraes and Facundo Pérez Aznar[3] competently describe – but also a mosaic of non-state actors. By implication, there is a Latin American mosaic of narratives embedding the different theories and doctrines – and which, today, tends to converge towards the clash between international investment law on the one hand, and international human rights law or sustainable development, on the other. Each of the actors that participate in this mosaic have their own identities and bring their own worldviews to bear on the meaning of international investments and of the international law as applied to these investments. From the geographies and histories of different states, the emerging but already sharp differences in investors, the common claims of civil society and its constant dialogue with other regions, to the traumatic experience of indigenous peoples – this Latin American mosaic emerges, in the following pages, as a force of resistance to, and accommodation of, the regime of international investment law.

The outcome is a volume that describes the complex roles that governments have played vis-à-vis foreign investors and investments,[4] the refreshing but

---

2 See Chapter 2 by Magdalena Bas in this volume.
3 See Chapter 3 by Henrique Choer Moraes and Facundo Pérez Aznar in this volume.
4 See Part I – The mosaic of states in this volume.

clashing forces that international organizations, corporations, civil society, and indigenous peoples have imprinted to the field;[5] the contribution that Latin America has made, sometimes inadvertently, to the development of the theory and practice of international investment law – notably in fields in which the Latin American experience has been traumatic: human rights and sustainable development.[6] All in all, in the different Latin Americas, the practice of international investment law is the vivid amalgamation, not uniform but sharply fragmentary, of the practice of the governments sometimes resisting, sometimes welcoming, the mainstream approaches; the practice of the lawyers assisting foreign investors from outside and within the region; and the practice of civil society, indigenous peoples and other actors in their struggle for human rights and sustainable development. To the theory of international investment law, Latin American scholars have been contributing for over a century – and resting on the shoulders of true giants, this volume humbly aims at pushing this contribution a little further.

Foreign investments in the Latin American mosaic

Flows of foreign direct investments with Latin America and the Caribbean have experienced a typical pattern of boom and bust.[7] In this decade alone, after suffering the impact of the Global Financial Crisis, investment inflows gained some momentum, only to be again affected, severely, by the COVID-19 pandemic.[8] Since the 1990s, when the region became progressively less dependent on foreign bank loans,[9] foreign direct investments have expanded significantly until 2012,[10] becoming an important element of the region's

---

5 See Part II – The mosaic of non-state actors in this volume.

6 See Part III – The Mosaic of Narratives in this volume.

7 There were upswings in inward flows of foreign direct investment that reached peaks in 1999 (above US$80 billion), 2008 (above US$130 billion), and 2012 (above US$210 billion), followed by periods of significant contraction. See CEPAL, *Foreign Direct Investment in Latin America and the Caribbean 2010* (CEPAL 2011); CEPAL, *La Inversión Extranjera En América Latina y El Caribe* (United Nations 2020).

8 CEPAL, *La Inversión Extranjera En América Latina y El Caribe* (n 7).

9 Nicoletta Batini, Eduardo Borensztein, and José Antonio Ocampo, "IMF Advice on Capital Flows to Latin America" (2020) BP/20–02/06 IEO Background Paper for IEO Evaluation of "IMF Advice on Capital Flows" (Washington: International Monetary Fund) para 3.

10 Inflows of foreign direct investment reached a maximum historical value in 2012 (above US$ 210 billion), which was also a result of the contraction of inflows to other regions caused by the Global Financial Crisis. Since 2012, there has been an almost uninterrupted contraction. See CEPAL, *La Inversión Extranjera En América Latina y El Caribe* (n 7).

gross domestic product,[11] and for several countries, a source of financing for the recurring current account deficits.[12] In other words, for some time now, Latin American governments seem to be promoting and relying on, foreign direct investments.[13] The main sources of foreign investment are the European Union and the US, followed by China. Among EU countries, France, Germany, Spain, the UK and Luxembourg have been the main sources.[14] Similarly, outflows of foreign direct investments rose to their peak in 2011 and have been falling progressively since then.[15] The fluctuations of the outflows of foreign direct investments can be attributed not only to the crises, but to other factors such as the impact that corruption cases had in the economic power of transnationals headquartered in Latin America.[16]

That said, the reality is much more complex than pictured above. Foreign direct investment inflows at the sub-regional and state level remain, as always, very heterogeneous.[17] While, at least up to the start of the pandemic, Central America and the Caribbean had been experiencing a growth in inflows of foreign direct investment, the situation was different in South America: inflows towards Brazil, Colombia and Paraguay had been growing but inflows to Argentina, Bolivia, Chile, Ecuador, Peru and Uruguay had been decreasing.[18] The effects of the pandemic will be felt differently in the region as some countries are more affected by it than others.[19] This heterogeneity is not only a reflection of macroeconomic development policies, but also of factors such as governance, efficiency of public institutions, perception of levels of corruption, regulatory and legal frameworks and political stability. While the European Union remains the main source of investments

---

11 The ratio of foreign direct investments income relative to the gross economic product has remained high in Latin America. OECD, CAF and CEPAL, *Latin American Economic Outlook 2018: Rethinking Institutions for Development* (OECD Publishing 2018) 101.

12 OECD, United Nations, CAF, European Commission, *Latin American Economic Outlook 2020: Digital Transformation for Building Back Better* (OECD Publishing 2020) 55–56 doi.org/10.1787/e6e864fb-en accessed 18 August 2020.

13 For a general discussion, Helmut Reisen, "Sustainable and Excessive Current Account Deficits" (1998) 25 *Empirica* 111; Douglas Alencar and others, "On Foreign Direct Investments and the Balance of Payments Constrained Growth Model in Latin America, 1990–2014" (2019) 72 *PSL Quarterly Review* 207.

14 CEPAL, *La Inversión Extranjera En América Latina y El Caribe* (n 7); OECD et al. (n 12).

15 CEPAL, *Foreign Direct Investment in Latin America and the Caribbean 2019* (CEPAL 2019) 84.

16 OECD, "FDI in Figures – Latin America" (2019); OECD, CAF and CEPAL (n 11) 12.

17 CEPAL, *La Inversión Extranjera En América Latina y El Caribe* (n 7).

18 Ibid.

19 For an initial overview, ibid.; OECD et al. (n 12).

in South America; the US remains as such in Central America, Mexico, and the Caribbean.[20] That most investors come from these regions is only a perpetuation of a long history. Yet, even here, the reality is more complex, and it is more accurate to speak of a triad of regions – Europe, the US and, still significantly behind, China.[21] The fact that Chinese companies often invest in the region through their European subsidiaries also make the definition of the sources more difficult.[22]

The main sectors receiving foreign investments – traditionally, services, manufacture and natural resources – vary in geography and in time.[23] Generally speaking, investments into extractive industries have been higher in the Andean region, Brazil and Central America than in other regions; into services, higher in Central America and the Caribbean, and the Andean region, than in other regions, and into manufacture, higher in Mexico, and Brazil, than in other places.[24] Recently, Brazil, Chile and Mexico have become a destination for investments in renewables,[25] and Central America, in medical apparel.[26]

The attitude towards foreign investments changes depending on the sector, the region, the history and, notably, on the actor in question, namely, governments, civil society, indigenous and local communities, and lawyers. But the attitude also fluctuates over time for an important actor – governments. Starting with the latter, throughout Latin American history, governments have been the main drivers of national development – and they have never succeeded in addressing the high levels of inequality in the region.[27] We can notice changes in the attitude of the same governments as the governing elites at times welcome and at times become suspicious of foreign investors. Maybe nothing illustrates this better with the nationalist and protectionist policies respecting public services and natural resources that prevailed in the region until the 1980s and that still prevails in some countries (Venezuela being the major illustration). As from the 1990s, with few exceptions, the general mood among Latin American governments has been favorable to attracting investors – but the general mood in society has not always matched that of governments.

20 CEPAL, *La Inversión Extranjera En América Latina y El Caribe* (n 7) 42.
21 OECD, CAF, and CEPAL (n 11).
22 CEPAL, *La Inversión Extranjera En América Latina y El Caribe* (n 7) 42–43.
23 Ibid. 33.
24 Ibid. 34.
25 Ibid. 40.
26 CEPAL, *La Inversión Extranjera En América Latina y El Caribe* (n 7).
27 For a detailed discussion, see Chapter 9 by Sufyan Droubi, Cecilia Juliana Flores Elizondo, and Raphael Heffron in this volume.

As from the 1990s, investors come to find a region that is still unstable, and that struggles with inequality. *Instability*, with all it encapsulates, from weak macro-economic foundations to weak political institutions, would place the investor in a clashing route not only with governments – but with parliaments, courts, and civil society. *Inequality* would become transparent in the contrast between foreign investors, protected by international standards and able to access international arbitration, and their local counterparts who had to be content with domestic law and courts; and, probably more poignantly, in the relationship between foreign investors and indigenous peoples and local communities. On the one hand, it is not possible to understand the dynamic between instability, inequality, and suspicion towards foreign investors without knowing the traumatic history of the relationship between foreign investors from *former* metropoles with the governments in the newly independent Latin American states. The Calvo tradition is able to provide such historical perspective.

However, on the other hand, within said dynamic lies another dimension of the Calvo tradition: throughout the decades, it came to resonate with what became long-held worldviews by different actors, some of whom most likely never heard of Calvo.[28] The 1990s governing elites who welcomed neoliberalism and had governments entering into bilateral investment agreements came to power in a region where nationalism, protectionism, and suspicion of foreign investors were still a reality in different parts of society, market, and the political elites. Nothing illustrates this better than Brazil: in the 1990s and early 2000s, the government managed to sign several agreements only to see Parliament refusing to ratify them (at least without substantial changes).[29] The narrative that parliamentarians espoused to justify their resistance to those agreements was, essentially, the same narrative that embedded the Calvo doctrine. At its heart, there was the need to ensure equality between national and foreign investors, and the defense of the capability of local courts to settle disputes between investors and the state. Similarly, when new governments arrived in Bolivia, Ecuador, and Venezuela, they did so on reasons that legally and ideologically resonate with the Calvo tradition.[30]

But instability and inequality also led to clashes between investors and the society at large – this is what happens in Argentina and Bolivia when the 1990s neoliberal experiment, which encompasses the privatization of

---

28 For a historiographic account of the Calvo doctrine, see Chapter 1 by Philip Burton and for a critical analysis, Chapter 14 by Fabian Cardenas and Jean d'Aspremont in this volume.

29 CEPAL, *La Inversión Extranjera En América Latina y El Caribe* (n 7) 42–43.

30 See Chapter 2 by Magdalena Bas in this volume.

public services, sinks, placing public opinion against foreign investors who had taken over the provision of such services from the government, only to face popular discontent over prices, when a new crisis emerged. But popular discontent with the *government* about the quality and the price of public services has a long history in the countries of the region – very recently, discontent led to traumatic clashes in, for instance, Brazil, with deep political repercussions.[31] When directed towards a *foreign* investor, who because it is protected by international law, manages to avoid accountability – at least, in the eyes of the population –[32] such discontent reverberates at other levels of the region's psyche. The Calvo doctrine, while providing legal arguments for grounding the actions of the resisting actors, also fits within their broader narrative, whose origins go beyond those of the Calvo doctrine.

It is ironic that, in legal terms, the historical instability and inequality often get diluted in doctrines and analyses that seem to think of Calvo tradition as a reality in itself and place the focus on the antagonism between Latin American governments and, their counterparts in Europe and North America and investors coming from the latter region. When trying to understand what the field of international investment law means on the ground, it is to the more harrowing relationship between investors and other non-state actors – such as indigenous peoples and local populations; as well as to the relationship between investors, who accept to take over from the government the provision of public services, with the consumers of these services; or to the relationship between the investors who are in sectors that affect public health, and the consumers of their products – that students of international investment law should turn their attention. On the ground, these actors resist the international investment regime. But in seeking legal arguments to defend their position, they also accommodate the regime. In this context, non-governmental organizations become important as actors giving visibility to indigenous peoples and local communities who have remained invisible, and as agents of the whole population. Non-governmental organizations become actors that resist investors on the ground. In resisting, their resistance resonates, at multiple levels, with the history of the region, notably in countries where indigenous peoples form a significant part of the population. But because non-governmental organizations also seek to speak for minorities and population before arbitration tribunals, as amici curiae,

---

31 Reuters Staff, "Bus Fare Protest in Brazil's Biggest City Turns Violent" *Reuters* (9 January 2016) www.reuters.com/article/us-brazil-protest-idUSKBN0UM2HY2016 0109 accessed 9 January 2021.

32 For a compelling account of the discontent towards foreign investors, in the region and beyond, see Haley Sweetland Edwards, *Shadow Courts: The Tribunals That Rule Global Trade* (Columbia Global Reports 2016).

they also become agents who accommodate the international investment regime.

A final actor needs highlighting. As the region receives more foreign investors, we can discern an increase in the number of lawyers seeking specialization in relevant legal fields, mainly in the North American but also in European universities, so as to come back and provide assistance to the investor interested in establishing in the region.[33] Mega-law and mega lawyering, to use Galanter's expression,[34] becomes a reality in Latin America. But it also becomes a reality in other fields of practice.[35] Of particular importance for the scope of this book, law students begin to seek specialization, often abroad, also in the US and Europe, in human rights, to work in non-governmental organizations. These contrasting interests will ensure that investors, non-governmental organizations, indigenous peoples, are assisted (which, however, should not be understood as equality of arms in the market and before the courts).[36] In legal terms, this leads to the development of the fields and, notably for our purposes, international investment law.

International investment law in the Latin American mosaic

The above clearly suggests the existence of different "Latin Americas."[37] But these different Latin Americas are not only different geographic regions – there is the Latin America of governments, the Latin America of investors, the Latin America of indigenous peoples, the Latin America of non-governmental organizations, the Latin America of lawyers who specialize in the fields such as international economic law or international human rights law, which clash among themselves. We prefer the expression mosaic to better describe this reality.

The book draws on the synergies and divergences among countries in the region to claim the existence of a mosaic of Latin American approaches

33 In fact, this is only part of a bigger reality that emerged with the redemocratization in the 1980s, with a significant increase in the number of lawyers and important changes in the curricula to respond to the deep changes in practice. Manuel Gómez and Rogelio Pérez-Perdomo, *Big Law in Latin America and Spain: Globalization and Adjustments in the Provision of High-End Legal Services* (Springer 2017).

34 Marc Galanter, "Mega-Law and Mega-Lawyering in the Contemporary United States" (1983) *The sociology of the professions* 152.

35 Gómez and Pérez-Perdomo (n 33) 6.

36 Sufyan Droubi, "Investment Facilitation Mechanisms and Access to Justice in Brazilian Investment Agreements: ASIL" (2020) 24 *ASIL Insights* www.asil.org/insights/volume/24/issue/9/investment-facilitation-mechanisms-and-access-justice-brazilian accessed 18 August 2020.

37 CEPAL 2018.

to international investment law in order to understand how these approaches have emerged and developed. The book comes at a moment in which some Latin American governments demonstrate a renewed interest in bilateral investment treaties. Ecuador is a case in point - from withdrawing from the ICSID Convention in 2009 as part of its strategy to exit the international investment regime, to rejoining the Convention after its ratification on 04 August 2021. Traditionally, international investment treaties are marked by investment protection and encompass clauses such as the most-favored nation treatment, national treatment, fair and equitable treatment, expropriation, prohibition of performance requirements, restriction on regulatory changes, free transfer of funds, elimination of national content requirements and, crucially, international arbitration as the mechanism for the settling of disputes between investors and their host states. There was an avalanche of unfavorable arbitration awards in the first decade of the new century,[38] which were delivered by tribunals operating under the law established by the traditional bilateral investment treaties that many Latin American governments had entered into in the preceding decades.

Latin American governments, such as the Argentinian, Bolivian, Ecuadorian, and Venezuelan had to live with the economic and social implications of what became highly unpopular international treaties.[39] Consequently, some of these governments withdrew from such treaties and rejected entering into new ones having the same traditional format.[40] However, this trend reverses from 2015, when many governments, now headed by a yet new generation of politicians, are faced once again with the conundrum of whether remaining or entering into bilateral investment treaties for the same purpose pursued by their 1980s and 90s counterparts, to attract international investments and foster economic growth, at a time marked by financial crises that deeply affect the region. But now the trend is different. While some countries, such as Brazil, adopt a radical new model that emphasizes facilitation over mere protection,[41] other countries, such as Argentina, Colombia and Ecuador, adopt the traditional model with cosmetic changes.[42] Hence, in the span of three decades, the region moved from

---

38 For a good overview of the impact of investor–state cases in Latin America, see Transnational Institute, "ISDS Impactos" (*ISDS America Latina*) https://isds-americ alatina.org/ accessed 9 January 2021.

39 Generally, ibid. (see case studies); Edwards (n 32).

40 See Chapters 2 by Magdalena Bas and 3 by Henrique Choer Moraes and Facundo Pérez Aznar in this volume.

41 See Chapters 4 by Leonardo V P de Oliveira and Marcus Spangenberger, and 5 by Luciana Ghiotto in this volume.

42 See Chapters 2 by Magdalena Bas and 3 by Henrique Choer Moraes and Facundo Pérez Aznar in this volume.

absorbing the mainstream model of bilateral investment treaties, to resisting it to accommodating it with changes.

Moreover, this volume is timely as some long-held criticisms that many in Latin America voiced against the law on international investments, such as the circumvention of the domestic courts and the differentiated treatment that it extends to foreign investors vis-à-vis domestic investors, are being echoed outside the region.[43] Indeed, a global dissatisfaction towards international investment law has not gone unnoticed.[44] Moreover, in this environment, it is worth noting that Latin American governments have been pursuing, and often leading multilateral efforts to implement, changes to the law on international investments. A notable example is the Joint Ministerial Statement on Investment Facilitation and development made at the Eleventh WTO Ministerial Conference in Buenos Aires 2017 by, inter alia, Argentina, Brazil, Chile, Colombia, Costa Rica, El Salvador, Guatemala, Guinea, Honduras, Mexico, Nicaragua, Panama, Paraguay, and Uruguay, and countries outside the region such as Australia, Canada, China, New Zealand, Nigeria, Pakistan, and Switzerland – as well as the European Union.[45]

Resisting: accommodating international investment law

This is not a volume on the theory of resistance; it is a volume about the manners in which resistance fosters the development of law. In the Latin American tradition, it is a volume that draws on real-life events, cases, and experiences. No chapter defines resistance, and in this introduction, we offer a basic definition and a basic framework that explains how resistance

---

43 In the US, see Wenhua Shan, "From North-South Divide to Private-Public Debate: Revival of the Calvo Doctrine and the Changing Landscape in International Investment Law Symposium on International Energy Law" (2006) 27 *Northwestern Journal of International Law & Business* 631; Wenhua Shan, "Is Calvo Dead?" (2007) 55 *The American Journal of Comparative Law* 123. In Europe, *Slovak Republic v Achmea BV*, Judgment, ECJ Case C-284/16 ECLI:EU:C:2018:158 (6 March 2018); *Opinion 1/17 of the Court (Full Court)* ECJ ECLI:EU:C:2019:341 (30 April 2019); Matthew Happold, "Belgium Asks European Court of Justice to Opine on Compatibility of Energy Charter Treaty's Investor-State Arbitration Provisions with EU Law" (*EJIL: Talk!*, 8 December 2020) www.ejiltalk.org/belgium-asks-european-court-of-justice-to-opine-on-compatibility-of-energy-charter-treatys-investor-state-arbitration-provisions-with-eu-law/ accessed 9 January 2021.
44 Muthucumaraswamy Sornarajah, *Resistance and Change in the International Law on Foreign Investment* (Cambridge University Press 2015); Edwards (n 32).
45 WTO, "Joint Ministerial Statement On Investment Facilitation For Development, WT/MIN(17)/59" https://docs.wto.org/dol2fe/Pages/FE_Search/FE_S_S009-DP.aspx?language=E&CatalogueIdList=240870 accessed 9 January 2021.

emerges in the subsequent chapters. In Latin America, resistance has been fundamental in shaping history, social, and economic relations, as well as *law*. The wave of new constitutions that came about after the period of dictatorships is evidence enough of this. For the different social actors, rights were won after much resistance. This could not be different in international law and of course international investment law.

Resistance to laws and commands emerges almost naturally, and manifests itself in different behavior along a spectrum, "from psychological processes of repression of feelings to open war."[46] Nonviolent resistance, which is of relevance here, is a rational, organized, and intentional effort to force a change in policy,[47] which the resisting actor believes to be unjust, illegitimate. Note how the history of inequality and instability, and the differences within Latin America, described above, help explaining the reasons of the resisting behavior. The first point that needs clarifying is what the object of resistance is. On the one hand, the object of the resistance arises clearly in some chapters, for instance, the investor–state arbitration model,[48] or the implementation of investment projects,[49] or certain proposals that international organizations make.[50] However, on the other hand, the object of the resistance is not so clearly articulated. For instance, there is the fact that the Calvo tradition resists the old Eurocentric view that places Latin American states at a lower level of civilization.[51] In short, this is resistance against inequality. A similar situation of inequality, but now affecting indigenous peoples will justify resistance by the latter against the foreign investor but also against the local governments who, replacing the old metropoles, continue to view indigenous peoples as non-civilized, and who authorize investment projects in indigenous lands without the necessary agreement of the affected people.[52] Even subtler, governments adopt defenses before investor–state arbitration tribunals that these governments embed in a narrative of resistance against illegitimate interference in their regulatory powers *by the tribunal* – notably, promotion of human rights

---

46 Sufyan Droubi, *Resisting United Nations Security Council Resolutions* (Routledge Taylor & Francis Group 2014) xviii.
47 Ibid.
48 See Chapters 2 by Magdalena Bas; 3 by Henrique Choer Moraes and Facundo Pérez Aznar; and 4 by Leonardo V P de Oliveira and Marcus Spangenberger in this volume.
49 This is addressed indirectly in Chapter 9 by Sufyan Droubi, Cecilia Juliana Flores Elizondo, and Raphael Heffron in this volume.
50 See Chapter 5 by Luciana Ghiotto in this volume.
51 See Chapters 1 by Philip Burton and 9 by Sufyan Droubi, Cecilia Juliana Flores Elizondo, and Raphael Heffron in this volume.
52 See Chapter 9 by Sufyan Droubi, Cecilia Juliana Flores Elizondo, and Raphael Heffron in this volume.

and the need for social license to operate become *reasons* for protecting their regulatory powers, thus instrumentalizing both human rights and sustainable development.[53]

Equally subtle is the emphasis that chapters place on the international investment *regime* or *system* that results from international investment treaties. While the concept of system is more loosely adopted in some chapters, the chapters that address the regime concept, draw, as we do in this introduction, on definitions found in international relations.[54] Be it as it may, what is important is that some chapters discuss resistance *to* the investment regime or system,[55] while others discuss resistance *within* the regime or the system.[56] We call the reader's attention to the processes that these chapters describe, and how they affect international investment law. For instance, resistance against the regime (or system) may result in proposals for the development of alternative institutions.[57] Resistance within the regime (or system) may translate into refusal of policies and rules,[58] or attrition between

---

53 See Chapters 10 by Rodrigo Polanco Lazo and Felipe Ferreira Catalán, 11 by Farouk El-Hosseny, Patrick Devine, and Ilan Brun-Vargas, 12 by Javier Echaide, and 13 by Sebastián Preller-Bórquez in this volume.

54 "International regimes are defined as principles, norms, rules, and decision-making procedures around which actor expectations converge in a given issue-area" Stephen D. Krasner, *International Regimes* (Cornell University Press 1983). Some authors have dealt with the international investment law regimes (Jeswald W. Salacuse, "The Emerging Global Regime for Investment" (2010) 51 *Harvard International Law Journal* 427; José E. Alvarez, *The Public International Law Regime Governing International Investment*, vol 344 (Martinus Nijhoff Publishers 2011); Beth A. Simmons, "Bargaining over BITs, Arbitrating Awards: The Regime for Protection and Promotion of International Investment Symposium: The Regime for International Investment – Foreign Direct Investment, Bilateral Investment Treaties, and Trade Agreements" (2014) 66 *World Politics* 12). Salacuse offers a clear definition that is centered on investment treaties (Jeswald W. Salacuse, *The Law of Investment Treaties* (OUP Oxford 2015). Chapters that openly adopt this definition are Chapter 2 by Magdalena Bas and Chapter 9 by Sufyan Droubi, Cecilia Juliana Flores Elizondo, and Raphael Heffron, while Chapters 7 by Claus von Wobeser, 5 by Luciana Ghiotto, and 13 by Sebastián Preller-Bórquez rely on this or similar definitions.

55 See Chapters 2 by Magdalena Bas and 9 by Sufyan Droubi, Cecilia Juliana Flores Elizondo and Raphael Heffron in this volume. Note that Chapter 3 by Henrique Choer Moraes and Facundo Pérez Aznar, and Chapter 7 by Claus von Wobeser rely on the concept of system.

56 See Chapters 5 by Luciana Ghiotto and 13 by Sebastián Preller-Bórquez in this volume.

57 See Chapters 2 by Magdalena Bas and 3 by Henrique Choer Moraes and Facundo Pérez Aznar – and Chapter 4 by Leonardo V P de Oliveira and Marcus Spangenberger in this volume.

58 See Chapters 5 by Luciana Ghiotto and 13 by Sebastián Preller-Bórquez in this volume.

participants in the regime,[59] or as defenses before investor–state arbitration tribunals.[60] Urueña and Prado-Uribe provide an excellent illustration of how resistance may fluctuate between resistance within the regime to resistance to the regime – in their chapter, they show how domestic courts may adopt either a private law or a public law framework when carrying out constitutional review of investment treaties, as the Colombian court has done, and how the resistance that results therefrom may become stronger as the court, adopting a public law framework, sees as its role the enforcement of constitutional – rather than international – law.[61] Also subtle is the manner that resistance may target the narratives that embed the investment regime.[62]

Another point of importance respects the definition of the identity of the different actors. State resistance may materialize as government resistance, as the chapters in Part I – The Mosaic of States, show – but as Urueña and Prada-Uribe explain, state resistance may result from the decisions of domestic courts. In both cases, the self-definition of the identity of the government, for instance, as a neoliberal or a socialist government, or a court, as a constitutional court, defines the strength of the resistance. Nevertheless, it should be clear by now that resistance is not merely understood as state resistance to the mainstream international investment law.[63] Rather, resistance has its origins both from states, as well as from certain non-state actors, such as corporations, social movements, non-governmental organizations, indigenous peoples, which, evidently, constitute different identity groups.[64] The definition of identities sometimes may become an issue in itself, given the implications in terms of establishing rights, such as is the case with indigenous peoples.[65] But the definition may also present problems for the analysis of different actors – should corporations, social movements and indigenous peoples be all defined as non-state actors?[66] Should corporations

---

59 Chapters 7 by Claus von Wobeser (mutual resistance between corporations and non-governmental organizations), 8 by Adoración Guamán (social resistance against governments and corporations) and 9 by Sufyan Droubi, Cecilia Juliana Flores Elizondo, and Raphael Heffron (indigenous peoples' resistance against governments and corporations).

60 Part III – The mosaic of narratives in this volume.

61 See Chapter 6 by René Urueña and María Angélica Prada-Uribe in this volume.

62 C.f. Chapter 1 by Philip Burton and, to an extent, Chapter 9 by Sufyan Droubi, Cecilia Juliana Flores Elizondo, and Raphael Heffron in this volume.

63 See the chapters in Part I – The Mosaic of States in this volume.

64 See the chapters in Part II – The mosaic of non-state actors in this volume.

65 See Chapter 9 by Sufyan Droubi, Cecilia Juliana Flores Elizondo, and Raphael Heffron in this volume.

66 Chapter 9 by Sufyan Droubi, Cecilia Juliana Flores Elizondo, and Raphael Heffron argue that indigenous peoples have acquired a status higher than that of corporations in international law.

be included in the concept of civil society?[67] We also underline that social movements and indigenous peoples are and see themselves as *international* actors. This allows, for instance, for cross-fertilization of ideas between civil society in Latin America and in Europe,[68] or for the status that indigenous peoples have acquired in international law.[69] Similarly, *Latin American* transnational corporations continue to be *transnational* corporations, responding to changes implemented by their peers elsewhere.[70] Moreover, Chapters 7 (corporations) and 8 (social movements) describe certain events, which for the editors, who come from a constructivist background, could be defined as changes in identities in response to social pressure – change in the identity of corporations (how under pressure corporations adopted corporate social responsibility) and social movements (how under social need they evolved from local to regional to trans-continental actors). Something similar is described in chapters in Part I (governments): new identities emerge over time as a result of developments on the ground, leading governments to reject and welcome and reject the regime of investment treaties.[71]

Resistance therefore should not be understood as a homogenous regional or state reaction to the mainstream European and North American-oriented approaches. The chapters in this volume are evidence that resistance comprises "a complex multitude of alternative visions of social relationships."[72] This complex network of alternative visions encompasses a wide range of worldviews and levels of resistance between mainstream approaches to international investment law and resisting states and non-state actors. In this network, the resisting actor may find itself working within the parameters created by the object of resistance,[73] for instance, the international investment regime. As Rajagopal explains,[74] actors can resist by creating alternative and culturally distinct realities;[75] and by treating resistance and

---

67 Adoración Guamán asks this question in Chapter 8.
68 See, especially, the Chapters 8 by Adoración Guamán and 9 by Sufyan Droubi, Cecilia Juliana Flores Elizondo, and Raphael Heffron in this volume.
69 See chapter by Sufyan Droubi, Cecilia Juliana Flores Elizondo, and Raphael Heffron in this volume.
70 See Chapter 7 by Claus von Wobeser in this volume.
71 See Part I – The mosaic of states in this volume.
72 Balakrishnan Rajagopal, *International Law from Below: Development, Social Movements and Third World Resistance* (Cambridge and New York; Cambridge University Press: 2003) at 11.
73 Ibid.
74 Ibid.
75 This tendency emerges most clearly in the Calvo tradition of articulating a narrative centered on equality of states and of respect for the domestic jurisdiction (Chapter 1 by Philip Burton and Chapter 14 by Fabian Cardenas and Jean d'Aspremont); the

the object of resistance as mutually constitutive and dialectical.[76] And so we arrive at the forms of resistance. We note that resistance is by no means equated to violent actions – and, as already noted, the volume is about nonviolent resistance. Albeit there are cases which chapters may discuss, in which violence is used by the resisting actors, this seems to be the outcome of tactical moves defined in response to the behavior of the object of resistance (investor or government).[77] But the book is not concerned with violent resistance, and the discussion on the topic is insignificant. Rather, it is what we call nonviolent, civil resistance that occupies most of the chapters: actions and discourses grounded on "rational, intentional and organised effort[s] to force change of policy,"[78] which policy the resisting actor considers unjust. In the chapters, this emerges notably as *accommodation*.

Gene Sharp argues that accommodation is one of the mechanisms of change in non-violent action, in which opponents agree to compromises with resisting actors, providing certain concessions to settle differences. So, Sharp argues, it is rarely the case that resistance aims at the disintegration of the opponent's regime;[79] and generally the chapters that ensue prove the point. Accommodation involves flexibility and compromises. Accommodation also represents the extent of *internalization* of international investment law in Latin America, a process that has not been homogenous, varying pursuant to the actors who put up resistance. When governments propose alternative political narratives and alternative institutions, which compete with the mainstream models, they accommodate international investment law. When governments make use of certain types of legal defenses before investment

---

impetus by certain governments to build Latin American institutions (Chapters 3 by Henrique Choer Moraes and Facundo Perez Aznar, and 4 by Leonardo V P de Oliveira and Marcus Spangenberger); the narratives that social movements articulate to emphasize the social and environmental costs of investments (Chapter 8 by Adoración Guaman), the open resistance that indigenous peoples put up against investments (Chapter 9 by Sufyan Droubi, Cecilia Juliana Flores Elizondo, and Raphael Heffron), and in certain doctrines, narratives and theories by Latin American scholars (Chapters 5 by Luciana Ghiotto, 6 by René Urueña and María Angélica Prada-Uribe, and 12 by Javier Echaide).

76 Emerging most clearly in the scholarly attempt to think developments in international investment law (Chapters 10 by Rodrigo Polanco Lazo and Felipe Ferreira Catalán, 11 by Farouk El-Hosseny, Patrick Devine and Ilan Brun-Vargas, and 13 by Sebastián Preller-Borquez).

77 As happens in some of the cases discussed in Chapter 9 by Sufyan Droubi, Cecilia Juliana Flores Elizondo, and Raphael Heffron.

78 Droubi (n 46) xviii.

79 For a full account of the four mechanisms of change in non-violent action, see: Gene Sharp, *There are Realistic Alternatives, Appendix One: Glossary of Important Terms in Non-Violent Struggle* (Albert Einstein Institution 2003).

arbitration tribunals, they accommodate international investment law. When non-governmental organizations and, alas, indigenous peoples resist the investor on the ground, but make use of amici curiae to make their case for the arbitration tribunal, they accommodate international investment law. Through these perspectives, both state and non-state actors promote debate within and beyond the region,[80] a debate that often goes beyond balancing their interests in order to reflect their respective identities. From resistance to accommodation represents an ongoing process that injects dynamism to the practice and interpretation of the law of foreign investment within the region, and its impact on international investment law at the global level.

The articulation of alternative political narratives is a key element in the development of international law and institutions.[81] Part III of this book illustrates the power that alternative narratives grounded on human rights and sustainable development can have as forces of change, embedding and giving meaning to legal theories and defenses before arbitration tribunals. Read in conjunction with Parts I and II, Part III of this book sheds light on diverse alternative political narratives that have emerged as resistance in Latin America, their struggles and development, and the debates arising therefrom.[82] These narratives, whilst not exhaustive, show that Latin America, far from being a passive receptor of the law of foreign investment, has contributed to the development of international investment law. Hence, storytelling in international investment law needs to be addressed to explore how alternative political narratives emerge and develop, and the extent to which these narratives are capable of constituting the kind of resistance that is able to challenge current mainstream approaches.

So it is that the reference to "the political" in the articulation of alternative narratives must not be understood restrictively to mean state-centered narratives, i.e. mainly those arising from legislative procedures.[83] In addition

---

80 For a general account of regional approaches and their significance in comparative international law, please see: Anthea Roberts, Paul B Stephen, Pierre-Hugues Verdier, and Mila Versteeg, "Comparative International Law: Framing the Field" (2015) 109 (3) *American Journal of International Law* 467, 474.

81 For an account of narratives in international law, see for example: Julia Otten, "Narratives in International Law" (2016) 99 (3) *Critical Quarterly for Legislation and Law* 187, 216. Otten acknowledges the use of narrative as a means of "persuad[ing] audiences with a particular reading of international law," exemplified in the context of collective security. Otten recognizes the conflict of narratives from diverse interpretative communities, but mainly within different legal interpretative approaches (e.g. feminist or post-colonial approaches) rather than emerging from an array of political sources.

82 See chapters in Part III – The mosaic of narratives in this volume.

83 Balakrishnan Rajagopal, *International Law from Below: Development, Social Movements and Third World Resistance* (Cambridge University Press 2003) at 244.

to formal spheres, "the political" refers to a broader decentered phenomenon comprising power struggles occurring in the private, social, economic, and cultural spheres. The alternative narratives that emerge from struggles against "meaning and values" in mainstream culture are thus political.[84] As such, cultural politics occurs when social actors, which are formed by and constitute diverse cultural values and practices, conflict amongst themselves.[85] Cultural struggles are considered political because their objective is to reformulate social power.[86]

In this context, alternative political narratives can be articulated based upon legal frameworks such as human rights, theoretical approaches, or social movements. Whilst some authors use the word "narrative" to articulate the use of doctrinal and theoretical approaches to balance international investment law,[87] other authors are more subtle in the articulation of their approaches as narratives.[88] As such, the human rights dimension, particularly through arbitral tribunals, has become a powerful resistance narrative against international investment law, capable of providing a balancing instrument to promote consistency between the two systems,[89] in which arbitral tribunals have found ways, within the limits of traditional structures, to accommodate pressures from the dialectic between human rights and international investment law.[90] However, as Echaide argues, the fulfilment of human rights is an obligation to the state, and not a mere defense (to which it should not be reduced) in investment arbitral tribunals.[91] Beyond balancing rights, there is a need to break the fragmentation between regimes in order to establish the concurrent responsibility of the state and investors.[92] Besides human rights, authors foreground resistance narratives

---

84 Ibid.
85 Sonia Alvarez, Evelina Dagnino, and Arturo Escobar (Eds.) (1998) *Cultures of Politics/ Politics of Cultures: Re-visioning Latin American Social Movements* (Westview Press) cited in Balakrishnan Rajagopal, *International Law from Below: Development, Social Movements and Third World Resistance* (Cambridge University Press: 2003) 244. For an account of the cultural context in social movements, see: James Jasper and Francesca Polletta, "The Cultural Context of Social Movements," in David A Snow, Sarah A Soule, Haspeter Kriesi and Holly McCammon (Eds.) *The Wiley Blackwell Companion to Social Movements* (2nd Edition, John Wiley & Sons Ltd 2019) 63–78.
86 Ibid.
87 See Chapter 13 by Sebastián Preller-Bórquez in this volume.
88 See Chapters 10 by Rodrigo Polanco Lazo and Felipe Ferreira Catalán and 11 by Farouk El-Hosseny, Patrick Devine and Brun-Vargas in this volume.
89 See Chapter 10 by Rodrigo Polanco Lazo and Felipe Ferreira Catalán in this volume.
90 See Chapter 11 by Farouk El-Hosseny, Patrick Devine and Ilan Brun-Vargas in this volume.
91 See Chapter 12 by Javier Echaide in this volume.
92 Ibid.

on sustainable development, in which the narrative of balance inherent to the concept of sustainable development offers a tool to accommodate social and environmental concerns in the international investment regime.[93] An interesting thesis that emerges from all this – which neither we nor the authors pursue – is whether, and if so, to what extent, this dynamic of accommodation fosters the de-fragmentation of international law.[94]

However, whilst some alternative narratives will be capable of gaining support and strength to counteract international investment law, others will not have such force despite the validity and nature of their claims. Studies note that the success of narratives depend on storytelling – for instance, the content of the story, its evaluation, and the appropriate manner and place to tell the story.[95] Human rights arguments recently have been gaining traction in arbitral tribunals,[96] but with them, there are a number of narratives that have emerged in terms of the environment, the role of foreign investment in the promotion of development and so on. The emergence of alternative political narratives, and the diversity of interests and values embedded therein, raises questions about coherence. Studies on narratives have shown that ambiguity in storytelling could be a powerful instrument to retain solidarity and to counteract opposing views.[97] In Chapter 14, Cardenas and d'Aspremont argue that ambivalence has enabled international investment law to accommodate both universality and resistance thereto. Ambiguity, rather than seen as a reflection of inconsistency and disorganization, is a powerful means towards resisting and accommodating international investment law, one in which Latin America has significantly contributed to.

The contributions

The book is organized in three parts, which address the diverse Latin Americas – or the Latin American mosaic – in terms of states (*Part I – The*

---

93 See Chapter 13 by Sebastián Preller-Bórquez in this volume.
94 Chapter 12 by Javier Echaide brings a critical assessment on fragmentation and argues that investor–state arbitration tribunals, even those recognizing the need to respect human rights, have decided against states, mainly as a result of prioritizing the international investment law regime. Echaide advocates for a hermeneutic interpretation and the possibility of affirming concurrent responsibilities, which are not yet explored by tribunals.
95 Francesca Polletta, Pang C. B. Chen, Beth G. Gardner and Alice Motes, "The Sociology of Storytelling" (2011) 37 *Annual Review of Sociology* 109.
96 See Chapters 10 by Rodrigo Polanco Lazo and Felipe Ferreira Catalán; and 11 by Farouk El-Hosseny, Patrick Devine, and Ilan Brun-Vargas in this volume.
97 Polletta and others (n 95).

Mosaic of States), non-state actors (*Part II – The mosaic of non-state actors*), and narratives (*Part III – The mosaic of narratives*). Evidently, there is some overlapping of topics between these parts – but the attentive reader will notice substantial differences in the manner that topics are studied in different parts. So, Parts I (*The mosaic of states*) and II (*The Mosaic of Non-State Actors*) bring to light the diverse group identities and the manner that they resist and accommodate international investment law. As we move to Part III (*Mosaic of Narratives*) the emphasis is placed on how narratives are articulated both *within* ISDS and *about* ISDS. We avoided addressing narratives about isolated standards as there is a lot already written on this. Throughout the chapters, two main themes are recurrent – human rights and sustainable development – which only reflect the high interest that, currently, governments, practitioners, activists, and scholars from the region have on them.

Part I opens with a chapter by Philip Burton addressing the great debate generated by the Calvo Doctrine. Chapter 1 offers an opening for the whole volume and not just for Part I. Burton attempts to provide a constructivist history of the great debate surrounding the Calvo doctrine, tracing the ways that jurists and diplomats invoked and attacked Calvo, and the ways participants sought to clothe their preferences in the language of universalism, while seeking to expose the particularist predilections of their rivals. This focus on the "historiographical Calvo," as opposed to the "historical Calvo," provides insight into the rhetorical strategies of the protagonists and antagonists of reformist projects in international law. This analysis of the "great debate" regarding the level of protection international law ought to offer foreign investors is structured by the transition between different institutional fora – clarifying much of the dynamics that resulted in the current mosaic that Part I describes. Starting in 1889, the analysis begins with the first Pan-American Conference and concludes in 1965 with the conclusion of the Convention establishing the International Centre for the Settlement of Investment Disputes. Unlike conventional accounts of the historical antecedents of what is, today, referred to as "international investment law," Chapter 1 decenters the arbitral tribunal (as later chapters also do) – the paradigmatic institution of modern investment law – from its ascribed place as the locus of legal development. Despite the indisputable importance of arbitral decisions, Burton argues that the basic structure of arbitral dispute resolution predisposes historical accounts towards a depiction of Latin American "resistance" as a rear-guard action; ad-hoc, disaggregated, and reactive. Focusing on the advocacy of reform projects through collective institutional forums not only facilitates a more coherent history of those projects but offers greater utility in the context of the present volume on the contemporary prospects of Latin American resistance and accommodation.

In Chapter 2, Magdalena Bas addresses the current South American mosaic of states. Drawing on the theory of international regimes, Chapter 2 develops a typology that organizes states into four groups based upon the different behaviors, which South American states have adopted in the last decades, towards the international investment regime and, precisely, towards the investor–state dispute settlement regime. As such, the typology categorizes states as *members*, states that are part of the regime and which have not substantially changed their attitude towards the regime (for instance, Argentina); *confronters*, namely, states that, without abandoning the international investment regime, came to adopt a different, more confrontational attitude towards it; *outsider*, to wit, the only state that has historically been located outside the regime (Brazil); and, *dissidents*, states that having been part of the regime withdrew from it (Bolivia and Venezuela and, for a moment, also Ecuador). Bas explores the positions of South American states regarding the investor–state dispute settlement regime, their basis and the reasons that led to its manifestations in the present. It argues that, historically, South America has moved from resistance to accommodation and from accommodation to fragmentation in relation to the regime created by the US and Europe, leading to a three-color mosaic – *members*, the *outsider*, and *dissidents*. The chapter concludes that, despite being an outsider, Brazil is the only state in the region that has already taken steps to reshape the traditional regime.

Looking at the same reality, from a different perspective, Henrique Choer Moraes and Facundo Pérez Aznar, in Chapter 3, address the pluralist approaches to dispute settlement mechanisms in Latin America. In the current period of regulatory experimentalism in international investment rule making, Moraes and Pérez Aznar argue that Latin America represents a clear example of pluralism, as countries in the region adopt a wide array of approaches to investment arbitration. The chapter charts the range of Latin American attitudes to investment arbitration, from the "modernizing remainers" to the "exiters," with "creative entrants" in between. Moraes and Pérez Aznar note a remarkable feature of the Latin American pluralism, the same country adopting different approaches to investment arbitration. In order to capture the full extent of pluralism in the region, Chapter 3 explores the different variations in approaches that can be identified across Latin American countries. The picture that emerges shows that Latin America is a laboratory of investment arbitration options, ranging from traditional investor–state dispute settlement through to no investor–state dispute settlement, from conditioned investor–state dispute settlement to state–state dispute settlement and to permanent investment tribunals.

Chapter 4, by Leonardo V P de Oliveira and Marcus Spangenberger, analyzes the new Brazilian investment agreement against the backdrop of the mosaic of international investment treaties in the region. Several Latin

American countries have been signatories to investment treaties and pro-tagonists in investment disputes. Nevertheless, the authors note, the biggest economy in Latin America does not fit such profile. Although Brazil signed 14 bilateral investment treaties in the nineties, it has never ratified a single one. Be that as it may, such position has never hindered the injection of for-eign investments into Brazil. However, Oliveira and Spangenberger argue, the scenario has now changed. In the courtyard of multinationals, Brazilian companies unmistakably have their share and are seeking protection to their international investments. But rather than jumping on the bandwagon of existing BIT regulations, Brazil chose to go down a different path. Since 2015, it has signed thirteen international investment agreements called Cooperation and Facilitation Investment Agreement. In the new approach, Brazil is seeking to balance investor protection with state regulatory pow-ers. The Brazilian model is structured under three main pillars: investment cooperation and facilitation; improved institutional governance and risk mitigation, with dispute prevention and settlement. Although this structure is not entirely new to international investment agreements, it brought new components to its content, limiting the rights of the investor towards a pri-marily diplomatic dispute resolution mechanism compared to most com-mon Latin American BITs. Therefore, from the evaluation of the Brazilian investment agreement, Chapter 4 assesses whether the Brazilian model can serve as a model for other Latin American countries.

Chapter 5 helps answer this question. Luciana Ghiotto provides a crit-ical approach to the investment facilitation debate, and throws light onto the different attitudes states manifest, often in international organizations, towards the investment facilitation model. In recent years, Ghiotto recalls, there have been many proposals for the reform of the investment protection regime, and one of such proposals entertains the adoption of investment facilitation rules. However, investment facilitation, as Ghiotto brilliantly explains, remains an indeterminate concept, whose objective is the simpli-fication of all administrative procedures to allow the free entrance, devel-opment, and exit of foreign investors from the host country. Investment facilitation encompasses three issues, namely, transparency, and predict-ability, commitment with stakeholders and regulatory cooperation. The centrality of regulatory cooperation connects to the notion of "good regu-latory practices" pushed by the Organisation for Economic Cooperation and Development. Ghiotto identifies a tension in the investment facilita-tion debate, especially between the concepts of "public policy space" on the road towards sustainable development proposed by the UNCTAD, and the notion of "good regulatory practices" of the OECD. Both categories can be considered as contradictory to the existence of sustainable foreign investment. Ghiotto's chapter could have been comfortably placed in Part II (as it deals with international organizations) or especially in Part III (as it addresses different narratives), but coming in Part I it strengthens the discussion about the Latin American mosaic at the same time as it helps set the grounds for some of the discussion that later chapters articulate.

Part I closes with Chapter 6 by René Urueña and María Angélica Prada-Uribe, which moves the focus away from governments and towards domestic courts. Urueña and Prada-Uribe explain how the *transformative constitutionalism* – as developed by constitutional courts in the region and by the Inter-American Court of Human Rights – may act as a mechanism for resisting and shaping international investment law. In a carefully articulated case study, the authors show how transformative constitutionalism create substantive limits on the fair and equitable standard of treatment – and they explain the procedural venues (both domestic and international) through which such limits can be imposed. Chapter 6 describes the public/private divide in investment arbitration and its interaction with fair and equitable treatment as a platform for transforming the investment arbitration regime in a decentralized mechanism of international public power. The authors turn to the interaction between the Colombian constitutional jurisdiction and the investment regime, before suggesting that the discussion on the public–private divide of international investment arbitration is today more relevant than ever, as it is instrumental in defining the appropriate standard of domestic constitutional review to be applied vis-à-vis the international investment regime. A private law mindset of the international investment regime requires accommodation of the domestic legal system, while a public law mindset opens a door for resistance through a broader interaction between the national and the transnational spheres. In this last scenario, constitutional courts need to give precise orders to the executive branch regarding the standards or wording that needs to be modified in the investment treaties. By not doing so, the authors conclude, domestic Courts fail to create a dialogue between constitutional law and the investment regime which may foster a more democratic investment regime.

Part II opens with Chapter 7 by Claus von Wobeser, who argues that multinational corporations are the most important vehicle of global trade and international investment in today's globalized economy, which they help shape, and that they are a central actor in the development of international investment law. The chapter describes the corporate stakeholder and its characteristics, interests, and role in the international investment law regime in Latin America. It begins by discussing the characteristics of the corporate stakeholder as a participant in the regime and the emergence of new corporate stakeholders. It argues that the corporate stakeholder and its interests are much more nuanced and diverse than the traditional conception of hostility between multinational corporations and the other systemic actors would suggest. The chapter adopts the perspective of the multinational enterprises towards international investment law and discusses whether, and if so, to what extent, corporations care about investment treaties and the availability of investor–state dispute resolution when making decisions on foreign direct investment. Wobeser submits that corporations care generally about the protection of property rights and investment safety, which are objectives that can be secured by several means, not limited to bilateral investment treaties and investor–state dispute settlement. In the final section, the chapter discusses some of the ways in which corporations have accommodated the narratives promoted by other systemic actors and how these developments may contribute to norm creation in international investment law.

In Chapter 8, Adoración Guamán offers an account of the role of civil society in international trade and investment agreements, which has increased in both quantity and quality. The increasing number of areas covered by "new generation agreements" has led to the popular rejection of these agreements, a rejection mainly promoted by social movements and groups. As such, negotiating parties have reacted by approaching civil society in order to incorporate civil society's requests, either in real or rhetorical ways, within international trade and investment agreements. The negotiation of agreements such as NAFTA, TTIP, and CETA shows that the most significant role of civil society has been the organization of strategies to resist these agreements. But there are other interactions that emerge – from consultations during negotiations to the use of dispute settlement mechanisms in these agreements. The chapter addresses the interaction of civil society from the 1980s to date, focusing on cases related to Latin America, as well as the most recent experiences of the interrelation between European social movements and international trade and investment agreements promoted by the European Union. Guamán argues that there is a global character in social movements, which is reflected in the transcontinental influence between the movements that organize in Latin America and Europe. The similarities in discourse and strategies between resistance campaigns against international and investment agreements in Latin America and Europe, and the cross-participation of actors, enables a permanent transcontinental learning experience. Guamán submits that the complex relationship between civil society and international trade and investment agreements evidences a relationship of resistance and accommodation. As such, demonstrations against these agreements are used in conjunction with mechanisms established by negotiating parties. Whilst these mechanisms are created to reduce social demonstrations against agreements, and to increase their legitimacy, the introduction of these mechanisms is insufficient to provide an adequate settlement of civil society requests. However, as the cases of Ecuador and

Peru demonstrate, the mechanisms incorporated into trade and investment agreements can serve to create transnational links, as well as to denounce breaches of social laws along with those related to human rights generally.

Moving forward in the analysis of other non-state actors, Chapter 9 by Sufyan Droubi, Cecilia Juliana Flores Elizondo, and Raphael Heffron defines the invisibility and inequality that affect indigenous peoples as a problem also for international investment law. The chapter argues that the international investment law regime perpetuates both invisibility and inequality. The regime perpetuates invisibility because it is firmly grounded on the principle that governments represent all the peoples in its territory, and inequality, on the strong protection of investors. From this perspective, the authors argue, two questions arise for the international investment lawyer: what to do when the facts of a case, for instance mounting resistance, make it clear that the local government does not represent indigenous peoples; and what to do when the promotion of sustainable development for indigenous peoples clashes with the protection of investors. The chapter addresses these questions through the deconstruction of the mainstream concept of statehood and of the neoliberal belief that the protection of investors reverts to continuous development for all. The chapter draws on critical statehood scholarship, on critical development theories, and on energy justice studies to bring visibility and justice to indigenous peoples and to affirm them as full participants, on their own terms, in international investment law. On a theoretical level, this is a conceptual chapter that falls within socially informed critiques to international law.

Part III opens with Chapter 10 by Polanco Lazo and Ferreira Catalán, who argue that the relationship between investment and human rights represents a troublesome matter to the states, especially at international level, as governments must balance their compliance with international obligations under human rights instruments, with the protection of investors guaranteed by international investment agreements. Human rights and investment law are usually presented as opposing fields with colliding interests as well as contradictory rules and regulations. International investment agreements are usually characterized as a tool that favors businesses, which in turn, allow the special interests of foreign investor to triumph over any other public policy concern of host states. Some of the alleged threats posed by international investment agreements to human rights range from concerns regarding a "regulatory chill" effect when pursuing human rights-related policies, to the lack of transparency and legitimacy of the investor–state dispute settlement. Focusing on Latin America, the chapter argues that a human rights dimension can be recognized in international investment law. Furthermore, the authors claim that the evolution of international investment agreements is not necessarily in opposition with human rights protection, and that there are more connecting points rather than conflicting ones. The chapter shows that international investment agreements have introduced several protections already included in human rights instruments and have provided them with a mechanism that allows their enforceability.

Farouk El-Hosseny, Patrick Devine, and Ilan Brun-Vargas continue on the topic of human rights. Chapter 11 looks at the dialectic between international investment law and human rights, which is more effervescent than ever. This is evidenced by a myriad of recently negotiated international instruments and an increasingly sizeable body of arbitral jurisprudence. On both fronts, the authors claim, Latin America is very much at the fore. The significance of the extractive sector to the region's economy and the pervasiveness of indigenous groups, amongst other factors, make it an obvious fertile ground for that dialectic to play out. This is notwithstanding the fact that human rights are typically absent from international investment agreements, as will be shown at the beginning of this chapter. A new generation of agreements has given, however, bearing to human rights with the aim of accommodating them within the broader goal of the promotion and protection of foreign investment. This chapter will then provide a survey of the latest jurisprudence, touching on human rights in investment treaty arbitration, the most recent of which involve Latin American states, and outline the various approaches which have been adopted by tribunals when faced with that dialectic. The chapter finally questions whether investment treaty tribunals are proving responsive to hitherto new pressures arising from the exponential emphasis on human rights.

Further into the analysis of human rights issues, in Chapter 12, Javier Echaide gives an account of the impact of international investments on the human right to water, which has been internationally recognized as an independent and positive human right since 2010, with the adoption of Resolution 64/292 of the United Nations General Assembly. However, the realization of this right has not been free of tension and contradictions, because factors such as the fragmentation of the international system, the different levels of development – especially in the post-Cold War context, the rise of neoliberalism and the opening of markets, have led to a legal framework for international public development that favors the transnational private capital, and to a dispute resolution system that favors multinational corporations through international arbitration by institutions such as ICSID. The case of drinking water and sanitation, particularly in respect to Argentina, which the chapter discusses, illustrates the tensions and contradictions in the realization of the right. While UNGA Resolution 64/292 recognizes that access to drinking water in sufficient quantity and quality is a basic and universal human right, the international investment law regime jeopardizes the effectiveness of such recognition.

In Chapter 13, Sebastián Preller-Bórquez addresses how the sustainable development narrative assists in the construction of successful arguments when governments defend the measures they adopt as responses to the investor's failure to attain social license. The author shows that, in the narrative of balance subjacent to sustainable development, host states may find a way to resist the mainstream rules of international investment law mostly established for the protection of foreign investors rather than for the protection of local communities and the environment. Thus, the sustainable development narrative of balance may provide a tool for host states to accommodate social and environmental concerns in a regime that appears to be mostly designed to protect investors engaging in transnational businesses. The chapter begins with an explanation of the expected role of host states and the paradigm of the protection of the investment as identified in current foreign investment regimes. It then addresses the legal basis found in international law for the creation of obligations relating to the attainment of social license and their relationship with sustainable development. The chapter then carries out some case studies in which the measures taken by the host state based on the alleged failure of the investor to comply with its obligation to attain social license are reviewed in order to determine the responsibility of the former. In so doing, Preller-Bórquez explores the place where the reasoning of arbitration tribunals intersects with the function contended by the sustainable development narrative of balance. The author finally discusses the application of the contributory fault standard and the potential use that the sustainable development narrative of balance may have to this end by providing a comprehensive assessment of the investor's obligation to attain social license.

The volume closes with chapter 14 by Fabian Cardenas and Jean d'Aspremont, who argue that international investment law does what it does by virtue of its ambivalent relationship towards universality. With a specific emphasis on Latin American legal thought and practice, the chapter shows how international investment law comes to simultaneously accommodate claims of universality as well as resistance thereto. Cardenas and d'Aspremont explain how the sources of metaphoric discourse enable the simultaneous vindication of both universality and resistance to universality. Then, they elaborate on how the enabling of an ambiguous engagement with universality came to inform the systematic use and espousal of the sources of international law in international legal thought and practice in Latin America. The attention turns to how this ambivalence manifests itself in the way in which the content is allocated to the concepts of international investment law like the international minimum standard and the standard of compensation. The chapter ends with a few concluding remarks on how such ambivalence towards universality is not accidental and makes the claim that resistance to universality is a form of cynicism at the service of universality itself.

This volume would not have been possible without the effort of the contributors and the support from our and partner institutions. The Manchester International Law Centre provided us with the means to start working on the project that resulted in this volume. We are thankful to Jean d'Aspremont and Iain Scobbie for all their motivation and support. The University of Dundee provided the funds for the first seminar, which allowed for many of the contributors to come to Dundee in the Summer of 2018; and provided travel grants that allowed some participants to attend the second seminar in Buenos Aires in the summer of 2019. The second seminar would not have been possible without the personal involvement of colleagues from the International Investments in Latin America Network, Luciana Ghiotto and Javier Echaide, and without the financial support of the Universidad Nacional de San Martin and of the Friedrich Ebert Foundation. Many people have helped us bring the book to fruition, and we are especially thankful to Sarah Hendry, Dean of the Dundee Law School, University of Dundee, who has been a supporter of this project since it's early days; to Naiara Correa Nogueira de Souza, who has provided assistance at every stage of the editorial process. We are also thankful to contributors without whom the completion of this book would not have been possible. Finally, we would like to thank the Manchester University Press, for its invaluable help and support, and for its professionalism, throughout.

Part I

The mosaic of states

[52]

1

Constructing the Calvo Doctrine: Claims to universality and charges of particularism

Philip Burton

Si como argentino acato la ley de mi país, como autor de un libro de doctrina universal he debido colocarme bajo el punto de vista de la ciencia, buscando, si no el modo de uniformar el principio, al menos de conciliar los intereses de todos los pueblos.[1]

Introduction

The Calvo Doctrine has been described as "one of the most controversial clauses in the Law of Nations."[2] Advanced in order to prevent abuses of diplomatic protection, critics contended that "it would also eliminate the institution itself without substituting an acceptable alternative."[3] At the height of the controversy, scholars were moved to decry that "[t]he far-reaching implications of this doctrine are so sinister and so deplorable that it should be resisted by the profession with every means at its command"![4] Nevertheless, despite, or perhaps in despite of, the controversy it elicited, [t]he Calvo Doctrine would "enter the collective psyche of Latin American (sic) and leave

---

1 "As an Argentinean I comply with the law of my country, but as an author of a book of universal jurisprudence, I have had to situate myself under a scientific point of view, seeking, if not a mode to uniform the principles, at least to reconcile the interests of all peoples." Carlos Calvo, "Polémica Calvo-Alcorta" (1883) 8 *Nueva Revista de Buenos Aires* 629, 633 (as cited in Arnulf Becker Lorca, "Universal International Law: Nineteenth-Century Histories of Imposition and Appropriation" (2010) 51 *Harvard Journal of International Law* 475, 522).

2 Manuel R. Garcia-Mora, "The Calvo Clause in Latin American Constitutions and International Law" (1949) 33 *Marq. L. Rev.* 205, 205.

3 Donald Shea, *The Calvo Clause: A Problem of Inter-American and International Law and Diplomacy* (University of Minnesota Press 1955) 20.

4 Alwyn V. Freeman, "Recent Aspects of the Calvo Doctrine and the Challenge to International Law" (1946) 40 *American Journal of International Law* 121, 125.

its mark well into the late twentieth century."[5] While the Calvo Doctrine never secured "mainstream" acceptance in international law, it is enjoying something of a renaissance in contemporary practice, with parallels emerging in increasingly surprising places.[6]

The remarkable intensity of the controversy surrounding the Calvo Doctrine was reflective of its emblematic significance to the first sustained attempt by post-colonial states to resist and reform the world order through international legal discourse. This chapter attempts to provide a constructivist history of this prolonged engagement, tracing the ways that jurists and diplomats invoked and attacked Calvo. The key objective of the study is to trace how participants sought to clothe their preferences in the language of universalism, while seeking to expose the particularist predilections of their rivals. This focus on the "historiographical Calvo," as opposed to the "historical Calvo," provides insight into the rhetorical strategies of the protagonists and antagonists of reformist projects in international law.

This analysis of the "great debate" regarding the level of protection international law ought to offer foreign investors is structured by the transition between different institutional forums. Starting in 1889, the analysis begins with the first Pan-American Conference and concludes in 1965 with conclusion of the Convention establishing the International Centre for the Settlement of Investment Disputes.[7] Unlike conventional accounts of the historical antecedents of what is, today, referred to as "international investment law," the present chapter decenters the arbitral tribunal – the paradigmatic institution of modern investment law – from its ascribed place as the locus of legal development. Despite the indisputable importance of arbitral decisions, it is argued that the basic structure of arbitral dispute resolution – in particular, the vesting of the right of initiative with the investor (or the home state of the investor) – predisposes historical accounts towards a depiction of Latin American "resistance" as a rear-guard action; ad-hoc, disaggregated, and reactive. Focusing on the advocacy of reform projects through collective institutional forums not only facilitates a more coherent history of those projects, but, it is hoped, offers greater utility in the context

---

5 Jan Paulsson, *Denial of Justice in International Law* (Cambridge University Press 2005) 20.

6 See, e.g., Rodrigo Polanco Lazo, "The No of Tokyo Revisited: Or How Developed Countries Learned to Start Worrying and Love the Calvo Doctrine" (2015) 30 *ICSID Review* 172.

7 Convention on the Settlement of Investment Disputes Between States and Nationals of Other States (signed 18 March 1965, entered into force 14 October 1966) 575 UNTS 159.

of the present volume on the contemporary prospects of Latin American resistance and accommodation.

Fixing the lens

Amidst a pervasive sense of "backlash,"[8] Latin American states are once more at the heart of resistance against international investment law.[9] This trend is most starkly illustrated by the withdrawal of Bolivia, Ecuador, and Venezuela from the ICSID Convention.[10] Less dramatically, but perhaps more significantly in the long term, the Union of South American Nation's (UNASUR) adoption of a final text for an Arbitration Centre presents a challenge to ICSID's hegemony over investor state dispute settlement, potentially opening the door to normative divergence within investment law.[11] In what ways, if any, can a study of the Calvo Doctrine shed on these contemporary challenges to the status quo?

The fundamental transformation that international investment law has undergone since the establishment of ICSID[12] means that we must be, at least, skeptical regarding the reliability of Calvo as guide to contemporary trends.[13] The underlying geology may be unchanged but a century and a half of legal, economic, and institutional development has altered the terrain. Indeed, it is plausible to suggest that the genesis of the discipline of "international investment law" occurred as recently as the early 1990s, with

---

8 Michael Waibel, *The Backlash against Investment Arbitration: Perceptions and Reality* (Kluwer Law International BV 2010); Muthucumaraswamy Sornarajah, *Resistance and Change in the International Law on Foreign Investment* (Cambridge University Press 2015).

9 See, e.g., Asha Kaushal, "Revisiting History: How the Past Matters for the Present Backlash Against the Foreign Investment Regime" (2009) 50 *Harvard International Law Journal* 491; Katia Fach Gomez, "Latin America and ICSID: David versus Goliath" (2011) 17 *Law & Bus. Rev. Am.* 195; Katia Fach Gómez and Catharine Titi, "International Investment Law and ISDS: Mapping Contemporary Latin America" (2016) *The Journal of World Investment & Trade* 515; Ignacio A Vincentelli, "The Uncertain Future of ICSID in Latin America" (2010) 16 *Law & Bus. Rev. Am.* 409; David Ma, "A BIT Unfair? An Illustration of the Backlash Against International Arbitration in Latin America" (2012) 2 *Journal of Dispute Resolution* 571.

10 Vincentelli (n 9) 425 et seq. It should be noted that on 21 June 2021 Ecuador resigned the ICSID Convention, which was ratified on 4 August 2021 and entered into force on 03 September 2021.

11 Fach Gómez and Titi (n 9) 518 et seq.

12 See, generally, Antonio R Parra, *The History of ICSID* (Second Edition, Oxford University Press 2017).

13 Quentin Skinner, "Meaning and Understanding in the History of Ideas" (1969) 8 *History and Theory* 3.

the emergence of "arbitration without privity."[14] Both the brevity of the lifespan of international investment law and the exponential, transformative growth the subject has undergone in recent decades have contributed to a pervasive disciplinary "presentism."[15] That is not to say that investment lawyers lack interest in the past. However, the wider historical turn in international legal scholarship has been comparatively slow to spread to investment law.[16]

Nevertheless, historical research in international investment law is now burgeoning. Beyond purely historical research, intended to reconstruct the past on its own terms, "history" has been put to work in two discrete senses within investment law discourse. Firstly, doctrinal scholars are increasingly taking the historical origins of modern rules and principles seriously.[17] By doing so, doctrinal history can influence the present by offering the potential of a deeper understanding of precedents or a more critical assessment of the existence and content of customary rules. In this sense, "[i]nternational lawyers are all historians of sorts."[18] Recent years have seen a series of studies that organize their examination of the genealogies and contemporary meanings of investment law concepts and doctrines through the prism of Calvo.[19]

---

14 Jan Paulsson, "Arbitration Without Privity" (1995) 10 *ICSID Review – Foreign Investment Law Journal* 232.
15 Stephan W. Schill, "International Investment Law and History: An Introduction" in Stephan Schill, Christian Tams, and Rainer Hofmann, *International Investment Law and History* (Edward Elgar Publishing 2018) 3.
16 See, e.g., Matthew Craven, "Theorising the Turn to History in International Law" in Anne Orford, Florian Hoffmann, and Martin Clark (eds), *Oxford Handbook of the Theory of International Law* (Oxford University Press 2016); Thomas Skouteris, "The Turn to History in International Law" (2005) 16 *Journal of International Law* 539; George Rodrigo Bandeira Galindo, "Martti Koskenniemi and the Historiographical Turn in International Law" (2005) 16 *European Journal of International Law* 539.
17 See, e.g., Martins Paparinskis, *The International Minimum Standard and Fair and Equitable Treatment* (Oxford University Press 2013); Paulsson (n 5).
18 Jean d'Aspremont, "Critical Histories of International Law and the Repression of Disciplinary Imagination" (2019) 7 *London Review of International Law* 89, 89; Rose Parfitt, "The Spectre of Sources" (2014) 25 *European Journal of International Law* 297, 298.
19 Christoph Schreuer, "Calvo's Grandchildren: The Return of Local Remedies in Investment Arbitration" (2005) 4 *The Law & Practice of International Courts and Tribunals* 1; Denise Manning-Cabrol, "The Imminent Death of the Calvo Clause and the Rebirth of the Calvo Principle: Equality of Foreign and National Investors" (1994) 26 *Law & Pol'y Int'l Bus.* 1169; Wenhua Shan, "Is Calvo Dead?" (2007) 55 *The American Journal of Comparative Law* 123; Polanco Lazo (n 6); Bernardo M. Cremades, "Resurgence of the Calvo Doctrine in Latin America" (2006) 7 *Bus. L. Int'l* 53.

Secondly, historical narratives are also used in order to shed light on the "nature" of contemporary international investment law.[20] This narrational form of history generally follows one of two rival "master narratives," the proponents of which are labelled by Kulick as "Friends of Investment" and "Backlashers."[21] For the "Friends of Investment," historical analysis has been used to tell a story of progress.[22] Despite international investment law's "original sin" – its historical foundations in colonialism and violence – successive reforms in the past half century have redeemed the discipline. The "Backlashers," conversely, argue that these colonial origins created "blind spots" and biases which subsequent reforms have uncritically reproduced.[23] The Calvo Doctrine is a key "marker" in the disciplinary history and, accordingly, it features prominently in both accounts.[24] Clearly, though, the two accounts diverge regarding the lessons to be drawn from the episode. For example, according to Miles, the prevailing economic and political conditions of the nineteenth century "enabled capital-exporting states to exert control over the content of the rules, the framing of foreign investment protection within the doctrine of state responsibility, and methods of implementation."[25] The legal regime favored the "protection of the investor, enmeshed the interests of state and investor within the operation of diplomatic protection, and legitimised military intervention against host states."[26] In light of this diagnosis Calvo is read as an attempt "to counteract [the] imbalance" which, ultimately, was quashed "by capital-exporting states through legal discourse, arbitration, and use of force."[27] Jan Paulsson starts from a similar portrayal of the exploitative nature of nineteenth-century rules protecting foreign property. However, for Paulsson, "[s]trict adherence to the Calvo Doctrine was understandable when international law offered no options

---

20 For a defense of this historical method, see Anne Orford, "On International Legal Method" (2013) 1 *London Review of International Law* 166.

21 Andreas Kulick, "Narrating Narratives of International Investment Law: History and Epistemic Forces" in Stephan Schill, Christian Tams, and Rainer Hofmann, *International Investment Law and History* (Edward Elgar Publishing 2018).

22 Thomas Skouteris, *The Notion of Progress in International Law Discourse* (TMC Asser Press 2010).

23 See, e.g., Antony Anghie, *Imperialism, Sovereignty and the Making of International Law* (Cambridge University Press 2007). C.f. d'Aspremont (n 18); Jörg Kammerhofer, "The Challenges of History in International Investment Law: A View from Legal Theory" in Stephan Schill, Christian Tams, and Rainer Hofmann, *International Investment Law and History* (Edward Elgar Publishing 2018).

24 d'Aspremont (n 18) 94.

25 Kate Miles, *The Origins of International Investment Law: Empire, Environment and the Safeguarding of Capital* (Cambridge University Press 2013) 69.

26 Ibid.

27 Ibid 69–70.

other than local courts or foreign warships."[28] In other words, the Calvo Doctrine was a response to the partial development of international law, as opposed to a subaltern response to a distributive order which favored the holders of capital.

The "master narratives" of "original sin" and "sinner redeemed" have formed the primary axis of historiographic debates since the historical turn in international law. However, I am skeptical regarding the extent to which an analysis of these narratives may fruitfully contribute to the focus of this collection; namely Latin American resistance and accommodation in the context of contemporary international investment law. Instead, I want to draw out an aspect of the focus of this volume that is left unsaid: resistance and accommodation in relation to what or whom? The substitution of "Latin American" for "international" to qualify the nature of the "investment law" implies we are concerned with continental adjustment within a universal regime. However, the reductivity of such an answer is neatly illustrated if we consider one of the appellations for the broader order that contemporary (global) investment law is nested within: "the Washington consensus." Alternating where emphasis placed between the two constituent terms of this appellation highlights alternatively the universality of this regime or its close relationship with a (particularist) hegemonic structure. This dynamic is the focus of this chapter. I want to use a constructivist historical methodology to examine two rival ways of describing Calvo within historical narratives, focusing, in particular, on the way that participants invoke the ideal of the universal.[29] Supporters present Calvo as a pacifist and an internationalist, committed to the rule of law and adjudication between states. Critics present him as a national chauvinist, who sought to pervert the basic structure of international law by elevating municipal law above international law. The debate essentially boils down to competing and contradictory attempts to articulate participants' own particular interests in universal terms. Just as proponents of the two rival narratives advance their interests in terms of universal values, they seek to expose the particular interests being advanced by their rivals, i.e. "imperialism" or "lawless tyranny."[30]

In analyzing this historiography, I am principally concerned with the "epistemic community" of jurists who invoked Calvo in their writings. In particular, those who participated in the discursive community which narrated the repeated attempts to inscribe the Calvo Doctrine in positive

---

28 Paulsson (n 5) 22.

29 See, e.g., Kulick (n 21); d'Aspremont (n 18).

30 See, generally, Duncan Kennedy, "The Hermeneutic of Suspicion in Contemporary American Legal Thought" (2014) 25 *Law and Critique* 91.

international law. As such, national legal rules (i.e. "Calvo Clauses") and the decisions of arbitral tribunals (largely concerning the lawfulness of Calvo Clauses) fall outside the ambit of this study. The intention is neither to simply produce a diplomatic history of conferences, nor to arrive at any precise conception of "what the law was" at any given point in this history. Indeed, "the orthodox approach to the sources of international law is incapable of reflecting the complexity of international legal interaction."[31] The analysis is principally focused on the controversies around law-making processes and the ways that jurists narrated these controversies. Geographically, the study focuses primarily on the Americas given both the nature of the present volume and the fact that the controversy enjoyed far greater salience in the Americas.[32] Temporally, the study spans from 1889–1965, beginning with the earliest meetings of the Pan-American Conference system and concluding with the drafting of the Washington Convention. Reading discourses of reform in conjunction with the succession of institutional orders spanning this era facilitates an understanding into the ways that the basic institutional context affects the bargaining positions and plausible objectives of diverse participants. It must be acknowledged from the outset that my personal limitations as a monolingual anglophone researcher mean that this study cannot make claim to exhaustiveness nor "universality."[33]

Calvo and "his" doctrine

In many ways a "hero of his time," Carlos Calvo's career as a diplomat and scholar coincided with the universalization and professionalization of international law.[34] Like many of his "semi-peripheral" contemporaries, Calvo was active in European diplomatic and academic circles.[35] In both capacities Calvo was a constant advocate for Latin American "civilization," seeking to demonstrate parity between the American republics and the established European states. Amongst contemporaries there was widespread recognition of Calvo's contribution to the development of international law; however, that contribution was understood in terms of

---

31 Parfitt (n 18) 304.
32 Shea (n 3) 7.
33 Parfitt (n 18) 301.
34 Martti Koskenniemi, *The Gentle Civilizer of Nations: The Rise and Fall of International Law 1870–1960* (Cambridge University Press 2001). Indeed, Calvo was one of the "men of 1873" who founded the *Institut de Droit Internationale*.
35 Becker Lorca, "Universal International Law: Nineteenth-Century Histories of Imposition and Appropriation" (n 1) 496.

compiling and systematizing international law. An editorial marking his passing (rather ungenerously) described Calvo as "neither a thinker nor an artist."[36] This section is intended to provide a *precis* of the context and content of the Calvo Doctrine. It is not my intention to arrive at any authoritative interpretation of the (notoriously vague) doctrine, but rather to survey its broad contours and sketch the principal ways that it has been understood.

Calvo formulated the assemblage that has come to be referred to as the "Calvo Doctrine" against the backdrop of repeated interventions (primarily) by European powers in Latin America. Such interventions were premised on the prevailing view (in Europe) of Southern American states as:

> imperfect, bankrupted republics, which because of social and political instability and unrest, their failure to honour their debts, ensure personal security and provide proper police protection, and their inefficient and slow court system, were not to be considered equal to the countries of Europe.[37]

Coercive interventions varied in intensity, with extreme cases resulting in the occupation of entire states.[38] Armed force, or the threat of force, were frequently used to secure the payment of reparations, "consent" to treaties and submission to arbitration. Unsurprisingly, interpretations of the severity and impact of these interventions differed. Amongst Latin American scholars, they were widely characterized as an "exhibition of international lawlessness ... a most sinister chapter in the relations of the strong toward the weak."[39] Outside observers were often more sanguine: coercive diplomatic interposition was preferable to direct colonial rule or concessionary regimes.[40]

Interventions in Latin America by European states were clothed in legal discourse, principally through the institution of diplomatic protection. Diplomatic interposition could be invoked by the "home" state if treatment of its nationals at the hands of a third state fell below a certain threshold, referred to as the "international minimum standard." The rules regarding the protection of aliens were understood to be near exclusively customary

---

36 Editorial, "Carlos Calvo" (1907) 1 *American Journal of International Law* 137, 138.
37 Horacio A Grigera Naón, "Arbitration and Latin America: Progress and Setbacks 2004 Freshfields Lecture" (2005) 21 *Arbitration International* 127, 131 (citing Thiers, Minister of Napoleon III).
38 The French establishment of a client state in Mexico (1861–1867) was the most dramatic example.
39 Julius Irizarry y Puente, "The Concept of 'Denial of Justice' in Latin America" (1944) *Michigan Law Review* 383, 387.
40 Frederick Sherwood Dunn, *The Protection of Nationals: A Study in the Application of International Law* (The Johns Hopkins Press 1932) 57.

in nature.[41] The most authoritative recital of the customary international standard stated that:

> [T]reatment of an alien, in order to constitute an international delinquency, should amount to an outrage, to bad faith, to wilful neglect of duty, or to an insufficiency of governmental action so far short of international standards, that every reasonable and impartial man would readily recognize its insufficiency.[42]

The content of the norm is vague and self-referential. Moreover, attempting to ground it within any conventional theory of sources is similarly problematic. For example, Root pointed to a "general acceptance by all civilized countries as to form a part of the international law of the world."[43] On what basis could the standard be understood as binding in relation to the "non-civilized" states, against which it was invariably invoked? This was compounded by the fact that, once the international minimum standard was accepted as the customary rule, the basic (voluntarist) framework of international law undermined attempts to attack diplomatic protection "from the inside." Anyone questioning the validity of the customary rule – in particular the degree that it was consensual – had to explain away a wide range of circumstances where the rule had been "enforced." The most obvious rejoinder, that such enforcement was premised on military coercion rather than free consent, was met with the response that international law did not curtail the right of states to employ force to enforce their claims. Arbitration did play an important role within this apparatus of enforcement. Between 1839 and 1910, Latin American states participated in close to 80 arbitrations with European states, around 40 with the United States, and a further 40 amongst themselves.[44] However, arbitration was frequently a consequence of the use of force rather than an alternative to it.

In this context, Calvo reconceptualized international law in order to offer greater protection to Latin American states. The principle vehicle for this project was the general treatise "International Law: Theory and Practice" initially published in 1868 in Spanish.[45] The fifth edition,[46] published in

41 Kenneth J Vandevelde, "A Brief History of International Investment Agreements" (2005) 12 *UC Davis Journal of International Law and Policy* 157, 159.

42 *L. F. H. Neer and Pauline Neer (U.S.A.) v. United Mexican States*, Mexico/USA General Claims Commission (Decision, 15 October 1926) 4 RIAA 60, 61–62.

43 Elihu Root, "The Basis of Protection of Citizens Abroad" (1910) 4 *American Journal of International Law* 517, 521. See, generally, Paparinskis (n 17) 40.

44 Lionel M Summers, "Arbitration and Latin America" (1972) 3 *Cal. W. Int'l LJ* 1, 7.

45 Carlos Calvo, *Derecho Internacional: Teórico y Práctico De Europa y América* (A Durand et Pedone-Lauriel 1868).

46 Carlos Calvo, *Le Droit International Theorique Et Pratique* (A Rousseau 1896).

French, is generally regarded as containing the most comprehensive and coherent statement of the doctrine.[47] For present purposes I want to distinguish between narrower and broader "versions" of the Calvo Doctrine which have been reproduced in subsequent literature. Donald Shea, the preeminent anglophone authority on the subject, provides us with the leading statement of the narrow version.[48] According to Shea "two concepts of non-intervention and absolute equality of foreign nationals are the essence of the Calvo doctrine."[49] However, with the virtue of concision comes the vice of vagueness.

> Even when [Calvo] is advocating the principles of the famous doctrine that bears his name, he falls into inconsistencies and qualifications that tend somewhat to undermine the current interpretation and application of his views.[50]

In constructing this formulation, Shea cites a variety of passages drawn from volumes I, III, and VI of Calvo's study.[51] The passages appear under a variety of headings, including relatively arcane topics such as the topic of state responsibility for violence carried out during revolutions. There is, therefore, controversy regarding which principles Calvo regarded as general and which were context specific.[52] The charge of vagueness is further supported by apparent equivocation, with Calvo endorsing the exclusive jurisdiction of national courts over claims in certain passages but, elsewhere,

47 See, e.g., Garcia-Mora (n 2) 206.
48 Indeed, in subsequent (anglophone) scholarship Shea's monograph is cited as frequently as Calvo's treatise regarding the content of the Calvo Doctrine. Even amongst those who cite Calvo, there is a tendency to follow Shea's formulation.
49 Shea (n 3) 19–20. "The responsibility of governments towards foreigners cannot be greater than that which these governments have toward their own citizens." Calvo, *Le droit internationale théoretique et practique* (5th ed) III, p. 138 (translation provided by Shea, p. 19). Additionally, assigning responsibility to host states for injuries to foreign nationals would:

"create an exorbitant and fatal privilege, essentially favourable to the powerful states and injurious to the weaker nations, establishing an unjustifiable inequality between nationals and foreigners. From another standpoint, in sanctioning the doctrine that we are combating, one would deal, although indirectly, a strong blow to one of the constituent elements of the independence of nations, that of territorial jurisdiction; here is, in effect the real extent, the true significance of such frequent recourse to diplomatic channels to resolve the questions which from their nature and the circumstances in the middle of which they arise come under the exclusive domain of ordinary tribunals." (Ibid., 142).

50 Ibid. 17.
51 Shea, pp. 17–19.
52 Compare, for example, the differing significance placed on this esoteric structure by Borchard, *Diplomatic Protection*, p. 793 and Freeman "Recent aspects" pp. 132–133.

acknowledging that international responsibility could still arise when the host state's conduct fell below the internationally recognized standard.[53] More generally, Calvo's alleged support for exclusive jurisdiction is difficult to square with his positive appraisal of international arbitral decisions regarding the rights of non-nationals.[54]

While critics have tended to interpret these apparent contradictions as inconsistencies, more sympathetic commentators have taken a broader view of what Calvo's project entailed. Accordingly, it is argued that critics fail to take into account the extent to which the doctrine was formulated as a response to the threat of armed force.[55] Or the extent to which it was framed as a claim for inclusion within the law of nations (the international law which applied between European states).[56] Grigera Naón provides a veritable panorama of the various ends that Calvo aspired to further, highlighting how the doctrine sought to:

> exclude the threat or use of force and armed intervention or diplomatic coercion in support of the claims of private persons exerted by their home countries, to further the peaceful resolution of disputes, including by resorting to arbitration freely agreed by the host state... to affirm the principle of the equality of states.[57]

Seen from this broader perspective, the apparent contradictions in Calvo's doctrine fade to the background. Calvo's views on limits of diplomatic protection are not free from contradiction because they are not an "end" in and of themselves. They are in the service of far greater objectives. Seen from this perspective, Calvo is no parochial adherent of unfettered sovereignty, but rather a critic of the false universalism of contemporaneous international law and adherent to, what might be termed today, a "thick" conception of the international rule of law.

The universal and the particular

In sketching out the rough dimensions of this study, I have repeatedly invoked the ideal of "the universal" and its antonym "the particular" without substantiating how these terms are understood. The present section seeks to redress this. The notion of "universalism" is perhaps the most essential

53 Calvo, *Le droit internationale théoretique et practique* (5th ed) III, p. 134.
54 Grigera Naón (n 37) 135.
55 James Thuo Gathii, "War's Legacy in International Investment Law" (2009) 11 *International Community Law Review* 353, 355.
56 Becker Lorca, "Universal International Law: Nineteenth-Century Histories of Imposition and Appropriation" (n 1) 477; Shan (n 19).
57 Grigera Naón (n 37) 139.

element in the ideology of international law.[58] Although the concept of universalism is by no means unique to European thought, the genealogy of the universalist strand in international legal theory is rooted in Enlightenment rationalism.[59] It is broadly accepted that the "Public Law of Europe" was "geographically universalized" through colonial processes, involving trade, the acquisition of land, and the subjugation of non-European peoples.[60] Jurists did not think "of Europe in merely local terms, but generalized it into a representative of the universal."[61] A growing awareness of this history has contributed to an increasing skepticism regarding explicit claims to, and underlying assumptions of, universalism.[62]

Third World Approaches to International Law ("TWAIL") scholarship has provided ample illustration of how this dynamic operates, demonstrating that formally neutral "universal" concepts serve the interests of the powerful.[63] However, this engagement has not invariably led to a renunciation of the universality of law *per se*, but rather a re-appropriation.[64]

---

58 Jennifer Pitts, "Empire and Legal Universalisms in the Eighteenth Century" (2012) 117 *The American Historical Review* 92; Becker Lorca, "Universal International Law: Nineteenth-Century Histories of Imposition and Appropriation" (n 1) 475.

59 Emmanuelle Jouannet, "Universalism and Imperialism: The True-False Paradox of International Law?" (2007) 18 *European Journal of International Law* 379.

60 Becker Lorca, "Universal International Law: Nineteenth-Century Histories of Imposition and Appropriation" (n 1) 477. See generally, Anghie (n 23); Jennifer Pitts, *Boundaries of the International: Law and Empire* (Harvard University Press 2018); Lauren Benton and Lisa Ford, *Rage for Order* (Harvard University Press 2016). With respect to international investment law, see Miles (n 25). With respect to the role of international institutions in these processes, see Guy Fiti Sinclair, "State Formation, Liberal Reform and the Growth of International Organizations" (2015) 26 *European Journal of International Law* 445.

61 Martti Koskenniemi, "International Law in Europe: Between Tradition and Renewal" (2005) 16 *European Journal of International Law* 113, 114.

62 See, for example, Koskenniemi (n 61). While initially, this critique was developed by radical and peripheral voices, it is increasingly voiced in mainstream scholarship; see for example, Anthea Roberts, *Is International Law International?* (Oxford University Press 2017).

63 The best example remains Anghie's study on the history of the concept of sovereignty. Anghie (n 23). More generally, see Bhupinder S Chimni, "Third World Approaches to International Law: A Manifesto" (2006) 8 *Int'l Comm. L. Rev.* 3; James Thuo Gathii, "TWAIL: A Brief History of Its Origins, Its Decentralized Network, and a Tentative Bibliography" (2011) 3 *Trade L. & Dev.* 26.

64 Arnulf Becker Lorca, *Mestizo International Law* (Cambridge University Press 2014); Luis Eslava and Sundhya Pahuja, "Between Resistance and Reform: TWAIL and the Universality of International Law Special Issue: Third World Approaches to International Law" (2011) 3 *Trade, Law and Development* [xiii]; Guy Fiti Sinclair, "Towards a Postcolonial Genealogy of International Organizations Law" (2018) 31 *Leiden Journal of International Law* 841.

For example, while international law effectively condemned Latin American states to second-class citizenship in the "international community," it nevertheless "represented the best hope for restraining the use of force against them by countries with more military power than they had."[65] Simply abandoning international law created a risk that, like the overwhelming majority of the non-European world, Latin America would be subject to territorial occupation or humiliating concessionary regimes.[66] However, international law proved a flexible tool in the hands of non-European jurists. Indeed "[a]fter becoming versed in Western legal discourse, these semi-peripheral lawyers used it to engage in disciplinary debates, arguing for rules and doctrines that served the interests of their states."[67] Resistance to Euro-centric claims of universalism therefore typically contain two elements: firstly, the particularism underlying the claim to universality is exposed and secondly a competing vision of the universal is advanced. Often "Euro-centric" claims to universality are expressed through the promulgation of a rule, while peripheral resistance focuses on the universality of sovereignty – with a particular emphasis on sovereign equality.[68]

Crucially, this paper maintains that no single narrative can have an exhaustive claim to truth. "What is 'imaginary' about any narrative representation is the illusion of a centered consciousness capable of looking out on the world, apprehending its structure and processes, and representing them to itself."[69] There is no necessary, prefigured determination of which conception of international law – either the orthodox rules on diplomatic protection or Calvo's heresy – had a better claim to represent the universal and which merely served particular interests. While both accounts claim to speak on behalf of the universal, "the Calvo Doctrine replaced one form of unilateralism with another."[70] In order to substantiate this, I want to tease out the play of "the universal" and "the

---

65 Gathii (n 55) 356.
66 Dunn (n 40) 57. More generally, on the concessionary regimes, see Turan Kayaoglu and Turan Kayaoğlu, *Legal Imperialism: Sovereignty and Extraterritoriality in Japan, the Ottoman Empire, and China* (Cambridge University Press 2010); Umut Özsu, "The Ottoman Empire, the Origins of Extraterritoriality, and International Legal Theory" in Anne Orford, Florian Hoffmann and Martin Clark (eds), *The Oxford Handbook of the Theory of International Law* (Oxford University Press Oxford 2016).
67 Becker Lorca, "Universal International Law: Nineteenth-Century Histories of Imposition and Appropriation" (n 1) 478.
68 Frank Griffith Dawson, "Contributions of Lesser Developed Nations to International Law: The Latin American Experience" (1981) 13 *Case W. Res. J. Int'l L.* 37, 38.
69 Hayden White, "The Question of Narrative in Contemporary Historical Theory" (1984) 23 *History and Theory* 1, 14.
70 Paulsson (n 5) 22.

particular" within the Calvo Doctrine across three vectors: subjecthood in domestic law; subjecthood in international law; and regional variation in international law.

Firstly, the Calvo Doctrine was rooted in the notion of a single, universal standard applying to all individuals within a given polity. Borchard, the pre-eminent authority on diplomatic protection within the time frame of this study, was broadly sympathetic to Latin American states and (moderately) critical of the bind that the rules in force put them in. It was "unfair to these exploited countries" that they were forced to put foreigners in such a "favored position that their presence becomes a continual potential menace."[71] From this perspective, a universal rule establishing equality within states appears most equitable. However, for critics, insistence on strict equality "ignore[s] the reality that the foreign investor is not in the same position as a citizen of the host country."[72] An international minimum standard – for all aliens – thus appears to be the best way to ensure a universally fair rule. There is no self-evident way to determine which of these two contradictory propositions has a better claim to "universality."

Secondly, the Calvo Doctrine was based on a conception of international law as a universal set of rules, applicable to all civilized states. In this respect, he was safely within the mainstream of contemporary legal thought: the key difference was where the line should be drawn. Calvo sought to demonstrate that the Latin American republics satisfied the now notorious "standard of civilization," which functioned as the rule of inclusion for the community of states.[73] In asserting the civilization of Latin American states, Calvo explicitly distinguished the Latin American republics, populated by European settlers, from "uncivilized" peoples.[74] As such, Calvo's "universalism" should not be romanticized. Likewise, in his treatment of the rules regarding intervention, Calvo is willing to cede that intervention was permissible under international law. Lawful interventions in Europe (for example, in support of Greek independence) were based on "sound reason and equity" and were

---

71 Edwin Montefiore Borchard, *The Diplomatic Protection of Citizens Abroad* (Banks Law Publishing Company 1915) 859.

72 William D Rogers, "Of Missionaries, Fanatics, and Lawyers: Some Thoughts on Investment Disputes in the Americas" (1978) 72 *The American Journal of International Law* 1, 4. This point may be rejoined by stating that the alien had foreknowledge of this prior to deciding to settle or invest within a given territory.

73 See, generally, Anghie (n 23); Georg Schwarzenberger, "The Standard of Civilisation in International Law" (1955) 8 *Current Legal Problems* 212.

74 Becker Lorca, "Universal International Law: Nineteenth-Century Histories of Imposition and Appropriation" (n 1) 499. In doing so, Calvo corresponded to the general tendency, on the part of nineteenth-century semi-peripheral jurists, to challenge placement on the spectrum of civilization as opposed to the existence of civilization as an operative concept in general (ibid. 496).

"favourable to the development of civilization."[75] By contrast, it was impossible to identify "a single serious and legitimate reason that could justify up to a certain point the European interferences in the domestic affairs of the Americas."[76] Again, Calvo is not opposed to intervention in order to further a notion of civilization founded upon a racial and confessional hierarchy; he was merely making the case for the American republics to be counted as civilized states. Regarding the use of force to secure recompense to private claimants, Calvo argued:

> According to strict international law, the recovery of debts and the pursuit of private claims does not justify *de plano* the armed intervention of governments, and, since European states invariably follow this rule in their reciprocal relations, there is no reason why they should not also impose it upon themselves in their relations with the nations of the new world.[77]

It is difficult to escape the sense that Calvo was a reluctant radical, seeking to highlight European hypocrisy rather than found a heresy. Amongst critics, however, Calvo's attempt to secure Latin American inclusion within the "universal"(/inter-European) principles regarding diplomatic intervention was read as an attempt to elevate the state above international law, to leave foreign investors without redress against the caprices of local corruption and tyranny.

The final vector charting the play of the concepts of the universal and the particular concerns the existence and nature of regional variants of international law. Calvo is central to the idea of a Latin American international law, described by modern scholars as a "Creole legal consciousness"[78] or "Mestizo International law."[79] Despite the fact that the Calvo doctrine would go on to be regarded as one of the principal achievements of Latin American international law, Calvo rejected the potential for regional variants of international law. Indeed, in the wake of criticisms that his text failed to emphasize sufficiently the separate nature of Latin American international law, Calvo denied the existence of Latin American international as separate from "international law" because international law was, by necessity, universal (at least amongst the civilized states).[80]

75 5th edition vol 1. 323 cited in ibid. 493.
76 Ibid.
77 Calvo, *Le droit internationale théoretique et practique*, Vol 1, 351.
78 Liliana Obregón, "Latin American International Law" in David Armstrong (ed), *Routledge Handbook of International Law* (Routledge 2009) 155.
79 Becker Lorca, *Mestizo International Law* (n 64).
80 Almacio Alcortas, La Ciencia del Derecho Internacional, 7 *Nueva Revista de Buenos Aires* 575 (1883), Arnulf Becker Lorca, "International Law in Latin America or Latin American International Law? Rise, Fall, and Retrieval of a Tradition of Legal Thinking and Political Imagination" (2006) 47 *Harv. Int'l LJ* 283, 299.

Inscribing the Calvo Doctrine in international law

Between the Washington Conference of 1889 and the Washington Convention of 1965, Latin American states made repeated attempts to reform international law with the ambition of bringing it more closely in line with the Calvo Doctrine. The analysis proceeds to divide this "prehistory" of investment into three (fuzzy) epochs, with each nested within an institutional context and representing a particular configuration of "the debate." The analysis begins by following the endeavors of Latin American jurists and diplomats at the first Pan-American Conferences and the second Hague Conference as they sought to place limits on the ability of states to press claims through the use of force. It then examines the technical emphasis of inter-war codification projects seeking to determine the nature and limits of state responsibility. Lastly, the chapter traces the rise of ideological expropriation, the emergence of "investment" and the establishment of ICSID.

Belle Époque: limiting the use of force (1889–1914)

While the basic structure of international law made it nigh impossible for any single state to challenge the orthodox rules of diplomatic protection, the emergence of international institutions gave Latin American states a collective platform to advocate reform. This opportunity would be seized immediately. For present purposes two developments are particularly salient. At the hemispheric level, the Washington Conference of 1889–90 represented the first occasion in which all independent states in the American hemisphere attended a diplomatic conference.[81] As such, the OAS today presents the Conference as its genesis.[82] Globally, the 1907 Hague Peace Conference marked the first occasion that Latin American states participated in a major European conference. Not only did the 1907 Conference strive for universal participation, its procedural egalitarianism meant that "semi-peripheral" states enjoyed genuine voice.

Set by the United States, the agenda of the Washington Conference was primarily commercial, with the principal intention being to establish a

---

81 The inclusion of the United States in Pan-American institutions has been argued to constitute a break in the historiography of Latin American international law. See, e.g., Héctor Gros Espiell, "La Doctrine Du Droit International En Amerique Latine Avant La Premiere Conference Panamericaine (Washington, 1889)" (2001) 3 *J. Hist. Int'l L.* 1.

82 See, e.g., "OAS: Our History" www.oas.org/en/about/our_history.asp accessed 20 January 2020. For an overview of Bolivarian Pan-Americanism, see Alejandro Alvarez, "Latin America and International Law" (1909) 3 *American Journal of International Law* 269, 277 et seq.

"Zollverein between the nations of America."[83] As such, the issue of the diplomatic protection of citizens abroad was not included.[84] Nevertheless, the delegates adopted a recommendation emphasizing the principle of strict equal treatment (e.g. both a floor and a ceiling) between nationals and aliens.

> (1) Foreigners are entitled to enjoy all the civil rights enjoyed by natives; and they shall be accorded all the benefits of said rights in all that is essential as well as in the form or procedure, and the legal remedies incident thereto, absolutely in like manner as said natives.

> (2) A nation has not, nor recognizes in favor to foreigners, any other obligations or responsibilities than those which in favor of the natives are established in like cases by the constitution and the laws.[85]

The Recommendation was only endorsed by six of the eighteen states. The United States – the sole explicit dissenter – submitted a separate minority report.[86]

The theme was resumed at the second International Conference of American States, held in Mexico City (1901–02). In Mexico City proponents of the Calvo Doctrine were, at least partially, successful in realizing the clause in a binding treaty: The Convention on the Rights of Aliens.[87] Article 2 restated the strict equality principle.[88] According to Article 3:

> Whenever an alien shall have claims or complaints of a civil, criminal or administrative order against a State, or its citizens, he shall present his claims to a competent court of the country, and such claims shall not be made, through diplomatic channels, except in the cases where there shall have been, on the part of the court, a manifest denial of justice, or unusual delay, or evident violation of the principles of international law.[89]

---

83 Joaquin D Casasus and others, "The Pan-American Conferences and Their Significance" (1906) 27 *The Annals of the American Academy of Political and Social Science* 1, 7.

84 James Brown Scott, *The International Conferences of American States, 1889–1928: A Collection of the Conventions, Recommendations, Resolutions, Reports, and Motions Adopted by the First Six International Conferences of the American States, and Documents Relating to the Organization of the Conferences* (Oxford University Press, 1931) 5–6.

85 Ibid. 45.

86 Ibid.

87 Convention Relative to the Rights of Aliens, signed 29 January 1902, ibid. 90–91. The treaty was signed by Argentina, Bolivia, Chile, Colombia, Costa Rica, Dominican Republic, Ecuador, Guatemala, Honduras, Mexico, Nicaragua, Paraguay, Peru, El Salvador, Uruguay. Of those states present, only the United States and Haiti declined to do so. Nevertheless, the treaty was only ratified by Bolivia, Colombia, Ecuador, Guatemala, Honduras, Nicaragua, El Salvador.

88 Article 2 ibid. 91.

89 Article 3 ibid.

This provision, essentially restating the requirement of exhaustion of local remedies in the contemporary law of diplomatic protection, was hardly innovative. In his 1915 treatise *The Diplomatic Protection of Citizens Abroad*, Borchard had observed that the principle of exhaustion of local remedies was "so thoroughly established that the detailed citation of authorities seems hardly necessary."[90] However, the US abstained from the drafting of the Treaty and refused to ratify it.[91] In addition to the Convention intended to establish the applicable law regarding the rights of aliens, states present at the 1901–02 Conference also drafted a dispute settlement convention.[92] According to the Convention, the states parties agreed to submit all financial claims from one another's nationals, provided the dispute could not be settled by diplomatic representations, to the Permanent Court of Arbitration.[93]

The prominence of the debate regarding the protection of aliens rose dramatically in the conferences convened after the Venezuelan Crisis of 1902–1903.[94] The crisis was precipitated by the refusal of Cipriano Castro, the Venezuelan President, to repay foreign debts. After failing to peacefully persuade Castro to settle the dispute through arbitration, Britain, Germany, and Italy blockaded the ports of Venezuela. The Venezuelan Crisis galvanized Latin American international lawyers. Calvo dispatched a series of letters to the leading European jurists in the hope of establishing a consensus against the legality of such actions.[95] The Argentine Minister of Foreign Affairs, Luis Drago, sent a famous memorandum to Washington criticizing the actions, and asserting that the use of force should not be employed to recover debt.[96] The "Drago Doctrine," as this assertion came to be known,

90 Borchard (n 71) 818.
91 This refusal was not an isolated occurrence. Writing in 1915 regarding clauses requiring an exhaustion of local remedies, Borchard observed that "[n]either the United States nor Great Britain appears to have consented to enter into such a treaty stipulation with a Latin-American state." Ibid. 820.
92 *Convention between the Argentine Republic, Bolivia, Chile, Colombia, Costa Rica, the Dominican Republic, Ecuador, Guatemala, Haiti, Honduras, Mexico, Nicaragua, Paraguay, Peru, El Salvador, the United States and Uruguay relative to the Arbitration of Pecuniary Claims* (signed 30 January 1902) 190 CTS 479; Scott, *The International Conferences of American States, 1889–1928* (n 84) 104–105. It was ratified by Colombia, Costa Rica, Ecuador, Guatemala, Honduras, Mexico, Peru, El Salvador, and United States of America.
93 Articles 1 and 2, ibid. 104.
94 See, generally, George Winfield Scott, "Hague Convention Restricting the Use of Force to Recover on Contract Claims" (1908) 2 *American Journal of International Law* 78, 81–82.
95 Freeman (n 4) 133.
96 House Doc. of 58th Congress, 2d session (1903–04), pp. 1–5.

was narrower than the Calvo Doctrine.[97] Moreover, it was founded on a different conceptual basis.[98] Nevertheless, they shared a common emphasis on prohibiting the use of force in order enforce private law claims.[99]

The Drago note had a transformative effect on the US administration's policy towards Latin America. As late as 1901, Theodore Roosevelt had stated that "if any South American country misbehaves toward any European country, let the European country spank it."[100] However, Drago framed the issue of European interventions as a threat to American independence, deliberately invoking the Monroe Doctrine.[101] In response to this plea, "President Roosevelt pronounced himself with his wonted vigor in favour of the Drago Doctrine."[102] Enlisting US support was a double-edged sword. Roosevelt's position did shift towards greater hemispheric solidarity. However, this "solidarity" was diminished by the attachment of the "Roosevelt Corollary" whereby the US claimed a right of pre-emptive intervention to forestall European interference in Latin America.[103] Nevertheless, US support paved the way for a renewed attempt to secure international recognition for the Calvo Doctrine. At the third International Conference of American States, held in Rio de Janeiro in 1906, a resolution was passed recommending that the matter be raised at the Second Peace Conference at The Hague.[104]

The 1907 Hague Peace Conference was the first occasion in which Latin American states participated *en masse* in a major European conference. Not without condescension, Albert de Lapradelle and Ellery Stowell observed:

> For the first time Europe found herself face to face with Latin America, whose activities were to be no longer confined to the American questions treated in her Pan-American Conferences. Great was the curiosity as to what would be

---

97 See, generally, Luis M Drago, "State Loans in Their Relation to International Policy 1" (1907) 1 *American Journal of International Law* 692; Luis M. Drago and H. Edward Nettles, "The Drago Doctrine in International Law and Politics" (1928) 8 *The Hispanic American Historical Review* 204; Amos S. Hershey, "The Calvo and Drago Doctrines" (1907) 1 *American Journal of International Law* 26.

98 See, e.g., Hershey (n 97) 29.

99 Grigera Naón (n 37) 139.

100 Edward S Kaplan, *US Imperialism in Latin America: Bryan's Challenges and Contributions, 1900–1920*, vol 35 (Greenwood Publishing Group 1998) 16.

101 Scott, "Hague Convention Restricting the Use of Force to Recover on Contract Claims" (n 94) 83.

102 Hershey (n 97) 30.

103 Matthias Maass, "Catalyst for the Roosevelt Corollary: Arbitrating the 1902–1903 Venezuela Crisis and Its Impact on the Development of the Roosevelt Corollary to the Monroe Doctrine" (2009) 20 *Diplomacy & Statecraft* 383.

104 Scott, *The International Conferences of American States, 1889–1928* (n 84) 135–136.

the attitude of this score of new comers towards Europe; the United States and one another.[105]

However, it was precisely "the American questions" that the Latin American states would bring to The Hague.[106] On the basis of the resolution adopted in Rio de Janeiro, Porter, the US representative, put forward a draft convention on recovery of debts. The final text would differ significantly from Drago's original vision. Article 1 of the Convention stated that:

> The Contracting Powers agree not to have recourse to armed force for the recovery of contract debts claimed from the Government of one country by the Government of other country as being due to its nationals.

> This undertaking is, however, not applicable when the debtor State refuses or neglects to reply to an offer of arbitration, or, after accepting the offer, prevents any *compromis* from being agreed on, or, after the arbitration, fails to submit to the award.[107]

Far from preventing or prohibiting states from forcibly intervening to secure to repayment of debt, the "Porter Proposition" actually provided an explicit basis for forcible intervention if the defaulting state sought to refuse or frustrate an "offer" of arbitration. Unsurprisingly, Venezuela refused to sign the Convention. The majority of Latin American states, taking lead from Drago himself, acceded subject to the reservations that domestic remedies had to be exhausted before resorting to arbitration and that defaulting on debts was never a lawful justification for the use of force.[108]

Calvo, Drago, and the Hague Conference claims provided a rich stream of materials for discussion in the earliest editions of the *American Journal of International Law*. Amongst US commentators, the 1907 Hague Convention (II) was widely celebrated both as an advance for the cause of international

---

105 AG De Lapradelle and Ellery C Stowell, "Latin America at the Hague Conference" (1908) 17 *The Yale Law Journal* 270, 271.

106 In addition to seeking limits to diplomatic interposition, the Latin American delegates fought for a muscular conception of sovereign equality. In particular, their unwillingness to accept that the "Great Powers" ought to receive preferential treatment with regards the appointment of judges meant that plans for Permanent Court of Arbitral Justice Collapsed. See, e.g., Gerry Simpson, *Great Powers and Outlaw States: Unequal Sovereigns in the International Legal Order* (Cambridge University Press 2004) 146.

107 Limitation of Employment of Force for Recovery of Contract Debts (Hague, II); 18 October 1907.

108 Scott, "Hague Convention Restricting the Use of Force to Recover on Contract Claims" (n 94) 89; It should be emphasized that not all Latin American states supported the Drago doctrine. Brazil, in particular, vehemently criticized the proposals at the Conference. De Lapradelle and Stowell (n 105) 274. As did Alejandro Alvarez, perhaps the most distinguished proponent of Latin American international law. Alvarez (n 82).

arbitration and a triumph of US diplomacy. George Scott, for example, noted the origins of the proposal in the letter of Drago and the dissatisfaction of the Latin American states with the final outcome. However, Scott did not dwell on the transformation of the proposal in the hands of US statesmen, simply noting that the Convention failed "to embody what [Drago] sought."[109] Rather than celebrating a treaty prohibiting the use of force to settle private law claims, Scott viewed the outcome as "the first convention involving obligatory arbitration adopted by a Hague conference and recommended to the states of the world for ratification."[110] Of course, arbitration was only obligatory in so far as the state in question had reasons to fear the threat of coercive intervention. George Scott clearly viewed outcome of the Conference through the prism of US diplomacy and prestige:

> [f]rom the first introduction in the conference, the *American* proposal enjoyed the almost unqualified approval of the delegations of Germany, Great Britain, France, Japan, Russia, Italy, Austria-Hungary, Portugal, and Spain.[111]

With respect to the Calvo Doctrine, the tone adopted by US jurists was sympathetic, if paternalistic, towards the plight of Latin American states. However, in the final analysis scholars were near unanimous in their criticism. Hershey is illustrative in both regards. Frequently, claims by aliens seeking international protection "are bottomed on fraud and tainted with illegality and injustice."[112] As such, "[b]oth the wider Calvo and the narrower Drago Doctrines are essentially sound in principle and expedient as policy."[113] However, "Calvo goes too far in condemning diplomatic interposition or the presentation of claims [...] and he does not sufficiently allow for exceptions to general rules or principles."[114]

The universality of international law was vigorously asserted. Calvo's critique of the double standard imposed by the rules on diplomatic protection was refuted in one of two ways. George Scott pointed to the formal equality of the legal order:

> The debtor states would do well to remember that though international law postulates the equal independence of states and the equality of their rights and obligations under its rules, it, has, as yet, developed no formal superior

---

109 Scott, "Hague Convention Restricting the Use of Force to Recover on Contract Claims" (n 94) 89; See, also, James Brown Scott, "The Work of the Second Hague Peace Conference" (1908) 2 *American Journal of International Law* 1.

110 Scott, "Hague Convention Restricting the Use of Force to Recover on Contract Claims" (n 94) 89.

111 Ibid. 80 (emphasis added).

112 Hershey (n 97) 44.

113 Ibid. 43.

114 Ibid.

judicial or administrative authority, and that, as a consequence, to every state is accorded the right to determine for itself whether its international rights have been invaded [...] The use of force is a recognized legal remedy by which states may settle their differences.[115]

The stark discrepancy between the ways that diplomatic claims were asserted in Europe and in Latin America, in other words the distributive consequences of the norm, is irrelevant.

Others tackled the charge of double standards more directly, whilst still asserting the universality of international law. In order to do so, commentators invoked the standard of civilization. Hershey, for example, observed that the "judicial tribunals in certain portions of Central America are notoriously inadequate for the impartial and effective administration of justice."[116] Borchard spoke plainly on the implications of this:

> these countries in effect deny that the states of Latin-America have reached that stage in the administration of civilized justice which would warrant a complete and final surrender of the rights of their subjects to the determination of the local courts.[117]

In other words, international law was universal in the sense that its rules were generally formulated. However, the application of those rules to a given state was conditioned upon its ability to demonstrate to "the European countries" that its legal system was sufficiently commensurable to those of Europe.[118] Only once European states "recognize[d] and admit[ted] the ability of their courts to perform their full international duty as measured by the standards of international law" would Latin American states be fully embraced within the "international community."[119] For both Hershey and Borchard, until European states acknowledged that Latin American legal systems had reached the requisite degree of "civilization," claims should be settled by arbitration.[120]

Interwar codification: state responsibility and denial of justice (1919–1938)

The establishment of the League involved a compromise between the ideals of universality and equality on the one hand and, on the other, the uneven

---

115 Scott, "Hague Convention Restricting the Use of Force to Recover on Contract Claims" (n 94) 85.
116 Hershey (n 97) 45.
117 Borchard (n 71) 857–858.
118 Ibid. 859.
119 Ibid.; See, generally, Paparinskis (n 17) 40.
120 Borchard (n 71) 859; Hershey (n 97) 44.

distribution of material power and the persistent ideology of "civilization."[121] On the whole, Latin American states were beneficiaries of this bargain. The adoption of the Covenant introduced significant changes, in particular it placed further limitations on the right to use force.[122] Successive erosions into the liberty to employ force "shifted the concerns of weak, mostly non-Western countries from the fear of forcible interventions to the bias against them in the rules, processes, and outcomes of arbitral forums."[123] In other areas, little changed. Indeed, the Advisory Committee of Jurists, tasked with drafting the Statute of the Permanent Court of International Justice, proposed that "[a] new interstate Conference" ought to be established "to carry on the work of the two first Conferences at the Hague."[124] Key among these topics was state responsibility.[125] The establishment of standing arbitral commissions in the aftermath of the Mexican revolution[126] in 1917 and the

---

121 For a selection of recent views on the nature of this compromise, compare Thomas Grant, "The League of Nations as a Universal Organization" in Michel Erpelding, Burkhard Hess and Hélène Ruiz Fabri (eds), *Peace Through Law: The Versailles Peace Treaty and Dispute Settlement After World War I* (Nomos 2019); Rose Parfitt, "Empire Des Negres Blancs: The Hybridity of International Personality and the Abyssinia Crisis of 1935–36" (2011) 24 *Leiden Journal of International Law* 849; Natasha Wheatley, "Spectral Legal Personality in Interwar International Law: On New Ways of Not Being a State" (2017) 35 *Law and History Review* 753.

122 Articles 12–16, Covenant of the League of Nations (adopted 28 June 1919, entered into force 10 January 1920) 108 LNTS 188, UKTS 4, 225 CTS 195. See, also, Treaty between the United States and other Powers Providing for the Renunciation of War as an Instrument of National Policy (signed 27 August 1928, entered into force 24 July 1929) 94 LNTS 57, 46 Stat 2343, TS No 796 ("Kellogg–Briand Pact"). Note the distinction between prohibition of "war" in the Covenant and Kellogg–Briand Pact, as opposed to the notion of "force" employed in the 1907 Hague (II) Convention and in Article 2(4) of the Charter of the United Nations. On this distinction, see, e.g., Georg Schwarzenberger, "Jus Pacis Ac Belli? Prolegomena to a Sociology of International Law" (1943) 37 *The American Journal of International Law* 460, 417 et seq.

123 Gathii (n 55) 358.

124 "Resolution of the Advisory Committee of Jurists, 24 July 1920" (1947) 41 *American Journal of International Law* 102, 102.

125 Increasingly, scholars began to distinguish state responsibility (the secondary rules, primarily governing attribution) from rules regarding the treatment of aliens. James Crawford, *State Responsibility: The General Part* (Cambridge University Press 2013) 22–26.

126 Jacobus Gijsbertus Beus, *The Jurisprudence of the General Claims Commission, United States and Mexico under the Convention of September 8, 1923* (Springer 2012); Jean d'Aspremont, "The General Claims Commission (Mexico and the United States) and the Invention of International Responsibility" in Ignacio de la Rasilla and Jorge E Viñuales (eds), *Experiments in international adjudication: historical accounts* (Cambridge University Press 2019).

Paris Peace Treaties[127] produced a growing body of judicial consideration of the law. While global efforts to resolve the treatment of aliens would ultimately founder, at a hemispheric level the Montevideo Convention of 1933 represented the highwater mark of consensus in the Americas regarding the treatment of aliens.

At the fifth session of the League of Nations Assembly, a resolution was adopted requesting that the Council convene a committee of experts tasked with identifying areas of international law which were "sufficiently ripe" for the organization of "conferences for their solution."[128] The topic of responsibility for states for injuries to aliens was assigned to a Sub-Committee led by Salvadorian jurist Gustavo Guerrero.[129] The influence of the Calvo doctrine on the final report is apparent. In the first place, Guerrero was at pains to emphasize that international law acquired its "binding character" through the "free consent" of "all States and not merely the consent of some."[130] Pointedly, the report stated that "the unilateral will of one State or the collective will of a number of States is not sufficient to create legal rules binding on the whole community of States."[131]

Individuals had certain rights – to life, liberty, and property – which required protection wherever they resided.[132] Ensuring the protection of these rights was the key element of the international minimum standard. However, Guerrero argued that the principle of equal treatment constituted both a floor and a ceiling. The "will of the community of peoples":

> accepts the above-mentioned rights as being the minimum which a State should accord to foreigners in its territory, but it does not thereby recognise the right to claim for the foreigner more favourable treatment than is accorded

---

127 See, generally, Marta Requejo Isidro and Burkhard Hess, "International Adjudication of Private Rights: The Mixed Arbitral Tribunals in the Peace Treaties of 1919–1922," *Peace Through Law* (Nomos Verlagsgesellschaft mbH & Co KG 2019); Michel Erpelding, "Local International Adjudication: The Groundbreaking 'Experiment'of the Arbitral Tribunal for Upper Silesia," *Peace Through Law* (Nomos Verlagsgesellschaft mbH & Co KG 2019); Andrew Martin, "Private Property, Rights, and Interests in the Paris Peace Treaties" (1947) 24 *Brit. YB Int'l L.* 273.

128 "Resolution Adopted by the Assembly of the League of Nations, 22 September 1924" (1926) 20 *American Journal of International Law* 1, 2–3.

129 The remainder of the Sub-Committee was composed of De Vischer and Wang Chung-Hui. However, the former was unable to take part in the preparation of the report and the latter did not take part in the final drafting of the text. "Questionnaire No. 4: Responsibility of States for Damage Done in Their Territories to the Person or Property of Foreigners" (1926) 20 *The American Journal of International Law* 176, 176 ("Guerrero Report").

130 Ibid. 179.

131 Ibid.

132 Ibid. 182.

to nationals. The maximum that may be claimed for a foreigner is civil equality with national... In any case, a State owes nothing more than that to foreigners, and any pretension on the contrary would be inadmissible and unjust both morally and juridically.[133]

Crucially, the protection of these rights was "exclusively" a matter for the "State in the territory of which the foreigner happens to be."[134] This was a consequence of the fact that "[p]rotection involves certain positive acts that can only be performed by the State possessing the sovereignty."[135] All delicts or injuries suffered by foreigners were to be resolved through the national legal system. Just as foreigners were entitled to equal treatment with respect to the content of rights, they were entitled to equal treatment with respect to judicial protection of rights.[136] Failure to do so would result in a denial of justice. As such, "a State, in so far as it is bound to afford judicial protection, incurs international responsibility only if it has been guilty of a *denial of justice*."[137] The Guerrero Report represent a bold claim for Latin American equality and inclusion within a single universal set of rules on diplomatic interposition. Outside of Latin America, the report was a "lightning-rod."[138]

The League's efforts to codify the law of state responsibility culminated in the 1930 Conference for the Codification of International Law.[139] The Third Committee of the Conference, under the chairmanship of Basdevant, was assigned the task of preparing a text on the law of state responsibility. The preparatory work for the Conference was undertaken by a Committee which met in 1928–29 and laid out 33 Bases of Discussion. The discrepancy between the Guerrero Report and the Bases of Discussion arguably "handicapped" the Conference "from the start."[140] A preliminary debate regarding the sources of international law, with smaller states seeking to

133 Ibid.
134 Ibid.
135 Ibid.
136 Ibid. 192.
137 Ibid., p. 193 (emphasis original). Guerrero's concept of denial of justice is significantly narrower than contemporaries, including Latin Americans. See Irizarry y Puente (n 39) 384. More generally, see, e.g., Clyde Eagleton, "Denial of Justice in International Law" (1928) 22 *American Journal of International Law* 538; Gerald G. Fitzmaurice, "The Meaning of the Term Denial of Justice" (1932) 13 *Brit. YB Int'l L.* 93.
138 Paulsson (n 5) 24.
139 Shabtai Rosenne, *League of Nations Conference for the Codification of International Law (1930)* (Oceana Dobbs Ferry 1975).
140 Edwin M Borchard, "'Responsibility of States,' at the Hague Codification Conference" (1930) 24 *American Journal of International Law* 517, 517.

minimize the role of non-consensual sources such as general principles of international law and judicial decisions, provided an indication of the breadth of dissensus.[141] In addition, controversy regarding the exhaustion of local remedies resurfaced, with many European states joining calls for robust protection for the integrity of local law.[142]

Ultimately, the conference broke down over controversy of whether foreign investors could be entitled to a higher standard of protection than nationals under any circumstances.[143] A significant minority of states, large enough to prevent the Conference from reaching the requisite two-thirds majority, demanded that equal treatment was an absolute standard. At the League of Nations, the resistance was led by Wu Chaoshu, the Chinese representative. In this way, the Latin American resistance began to spread across the globe, prefiguring the non-aligned movement's resistance to foreign investment law in the post-war.

Beyond the controversy regarding the absoluteness of the principle of equal treatment with nationals, the Conference struggled to reach any consensus on what constituted a denial of justice. In principle, there were two opposing positions. For Guerrero and his sympathizers, the norm against denial of justice guaranteed the integrity of judicial and administrative processes. Conversely, more orthodox scholars argued that denial of justice encompassed a wider range of sins, including certain substantive acts which were wrongs in and of themselves. In light of this disagreement, scholars published a series of articles which purported to resolve this controversy through the application of legal science. By comparison to prior scholarly commentary, this vein of literature was far more technical and prioritized arbitral decisions over other sources of law. Calvo was far less prominent in debates during the inter-war than he was prior to the First World War or in the years after the Second.

Despite largely conforming to the new, technical approach, Fitzmaurice raises the underlying political economy of the dispute to the surface. The causes of this disagreement were, according to Fitzmaurice, "of a political rather than a legal character."[144] Namely, the fact that the states present could be divided into two groups:

> The first group consists of "creditor" or "plaintiff" states, whose independence and civilization are established, whose institutions are strong and whose courts relatively impartial, who lend money to other countries for their development and whose nationals are accustomed to carry on business abroad. The other group

141 Ibid. 521; Paparinskis (n 17) 45.
142 Borchard (n 140) 525.
143 Ibid 537–538.
144 Fitzmaurice (n 137) 93.

consists of "debtor" or "defendant" states, whose independence and civilization are relatively recent, whose institutions are often weak and whose courts are not infrequently under the control of the executive or at the service of purely national interests, who borrow money for their development and are largely aided therein by the knowledge and experience of foreigners. The combination, in this latter group of countries, of the presence of numbers of foreigners carrying on business with the existence of weak or corrupt courts and institutions at whose hands they suffer, has led to a multiplicity of claims on the part of the governments of the former states against the latter.[145]

Fitzmaurice's emphasis on the "creditor" and "debtor" states highlights the essentially distributive nature of the disagreement. These statuses are substantively opposed to one another and it is clear that a "universal" solution would have to strike an appropriate balance between respective rights and duties. Nevertheless, the concept of "civilization" remains central and entails no equivalent requirement of reciprocity. There is no need to "balance" the respective rights of the "civilized" and the "uncivilized" because of the underlying assumption that international law is a "civilizing" force: its function is to transform the uncivilized states into civilized ones. As such, a "universal" rule can only come about once states attain a certain level of "civilization;" defined by reference to the development of European states. Despite acknowledging that Latin American states may legitimately feel "that the existing law had gone beyond what they considered just,"[146] Borchard ultimately arrived at a similar conclusion.[147]

During the interwar, global efforts to codify the rules of state responsibility in general, and in relation to foreigners in particular, foundered. However, at a hemispheric level, proponents of the Calvo doctrine enjoyed far greater success – in particular with respect to the drafting and ratification of the Montevideo Convention on the Rights and Duties of States.[148] The Montevideo Convention coincided with the election of Franklin D. Roosevelt who, in stark contrast to his namesake, wholeheartedly embraced a policy of non-intervention in Latin America.[149] While the Montevideo Convention's

---

145 Ibid.
146 Borchard (n 140) 521.
147 Ibid. 537.
148 Montevideo Convention on the Rights and Duties of States (adopted 26 December 1933, entered into force 26 December 1934) *International Conferences of American States, First Supplement, 1933–1940* (Carnegie Endowment for International Peace 1940) 121–123.
149 See, generally, Irwin Gellman, *Good Neighbor Diplomacy: United States Policies in Latin America, 1933–1945* (JHU Press 2019).

fame was secured by its definition of a state,[150] its significance for the Latin American participants was to be found in Articles 8 and 9. Article 8 affirmed that: "No state has the right to intervene in the internal or external affairs of another." Article 9 emphasized that: "Nationals and foreigners are under the same protection of the law and the foreigners may not claim rights other or more extensive than those of nationals." The Montevideo Convention represented a "sweeping triumph for Latin American jurisprudence and diplomacy on both of the cardinal principles of the Calvo doctrine."[151] This success was followed up at the Buenos Aires Conference of 1936, where the US accepted, without reservation, the 1936 Additional Protocol Relative to Non-Intervention, which stated:

> The High Contracting Parties declare inadmissible the intervention of any one of them, directly or indirectly, and for whatever reason, in the internal or external affairs of any of the other Parties.[152]

Nevertheless, while it became common place for Latin American jurists to assert that equal treatment was now a rule of international law (at least amongst American states), the US maintained its advocacy of the minimum standards rule.[153]

The institutional context of the interwar, in particular the increasingly restrictive regulation of the use of force, resulted in a shift in the terms of the debate. The attempts to codify the rules on responsibility of states towards foreign nationals, centered around, but not confined to, Geneva, saw debates shift away from broad principles towards technical solutions. In particular, the concept of denial of justice received close attention. However, attempts to find a technical solution merely shifted the locus of the debate, namely whether the concept of denial of justice encompassed substantive as well as procedural standards. This work would fizzle out against a backdrop of political expropriations and investment law would not return to this degree of technical sophistication until the 1990s.

Expropriation and institutionalization (1938–1965)

The codification projects of the interwar were, for the most part, rooted in the classic framework of diplomatic protection: they were concerned with

---

150 See, for example, James Crawford, *The creation of states in international law* (Oxford University Press 2006), p 45 *et seq.*

151 Shea (n 3) 82.

152 Article 1, Additional Protocol Relative to Non-intervention *International Conferences of American States, First Supplement, 1933–1940* (n 148) 191.

153 Shea (n 3) 82–83.

maltreatment of foreigners in general, rather than foreign direct investment *per se*. However, in parallel to deliberations regarding the state responsibility and denial of justice, a series of expropriations transformed the nature of the debate.[154] The emergence of political expropriations, initially at least, did not significantly alter the basic conceptual framework of diplomatic protection.[155] Arbitral proceedings carried out by the US–Mexico claims commission produced important statements on the content of the international minimum standard, the scope of the concept of denial of justice, the validity of Calvo clauses in contracts as well as contributing to the development of the secondary rules of state responsibility. Within the literature, scholars debated the degree to which the international minimum standard embraced a normative concept of property.[156]

---

154 The Mexican and Russian Revolutions of 1917 were the earliest examples. The territorial settlement arrived at in the Peace Treaties contained numerous provisions regarding expropriation. In particular, Article 6 of the Geneva Convention concerning Upper Silesia, 15 May 1922: "Poland may expropriate in Polish Upper Silesia in conformity with the provisions of articles 7 to 23 undertakings belonging to the category of major industries including mineral deposits and rural estates. Except as provided in these clauses, the property, rights and interests of German nationals or of companies controlled by German nationals may not be liquidated in Polish Upper Silesia." See further *Certain German Interests in Polish Upper* Silesia *(Germany v Poland)* (Merits) [1926] PCIJ Series A No 7; *Factory at Chorzów (Germany v Poland)* (Judgment, Claim for Indemnity, Merits, Judgment No 13) [1928] PCIJ Series A No 17. See also Article 250 Treaty of Peace between the Allied and Associated Powers and Hungary and Protocol and Declaration (signed 4 June 1920) (1921) 15.1 AJIL 1: "...the property, rights and interests of Hungarian nationals or companies controlled by them situated in the territories which formed part of the former Austro-Hungarian Monarchy shall not be subject to retention or liquidation in accordance with these provisions." See also, Article 3 of the Minority Treaty between the Principal Allied and Associated Powers and Rumania (signed 9 December 1919) AJIL 1920, Vol. 14, No. 4, Supplement Official Documents (Oct. 1920), pp 324–332. See, generally, Francis Deák, "The Rumanian-Hungarian Dispute before the Council of the League of Nations" (1927) 16 *Calif. L. Rev.* 120.
155 John H. Herz, "Expropriation of Foreign Property" (1941) 35 *The American Journal of International Law* 243, 243; Paparinskis (n 17) 46–48; Andrea Leiter, "The Silent Impact of the 1917 Revolutions on International Investment Law: And What It Tells Us about Reforming the System" (2017) 6 *ESIL Reflections* 1.
156 Anderson's "examination of the fundamental laws of ... all of the elder members of the family of nations" revealed "a profound respect among them for the sanctity of private property." The absolute concept of property was "inherent" and a "universally recognised standard of justice." Chandler P. Anderson, "Basis of the Law against Confiscating Foreign-Owned Property" (1927) 21 *The American Journal of International Law* 525, 525–526; others recognized that encompassing a normative concept of property would "give dominant nations of western civilization a veto power over attempts by other nations to make changes in their economic structure

However, in the longer term, political expropriations would have profound effects which, cumulatively, would constitute of the emerging field of investment law.[157] Debates regarding the appropriate degree of compensation, which were present in but largely peripheral to interwar discourses, would become salient.[158] Indeed, the politicization of the concept of "property" led to the adoption of the language of "investment," with its dual implications of economic benefit for the "host" and profitable returns for the investor.[159] This shift coincided with a diminishment of the role of Latin American states as agents of change in international law: the Soviet Union, a pariah for much of the interwar, was now a superpower and the process of post-war decolonization created new generations of states seeking economic, as well as political, self-determination.[160] Thus, the mantle of norm-pioneers shifted.[161] The post-war period also witnessed a decline in

as may seem advisable in particular instances. It seems to stand in the way of progress in social reform in those states in which foreigners have acquired vested property interests, and to perpetuate the status quo in favour of the propertied classes." Frederick Sherwood Dunn, "International Law and Private Property Rights" (1928) 28 *Columbia Law Review* 166, 178; see, also, Alexander P. Fachiri, "Expropriation and International Law" (1925) 6 *Brit. YB Int'l L.* 159; John Fischer Williams, "International Law and the Property of Aliens" (1928) 9 *Brit. YB Int'l L.* 1.

157 See, generally, Robert Yewdall Jennings, *General Course on Principles of International Law* (Recueil des Cours de l'Académie de Droit International (Martinus Nijhoff) 1967) 473 et seq.

158 Paparinskis (n 17) 33; Rudolf Dolzer, "New Foundations of the Law of Expropriation of Alien Property" (1981) 75 *American Journal of International Law* 553.

159 Leiter (n 155).

160 In many ways the concept of a state employed in Soviet international law discourse closely resembled that adopted by Calvo. C.f. Mintauts Chakste, "Soviet Concepts of the State, International Law and Sovereignty" (1949) 43 *American Journal of International Law* 21; Becker Lorca, "Universal International Law: Nineteenth-Century Histories of Imposition and Appropriation" (n 1) 492 et seq.

161 See, generally, Nico Schrijver, *Sovereignty over Natural Resources: Balancing Rights and Duties*, vol 4 (Cambridge University Press 1997); James N Hyde, "Permanent Sovereignty over Natural Wealth and Resources" (1956) 50 *American Journal of International Law* 854; Stephen M Schwebel, "The Story of the UN's Declaration on Permanent Sovereignty over Natural Resources" (1963) 49 *American Bar Association Journal* 463; Karol N Gess, "Permanent Sovereignty over Natural Resources: An Analytical Review of the United Nations Declaration and Its Genesis" (1964) 13 *International & Comparative Law Quarterly* 398; P. J. O'Keefe, "The United Nations and Permanent Sovereignty over Natural Resources" (1974) 8 *Journal of World Trade* 239. Likewise, jurists from the newly independent states increasingly became the key scholarly interlocuters. See, e.g., S. N. Guha Roy, "Is the Law of Responsibility of States for Injuries to Aliens a Part of Universal International Law?" (1961) 55 *American Journal of International* Law 863; Ram Prakash Anand, *New States and International Law* (Vikas Publishing House 1972) 39 et seq.

the vitality of idea of a Latin American international law.[162] As such, many of the developments in this transformative period lie beyond the scope of this chapter. Rather than providing a comprehensive account, two discrete episodes will be discussed. The first examines the "Cárdenas doctrine" as a radical reinterpretation of Calvo. The second brings the chapter to a close by examining the famous "*No de Tokyo.*"

At least initially, the majority of proponents of the Calvo Doctrine, like Calvo himself, were classic liberals.[163] However, the leftward turn of the Mexican revolutionary state under the Presidency of Lázaro Cárdenas (1934–1940) led to a new wave of nationalization programs, principally regarding agrarian properties and oil facilities.[164] Cárdenas' nationalizations provided the context for US Secretary of State Corder Hull's famous assertion that international law required full – prompt, adequate, and effective – compensation. As part of this discourse, Cárdenas outlined the "Cárdenas Doctrine," which unequivocally denied the right of foreigners to benefit from diplomatic protection. The essence was that:

> Nationality, as a personal status, has full juridical effect only within local jurisdiction. It lacks extraterritoriality, and its effects are therefore suspended in every instance when a moral and physical person moves to foreign soil to develop investments, commercial undertakings, or for pecuniary gain, or for the purpose of establishing oneself in the midst of a hospitable state, which, as a consequence, should afford every facility and guarantees to those who immigrate lawfully to its territory with these intentions, in order that they may acquire the status of nationality on terms of civil equality respecting the rights and obligations of its own citizens.[165]

While clearly encompassing elements of the Calvo Doctrine (strict equality between nationals and foreigners), the Cárdenas Doctrine clearly goes further (eliminating rather than curtailing diplomatic protection). The Cárdenas Doctrine thus represented the realization of the specter of Calvo which had, hitherto, merely existed in the imaginations of North Atlantic critics.[166] At a

---

162 Obregón (n 78) 154; Becker Lorca, "International Law in Latin America or Latin American International Law? Rise, Fall, and Retrieval of a Tradition of Legal Thinking and Political Imagination" (n 80) 294.

163 Grigera Naón (n 37) 140.

164 See, e.g., Lester H Woolsey, "The Expropriation of Oil Properties by Mexico" (1938) 32 *American Journal of International Law* 519.

165 This formulation was drafted by Juan Manuel Alvarez del Castillo, Francisco Arellano Belloc, and Luciano Castillo. As cited by Philip Marshall Brown, 'The "Cardenas Doctrine"' (1940) 34 *American Journal of International Law* 300, 300.

166 See, e.g., James L. Brierly, *The Law of Nations* (2nd edition, Oxford University Press 1938) 181–183.

series of conferences held in the 1940s, Mexican lawyers attacked the institution of diplomatic protection in new ways. Instead of seeking acceptance of a treaty recognizing the Calvo Doctrine, they argued that the developments, charted above, had established the doctrine as positive international law.[167] This new approach was led by Ramón Beteta Quintana, the Mexican representative at the Eighth American Scientific Congress[168] and Alfonso García Robles at the 1944 and 1945 Inter-American Bar Association Conferences. Within the context of this chapter, I want to focus principally on the debates at the Inter-American Bar Association Conferences. Here, proposals to eliminate, or at least severely curtail, diplomatic protection would be offset by the establishment of a universally applicable, international system that would protect the rights of all individuals, irrespective of ties of nationality.

At the Inter-American Bar Conference of 1944, Latin American jurists came extremely close to securing a prestigious endorsement of the Calvo Doctrine. At the conference, García Robles delivered "perhaps the best presentation of the legal arguments for the Latin American viewpoint on diplomatic protection and the Calvo Clause."[169] In his address to the Conference, García Robles frankly stated that "diplomatic protection is an artificial creation constructed in the nineteenth century for expansionist purposes."[170] However, the developments, charted above, meant that claims of diplomatic intervention "have lost in America all legal foundation."[171] Crucially, García Robles argued for the creation of an international system to protect individuals' fundamental rights, irrespective of whether they resided within their state of nationality or elsewhere. García Robles' "brilliant address" had a profound effect on the participants at the Conference, persuading many, including Frederic Coudert, the then president of the American Society of International Law.[172]

The matter was referred to the Committee on Post-War Problems, resulting in the Riesco-Coudert-García Robles draft resolution.[173] The draft resolution argued for the replacement of diplomatic protection with a

---

167 Shea (n 3) 89–90.
168 Ramón Beteta Quintana and Ernesto Henríquez, "La Protección Diplomàtica de los Intereses Pecuniarios Extranjeros en los Estados de América" Paul H Oehser (ed), *Proceedings of the Eighth American Scientific Congress*, vol X (Dept of State 1941) 27 especially 30–34, 40, 47. C.f. Edwin Borchard "Remarks on papers of Dr. Betata and Dr. Cruchaga Ossa," ibid. 69.
169 Shea (n 3) 91.
170 Mimeographed copy of García Robles' Address at the 1944 Inter-American Bar Association Conference, p 28 (as cited by Freeman (n 4) 138.).
171 Ibid. 2.
172 Shea (n 3) 91.
173 Full text of the resolution is cited in ibid 92–93.

new international system to ensure the protection of the "Rights of Man." Diplomatic protection was to be maintained until such time as this system could be established, but limited to "well defined cases of denial of justice, restrictively interpreted." Moreover, the resolution asserted that, given the maturation of republican governance on the continent, all American states had attained a "reasonable standard of civilised justice." As such, "equality of rights with the national is the maximum limit to which a foreigner may aspire." Lastly, American states were urged to sign a convention recognizing the "integral validity" of the Calvo Clause.

Despite its initial popularity, the resolution was deferred for further consideration. At the Fourth Conference of the Inter-American Bar Association, the matter was again referred to the Committee on post-war problems, where the President asserted that while the resolution "would receive nearly the unanimous approval of the members of the association," it was unlikely to secure the "universal acceptance of the governments of the American Republics."[174] Ultimately, the conference concluded that "although legal in form, [the issue] is so mixed with political subjects that no resolution should be adopted."[175]

Outside of the conference, the latest attempts to secure recognition for the Calvo Doctrine were met with strident condemnation. For Freeman, a participant of the Inter-American Bar Association Conferences, the Calvo Doctrine was " 'anachronistic,' 'totalitarian,' and antiliberal, it is the dogma of extreme sovereignty."[176] Moreover:

> So repeatedly have these arguments been rejected by international tribunals, and so overwhelmingly have they been condemned by publicists outside Latin-America – as well as by some Latin-American writers themselves – that their persistent espousal can only be explained in the light of hopeful self-interest.[177]

Freeman was similarly scathing of the universal solution proposed by García Robles: the creation of an international system to ensure the "rights of man."

> To one unfamiliar with the origin, antecedents, and history of this attractively phrased proposal, it might appear as a desirable, albeit revolutionary, doctrine, the aims of which are of the most laudable order. A closer analysis of the three points of the resolution, when read as a whole reveals, however, that its purpose is quite other than what on the surface seems to be a noble effort to elevate the position of the individual in international law.[178]

---

174 Ibid. 94.
175 Resolution No. 48 Cuarta Conferencia, III, p 1604 (translated ibid. 95.)
176 Freeman (n 4) 139.
177 Ibid. 123–124 (footnotes excluded).
178 Ibid. 122.

Despite the clear universalism of García Robles' proposal, mooted to apply to all individuals within all states, for Freeman it is merely a mask.[179] The concept, or perhaps the conceit, of an international system for human rights protection is simply the latest attempt, on the part of Latin American states, to escape from the international rule of law. However, Freeman does not appear unduly troubled by the question of whether the existing system of diplomatic protection was maintained by the "persistent" enforcement, by capital exporting states in light of their own self-interest.

The dynamics of the post-war international order created a volatile climate for international investment. In response, North Atlantic states began to develop a range of instruments, including the modern bilateral investment treaty and a draft multilateral investment treaty. However, mirroring the division between substance and dispute settlement from the earliest Inter-American Conventions, the proposal which gained greatest traction was the World Bank's suggestion to establish an international center for investment arbitration.[180] This process would ultimately lead to the establishment of ICSID in 1966. The World Bank's proposal consciously avoided any discussion of the content of the international rules governing foreign-owned property. Broches, the General Counsel of the World Bank and chief architect of the Convention, deliberately avoided making any reference to the recently adopted General Assembly resolution on Permanent Sovereignty over Natural Resources.[181] Crucially, unlike previous conventions adopted at the World Bank, the drafting of the Washington Convention was, at least superficially, inclusive. "The main voices in its drafting could not be Executive Directors from capital-exporting states, because the proposal's success rested upon the perceptions of capital-importing states."[182] Nevertheless, final authority to amend the text lay solely in the hands of Broches.

---

179 It is ironic that, across the Atlantic, Friedrich von Hayek was developing a similar proposal, but to opposite ends. See, generally, Quinn Slobodian, *Globalists. The End of Empire and the Birth of Neoliberalism* (Harvard University Press 2018).

180 See, generally, Taylor St John, "Enriching Law with Political History: A Case Study on the Creation of the ICSID Convention" in Stephan Schill, Christian Tams, and Rainer Hofmann, *International Investment Law and History* (Edward Elgar Publishing 2018); Parra (n 12).

181 UNGA Res. 1803 (XVII) 14 December 1962. Andreas F. Lowenfeld, "The ICSID Convention: Origins and Transformation" (2009) 38 *Ga. J. Int'l & Comp. L.* 47, 49. Likewise, the US delegates at the Santiago meeting avoided proselytizing about the perceived benefits of the substantive aspects of the "United States doctrine." Ibid. 53.

182 St John (n 180) 316.

The proposal for ICSID was justified in terms that directly addressed the concerns expressed in the Calvo Doctrine. At the heart of the proposal, as presented by Broches, was the elimination of diplomatic protection with respect to investment:

> If the parties had agreed to use the services of the Center for arbitration as the sole means of settling their dispute, the government party should not be permitted to refer the private party to the government's national courts, and the private party should not be permitted to seek the protection of its own government and that government would not be entitled to give such protection.[183]

In exchange for abandoning national jurisdiction, states would be offered the opportunity to eliminate diplomatic interposition. Ultimately, however "modest" the proposals appeared to proponents,[184] they proved too rich for Latin American states to stomach. Speaking on behalf of a group of predominantly Latin American states, Félix Ruiz, the Chilean Governor of the World Bank, emphatically rejected the proposals in terms that echoed Calvo. The text of this rejection is worth quoting at length.

> We consider undesirable the resolution ... which recommends [...] the drafting of an international agreement to create a center for conciliation and arbitration to which foreign private investors could have recourse for the settlement of their disputes with governments of member countries, without necessarily having to exhaust the formalities and procedures of the national tribunals...

> The legal and constitutional systems of all Latin American countries that are members of the Bank offer the foreign investor at the present time the same rights and protection as their own nationals...

> The new system that has been suggested would give the foreign investor, by virtue of the fact that he is a foreigner, the right to sue a sovereign state outside its national territory, dispensing with the courts of law. This provision is contrary to the accepted legal principles of our countries and, de facto, would confer a privilege on the foreign investor, placing the nationals of the country concerned in a position of inferiority.[185]

The Washington Convention would eliminate diplomatic interposition, lifting the burden of uneven and intrusive enforcement of the international minimum standard. However, it further entrenched the differentiation between nationals and foreigners. While the Convention, in and of itself,

---

183 *History of the ICSID Convention (Vol II)* (International Centre for Settlement of Investment Disputes 1968) 80.
184 Lowenfeld (n 181) 54.
185 *History of the ICSID Convention (Vol II)* (n 183) 606.

did not necessarily entail that foreign investors would be subject to different rules, it ensured that, as a minimum, they would enjoy greater procedural protections.

Concluding remarks

The post-war period witnessed a crucial change in the way that anglophone scholars narrated the "great debate" regarding whether and to what extent international law should protect foreign investors. Calvo reappears, more prominent than ever, but he reappears as a historicized figure. As mentioned above, post war jurists sought to expose the contradictions in Calvo's work.[186] What really constituted intervention? Did the Calvo Doctrine merely seek to preclude coercive interventions or diplomatic representations also impermissible? What about the submission of a dispute to international arbitration? Nevertheless, despite this apparent vagueness, post-war commentators were sufficiently able to distil the "correct" interpretation of Calvo to critique contemporaneous heretics. In other words, contemporary Latin Americans were betraying the original intentions of their "patron saint."[187] Calvo was thus cast as the bumbling but, crucially, respectable face of Latin American dissent.[188] The conscious historicization of Calvo also performed an additional function; enabling anglophone commentators to distinguish between the past, where historical injustice could be acknowledged, and the present where fears were misguided. Lastly, this historicization is curiously bounded. In an article lamenting Latin American States' unwillingness to accede to the Washington Convention, Broches conceded that "[t]he history of foreign investment in Latin America has not always been a happy one."[189] This history, in the eyes of Broches, is particular to Latin America. As if no one else had been involved!

This historiography of Calvo, and the evolving ways he was invoked within anglophone debates regarding the protection of foreign investors, undermines the notion that any particular position can ever do anything more than aspire to universality. However, as investment law has developed into a genuinely universal system, eroding the distinctions between capital

---

186 See, for example, Shea (n 3) 17.
187 Freeman (n 4) 132. See also Shea (n 3) 17; Richard B. Lillich, "The Diplomatic Protection of Nationals Abroad: An Elementary Principle of International Law Under Attack" (1975) 69 *American Journal of International Law* 359, 361.
188 C.f. Freeman (n 4) 132 et seq; Rogers (n 72).
189 Aron Broches, "The Convention on the Settlement of Investment Disputes" (1965) 9 *Section of International and Comparative Law Bulletin* 11, 15.

importers and exporters, the ideas at the heart of the Calvo Doctrine are finding new audiences. Calvo's relevance to the successive iterations of the debate regarding the degree of protection foreign investors ought to enjoy has waxed and waned. An innovator worthy of serious consideration in his lifetime, Calvo faded from view amidst the technically of interwar reform. In the post-war, Calvo was restored in anglophone scholarship, no longer an opponent but as means to reproach his wayward successors. Today, Calvo has been elevated to the position of a "Grandfather" of investment law,[190] reflecting a discipline in search of historical prestige and contemporary legitimacy.

190 Schreuer (n 19).

2

Calvo Doctrine and the South American mosaic: Members, dissidents, and an outsider

Magdalena Bas

Introduction

Drawing on theory of international regimes,[1] I argue that the states members of the international investment regime converge around the fundamental principle of investment promotion and protection. That is, the home state ensures protection for the investments of its nationals while host states establish instruments that provide legal certainty to the foreign investor as a way to promote the reception of foreign capital. Although the international investment regime of investor–state dispute settlement emerges as a European–American creation, it expanded globally and its principles and rules are applicable throughout the world, with few exceptions. The fundamental principle is complemented by others that regulate the behavior of the main actors linked to foreign investment, that is, states and investors. Some of the principles deriving therefrom are national treatment; fair and equitable treatment; guarantee and compensation for expropriation; guarantee of free transfer of funds and transfer of capital and profits abroad; and investor–state dispute settlement (ISDS) insofar as states consent to ascribe to investor–state arbitration in international investment agreements or contracts.[2] Therefore, ISDS regime is a regime under international investment regime, characterized by four principles: investors have locus standi

---

1 International regimes are "a set of mutual expectations, rules and regulations, plans, organizational energies and financial commitments, which have been accepted by a group of states." John Ruggie, "International Responses to Technology: Concepts and Trends" (1975) 29 (3) *International Organization* 557 www.jstor.org/stable/2706342. Thus, in international regimes, "actors' expectations converge in a given area of international relations," in this case, protection and promotion of foreign investment. Stephen D. Krasner, "Structural Causes and Regime Consequences: Regimes as Intervening Variables" (1982) 36 *International Organizations* 186.

2 Magdalena Bas, "Régimen De Solución De Controversias Inversor-Estados: ¿Resistencias Del Modelo Relacional En Un Marco Institucional De Las Relaciones Internacionales?" (2018) 27 (54) *Relaciones internacionales* 163.

and ius standi (not states); exhaustion of local remedies is not the rule; ad hoc arbitration (not permanent courts[3]); absence of an appeal mechanism for awards.

Under customary international law, states have the right to regulate foreign investment in their territory, as a direct expression of their sovereignty;[4] consequently, they are also able to decide whether or not to be members of the international investment regime or the ISDS regime.[5] Having the different state behaviors in mind, I developed a typology that organizes states in four groups, considering whether or not they are part of the ISDS regime and the existence or not of changes in their position regarding the regime. The groups are: *members*, i.e., the states that are part of the regime and did not present changes in their position (residual figure); *confronters*, which are the states that, without abandoning the regime, present changes in their original position, especially by the proposal of an alternative or parallel regime or by seeking a complex access to the current one;[6] *outsiders*, namely, states that historically were located outside the regime (for instance, Brazil); and *dissidents* or states that were part of the regime and changed their position upon withdrawing from it.[7]

Historically, South America moved from resistance to accommodation to the international investment regime. However, since the first decade of the twenty-first century the states have grouped into three: members, outsider, and dissidents. There is no example of confronters as the group has emerged in the last five years in other parts of the world (Europe and Asia). With these ideas in mind, this chapter aims to analyze the positions of South

---

3 The International Center for Settlement of Investor–State Disputes (ICSID) or the Permanent Court of Arbitration are not permanent tribunals, they manage ad hoc tribunals.

4 Rudolf Dolzer and Christoph Scheuer, *Principles of International Investment Law* (Oxford University Press 2012).

5 Magdalena Bas, *América Del Sur Ante Los Tratados Bilaterales De Inversión: ¿Hacia Un Retorno Del Estado En La Solución De Controversias?* (Universidad de la República, Comisión Sectorial de Investigación Científica 2017).

6 For instance, Bilateral Investment Treaty Between The Government of The Republic Of India and [...] (adopted 28 December 2015) (*India Model BIT (2015)* and the Agreement for the termination of Bilateral Investment Treaties between the Member States of the European Union SN/4656/2019/INIT 169 *OJL* 1 29.5.2020 pp. 1–41.

7 Examples are Bolivia, Ecuador (2009–2021), and Venezuela, and closer to the outsider ones but with dissident characteristics is South Africa that did not signed or adhered to the International Center for Settlement of Investment Disputes (ICSID) Convention. See Magdalena Bas, "Acuerdo Mercosur-Unión Europea: Sombras y Ausencia De La Solución De Controversias Inversor-Estado" (2019) 21 *(Segunda época) Documentos De Trabajo (Fundación Carolina)* 1.

American states regarding ISDS regime, their basis and the reasons that led to its manifestation in the present.

From the Calvo doctrine to the South American mosaic

Until the 1980s, South America presented a uniform position against international investor–state arbitration, a position based on its identification with the Calvo doctrine, and which generated an obvious differentiation from the rest of the states or groups of states across the globe. The aforementioned doctrine, elaborated in 1868 by the Argentine jurist Carlos Calvo and later incorporated into several South American constitutions, was based on the principles of sovereign equality, non-intervention and equal treatment between foreigners and nationals.[8] States, as sovereigns, had the right to freely determine their internal and external policies, without foreign interference, and given that foreigners had equal rights to nationals; foreigners had to exhaust all the resources of domestic jurisdiction before requesting the diplomatic protection of the state of their nationality in order to enforce the international responsibility of the other state.[9]

Diplomatic protection establishes that the state of the nationality of the affected individual, and not the individual, is the one who makes the claim against the non-compliant state.[10] Currently, unlike what happened during the development and consolidation of the Calvo doctrine, the majority of the scholars, as well as the Draft articles on diplomatic protection (United Nations International Law Commission),[11] condition the exercise of diplomatic protection to the affected individual having a nationality link with the complaining state, as well as to the exhaustion of domestic remedies.[12]

---

8 Francesco Tamburini, "Historia y Destino De La Doctrina Calvo: ¿Actualidad u Obsolescencia Del Pensamiento De Carlos Calvo?" (2002) 24 *Revista de estudios histórico-jurídicos* 81.

9 Francesco Tamburini, "Historia y Destino De La Doctrina Calvo: ¿Actualidad u Obsolescencia Del Pensamiento De Carlos Calvo?" (2002) 24 *Revista de estudios histórico-jurídicos* 81.

10 Helena Torroja Mateu, "Protección Diplomática" Victor M Sánchez (ed), *Derecho Internacional Público* (Huygens Editorial 2010) 317.

11 ILC, Draft Articles on Diplomatic Protection adopted by the Drafting Committee on second reading in 2006, UN Doc A/CN.4/L.684, UN Doc A/61/10, 16, GAOR 61st Session Supp 10.

12 There are dissenting views despite the fact that the Draft Articles of Diplomatic Protection confirm that nationality is the only link. Helena Torroja Mateu, "Protección Diplomática" Victor M. Sánchez (ed), *Derecho Internacional Público* (Huygens Editorial 2010) 322.

With regard to the protection of foreign investments, this limitation implies the exhaustion of domestic jurisdiction as a condition for the foreign investor to initiate arbitration against the host state. A more restricted version of the Calvo doctrine, included in different contracts between foreign investors and South American states, is the so-called "Calvo clause." This provision determines that the investor is not entitled to resort to the diplomatic protection of the home state, whether implemented or not through peaceful means of international dispute resolution.[13] It should be noted that at the time Calvo articulated his theory, the prohibition of the use or threat of force in relations between states did not constitute a principle of public international law.

At the multilateral level South American uniqueness acquires special value against the draft of ICSID Convention that established ad hoc international arbitration as a mechanism for the resolution of investor–state disputes prepared by the World Bank.[14] The purpose was the constitution of an institution that facilitated a platform and a framework for arbitrations under a series of parameters, that is, disputes between a national investor of a state signatory of the aforementioned agreement and a state also signatory, directly related to an investment, as long as it consents to jurisdiction in writing. The one who initiated the arbitration was necessarily the foreign investor whose protections allegedly had been breached by the host state, which was obliged to provide them, and not vice versa. Nothing is established with respect to the obligation to exhaust domestic jurisdiction.

At the annual meeting of the Board of Governors of the World Bank on 9 September 1964 in the city of Tokyo, moved by the legal tradition around the Calvo doctrine and therefore in protection of constitutional premises, nineteen South American states,[15] together with Iraq and the Philippines voted against the preliminary draft of the ICSID Convention.[16] In the speech made by the representative of Chile on the Board of Governors, the main points of the above are summarized in the well-known "El No de Tokyo,"[17] in particular the fact that

---

13 Rodrigo Polanco, "Lecciones Aprendidas y Lecciones Por Aprender: ¿Qué Pueden Aprender Los Países Desarrollados De La Experiencia De Latinoamérica En Disputas Sobre Inversión Extranjera?" (2014) 20th Seminar in Latin America on Constitutional and Political Theory (SELA – Seminario en Latinoamérica de Teoría Constitucional y Política), Yale University Lima.

14 Convention on the Settlement of Investment Disputes Between States and Nationals of Other States (signed 18 March 1965, entered into force 14 October 1966) 575 UNTS 159, 4 ILM 532.

15 Argentina, Bolivia, Brazil, Chile, Colombia, Costa Rica, Dominican Republic, Ecuador, El Salvador, Guatemala, Haiti, Honduras, Mexico, Nicaragua, Panama, Paraguay, Peru, Uruguay, and Venezuela.

16 Christoph H. Schreuer, *The ICSID Convention: A Commentary* (2nd edition, Cambridge University Press 2009). See Chapter 1 by Philip Burton in this volume.

17 See Chapter 1 by Philip Burton in this volume.

the new system that has been suggested would give the foreign investor, only by virtue of the fact that he is a foreigner, the right to sue a sovereign state outside its national territory, regardless of its courts of justice. This provision is contrary to the accepted legal principles of our countries and, in fact, would grant a privilege to the foreign investor, placing the nationals of the country in question in a position of inferiority.[18]

Even without the support of the South American states, the Convention establishing the ICSID was approved and entered into force in 1966. With the Washington consensus, "El No de Tokyo" began to be reversed in most of the South American states. As of October 2019, there are seven South American states that are part of the ICSID Convention (see Table 2.1), also Philippines, Iraq, and Mexico. The exception is still Brazil, which has never acceded to the agreement and the Dominican Republic, which acceded to it in 2000 but failed to ratify it. Additionally, the agreement has been withdrawn by Bolivia, Venezuela and Ecuador, but the latter ratified the ICSID Convention again in August 2021.

The Washington consensus is a package of macroeconomic measures promoted by the International Monetary Fund, the World Bank, and the United States Department of the Treasury, all institutions based in the city of Washington, hence its denomination.[19] Therefore, the proposed package created the favorable climate for the neoliberal governments of the 1990s to begin the practice of signing BITs and their adherence to the ICSID Convention.[20] BITs are presented as instruments capable of counteracting political or non-commercial risks, especially in developing countries, avoiding any change in national legislation that is likely to affect such investments,

18 Original quotation: *"El nuevo sistema que se ha sugerido daría al inversionista extranjero, sólo en virtud del hecho de que es un extranjero, el derecho a demandar a un Estado soberano fuera de su territorio nacional, prescindiendo de sus tribunales de justicia. Esta disposición es contraria a los principios jurídicos aceptados de nuestros países y, de hecho, otorgaría un privilegio al inversionista extranjero, colocando a los nacionales del país de que se trate en una posición de inferioridad."* Cited in Rodrigo Polanco, "Lecciones Aprendidas y Lecciones Por Aprender: ¿Qué Pueden Aprender Los Países Desarrollados De La Experiencia De Latinoamérica En Disputas Sobre Inversión Extranjera?" (2014) 20th Seminar in Latin America on Constitutional and Political Theory (SELA – Seminario en Latinoamérica de Teoría Constitucional y Política), Yale University Lima.

19 The ten points of the agenda are: 1) Fiscal discipline; 2) Reorganization of public spending priorities; 3) Tax reform; 4) Financial liberalization; 5) Competitive exchange rate; 6) Trade liberalization; 7) Liberalization of foreign direct investment; 8) Privatizations; 9) Deregulation; and 10) Property rights insured. Rubi Martínez Rangel and Ernesto S. Reyes Garmendia, "El Consenso De Washington: La Instauración De Las Políticas Neoliberales En América Latina" (2012) 37 *Política y cultura* 35.

20 See Chapter 9 by Sufyan Droubi, Cecilia Juliana Flores Elizondo, and Raphael Heffron in this volume.

Table 2.1 Status of ratifications of the Washington Convention by South American state

State	Access	Deposit	Enter into force	Observations
Argentina	21 May 1991	19 October 1994	18 November 1994	–
Bolivia	3 May 1991	23 June 1995	23 July 1995	Terminated by unilateral withdrawal notified on 1 May 2007
Brazil	–	–	–	–
Chile	25 January 1991	24 September 1991	24 October 1991	–
Colombia	18 May 1993	15 July 1997	14 August 1997	–
Ecuador	15 January 1986	15 January 1986	14 February 1986	Terminated by unilateral withdrawal notified on 2 July 2009, (re)signed on 21 June 2021 (ratified 04 August 2021)
Guyana	3 July 1969	11 July 1969	10 August 1969	–
Paraguay	27 July 1981	7 January 1983	6 February 1983	–
Peru	4 September 1991	9 August 1993	8 September 1993	–
Suriname	–	–	–	–
Uruguay	28 May 1992	9 August 2000	8 September 2000	–
Venezuela	18 August 1993	2 May 1995	1 June 1995	Terminated by unilateral withdrawal notified on 24 January 2012

Source: Prepared by the author based on ICSID data. Date of consultation: 28 October 2021.

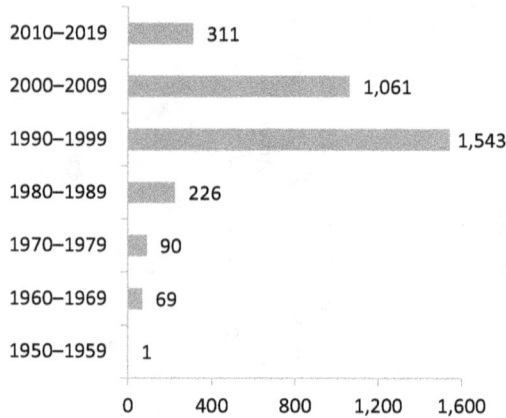

Figure 2.1 Number of BITs signed by decade

and generating a climate of political security for the investor.[21] Also, the failed attempt to conclude the Multilateral Investment Agreement promoted by the Organization for Cooperation and Development in 1995,[22] a treaty that sought to link even non-member states of the organization, led to the signing of a greater number of BITs (see Figure 2.1).

Although the last draft of the Multilateral Investment Agreement[23] has the structure of the investment treaties signed in the 1990s, especially of the North American Free Trade Agreement, it had a strong resistance. Three

---

21 Déborah B. de Azevedo, "Os Acordos Para a Promoção e a Proteção Recíproca De Investimentos Assinados Pelo Brasil" (2001) Câmara dos Deputados, Brasil https://bd.camara.leg.br/bd/handle/bdcamara/2542 accessed 17 April 2021.

22 OECD. "The Multilateral Agreement on Investment Draft Consolidated Text" DAFFE/MAI(98)7/REV1, 22 April 1998 www1.oecd.org/daf/mai/pdf/ng/ng987r1e.pdf accessed 2 March 2021.

23 Its provisions were grouped into the following points: 1) General provisions; 2) Scope of application, including a broad definition of investment; 3) Treatment of investors and investments, including the most favored nation treatment, national treatment, transparency, no reduction of the minimum standard in labor or environmental matters, etc.; 4) Protection of investments – that is, guarantees and compensation for expropriation, guarantees of free transfer of funds and transfer of capital and profits abroad, and protection of existing investments; 5) State–state and investor–state dispute settlement (domestic jurisdiction or international arbitration under the ICSID Arbitration Rules, the Additional ICSID Mechanism, the UNCITRAL Arbitration Rules, or the ICC Arbitration Rules.); 6) Exceptions and safeguards; 7) Specific provisions for financial services; 8) Specific tax provisions; 9) Exceptions by state; 10) Relationship with other international treaties, citing only the International Monetary Fund Agreement and the OECD Guidelines on multinational companies, although the latter is not an international treaty; 11) Implementation and operation; and, 12) Final provisions.

were the most controversial issues: the compatibility of the agreement with the previous regional integration treaties; the ambiguity of social, labor, and environmental aspects and the wide scope for interpretation when claiming their protection; and, the situation of the cultural sector which was treated as an industry and did not contemplate the protection of cultural and linguistic diversity.[24] The resistance came both from developing states and some European States, particularly pointing out the concern of the threat to sovereignty.

Faced with the failure of the Multilateral Investment Agreement, the boom in bilateral agreements was strengthened. As Fontoura Costa points out,[25] the 1990s coincides with the largest number of BITs entered into by states traditionally in favor of the Calvo doctrine. Of the 203 BITs held in the South American states as of 31 December 2018, whether they are in force or not, 155 were signed in the 1990s. Argentina stands out, with 55 BITs entered into in that decade and only 6 in other periods (see Figure 2.2).

The first decade of the twenty-first century and the following years have been characterized by a significant increase in the number of investment claims against the South American states, many of them claiming substantial compensation. As an example, in *Occidental v. Ecuador*,[26] the compensation reached almost 1800 million dollars. Particularly, those claims that question new domestic legislation regarding sensitive sectors such as oil, gas, and mining, electricity and other sources of energy, water and sanitation services, finance, debt instruments, among others, stand out. These sectors involve issues that are not exclusively in the economic field, but that overflow into other areas of law, such as human rights (access to water, public health, environment, etc.).[27]

It is in this context that the South American states broke their traditional monolithic position against the ISDS regime. Thus, drawing on the theory of international regimes, I argue that the continent is divided into three groups: members of the regime, dissidents and the outsider. In the case of members, their expectations converge on the protection of investments, which implies the existence of dispute resolution mechanisms, usually ad

24 Maria Rosa Borrás, "El Trasfondo Del Acuerdo Multilateral De Inversiones (AMI): Un Proyecto Político De Graves Consecuencias Antidemocráticas" (1998) 72 *Mientras tanto* 26.

25 José Augusto Fontoura Costa, *Direito Internacional Do Investimento Estrangeiro* (Jurúa Editorial 2010).

26 *Occidental Petroleum Corporation and Occidental Exploration and Production Company v. Republic of Ecuador (II)*, ICSID Case No. ARB/06/11 (Award, 5 October 2012).

27 See Chapters 9 by Sufyan Droubi, Cecilia Juliana Flores Elizondo, and Raphael Heffron, and 12 by Javier Echaide in this volume.

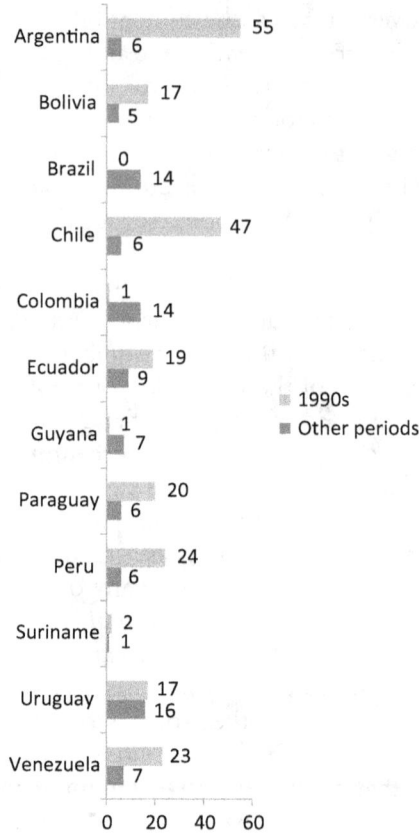

Figure 2.2 Number of BITs celebrated by South American states in the 1990s compared to other periods

hoc arbitration. To be members to the system, states sign BITs and, usually, the ICSID Convention, as ICSID arbitration is the most used dispute resolution mechanism. Examples of this category of states are Argentina, Chile, Colombia, Paraguay, Peru, and Uruguay. In relation to the following group of states, the outsiders are those who understand that the benefits received once incorporated into the regime, are not greater or equal to those received before their incorporation and choose to remain outside. Therefore, they do not sign the ICSID Convention or BITs. This group is formed by a single state: Brazil. Finally, the dissidents are those states that at one time were members of the regime but decided to cease to be, withdrawing the BITs in force and from the ICSID Convention. The withdrawal process is motivated by the perception that the costs of remaining in the regime are greater than those of being outside the regime. This is the case in Bolivia, Ecuador (2009–2021), and Venezuela.

Members: the special situation of Argentina

Among the members, Argentina's position regarding the investor–state dispute resolution regime deserves a particular analysis since it is the most sued state in South America and the world, with 61 known disputes against it as of 31 December 2018.[28] Likewise, Argentina is the state with the highest number of BITs in force in South America: 50 of the 61 agreements signed. Argentina's experience in the investor–state dispute resolution regime undergoes three stages, namely, adherence to the Washington consensus (1990–2002); abandonment of the practice of signing new BITs but maintaining membership in the ICSID and renewing the BITs in force (2003–2015); and return to the signature of BITs (2016–2019).

The first stage coincides with the two presidential periods of Carlos Menem (1989–1999) during which Argentina signed 53 BITs. This practice is motivated by the privatization process, especially of public services, the ideological belief in the advantages of greater openness of the economy, the international trend towards the signing of BITs driven by the Washington consensus, and the need for legal instruments that provide greater legal certainty to foreign investors.[29] It is for this last point that 41 of the BITs that were held in this period do not require the exhaustion of domestic remedies, marking a clear break from the traditional Calvo doctrine.

The economic crisis of December 2001 and the measures taken to mitigate its negative consequences marked the breaking point of the stage of adherence to the Washington consensus. The Public Emergency and Exchange Regime Reform Act[30] introduced a series of measures intended to convert into pesos the prices and tariffs in public contracts, at a parity of one peso, one dollar. These measures derived in 37 claims against Argentina. These claims were lodged by privatized public services companies regarding fair and equitable treatment, less favorable treatment than that granted to

---

28 UNCTAD, *Investment Policy Hub*. https://investmentpolicy.unctad.org/ accessed 21 de abril de 2019.

29 Ricardo Beltramino, "Promoción De Inversiones En Los Acuerdos De Inversiones Firmados Por Argentina" (2010) *Documento de trabajo* Nro 49 http://rrii.flacso.org. ar/wp-content/uploads/2010/06/FLA_Doc49.pdf

30 Argentina, *Public Emergency and Exchange Regime Reform Act* (2002). Ley de Emergencia Publica y de Reforma del Régimen Cambiario de 6 enero de 2002. Boletín Oficial, 7 de enero de 2002.

national investors and indirect expropriation in relation to the provision of public services such as gas and water and sanitation.[31]

The second stage, which covers the years 2003 to 2015 (governments of Néstor Kirchner and Cristina Fernández), exposes a structural change in the country, leaving the tendency to negotiate and ratify new BITs. Only the treaty with Panama was modified in 2004 and the treaty with Senegal came into force in 2010 with the ratification of the African nation.[32] However, all the BITs were renewed and Argentina remained a member of the ICSID. It is not a stage of break, but of maintaining the status quo without deepening it, in other words, following the theory of international regimes, Argentina remains as a member of the investor–state dispute resolution regime but with conditions.

Notwithstanding the foregoing, during the period 2003–2015, various projects were presented in the Lower House (*Camara de Diputados*) proposing the withdrawal from the regime, either through the denunciation of the ICSID Washington Convention or the BITs in force, or the declaration of absolute nullity of the mentioned rules. The first group of projects presented to the Lower House was based on the characteristics of the clauses usually included in BITs, especially the stability clause, the umbrella clause and the MFN treatment, and the waiver of sovereignty relative to the territorial jurisdiction of the national courts, in favor of the ICSID or other international arbitral tribunals. The second group of projects started from a different base; they considered that the BITs were absolutely null as they collided with the constitutional provisions that provide for the jurisdiction of the local courts in all matters provided for in the Argentine Constitution (1994), such as borrowing on credit of the Nation and arranging the payment of the internal and external debt of the Nation,[33] since they are treated with supra-legal but infra-constitutional status.[34]

---

31 For instance: *Azurix Corp. v. Argentine Republic (I)*, ICSID Case No. ARB/01/12 (Award, 14 July 2006); CMS *Gas Transmission Company v. The Argentine Republic*, ICSID Case No. ARB/01/8 (Award, 12 May 2005); *Urbaser S.A. and Consorcio de Aguas Bilbao Biskaia, Bilbao Biskaia Ur Partzuergoa v. Argentine Republic*, ICSID Case No. ARB/07/26 (Award, 8 December 2016).

32 Agreement between the Argentine Republic and the Republic of Panama for the Reciprocal Promotion and Protection of Investments (signed 10 May 1996, entered into force 22 June 1998); Agreement between the Argentine Republic and the Republic of Senegal for the Promotion and Protection of Investment (signed 6 April 1993, entered into force 1 February 2010).

33 Argentina Constitution 1853 (reinst. 1983, rev. 1994) articles 75.4, 75.7, 116 and 117.

34 Liliana Costante, "Soberanía Nacional vs. CIADI: ¿Estados o Mercados?" (2012) 1 (2) *Revista de Derecho Público* 59.

Finally, the trilogy closes with the government of Mauricio Macri that in 2016 resumed the practice of signing BITs.[35] The signing of a fewer number of BITs than in the menemist stage has a pragmatic explanation: Argentina already had agreements in force with the main economies of the world.

The dissidents: the case of Ecuador

Ecuador followed the path initiated in 2007 by Bolivia, and between 2008 and 2009 embarked on a process of termination of the BITs in force and withdrawal from the ICSID. In January 2008, Ecuador notified the termination of nine of the 26 BITs in force, those under which no reciprocal investments had been recorded. These are the agreements concluded with Cuba, El Salvador, Guatemala, Honduras, Nicaragua, Paraguay, Dominican Republic, Romania, and Uruguay.[36] Likewise, the ICSID withdrawal was formalized on 2 July 2009.

The context in which the process of recovery of autonomy begins has legal roots, especially in relation to the constitutional reform of 2008. The new Constitution enshrined rights of nature for the first time and established the jurisdiction of South American regional organizations for disputes involving the state.[37] According to Cervantes,[38] this is a relative isolation clause, because unlike Bolivia – whose Constitution provides an exception to the general rule – treaties that include dispute resolution between states and citizens in South America have to be resolved in regional arbitration instances or by jurisdictional designation bodies of the signatory countries.

The high compensation amounts claimed by foreign investors around the oil sector consolidated the perfect breeding ground for decision-making in this matter. Among others, the *Chevron v. Ecuador* (Chevron II) case stands out with a request for the Tribunal inter alia to hold Ecuador (or Petroecuador) exclusively liable for the judgment in the Lago Agrio Litigation before the Ecuadorian courts, which judgment held *Chevron*

---

35 Agreement for the Reciprocal Promotion and Protection of Investments between the Argentine Republic and the State of Qatar (signed 6 November 2016); Agreement for the Reciprocal Promotion and Protection of Investments between the Argentine Republic and the United Arab Emirates (signed 14 April 2018); Agreement between the Argentine Republic and Japan for the Promotion and Protection of Investment (signed 1 December 2018).

36 Gustavo Guerra Bello, "Las Disposiciones Legales Que Desarrollan Los Preceptos Constituciones Sobre La Inversión Privada Extranjera En El Ecuador" (2012) 17 *Foro, Revista de Derecho* 31.

37 Ecuador Constitution 2008 (rev. 2015) article 422.

38 Andrés Cervantes Valarezo, "Nuevo Constitucionalismo Latinoamericano y Arbitraje De Inversión" (2017) 30 *Spain Arbitration Review: revista del Club Español del Arbitraje* 81.

liable for damages amount $9,500 million.[39] This is one of the most emblematic cases of the investor–state dispute resolution regime, not just because of the collision between investment protection and environmental protection regulations, but also because of the environmental (pollution in rivers and soils) and human costs (communities that were affected in social and cultural terms: displacement, impact on their customs and productive activities). However, Chevron II is not an isolated case, but is part of a series of domestic and international jurisdictional processes that took place in the United States, Ecuador, and the Permanent Court of Arbitration, due to the responsibility for contamination in an area of approximately 20,000 km sq in Lake Agrio region (Napo, eastern Ecuador) for oil exploration and production (1964–1992) and the consequent environmental remediation program developed by a business consortium of which Texaco was part and in charge of its operation until 1990.

Ecuador complemented the process initiated with the enactment of the 2008 Constitution with changes to its domestic structures in order to solidify its position towards the recovery of autonomy. In accordance with the Constitution, and based on neo-constitutionalist foundations, in order to withdraw BITs Ecuador must follow the following stages: Office of the Presidency to the Constitutional Court requesting that it pronounce on the complaint; Opinion of the Constitutional Court; Office of the Presidency to the National Assembly requesting the complaint based on the opinion of the Constitutional Court; Report of the Permanent Specialised Commission on Sovereignty, Integration, International Relations and Integral Security of the National Assembly; Resolution of the Plenary of the National Assembly based on the report of the specialized Commission; and Written notification to the other party in the BIT. The first agreement to complete the procedure was the Ecuador–Finland BIT.[40]

Finally, the changes to domestic structures were completed with the creation of the Citizens' Commission for a Comprehensive Audit of Investment Protection Treaties and of the International Arbitration System on Investments (CAITISA).[41] It comprised four experts or researchers in

39 *Chevron Corporation and Texaco Petroleum Company v. The Republic of Ecuador (II)*, PCA Case No. 2009–23 (Claimant's Notice of Arbitration, 23 September 2009).
40 Agreement between the Government of the Republic of Finland and the Government of the Republic of Ecuador on the promotion and protection of investments (signed 18 April 2001, entered into force 16 December 2001; see Chapter 6 by René Ureña and María Angélica Prada-Uribe in this volume (in relation to transformative constitutionalism in Latin America).
41 Decreto Ejecutivo 1506 de 06 de mayo de 2013, crea la Comisión para la Auditoría Integral Ciudadana de los Tratados de Protección Recíproca de Inversiones y del Sistema de Arbitraje Internacional en Materia de Inversiones CAITISA. Registro Oficial No 958, martes 21 de mayo de 2013.

matters of investments and International Law linked to civil society organizations, and four representatives of Ecuador. CAITISA has competence to study the BITs and other international agreements in force, rules of international investment arbitration and disputes against Ecuador, among others.

President Rafael Correa received the final report on 8 May 2017, a few days before the end of his term (24 May 2017). It established that the BITs concluded by Ecuador contained provisions incompatible with the current Constitution as well as other norms of domestic law. In particular, the agreements contained provisions regarding the submission of the state to international arbitration jurisdiction; the differential treatment between foreign and domestic investors, giving them the possibility to access to international arbitration; and the indirect expropriation clauses that go against the right of expropriation and nationalization. The report also identified that the payments made by Ecuador for negative awards and expenses of lawyers and administrative arbitrations reached $1,498 million, equivalent to 5.6 percent of the general budget of the state for the year 2017.[42]

Therefore, the CAITISA recommended the withdrawal of BITs in force and the negotiation of new contracts with foreign investors. Additionally, it proposed an alternative model of investment treaty that establishes the right to regulate the state; excludes or reconsiders the privileges granted so far to foreign investors (national treatment, fair and equitable treatment, indirect expropriation, etc.); and establishes as obligatory the domestic jurisdiction for the resolution of disputes, within the main points to highlight.[43] In light of the above, on 3 May 2017 the Plenary of the National Assembly approved the denunciation of the twelve BITs that had not reached that stage (BITs with Argentina, Bolivia, Canada, Chile, China, Spain, United States, Italy, Netherlands, Peru, Switzerland, and Venezuela) (see Table 2.2).

Thus, the path seemed solidly marked towards the exclusion of the investor–state dispute resolution regime; even the new bilateral investment agreement model developed by the Foreign Ministry is presented with the aim of renegotiating the agreements denounced from a strategy that gives priority to the national interest. However, a few months later, attempts were made to reverse the path travelled, with most of these

---

42 CAITISA. "Informe Ejecutivo. Auditoría Integral Ciudadana De Los Tratados De Protección Recíproca De Inversiones y Del Sistema De Arbitraje En Materia De Inversiones En Ecuador" (2017) 94–95 http://caitisa.org/index.php/home/enlaces-de-interes accessed 2 March 2021.

43 CAITISA. "Informe Ejecutivo. Auditoría Integral Ciudadana De Los Tratados De Protección Recíproca De Inversiones y Del Sistema De Arbitraje En Materia De Inversiones En Ecuador" (2017) 99–105 http://caitisa.org/index.php/home/enlaces-de-interes accessed 2 March 2021.

attempts taking place on 28 June 2018, when the National Assembly sent a question to the Constitutional Court of Ecuador as to whether Article 422 of the Constitution also included the resolution of disputes within a BIT, since the regulation could be interpreted as referring only to commercial treaties and not investment.

Additionally, on 7 August 2018, the National Assembly of Ecuador approved the new Organic Acts for productive development, investment attraction, job creation, and fiscal stability and balance. Article 37 modifies the Organic Code of Production, Commerce and Investments, by establishing the obligation to agree on national or international arbitration for the resolution of disputes within the framework of investment contracts. If the contracts exceed $10,000 million, the dispute must be resolved in accordance with the UNCITRAL Rules in the Permanent Court of Arbitration, the International Chamber of Commerce (ICC) Rules, or the Interamerican Commercial Arbitration Commission, among others. The law incorporates the text of President Moreno's partial veto regarding international investment arbitration.[44] During the Lasso Administration, on 4 August 2021, Ecuador deposited its instrument of ratification of the ICSID Convention, entering into force 30 days after. With this step, Ecuador returned to be a member of the regime.

The outsider: the Brazilian state policy

Brazil is a paradigmatic state in South America since historically it has behaved as an outsider to the international investment protection regime in general, and the investor–state dispute resolution regime. Even when a new model of bilateral agreement, Cooperation and Facilitation Investment Agreements (CFIA), has been drafted in recent years, it excludes the questioned investor–state arbitration. Likewise, it should be noted that it has marked its regional leadership by transmitting the imprint of the CFIA model to relations between Mercosur members with the conclusion of the intra-Mercosur Investment Cooperation and Facilitation Protocol (7 April 2017).[45]

---

44 President of the Republic of Ecuador, Official Communication T.315-SCJ-l8–0543 (18 July 2018) www.asambleanacional.gob.ec/sites/default/files/private/asamblea-nacional/filesasambleanacionalnameuid-29/Leyes%202013–2017/563-fomento/op-fomento-productivo-17–07–2018.pdf accessed 2 March 2021.

45 See Chapters 3 by Henrique Choer Moraes and Facundo Pérez Aznar, and 4 by Leonardo V P de Oliveira and Marcus Spangenberger in this volume.

Table 2.2 BITs terminated by unilateral withdrawal of Ecuador

No.	Part	Signature	Enter into force	Termination	Sunset clause
1	Argentina	18/02/1994	01/12/1995	18/05/2018	15 years
2	Bolivia	25/05/1995	15/08/1997	19/05/2018	10 years
3	Canada	29/04/1996	06/06/1997	19/05/2018	15 years
4	Chile	23/10/1993	21/02/1996	19/05/2018	10 years
5	China	21/03/1994	01/07/1997	19/05/2018	10 years
6	Cuba	25/05/1995	15/08/1997	18/01/2008	10 years
7	Dominican Republic	26/06/1998	21/06/1999	18/01/2008	5 years
8	El Salvador	16/05/1994	14/01/1996	18/01/2008	10 years
9	Finland	18/04/2001	16/12/2001	09/12/2010	10 years
10	France	07/09/1994	10/06/1996	18/05/2018	15 years
11	Germany	21/03/1996	12/02/1999	18/05/2018	15 years
12	Guatemala	14/08/2002	25/05/2005	18/01/2008	10 years
13	Honduras	26/06/2000	11/04/2005	18/01/2008	10 years
14	Nicaragua	02/06/2000	21/05/2001	18/01/2008	10 years
15	Paraguay	28/01/1994	18/09/1995	18/01/2008	10 years
16	Peru	07/04/1999	09/12/1999	19/11/2017	10 years
17	Rumania	21/03/1996	18/07/1997	18/01/2008	10 years
18	Sweden	31/05/2001	01/03/2002	18/05/2018	15 years
19	Switzerland	02/05/1968	09/11/1969	11/09/2018	10 years
20	United Kingdom	10/05/1994	24/08/1995	18/05/2018	15 years
21	United States	27/08/1993	11/05/1997	18/05/2018	10 years
22	Uruguay	31/07/1985	31/07/1985	18/01/2008	No sunset clause
23	Venezuela	18/11/1993	01/02/1995	19/05/2018	10 years

Source: Prepared by the author based on data from UNCTAD Investment Policy Hub (21 April 2019).

Initially, Brazil was also part of the South American process of the 1990s, aimed at the signing of BITs within the framework of the Washington consensus. In this regard, in addition to adhering to the Convention establishing the Multilateral Investment Guarantee Agency (Seoul, 1985) in 1994, it signed 14 agreements with: Belgium and Luxembourg; Chile; Cuba; Denmark; Finland; France; Germany; Italy; Netherlands; Portugal; Republic of Korea; Switzerland; United Kingdom, and Venezuela. After the first six agreements were sent by the Executive Power to Congress for approval,[46] in March 2002 an Interministerial Working Group was created to analyze their compatibility with the domestic legal system. The Group determined that it was convenient to withdraw the agreements from the legislative discussion, which happened in December 2002.[47]

De Azevedo stresses that the inconveniences for the approval of BITs by the Congress was related to autonomy.[48] The author emphasizes that the aforementioned treaties commit the state for very long periods, create risks in the balance of payments for consecrating the free transfer of capital, in addition to presenting constitutional problems when establishing a jurisdiction different from the domestic one for the resolution of disputes between investors and the state. Furthermore, these treaties provide privileges to foreign investors to the detriment of the national by giving them the right to initiate an international arbitration against the state.

Framed in a flow of investments that had stopped being unidirectional to become bidirectional, and a foreign policy of strong south–south relationships,[49] in 2015 Brazil consolidated its autonomous position by presenting an alternative legal instrument to BITs. After a twelve-year process of negotiation, the directorate of the Ministry of Foreign Trade of the Ministry of Development, Industry and Commerce presented the new investment treaty model: the CFIA. The new model treaty is part of the global trend, especially in the field of international trade and, as Ghiotto

---

46 In 1996, BITs with Switzerland, Portugal, Chile, and the United Kingdom; and in 2000, with France and Germany

47 Esteban Actis, "Brasil y La Promoción De Tratados Bilaterales De Inversión: El Fin De La Disyuntiva" (2014) 6 (1) *Escuela de Asuntos Interncionales, Latin American Journal of International Affairs* 18.

48 Déborah B. de Azevedo, "Os Acordos Para a Promoção e a Proteção Recíproca De Investimentos Assinados Pelo Brasil" (2001) Câmara dos Deputados, Brasil.

49 Michelle Ratton Sanchez Badin and Fabio Morosini, "Navigating between Resistance and Conformity with the International Investment Regime," Fabio Morosini and Michelle Ratton Sanchez Badin (ed), *Reconceptualizing International Investment Law from the global south* (Cambridge University Press 2017).

explains, the new model is related to "the simplification of administrative procedures and, especially, [to the simplification] of regulatory processes for foreign investors and economic operators, in order to ease the regulatory burden."[50]

With regard to dispute resolution, a decisive aspect for the non-approval of the previous BITs by the Brazilian Congress, the new treaty model is innovative by excluding investor–state dispute resolution mechanisms, incorporating a system of prevention of state–state disputes based on an institutional governance: 1) Focal Points or Ombudsman in each state for the prevention of disputes and facilitation of its resolution; 2) a Joint Committee, composed of government representatives of both states, which is responsible for assessing the dispute through consultations and negotiations between the parties, as a prerequisite for the start of the state–state arbitration. Each agreement presents particularities in relation to the mechanisms or institutions for interstate arbitration.

In short, the CFIAs solve part of the problems that traditionally concern the BITs, that is, they mitigate the risks and eventual controversies with the presence of the Ombudsman; and eliminate the typical draconian clauses that give foreign investors greater advantages over national ones by giving them the unilateral possibility of presenting actions before international arbitral tribunals.[51] Domestic jurisdiction, in accordance with the constitutional provisions, remains the existing option for the resolution of disputes initiated by foreign investors, confirming that the defense of state autonomy is a key part of Brazilian foreign investment policy. In the region, the Intra-Mercosur Cooperation and Facilitation Investment Protocol[52] follows Brazil's CFIA model and introduced the idea of investment cooperation and facilitation as an alternative to the classic investment promotion and protection in BITs or

---

50 Original quotation: *"la simplificación de los trámites administrativos y, especialmente de los procesos regulatorios para los inversores extranjeros y operadores económicos, con el fin de alivianar la carga regulatoria"* Luciana Ghiotto, "Una Revisión Crítica Del Debate Sobre Facilitación De Inversiones" [2018] 9 *Investment Treaty News* 4 www.iisd.org/itn/es/2018/10/17/a-critical-review-of-debate-investment-facilitation-luciana-ghiotto/. See also Chapter 5 by Luciana Ghiotto in this volume.

51 Esteban Actis, "Brasil frente al orden internacional liberal (2011–2013): los límites de la posición reformista a la luz del régimen internacional de inversiones" (2015) 6 (1) *Mural Internacional* 22.

52 Intra-MERCOSUR Cooperation and Facilitation Investment Protocol (signed 7 April 2017, entered in force 30 July 2019) (*Intra-MERCOSUR Investment Facilitation Protocol (2017)*).

the Protocol of Colonia (1994)[53] that replicated BITs model. The new regional text is a proof of Brazil's regional leadership in this area, a leadership that has extended to the multilateral level with the draft of a multilateral agreement on investment facilitation proposed to the World Trade Organization (WTO).[54] The text does not include ISDS mechanisms and provides that disputes that may arise between states parties will be addressed under the WTO system under Articles XXII and XXIII of the General Agreement on Tariff and Trade and the Dispute Settlement Understanding, except for the suspension of concessions under another agreement.[55]

Other WTO members have also submitted proposals under the umbrella of investment facilitation, such as Russia;[56] Mexico, Indonesia, Korea, Turkey, and Australia;[57] China;[58] Argentina, and Brazil.[59] It is relevant to point out that Russian's draft proposes domestic jurisdiction as a sole mechanism for dispute resolution, which is a return to the Calvo doctrine.

Concluding remarks

Although the ISDS regime was a creation of the United States and Europe, South America marked its own imprint during the stage of the Calvo doctrine and "El No de Tokyo," being a region that for almost three decades resisted the hegemonic regime. The late incorporation of the region into the regime (1990s) goes hand in hand with the Washington consensus and brings with it the proliferation of BITs, especially with European countries and the United States. Thus, the continent's position went from resistance to accommodation. The first decade of the twenty-first century presents ruptures in the continent that form a new mosaic of states divided in three groups.

53 Protocolo de Colonia para la Promoción y Protección Recíproca de Inversiones en el MERCOSUR (signed 17 January 1994) MERCOSUR/CMC/DEC No 11/93.
54 Structured discussions on investment facilitation, Communication from Brazil. Document JOB/GC/169 (1 February 2018) https://docs.wto.org/
55 *Intra-MERCOSUR Investment Facilitation Protocol (2017)* (n 52) article 22(3)(c)
56 Communication from the Russian Federation, Investment Policy Discussion Group. Document JOB/GC/120 (31 March 2017) https://docs.wto.org/
57 MIKTA Investment Workshop Reflections, Communication from Mexico, Indonesia, Korea, Turkey, and Australia (MIKTA). Document JOB/GC/121 (6 April 2017) https://docs.wto.org/
58 Possible Elements of Investment Facilitation, Communication from China. Document JOB/GC/123 (26 April 2017) https://docs.wto.org/
59 Possible Elements of a WTO Instrument on Investment Facilitation, Communication from Argentina and Brazil. Document JOB/GC/124 (26 April 2017) https://docs.wto.org/

Brazil continues to be the exception to the regime and the continent, in its role as the outsider. Likewise, since 2015 it proposes the signing of the CPFIs at the bilateral level, a model on which the Intra-Mercosur Investment Cooperation and Facilitation Protocol, as well as the proposal at the WTO, were based. In this way, Brazil is consolidated as an actor that seeks to reshape the regime both bilaterally, regionally and multilaterally. Additionally, three states of the region began to present movements with respect to the initial positions: Bolivia (2007), Ecuador (2009–2021), and Venezuela (2012). The basis for the withdrawal of the regime is conjunctural (claims in extractive sectors and linked to environmental protection), legal (new constitutional provisions) and ideological. Finally, the rest of the states still maintain their status as members, but some voices have raised doubts in regard to disputes related to human rights issues (example: water and sanitation in Argentina, public health in Uruguay, etc.).

From the previous analysis, two conclusions can be reached. First, the signing, termination, or renegotiation of international agreements is the way that allows states to protect their policy space and recuperate their "domains of power."[60] This behavior reinforces the idea that the state cannot be limited to declining significance and a reduction in its ability to regulate is not explained solely because it operates in a globalized world.[61] Faced with an international regime that conditions or erodes policy space, the states seek ways to regain or maintain their regulatory powers.

Agreements such as CFIA are an alternative to rebalancing the current regime, avoiding the conditioning of state sovereignty in the face of the claims by foreign investors. Internationally, there are other examples such as India's 2016 BIT model,[62] with a complex system that avoids direct passage to international arbitral jurisdiction and strengthens domestic jurisdiction. However, other alternatives do not go so far as to exclude investor–state arbitration mechanisms as in CFIA.

The second element that emerges from the proposed typology is that the existence of emblematic disputes boosted the withdrawal from the regime. In the case of Brazil, although it still remains as the outsider, the CFIA model represents an important alternative to the regime as they exclude ISDS, focusing on alternative dispute resolution mechanisms and interstate

---

60 Susan Strange, *The Retreat of the State. The diffusion of power in the world economy* (Cambridge University Press 1996) 65.

61 Saskia Sassen, *¿Perdiendo el control? La soberanía en la era de la globalización* (Barcelona: Belaterra 2001) 45

62 *India Model BIT (2015)* (n 6).

arbitration. Furthermore, CFIA model has now been regionalized with the Intra-Mercosur Investment Cooperation and Facilitation Protocol and it could be multilateralized if the draft issued to the WTO enters into force.

To sum up, currently South America is a three-color mosaic, a continent that moves from resistance to accommodation, and from accommodation to fragmentation regarding a regime created by the United States and Europe. Currently, Brazil, despite being an outsider to the traditional regime, is the only state in the region that has already taken firm steps to reshape it.

3

Pluralist approaches to dispute settlement mechanisms

Henrique Choer Moraes[1] and Facundo Pérez Aznar

Introduction

International investment law is witnessing an unprecedented level of experimentalism. This is a significant development given the considerable period of time in which investment governance derived predominantly from agreements incorporating standard provisions of Bilateral Investment Treaties (BITs).[2] Prominent among these provisions were those allowing for investor–State dispute settlement (ISDS) through arbitration.

In a number of high-profile ISDS cases arbitrators recognized investors' right to compensation as a result of regulations or other state measures in areas such as public health, environment protection, and financial stability. As a reaction, states – developing and developed alike – have been working to repurpose[3] investment treaties in order to reassert control[4] over investment rules. To the extent that a common direction can be discerned in this trend it is that states have been seeking to tilt the balance farther from the interests of investors and towards the public interest.

This movement has taken many shapes, ranging from modifications on standards of investment protection to the rejection of investment treaties altogether. Despite the different approaches taken by states, the main focus

---

1 The views and opinions expressed in this chapter are the sole responsibility of the author and do not necessarily reflect the positions of the government of Brazil.

2 Despite occasional differences across (often national) models of investment agreements, BITs tend to share key provisions and "are the most important source of contemporary international investment law" (Rudolf Dolzer and Christoph Schreuer, *Principles of International Investment Law* (2nd edn Oxford University Press 2012) 13).

3 Wolfgang Alschner, "The global laboratory of investment law reform alternatives" (2018) 112 *AJIL Unbound* 237.

4 Andreas Kulick, "Reassertion of control: an introduction" *in* Andreas Kulick (ed), *Reassertion of Control Over the Investment Treaty Regime* (Cambridge University Press 2017) 10.

has ultimately been to constrain the room of maneuver of investment arbitrators. While no solution has gathered enough level of convergence to replace the BIT,[5] it is likely that we enter a period of fragmentation[6] and pluralism where a number of different approaches co-exist with the BIT, which no longer occupies a position of virtual exclusivity.

Latin America seems to corroborate the trend towards pluralism in investment treaties, and investment arbitration in particular. Perhaps more than any other region in the world, it displays a significant diversity of approaches to investment arbitration – in some ways it represents a microcosm of the reform of investment agreements.

This chapter argues that, as it stands today, investment arbitration in Latin America is marked by pluralism, instead of the predominance of any one solution. In order to substantiate this claim, the next section looks at the attitudes of Latin American countries towards investment arbitration and proposes categories under which to place countries of the region. The objective of this exercise is to show how wide is the spectrum of approaches adopted by Latin American countries regarding investment arbitration rather than to seek to fit them neatly and exclusively under any of these categories.

The subsequent section rolls out the elements showing that pluralism is the prevailing approach to investment arbitration in Latin America. It argues that each Latin American country today often adopts varied solutions to investment arbitration, making any attempt to categorize their approach necessarily a partial depiction of reality.

The final section presents concluding remarks, among them the finding that pluralism in Latin America does not emerge from a constellation of different solutions to investment arbitration, each promoted by an individual country in the region. With the exception of Brazil – which crafted its own investment treaty model and has used no other until now – this is not how pluralism plays out in Latin America. Instead, it is expressed by different approaches to investment arbitration often adopted *by the same country* depending on their investment treaty partner. In this sense, pluralism implies also the fragmentation of investment arbitration disciplines within the portfolio of agreements of one single country.

Whether Latin American pluralism foreshadows the evolution of investment law on a global scale remains to be seen. Still, the wide range of options towards investment arbitration identified in Latin America – from

---

5 Anthea Roberts, "Incremental, systemic, and paradigmatic reform of investor-state arbitration" (2018) 112 (3) *American Journal of International Law* 410.

6 Catharine Titi, "Who's afraid of reform? Beware the risk of fragmentation" (2018) 112 *American Journal of International Law* 232.

the rejection of ICSID and of BITs to the resort to state-to-state arbitration – can certainly provide elements for other regions as they examine options to reform their investment treaties.

Latin American attitudes towards investment arbitration

It is misleading to try to pin down a Latin American approach to investment arbitration,[7] let alone to discern principles[8] or propose overarching models that would tie together the different views across the region.

However tempting it might be for analysts to attach labels such as "hostility"[9] to the attitude of the region to investment arbitration, the reality has always been more nuanced: for instance, of the two main recipients of foreign direct investment (FDI) in Latin America,[10] Brazil has never ratified a traditional BIT and Mexico only in 2018 recognized the jurisdiction of the International Center for the Settlement of Investment Disputes (ICSID). This goes some way in challenging the view that investment-friendly regulatory investments would require the endorsement of a single approach. If ever the Calvo doctrine had any explanatory power in making sense of Latin American views on investment regulation, this does not seem to be the case anymore. Instead, Latin American countries currently stand at different positions when it comes to investment arbitration.

---

7 Catharine Titi, "Investment arbitration in Latin America: The uncertain veracity of preconceived ideas" (2014) 30 (2) *Arbitration International* 357; Katia Fach Gómez and Catharine Titi, "International investment law and ISDS: Mapping contemporary Latin America" (2016) 17 (4) *Journal of World Investment and Trade* 534; Rodrigo Polanco Lazo, "Two worlds apart: the changing features of international investment agreements in Latin America" *in* Attila Tanzi, Alessandra Asteriti, Rodrigo Polanco Lazo, and Paolo Turrini (eds) *International Investment Law in Latin America: Problems and Prospects* (Brill 2016) 97.

8 For example, see José Gustavo Prieto Muñoz, "The rise of common principles for investment in Latin America: Proposing a methodological shift for investor-state dispute settlement" (2016) 17 (4) *Journal of World Investment & Trade* 614.

9 Such as in Carlos Bellei Tagle, "Arbitraje de inversiones en América Latina: de la hostilidad a la búsqueda de nuevas alternativas" *in* Attila Tanzi, Alessandra Asteriti, Rodrigo Polanco Lazo, and Paolo Turrini (eds) *International Investment Law in Latin America: Problems and Prospects* (Brill 2016) 98.

10 Inflows of FDI in the two economies have been the following in recent years: Brazil: US$ 76 billion (2012), US$ 53 billion (2013), US$ 73 billion (2014), US$ 64 billion (2015), US$ 58 billion (2016), and US$ 62 billion (2017). Mexico: US$ 21 billion (2012), US$ 48 billion (2013), US$ 28 billion (2014), US$ 34 billion (2015), US$ 29 billion (2016), and US$ 29 billion (2017). (UNCTAD, *World Investment Report 2018*, Annex table 1, p 186 https://unctad.org/system/files/official-document/wir2018_en.pdf accessed 2 March 2021).

The mosaic of states

Table 3.1 Latin America – ISDS cases

Country	Cases as respondent
Argentina	60
Belize	3
Bolivia	14
Chile	5
Colombia	11
Costa Rica	9
Dominican Republic	6
Ecuador	23
El Salvador	3
Guatemala	4
Guyana	1
Honduras	1
Mexico	28
Nicaragua	2
Panama	8
Paraguay	3
Peru	15
Uruguay	4
Venezuela	45
TOTAL	*245*
TOTAL WORLD	*904*

Source: UNCTAD (31 July, 2018)

Still, it is accurate to point to a general discontent in the region with respect to the perceived lack of balance in international investment rules[11] – a sentiment that, despite being globally shared in varying degrees, is particularly acute in Latin America, whose countries have been on the respondent position in more than a quarter of all known investment arbitrations (see Table 3.1).

11 María José Luque Macías, "Reliance on alternative methods for investment protection through national laws, investment contracts, and regional institutions in Latin America" *in* Steffen Hindelang and Markus Krajewski (eds) *Shifting Paradigms in International Investment Law* (Oxford University Press 2016) 292.

With the sole intention of providing a minimally organized map of the attitudes in Latin America towards investment arbitration, countries in the region could be roughly placed under the following positions (drawing on a recent, but unrelated, debate): *modernizing remainers, exiters,* and *creative entrants.*[12] Each categorization takes into account what seems to be the predominant approach of each individual Latin American country to investment arbitration, judged by either their treaty practice, particularly more recent agreements, or by state decisions or measures that point to a given preference regarding investment arbitration.

Modernizing remainers: persisting trust in investment arbitration, but with updated rules

This subset includes Latin American countries that remain committed to signing BITs, and to accepting ISDS mechanisms to settle investment disputes. Among the countries in this position are Argentina, Chile, Colombia, Costa Rica, Peru, and Mexico.

The case of Argentina is particularly noteworthy: despite the significant number of investment arbitrations in which it has been involved as respondent (60 cases as of 31 July 2018[13]), Argentina remains a stakeholder of the BIT-format. In 2017, after roughly 15 years without negotiating any BIT, Argentina went back to the negotiating table to sign two new BITs[14] and to renegotiate some of the old BITs in its portfolio. One of the new treaties, with Qatar, follows the standard provisions of traditional investment agreements.

Argentina is a case in point of another feature of *modernizing remainers*, namely the intention to operate incremental changes to the language of provisions in investment agreements. Accordingly, in the FTA with Chile signed

---

12 The proposed categories draw loosely on those put forward by Roberts (note 5, above) of "incrementalists," "systemic reformers," and "paradigmatic reformers," but they differ in the following aspects: (i) Roberts' categories seem to imply that each actor adopts one preference to regulate investment arbitration (e.g., to institute a permanent court) and consistently pursues this preference. This is clearly not the case with most of Latin American countries, which are not always in a position to impose their preferences on their treaty partners and instead accept the preferences of others; (ii) despite covering a broad range of positions regarding investment arbitration, Roberts' categories do not seem to capture the position of the "exiters," which could hardly fit under the same position of what she considers "paradigmatic reformers" –where Brazil, for example, would fit.

13 See   https://investmentpolicyhub.unctad.org/ISDS/CountryCases/8?partyRole=2 accessed 9 December 2018.

14 Facundo Pérez-Aznar, "The recent Argentina-Qatar BIT and the challenges of investment negotiations" *Investment Treaty News* (12 June 2017) www.iisd.org/itn/2017/06/12/recent-argentina-qatar-bit-challenges-investment-negotiations-facundo-perez-aznar/ accessed 9 December 2018.

in 2017, Argentina innovated in comparison to its previous investment agreements by introducing provisions such as: (i) non-conforming measures; (ii) denial of benefits; (iii) right to regulate; and (iv) the duty imposed on investors to comply with the legislation of the host state.

Concerning directly the regulation of dispute settlement, the Argentina–Chile FTA includes innovative clauses such as: (i) the possibility to resort to mediation; (ii) the duty to disclose the existence of third-party funders; (iii) the duty of the tribunal to decide on objections related to its competence or its jurisdiction as a preliminary matter; and (iv) the challenge of arbitrators when there are justifiable doubts as to their impartiality or independence. In these latter provisions particularly, it is clear to observe how Argentina sought to react to lessons learned in its trajectory with investment arbitration.[15]

In many ways, Chile provides the text-book case of a *modernizing remainer* in that it has retained its support for investment treaties, including investment arbitration, while allowing for incremental updates. Some of the refinements to Chilean investment treaties have resulted from changes adopted by players such as European countries or the US. Thus, Chile's approach to investment lawmaking has been described as moving from an initial period where it has followed, in general, the "Dutch gold standard" then favored by European countries to an updated "NAFTA Model"[16] that emerged with the 2003 Chile–US FTA.

In a more institutional development, some Latin American countries are introducing domestic mechanisms to reinforce their capacity to respond to investment arbitrations, in order to ensure coordinated action by the government before international arbitrators. A case in this direction is that

---

15 See, among others, *Compañía de Aguas del Aconquija S.A. and Vivendi Universal S.A. (formerly Compañía de Aguas del Aconquija, S.A. and Compagnie Générale des Eaux) v. Argentine Republic (I)*, ICSID Case No. ARB/97/3 (Decision on the Challenge to the President of the Committee, 3 October 2001); *Suez, Sociedad General de Aguas de Barcelona, S.A. and Interagua Servicios Integrales de Agua, S.A. v. Argentine Republic (formerly Aguas Provinciales de Santa Fe, Suez, Sociedad General de Aguas de Barcelona y Interagua Servicios Integrales de Agua) v Argentina*, ICSID Case No. ARB/03/17 and *Suez, Sociedad General de Aguas de Barcelona, S.A. and Vivendi Universal, S.A. (formerly Aguas Argentinas, S.A., Suez, Sociedad General de Aguas de Barcelona, S.A. and Vivendi Universal, S.A.) v. Argentine Republic (II)*, ICSID Case No. ARB/03/19 (Decision on the Proposal for the Disqualification of a Member of the Arbitral Tribunal, 22 October 2007); *National Grid PLC v. The Argentine Republic*, UNCITRAL (Decision on the Challenge to Mr Judd L. Kessler, 3 December 2007).

16 Rodrigo Polanco Lazo, "The Chilean experice in South-South investment and trade agreements" *in* Fabio Morosini and Michelle Ratton Sanchez (eds) *Reconceptualizing International Investment Law from the Global South* (Cambridge 2017) 117; Gonzalo Biggs, "The Latin American treatment of international arbitration and foreign investments and the Chile-U.S. Free Trade Agreement" (2004) 19 (1) *ICSID Review* 61.

of Colombia, which introduced in 2013 a high-level government forum to direct Colombia's responses to investment disputes (*Instancia de Alto Nivel de Gobierno para la atención de controversias internacionales de inversión*[17]).

These cases show that, despite maintaining the preference for entering into international agreements following the traditional approach, including ISDS, these Latin American countries have been tweaking the rules and institutions so as to rebalance the state–investor relationship, often as a response to the (direct or indirect) experience with investment arbitrations.

Exiters: abandoning investment arbitration commitments

The second category, unique to Latin America, is comprised of countries that have abandoned investment arbitration by withdrawing their recognition to the jurisdiction of the ICSID and, simultaneously, but in different degrees, have denounced their BITs. This is the category formed by Bolivia, Ecuador, and Venezuela, which have respectively denounced the 1965 Washington Convention ("ICSID Convention") in May 2007, July 2009 and January 2012.[18] In so doing, these countries have sought to remove from investors' reach the recourse to one of the main settings of investment arbitration.

Aside from exiting the ICSID, these countries have also set off to denounce most of or some of their investment agreements,[19] which evidently curtails the capacity of investors to subject cases to investment arbitrations. In this strategy, the *exiters* are not an isolated example, as countries elsewhere – such

17 Established by Decree 1939 of 9 September 2013. See also "El Arbitramento y la Agencia Nacional de Defensa Jurídica del Estado" www.oas.org/juridico/PDFs/mesicic5_col_andje_anex1.pdf accessed 9 December 2018.

18 See ICSID, "Lista de Estados Contratantes y signatarios del Convenio (al 27 de agosto de 2018)", https://icsid.worldbank.org/en/Documents/icsiddocs/Lista%20de%20Estados%20Contratantes%20y%20Signatarios%20del%20Convenio-%20Latest.pdf accessed 9 December 2018.

19 "Ecuador denounces its remaining 16 BITs and publishes CAITISA audit report," *Investment Treaty News*, 12 June 2017, www.iisd.org/itn/2017/06/12/ecuador-denounces-its-remaining-16-bits-and-publishes-caitisa-audit-report/ accessed 9 December 2018; Aldo Orellana López, "Bolivia denounces its Bilateral Investment Treaties and attempts to put an end to the Power of Corporations to sue the country in International Tribunals" http://justinvestment.org/wp-content/uploads/2014/07/Bolivia-denounces-its-Bilateral-Investment-Treaties-and-attempts-to-put-an-end-to-the-Power-of-Corporations-to-sue-the-country-in-International-Tribunals1.pdf accessed 9 December 2018; Venezuela has denounced its BIT with the Netherlands (Rodrigo Javier Polanco, "Beyond ICSID arbitration – The Centre for Settlement of Investment Disputes of UNASUR" in Andrea Bjorklund, *Yearbook on International Investment Law and Policy* 2014–2015, p. 375). Ecuador rejoined the ICSID Convention whilst the book was in Press, which does not affect the argument of the chapter.

as South Africa, India and Indonesia – have also denounced all or some of their treaties or let them expire.

Exiters, then, stand out for their active rejection of a system of investment arbitration that they see as detrimental to their interests, which, for this reason, is no longer worthy of their participation. This does not mean, nevertheless, that *exiters* are averse to investment arbitration as a dispute settlement mechanism, as will be explored later in this chapter.

Creative entrants: accepting investment arbitration, but under new rules

The last category is arguably also uniquely Latin American and is comprised by Brazil. It is a stand-alone category given the particular features of the approach adopted by Brazil with its model of investment treaty, the Cooperation and Facilitation Investment Agreement (CFIA).

Brazil is one of the few countries in the world never to have ratified a traditional BIT – although it signed some agreements in the 1990s they have not been ratified[20] – and only in 2015 signed its first investment agreement. When it did so, it was within the terms stipulated in the CFIA, which significantly departs from the traditional BIT, among others by not providing for ISDS mechanisms.[21] Interestingly, though, the CFIA does not do away with investment arbitration, given that the Brazilian treaties provide for (state-to-state) arbitration, even though not investor–state arbitration.

Since the first CFIA, with Angola in 2015, Brazil has signed investment agreements with the whole of South America – with the exception of Bolivia and Venezuela. It is in the process of negotiating an agreement with Ecuador. It has also signed a CFIA with Mexico. Outside of Latin America, CFIAs have been signed with Ethiopia, Malawi, and Mozambique, and negotiated with India, though not signed yet.

The category singly led by Brazil is characterized not so much by the late entrance in the universe of investment agreements, but by the capacity to craft its own innovative approach to these agreements and, until now, to disseminate it particularly to Latin America.

20 Martino Maggetti and Henrique Choer Moraes, "The Policy-Making of Investment Treaties in Brazil: Policy Learning in the Context of Late Adoption," *in* Claire A Dunlop (ed), *Learning in public policy: analysis, modes and outcomes* (Palgrave 2018) 295. See Chapter 4 by Leonardo V P de Oliveira and Marcus Spangenberger in this volume.

21 Henrique Choer Moraes and Felipe Hees, "Breaking the BIT mold: Brazil's pioneering approach to investment agreements" (2018) 112 *AJIL Unbound* 197.

Pluralism in Latin American approaches to investment arbitration

The categories outlined above are not meant to contain the variety of approaches to investment arbitration that can be witnessed in the Latin American practice. Instead, pluralism is the defining mark of countries in the region, and, as this section explores in more detail, it is often the case that one country adopts a plurality of approaches.

Therefore, countries tagged as *modernizing remainers* behave as *creative entrants*, at the same time that *exiters* behave as *modernizing remainers*. Even Brazil, a *creative entrant*, can be spotted behaving as a *modernizing remainer*. What is more, within this latter realm, there are different shades of modernization that *remainers* endorse, often as a result of interactions of actors from outside Latin America.

A spectrum of positions varying according to state control over investment arbitration

Looking at the current positions of Latin American countries regarding investment arbitration, a spectrum can be drawn considering as a vector the degree of control exerted by states over investment arbitration. This degree of control would imply states exert more influence over investment arbitration than they currently enjoy. It would thus include, among others, the capacity to appoint arbitrators, to challenge arbitrators and to agree on binding interpretations of provisions of investment treaties.

This spectrum would include both (i) the traditional ISDS mechanisms (where arguably state control over arbitration is minimal), and the more disruptive options of (ii) the outright rejection of a key investment arbitration forum such as the ICSID often coupled with the denouncing of BITs (which accords states some level of control over the very possibility for investors to resort to investment arbitration to address grievances they ascribe to the host state).

It would also include the following options: (iii) conditioned and/or sectorial recourse to ISDS, as recently negotiated by Mexico and the US within the USMCA, the new edition of NAFTA; (iv) recourse to a permanent investment tribunal, as proposed by the European Union (EU) and Canada, in which investors might file complaints against states, but the former hold the exclusive competence to appoint the judges; and (v) state-to-state arbitration, as provided for in the Brazilian CFIA.

While no country adopts all of these possibilities, Mexico is perhaps the one that best epitomizes the notion of Latin American pluralism to investment arbitration articulated in this chapter (Figure 3.1).

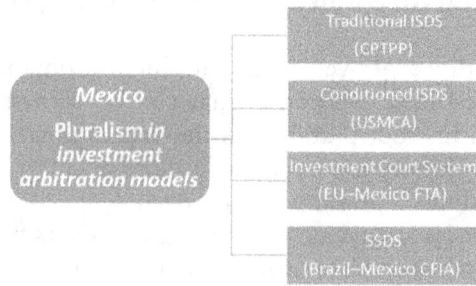

Figure 3.1 Pluralism in investment arbitration models

Although Mexico has been signing investment agreements with traditional ISDS mechanisms, it has recently started to diversify its portfolio as it negotiated treaties with Brazil, the European Union, and the US. It has started to apply the "à la carte approach, depending on the demands of the other Contracting Parties."[22]

In the CFIA signed with Brazil,[23] Mexico accepted the state-to-state dispute settlement that is a key feature of the Brazilian approach. In its turn, in the modernization of its free trade agreement with the EU, Mexico has agreed to the set-up of the Investment Court System,[24] a permanent forum to settle investor–state disputes promoted by the EU in its regional agreements. More recently, in the framework of the renegotiation of NAFTA, Mexico accepted an ISDS mechanism with the US that is limited and subject to conditions in some cases, as explained below.

Positions of Latin American countries across the spectrum: pluralism in action

Projecting the practice of other Latin American countries across the spectrum outlined above provides concrete examples of pluralist approaches to investment arbitration. The cases below are not meant to exhaust all the

---

22 Nikos Lavranos, "Beyond USMCA: ISDS à la carte", Kluwer Arbitration Blog, 8 October 2018 http://arbitrationblog.kluwerarbitration.com/2018/10/08/beyond-usmca-isds-la-carte/ accessed 9 December 2018.

23 Cooperation and Investment Facilitation Agreement between the Federative Republic of Brazil and the United Mexican States (signed 26 May 2015).

24 European Commission, "EU and Mexico reach new agreement on trade", press release of 21 April 2018 http://trade.ec.europa.eu/doclib/press/index.cfm?id=1830 accessed 9 December 2018.

existing possibilities of investment arbitration, but rather to showcase the variety of approaches in the region.

Traditional ISDS

Unsurprisingly, this approach is adopted by the *modernizing remainers*. These countries do not seem to take issue with the possibility of investors to file claims against states, although they might have an interest in refining the disciplines on ISDS to address concerns that have been raised over the years with respect to procedural questions such as the appointment, independence, and impartiality of arbitrators, as well as with substantive rules laying out standards of protection of investors.

What may seem somewhat counter-intuitive is that *exiters* might also find themselves subject to ISDS mechanisms, albeit within a different institutional structure. This might be particularly the case depending on the evolution of the negotiations for the establishment of the UNASUR Center for the Settlement of Investment Disputes. In the current version of the draft,[25] the Centre provides for the possibility that investors file claims against states, including possibly Bolivia, Ecuador, and Venezuela. Of course, this possibility now hinges on the future steps in this negotiation and, more crucially, on the future of the UNASUR itself.

Exiters may also be subject to ISDS mechanisms as a result of sunset clauses in BITs they have denounced, which continue to produce effects for a predetermined number of years after the termination of the treaty.

Conditioned/sectorial ISDS

So far, the main example under this approach to investment arbitration is the recently negotiated update of the NAFTA – the USMCA.[26] The disciplines governing investment disputes between the US and Mexico introduce a number of conditions and limitations that constrain the traditional wide scope for ISDS.

Notably, the US and Mexico agreed that ISDS is available provided the claimant resorts to national remedies first.[27] Furthermore, other limitations

25 An unofficial translation of 2014 Draft Constitutive Agreement of the Centre for the Settlement of Investment Disputes of the UNASUR has been prepared by Maria Sarmiento and is available at https://papers.ssrn.com/sol3/papers.cfm?abstract_id=2703651 accessed 9 December 2018.

26 For comments on the ISDS aspects of the USMCA, see, among others, Congressional Research Service, "Proposed U.S.-Mexico-Canada (USMCA) Trade Agreement," 30 November 2018, https://fas.org/sgp/crs/row/IF10997.pdf accessed 9 December 2018; and Nathalie Bernasconi-Osterwalder, "USMCA Curbs How Much Investors Can Sue Countries – Sort of" www.iisd.org/library/usmca-investors accessed 9 December 2018.

27 Annex 14-D, Article 5.1 (a) and (b). Agreement between the United States of America, the United Mexican States, and Canada (signed 30 November 2018, entered into force 1 July 2020) *(USMCA 2018)*.

apply, such as a restriction on the standards that can lead to a dispute (e.g., claims based on indirect expropriation are excluded).[28] Nevertheless, for claims emerging from government contracts in the oil, natural gas, power generation, infrastructure, transport and telecommunications sectors, such conditions are not applicable.[29]

Permanent investment court

This option of investment agreement is more common than would be imagined. Mexico is the most recent Latin American country to include this option of investment dispute settlement within its portfolio, following a commitment deriving from the modernization of its FTA with the EU.

Following other EU FTA partners such as Canada, Mexico agreed to subject investment disputes to the so-called Investment Court System (ICS), whereby a public investment court of first instance and an appeal jurisdiction are established to hear claims submitted by investors against a state party to the FTA.[30]

Chile might follow suit. In the framework of the modernization of its FTA with the EU, launched in 2018, it is expected that the European Commission also seeks Chilean endorsement to the ICS, according to the negotiating positions of the EU.[31]

But it is not only the EU that is responsible for introducing in the region the possibility of submitting investment claims to a permanent court. Within the MERCOSUR Protocol on Investment Facilitation and Cooperation, Argentina, Brazil, Paraguay, and Uruguay recognized that the permanent review procedure existing in MERCOSUR, under the Olivos Protocol, be applied also to investment cases emerging from the Protocol.[32]

State-to-state investment arbitration

This is the approach adopted by the Brazilian model investment agreement. As a consequence of Brazil having signed CFIAs with a number of countries

---

28 Ibid. Annex 14-D, Article 3.1(b)(i)(B).
29 Ibid. Annex 14-E.
30 European Commission, "Commission proposes new Investment Court System for TTIP and other EU trade and investment negotiations," press release of 16 September 2015, http://europa.eu/rapid/press-release_IP-15-5651_en.htm accessed 9 December 2018.
31 See the "Impact assessment of the EU-Chile agreement" https://eur-lex.europa.eu/legal-content/en/TXT/?uri=CELEX%3A52017SC0172 accessed 9 December 2018.
32 Facundo Pérez-Aznar and Henrique Choer Moraes, "The MERCOSUR Protocol on Investment Cooperation and Facilitation: regionalizing an innovative approach to investment agreements" *EJIL Talk!* 12 September 2017 www.ejiltalk.org/the-mercosur-protocol-on-investment-cooperation-and-facilitation-regionalizing-an-innovative-approach-to-investment-agreements/ accessed 9 December 2018.

in Latin America, today Argentina, Chile, Colombia, Mexico, Paraguay, Peru, and Uruguay have included in their portfolios the recourse to state-to-state dispute settlement for investment disputes arising with Brazil.

It is worth mentioning that, following the signature of the MERCOSUR Protocol, Argentina, Paraguay, and Uruguay agreed to subject investment disputes among themselves to state-to-state investment arbitration, in what amounts to the first example of the regionalization of the Brazilian approach.[33]

Exiting ICSID and denouncing of BITs

Finally, there is also the approach adopted by the *exiters*, namely to reject the jurisdiction of a key setting for investment arbitration such as the ICSID and to, in different degrees, terminate BITs. This step is meaningful because it evidences an unprecedented change of heart in countries, which opted for going back on their previous decisions to recognize the authority of a forum for investment arbitration, thereby affecting in some ways the legitimacy of the system.

Still, as argued above, this step does not necessarily imply a rejection of investment arbitration *per se*, as the *exiters* might continue to be subject to ISDS in the BITs that are still in force and provide for other fora apart from ICSID or are actively promoting ISDS mechanisms, such as the UNASUR Centre. An interesting case is that of Ecuador. After Ecuador's denunciation of the ICSID Convention and the withdrawal from its BITs in May 2018, the new Ecuadorian government that took office some days later announced that it may renegotiate and renew these BITs and even readopt the ICSID Convention.[34]

While these approaches to investment arbitration across some Latin American countries might not exhaust all the possibilities, they offer a clear manifestation of pluralism (Table 3.2), to such an extent that might not be rivalled by any other region.

Concluding remarks

Examining different design options for investment dispute settlement, Puig and Shaffer have recently found that "[m]aintaining flexibility will be key, a flexibility that permits states facing different challenges to select from a menu

---

33 See Facundo Pérez-Aznar and Henrique Choer Moraes, note 32 above.

34 Facundo Pérez-Aznar, "Recent Trends in Investment Law and Policy in Latin America," in Lisa E. Sachs and Lise Johnson (eds) *Yearbook on International Investment Law & Policy 2017–2018* (Oxford University Press) 273–288, 278.

Table 3.2 Latin America: different shades of investment arbitration

Traditional ISDS	Exiting ICSID/denouncing BITs	Conditioned/sectorial ISDS	Permanent court	SSDS
Argentina Chile Colombia Mexico Peru	Bolivia [Ecuador] Venezuela	Mexico (USMCA)	Mexico (EU-FTA)	Brazil
				IIAs with Brazil: Argentina Chile Colombia Mexico Paraguay Peru Uruguay
				MERCOSUR Protocol: Argentina, Paraguay & Uruguay (among each other)
Bolivia Ecuador Venezuela			Chile (future EU-FTA)	
			MERCOSUR Protocol (appeals' jurisdiction)	
[UNASUR Center]				[UNASUR Center]

Level of state control over investment arbitration

of imperfect alternatives in light of their trade-offs. That flexibility should include experimentation with different complementarity mechanisms."[35] In varying degrees, Latin American countries might be doing just that as they increasingly adopt different options of investment arbitration into their investment agreement. In Latin America, flexibility means pluralism of approaches. And, as explained in this chapter, pluralism means diverse solutions for investment arbitration inside the portfolio of a single country. It remains to be seen which reasons account for this pluralism, whether it reflects the conviction that this is the best approach, a pragmatic option or simply a lack of economic or political power to develop and sustain alternative options.

Irrespective of whether these varied options emerge from solutions originally conceived in Latin America or reflect the preferences of extra-regional treaty partners, Latin America today is doubtless a laboratory of pluralism in investment arbitration. While it remains elusive to discern a proper Latin American approach to investment arbitration, paradoxically the most common approach across countries in the region is the plurality of options.

And pluralism might as well be the direction towards which the reform of investment agreements might lead,[36] as states look for options to bring the balance closer to the center between public and investor's interests. In this sense, the Latin American experience might provide relevant inputs for the evolution of the global rules on investment.

35 Sergio Puig and Gregory Shaffer, "Imperfect alternatives: institutional choice and the reform of investment law" (2018) 112 (3) *American Journal of International Law* 409.
36 Anthea Roberts, "Incremental, systemic, and paradigmatic reform of investor–state arbitration," note 5 above, p. 431.

4

The Brazilian Cooperation and Facilitation Investment Agreement as a model for Latin America

Leonardo V P de Oliveira and Marcus Spangenberger

Introduction

Foreign direct investment (FDI) and the regulation of investment law in Latin America is not a new phenomenon.[1] There are several regional agreements, as well as bilateral investment treaties (BIT), regulating FDI and also, if a dispute regarding FDI arises, how parties can seek redress. Although many Latin American countries have been signatories to investment treaties and protagonists in investment disputes,[2] Brazil has always been the "odd one out" when it comes to BITs.[3] It signed 14 BITs in the 1990s, but it never ratified a single one.[4] Such approach would lead to a conclusion that Brazil is a resilient country with inwards policies, contrary to any type of internationalization of its trade. This logic does not apply to Brazil. Despite its refusal to accept the well-established format of FDI agreements,[5] such position has never hindered the injection of FDI into Brazil. Nevertheless,

---

1   Daniela Campello and Leany Lemos, "The non-ratification of bilateral investment treaties in Brazil: a story of conflict in a land of cooperation" (2015) 22(5) *Review of International Political Economy*, 1055, 1059.

2   For a perspective between Latin America and ICSID see Katia Fach Gomez, "Latin America and ICSID: David versus Goliath" (2011) 17 *Law & Bus Rev Am*, 195.

3   See Chapter 2 by Magdalena Bas and Chapter 3 by Henrique Choer Moraes and Facundo Pérez Aznar in this volume.

4   In the period between 1994 and 1999, Brazil signed agreements on the promotion and protection of investments with Chile, Portugal, Switzerland, United Kingdom, Denmark, Finland, France, Germany, Italy, South Korea, Venezuela, Cuba, the Netherlands, and the Belgium Luxembourg Economic Union. See UNCTAD, Investment Policy Hub https://investmentpolicy.unctad.org/international-investment-agreements/countries/27/brazil accessed 22 October 2021.

5   In this chapter, it is understood that the well-established format for FDI will be the one including arbitration as a dispute settlement system as well as the common clauses in

due to the increase of Brazilian outbound investments, the scenario has now changed. But, rather than jumping on the bandwagon of existing BIT regulations, Brazil chose to go down a different path. Brazil created a different type of international investment agreement called the Cooperation and Facilitation Investment Agreement (CFIA), which is the template for Brazilian BITs. Since 2015, it has already signed thirteen CFIAs.[6] The new method aims at finding equilibrium between investor protection and the state's regulatory powers. The CFIA's innovations can be found in its three main pillars: investment cooperation and facilitation; improved institutional governance and risk mitigation; and dispute prevention and settlement.

At the same time, Latin America is going through a process of reformulation concerning FDI. On the one hand you have countries repealing the Convention of the International Centre for Settlement of Investment Disputes (ICSID), seeing FDI as imperialism;[7] on the other hand, there are countries embracing FDI and therefore, these countries have formed regional alliances outside Latin America.[8] As a result, Brazil being a country with an important position in Latin America, its CFIA is timely and follows a movement towards state-driven arbitration in international investment law. Moreover, recently, Brazil ceased to be just famous for beautiful landscape and Carnival. Brazilian multinationals have been investing heavily abroad,[9] changing Brazil's position from "not a serious country,"[10] to a promoter of footwear fashion.[11] But, could Brazil's CFIA

BITs such as most favored nation clauses, national treatment and direct and indirect expropriation.

6   Brazil signed CFIAs with Angola, Chile, Colombia, Ecuador, Ethiopia, Guyana, India, Malawi, Mexico, Morocco, Mozambique, Suriname and United Arab Emirates. UNCTAD (n 4).

7   This is the policy adopted once by Ecuador and continued to be employed by Venezuela and Bolivia.

8   This is the case of Mexico, Chile, and Peru.

9   Juciara Nunes de Alcântara, Caroline Mendonça Nogueira Paiva, Nádia Campos Pereira Bruhn, Heloísa Rosa de Carvalho, and Cristina Lelis Leal Calegario, "Brazilian OFDI Determinants" (2016) 17(3) *Latin American Business Review*, 177, 180.

10 See Eul-Soo Pang, "Brazil Is Not a Serious Country," in *The International Political Economy of Transformation in Argentina, Brazil, and Chile since 1960. International Political Economy Series* (Palgrave Macmillan, 2002).

11 See Susana Costa e Silva, Maria João Sousa and Fernando Freyre Filho, "Understanding the Internationalisation Process of Havaianas: The Important Role of the Brand" (2010) 6, *Revista de Encontros Científicos – Tourism & Management Studies*, 118.

be a model for other Latin American countries? Or a model for investment disputes in general? To answer these questions, this chapter will first assess the relation between Brazil and FDI to explain the CFIA's origin and its regulations. After such analysis, a non-exhaustive scenario of international investment law in Latin America will be presented, followed by an assessment of the CFIA in the Latin American context. The chapter will conclude that although the Brazilian initiative is commendable, the FDI scene in Latina America is divided between resistance and accommodation of Western ideas, making the Brazilian model a Brazilian product to protect Brazilian companies. For the purposes of this chapter, Latin America will be understood to include South and Central America, including Mexico, as well as the Caribbean.[12]

Brazil and the regulation of FDI

When it comes to the effectiveness of investment treaties to promote FDI, Brazil has been looked upon as a counterexample for those who argue that BITs are neither required nor effective for boosting foreign investment.[13] That is why Brazil seems to have questioned, or at least challenged, the long-established interaction between the number of BITs a country has ratified and the intensity of FDI.[14] Despite the wave of adherences to BITs by other Latin American countries, which acted on the assumption that the BITs would be the key to attracting foreign investment and provide investors with greater legal security, Brazil remained outside this system.[15] Instead, foreign nationals would receive the same treatment as did nationals. In the 1960s, Brazil's view of an international investment regime was in line with the majority of Latin

---

12 In terms of the Caribbean, the authors exclude the islands that are unincorporated territories of the United States of America; British Overseas Territories; French Overseas Collectives and constituencies countries of the Kingdom of the Netherlands.

13 Joaquim P. Muniz, Kabir A. N. Duggal and Luis A. S. Peretti, "The New Brazilian BIT on Cooperation and Facilitation of Investments: A New Approach in Times of Change" (2017) 32 *ICSID Review – Foreign Investment Law Journal* 404, 405.

14 Daniel de Andrade Levy, "The ICSID Convention and Non-contracting States: The Brazilian Position Methaphor" in Crina Baltag (ed), *ICSID Convention after 50 Years* (Wolters Kluwer Law & Business 2017) 512. See also Chapter 7 by Claus von Wobeser in this volume.

15 Michelle Ratton Sanchez Badin and Fabio Morosini, "Navigating between Resistance and Conformity with the International Investment Regime, The Brazilian Agreements on Cooperation and Facilitation of Investment (ACFIs)," in Fabio Morosini and Michelle Ratton Sanchez Badin, *Reconceptualizing International Investment Law from the Global South* (Cambridge University Press 2017) 221.

American countries.[16] This view was based on the so-called Calvo doctrine linked to the Latin American jurist and diplomat Carlos Calvo.[17] Its aim was to secure that foreigners were not treated better than nationals. Thus, national treatment was intended to limit, not broaden, foreigners' rights.[18] This attitude against the investment protection regime resulted in the vote against the adoption of the International Bank for Reconstruction and Development Board of Governors Resolution No. 214 by 19 countries, including Brazil, in 1964, which subsequently allowed the formulation of ICSID in the "*El no de Tokio.*"[19] The international center proposed by the World Bank was responsible for institutionalizing investor–state arbitration.[20] Thus, since the creation of ICSID by the Washington Convention in 1965, Brazilian resistance to the international investment regime has been perceived.[21]

Even in the 1990s – when most Latin American countries were competing for capital through liberal investment treaties – contrary to their reluctance in the 1960s, Brazil resisted ratifying such agreements.[22] Especially, it did not follow the example of Argentina, Bolivia, Ecuador, and Venezuela, which, by August 1995, had all ratified the ICSID Convention.[23] Further, between 1995 and 1999, Brazil signed 14

16 Marc Bungenberg, Jörn Griebel, Stephan Hobe, and August Reinisch, *International Investment Law: A Handbook* (Bloomsbury Publishing Plc 2015) 158 and Catharine Titi, "International Investment Law and the Protection of Foreign Investment in Brazil" (2016) 2 *Transnational Dispute Management*, Special Issue on Latin America vol. 1 (eds Ignacio Torterola and Quinn Smith) https://ssrn.com/abstract=2786967 accessed 25 April 2018.

17 Carlos Calvo fought for the right of newly independent states to be free of such intervention by foreign powers, promoting the so-called Calvo doctrine, whereby foreign investors should be in no better position than local investors, with their rights and obligations to be determined through an exclusive jurisdiction of the courts of that state. This thesis was first published in 1868 in the seminal Calvo, *Derecho internacional teórico y páctico de Europa y América* (Paris, 1868). See Chapter 1 by Philip Burton in this volume.

18 Titi (n 16) 3; Bungenberg et al. (n 16) 848.

19 Titi (n 16) 4.

20 Nitish Monebhurrun, "Novelty in International Investment Law: The Brazilian Agreement on Cooperation and Facilitation of Investments as a Different International Investment Agreement Model" (2017) 8 *Journal of International Dispute Settlement* 79, 82.

21 Vivian Gabriel, "The New Brazilian Cooperation and Facilitation Investment Agreement: An Analysis of the Conflict Resolution Mechanism in Light of the Theory of the Shadow of the Law" (2016) 34 *Conflict Resolution Quarterly* 141, 143.

22 Ratton et al. (n 14) 221.

23 List of Contracting States and other Signatories of the Convention (as of 11 January 2018), ICSID/3, in https://icsid.worldbank.org/en/Documents/icsiddocs/List%20 of%20Contracting%20States%20and%20Other%20Signatories%20of%20 the%20Convention%20-%20Latest.pdf accessed 10 May 2018.

BITs.[24] But despite the apparent governmental support for the idea of BITs, none of these treaties was ratified by congress and therefore, these agreements did not enter into force. Moreover, in 2002, the government withdrew from congress its requests to obtain the approval of six more BITs (with Portugal, Chile, the United Kingdom, Switzerland, France, and Germany).[25] The same happened to two protocols[26] that Brazil signed in 1994 in the context of Mercosur, namely the Colonia Protocol for the Promotion and Reciprocal Protection of Investments within Mercosur Member States and the Buenos Aires Protocol for the Promotion and Reciprocal Protection of Investments for non-Member States of Mercosur. Of the two protocols, only the latter was submitted to the Brazilian congress for approval and later withdrawn.[27]

This Brazilian skepticism towards the international investment regime has always been driven by two major factors. First, the international adjudication of investment disputes was seen contrary to the state's monopoly over the administration of justice.[28] Second, international investment treaties would place foreign investors in a privileged position vis-à-vis domestic investors, thus violating the principle of equality before the law.[29] Interestingly, this same argument relates to criticisms currently raised in the European Union (EU); for instance, although the European Parliament referred to substantive standards rather than the investment dispute settlement mechanism, it underlined that EU investment agreements must provide protection no higher than that afforded by EU law.[30]

Despite all the resistance to the international investment regime, Brazil is an exception. It has been able to attract FDI without being part of the

---

24 See ft 3; only six of the fourteen BITs of the first generation were sent to Congress for approval, only to be withdrawn later. The remaining eight were never even sent to Congress for ratification.

25 Muniz et al. (n 13) 405.

26 Protocol of Colonia on the Reciprocal Promotion and Protection of Investments in MERCOSUR (Protocolo de Colonia para la Promoción y Protección Recíproca de Inversiones en el MERCOSUR) (signed 17 January 1994) MERCOSUR/CMC/DEC No 11/93.

27 Titi (n 16) 7.

28 ICSID, Documents Concerning the Origin and Formulation of the Convention on the Settlement of Investment Disputes between States and Nationals of Other States, Vol. II–I (1967), p 306.

29 Titi (n 16) 5.

30 Regulation (EU) No 912/2014 of the European Parliament and of the Council establishing a framework for managing financial responsibility linked to investor-to-state dispute settlement tribunals established by international agreements to which the European Union is party, *OJ L* 257, 28.8.2014, pp. 121–134, recital 4.

international investment regime.[31] In the last decade, Brazil became the world's ninth largest economy.[32] Not only has Brazil established itself as a highly attractive investment destination, but it has been and remains the largest recipient of FDI in South America,[33] especially for capital from developed countries.[34] In the first decade of the 2000s, this process advanced even more, notwithstanding the global economic crisis beginning in 2008. The amounts of FDI recorded in 2012, 2013 and 2014 remained above US$60 billion annually, a level reached only in 2011.[35]

In 2016, an economic recession arose in Latin America and the Caribbean which, coupled with weak commodities prices for the region's principal exports, factored heavily in the decline in FDI flows to the region (down 19 percent to US$135 billion).[36] Even though there were sizable falls in FDIs in Brazil from US$65 billion in 2015 to around US$50 billion in 2016, the country kept a high level of foreign investments compared to other strong Latin American economies such as Chile, which dropped from US$16 billion in 2015 to an estimated US$11 billion in 2016.[37] Further, even in Central America, despite its relatively stronger economic performance, flows diminished by 20 percent[38] in Mexico from US$33 billion in 2015 to US$26 billion in 2016.[39] These figures prove that Brazil has been and remains a highly attractive FDI destination; but now the focus has changed. As the investments of Brazilian companies abroad grew, the lack of regulatory framework for FDI made such companies vulnerable to policy changes in the place of investment.

Since Brazil remained the only South American country without BITs, Brazilian investors found themselves in an unfavorable position when investing abroad, as they were unable to benefit from protections typically covered

---

31 See Chapter 7 by Claus von Wobeser in this volume.
32 CIA World Fact Book www.cia.gov/library/publications/the-world-factbook/rankorder/2001rank.html accessed 2 June 2018.
33 Bungenberg et al. (n 16) 219.
34 Gabriel (21) 142.
35 Confederação Nacional da Indústria. 2015. Investimentos Estrangeiros Diretos no Brasil – 2014 os Regimes e Políticas de IED: tendências recentes no mundo e no Brasil. Brasília: CNIibid. https://static-cms-si.s3.amazonaws.com/media/filer_public/7b/db/7bdb4b72–80e9–4256-a0c8–79b6188d5266/investimentos_estrangeiros_diretos_no_brasil_2014.pdf accessed 18 June 2018.
36 United Nations Publications (ed), *Foreign Direct Investment in Latin America and the Caribbean: 2016* (English edition, United Nations 2016).
37 Ibid.
38 Ibid.
39 UNCTAD, "Global FDI flows slip in 2016, Modest recovery expected in 2017" (1 February 2017) http://unctad.org/en/PublicationsLibrary/webdiaeia2017d1_en.pdf accessed 17 March 2018.

by BITs, which investors from other countries may be able to benefit from. As a result, there was a concern regarding the country's lack of an outward foreign investment policy.[40] The vulnerability of Brazilian transnational companies was exemplified by two major incidents that struck two major Brazilian market players in Latin America. In 2006, the leading Brazilian company for natural gas, Petróleo Brasileiro SA – Petrobras – had two of its Petron Bataan refineries expropriated by the Bolivian government. On 1 May 2006, President Evo Morales issued the "Nationalization" Supreme Decree No 28701, through which the state effectively took control of the entire commercial and production chain of the oil and gas sector.[41] The Bolivian government demanded that foreign companies renegotiate their contracts with Bolivia so that Yacimientos Petroliferos Fiscales Bolivianos, the state-owned oil and gas company, could hold the majority shareholder control in Bolivian oil and gas trade. By the time of the Decree's enactment there were six subsidiaries of Petrobras in Bolivia.[42]

The move astonished Brazilian President Luiz Inácio Lula da Silva's government, which considered itself friendly towards Bolivia's President Evo Morales. However, energy security constraints limited Brazil's margin to maneuver.[43] Therefore, the Brazilian government took a cautious approach both to negotiations over the effects of nationalization on Petrobras's assets in Bolivia and the price of Bolivian gas exports to Brazil.[44] It recognized Bolivia's right to nationalize and ruled out retaliation.[45] On 10 May 2007, the Brazilian government announced the conclusion of a contract between Petrobras and Bolivia whereby the Brazilian company would receive US$12 million for selling its assets in its Bolivian refineries. Until then, besides the US$104 million used in the purchase

40 Lucas Bento, "Time to join the 'Bit Club'? Promoting and Protecting Brazilian Investments Abroad" (2013) 24 (2) *American Review of International Arbitration* 271, 324.

41 Bolivia, *Supreme Decree* 28701 (2006). Paulo Prada, "Bolivian Nationalizes the Oil and Gas Sector" *The New York Times* (2 May 2006) www.nytimes.com/2006/05/02/world/americas/02bolivia.html accessed 4 November 2018.

42 Marilda Rosado de Sá Ribeiro, "Sovereignty over Natural Resources Investment Law and Expropriation: The Case of Bolivia and Brazil" (2009) 2 *The Journal of World Energy Law & Business* 129.

43 Dan Keane, "Bolivia, Firms Reach Deal Nationalizing Oil and Gas" (30 October 2006) www.washingtonpost.com/wp-dyn/content/article/2006/10/29/AR2006102900937.html accessed 4 November 2018.

44 "Bolívia reduz pobreza e pobreza extrema através de programas sociais" (*ISTOÉ Independente*, 17 October 2016) https://istoe.com.br/bolivia-reduz-pobreza-e-pobreza-extrema-atraves-de-programas-sociais/ accessed 4 November 2018.

45 Ian Bremmer and Preston Keat, *The Fat Tail: The Power of Political Knowledge for Strategic Investing* (Oxford University Press 2010) 128.

refineries, Petrobras had invested US$30 million in Bolivian-related investments. Due to this expropriation, Petrobras's investments outside of Brazilian territory are now concentrated in Petrobras International Braspetro BV, an incorporated subsidiary with headquarters in the Netherlands, which is considered native to that country and therefore able to rely on Dutch BITs.[46]

A similar case occurred a year later in Ecuador. In 2008, Odebrecht, a Brazilian engineering and construction company, was forced to withdraw its operations from Ecuador.[47] The Ecuadorian government decided to issue executive decrees that ordered the militarization of Odebrecht's camps and offices, the termination of all its agreements with the Ecuadorian government, and the revocation of Odebrecht executive officers' and employees' visas. In the process, the Ecuadorean military seized over US$800 million of Oderbrecht's assets.[48] The Ecuadorian President, Rafael Correa, declared that his country would not compensate the company for what it had built;[49] furthermore, he also refused to repay the US$243 million loan that Brazil's National Bank of Economic and Social Development gave to Ecuador to finance the activities of Odebrecht. The decision led Brazil to recall its ambassador in Ecuador.[50] When Ecuador seized Oderbrecht's assets in 2008, and when Bolivia expropriated Petrobras' plant in 2006, there were no direct means of international redress against the host states other than going to the respective countries' courts. They became subject to political and diplomatic processes which were slow and provided no guarantee for compensation.

Brazil's new status as a capital exporter, the aforementioned cases and an increasing presence of Brazilian multinationals in many African countries motivated the Brazilian National Confederation of Industries, the Federation of Industries São Paulo, and many Brazilian multinational companies to influence national policies on foreign investment protection abroad. Due to this support, in 2015 the Brazilian government designed a new model investment agreement titled the Cooperation and Facilitation Investment

---

46 Sá Ribeiro (n 42) 132.
47 See BNamericas, "Odebrecht reportedly paid bribes for Ecuador water projects" (18 December 2018) www.bnamericas.com/en/news/odebrecht-reportedly-paid-bribes-for-ecuador-water-projects accessed 2 March 2021.
48 Bento (n 40) 16; Huub Ruël, *International Business Diplomacy: How Can Multinational Corporations Deal with Global Challenges?* (Emerald Group Publishing 2017) 232.
49 "Odebrecht: 'Usina Trabalhou Acima Da Capacidade' " BBCBrasil.Com, Reporter BBC |www.bbc.com/portuguese/reporterbbc/story/2008/09/080925_odebrecht_equador_cq.shtml accessed 4 November 2018.
50 Pía Riggirozzi and Diana Tussie, *The Rise of Post-Hegemonic Regionalism: The Case of Latin America* (Springer Science & Business Media 2012) 175.

Agreement (CFIA).[51] At the core of this agreement lies the mitigation of risks and the prevention of investment disputes with a dispute settlement system formed by a negotiating phase.[52] The focus of the Brazilian agreement thereby lays on a state-to-state dispute settlement process that is similar to traditional diplomatic protection. This is unlike traditional BIT procedures. Such a system contradicts the trend of judicialization of foreign investment law and the concomitant growing role of private entities in international law over the past century.[53]

The atypical Brazilian investment agreement

The CFIA stands out compared to the BITs signed by Brazil in the 1990s.[54] Undoubtedly, it marks an evolution in international investment law by taking decades of investment law practice and doctrine into account and forming a new role model for the investment protection regime. The Brazilian investment protection regime, thereby, can be divided into three main pillars: substantive protection; institutional governance; and dispute prevention and resolution.[55] Although this structure is not entirely new to international investment agreements,[56] the Model CFIA includes new provisions in contrast to the widespread BITs. Constant cooperation among governmental agencies,[57] mediated by diplomatic action,[58] deference to domestic legislation, and balanced obligations between foreign and domestic investors[59] as well as between investor and host state can be considered the leading notions behind this model arrangement.[60]

Substantive protection

The most distinctive characteristic about the CFIA is the absence of classical private international investment protection provisions compared to common

---

51 Monebhurrun (n 20) 82; Gabriel (n 21) 141–142.
52 Gabriel (n 21) 142.
53 David M. Trubek and Sonia E. Rolland, "Legal Innovation in Investment Law: Rhetoric and Practice in the South" (2017) 39 (2), *University of Pennsylvania Journal of International Law* 355.
54 The full English text of the model agreement is available at UNCTAD's Investment Hub Policy https://investmentpolicy.unctad.org/international-investment-agreements/treaty-files/4786/download accessed 2 June 2018.
55 Muniz et al. (n 13) 406–407; Ratton et al. (n 15) 223 and Monebhurrun (n 20) 83–85.
56 Titi (n 16) 9.
57 2015 Model Investment Agreement (n 54) Art 17.
58 Ibid. (n 54) Art 18 and 22.
59 Ibid. (n 54) Art 14–16.
60 Ratton et al. (n 15) 224.

international investment agreements. This characteristic is a result of Brazil's historically grown skepticism towards the international investment regime. So classical provisions such as the fair and equitable treatment standard, an investor–state dispute settlement mechanism, as well as provisions concerning indirect expropriation, are missing in the model agreement. Also, the CFIA does not contain an observance of undertakings or an umbrella clause.[61] While these international standards might be seen as an effective tool for the protection of investors, they can be used to limit host states' right to regulate in the public interest.[62] Since the CFIA is meant to stand out as an alternative to standard international practice, it is no surprise that Brazil went down this path in order to strengthen the position of the host state.

However, it is noticeable that one of the components of the fair and equal treatment is included in Article 9 of the Model CFIA. This states that all the regulatory measures regarding investments must be administered in an objective, reasonable and impartial manner, in line with each party's domestic legal system.[63] These obligations, as well as the publication of all laws and regulations affecting any provision of the CFIA, are made to guarantee transparency. Even further, the host state must enable the interested stakeholders to voice out their opinion on investment-related measures. Therefore, Article 9 of the Model CFIA includes at least some of the elements of a fair and equitable treatment standard into the agreement. Parallels can be drawn to Article 10.1 of the Energy Charter Treaty as a common example of the equalization of transparency and the means of fairness and equitability in the international investment regime.[64]

61 Muniz et al. (n 3) 412; Monebhurrun (n 20) 93.
62 Ratton et al. (n 15) 229.
63 The full wording of the provision declares: "Each Party shall ensure that its laws, regulations, procedures and general administrative resolutions related to any matter covered by this Agreement, in particular regarding qualification, licensing and certification, are published without delay and, when possible, in electronic format, as to allow interested persons of the other Party to be aware of such information."
64 Article 10.1 of the Energy Charter Treaty (adopted 17 December 1994, entered into force 16 April 1998) 2080 UNTS 95 states: "Each Contracting Party shall, in accordance with the provisions of this Treaty, encourage and create stable, equitable, favourable and transparent conditions for Investors of other Contracting Parties to make Investments in its Area. Such conditions shall include a commitment to accord at all times to Investments of Investors of other Contracting Parties fair and equitable treatment. Such Investments shall also enjoy the most constant protection and security and no Contracting Party shall in any way impair by unreasonable or discriminatory measures their management, maintenance, use, enjoyment or disposal. In no case shall such Investments be accorded treatment less favourable than that required by international law, including treaty obligations. Each Contracting Party shall observe any obligations it has entered into with an Investor or an Investment of an Investor of any other Contracting Party."

Even the most favored nation clause (MFN) – another common standard of protection in international investment law – has been pruned to fit Brazil's ideology of international investment law. The goal of MFN clauses in treaties is to ensure that the relevant parties treat each other in a manner at least as favorable as they treat third parties. The normal effect of an MFN clause in a BIT is to widen the rights of the investor.[65] The Model CFIA contains such a traditional MFN clause in Article 6.1: "Each Party shall accord to investors of another Party treatment no less favourable than that it accords, in like circumstances, to investors of any non-Party." A similar provision in Article 6.2 of the Model CFIA extends this treatment to "investments of investors of the other party." Nevertheless, Article 6.3(ii) of the Model CFIA limits the mentioned articles in relation to the benefits that may be derived from "any agreement for regional economic integration, free trade area, customs union or common market, of which a Party is a member." In Article 6.3(i), the scope of the MFN is narrowed down even further. The clause excludes the benefits deriving from regional economic integration as well as the "provisions relating to investment dispute settlement." This provision prevents investors from relying on investor–state dispute settlement by operation of the MFN clause.[66]

Regarding expropriation, the CFIA does not fulfil the minimum standard granted by BITs standard regulations. Most modern BITs apply to direct, indirect, and creeping expropriation. Their scope is usually limited either by the definition of certain situations or by carve-outs. Consistent with its goal to persevere the regulatory freedom on the contracting state, Article 7 of the Model CFIA excludes from its scope all indirect or creeping expropriations. The agreement, therefore, applies only to direct takings, and confers policy powers to the host state.[67] In addition, the Model CFIA names certain measures that are carved from the regulations on expropriation. It also opens up space to define general exceptions that influence the content of expropriation. Among the exception clauses are those concerning tax and prudential measures, national security, and others referring to a broader notion of the right to regulate when dealing with environmental, health, and labor policies.[68] Article 7.1 of the Model CFIA sets forth the conditions for lawful direct expropriations, stating that direct expropriations can only be

65 Rudolf Dolzer and Christoph Schreuer, *Principles of International Investment Law* (2nd edn, Oxford University Press 2012) 206.

66 Muniz et al. (n 13) 410; Catharine Titi, "Most-Favoured-Nation Treatment: Survival Clauses and Reform of International Investment Law" (2016) 33(5) *Journal of International Arbitration*, 425 and Ratton et al. (n 15) 228.

67 Ratton et al. (n 15) 229.

68 Ratton et al. (n 15) 229–230.

justified if they are "for a public purpose or necessity or when justified as social interest," carried out "in a non-discriminatory manner," and if they require "payment of effective compensation [...] in accordance with due process of law."[69]

In addition to the aforementioned novelties, Article 14 of the Model CFIA, provides for a new trend in investment treaty drafting. The agreement commits companies to make sure that their investments fulfil corporate social responsibility (CSR) obligations. The investments shall be in line with, and contribute to, the objective of sustainable development of the host state and the local community. The implementation and execution of these standards depend on the investor's voluntary conduct. The enforcement of these obligations are, however, essentially based on domestic supervision by the host state, given that they were explicitly excluded from arbitration in Article 24.3 of the Model CFIA.[70] The CSR shall encourage foreign investors to respect human rights and environmental laws in the host state.[71] Still in the logic of a voluntary conduct, the investor must also refrain from seeking or accepting any kind of exemption which would not be in line with the host states' laws on environment, health and security issues, financial incentives, and right of workers. The bottom line is that the CSR mainly tries to mitigate the risk of the parties through these regulations.[72]

Institutional governance

The CFIA does not merely provide for dispute resolution but has an entire chapter devoted to "Institutional Governance and Dispute Prevention." Thus, two types of institutions govern the agreement. On the one hand, a joint committee for the administration of the agreement composed of government representatives of both parties works towards implementing the concluded CFIA. The committee shall resolve any issues or disputes concerning an investment in an amicable manner. It operates on a state-to-state level.[73] On the other hand, in addition to the joint committee, the CFIA institutes national focal points or ombudsmen on an investor–state level. Thereby, the main task for the national focal points or ombudsmen

---

69 Muniz et al. (n 13) 412.
70 Ratton et al. (n 15) 231.
71 "The Brazilian Agreement on Cooperation and Facilitation of Investments (ACFI): A New Formula for International Investment Agreements? – Investment Treaty News" www.iisd.org/itn/2015/08/04/the-brazilian-agreement-on-cooperation-and-facilitation-of-investments-acfi-a-new-formula-for-international-investment-agreements/ accessed 3 May 2018.
72 Monebhurrun (n 20) 96.
73 Ibid. 83–84; Muniz et al. (n 13) 413; Ratton et al. (n 15) 226.

is to provide support for investors from the other party in its territory. The creation and regulation of the focal points, or rather ombudsmen, depend on each party's domestic regulation and will be generally formed as an agency. In the case of Brazil, the regulation of the ombudsman is linked to the Chamber of Foreign Trade as an interministerial body. The CFIA also includes provisions regulating the exchange of information regarding the regulatory and policy framework for investment, promoting transparency and accessibility of information relevant for investment initiatives and envisaging an Agenda for Further Investment Cooperation and Facilitation that paves the way for future initiatives.[74]

Dispute prevention and resolution

The main objective of the agreement, based on its core conception of cooperation, is to provide mechanisms to prevent disputes. The design of these mechanisms also brings the states to the front line in dealing with the internal challenges related to the implementation of the agreement.[75] By emphasizing dispute prevention, Brazil developed an innovative set of institutional mechanisms to pursue that goal. The Model CFIA presents three different levels of dispute resolution. The basis of this mechanism is formed by the focal point or ombudspersons. On the second level, the consultation and negotiation between the parties and the joint committee is the further escalating measure. Finally, if the aforementioned mechanisms fail, the arbitration between the contracting parties is the last instance to resolve any matters arising.[76]

On the first level of dispute prevention,[77] the permanent institutional body articulates the different constituencies from the representatives of the parties to the private sector, as well as governmental and non-governmental interested bodies. Any investor and/or representative of a party will bring the issue to the ombudsman level before taking a formal claim to the joint committee. The joint committee is, however, the first mandatory instance for addressing an investor claim based on the CFIA commitments. The joint committee is a governance structure composed by representatives of the parties to the agreements. Accordingly, from the dispute prevention perspective, it is the forum for consultations and negotiations between the parties. The CFIA declares that a formal notice to the joint committee is due by submitting a claim on behalf of an investor. At this stage, representatives of the

---

74 Monebhurrun (n 20) 85 et seq; Muniz et al. (n 13) 413; Ratton et al. (n 15) 227.
75 Ratton et al. (15) 232.
76 Ibid. 233–235; Muniz et al. (n 13) 414.
77 2015 Model Investment Agreement (n 54) Art 17.

interested investor and of the governmental or non-governmental entities involved in the measure or situation under consultation shall participate in the bilateral meetings[78] held by the joint committee.[79]

If the disputes are not resolved through dialogue and bilateral consultations, the contracting parties can initiate state-to-state arbitration through the provision included in Article 24 of the Model CFIA.[80] As a result, a tribunal comprised of three arbitrators is assigned with resolving the dispute, provided that not more than five years have elapsed since the investor knew or should have known of the facts giving rise to the dispute. The arbitration process commences with the filing of a notice of arbitration, after which each party appoints one arbitrator and both of the selected arbitrators agree on the appointment of a chairperson. If appointments are not concluded, the Secretary General of the International Court of Justice shall make the appointment. The tribunal is empowered to determine its own procedure or to adopt the United Nations Commission on International Trade Law arbitration rules; it shall render a decision by majority vote in accordance with the CFIA and the applicable principles and rules of international law as recognized by both parties. The outcome of the case can be a dismissal by the tribunal or any monetary compensation to the investor which ultimately has to be followed.[81] The result of the CFIA mechanism is that the investor can only influence the process to a certain degree. The final resolution of any arising problems will be found on a state-to-state level by the contracting parties.

Current investment scenario in Latin America

The contemporary investment law scenario in Latin America is a competitive one. There are too many forms of FDI regulation in place. From Central America, the Caribbean and South America, regional, independent, and international agreements have been employed to regulate investment. Such variety would represent diversity and opportunity for Latin America; nonetheless, the reality seems more like a series of different frameworks aiming at achieving a particular ideology. The most common investment

---

78 Article 17.3 states: "The Joint Committee shall meet at such times, in such places and through such means as the Parties may agree. Meetings shall be held at least once a year, with alternating chairmanships between the Parties."

79 Ratton et al. (n 15) 233.

80 Article 24.1 states: "Once the procedure under paragraph 3 of Article 23 has been exhausted and the dispute has not been resolved, either Party may submit the dispute to an ad hoc Arbitral Tribunal, in accordance with the provisions of this Article. Alternatively, the Parties may choose, by mutual agreement, to submit the dispute to a permanent arbitration institution for settlement of investment disputes. Unless the Parties decide otherwise, such institution shall apply the provisions of this Section."

81 Muniz et al. (n 13) 32.

agreements adopted by Latin American countries are BITs. There are different types of BITs throughout Latin America with one common pattern; most of them are subject to ICSID for dispute resolution. Exceptions can be found in Brazil, Suriname, Antigua and Barbuda, and Dominica, none of which have adhered to the ICSID Convention.[82] There are some islands in the Caribbean that are not signatories to the ICSID Convention; however, they are territories of other sovereignties.[83] Lastly, Venezuela, Ecuador and Bolivia were signatories but they all have withdrawn from the Convention, but Ecuador re-adhered to it in 2021.[84]

The approach to ICSID in Latin America generates mixed feelings. Countries such as Chile have used ICSID with positive and negative results. Chile has been the respondent in four ICSID cases;[85] it has been the home state of the investor in seven ICSID cases;[86] as a respondent, it had three decisions in its favor; and as a home state of the investor, it had four decisions in its favor.[87] The Chilean perspective is rather unique. Chile went

---

82 List of Contracting States and other Signatories of the Convention (n 23).

83 Puerto Rico and the United States Virgin Islands are an unincorporated territory of the United States of America. The Virgin British Islands, Anguila, Cayman Islands, and Montserrat are part of the British Overseas Territories. Saint Martin, Martinique, and Guadeloupe are part of the French Overseas Collectives. St Maarten, Bonaire, Curacao, and Aruba are constituencies' countries of the Kingdom of the Netherlands. All the places mentioned here are not on the ICISD list of contracting states and other signatories of the convention.

84 List of Contracting States and other Signatories of the Convention (n 23). Venezuela withdrew on 25 July 2012, Ecuador withdrew on 7 January 2010 and re-adhered to it on 21 June 2021, and Bolivia withdrew on 3 November 2007.

85 They are: *MTD Equity Sdn. Bhd. and MTD Chile S.A. v. Chile*, ICSID Case No. ARB/01/7 (Award, 25 May 2004); *Víctor Pey Casado and President Allende Foundation v. Republic of Chile*, ICSID Case No. ARB/98/2 (Award, 8 May 2008); *Sociedad Anónima Eduardo Vieira v. Republic of Chile*, ICSID Case No. ARB/04/7 (Award, 21 August 2007) and *Carlos Ríos and Francisco Ríos v. Republic of Chile*, ICSID Case No. ARB/17/16 (Award, 11 January 2021) (*Ríos v Chile* (Award 2021)).

86 They are: *Empresa Nacional de Electricidad S.A. v. Argentine Republic*, ICSID Case No. ARB/99/4 (*Nacional de Electricidad v Argentina*); *Industria Nacional de Alimentos, S.A. and Indalsa Perú, S.A. (formerly Empresas Lucchetti, S.A. and Lucchetti Perú, S.A.) v. Republic of Peru*, ICSID Case No. ARB/03/4; *Chilectra S.A., Elesur S.A., Empresa Nacional de Electrecidad S.A., and Enersis S.A. v. Argentine Republic*, ICSID Case No. ARB/03/21 (*Chilectra v Argentina*); *Compañía General de Electricidad S.A. and CGE Argentina S.A. v. Argentine Republic*, ICSID Case No. ARB/05/2 (*General de Electricidad v Argentina*); *Quiborax S.A., Non-Metallic Minerals S.A. v. Plurinational State of Bolivia*, ICSID Case No. ARB/06/2 and *Flughafen Zürich A.G. and Gestión e Ingenería IDC S.A. v. Bolivarian Republic of Venezuela*, ICSID Case No. ARB/10/19.

87 As the respondent, the case of *Ríos v Chile* (Award 2021) (n 85); and as the home State of the investor, two cases were discontinued *Chilectra v Argentina*

through a military dictatorship in the twentieth century, but when democracy was restored in the 1990s, it adopted an open policy regionalism to reconcile regional integration with globalization.[88] This led to several agreements, bilateral and multilateral, with different trading partners, resulting in a network of investment treaties.[89] For Chile, such approach was successful but the same cannot be said about other Latin American countries such as Argentina which might not see ICSID as a great experience.[90] Argentina holds the record of 62 ICSID cases as the respondent.[91] Such a negative record led to rumors that Argentina would be withdrawing from ICSID.[92] Ironically, it remains a signatory to the Convention having its last case started in 2019.[93] Even though Venezuela, Ecuador, and Bolivia do not have the same case record as Argentina, these countries decided to denounce the Convention. As opposed to Argentina, the three countries have adopted policies conflicting directly with the liberalism embodied

(n 86) (Discontinuance Order 2017) and *Nacional de Electricidad v Argentina* (n 86) (Discontinuance Order 2001) and one settled, *General de Electricidad v Argentina* (n 86) (Discontinuance Order 2009).

88 Rodrigo Polanco Lazo, "The Chilean Experience in South-South Investment and Trade Agreements," in Fabio Morosini and Michelle Ratton Sanchez Badin (eds), *Reconceptualizing International Investment Law from the Global South* (CUP, 2017), pp 100–101.

89 Since 1991 Chile has concluded 55 BITs and 32 Treaties with investment provisions. In http://investmentpolicyhub.unctad.org/IIA/CountryOtherIias/41#iiaInnerMen, accessed 10 May 2018.

90 See Carlos E. Alfaro and Pedro M. Lorenti, "The Growing Opposition of Argentina to ICSID Arbitral Tribunals: A Conflict between International and Domestic Law" (2005) 6 *Journal of World Investment & Trade* 417; Charity L. Goodman, "Uncharted Waters: Financial Crisis and Enforcement of ICSID Awards in Argentina" (2007), 28 *University of Pennsylvania Journal International Economic Law* 449 and William W. Burke-White, "The Argentine Financial Crisis: State Liability under BITs and the Legitimacy of the ICSID System" (2008) 3 *Asian Journal of WTO & International Health Law & Policy* 199.

91 In UNCTAD, Investment Policy Hub "Argentina" https://investmentpolicy.unctad.org/investment-dispute-settlement/country/8/argentina accessed 26 October 2021.

92 See Eric David Kasenetz, "Desperate Times Call for Desperate Measures: The Aftermath of Argentina's State of Necessity & the Current Fight in the ICSID" (2010) 41 *George Washington International Law Review* 709, 745; Oscar Lopez, "Smart Move: Argentina to Leave the ICSID" (2013) 1 *Cornell International Law Journal Online*, 121 and "Argentina in the Process of Quitting from World Bank Investment Disputes Centre," MERCOPRESS, in http://en.mercopress.com/2013/01/31/argentina-in-the-process-of-quitting-from-world-bank-investment-disputes-centre accessed 11 May 2018.

93 See *Nationale-Nederlanden Holdinvest B.V., Nationale-Nederlanden Intertrust B.V., NN Insurance International B.V., Orígenes AFJP S.A. (en liquidación) v. Argentine Republic* (ICSID Case No. ARB/19/11).

in the ICSID framework.[94] This resistance to FDI started in Bolivia, after President Evo Morales took office. He renationalized several industries and, in 2007, Bolivia notified the World Bank to inform its denunciation of ICSID. The reasons for the withdrawal were to maintain the sovereignty of Bolivia and to avoid international arbitration as a method to solve disputes involving Bolivia and investors.[95] Ecuador followed in 2010, when President Rafael Correa adopted similar policies to Bolivia and considered ICISD as a form of control over countries that needed to be set free.[96] Last, Venezuela left ICSID in 2012 when President Hugo Chavez was still in power. The rhetoric was similar; all countries opposed a neoliberal agenda and acted to renationalize companies controlled by foreign investors.[97] Hence, ICSID was an obstacle to the policies of the three countries as it excluded the power of national courts to decide any dispute regarding investment agreements and it provided for a platform to seek compensation for the countries' new policies. Strangely, Morales nationalized companies that were not protected by ICSID such as Petrobras refineries in Bolivia and Correa adopted a similar practice to Odebrecht in Ecuador, bringing doubt as to whether this was a move solely against the neoliberal ideas or a subterfuge to repatriate assets.

94 Such view can be extracted by the preamble of the ICSID convention when it declares that "while such disputes would usually be subject to national legal processes, international methods of settlement may be appropriate in certain cases."

95 Investment Treaty News reported on 9 May 2007 that Evo Morales stated that Bolivia "emphatically reject the legal, media and diplomatic pressure of some multinationals that … resist the sovereign rulings of countries, making threats and initiating suits in international arbitration." Moreover, according to the Bolivia's Charge d'Affaires for Trade with the Ministry of Foreign Affairs in La Paz, Bolivia wanted to revise 24 BITs to limit "the definition of an investment to those that 'truly generate a value to the country.'" In www.iisd.org/itn/wp-content/uploads/2010/10/itn_may9_2007.pdf accessed 14 May 2018.

96 Investment Treaty News reported on 8 June 2009 that Rafael Correa declared that departing from ICSID represented "the liberation of our countries because this signifies colonialism, slavery with respect to transnationals, with respect to Washington, with respect to the World Bank and we cannot tolerate this." In www.iisd.org/itn/2009/06/05/ecuador-continues-exit-from-icsid/ accessed 14 May 2018. Ironically, Ecuador has recently decided to rejoin ICSID. Under a new administration which opposes Correa's perspective, Ecuador decided that it needed to return to ICSID to bring back more foreign investment. See Gustavo Prieto, 'Ecuador Returns to the ICSID Convention: A Brief Assessment of Its Decade-Long International Investment Law "Exit Strategy"' (EJIL: Talk!, 19 July 2021) <https://www.ejiltalk.org/ecuador-returns-to-the-icsid-convention-a-brief-assessment-of-its-decade-long-international-investment-law-exit-strategy/> accessed 14 November 2021.

97 Steve Ellner, "Distinguishing Features of Latin America's New Left in Power, The Chavez, Morales and Correa Governments" (2012) 39(1) *Latin American Perspectives*, 96, 102.

The approach implemented by Ecuador, Venezuela, and Bolivia can also find its roots in the formation of Bolivarian Alliance for the Peoples of Our America (ALBA).[98] This organization was formed in 2004 between Venezuela and Cuba.[99] In 2005, the final declaration of the first ALBA meeting laid down its ethos, that is, to promote the ideology of Simón Bolívar and José Martí.[100] In effect, ALBA's purpose is to challenge neoliberalism by concentrating the monopoly of essential services in the government's hands instead of allowing the private sector to operate social services.[101] However, ALBA is not the only regional block in Latin America. As a result of the second wave of regionalism that has been observed and implemented by Latin American countries, several regional agreements promoting integration in Latin America came to life.[102]

In the Caribbean, CARICOM[103] was established in 1973 targeting "the economic integration of the Member States by the establishment of a

---

98 Daniel de Andrade Levy and Rodrigo Moreira, "ICSID in Latin America: Where Does Brazil Stand?" in Daniel de Andrade Levy, Ana Gerdau de Borja & Adriana Noemi Pucci (eds) *Investment Protection in Brazil* (Kluwer 2014) 25.

99 Agreement for the ALBA Application (signed 14 December 2004), https://web.arch ive.org/web/20170512125915/http://alba-tcp.org/en/contenido/agreement-alba-application accessed 20 April 2021.

100 The text of the final declaration expressed: "we fully agree that the ALBA will not become a reality with mercantilist ideas or the selfish interests of business profitability or national benefit to the detriment of other peoples. Only a broad Latin Americanist vision, which acknowledges the impossibility of our countries' developing and being truly independent in an isolated manner, will be capable of achieving what Bolívar called 'to see the formation in the Americas of the greatest nation in the world, not so much for its size and riches as for its freedom and glory,' and that Martí conceived of as 'Our America,' to differentiate it from the other America, the expansionist one with imperialist appetites." In www.anti-imperialist.org/cuba-venezuela_5-7-05.htm accessed 14 May 2018.

101 Paul Kellogg, "Regional Integration in Lain America: Dawn of Alternative to Neoliberalism?" (2007) 29(2) *New Political Science*, 187–209, 205.

102 According to Belisa Esteca Eleoterio and Alebe Linhares Mesquita, "The Twenty-First Century Regionalism: Brazil and Mercosur in the New International Scenario," in Giovanna Adinolfi, Freya Baetens, Jose Caiado, Angela Lupone, and Anna G. Micara (eds), *International Economic Law, Contemporary Issues* (Springer 2017) 101, there were two well-defined waves of regionalism. The first occurred after World War II with the formation of the European Economic Community and the second during the 1990s with the formation of NAFTA, Mercosur, ASEAN etc.

103 According to its website, "[s]tretching from The Bahamas in the north to Suriname and Guyana in South America, CARICOM comprises states that are considered developing countries, and except for Belize, in Central America and Guyana and Suriname in South America, all Members and Associate Members are island states." This integration has as its core value "winning hearts and minds to work towards a robust and inclusive Caribbean Community, able to work together to preserve the gains of regional integration and address the current challenges of economic recovery and growth and sustainable human development." In www.caricom.org/ accessed 1 July 2018.

common market regime."[104] CARICOM has five free trade agreements with the following countries: the Dominican Republic; Costa Rica; Colombia; Venezuela; and Cuba. Except for the agreement with Colombia, all the others have an express provision about investment.[105] All agreements embrace the ideas of national treatment, MFN, and transparency. The difference between the agreements can be found in relation to the settlement of disputes. With Costa Rica, ICSID is applicable, while with the other countries, a Joint Commission or a Joint Council is formed to resolve disputes if the parties cannot reach an agreement.[106] The Dominican Republic has another agreement with the United States, Costa Rica, El Salvador, Guatemala, Honduras, and Nicaragua called CAFTA DR. Chapter 10 of the agreement provides for the regulation of foreign investment. The settlement of disputes is made through ICSID and national treatment, MFN, and transparency are also principles applied in the agreement. Moving to countries bordering the Pacific Ocean, Mexico, Peru, Chile, and Colombia formed the Pacific Alliance on 28 April 2011. The aim of the integration is to provide for an area of free movement of people, goods, services, and capital.[107] In relation to investments, it adopts the well-established format of FDI rules and for settlement of disputes, ICSID is the chosen method.[108]

Another agreement involving Mexico is the old North America Free Trade Agreement (NAFTA), now called the United States–Mexico–Canada Agreement (USMCA). Chapter 11 of the NAFTA agreement regulated foreign investment in a similar manner to the CAFTA DR format; however, the

---

104 Article 49(a) of the Treaty Establishing the Caribbean Community (signed 4 July 1973, entered into force 1 August 1973) 946 UNTS 17, UN Reg No I-13489.

105 With the Dominican Republic, annex III provides for a Reciprocal Promotion and Protection of Investments, Agreement Establishing the Free Trade Area between the Caribbean Community (CARICOM) and the Dominican Republic (signed 22 August 1998, entered into force 5 February 2002) (CARICOM – Dominican Republic FTA). With Costa Rica, Chapter X talks about investment, Free Trade Agreement between the Caribbean Community (CARICOM) and Costa Rica (signed 09 March 2004, entered into force 15 November 2005) (CARICOM – Costa Rica FTA). The Cuban agreement provides for Investments in Article 17 while the Venezuelan does in Article 9: Trade and Economic Cooperation Agreement between CARICOM and Cuba (signed 5 July 2000, entered into force 1 January 2001) (CARICOM – Cuba Cooperation Agreement) and Agreement between the Caribbean Community (CARICOM) and Venezuela on Trade and Investment (signed 13 October 1992; entered into force 1 January 1993) (CARICOM – Venezuela FTA) respectively.

106 For Costa Rica, see Article XII CARICOM – Costa Rica FTA (n 105); for Venezuela, see Article 17 CARICOM – Venezuela FTA (n 105), and for Cuba, see Article 24 CARICOM – Cuba Cooperation Agreement (n 105).

107 Article 3 1(a) of the Acuerdo Marco de la Alianza del Pacifico entre la República de Colombia, la República de Chile, los Estados Unidos Mexicanos y la República del Perú (signed 6 de junio de 2012).

108 See Chapter 10 of the Protocolo Adicional al Acuerdo Marco de la Alianza del Pacífico (signed 10 February 2014, entered into force 1 May 2016).

USMCA presents a new scenario. Now, Chapter 14 of USMCA provides for investment with common clauses such as national treatment,[109] MFN,[110] expropriation and compensation,[111] and a CSR clause.[112] But, when it comes to dispute resolution, it determines that Chapter 11 of NAFTA can only be employed up to three years after NAFTA's termination. This is called the Legacy Investment Claims and Pending Claims and once NAFTA's directives are no longer in place, a new set of rules limiting arbitration will replace the old system of dispute resolution. Article 14.2 of USMCA determines that investors can only start arbitration in Mexico–United States Investment Dispute and Mexico–United States Investment Disputes Related to Covered Government Contracts.[113] For the Mexico–United States Investment Dispute, before arbitration can be triggered, a consultation and negotiation should be employed to resolve the dispute.[114] If no agreement is reached, claimant or respondent could have the dispute arbitrated for breach of national treatment, MFN, expropriation and compensation and loss or damage by reason of treaty breach.[115] The claim will be referred to ICSID or UNCITRAL. The same rules apply to Mexico–United States Investment Disputes Related to Covered Government Contracts but the treaty breach has to be related to a government contract.[116] An innovative feature of USMCA is the requirement to go to court before arbitrating. The American and Mexican claimants have to initiate legal proceedings before a court or an administrative tribunal and they can only resort to arbitration if proceedings have not been decided or 30 months have passed since they commenced.[117]

---

109 Agreement between the United States of America, the United Mexican States, and Canada (signed 30 November 2018, entered into force 1 July 2020) Chapter 14, Article 14.4.

110 Ibid., Article 14.5.

111 Ibid., Article 14.8.

112 Ibid., Article 14.17.

113 Article 14.2(4) states: "For greater certainty, an investor may only submit a claim to arbitration under this Chapter as provided under Annex 14-C (Legacy Investment Claims and Pending Claims), Annex 14-D (Mexico–United States Investment Disputes), or Annex 14-E (Mexico–United States Investment Disputes Related to Covered Government Contracts)."

114 Annex 14-D, Article 2.

115 Ibid., Article 3.

116 Annex 14-E.

117 Annex 14-D, Article 5 declares: "Article 5: Conditions and Limitations on Consent 1. No claim shall be submitted to arbitration under this Annex unless: (a) the claimant (for claims brought under Article 3.1(a) (Submission of a Claim)) and the claimant or the enterprise (for claims brought under Article 3.1(b)) first initiated a proceeding before a competent court or administrative tribunal of the respondent with respect to the measures alleged to constitute a breach referred to in Article 3 (Submission of a Claim to Arbitration); (b) the claimant or the enterprise obtained a final decision from a court of last resort of the respondent or 30 months have elapsed from the date the proceeding in subparagraph (a) was initiated."

Regionalism involving Brazil can be found in the South Common Market (Mercosur) and in the Union of the South American Nations (UNASUR). Mercosur is a common market formed by Brazil, Argentina, Paraguay Uruguay, Bolivia, and Venezuela.[118] Although the treaty creating Mercosur was signed in 1991, its regulation of investment is rather new, being introduced in 2017.[119] The surprising aspect of this agreement is that it follows the steps of the Brazilian CFIA. Therefore, on one side it rejects the BITs view of fair and equitable treatment, full protection and security clauses.[120] It also excludes the protection against indirect expropriation.[121] On the other side, it embraces access to justice and due process,[122] it foments CSR,[123] it provides for an ombudsman to assist foreign investors[124] and a system to prevent disputes.[125] If a dispute cannot be settled, the Mercosur Olivos Protocol for the Settlement of Disputes will apply and the parties can resort to state-to-state negotiations or a state-to-state arbitration.[126] As can be seen, the options in Mercosur are also within the Latin America view of resistance to mainstream approaches. However, the refusal is partial. Instead of having a traditional investment framework, it provides remedies in a state-to-state level, accommodating the need for investors to have some protection over their investment.

UNSAUR is actually defunct: in 2018, Argentina, Brazil, Chile, Colombia, Paraguay and Peru suspended their participation in, and later on, Brazil, Ecuador and Uruguay declared their intention to withdraw from, the organization - and while UNASUR was a functioning organization, the regulation of

---

118 Venezuela had its membership suspended on 5 August 2017 for breaching the Mercosur Protocol of Ushuaia which established the Democratic Commitment of Mercosur. In www.mercosur.int/innovaportal/v/8470/12/innova.front/decis%C3%A3o-sobre-a-suspens%C3%A3o-da-republica-bolivariana-da-venezuela-no-mercosul accessed 20 May 2018.

119 This was done by the Intra-MERCOSUR Cooperation and Facilitation Investment Protocol (signed 7 April 2017, entered into force 30 July 2019) (Intra-MERCOSUR Investment Facilitation Protocol (2017)). For the initial attempts in creating an investment agreement in Mercosur see James D. Fry and Juan Ignacio Stampalija, "Towards an Agreement on Investment in Mercosur: Conflict and Complementarity of International Investment Law and International Trade-in-Services Law" (2012) 13, *The Journal of World Investment & Trade*, 556.

120 Intra-MERCOSUR Investment Facilitation Protocol (2017) (n 119), Article 4.3.

121 Ibid., Article 6.6l.

122 Ibid., Articles 4.2 and 4.3.

123 Ibid., Article 14.

124 Ibid., Article 18.

125 Ibid., Article 23.

126 Articles 4 and 9 of the Olivos Protocol for the Settlement of Disputes in MERCOSUR (signed 18 February 2002, entered into force 1 January 2004) 2251 UNTS 243, UN Reg No A-37341 (2003) 42 ILM 2.

investment was tendered by Ecuador.[127] More precisely, to oppose the ICSID structure, Ecuador made a proposal for the creation of an investment center to settle disputes.[128] A working group was established in 2008 to develop a mechanism to settle investment disputes in UNASUR.[129] In 2012, a first draft of the agreement was presented at the IV meeting of the working group. Another draft was presented in 2014, but no final version has been accepted by all UNASUR members.[130] The new system wanted to use facilitation in conflict resolution. It recommended a procedure in which a party may ask assistance from the center to reach an amicable solution to a dispute as long as the investment agreement provides for consultation and negotiation as a system to solve disputes.[131] Additional to facilitation, conciliation could be done by requesting it to be established by the executive secretary of the center.[132] Finally, parties could request that a dispute be submitted to arbitration.[133]

127 See Katia Fach Gómez and Catharine Titi, "UNASUR Centre for the Settlement of Investment Disputes: Comments on the Draft Constitutive Agreement," Investment Treaty News, in www.iisd.org/itn/2016/08/10/unasur-centre-for-the-settlement-of-investment-disputes-comments-on-the-draft-constitutive-agreement-katia-fach-gomez-catharine-titi/ accessed 21 May 2018; Lisandra Paraguassu, 'Six South American Nations Suspend Membership of Anti-U.S. Bloc' *Reuters* (20 April 2018) <https://www.reuters.com/article/us-unasur-membership-idUSKBN1HR2P6> accessed 14 November 2021; Sara España, 'Ecuador se retira de Unasur y abre la puerta a nuevas iniciativas de integración' *El País* (Madrid, 14 March 2019) <https://elpais.com/internacional/2019/03/14/america/1552524533_446745.html> accessed 14 November 2021; El País, 'Gobierno Anunció El Retiro de Uruguay de La Unasur y El Reingreso al TIAR - Información - 10/03/2020 - EL PAÍS Uruguay' *El País* (Montevideo, 10 March 2020) <https://www.elpais.com.uy/informacion/politica/gobierno-anuncio-retiro-uruguay-unasur-reingreso-tiar.html> accessed 14 November 2021; Eliane Oliveira and Marina Gonçalves, 'Governo Bolsonaro enterra Unasul criada por Lula e adere a novo organismo regional' *O Globo* (7 March 2019) <https://oglobo.globo.com/mundo/governo-bolsonaro-enterra-unasul-criada-por-lula-adere-novo-organismo-regional-23505468> accessed 14 November 2021.
128 Silvia Karina Fiezzoni, "The Challenge of UNASUR Member Countries to Replace ICSID Arbitration" (2011) 2, *Beijing Law Review*, 134.
129 This was done by the foreign ministers of UNASUR in a meeting in Colombia. In https://repo.unasursg.org/alfresco/service/unasursg/documents/content/los_ministros_de_relaciones_exteriores_de_america_del_sur_resuelven_crear_un_grupo_de_trabajo_con_miras_a_la_constitucion_de_un_mecanismo_para_solucion_de_controversias_en_materia_de_inversiones_en_el_marco_de_unasur.pdf?noderef=55ad4a66-069a-4da6-9dc3-db570c58ddcd accessed 21 May 2018.
130 The last meeting of the working group, the fourteenth meeting, was held on 31 March 2016. In https://repo.unasursg.org/alfresco/service/unasursg/documents/content/decima_cuarta_reunion_del_grupo_de_trabajo_de_expertos_de_alto_nivel_sobre_solucion_de_controversias_en_materia_de_inversiones_de_unasur_acta.pdf?noderef=42dd7b23-19c6-4252-abd1-654d895d8a2c accessed 21 May 2018.
131 Article 11 of the 2014 draft proposal.
132 Article 12 of the 2014 draft proposal.
133 Article 13 of the 2014 draft proposal.

A feature in the UNASUR arbitration was the possibility to present an appeal to the arbitral award in two circumstances: an error in the application or interpretation of the law applicable to the dispute and a manifest error in the appreciation of facts, which negatively influenced the assessment of evidence that would have otherwise changed the award.[134] Even though the initiative presents different options, the proposal has a discouraging provision stating that in disputes between an investor and a state, the latter can demand the exhaustion of domestic administrative and judicial remedies before resorting to the center's system of dispute resolution.[135] Not all legal systems have a fast and efficient judiciary. Therefore, the idea is a disservice to the ethos of the center as it could take a long time to go through all domestic administrative and judicial spheres of a country. Conversely, this might have been the goal of the agreement; that is, to create obstacles so parties will opt out from using arbitration and will try to settle any impasse amicably.

The examples presented above are samples of some of the structures adopted in Latin America.[136] Besides the BITs covered by ICSID, there are other investment treaties relying on ad hoc arbitration or another institutional arbitration such as the International Centre of Commerce, the Stockholm Chamber of Commerce, and the Permanent Court of Arbitration.[137] To put it briefly, there is a myriad of agreements in Latin America tailored for the ideology of each regional bloc. The positive aspect of such diversity is questionable. Looking at FDI policies, each country, or regional block, has a different objective. Chile has a welcoming policy towards FDI,[138] it

---

134 Article 31 of the 2014 draft proposal.

135 Article 5(10) of the 2014 draft proposal.

136 A list of all agreements, regional, bilateral or multilateral can be found in the Foreign Trade Information System of the Organization of American States in www.sice.oas.org/.

137 For instance, in the Permanent Court of Arbitration, Ecuador has three cases, *Merck Sharpe & Dohme (I.A.) Corporation v. The Republic of Ecuador*, PCA Case No. 2012–10; *Albacora S.A. v. Republic of Ecuador*, PCA Case No. 2016–11; and *Chevron Corporation and Texaco Petroleum Company v. The Republic of Ecuador (II)*, PCA Case No. 2009–23; Venezuela has two, *Venezuela US, S.R.L. v. Bolivarian Republic of Venezuela*, PCA Case No. 2013–34; and *Manuel García Armas, Pedro García Armas, Sebastián García Armas, Domingo García Armas, Manuel García Piñero, Margaret García Piñero, Alicia García González, Domingo García Cámara, Carmen García Cámara v. Bolivarian Republic of Venezuela*, PCA Case No. 2016–08; and Bolivia has two cases, *Glencore Finance (Bermuda) Ltd. v. Plurinational State of Bolivia*, PCA Case No. 2016–39, and *South American Silver Limited v. The Plurinational State of Bolivia*, PCA Case No. 2013–15.

138 See OECD, *Diagnostic of Chile's Engagement in Global Value Chains* (OECD Publishing, 2015) www.oecd.org/chile/diagnostic-chile-gvc-2015.pdf accessed 8 November 2018.

has a relative good experience with FDI dispute settlement and has tried to merge regionalism with globalization. Argentina incorporated a neoliberal agenda in the 1990s but since the beginning of this century, its economy has been unstable.[139] However, it has not rejected the Western FDI framework. ALBA is an alliance and it does not adhere or produce FDI instruments; nevertheless, it presents an ideology that guides its members against ICSID, which can be seen by the fact that it has as its members anti-ICSID countries. Be that as it may, even at ALBA it is hard to find cohesion because in August 2018, Ecuador withdrew from the organization.[140] Moreover, when Ecuador was contrary to FDI, it tried to create a system to oppose ICSID. In the meantime, MERCOSUR is trying to follow the Brazilian CFIA model, and Mexico, in the USMCA system, is adhering to the new American policies towards FDI. Too many systems will render some frameworks obsolete. Furthermore, creating formats fit for a local policy will only work if the specific country has bargaining power in transacting. Otherwise, instead of encouraging trade, isolation and introspection are likely to be the outcomes of so many options.

The Brazilian CFIA as an alternative for investment in Latin America

With the variety of models regulating investment in Latin America, the Brazilian CFIA could present a new framework to Latin American countries resisting ICSID or the like. The BIT system together with ICSID has encountered obstacles that go beyond ALBA members. Australia decided that it will no longer adopt arbitration to settle disputes involving its BITs.[141] The move

---

139 Martha Martínez Licetti, Mariana Iootty, Tanja Goodwin, and José Signoret, *Strengthening Argentina's Integration into the Global Economy: Policy Proposals for Trade, Investment, and Competition* (World Bank, 2018) https://openknowle dge.worldbank.org/handle/10986/29645 License: CC BY 3.0 IGO, accessed 8 November 2018.

140 "Ecuador deja la Alba al no concordar con sus principios" *El Telégrafo* (24 August 2018) www.eltelegrafo.com.ec/noticias/politica/3/onu-venezolanos-acogida-refugia-dos accessed 9 November 2018.

141 See Gillard Government Trade Policy Statement: Trading our way to more jobs and prosperity, April 2011, in http://blogs.usyd.edu.au/japaneselaw/2011_Gillard%20G ovt%20Trade%20Policy%20Statement.pdf accessed 30 May 2018, page 14 where it states: "In the past, Australian Governments have sought the inclusion of investor–state dispute resolution procedures in trade agreements with developing countries at the behest of Australian businesses. The Gillard Government will discontinue this practice. If Australian businesses are concerned about sovereign risk in Australian trading partner countries, they will need to make their own assessments about whether they want to commit to investing in those countries."

is a reaction to the case of *Philip Morris Asia Limited v The Commonwealth of Australia*[142] which challenged Australia's Tobacco Plain Packaging Act 2011;[143] added to the fact that "there are growing doubts about the perceived economic merits of trade and investment arbitration."[144] The EU has taken a similar approach and in its latest trade agreements with Canada and Vietnam, it is proposing the creation of an investment court system.[145] Therefore, in this scenario, Brazil's vision appears innovative and bold. Nevertheless, the framework presented reflects more a necessity for Brazil to enter the investment protection world and as a result, to give assurances to its own companies.

In a sense, the Brazilian CFIA is already a model for some Latin American countries because the Mercosur's Protocol on Investment Cooperation and Facilitation is mirrored in the Brazilian CFIA. This is not a mere coincidence as within Mercosur Brazil has a leadership position. Nevertheless, even though the country is a world top ten economy,[146] within Latin America, the tale is not the same. Brazil can exercise influence but not as the main leader; additionally, Brazil's policy is not always in line with the politics of other Latin American countries.[147]

Be that as it may, so far, Brazil has signed CFIAs with six Latin American countries that are familiar with the ICSID system and the well-established BIT. This mirrors an acceptance to the new model but no standardization.

---

142 *Philip Morris Asia Limited v. The Commonwealth of Australia*, UNCITRAL, PCA Case No. 2012–12 (*Philip Morris Asia v Australia*).

143 The claim argued that "[t]he plain packaging legislation bars the use of intellectual property on tobacco products and packaging, transforming [the Claimant's subsidiary in Australia] from a manufacturer of branded products to a manufacturer of commoditized products with the consequential effect of substantially diminishing the value of [the Claimant's] investments in Australia." *Philip Morris Asia v. Australia* (n 142) (Notice of Arbitration, 21 November 2011). The tribunal concluded that the claims raised were inadmissible and therefore, it had no jurisdiction over the dispute. See *Philip Morris Asia v Austalia* (n 142) (Award on Jurisdiction 2015) (n 142).

144 Leon E Trakman, "Australia's Rejection of Investor-State Arbitration: A Sign of Global Change" in Leon E. Trakman and Nicola Ranieri (eds), *Regionalism in International Investment Law* (Oxford University Press 2013), 348.

145 See August Reinisch, "Will the EU's Proposal Concerning an Investment Court System for CETA and TTIP Lead to Enforceable Awards? – The Limits of Modifying the ICSID Convention and the Nature of Investment Arbitration" (2016) 19, *Journal of International Economic Law*, 2016, 761 and Freya Baetens, "The European Union's Proposed Investment Court System: Addressing Criticisms of Investor-State Arbitration While Raising New Challenges" (2016) 43(4) *Legal Issues of Economic Integration*, 367.

146 CIA World Fact Book (n 32).

147 See Levy et al. (n 85) and Badin et al. (n 10).

On the contrary, four out of the six countries have agreed to different frameworks and are open to a diverse portfolio of investment agreements.[148] The initial political situation in Brazil was to reject the FDI framework. Brazil signed several BITs but never ratified them. Eventually, Brazilian companies started to invest abroad, the economy grew, and Brazil became an exporter of investment as opposed to just a recipient of investment. Such events promoted a change; however, the modification needed to be done in a Brazilian way, that is, Brazil could not now turn a blind eye to the past and adhere to the mainstream BIT model. Hence, what Brazil did was to create a framework that would be acceptable internally and externally. Internally, because it proposes a system different from what has already been rejected; and externally, because it distances itself from ICSID. The latter position is materialized through the countries with which Brazil has already concluded a CFIA. These countries are all developing economies, and once the South American nations are excluded, other signatories are from Africa, Middle East and Central Asia, regions which Brazilian companies operate or want to operate.[149] Thus, at first sight, the CFIAs concluded were primarily made to protect outbound investments from Brazil as some of the counterparties of the agreements themselves do not have much investment in Brazil.

Moreover, when it comes to trade deals and regulation of investments, Latin America has a plethora of frameworks. Despite the efforts of the trade blocs such as the Pacific Alliance, the defunct UNASUR, Mercosur, and CARICOM to harmonize trade, each group is pursuing local interests that do not reflect a will for Latin American integration. Otherwise, perhaps, there would be no need for so many regional agreements. Also, some countries – such as Mexico, Chile, and Peru – appear to be comfortable with the ICSID system.[150] The political regimes in Latin America are so diverse that despite the existing regional efforts, it is unlikely that Latin America can agree on a common standard.

Another question that will be answered through time is if Western countries that heavily invest in Brazil will adhere to CFIA. Even though the ICSID

---

148 Mexico, Chile, and Peru are part of the TPP. Mexico is part of NAFTA and the three countries together with Colombia are part of the Pacific Alliance. Moreover, all four countries are signatory to the ICSID convention. See Chapter 3 by Henrique Choer Moraes and Facundo Pérez Aznar in this volume.

149 See "A new Atlantic alliance," *The Economist* (London, 10 November 2012) www.economist.com/business/2012/11/10/a-new-atlantic-alliance accessed 2 March 2021.

150 Mexico signed the ICSID on 11 January 2018 and it entered into force on 26 August 2018. Chile did not have a bad experience with ICSID.

model is being criticized,[151] it is still the most common method to solve investment disputes. Additionally, CFIA's exclusion of ICSID is not exceptional. The CARICOM has a system of Joint Commission or a Joint Council to solve disputes that avoid the investor–state arbitration. Outside Latin America, the EU is also working on establishing an investment court. What makes it different is its suitability to Brazil. As Brazil is an attractive place for FDI, the country has some bargaining power to implement a bespoke arrangement for investment. But until the CFIA can be deemed successful, ICSID will remain in place. Perhaps, the ALBA countries could embrace the CFIA style as it counterposes ICSID, but Latin America seems far from reaching a homogeneous format of FDI.

Concluding remarks

The Brazilian CFIA comes at an interesting moment for FDI. It represents the debut for Brazil in the FDI scenario. It is also an opportunity for developing economies wishing to be recipients of Brazilian FDI or to encourage investment in Brazil, and to have some protection in its endeavors. As Latin America has been dealing with FDI and its dispute resolution system since the 1990s, it was the right time for Brazil to position itself in this arena. Be that as it may, the situation in Latin America is far from stable when it comes to FDI. The revival of the Calvo doctrine and the "us against them" ideology runs contrary to the idea of integration that is needed in Latin America. The reality is that Latin America tends to have policies resisting and accommodating FDI and that is the Brazilian case. It resisted the FDI framework for years but when it became necessary to provide protection to its companies, it decided to accommodate, that is, create its own system which derives, in part, from the well-established Western view of FDI.

It is natural that similitudes in Latin America would bring countries together, but recently, the myriad of arrangements resembles groups forming against the threat of each other.[152] The CFIA could be a good model for

---

151 See Muthucumaraswamy Sornarajah, "The case Against a Regime on International Investment Law," in Leon E. Trakman and Nicola Ranieri (eds), *Regionalism in International Investment Law* (Oxford University Press 2013); Caroline Foster, "A New Stratosphere? Investment Treaty Arbitration as 'Internationalized Public Law'" (2015) 64, *International Comparative Law Quarterly*, 461; and Nicolás M. Perrone, "The Emerging Global Right to Investment: Understanding the Reasoning behind Foreign Investor Rights" (2017) 8, *Journal of International Dispute Settlement*, 673.

152 C.f. Chapter 2 by Magdalena Bas and Chapter 3 by Henrique Choer Moraes and Facundo Perez Aznar in this volume.

Latin America. It certainly would make some of the anti-ICSID countries feel more comfortable with the settlement of disputes. The state-to-state arbitration, in theory, would provide a different spectrum and exclude the ideas of an arbitral tribunal protecting foreign multinationals and interfering in domestic sovereignty. But even so, the imperialist argument could still be raised due to the economic position of one of the state parties in the arbitration. In any case, a state-to-state arbitration would appear more transparent as there would be a stronger public pressure to make the proceedings public.

The Brazilian initiative is good for Brazil, and it can be good for Latin America if there is a will to act together. However, nowadays, Latin American countries acting as a team seems more symbolic than real. It is hard to see a true intention to work together. The changes are happening so often and so fast that by the time this book has been published, it is likely that new blocks might be formed and more countries will have withdrawn from regional agreements. As a result, it is difficult to aspire a true willingness amongst Latin American countries to work together. What is clear is that different blocks are formed to either resist or accommodate foreign influence. If the CFIA proves to be successful, perhaps a movement for its expansion should be made, though, for the moment, it is an investment agreement made in Brazil for Brazil.

5

Foreign investment and regulatory governance: A critical approach to investment facilitation debate

Luciana Ghiotto

Introduction

For the past three decades we have witnessed the signing of multiple bilateral investment treaties (BIT) and free trade agreements (FTA) with investment provisions all over the world. These treaties include a number of clauses that protect foreign investment against the action of states that could affect their investment and their right to profit in any way. These clauses usually include national treatment, most favored nation, fair and equitable treatment, expropriation (direct and indirect), and the investor–state dispute settlement (ISDS) mechanism. The result of the signing of these treaties has been the development of what Jagdish Bhagwati called a "spaghetti bowl of treaties"[1] that has created a phenomenon of lack of governance of global investment protection rules and a flourishing of ISDS cases against developed and non-developed states all over the world.

This lack of multilateral governance has been a concern for the United Nations Conference on Trade and Development (UNCTAD) for the past ten years. According to this organization, nearly 3,000 BITs have created a kind of "governance chaos" of investment protection rules.[2] This is why UNCTAD has proposed that states renegotiate the old-generation of BITs, that is to say, treaties signed in the nineties, and make them more "modern"

---

1 Jagdish Bhagwati "US Trade Policy: The Infatuation with FTAs" (1995) Discussion Paper Series No. 726 https://academiccommons.columbia.edu/doi/10.7916/D8QF9 1BB/download accessed 2 March 2021.
2 Luciana Ghiotto, "¿UNCTAD pro-desarrollo o pro-liberalización? Un estudio de los cambios en el organismo a la luz de las políticas sobre inversiones" in Echaide (ed) *Inversiones extranjeras y responsabilidad social de las empresas; problemáticas en torno al CIADI, los TBI y los Derechos Humanos* (Buenos Aires, Ediciones BdeF 2017).

by including sustainable development oriented dispositions, as well as putting public policy space at the heart of the new treaties.[3]

New trends in foreign investment treatment have not particularly improved this "chaos." For the past decade, states have taken different paths to address the multiplication of treaties. This has been clear in Latin America, where governments have followed different approaches regarding how to engage with the existing BITs. On the one hand, the most radical approach has been the cases of Ecuador, Bolivia, and Venezuela, as they terminated many (or all) of their BITs and also withdrew from the International Centre for Settlement of Investment Disputes (ICSID). On the other hand, many new BIT models have popped up, where some of the new treaties have been presented by governments as "new generation" treaties,[4] but these still include the problematic clauses that have put countries like Argentina in the top of the ranking of ISDS cases. So some of the countries have found a way to accommodate to the new trends, instead of entering into a debate on how these treaties have affected their regulatory capacity.

This chapter focuses on the debate that arose in 2012, which is on investment facilitation rules. The investment facilitation debate came to light in the multilateral forums, especially in the World Trade Organization (WTO) and G20. Also, UNCTAD and the Organisation for Economic Cooperation and Development (OECD) have been working on different aspects of this new topic. However, first of all, it should be said that investment facilitation does not focus on protection rights for foreign investments but it sticks to facilitation rules. This difference has been presented by some of the proposing countries (like China) as a point that overcomes many of the investment protection system problems.[5] This proposal is rather new, and thus, it still is very much unknown to the public, policymakers, and also to academia. The changes to the system are moving fast, and the analysis capacity is not yet keeping up with these variations.

As will be explained, the investment facilitation proposal focuses on three issues: 1) transparency and predictability; 2) commitment with stakeholders;

---

3 UNCTAD "Recent developments in the international investment regime" (2018) IIA Issues Note, Issue 1.
4 Examples of this are the new Agreement for the Reciprocal Promotion and Protection of Investments between the Argentine Republic and the State of Qatar (signed 6 November 2016), Agreement between the Argentine Republic and Japan for the Promotion and Protection of Investment (signed 1 December 2018) and Agreement for the Reciprocal Promotion and Protection of Investments between the Argentine Republic and the United Arab Emirates (signed 14 April 2018). These treaties are not in force (as of January 2021).
5 Kavaljit Singh, "Do we need a Multilateral Instrument on Investment Facilitation?" (2017) 19 Madhyam Briefing Papers.

and, 3) regulatory cooperation. The definition of investment facilitation is loose and indeterminate, as its main aim is the simplification of all administrative procedures in the host country to allow the free entrance, development, and exit of foreign investors.

A problem emerges when we see one of the main components of investment facilitation which is regulatory cooperation. It is presented as a way of guaranteeing transparency and commitment to stakeholders, as it demands that states make public and available for the discussion of stakeholders all their existing regulations on foreign investments, as well as all the planned changes to their regulation. Regulatory cooperation is part of the concept of "good regulatory practices" which has been pushed internationally by the Organisation for Economic Cooperation and Development (OECD). This concept comes from the OECD's work since 2012, with the recommendation of the Council on Regulatory Policy and Governance for countries to "[d]evelop a consistent policy covering the role and functions of regulatory agencies in order to provide greater confidence that regulatory decisions are made on an objective, impartial and consistent basis, without conflict of interest, bias or improper influence."[6] The focus is set on efficient and effective regulators and regulations.

The set of rules that contain regulatory cooperation mechanisms have the objective of reducing operating costs for investors. These instruments are central to all mega-regional agreements signed or negotiated as of 2012, as they not only incorporate trade liberalization and investment provisions, but also include the "issues behind the borders," that is, regulatory issues. Investment Facilitation rules are a way to intervene in the regulatory process of states through the establishment of the obligation to open up the regulatory process to the private sector, and even to other states.

It can be argued that the notion of good regulatory practices is a way of shrinking policy space, and of giving enhanced decision capabilities to private stakeholders in the investment process. Under the title of "transparency" and "administrative procedures" we find issues related not to trade or investment, but to the restriction of regulatory space. In this article, we argue that the notions included in the investment facilitation concept have formed a mechanism that operates at the core of domestic regulatory processes. This implies not only a set of clauses on the treatment to be given to foreign investors, like those contained in "old" investment treaties, but also processes for the design of rules and laws that directly affect (or benefit) investors and investment projects.

6 OECD, *Recommendation of the Council on Regulatory Policy and Governance* (2012) Regulatory Process, 4.

In the same way, we find that there is a tension that can be identified in the investment facilitation debate, especially between the two concepts presented here: on the one hand, the UNCTAD proposal for the investment regime reform which includes the need for "public policy space" on the road towards sustainable development and sustainable investment. On the other hand, we find the core element of investment facilitation which is the notion of "good regulatory practices" proposed by the OECD. Both categories can be considered as contradictory to the existence of policy space for regulation, in accordance to sustainable development goals. We find that this tension arising between both concepts is an expression of the tensions existing in the current process of reform of the investment protection regime in a global scale.

The investment facilitation debate

The debate on investment facilitation is relatively new, though it has intensified since Brazil, Argentina, Russia, China, and the MIKTA countries (Mexico, Indonesia, Korea, Turkey, and Australia) started to promote it at a multilateral level.[7] In 2017, these countries submitted their proposals to include investment facilitation in the eleventh WTO Ministerial Conference that took place in Buenos Aires, but other countries such as the United States, South Africa, India and the countries of the Bolivarian Alliance for the Peoples of our America (ALBA, in its Spanish acronym) (Bolivia, Cuba, and Venezuela) blocked its inclusion. For its part, China also promoted this proposal in the organization process of the G20 summit in Hamburg (2017),

---

7 The proposals submitted to the General Council of the WTO are: Communication from the Russian Federation, Investment Policy Discussion Group. Document JOB/GC/120 (31 March 2017) https://docs.wto.org/ *(Russia Communication JOB/GC/120)*; MIKTA Investment Workshop Reflections, Communication from Mexico, Indonesia, Korea, Turkey, and Australia (MIKTA). Document JOB/GC/121 (6 April 2017) https://docs.wto.org/; Proposal for a WTO Informal Dialogue on Investment Facilitation for Development, Joint Communication form the Friends of Investment Facilitation for Development (FIFD). Document JOB/GC/122 (26 April 2017) https://docs.wto.org/; Possible Elements of Investment Facilitation, Communication from China. Document JOB/GC/123 (26 April 2017) https://docs.wto.org/ *(China Communication JOB/GC/123)*; Possible Elements of a WTO Instrument on Investment Facilitation, Communication from Argentina and Brazil. Document JOB/GC/124 (26 April 2017) https://docs.wto.org/ *(Argentina and Brazil Communication JOB/GC/124)*; Structured discussions on investment facilitation, Communication from Brazil. Document JOB/GC/169 (1 February 2018) https://docs.wto.org/. See Joe Zhang *Investment Facilitation: Making sense of concepts, discussions and processes* (10 July 2018) www.iisd.org/system/files/publications/investment-facilitation-webinar-background.pdf accessed 2 March 2021. See Chapter 2 by Magdalena Bas in this volume.

but it was also blocked on that occasion.[8] In the Buenos Aires Ministerial, a group of countries created a Joint Initiative on Investment Facilitation,[9] which was opposed by several countries. Nonetheless, the group was able to create an agenda of meetings for the last months of 2019, which took place in Geneva. Thus, although slowly and with some opposition, the debate on investment facilitation keeps moving forward.

Investment facilitation is a vague and broad term. It encompasses regulatory actions, institutional roles and administrative procedures with the aim of facilitating the entry, operation, and exit of investors. There is neither a common definition nor a list of rules to facilitate investments.[10] So far, investment facilitation is seen as a group of principles, including "transparency," "consistency," and "predictability," aimed at changing some national regulations in order to ease investment flows.

The investment facilitation proposal differs radically from investment protection rules present in the "old" BITs signed in the nineties. Investment protection clauses have been highly questioned in recent years,[11] especially the inclusion of some clauses such as Fair and Equitable Treatment, Non-discriminatory Treatment, and Indirect Expropriation. The inclusion of ISDS and the proliferation of investor claims against states have also received criticism, as this mechanism is understood as a generator of a "chilling effect" on state regulation.[12] Thus, facilitation does not detail a system of protection for investments, but it does establish a series of changes that states must make, both of their administrative procedures and regulations regarding foreign investments. It is therefore a kind of indirect obligation that affects fully the design of state regulations.

Therefore, investment facilitation is not the same as investment protection. Facilitation involves a central idea: the trend toward simplifying

---

8 Luciana Ghiotto, "*La negociación sobre reglas de facilitación multilateral de las inversiones*" (2017), Working Paper, Transnational Institute (TNI) www.tni.org/es/publicacion/la-negociacion-sobre-reglas-para-la-facilitacion-multilateral-de-las-inversiones accessed 2 March 2021.

9 Kinda Mohamadieh, "Investment Facilitation – Another Plurilateral Initiative at the WTO and its Potential Implications" (2019), Third World Network, Briefing Paper 102, October.

10 See Kinda Mohamadieh, "Reflections on the Discussion of Investment Facilitation" (2017) 8 Investment Policy Brief; and Singh (n 5).

11 Muthucumaraswamy Sornarajah, *The international Law on Foreign Investment* (Cambridge University Press 2010); and Lauge Poulsen, "The Importance of BITs for Foreign Direct Investment and Political Risk Insurance: Revisiting the Evidence" (2010) *Yearbook on International Investment Law and Policy 2009/2010* (Oxford University Press).

12 Pia Eberhardt, "Investment protection at a crossroads: the TTIP and the future of International Investment Law" (2014); Dialogue on Globalization/ International Political Analysis, Friedrich Ebert Foundation.

administrative procedures, and especially regulatory processes for foreign investors and economic operators, in order to reduce the "regulatory burden." For example, in the Transatlantic Trade and Investment Partnership (TTIP), tariffs between the United States and the EU are already low (on average 4 percent), and it is understood that dealing with unnecessary bureaucracy can add a tariff-equivalent of 10–20 percent to the price of goods.[13] Also, the Inter-American Development Bank (BID) understands that the absence of digital channels for the submission of investment proposals make citizens, corporations, and public administration lose time, money, and productivity, increasing the risk of corruption.[14] In other words, this proposal is focused on the reduction of transaction costs for foreign investors and operators through the transformation of domestic administrative processes. This was also the focus of the debate within the WTO regarding the Trade Facilitation Agreement which implies, among other things, the facilitation, modernization and harmonization of export and import procedures, for example, by means of measures for effective cooperation among customs authorities and the creation of the *single window* for trade operators.

Besides the administrative simplification for investors, all the investment facilitation proposals submitted at global forums include mechanisms that are an essential part of regulatory cooperation, such as transparency. In this debate, foreign investors (private sector entities or other states) would have the opportunity to participate in the design process of new regulations that affect foreign investment. This poses a high risk of undermining social, environmental, and human rights standards if there is pressure exerted by the private sector[15] in its search for reducing transaction costs and expanding its scope of action within national territories.

Regulatory cooperation: the heart of the debate on investment facilitation

Investment facilitation establishes a series of changes that states must introduce in their administrative procedures as well as in the regulations on

---

13 Peter Mumford, "Regulatory Coherence: blending trade and regulatory policy" (2014) 10 (4) *Policy Quarterly*.

14 Benjamin Roseth, Angela Reyes, and Carlos Santiso, *El fin del trámite eterno; ciudadanos, burocracia y gobierno digital* (BID, New York 2018).

15 European Environmental Citizens Organization for Standardisation, *Mutual recognition of standards in TTIP: Another threat to citizens' welfare and the environment* (2016), retrieved from http://ecostandard.org/wp-content/uploads/ECOS-2016-POS-002-TTIP.pdf accessed 2 March 2021.

foreign investments. In investment facilitation, we find a new form of regulatory cooperation which shows a trend toward *standardization* and *reconciliation* of regulatory systems and processes. Hence, the focus is not on the rules themselves, but on administrative procedures to enforce those rules. It is about minimizing future regulatory barriers by means of joint procedures.[16] Thus, it is about reducing costs for economic operators, focused on the "burden" posed by public regulations.

Regulatory cooperation has already been included in new mega-regional treaties, such as the Comprehensive and Progressive Agreement for Trans Pacific Partnership (CPTPP) and the TTIP, as well as the FTA between the European Union and Canada (CETA). It is also present in the process of convergence between the Pacific Alliance and the Southern Common Market (MERCOSUR), such as the Argentina–Chile FTA, under the title Technical Barriers to Trade.[17] Some elements also appear in the recently negotiated EU–MERCOSUR association agreement.[18] Regulatory cooperation has also been promoted by the Juncker Commission in the EU since 2014 under the title Better Regulation. This issue is directly related to what the OECD considers as "good regulatory practices," pursuing the following principles: transparency; consultation; impact assessments; and maximization of benefits.

Many of these principles also appear in the investment facilitation proposals submitted to the WTO in 2017, which underline that regulatory cooperation is the most powerful tool for debate. It involves a series of common principles for investors to have a "stable, predictable and effective" framework, according to the proposal presented by Brazil and Argentina.[19] Meanwhile, China and Russia support the idea that these mechanisms can "promote the establishment of clear and consistent criteria and procedures for the process of selection, evaluation and approval of investments."[20]

It is interesting to see that while Argentina and Brazil prepared a proposal on the issue (as part of the "Friends of investment facilitation for development" group that also included Colombia and Mexico) other Latin

16 Anne Meuwese, "Constitutional aspects of regulatory coherence in TTIP: an EU perspective" (2015) 78 *Law and Contemporary Problems*.

17 Luciana Ghiotto and Patricio López, "El Tratado de Libre Comercio Chile-Argentina: el camino a un retorno encubierto del ALCA" (2018) ALAI América Latina, in: www.alainet.org/es/articulo/194817 accessed 2 March 2021.

18 Luciana Ghiotto and Javier Echaide, "Analysis of the agreement between the European Union and Mercosur" (2019) Study, Brussels, The Greens in Parliament & Powershift, *in press*.

19 *Argentina and Brazil Communication JOB/GC/124* (n 7).

20 *Russia Communication JOB/GC/120* (n 7); *China Communication JOB/GC/123* (n 7).

American countries have resisted this in the WTO. Especially, Bolivia, Venezuela, and Ecuador spoke against the proposal in the WTO General Council in 2017. Their explanation for the refusal was focused on the lack of consensus to bring about the investment agenda to the WTO.[21] Also, other countries as South Africa and Uganda were against the proposal. South Africa argued against the creation of a Joint Initiative on Investment Facilitation in Buenos Aires.[22]

Following the proposals presented at the WTO, we find that the main principles of investment facilitation are:

a) "Transparency" and "commitment with stakeholders": These principles refer to the generation of a "transparent, stable and predictable regulatory framework for investors, without questioning the right of members to regulate" (Russia).[23] The term transparency appears as the need for States to make publicly known all laws, regulations, judicial decisions and administrative regulations that have to do with foreign investment. For example, under the TTIP, this mechanism is included as the notice-and-comment system, which implies that stakeholders can make their own proposals and they must be invited to present their comments on regulations through contact points. The comments of these sectors have to be "taken into account."[24] Also, China's proposal includes "improving the transparency of the investment policy framework," and "improving the efficiency of investment-related administrative procedures."[25] It also states that: "all investment laws and regulations must be made publicly available to interested parties including electronic means."[26] States should also establish a database of laws and regulations that affect foreign investment.

b) Simplification of administrative processes: Simplification means that investors can operate their investment more easily; they will find lighter administrative procedures and a quicker access to permits. All of the proposals state the need for the implementation of a single window for procedures and the creation of a single institution for procedures, as well as guarantee access to an online system with all the necessary information for the establishment of

---

21 Ghiotto (n 8).
22 Kinda Mohamadieh, "Investment Facilitation – Another Plurilateral Initiative at the WTO and its Potential Implications" (2019) 102 Third World Network, Briefing Paper 102.
23 *Russia Communication JOB/GC/120* (n 7).
24 Kenneth Haar "Cooperating to deregulate" (2015), Corporate Europe Observatory (CEO), in https://corporateeurope.org/international-trade/2015/11/cooperating-deregulate accessed 2 March 2021.
25 *China Communication JOB/GC/123* (n 7).
26 Ibid.

an investment. This principle even includes the establishment of a set of common rules on the processing of investment orders and the delivery of permits. The proposal from Brazil and Argentina explains that simplification will create a "stable, predictable and efficient" framework.[27] The proposals of China and Russia add that this will "encourage the establishment of clear and consistent criteria and procedures for the process of selection, evaluation and approval of the investment."[28]

c) Regulatory cooperation: The concept of cooperation appears many times in all of the proposals. For China, investment facilitation should encourage and foster institutional cooperation and coordination among members' domestic regulatory authorities and establish a "one-stop" approval institution where possible.[29] Also, it should clarify roles and accountability of different levels of government, and of various agencies, where more than one agency is involved in the investment screening process.[30] Brazil and Argentina's proposal focuses on cooperation among competent authorities;[31] the areas for cooperation under this provision could include exchange of information on procedural requirements and associated formalities and documentation. Other areas of cooperation could address the sharing of experiences regarding implementation, best practices for collection and compilation of data relating to investment, exchange of statistics as well as technical guidance or assistance and support for capacity building for small and medium enterprises.

In summary, all the proposals coincide in the following points: 1) the concept of transparency implies publicizing the existing (and future) regulatory frameworks corresponding to foreign investment; 2) stakeholders should have the opportunity to comment on new laws, regulations, and policies proposed by a state, as well as on changes to previously existing regulations; 3) states are expected to make required changes in their regulatory framework on foreign investments in order to simplify and facilitate the arrival, operation, and exit of investors; 4) states are expected to modify their internal administrative processes in order to simplify the process and the selection criteria for investors. As can be seen, all of these elements work together. They all aim for the same thing: the changing of administrative procedures inside states in order to facilitate the operation of foreign investors.

27 *Argentina and Brazil Communication JOB/GC/124* (n 7).
28 *Russia Communication JOB/GC/120* (n 7); *China Communication JOB/GC/123* (n 7).
29 *China Communication JOB/GC/123* (n 7)
30 Ibid.
31 *Argentina and Brazil Communication JOB/GC/124* (n 7).

Cooperation among states is understood as the sharing of experiences that will help achieve better regulations. We argue that this kind of cooperation could result in comprehensive changes in decision making, leading to a hyper-deregulation process.[32] So states are supposed to copy what other states have already done, especially the case of the United States, as much of the essence of facilitation comes from its model.[33] The 1974 Trade Act (with its incorporation of all-business advisory committees in the development of US trade policy) and Executive Order 12866 of 1993 requires the federal agencies to do a cost–benefit analysis and risk assessment of all proposed rules, including their impact on trade. Also, in the 1994 North American Free Trade Agreement (NAFTA) many elements of Regulatory Cooperation were included, expanding these commitments to Canada and Mexico. In the EU, the Juncker "Better Regulation" project moved in the same direction.

This means that the main objective of *better regulation* is to facilitate operations for the private sector, not for citizens. Instead of referring to the benefits of certain regulations, as protection of consumers' rights, health or the environment, this idea of cooperation focuses on the need to make regulations more flexible and according to the need of stakeholders, which is mainly a quicker access to profit. This implies that the private sector would have a decisive weight in the legislation of a country, intervening directly in the creation of regulatory frameworks. As public regulations tend to be considered a "burden" for private sector, and economic operators would certainly prefer free markets with no state intervention, it is certain that we are witnessing a tendency towards more and more deregulation.

In short, it is not just about facilitating investments with simpler administrative mechanisms, but that foreign investors (other states or the private sector) can have an impact on the regulatory mechanism of each State. Yet, in the case of investment facilitation, none of the abovementioned proposals explain how this process would be implemented; this is why there is a dangerous definition gap in an issue as relevant as foreign investment regulation.

UNCTAD's "public policy space" and OECD's "good regulatory practices"

Following this explanation, we find that investment facilitation core elements have a direct relationship to the concept of "good regulatory practice" promoted by the OECD. This notion entails the changes in regulative and

32 Haar (n 24).
33 Stuart Trew, "International regulatory cooperation and the public good" (2019), Report, PowerShift, Canadian Centre for Policy Alternatives and Transnational Institute.

administrative procedures in order to make regulation more efficient and effective, which we have seen is the key point of regulatory cooperation and of the investment facilitation debate. The role of stakeholders in the revision of existing regulation and the creation of new one is central to the proposal.

But we also understand that the notion of good regulatory practices collides with the proposal upheld by UNCTAD regarding the need to incorporate the concept of "public policy space" in the foreign investment rules. We see that while UNCTAD is currently recommending governments renegotiate their old treaties in order to incorporate sustainable development elements that would guarantee a good quality of foreign investment, OECD focuses on the quality of regulation in itself. OECD's concept introduces the requirement for regulatory reform according to investor's needs in order to facilitate the arrival, operation, and exit of any type of investment. So, while UNCTAD would support the idea that governments regulate in order to see which type of investment is desirable in order to accompany a national process of sustainable development, the OECD proposal defends the need to liberalize and facilitate the operation of any investment, no matter what kind or for what purpose. In sum, we find a tension between both concepts, which actually shows the tensions in current processes of reform of the investment protection regime. We understand that the relationship between the two concepts should be more thoroughly studied, but we provide here some key elements for its understanding.

Since 2003, the UNCTAD started questioning the causal relationship established between the signing of BITs and the arrival of foreign investment.[34] A shift in the UNCTAD policy became evident, putting the question of state policy at the center of investment protection policies, especially for developing countries.[35] The UNCTAD examined the type of investment that had reached the least industrialized economies, and explained that these countries should start focusing on the arrival of investments that were useful for sustainable development policies. The *World Investment Report* of 2003 argues that passive liberalization is not enough to attract foreign investment and profit from it.

From there, the UNCTAD launched the concept of "national policy space" and this has been the core policy of the organization regarding foreign direct investment (FDI) ever since. This category deals with the explicit recognition of the right of sovereign states to regulate, which is a basic function in the control over its territory: "The concept of 'national policy space' and the flexibility it affords to governments to pursue development-oriented FDI policies is the operational bridge between the differing perspectives of

---

34 UNCTAD *World Investment Report; FDI Policies for Development: National and International Perspectives* (2003), United Nations, New York & Geneva.
35 Ghiotto (n 2).

host countries, home countries and investors."[36] The challenge for developing countries would be to find an adequate balance between liberalization and national sustainable development policy.

So, in a context of increasing liberalization, states must be able to regulate in order to maximize the benefits of such opening and minimize the negative effects, since the free market "does not always ensure efficient and equitable results, particularly in developing countries that have weak markets and institutions."[37] But the centrality of policy space coexists with the process of liberalization of the economies so as to attract FDI. This means that liberalization is not in question. In this regard, the UNCTAD has worked in recent years to propose a reform of the international investment protection system, encouraging countries to carry out more aggressive negotiations of their investment protection treaties, where countries negotiate the clauses that best suit each other.[38] Nonetheless, the agency recognizes that many countries are not in a position to carry out such aggressive negotiations, and that they end up succumbing to the needs of capital exporting countries.

The concept of "public policy space" was condensed into the New Generation of Investment Policies.[39] The promotion of these policies is based on the recognition of the need for investment to be accompanied by two elements: 1) inclusive growth; and 2) sustainable development. These two points would be essential to attract foreign investment, as well as to benefit from it. With this policy, the UNCTAD puts the accent on the qualitative aspect of investment, and not so much on the quantitative aspect, which would have implied promoting the attraction of any type of investment. The qualitative aspect implies the possibility of generating a process of "responsible investments," following the line of Corporate Responsibility.[40]

Conversely, the OECD has been a pioneer in the regulatory reform. Already in 1995, this organization launched the Recommendations on Improving the Quality of Government Regulation and then in 1997 the Policy Recommendations on Regulatory Reform. The Recommendations of 1995 suggested that governments, which had cut the size of their budgets due to neoliberal policies, should "learn to do more with less," which included establishing more orderly and predictable decision processes,

---

36 UNCTAD (n 34), 145.

37 UNCTAD (n 34), 86.

38 UNCTAD "International Investment Policymaking in Transition: Challenges and Opportunities of Treaty Renewal" (2013), *IIA Issue Notes*, 4/2013, and UNCTAD "Recent developments in the international investment regime" (2018), IIA Issues Note, Issue 1, May 2018.

39 UNCTAD (n 38), 2013.

40 Marcelo Saguier and Luciana Ghiotto, "Las empresas transnacionales: un punto de encuentro para la Economía Política Internacional en América Latina" (2018) 30 (2) *Desafíos* 159, 190.

identifying regulations that were outdated or unnecessary, and making government actions more transparent.[41]

More recently, the OECD launched in 2012 the ultimate document on regulation: the Recommendations of the Council on Regulatory Policy and Governance, which aimed at assisting members and non-members in "building and strengthening capacity for regulatory quality and regulatory reform."[42] The main point of discussion has to do with the concept of "good regulation." In the words of Angel Gurría, Secretary-General of OECD in 2012, the global financial and economic crisis uncovered major failings in governance and regulation, which undermined trust in public and private institutions alike. So, in order to re-inject confidence and restore growth, the OECD recommends members adopt a well-functioning national regulatory framework. The motto "better regulation for a better life" shows the idea that is being pushed forward: that there is a direct relationship between regulatory processes and economic prosperity and welfare.[43] In sum, regulatory reform would improve social well-being, an idea that scholars have very much discussed.[44]

In the document of 2012, the OECD recommends that governments understand that the main objective is to reach regulatory quality, and this is accomplished by adhering to "open government, including transparency and participation in the regulatory process to ensure that regulation serves the public interest and is informed by the legitimate needs of those interested in and affected by regulation."[45] Some concepts arise here that would need further explanation, although we do not find such explanations in the OECD documents. We refer to the notions of regulatory quality, of better regulation, and of public interest. The documents create a link between regulatory practices and the idea of good, which refers to a moral perspective that is never addressed. Also, we cannot find any references as to why the OECD members understand that regulatory reform would serve the public interest. Therefore, the concept of interest in itself needs more clarification. For example, can we say that the interests of a corporation investing on soil exploitation, and the interests of a community affected by this investment are the same? Which public interest would regulatory reform address? Who are the stakeholders and who says who they are? In the case of investment

41 Trew (n 33).
42 OECD *Recommendation of the Council on Regulatory Policy and Governance* (2012), Regulatory Process, Geneva; 1.
43 OECD (n 42), 3.
44 For discussions, see Meuwesse (n 16).
45 OECD (n 42), 4.

facilitation, the proposals do not say much on who will participate in rule-making (and how).

One key element of good regulatory practice is the Regulatory Impact Analysis. This analysis means that governments should adopt ex-ante impact assessments and include benefit–cost analyses that consider the welfare impacts of regulation. Also, the impact analysis implies the review and revision of existing regulations, which should indicate "the objective to improve the efficiency and effectiveness of the regulations, including better design of regulatory instruments and to lessen regulatory costs for citizens and businesses as part of a policy to promote economic efficiency."[46] So what is being pushed forward is the need not only to adopt the impact analysis before new regulation is acquired, but also the revision of existing regulation according to these analysis principles.

Scholars observe that the notion of "good regulatory practices" as articulated by the OECD refers mainly to the *proceduralization* of trade and investment issues.[47] That is to say, the focus is not set on the rules in themselves: it is the procedures by which these rules are obtained that become the object of cooperation. "The compatibility of domestic structures for producing rules and regulation becomes crucial to the success of regulatory cooperation as a pathway to further economic integration."[48] The compatibility or harmonization of regulation has become central. This process would help to address the problematic spaghetti bowl that Bhagwati referred to when analyzing the proliferation of BITs. From the point of view of investment rules, we can say that while the BITs of the nineties addressed the rules on foreign investment in themselves, aiming at liberalization of super-regulated economies, the current investment facilitation and regulatory cooperation rules crossed the frontiers and moved inside national regulations and procedures, focusing on the decision-making process.

Concluding remarks

The investment facilitation debate is here to stay. Even if it will not see concrete progress in the short term, it is a matter that deserves to be the focus of analysis by experts in the investment protection regime. As such, investment

---

46 OECD (n 42), 12.
47 Alberto Alemanno, "The Regulatory Cooperation Chapter of the Transatlantic Trade and Investment Partnership: Institutional Structures and Democratic Consequences" (2015) 18 (3) *Journal of International Economic Law* 625, 640; also Meuwesse (n 16) and Haar (n 24).
48 Meuwese (n 16), 153.

facilitation includes a topic that involves new FTAs as well as international forum debates, namely regulatory cooperation. This discussion is currently developing in forums such as the WTO and G20, as well as in the OECD and the UNCTAD, and at a regional level in the European Union and the Pacific Alliance. As we stated previously, it is also present in most new generation FTAs.

Particularly at the WTO, the introduction of investment facilitation would mean the "multilateralization" of the investment debate, which would bring substantial changes to member states' regulatory processes. Until now, the WTO has succeeded in removing trade barriers at the border level. But if investment facilitation is accepted as a multilateral agreement, this would imply the establishment of rules that reduce the administrative burden for foreign investors "behind the borders," leading to a movement toward harmonization of procedures for the adoption of domestic regulations in all member states. This would have an impact on the adoption of countries' domestic standards. Thus, "good regulatory practices" is now fighting directly against the non-tariff barriers that WTO has not been able to tackle.[49]

As already explained, the debates on facilitation, whether trade or investment, have moved the discussions to the regulation process level, that is, the heart of liberal democracy decision-making process. While the UNCTAD is heading to a process of re-discussing the bilateral treaties signed during the nineties, the OECD's "good regulatory practices" poses a new type of challenge to democratic decision making. While investment protection discusses laws at a national level, investment facilitation puts the focus on the same process by which rules are obtained. Even though investment facilitation seems to be innocuous, as it does not create a new set of rules on how states should protect foreign investment and solve arising disputes, this new discussion goes a step further, modifying regulatory processes and introducing stakeholders. This is why it can be argued that although the UNCTAD's idea is to broaden public policy space, the introduction of regulatory cooperation is actually a way of shrinking policy space as policy makers will have to discuss all new regulations (and existing ones) with private stakeholders. International trade and investment dispositions inevitably limit all states' decision-making. But good regulatory practices aim at changing the decision-making process in itself, making it more difficult for legislators to regulate in favor of human rights or the environment.

Also, some questions arise regarding why some states have been pushing in the different forums for the inclusion of investment facilitation rules, while others have been blocking the discussion. It can be argued that the

49 Alemanno (n 47).

recent debate on investment facilitation relates to the deep changes in the mode of capital accumulation in the past decades. From there we can understand that China is now very interested in facilitating trade and investments. On the other hand, China has not shown an offensive agenda in investment protection rules, as most of the investments that it does abroad are not from private corporations, but from state or mix enterprises.[50] So, a line of research should be started that studies the relationship between the investment facilitation proposal and the Chinese Belt and Road Initiative.

Finally, this debate has given way to more challenging questions than answers. Investment facilitation and regulatory cooperation are not matters of trade and investment technical rules, but they represent a political matter: under the name of "good" regulation, it has impact on existing regulatory processes, on democratic legitimacy and it directly transforms states' functions.

In this sense, the most affected nations would be those that have the highest thresholds. For example, countries with stricter regulations about the acceptance of an investment in areas considered strategic or with regulations that set performance requirements for foreign investors will be obligated to adjust their domestic laws to those of countries with more relaxed regulations. The effect of this would be a generalized "downward spiral," as the pressure exerted by the private sector would lead to undermining regulations in the investment sector at a global scale.

---

50 Ariel Slipak and Luciana Ghiotto, "América Latina en la Nueva Ruta de la Seda; El rol de las inversiones chinas en la región en un contexto de disputa interhegemónica" (2019) 4 (7), *Cuadernos de Estudios Latinoamericnos (CEL)*.

6

Domestic courts in the mosaic of states: Transformative constitutionalism and fair and equitable treatment

René Urueña and María Angélica Prada-Uribe

The fair and equitable principle (FET) is the most frequently used basis for investment claims[1] and the most used provision by investment tribunals to hold states liable.[2] As such, FET has become a central mechanism through which investment arbitration regulates state action by forcing the accommodation of the domestic legal system to international investment standards. Thus, functioning as a veritable technology of global governance, which has triggered questions of legitimacy, growing criticisms and resistance, when not an all-out backlash, to the international investment regime.[3]

This chapter explores the *domestic* life of FET in the context of Latin America, with a particular focus on constitutional adjudication in Colombia. Specifically, it focuses on transformative constitutionalism – as developed by both constitutional courts in the region (such as the Colombian Court) and by the InterAmerican Court of Human Rights – and discusses the potential for such a distinctively Latin America strand of constitutionalism to act as a mechanism for resisting and shaping international investment law by imposing substantive limits on FET, and the procedural venues (both domestic and international) through which such limits could be imposed.

The chapter proceeds as follows. The first section describes the public/private divide in investment arbitration and its interaction with FET as a platform for transforming the investment arbitration regime in a decentralized

---

1 UNCTAD, *Fair and Equitable Treatment*, UNCTAD Series on Issues in International Investment Agreements II (New York: United Nations Publications, 2012), 10.

2 UNCTAD, "Investor-State Dispute Settlement: Review of Developments in 2017, Issue 2," 2018, 5, https://unctad.org/en/PublicationsLibrary/diaepcbinf2018d2_en.pdf accessed 2 March 2021.

3 See, Michael Waibel, Asha Kaushal, Kyo-Hwa Liz Chung, and Claire Balchin, "The Backlash Against Investment Arbitration: Perceptions and Reality" in Asha Kaushal, Kyo-Hwa Liz Chung, and Claire Balchin (eds) *The Backlash Against Investment Arbitration: Perceptions and Reality* (Kluwer Law International 2010).

mechanism of international public power. Then, the second section focuses on interaction between the Colombian constitutional jurisdiction and the investment regime. Finally, the third section concludes suggesting, first, that the discussion on the public–private divide of international investment arbitration is today more relevant than ever, as it is instrumental in defining the appropriate standard of domestic constitutional review to be applied vis-à-vis the international investment regime. As will be shown, a private law mindset of the international investment regime requires accommodation of the domestic legal system, while a public law mindset opens a door for resistance through a broader interaction between the national and the transnational spheres. In this last scenario, constitutional courts need to give precise orders to the executive branch regarding the standards or wording that needs to be modified in the investment treaties. By not doing so, domestic Courts fail to create a dialogue between constitutional law and the investment regime which may foster a more democratic investment regime.

FET and investment arbitration as a decentralized mechanism of international public power

International investment arbitration is not only a system of private dispute resolution between investors and the host states, but a decentralized mechanism of international public power. Although the top-down exercise of public authority displayed by investment arbitration is supported in the overall system of international investment law, the FET standard has played a decisive role in the expansion of investment arbitration beyond a mere investor–state dispute settlement mechanism. FET has been included in most investment treaties and, despite the heterogeneity of treaty language and the ambiguity of its content, in the last two decades, investment case law has shed some light on the meaning and content of the standard.[4]

FET has been broadly interpreted by arbitral tribunals to include, at least, the following set of good governance standards: "(1) the requirement of stability, predictability and consistency of the legal framework (2) the

---

4 Sornarajah points out that "[i]n a leading article on the clause written in 1999, Vasciannie found it difficult to identify the content of the fair and equitable standard of treatment. Yet writing six years later, Schreuer maintained that the standard had been fleshed out with sufficient meaning within that period by arbitral awards." See Muthucumaraswamy Sornarajah, *Resistance and Change in the International Law on Foreign Investment* (Cambridge University Press 2015), 247. Similarly, Dolzer and Schreuer argue that "it is only since 2000 that investment tribunals have started giving content to the meaning of the standard." See, Rudolf Dolzer and Christoph Schreuer, *Principles of International Investment Law*, Second Edition (Oxford University Press 2012), 130.

protection of legitimate expectations (3) the requirement to grant procedural and administrative due process and the prohibition of denial of justice (4) the requirement of transparency, and (5) the requirement of reasonableness and proportionality."[5] Critics of this broader standard have pointed out to the obligations to protect the investors' legitimate expectations, and to provide a predictable and stable legal environment as the most controversial one because they "have arguably broadened the standard significantly from its original and intended scope."[6]

In response, some commentators have argued that a way to limit the broader interpretation of the FET is to link the standard to the customary international law minimum standard of treatment,[7] while others have advocated for the inclusion of general exception clauses in the investment treaties.[8] Both strategies have been incorporated in recent state practice, which has started to revise the language and content of the investment treaties to protect their regulatory power.[9] The modification of treaty language is fundamental for the incorporation of a public mindset into investment arbitration, because, despite the existence of international law arguments and tools

---

5 See Benedict Kingsbury and Stephan W. Schill, "Investor-State Arbitration as Governance: Fair and Equitable Treatment, Proportionality and the Emerging Global Administrative Law" (2009) *NYU School of Law, Public Law Research Paper 9–46*, 10. In a subsequent article Stepahn Schill adds the principle of legality and the protection against arbitrariness and discrimination. See Stephan W. Schill, "International Investment Law and the Rule of Law" (2017) *ACIL Research Paper 2017–15*, 9. See also, Stephan W. Schill, "Fair and Equitable Treatment under Investment Treaties as an Embodiment of the Rule of Law" (2016) 3 (5) *Transnational Dispute Management (TDM)*.

6 J. Roman Picherack, "The Expanding Scope of the Fair and Equitable Treatment Standard: Have Recent Tribunals Gone Too Far?" (2008) 9 (4) *The Journal of World Investment & Trade* 256.

7 Ibid.

8 See, Levent Sabanogullari, *General Exception Clauses in International Investment Law. The Recalibration of Investment Agreements via WTO-Based Flexibility* (Nomos Verlag 2018); Markus Krajewski, "Ensuring the Primacy of Human Rights in Trade and Investment Policies: Model Clauses for a UN Treaty on Transnational Corporations, Other Businesses and Human Rights" (CIDSE Private Sector Group, 2017), www.cidse.org/publications/business-and-human-rights/business-and-human-rights-frameworks/ensuring-the-primacy-of-human-rights-in-trade-and-investment-policies.html.

9 This is precisely what Mexico, Canada, and the United States did in the interpretative note to article 1105 of the NAFTA. See "Notes of Interpretation of Certain Chapter 11 Provisions," 31 July 2001, www.sice.oas.org/tpd/nafta/commission/ch11understanding_e.asp. See also the proposal made by the International Institute of Sustainable Development in its Model Investment Agreement, Howard Mann, Konrad von Moltke, Luke Eric Peterson, and Aaron Cosbey, *IISD Model International Agreement on Investment for Sustainable Development* (International Institute for Sustainable Development (IISD) 2005).

available for arbitrators – for example, to resort to Article 31(3)(c) of the Vienna Convention on the Law of Treaties to incorporate human rights obligations into the investment regimen,[10] they have been reluctant to use them unless (and even when) treaties contained a direct mandate to do so.[11]

However, the incorporation of treaty modifications has been unsystematic and dependent on the case-by-case negotiations carried out by the executive brands of governments. For this reason, critics of the international investment regime are increasingly advocating for the use of national jurisdictions as mechanism for resisting the expansive interpretation that arbitrators have given to the investment treaty obligations. This resort to national courts is possible because, although historically the power to negotiate and ratify treaties lies in the executive branch, modern constitutional arrangements have recognized that one of the ancillary powers of constitutional courts is to exercise the constitutional review – in some cases *ex-ante* and in other cases *ex-post* – of international treaties.[12]

The need to include the constitutional scale in the study of the impacts of the international investment regime on the protection of human rights is especially important in the Latin-American legal space,[13] which is characterized for a long tradition of dialogue between the national courts and the Inter-American System of Human Rights (IASHR).[14] In this sense, the

10 Vienna Convention on the Law of Treaties (signed 23 May 1969, entered into force 27 January 1980) 1155 UNTS 331. See Bruno Simma, "Foreign Investment Arbitration: A Place for Human Rights?" (2011) 60 (3) *International and Comparative Law Quarterly* 573, 596.

11 See Chapters 10 by Rodrigo Polanco Lazo and Felipe Ferreira Catalán and 11 by Farouk El-Hosseny, Patrick Devine, and Ilan Brun-Vargas in this volume.

12 According to Ginsburg and Elkins, by 2006, the second most frequent ancillary power of constitutional courts was the review of treaties (39 percent). See, Tom Ginsburg and Zachary Elkins, "Ancillary Powers of Constitutional Courts" (2008) 87 *Tex. L. Rev.* 1443.

13 This article is based on René Urueña's proposal that the relationship between international investment and human rights regime takes place in the "Latin-American legal space," which should be understood as a form of interaction among Systems and not in terms of contradiction or collision. See René Urueña, "Después de La Fragmentación: ICCAL, Derechos Humanos y Arbitraje de Inversiones," in Armin von Bogdandy, Pedro Salazar Ugarte, Mariela Morales Antoniazzi, and Franz Christian Ebert (eds) *El Constitucionalismo Transformador En América Latina y El Derecho Económico Internacional. De La Tensión Al Diálogo*, ed. Armin (Universidad Nacional Autónoma de México 2018).

14 Armin Von Bogdandy, Eduardo F. Mac Gregor, Mariela Morales Antoniazzi, Flavia Piovesan, and Ximena Soley, "Ius Constitutionale Commune En América Latina: A Regional Approach to Transformative Constitutionalism" in Armin von Bogdandy, Eduardo Ferrer Mac-Gregor, Mariela Morales Antoniazzi, and Flávia Piovesan (eds) *Transformative Constitutionalism in Latin America* (Oxford University Press 2017).

Latin-American legal space is a regulatory complex where the regimes of international investment arbitration and human rights interact with the domestic constitutional system of the states. In this space "institutions are dynamic, since they change and adapt in their interactions,"[15] and the international investment tribunals, the IASHR organs and the national courts (with emphasis on the constitutional ones) "enter as actors in a space where regulation is already being adopted, discussed, implemented and rejected."[16]

As will be discussed in the next section, the constitutional review of international treaties is a fundamental characteristic of Latin America's transformative constitutionalism, which can play a gatekeeping function of the public law rationality in the international investment regime.

FET and the public/private divide

The international investment system has been characterized by using two competing perspectives on the nature, function, principles, and objectives underlying investment arbitration.[17] The public–private distinction of international investment law is not a mere conceptual disagreement on how to examine and characterize the regime: it is a normative statement about how authority should be distributed at the transnational sphere. In consequence, this distinction has important implications not only for arbitral practice, but also for how power should be allocated across scales, in this case, between the constitutional and investment regimes.

Although the discussion regarding the public–private divide and its implications is not new, its effects for the domestic review of investment treaties and awards has been less discussed.

The discussion on the private–public divide and FET is important because each mindset favors a different approach to the allocation of authority at the transnational level. While the public law mindset favors allocation of power at the national level, the private law one favors its allocation at the international level. In practice, how authority is allocated

---

15 René Urueña, "Después de La Fragmentación: ICCAL, Derechos Humanos y Arbitraje de Inversiones (After Fragmentation: ICCAL, Human Rights and Investment Arbitration)" (2018) 30 *Max Planck Institute for Comparative Public Law & International Law (MPIL) Research Paper* 67.

16 Ibid. 68.

17 See Alex Mills, "The Public-Private Dualities of International Investment Law and Arbitration" in Chester Brown and Kate Miles (eds) *Evolution in Investment Treaty Law and Arbitration* (Cambridge University Press 2011) 97, 116.

determines the answer given by a system to the shifting demand for subsidiarity. In other words, while the private law mindset requires accommodation of the domestic legal system to the international investment regime, the public law mindset opens the possibility for resistance through the recognition of the public authority exercised at the domestic level. The academic and public policy discussion on this issue has been framed in terms of the standard of review that investment arbitration tribunals owe to the decisions and actions of the host state.[18] In this sense, a public-law mindset would promote a deferential standard when investment tribunals review domestic decisions, while a private-law mindset would prefer a non-deferential standard.[19]

As is explained in the table below, international investment arbitration has become a decentralized mechanism of international public power for four main reasons: (i) its legal regime and the parties to the dispute; (ii) the emergence of a system of quasi-judicial precedent; (iii) its underlying logic; and (iv) the expansion of its subject-matter jurisdiction. Although the international investment regimes, as a whole, works as a mechanism of international public authority, the FET standard has been its cornerstone because of its ability to limit the regulatory freedom of states.[20] In other words, the fair and equitable treatment has been the master tool through which investment arbitration has, in many cases, allocated authority at the international level by using a non-deferential standard to review states' actions in disputes that affect the public interest of the state and its citizens.

18 For a discussion on the standard of review that should be applied in investment treaty arbitration, see William W. Burke-White and Andreas Von Staden, "Private Litigation in a Public Sphere: The Standard of Review in Investor-State Arbitrations" (2010) 35 *Yale J. Int'l L.* 283; Caroline Henckels, "Indirect Expropriation and the Right to Regulate: Revisiting Proportionality Analysis and the Standard of Review in Investor-State Arbitration" (2012) 15 (1) *Journal of International Economic Law* 223, 255; Stephan W. Schill, "Deference in Investment Treaty Arbitration: Re-Conceptualizing the Standard of Review" (2012) 3 (3) *Journal of International Dispute Settlement* 577, 607; Anthea Roberts, "The Next Battleground: Standards of Review in Investment Treaty Arbitration" (2011) 16 *International Council for Commercial Arbitrations Congress Series* 170 https://papers.ssrn.com/abstract=2186208 accessed 2 March 2021.

19 René Urueña, "Subsidiarity and the Public-Private Distinction in Investment Treaty Arbitration" (2016) 79 *Law & Contemp. Probs.* 110.

20 Roland Kläger, "Fair and Equitable Treatment' and Sustainable Development" in Marie-Claire Cordonier Segger, Markus W. Gehring, and Andrew Newcombe (ed) *Sustainable Development in World Investment Law*, vol. 30, Global Trade Law Series (Kluwer Law International 2011) 251, 252.

Table 6.1 Differences between international investment arbitration and international commercial arbitration

Characteristics	International investment arbitration	International commercial arbitration
Logic of the mechanism	Decentralized exercise of public authority	Private dispute settlement
Sources of law	Public international law (custom, treaties and general principles of international law)	Contracts, principles of private law.
Consent	General and unqualified	Specific and contract-based
Actors	The state in its sovereign capacity	Private actors (the state in its private capacity)
Function of arbitration	Review of laws, public policies and judicial decisions	Settlement of commercial and private-interests disputes
Precedent	Quasi-judicial precedent	No precedent
Transparency	Public information in most cases	Confidentiality in most cases
Third party participation	Permitted but it is not mandatory	It is not permitted

The legal regime and the parties to the dispute in investment arbitration

The regime of international investment arbitration differs from international commercial arbitration in the nature of the parties to the dispute and the applicable substantive law. First, it is the state in its sovereign capacity that consents to the jurisdiction of the arbitral tribunal through the ratification of a treaty. This consent is of a general nature "because it authorizes the arbitration of any future dispute with any foreign investor in the state's territory,"[21] and, therefore, it contrasts with the specific consent granted

---

21 Gus Van Harten, "Private Authority and Transnational Governance: The Contours of the International System of Investor Protection" (2005) 12 (4) *Review of International Political Economy* 607.

in commercial contracts.[22] As a consequence, all sovereign acts of a state – which in other jurisdictions would be granted sovereign immunity – could be subjected to review by the investment arbitration tribunals.[23]

Furthermore, contrary to private law contracts, investment treaties are asymmetrical instruments;[24] in other words, they grant investor rights that can be protected before international tribunals,[25] while not imposing any obligations on them.[26] In consequence, only the state can be sued before investment tribunals, in opposition to commercial arbitration, in which each party of the contract is susceptible to becoming the applicant or respondent of a dispute.[27] Additionally, investment arbitration grants investors the power to directly present claims against the STATE without, in most cases, having to exhaust local remedies.

Second, since the investment system is mostly a treaty-based regime, arbitrators have relied on different sources and methods of interpretation of international law to determine the content of the rights and obligations contained in investment treaties,[28] instead of limiting their findings to the

---

22 See also, A. Claire Cutler, "Transformations in Statehood, the Investor-State Regime, and the New Constitutionalism" (2016) 23 *Ind. J. Global Legal Stud.* 105, 106.

23 Gus Van Harten, "The Public–Private Distinction in the International Arbitration of Individual Claims against the State," (2007) 56 (2) *International & Comparative Law Quarterly* 371, 393.

24 Although contract-based arbitration also exists, the investment regime is based on a network of bilateral and multilateral treaties that by 2018 had increased to over 3.000. See, UNCTAD, *World Investment Report 2018* (Geneva: United Nations, 2018), 88–91.

25 On the discussion of whether investment treaties grant direct or derivative rights, see, Zachary Douglas, "The Hybrid Foundations of Investment Treaty Arbitration" (2004) 74(1) *The British Year Book of International Law* 151.

26 José E. Alvarez, "Critical Theory and the North American Free Trade Agreement's Chapter Eleven" (1996) 28 (2) *The University of Miami Inter-American Law Review*, 308. Tarcisio Gazzini argues that there is not inherent asymmetry in investment treaties, since there is nothing in their nature that prevents states from imposing obligations to foreign investors. Even if this was true, in practice states have not included this kind of obligation in the text of investment treaties. See, Tarcisio Gazzini, "Bilateral Investment Treaties" in Tarcisio Gazzini and Eric De Brabandere (eds) *International Investment Law: The Sources of Rights and Obligations* (Martinus Nijhoff Publishers 2012), 107.

27 Anthea Roberts and Christina Trahanas, "Judicial Review of Investment Treaty Awards: BG Group v. Argentina" (2014) 108 (4) *American Journal of International Law* 11. See also, Gustavo Laborde, "The Case for Host State Claims in Investment Arbitration" (2010) 1 (1) *Journal of International Dispute Settlement* 97, 122.

28 On the sources of international investment law, see in general, Moshe Hirsch, "Sources of International Investment Law" in Andrea K. Bjorklund and August Reinisch (eds) *International Investment Law and Soft Law* (Edward Elgar Publishing 2012); Tarcisio Gazzini and Eric De Brabandere (eds) *International Investment Law. The Sources of Rights and Obligations* (Martinus Nijhoff Publishers 2012).

obligations and rights contained in private law instruments.[29] Although treaty law has played a pivotal role in the development of investment law, other sources of international law, such as custom, have become prominent in the interpretation and definition of the treaty standards like FET.

However, despite the public law nature of the international investment regime, its procedural rules and internal logic continue to be based on the paradigm of arbitration as a simple forum of private dispute settlement.[30] For example, the rules of procedure of UNCITRAL and ICSID were originally thought of as responding to a private justice system. This has generated a dual nature of the investment arbitration regime, which is, in turn, responsible for its legitimacy crisis. Only recently, and in response to growing criticism, the arbitration regime has modified some of its procedural rules; for example, allowing the intervention of third parties.

The emergence of a system of quasi-judicial precedent

The international investment law regime has been shaped, at the same time, through the proliferation of bilateral investment treaties (BITs) and the systematization of the incorporation of substantial and arbitration provisions, which has, according to some authors, led to the creation "of a web of substantive rules for the protection of foreign capital" akin to a process of multilateralization of investment protection.[31] Although the texts of investment treaties have been characterized for their shortness and vagueness, the fact that most treaties contained similar clauses and that many investment

29 See, Yuval Shany, "Contract Claims vs. Treaty Claims: Mapping Conflicts between ICSID Decisions on Multisourced Investment Claims" (2005) 99 (4) *American Journal of International Law* 835, 851.

30 René Urueña, "Subsidiarity and the Public-Private Distinction in Investment Treaty Arbitration" (2016) 79 *Law & Contemp. Probs.* 105. On a defense of the private paradigm of investment arbitration, see, Thomas W. Wälde, "Procedural Challenges in Investment Arbitration under the Shadow of the Dual Role of the State: Asymmetries and Tribunals' Duty to Ensure, pro-Actively, the Equality of Arms" (2010) 26 (1) *Arbitration International* 3, 42.

31 Jean d'Aspremont, "International Customary Investment Law: Story of a Paradox" in Tarcisio Gazzini and Eric De Brabandere (eds) *International Investment Law. The Sources of Rights and Obligations* (Leiden: Martinus Nijhoff Publishers 2012), 19. See also, Stephan W. Schill, *The Multilateralization of International Investment Law* (Cambridge University Press 2009); Anthea Roberts, "Clash of Paradigms: Actors and Analogies Shaping the Investment Treaty System" (2013) 107 (1) *American Journal of International Law* 53.

awards have been made public has led to the development of general princi-ples of international investment law.[32]

As a matter of fact, despite the existence of inconsistent and contra-dictory arbitral awards, the case law of investment arbitration has slowly but steadily developed into a system with "considerable convergence, and hence order, in the practice of arbitral decision-making."[33] In consequence, contrary to international commercial arbitration that does not recognize the principle of *stare decisis*, international investment arbitration's exercise of public power is supported by a system of quasi-judicial precedent.[34] This, in turn, has resulted in the development of investment law beyond the initial expectations of states.[35] A clear example of this is the FET standard, since states did not have any initial expectations of the expansion of this clause into, at least, the seven normative principles of good governance mentioned above.[36] Thus, investment law, primarily but not limited to FET, sets high behavioral standards that require states to behave in accordance with broad substantive and procedural rules developed through arbitral case law.[37]

A function of the system is to review national legislation and to limit the regulatory freedom of states

The third characteristic that makes investment arbitration a decentralized exercise of international public power is that its intrinsic function and

32 See, Rudof Dolzer and Christoph Schreuer, *Principles of International Investment Law* (Oxford University Press 2012).

33 Stephan W. Schill, "International Arbitrators as System-Builders" (2012) 106 *Proceedings of the Annual Meeting (American Society of International Law)* 295.

34 See, Andrea K. Bjorklund, "Investment Treaty Arbitral Decisions as Jurisprudence Constante" in Colin B. Picker, Isabella D. Bunn, and Douglas W. Arner (eds) *International Economic Law: The State and Future of the Discipline* (Hart Publishing 2008); Jeffrey P. Commission, "Precedent in Investment Treaty Arbitration-A Citation Analysis of a Developing Jurisprudence" (2007) 24 *J. Int'l Arb.* 129.

35 Anthea Roberts, "Divergence Between Investment and Commercial Arbitration" (2012) 106 *Proceedings of the Annual Meeting (American Society of International Law)* 298.

36 David Schneiderman, "Against Constitutional Excess: Tocquevillian Reflections on International Investment Law" (2018) 85 *U. Chi. L. Rev.* 599; Muthucumaraswamy Sornarajah, *Resistance and Change in the International Law on Foreign Investment* (Cambridge University Press 2015) 246–299.

37 See, René Urueña, "Of Precedents and Ideology: Law-Making by Investment Arbitration Tribunals" in Prabhakar Singh and Benoît Mayer (eds) *Critical International Law: Postrealism, Postcolonialism, and Transnationalism* (Oxford University Press 2014), 276–303. See also, Jeswald W. Salacuse, "The Emerging Global Regime for Investment" 51 (2010) *Harv. Int'l LJ* 427; Jeswald W Salacuse, *The Law of Investment Treaties* (Oxford University Press on Demand 2010); Stephan W. Schill, "International Arbitrators as System-Builders" (2012) 106 *Am. Soc'y Int'l L. Proc.* 296.

underlying logic necessarily lead to the judicial review of national legal systems (including laws, public policies, and domestic judicial decisions). The consequence of this exercise of authority over the sovereign power of state is the limitation of its regulatory power over foreign investment. This is happening because states usually breach (or comply with) their international obligations toward foreign investors through domestic regulations or public policies – in other words, the host state acts through its national legal instruments and, for that reason, reviewing its decisions is tantamount to reviewing its national laws and regulations.[38]

The authority exercised by investment arbitration over the regulatory power of states has two concrete effects that generate a mechanism of top-down governance that forces accommodation of state behavior and domestic legal systems to international investment standards. First, as a result of the review of state actions,[39] although arbitral tribunals cannot directly invalidate national regulations, they generate strong incentives for states to derogate their regulations or to avoid issuing new ones due to the risk of being sued before an investment tribunal.[40] This last effect is known as the "chilling effect" of international investment arbitration.[41] Second, by establishing behavioral standards, such as the good governance one in FET, towards which a state's action is measured, investment arbitration is currently resembling a constitutional or administrative adjudication mechanism.[42] The issue surrounding this exercise of top-down authority is not only the ability of arbitration tribunals to restrict the State's discretionary power, but the use of a strict standard of review and

---

38 René Urueña, "Subsidiarity and the Public-Private Distinction in Investment Treaty Arbitration" (2016) 79 *Law & Contemp. Probs.*

39 Lise Johnson, Lisa E. Sachs, and Jeffrey D. Sachs, "Investor-State Dispute Settlement, Public Interest and US Domestic Law" (Columbia Center on Sustainable Investment 2015), http://ccsi.columbia.edu/files/2015/05/Investor-State-Dispute-Settlement-Pub lic-Interest-and-U.S.-Domestic-Law-FINAL-May-19–8.pdf.

40 René Urueña, "Subsidiarity and the Public-Private Distinction in Investment Treaty Arbitration" (2016) 79 *Law & Contemp. Probs.* 102. See also, Tienhaara, Kyla, *The Expropriation of Environmental Governance: Protecting Foreign Investors at the Expense of Public Policy* (Cambridge University Press 2009).

41 See, Kyla Tienhaara, "Regulatory Chill and the Threat of Arbitration: A View from Political Science" in Chester Brown and Kate Miles (eds) *Evolution in Investment Treaty Law and Arbitration* (Cambridge University Press, 2011); Arseni Matveev, "Investor-State Dispute Settlement: The Evolving Balance between Investor Protection and State Sovereignty" (2015) 40 *UW Austl. L. Rev.* 348.

42 Gus Van Harten, *Investment Treaty Arbitration and Public Law* (Oxford University Press 2007); David Schneiderman, *Constitutionalizing Economic Globalization: Investment Rules and Democracy's Promise* (Cambridge University Press 2008).

low demand for subsidiarity justified through a private rationale of investment arbitration.[43]

The expansion of the subject matter jurisdiction towards collective and public interest disputes

The last element that makes the international investment regime a mechanism of decentralized international public authority is the expansion of its subject matter jurisdiction beyond the private interests of the foreign investors. The double fact that investment arbitration focuses on the states' actions performed under their sovereign capacity and that, as a consequence, it has turned into a mechanism of quasi-constitutional or administrative adjudication, has necessarily led the regime to deal with issues of public interest for states and communities such as the protection of human rights or the environment.[44] In this sense, the logic of investment arbitration as a mechanism of international public authority recognizes that, even if investment disputes arise out of a bilateral disagreement between the investor and the state, the decisions of the tribunals can have important impacts over community values and interests.[45] Throughout the existence of investment arbitration, arbitral awards have dealt with issues of public interest for states, communities, and civil society, such as: the regulation of public services (specially the access to drinking water[46]), measures to

---

43 René Urueña, "Subsidiarity and the Public-Private Distinction in Investment Treaty Arbitration" (2016) 79 *Law & Contemp. Probs.* 112. See, for instance, the cases of CMS, Enron, and Sempra, which are an example of judicial review through a private rationale. *CMS Gas Transmission Company v. The Argentine Republic*, ICSID Case No. ARB/01/8 (Award, 12 May 2005); *Enron Creditors Recovery Corporation (formerly Enron Corporation) and Ponderosa Assets, L.P. v. Argentine Republic*, ICSID Case No. ARB/01/3 (Award, 22 May 2007); *Sempra Energy International v. Argentine Republic*, ICSID Case No. ARB/02/16 (Award, 28 September 2007). For a defense of the strict standard of review used by investment tribunals in the so-called Argentina cases, see, José E. Álvarez and Kathryn Khamsi, "The Argentine Crisis and Foreign Investors: A Glimpse into the Heart of the Investment Regime" (2008) *The Yearbook on International Investment Law and Policy* 2008/2009 382–385.

44 Barnali Choudhury, "Recapturing Public Power: Is Investment Arbitration's Engagement of the Public Interest Contributing to the Democratic Deficit" (2008) 41 *Vand. J. Transnat'l L.* 775.

45 René Urueña, *No Citizens Here: Global Subjects and Participation in International Law* (Martinus Nijhoff Publishers 2012), 182. See also, Miles, Kate, "Reconceptualising International Investment Law: Bringing the Public Interest into Private Business" in Meredith Kolsky Lewis and Susy Frankel (eds) *International Economic Law and National Autonomy* (Cambridge University Press 2010).

46 Pierre Thielbörger, "The Human Right to Water Versus Investor Rights: Double-Dilemma or Pseudo-Conflict?" in Pierre-Marie Dupuy, Francesco Francioni and

alleviate economic crisis,[47] the protection of the environment,[48] the protection of public health,[49] the rights of indigenous and tribal communities,[50] among many others.[51]

Although investment arbitration has generally extended its scope towards collective interest disputes, those concerning FET violations are more likely to deal with countries' social, political, environmental, or other public interests because of its predisposition to review the state's public policies. An often-cited example of the impact of FET in public interest issues are the cases against Mexico dealing with hazardous landfills, in which foreign investors contested a series of norms issued to regulate sanitary landfills that, according to Mexico, sought to solve the adverse environmental effects caused by hazardous waste.[52] Another set of cases – among them *Glamis Gold v. the United States*,[53] and *Chevron and Texaco v. Ecuador*[54] – have involved disputes in which the rights of indigenous

Emst-Ulrich Petersmann (eds) *Human Rights in International Investment Law and Arbitration* (Oxford University Press 2009). See the following case, *Aguas del Tunari S.A. v. Republic of Bolivia*, ICSID Case No. ARB/02/3. See Chapter 12 by Javier Echaide in this volume.

47 See the above cited cases against Argentina, footnote 39.

48 *S.D. Myers, Inc. v. Government of Canada*, UNCITRAL (Partial Award, Merits, 13 November 2000) (*Myers v Canada* (Partial Award 2000)); *Compañia del Desarrollo de Santa Elena S.A. v. Republic of Costa Rica*, ICSID Case No. ARB/96/1 (Award, 17 February 2000).

49 *Chemtura Corporation v. Government of Canada*, UNCITRAL *(formerly Crompton Corporation v. Government of Canada)* (Award, 2 August 2010).

50 ICSID rejected the petition to participate presented by the ECCHR and the tribal leaders of four indigenous communities in Zimbabwe; see *Border Timbers Limited, Timber Products International (Private) Limited, and Hangani Development Co. (Private) Limited v. Republic of Zimbabwe*, ICSID Case No. ARB/10/25 (Procedural Order No. 2 concerning the non-disputing parties' application of 23 May 2012, 26 June 2012). Also see Chapter 9 by Sufyan Droubi, Cecilia Juliana Flores Elizondo, and Raphael Heffron in this volume.

51 For example, in the case of Piero Foreti and others against South Africa the arbitration tribunal had to review an affirmative action program that sought to address some of the injustices that took place during apartheid. See *Piero Foresti, Laura de Carli and others v. Republic of South Africa*, ICSID Case No. ARB(AF)/07/1 (Award, 4 August 2010).

52 See, *Metalclad Corporation v. The United Mexican States*, ICSID Case No. ARB(AF)/97/1 (Award, 30 August 2000); *Técnicas Medioambientales Tecmed v. United Mexican States*, ICSID Case No. ARB(AF)/00/2 (Award, 29 May 2003). For a similar case against Canada, see, for example, *Myers v Canada* (Partial Award 2000) (n 48).

53 *Glamis Gold Ltd. v. United States of America*, UNCITRAL (Award, 8 June 2009).

54 *Chevron Corporation and Texaco Petroleum Company v. The Republic of Ecuador (II)*, PCA Case No. 2009–23 (Claimants' Memorial on the Merits, 6 September 2010).

communities have been affected.[55] These are just some cases that show how investment arbitration ends up deciding about issues that are in their nature of particular public interest and, therefore, having effects beyond the resolution of the bilateral dispute between the foreign investor and the state.

Colombia is familiar with these problems of investment arbitration. Currently, the country is facing several processes before investment tribunals in which, necessarily, the arbitrators will have to decide upon issues of public interest for all Colombians. It is enough to recall the four cases brought by foreign mining companies against Colombia – (1) *Cosigo Resources, Ltd, Cosigo Resources Sucursal Colombia, Tobie Mining and Energy, Inc (Tobie Mining);*[56] (2) *Eco Oro Minerals Corp;*[57] (3) *Galway Gold;*[58] and (4) *Red Eagle*[59] – which deal with decisions made by the government to protect the environment. In fact, in the cases of *Galway Gold* and *Red Eagle*, the investors are challenging a decision of the Colombian Constitutional Court that had the effect of banning mining operations in the countries high wetlands (*páramos*). Furthermore, the case of *Cosigo Resources and Tobie Mining* also involves the rights of the indigenous communities that live in the national natural park Yaigoje-Apaporis, where the company is expecting to extract and exploit its natural resources.

As has already been mentioned, the legitimacy problem of investment–State arbitration lies not only in the arbitral practice of reviewing public interest issued when deciding upon an investment dispute, but in the predominance of a private law mindset in arbitral awards. As a result, in many cases, arbitral tribunals have refused to consider the public interest objectives that lie beneath the measures taken by States.[60]

---

55 Farouk El-Hosseny, *Civil Society in Investment Treaty Arbitration: Status and Prospects* (BRILL 2018) 164.

56 *Cosigo Resources, Ltd., Cosigo Resources Sucursal Colombia, Tobie Mining and Energy, Inc. v. Republic of Colombia*, UNCITRAL (Pending).

57 *Eco Oro Minerals Corp. v. Republic of Colombia*, ICSID Case No. ARB/16/41 (Pending).

58 *Galway Gold Inc. v. Republic of Colombia*, ICSID Case No. ARB/18/13 (Pending).

59 *Red Eagle Exploration Limited v. Republic of Colombia*, ICSID Case No. ARB/18/12 (Pending).

60 On the arguments used by investment tribunals to reject human rights arguments, see Moshe Hirsch "Investment Tribunals and Human Rights: Divergent Paths," in Pierre-Marie Dupuy, Francesco Francioni, and Emst-Ulrich Petersmann (eds) *Human Rights in International Investment Law and Arbitration* (Oxford University Press 2009). But also see Chapters 10 by Rodrigo Polanco Lazo and Felipe Ferreira Catalán and 11 by Farouk El-Hosseny, Patrick Devine, and Ilan Brun-Vargas in this volume.

The interaction between the Colombian constitutional jurisdiction and the investment regime

While the relationship between investment arbitration and the regulatory power of the State has been broadly studied, the interaction between the international investment regime and the decisions of national tribunals, especially constitutional ones, has received less attention until now. This is surprising, considering that one of the transformations in modern constitutionalism was the emergence of the constitutional review of treaties in order "to reconcile the sanctity of the domestic constitutional order with the constitutionally significant ramifications that can flow from treaty commitments."[61] In Latin America, the relationship between the international investment regime and the national constitutional regimes must be read in the context of the political project of transformative constitutionalism, which has been shaped through a multi-level dialogue (both horizontal and vertical) between the national constitutional systems and the Inter-American System of Human Rights.[62]

Due to its ability to limit the regulatory power of the state, investment arbitration is now perceived as an obstacle for the achievement of public interest objectives, such as the protection of the environment and human rights.[63] In Latin America, this means that investment arbitration could pose a threat to some of the transformative aspiration of the region's constitutionalism, such as the protection of human rights, the commitment towards overcoming inequality, the protection of indigenous people, the consolidation of democracy and the strengthening of the domestic institutions.[64] Constitutional courts have been, in many countries, passionate advocates of

---

61 Mario Mendez, "Constitutional Review of Treaties: Lessons for Comparative Constitutional Design and Practice" (2017) 15 (1) *International Journal of Constitutional Law* 95.
62 On the concept of transformative constitutionalism in Latin America, see, Armin Von Bogdandy, Eduardo F. Mac-Gregor, Mariela Morales Antoniazzi, and Flávia Piovesan (eds) *Transformative Constitutionalism in Latin America: The Emergence of a New Ius Commune* (Oxford University Press 2017).
63 See, for example, Kyla Susanne Tienhaara, *The Expropriation of Environmental Governance: Protecting Foreign Investors at the Expense of Public Policy* (Cambridge University 2009); Pierre-Marie Dupuy, Francesco Francioni, and Emst-Ulrich Petersmann (eds), *Human Rights in International Investment Law and Arbitration* (Oxford University Press 2009).
64 See the contributions in the book, Armin von Bogdandy, Pedro Salazar Ugarte, Mariela Morales Antoniazzi, and Franz Christian Ebert (eds) *El Constitucionalismo Transformador En América Latina y El Derecho Económico Internacional. De La Tensión Al Diálogo* (Universidad Nacional Autónoma de México, 2018).

transformative constitutionalism; for that reason, in the face of the decentralized public authority exercise by investment arbitration, constitutional courts are the natural gatekeepers of Latin America's constitutional promise towards vulnerable populations.

The Colombian Constitutional Court has been recognized as a champion of transformative constitutionalism in the region, and many of its decisions have been, in fact, groundbreaking in terms of the protection of human rights and the environment. The 1991 Colombian Constitution grants the Constitutional Court a broad authority in terms of the interpretation of the constitutional text, the protection of fundamental rights, the ex-ante review of international treaties and the constitutional review of national laws.[65] For this reason, it is most likely that the constitutional jurisdiction will, in many cases, end up playing a fundamental role in the implementation of the investment regime in the country.

If we understand the working of the investment regime in temporal terms, we can identify at least four stages in which the Colombian courts, especially the constitutional jurisdiction, could interact and, thus, impact the functioning and enforcement of the investment regime in the country: (i) the ex-ante and abstract constitutional review of treaties; (ii) the concurrent jurisdiction over investment-related disputes; (iii) the recognition and enforcement of arbitral awards; and (iv) the constitutional (and in some cases administrative) review of the national norms enacted to implement the decisions of the arbitral awards.[66] The existence of these four stages demonstrates the need for a mechanism that allows the domestic constitutional jurisdiction to communicate effectively with the international adjudication organs in investment-related disputes.

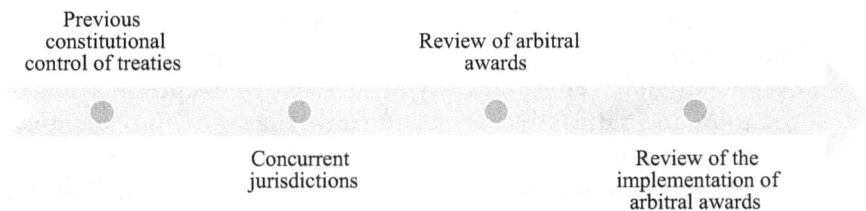

Previous
constitutional
control of treaties   Review of arbitral
                                       awards

        Concurrent   Review of the
        jurisdictions   implementation of
                                                arbitral awards

Figure 6.1 Spaces of interaction between the Colombian constitutional jurisdiction and the international investment regime

65 Colombia Constitution 1991 (rev. 2015) art 241.
66 See, Juan Camilo Fandiño-Bravo, "LL. M. Thesis: The Role of Constitutional Courts in International Investment Law and Investment Treaty Arbitration: A Latin American Perspective" (2014) 18 (1) *Max Planck Yearbook of United Nations Law Online* 667, 745.

Previous and abstract constitutional review of treaties: the need for concrete orders

The first stage in which constitutional courts may impact the international investment regime is through the exercise of the ex-ante constitutional review of investment treaties.[67] In Colombia, article 241(10) of the Political Constitution grants the Constitutional Court the competence to exercise a thorough, previous, and automatic review over international treaties and their approbatory laws. The constitutional review of treaties has five fundamental characteristics. First, it is previous, which means that it is necessarily exercised before the ratification of the instrument by the President, but after it has been discussed and approved through the enactment of a law by the Congress. Second, it is automatic. Once the law that approves the treaty has been issued, the constitutional jurisdiction is automatically triggered, and the President has six days to send the treaty and its approbatory law to the Court for their review. Third, it has an enabling function. Without a positive review of the Court the President does not have the authority to bind Colombia internationally through the ratification of a treaty. Fourth, it is preventive, since one of its objectives is to anticipate and prevent possible clashes between the international and constitutional obligations of the State. Fifth, it is comprehensive because the Court is called upon to analyze both formally and substantially the conformity of the treaty with the entirety of the Colombian constitutional framework.[68]

Because of all these characteristics, the ex-ante constitutional review is the ideal mechanism to generate a dialogue between the domestic jurisdiction and the international investment system since it can bar the executive power from ratifying investment treaties if the text does not reflect the minimum guarantees necessary to allow the state to protect public interest issues such as human rights and the environment. In other words, the constitutional review has the potential to resist the investment regime's top-down exercise of global governance by impacting the practice of states in the negotiation and ratification of investment obligations. In Colombia, the Constitutional Court has already used its power to order the modification of an obligation contained in an investment treaty for going against a constitutional disposition. In three cases awarded in the nineties, the Court

---

67 Ibid. 697. The following countries in Latin America also have constitutional review of treaties: Costa Rica (art. 10.b. of the Constitution), Bolivia (art. 202.9. of the Constitution), Ecuador (art. 438.1 of the Constitution), Perú (art. 200 of the Constitution); Chile (art. 93.1 of the Constitution).

68 Colombian Constitutional Court, *Sentencia C-286/15 Acuerdo Entre Colombia Y Japon Para La Liberacion, Promocion Y Protecction De Inversiones* www.corteconstitucional.gov.co/relatoria/providencia.aspx?buscar=c-286–15.

established that the bilateral investment treaties that Colombia negotiated with the United Kingdom, Peru and Spain were unconstitutional because of the expropriation clause, which prohibited expropriation without compensation.[69]

At the time, the Colombia Constitution authorized the government to expropriate without compensation for reasons of equity.[70] As a result of the constitutional review, these treaties never entered into force because the other state parties did not accept the modification of the expropriation provision ordered by the Court. In consequence, in 1999 the Congress modified article 58 of the Constitution to remove the legal institution of expropriation without compensation for reasons of equity.[71] This case of interaction between the Constitutional Court and the investment regime can be read as in dialogic terms. In this sense, the Court sent a clear message of resistance by rejecting the prohibition of expropriation without compensation because of its incompatibility with the Constitutional ordering the modification of the international standard. However, the investment regime answered by rejecting the constitutional demand and forcing the Colombian government to accommodate to the existing international standard by modifying its constitution if it wanted to join the system.

Although in this case the constitutional regime failed to impact international investment law, it is an example of the potential dialogue among regimes, which illustrates both the possibilities and limitations of resistance. Unfortunately, the subsequent Constitutional Court's practice has not been as effective in generating this type of interactions. In other cases, in which the Court has not found a blatant contradiction between the investment treaty and the constitution, it has authorized the President to ratify the treaty in the understanding that the relevant provisions should be interpreted following the constitutional interpretation made by the Court in its decision. For example, in several decisions, the Court found an apparent contradiction between the national treatment and most favored nation clauses with article 100 of the Constitution, which establishes that the law

---

69 See Colombian Constitutional Court, *Sentencia C-358/96 Tratado Internacional/ Inversion Extrajera* www.corteconstitucional.gov.co/relatoria/providencia.aspx? buscar=c-358-96 (Colombian Constitutional Court, Decision C-358/96 (1996)) respecting the Colombia–United Kingdom BIT; Colombian Constitutional Court, *Sentencia C-008/97 Convenio Con Peru Sovre Promocion Y Proteccion Reciproca de Inversiones* www.corteconstitucional.gov.co/relatoria/providencia.aspx?buscar=c-008-97 on the Colombia–Peru BIT; and Colombian Constitutional Court, *Sentencia C-494/98 Proyecto De Ley* www.corteconstitucional.gov.co/relatoria/providencia. aspx?buscar=c-494-98 regarding the Colombia–Spain BIT.
70 Article 59 of the Colombian Constitution.
71 Colombia, *Legislative Act 1* (1999).

can, for reasons of public order, deny or condition the exercise of certain civil rights to foreigners.[72]

However, in those cases, the Court did not directly order the President to take any action to guarantee that the national treatment and most favored nation clauses in the investment treaties would be interpreted on the light of article 100 of the Constitution. The problem with this second approach is that the decisions made by a domestic court do not have any effect before an international tribunal unless they are incorporated in the wording of the treaty or, at least, in an interpretative note to the relevant provisions. This is so because domestic law is seen as a mere "fact" in international dispute resolution,[73] as has been recognized by international courts[74] and investment arbitration awards.[75]

Unfortunately, the second approach taken by the Colombian Constitutional Court shows that it has applied a soft standard of constitutional review to investment treaties based on a mistaken view of investment arbitration as a mere mechanism of private dispute settlement (what we called above the private-law mindset), thus, maintaining the power dynamics that require the accommodation of the domestic system to the transnational investment regime. However, since the latter works as a mechanism of decentralized international public authority, "a public-law mindset favors allocating authority at the domestic level."[76] In practical terms, this would mean that, in order to push-back, constitutional courts need to exercise a strict constitutional review over the content investment treaties by explicitly ordering the modification of the treaty text if found that it may impede the protection of human rights or disproportionally limits State regulatory power in issues of public interest.[77]

---

72 Colombian Constitutional Court, Decision C-358 (1996) (n 69); Colombian Constitutional Court, *Sentencia C-199/12 Acuerdo Para Promocion Y Proteccion de Inversiones Entre La Republica de Colombia Y La Republica Popular De China* www.corteconstitucional.gov.co/relatoria/providencia.aspx?buscar=c-199–12 on the Colombia–China BIT.

73 See Laurence Boisson de Chazournes, "Fundamental Rights and International Arbitration: Arbitral Awards and Constitutional Law" in Albert Jan van den Berg (ed) *Arbitration Advocacy in Changing Times* (Wolters Kluwer Law & Business 2011).

74 Case concerning *Certain German Interests in Polish Upper* Silesia *(Germany v Poland)* (Merits) [1926] PCIJ Series A 7, 19; Case concerning Elettronica Sicula SpA (ELSI) (*United States v Italy*) (Judgment, Merits) [1989] ICJ Rep 15, para 73.

75 *Bernardus Henricus Funnekotter and others v. Republic of Zimbabwe*, ICSID Case No. ARB/05/6 (Award, 22 April 2009), para 103.

76 René Urueña, "Subsidiarity and the Public-Private Distinction in Investment Treaty Arbitration" (2016) 79 *Law & Contemp. Probs.* 110.

77 For a discussion on the content of the standard of constitutional review, see, René Urueña and María Angélica Prada-Uribe, "Constitucionalismo Transformador y Arbitraje de

These issues were the object of a heated debate between international lawyers, including the authors of this article, and State agents of the Colombia government during the process of prior constitutional review of the BIT between France and Colombia. After decades of a unified constitutional jurisprudence on the matter, the Court opened the door for the discussion of its precedent in a public hearing that took place in December 2018. Six months later, on the 6th of June 2019, the Constitutional Court issued a historical decision declaring the constitutionality of the treaty under review but conditioning its ratification to the issuance of a joint interpretative note by the parties to the treaty regarding the content of several dispositions of the agreement, including the FET clause.

In relation to the wording of the FET obligation, the Court found, among other issues, that the concept of "legitimate expectations" was a source of legal insecurity and uncertainty and, thus, required that its content be clarified through an interpretative note stating that legitimate expectations are "only derived from specific and repeated acts undertaken by the parties to this agreement which lead the investor to carry out or maintain the investment in good faith, and regarding abrupt and unexpected changes of the authorities that affect its investment."[78] The use of a stricter constitutional review that requires the negotiation of a joint interpretative note before ratification immediately opens a possibility for resistance by triggering a dialogue between the domestic and the transnational sphere. Now Colombia and France will have to reenter negotiations, and we will have to wait and see the effects that this decision might have in both State practice and future investment arbitration.

Concurrent jurisdiction over investment-related disputes

The consolidation of the investment regime meant a radical transformation of the international framework for the protection of foreigners by leading to the almost complete abandonment of the obligation to exhaust local remedies as a prerequisite for the admissibility of a claim before an international investment tribunal.[79] Although investment treaty practice varies a lot,

Inversión: Elementos Para Un Estándar de Revisión Constitucional Nacional Estricto (Transformative Constitutionalism and Investment Arbitration: Towards a Strict National Standard of Review)" (2019) 2019–5 *Max Planck Institute for Comparative Public Law & International Law (MPIL) Research Paper*.

78 Colombian Constitutional Court, *Sentencia C-252/19 Control De Constitucionalidad de Tratados Internacionales Y Sus Leyes Aprobatorias* www.corteconstitucional.gov.co/relatoria/providencia.aspx?buscar=c-252–19 respecting the Colombia–France BIT. Translation by the authors.

79 See, for example, art. 26 of the ICSID Convention.

nowadays only a few include a requirement to exhaust local remedies, while most include requirements for cooling periods, fork-in-the-road clauses or do not include any relevant provision on the matter.[80] Fork-in-the-road-dispositions seek to avoid the existence of concurrent process at the national and international level for the same issues; however, there have been cases in which, due to the absence of this disposition or because of the vague wording of the treaty, a national court and an international tribunal have been seized of disputes arising of the same facts.[81]

An example of a case of clashing jurisdictions was the dispute between GAMI and Mexico regarding the expropriation of sugar mills and the imposition of additional taxes to soft drinks sweetened using sugar and high fructose corn syrup, in which both the NAFTA investment arbitral tribunal and the Mexican Supreme Court issued decisions regarding the conflict.[82] Nevertheless, this instance of concurring jurisdiction is a case in which an investor has initiated parallel processes before both national and international jurisdiction to solve the same dispute with the host state. However, concurring jurisdictions may also arise when national courts are seized of the public interest side of a dispute between the investor and the State, without the investor being part of the proceeding. In these cases, the domestic jurisdiction may be triggered by citizens or communities seeking the protection of their fundamental or collective rights through, for example, the writ of amparo or class actions.

In Colombia, natural persons have access – in some cases even without the need of a lawyer – to different constitutional actions that pursue the protection of individual (in the case of the tutela writ or writ of amparo, as is called in other jurisdictions[83]) and collective rights (in the case of the popular and group actions).[84] In the absence of broader guarantees for the participation of third parties before investment arbitral tribunals, affected individuals and communities may try to exercise some form of resistance to the investment regime by using these constitutional actions, thus giving rise to concurrent jurisdictions when the investment

---

80 Rudolf Dolzer and Christoph Schreuer, *Principles of International Investment Law* (Oxford University Press 2012) 265.

81 Juan Camilo Fandiño-Bravo, "LL. M. Thesis: The Role of Constitutional Courts in International Investment Law and Investment Treaty Arbitration: A Latin American Perspective" (2014) 18 (1) *Max Planck Yearbook of United Nations Law Online* 717–718.

82 For an analysis of the cases, see, Sergio Puig, "Investor-State Tribunals and Constitutional Courts: The Mexican Sweeteners Saga" (2013) 5 (2) *Mexican Law Review* 199, 243.

83 Colombian Political Constitution, art. 86.

84 Colombian Political Constitution, art. 88 and Law 472 (1998).

dispute deals with issues that affect fundamental rights protected by the Colombian constitution. This is already happening in some of Colombia's investment disputes, especially in those cases that involve the exploitation of national resources by foreign investors. For example, in the case of Eco Oro Minerals Corp against Colombia, the arbitration tribunal will have to review a series of decisions of the Constitutional Court that prohibited mining operations in the high-wetland of Santurbán.[85] However, this strategy may prove less effective in shaping investment law, because, as mentioned before, domestic law is seen as a mere "fact" in international dispute resolution.

Implementation of the arbitral awards

More debated in the literature has been the role of national courts in the implementation of international arbitral awards. There are currently two different paths for the implementation of investment arbitral awards. On the one side, an award rendered by ICSID tribunals has to be recognized and implemented "as if it were a final judgment of a court in that State," as is mandated by article 54.1 of the ICSID Convention.[86] On the other side, all other international arbitral awards are subjected to the proceedings encompassed in the New York Convention, which opens a small door for the discussion before domestic courts of the recognition and implementation of the arbitral awards.[87] Due to the limited scope that the Convention gives to the challenge of awards, this legal mechanism has not proven effective to resist the international investment regime. Despite this, states have continuously sought the revision of investment arbitration awards before domestic jurisdictions.[88] Furthermore, several scholars argue that the door remains open for states to use arguments regarding the violation of human rights or the existence of public interests before national courts

---

85 See Colombian Constitutional Court, *Sentencia C-035/16 Normas Sobre Creacion Y Ampliacion de Areas de Reservas Estrategicas Mineras* www.corteconstitucional. gov.co/relatoria/providencia.aspx?buscar=c-035–16 and Colombian Constitutional Court, *Sentencia T-361/17 Derecho De Parcipacion En Materia Ambiental En El Marco De La Expedicion de Resolucion Que Delimito Paramo de Santurban Delemitacion Del Paramo De Santurban* www.corteconstitucional.gov.co/relatoria/ providencia.aspx?buscar=T-361–17.
86 See, articles 53–54 of the ICSID Convention.
87 Convention on the Recognition and Enforcement of Foreign Arbitral Awards (signed 10 June1958, entered into force 7 June 1959) (New York Convention (1958)).
88 The Canadian Courts used a similar argument to review the case of *Metalclad v. México*. See Supreme Court of British Columbia, *United Mexican States v. Metalclad Corp.*, 2001 B.C.S.C. 664 (2 May 2001).

to seek a decision denying the recognition and implementation of investment awards.[89]

In Colombia, the procedure for the recognition and execution of international awards covered by the New York Convention has been codified under
the Law 1563 of 2012, which established the National and International
Arbitration Statute. This law has as its main objective to incorporate into the
Colombian legal system the rules for the recognition and execution of arbitral awards of the New York Convention in order to respond to the critics
raised for the former use of the *exequátor* institution contained in the Civil
Procedural Code.[90] This law contains the same limited list of reasons for the
denial of recognition of awards.[91]

Regarding arbitral awards issued by ICSID tribunals, according to article 53
of the ICSID Convention, they should not be subjected to any additional legal
actions for their recognition and compliance with by the contracting states.
Nonetheless, in some states like Argentina, investment arbitration awards
have been challenged before national courts. In 2004 the Argentinean Supreme
Court of Justice issued a decision acknowledging the possibility to challenge
ICSID awards for constitutional reasons:

> [i]t cannot be licitly interpreted that the renunciation to appeal an arbitral decision
> is extended to cases in which the content of the issued award contradicts public
> order, since it is not logic to anticipate, when formulating a renunciation, that
> the arbitrators will adopt a decision with such vices. It is important to remember
> that the assessment of the facts and the regular application of the law are respon-
> sibilities of the arbitrators and, for that reason, the issued award should not be
> subject to appeal under such conditions, but, on the contrary, its decision can be
> challenged in cases of unconstitutionality, illegality or unreasonability.[92]

In Colombia, for instance, arbitral awards can be extraordinarily challenged
to protect fundamental rights using the *tutela* writ.[93] The Constitutional
Court has pointed out that "arbitral awards are equivalent to a judicial

---

89 Art. V(2)(b) of the New York Convention (1958) (n 87). See also, Audley Sheppard,
    "Interim ILA Report on Public Policy as a Bar to Enforcement of International
    Arbitral Awards" (2003) 19 (2) *Arbitration International* 217, 248.

90 Nicolás Lozada, "Diferencias entre exequátur y reconocimiento de laudos
    arbitrales internacionales," *Ámbito Jurídico* (blog), 5 February 2004, www.
    ambitojuridico.com/noticias/educacion-y-cultura/diferencias-entre-exequatur-
    y-reconocimiento-de-laudos-arbitrales.

91 Colombia, *Law 1563* (2012), art. 112.

92 Argentina Supreme Court of Justice, *José Cartellone Construcciones Civiles S.A. c/
    Hidroeléctrica Norpatagónica S.A. o Hidronor S.A. s/ proceso de conocimiento* (1
    June 2004) https://sjconsulta.csjn.gov.ar/sjconsulta/documentos/verDocumentoSuma
    rio.html?idDocumentoSumario=10488, para 14.

93 A constitutional action that any person can present before a Colombian judge to seek
    the protection of her fundamental rights. See art. 86 of the Colombian Constitution.

decision for the effects of the admissibility of the *tutela* writ. In effect, this constitutional mechanism is admissible against arbitral awards as long as they violate, threaten or affect the fundamental rights of the parties (to the arbitration) or third parties."[94] Since investment cases against Colombia are relatively new and no arbitral award has yet been issued, the use of the *tutela* action as a form of resisting the compliance with arbitral awards is still just a hypothetical. However, the possibility remains open, especially because ICSID awards are to be treated "as if it were a final judgment of a court in that State" (article 54 of the ICSID Convention) and in Colombia all judgments (except the ones that decide *tutela* actions) can be challenged using the writ of *tutela* if they violate fundamental rights. As has already been mentioned, in these cases the public-law mindset would require domestic courts to apply a non-deferential standard of review.[95]

Abstract control of the legislation that implements the arbitral award

Finally, in Colombia, the decision issued by the Constitutional Court regarding the *ex-ante* constitutional review of treaties has the effect of *prima facie res judicata*.[96] This means that the Constitutional Court recognizes that not all issues of constitutional relevance regarding the implementation of the investment treaty are solved at the stage of the previous constitutional review. This is especially the case of the implementation of the obligations derived from the treaty, including the ones established by investment awards, as has been established by the Court:

> In the same vein, the future legislative and administrative execution of the treaty should be in accordance with the Constitution. In effect, it is common that certain dispositions in the treaties have the character (...) of non-self-executing norms, this means that, in order to have full effect in the domestic legal system of a State, they need the pertinent normative development, as opposed

---

94 Colombian Constitutional Court, *Sentencia T-055/14 Accion De Tutela Contra Laudo Arbitral*, www.corteconstitucional.gov.co/relatoria/providencia.aspx?buscar=T-055–14.

95 For an example of a public-law mindset in the review of investment awards, see, *BG Grp. PLC v. Republic of Arg.*, 572 U.S 25, 134 S. Ct. 1198, 1215 (2014) (Roberts, J., dissenting).

96 Magdalena Correa, "El Control de Constitucionalidad de Los Acuerdos de Inversión En Colombia. Análisis Desde La Cláusula de Expropiación Indirecta" in Armin Von Bogdandy, Pedro Salazar Ugarte, Mariela Morales Antoniazzi, and Franz Christian Ebert (eds) *El Constitucionalismo Transformador En América Latina y El Derecho Económico Internacional. De La Tensión Al Diálogo* (Universidad Nacional Autónoma de México, 2018) 524–26.

to the ones that are self-executed. For that reason, those laws and regulations that allow for the rightful inner implementation of the free trade agreement should be subjected to the appropriate judicial control.[97]

By the same token, many times the investment awards require the implementation of legislative or administrative reforms for its compliance. Due to the doctrine of *prima facie res judicata*, those laws and administrative acts could also be subjected to constitutional (or administrative) review. Furthermore, in case of a possible threat or violation of human rights, these implementation norms could also be challenged using the writ of *tutela*, for example, in the case of the right to prior consultation of indigenous or Afro-Colombian communities.

Concluding remarks

This chapter explored the role that the constitutional jurisdiction may play vis-à-vis the possibility to resist or the need to accommodate the domestic legal system to the international investment regime in the Latin American legal space. The case of the Colombian Constitutional Court shows us how the dormant authority of constitutional tribunals may be awakened through the use of a stricter *ex-ante* constitutional review of investment treaties. As was shown in previous sections, other spaces of interaction between the domestic jurisdiction and the international investment regime are less effective at prompting a dialogue between both jurisdictions, and, thus, they are less likely to shape international investment law even if some forms of resistance are still possible.

Two major conclusions can be extracted from the arguments presented throughout this text regarding the importance of *ex-ante* constitutional review of investment treaties by constitutional tribunals. First, the discussion on the public–private divide of international investment arbitration continues to be relevant because it has direct effects on the level of constitutional review that domestic courts should apply vis-à-vis the international investment regime. As we have shown, the public-law mindset requires that domestic courts apply a non-deferential standard when reviewing investment awards and a strict standard of constitutional review when analyzing investment treaties.

97 Colombian Constitutional Court, *Sentencia C-608/10 Tratado De Libre Comercio Entre Canada Y La Republica de Colombia* www.corteconstitucional.gov.co/relatoria/providencia.aspx?buscar=C-608–10.

Second, when doing so, Constitutional Courts need to give precise orders to the executive branch regarding the standards or wording that needs to be modified in the treaty. By not doing so domestic Courts failed to effectively engage with the investment regime because domestic law is only taken into account by international courts as a matter of fact. For that reason, in order to create a dialogue between the constitutional and the investment regime that opens a window for a bottom-up transformation of international investment law, Constitutional Courts need to give direct orders to the executive branch – such as to renegotiate a standard contained in the treaty or to negotiate an interpretation note to clarify the content of a specific clause – when an investment treaty is found to go against constitutional rights and principles.

Part II

The mosaic of non-state actors

7

Corporations and international investment law in Latin America

Claus von Wobeser[1]

Introduction

Multinational corporations or enterprises (MNEs)[2] have arguably been a central actor in the development of international investment law (IIL) due to their dominant role in the foreign trade and investment landscapes. MNEs are by and large the most important vehicle of global trade and international investment in today's globalized economy, which they helped to shape.[3] Latin America and the significant growth experienced in several countries in the region, in turn, has been an important catalyst of foreign investment, and foreign investment has played a key role in the development and the economic life of the region.[4] In light of these considerations, combined with the fact that Latin American states have been among the most

1 The author would like to thank Katarina Lundahl and Valeria Bonechi for their excellent research and drafting assistance.
2 For the purposes of this chapter, multinational corporation, multinational enterprise, and transnational corporation are considered synonymous terms referring to a corporation that owns or controls production or service facilities outside the country in which it is based.
3 For instance, Bernard, Jensen, and Schott conclude that multinational enterprises mediate a substantial majority of US trade, as roughly 90 percent of US exports and imports in their sample flowed through multinational firms. See Andrew B. Bernard, J. Bradford Jensen and Peter K. Schott, "Importers, Exporters, and Multinationals: A Portrait of Firms in the U.S. that Trade Goods" (2005) National Bureau of Economic Research Working Paper 11404, 19, 54 www.nber.org/papers/w11404 accessed 10 August 2018.
4 United Nations Conference on Trade and Development (UNCTAD), "World Investment Report 2018: Investment and New Industrial Policies," Chapter 1, 3. In 2017, approximately 47 percent of global FDI inflows were received by developing economies and 22.5 percent of the inflows received by developing economies were received by Latin American and Caribbean states.

frequent respondents in investment-treaty arbitrations,[5] observing MNEs as stakeholders in the international investment regime in Latin America is a fruitful laboratory of IIL, both in terms of volume and content.

This chapter describes the corporate stakeholder and its characteristics, interests, and role in the IIL regime in Latin America. It begins by discussing the characteristics of the corporate stakeholder as a participant in the regime and the emergence of new corporate stakeholders. It is submitted that the corporate stakeholder and its interests are much more nuanced and diverse than the traditional conception of hostility between MNEs and the other systemic actors would suggest. Next, the chapter adopts the perspective of the MNE towards IIL and discusses whether and if so, to what extent, corporations care about investment treaties and the availability of investor–state dispute resolution (ISDS) when making decisions on foreign direct investment (FDI). It is submitted that corporations care generally about the protection of property rights and investment safety, which are objectives that can be secured by several means, not limited to bilateral investment treaties (BIT) and ISDS. In the final section, the chapter discusses some of the ways in which corporations have accommodated the narratives promoted by other systemic actors and how these developments may contribute to norm creation in IIL.

The corporate stakeholder

Traditional corporate management strives to generate revenue to shareholders. Although the ultimate objective of a corporation does not by any fact of nature have to be the generation of profit, to function and exist, corporate activities must at least have the result, if not the objective, of making money. All corporations share this nature. Behind this seeming uniformity of objectives, however, the corporate stakeholder in the IIL regime is anything but a uniform, homogenous actor with hostile interests vis-à-vis the other systemic actors.

Multitude of corporate stakeholders

Several corporate actors participate in the international investment regime behind the apparently uniform corporate veil and contribute to the corporate

---

5 United Nations Conference on Trade and Development (UNCTAD), "Investment Dispute Settlement Navigator" (*Investment Policy Hub*, 31 December 2017) http:// investmentpolicyhub.unctad.org/ISDS accessed 15 April 2018.

perspective in different ways. These actors include shareholders, managers, and corporate counsel.

First, shareholders are a particularly relevant category because shareholding or participation in a company is a form of protected investment under most investment treaty provisions.[6] Most investment treaties do not specify what type of equity instruments may constitute protected investments, but rather refer generally to shares, stocks and other forms of equity participation.[7] Other treaties provide additional details. For instance, Article 1139 of NAFTA specifies that "investment" includes equity and debt securities, which in turn include voting and non-voting shares, bonds, convertible debentures, stock options, and warrants.[8] Invariably, however, the definitions of protected investments are broad. This is accommodating to investors, including corporations, because foreign investment comes in many forms. The definition is also crucial to corporations because it allows them to structure their foreign investment in a way that allows the company to benefit from the substantive investment protections. The generally broad definitions of protected investments also mean that shareholders, or holders of other protected equity or debt instruments, can be seen as separate participants from the corporation.

Investment treaties also typically do not specify any percentage requirements for shareholding, ensuring that majority as well as minority and non-controlling interests are covered. Moreover, it has been considered that indirect participation is covered unless specifically excluded in the treaty definition.[9] Through indirect participation, layers of shareholders may become participants in the investment regime beyond the immediate shareholders of the affected company. Further, conflicts behind the corporate veil may arise between minority or non-controlling and majority shareholders, and shareholders at different levels vis-à-vis the affected corporation may pursue parallel and conflicting remedies for treaty violations.[10]

---

6 See generally Christoph Schreuer, "Shareholder Protection in International Investment Law" in Pierre Marie Dupuy, Bardo Fassbender, Malcolm N. Shaw, and Karl-Peter Sommermann (eds), *Common Values in International Law: Essays in Honour of Christian Tomuschat* (NP Engel Verlag 2006) 601–619; David Gaukrodger, "Investment Treaties and Shareholder Claims" (2014) OECD Working Papers on International Investment 2014/03 www.oecd.org/daf/inv/investment-policy/WP-2014–3.pdf accessed 15 August 2018.

7 See e.g. Energy Charter Treaty (adopted 17 December 1994, entered into force 16 April 1998) 2080 UNTS 95, art 1(6)(b).

8 North American Free Trade Agreement (signed 17 December 1992, entered into force 1 January 1994) 32 ILM 289, 605, art 1139.

9 *Siemens A.G. v. The Argentine Republic*, ICSID Case No. ARB/02/8 (Decision on Jurisdiction, 3 August 2004) [137].

10 Schreuer (n 6) 610.

Further, nationality is a relevant consideration to corporations that have arguably at times made creative use of forum shopping to obtain treaty benefits. A foreign shareholder in a domestic corporation in the host state may fulfil a nationality requirement in an investment treaty and have access to ISDS in cases where the corporation would not. It is also arguable that foreign shareholders may fulfil the nationality requirements under an investment treaty even if their participation in the affected company is through an intermediate company that does not fulfil the nationality requirement.[11]

The above considerations suggest that, in many cases, there is no such thing as a single, uniform corporate stakeholder, but rather various corporate actors that are all potential participants in the international investment regime.

Second, managers influence corporate FDI decisions and shape the corporate culture, which may vary greatly as to how accommodating the corporation is towards non-investment interests and corporate social responsibility issues. The sector, the level of risk aversion, the number of countries in which operations are conducted, and the nationality and attitudes of shareholders and managers, among a myriad of other factors, influence the characteristics of a corporation, which, in turn, influence how accommodating the corporation will be towards the narratives promoted by other systemic actors. For instance, corporations that value corporate social responsibility more highly may be more reluctant to engage in ISDS on issues that involve controversial public goods considerations, like health and environment, due to the potential reputational cost.

Similarly, the narrative of these corporations may find more synergies with the narratives of other systemic actors like NGOs, although the level of corporate social responsibility may be difficult to evaluate objectively, for instance a 2018 consumer survey in the United States found information age corporations like Amazon and Tesla among the multinational corporations to be perceived as the most socially responsible, while many banks and oil companies were among the companies perceived to be the least socially responsible.[12] Coincidentally, the banking and oil and gas industries rank among the top four industries where investor claims have been brought in Latin America.[13] Again, these considerations speak against the conception of a uniform corporate stakeholder.

---

11 Schreuer (n 6) 604–612.
12 The Harris Poll, "The Reputations of the Most Visible Companies" (2018) https://theharrispoll.com/reputation-quotient/ accessed 15 August 2018. For a discussion on the investor's need to obtain social license, see Chapter 13 by Sebastián Preller-Bórquez; for a discussion on the perspective of civil society, see Chapter 8 by Adoración Guamán, both in this volume.
13 Out of all investor–state claims brought against Latin American states, the top four economic sectors to which the investment at issue allegedly belongs are mining and

In terms of dispute resolution preferences, the sector of the corporation is also highly influential. For instance, the 2013 PwC and Queen Mary International Arbitration Survey on corporate preferences in international arbitration, although not distinguishing between commercial and investment arbitration, concluded that, while corporations generally view arbitration as well suited for their industries, the industries that viewed arbitration most favorably were the construction and energy industries. On the contrary, the financial services industry largely preferred litigation over arbitration.[14] These varying corporate preferences may imply that certain industries are more active participants in the regime than others and hence the corporate contributions to the making of IIL may be tilted towards sectors like construction and oil and gas.

In this context, it should also be noted that, from an economic perspective, corporations generally prefer to avoid dispute resolution (whether arbitration or litigation) because it implies an additional cost that reduces the value of the investment. In fact, of all investor–state cases concluded to date against Latin American states over 25 percent were settled during arbitration.[15] In addition, considering that many investment treaties provide for mandatory consultation or negotiation before a claim can be submitted to arbitration, a presumably large number of cases is settled before arbitration. Therefore, considering that settlement agreements are usually confidential, a significant portion of corporate participation in the regime does not have observable results or public manifestations.

Finally, corporate counsel influences the legal structures chosen to execute a foreign investment, the choice of whether to pursue a claim, the choice of the appropriate dispute resolution mechanism and strategy, and the formulation of the corporation's legal position in a given dispute. These considerations are key when it comes to the participation of corporations in the making of international investment law through their participation in investor–state dispute resolution. Although the final say in whether to initiate dispute resolution usually depends on the board of the corporation, once the decision to pursue arbitration or litigation has been taken, corporate counsel, in-house and external, arguably play an important role in the way in which corporations act as participants in the making of international investment law.

---

quarrying, electricity, gas, steam and air conditions supply, manufacturing, and financial and insurance activities. See UNCTAD (n 5).

14 PricewaterhouseCoopers and Queen Mary University of London, "Corporate Choices in International Arbitration: Industry Perspectives" (2013) 1, 4. www.pwc. com/gx/en/arbitration-dispute-resolution/assets/pwc-international-arbitration-study. pdf accessed 15 August 2018.

15 UNCTAD (n 5). Of 163 cases concluded against Latin American states (excluding the Caribbean), 41 were settled.

The importance of corporate counsel is magnified by the fact that corporate decisions on FDI or dispute resolution options and tactics are not readily available to the public. Virtually the only publicly available material to study the perspective of corporations in IIL is the documentation published in the course of investment arbitrations. This documentation is, of course, drafted by corporate counsel. The corporate perspectives available from ISDS documentation are therefore, in reality, perspectives of corporate counsel in the execution of a legal strategy chosen after the choice to pursue a claim has been made. It says little about how corporations view IIL and what role it plays in corporate decisions on FDI.

In summary, there is a myriad of corporate actors behind the seemingly uniform corporate veil who participate in the system and shape corporate perspectives towards IIL.

Corporations vis-à-vis other systemic actors

At a first glance, the relationship between MNEs and other actors in the regime in Latin America, particularly governments and NGOs, might seem one of hostility, especially in light of the long history of expropriations of foreign multinationals in the region and the traditional focus of IIL on the protection of investors.

The traditional dependency theory stemming from the Latin American experience with multinationals posits that MNEs are vehicles of foreign control and intervention that undermine sovereignty and distort development.[16] In reality, however, MNEs have both conflicting and converging interests with the other systemic actors.

Both governments and MNEs benefit from economic growth, which coincided globally with globalization and the expansion of MNE investment.[17] Both MNEs, NGOs, and regional international organizations care about topics like the rule of law, political stability, and low levels of corruption.[18] The agendas of everyone involved are advanced if these objectives are obtained.

---

16 Richard S. Weinert, "Multinationals in Latin America" (1976) 18 *Journal of Interamerican Studies and World Affairs*, 253; Russell Martin Moore, "Imperialism and Dependency in Latin America: A View of the New Reality of Multinational Investment" (1973) 15 *Journal of Interamerican Studies and World Affairs* 21, 32–33. C.f. Chapter 9 by Sufyan Droubi, Cecilia Juliana Flores Elizondo, and Raphael Heffron in this volume.
17 Weinert (n 16) 254.
18 These factors are among key considerations multinationals consider when making FDI decisions. See Nathan M. Jensen, Glen Biglaiser, Quan Li, Edmund Malesky, Pablo M. Pinto, Santiago M. Pinto, and Joseph L. Staats (eds) *Politics and Foreign Direct Investment* (University of Michigan Press 2012) 66.

There is also little evidence that multinationals, that are largely stateless these days, continue to act as vehicles of foreign influence and interference. While this was certainly true in the times of early multinationals like the Dutch East India Company that held delegated sovereign powers,[19] MNEs today are arguably more global and less aligned with the sovereign interests of any particular state. This challenges the idea that globalization today is synonymous with exclusively Western influence in the developing world.[20] If an MNE adopts a global viewpoint and coordinates activities in a way that avoids national bias, as many MNEs today do, they conflict with both their home state and their host states.[21] It would be an over-simplification to assume that MNE interests today are necessarily aligned with the interests of the home state, which, in many cases, may be difficult to identify in the first place.

In sum, corporate interests overlap with other systemic interests on several points, including conditions like adherence to the rule of law that are thought to promote FDI inflow. Although profit considerations may trump other interests in cases where non-investment and investment concerns clash explicitly, that is not to say that the corporate agenda is limited to economic concerns.

Corporations as participants in the IIL regime

Considering the role of MNEs in international trade and investment, the perspective of the MNE towards IIL is inherently accommodating: the system was created to uphold investors' rights. However, in the traditional positivist conception, corporations and other non-state actors are aliens in terms of international personality. Corporations are not subjects of international law and lack international legal personality. The fact that international investment law endows corporations with some of the aspects traditionally associated with international personality has sparked extensive debates, with the majority view concluding that corporations probably have some sort of limited, derived personality at least within IIL.[22] Notably,

---

19 Kate Miles, *The Origins of International Investment Law: Empire, Environment and the Safeguarding of Capital* (Cambridge University Press 2013) 33–34.

20 See e.g. Robert Reich, "The Increasing Irrelevance of Corporate Nationality" (*Robert Reich*, 28 July 2014) http://robertreich.org/post/93122315065 accessed 15 August 2018; Edward M. Graham, *Global Corporations and National Governments* (Institute for International Economics 1996) 33–35.

21 Moore (n 16) 33.

22 Vincent Chetail, "The Legal Personality of Multinational Corporations, State Responsibility and Due Diligence: The Way Forward" in Denis Alland, Vincent Chetail, Olivier de Frouville, and Jorge E. Viñuales (eds), *Unity and Diversity of International Law: Essays in Honour of Professor Pierre-Marie Dupuy* (Martinus Nijhoff Publishers 2014) 110–112.

corporations hold rights under IIL, be they direct or derivative, and they have a direct procedural right to enforce those rights through investor–state adjudication, independently of their host and home states. However, corporations arguably lack some of the other aspects traditionally associated with international legal personality, such as the ability to be the direct bearers of international obligations or to participate in the making of international law through the conclusion of treaties and customary international law.

However, as some prominent scholars have pointed out, focusing on the purported international personhood of corporations constitutes "intellectual baggage" that is insensitive to real-world practice and elicits misleading analogies.[23] Instead, corporations as well as other non-state actors should more practically be treated as participants in the international legal process.[24]

IIL is, of course, the specialized regime of international law that has allowed corporations to become participants in the international legal process. Their role as prominent claimants in investor–state adjudication makes them perhaps the most active participants in the making of international investment law although, as noted above, some corporations participate more actively than others.

As Alvarez notes in this context, corporate plaintiffs play a jurisgenerative role that is formally reserved to states throughout much of international law, including WTO law and dispute settlement, where corporations still need their home states to espouse their claim.[25] By creating the international investment regime through the nearly 2,300 bilateral investment treaties and 324 other treaties with investment provisions currently in force,[26] states essentially delegated some of their jurisgenerative power to investors, whereas the states themselves were left in the role of a passive defendant and their regulatory conduct subject to control through investor–state adjudication.[27] Ultimately, however, states hold the power to fundamentally

---

23 Jose E Alvarez, "Are Corporations 'Subjects' of International Law?" (2011) 9 *Santa Clara Journal of International Law* 1, 8, citing Rosalyn Higgins, *Problems and Process: International Law and How We Use It* (Oxford University Press 1994) 49–50.

24 Alvarez (n 23) 9. C.f. Chapter 9 by Sufyan Droubi, Cecilia Juliana Flores Elizondo, and Raphael Heffron in this volume.

25 Alvarez (n 23) 11.

26 According to UNCTAD, there are currently a total of 2,852 BITs and 417 treaties with investment protections (TIP). However, 2,298 BITs and 324 TIPs are in force. See United Nations Conference on Trade and Development (UNCTAD), "International Investment Agreements Navigator" (Investment Policy Hub, 31 December 2017) http://investmentpolicyhub.unctad.org/IIA accessed 18 April 2021.

27 See Gus Van Harten and Martin Loughlin, "Investment Treaty Arbitration as a Species of Global Administrative Law" (2006) 17 *The European Journal of International Law* 121.

shape the regime through the negotiation and re-negotiation of investment treaties and the creation of custom.

Multinational corporations vis-à-vis other investors are in a privileged position in the regime due to their wealth, organizational sophistication, and expertise in foreign investment. These advantages allow them to pursue costly investor–state claims. These claims, in turn, generate case law and contribute to the making of IIL. Although there is no doctrine of binding precedent in international law, previous case law is influential and may contribute to the generation of norms.[28] MNEs can therefore be seen as powerful participants in the making of IIL, even though corporations do not have formal personality in international law and decisions of investment tribunals are not binding precedents.

To summarize, just like states do not have a uniform character when it comes to international investment law, Latin America being a prime example of intra-regional splits in approaches, neither do corporations. Rather than one uniform corporate stakeholder, a myriad of corporate actors function as participants in the specialized regime of IIL and contribute to its law-making processes.

The emergence of new corporate stakeholders

The IIL regime emerged, and has developed until recent days, as a regime that served primarily the interests of capital-exporting states and their investors, with MNEs being the key vehicle of foreign investment.[29] As a consequence, the perspective of the corporation in the clash of narratives that has shaped the international investment regime has traditionally been represented by European and US MNEs. Similarly, while abundant literature emerged regarding the impact of inward FDI and MNEs on the Latin American economies, research in outward FDI and MNEs from developing economies, including Latin America, has not gained relevance until more recently.[30] However, this landscape has changed in important ways over the past few decades, which further diversifies the corporate stakeholder in the regime.

---

28 Jan Paulsson, "International Arbitration and the Generation of Legal Norms: Treaty Arbitration and International Law," in Albert Jan van den Berg (ed), *International Arbitration 2006: Back to Basics?* (Kluwer Law International 2007) 881. Paulsson notes that, "[i]t is pointless to resist the observation that precedents generate norms of international law. It is a fact of life before international courts and tribunals."

29 Miles (n 19) 2–3.

30 John D. Daniels, Jeffrey A. Krug and Len Trevino, "Foreign Direct Investment from Latin America and the Caribbean" (2007) 16 *Transnational Corporations* 27, 28.

First, the emergence of new multinationals from Latin America and other developing economies has altered the "global corporate chessboard" since the 2000s.[31] One of the key economic reasons for the long absence of the Latin American corporation from the international investment regime was the protectionist environment in many states in the region that prevented local corporations from creating internationally competitive products and the competencies necessary to extend their operations internationally.[32] As a consequence, it was not until the 1990s that some Latin American economies had stabilized their economies sufficiently to allow for increased FDI inflow. For instance, the shift in Mexican economic policy in the early 1990s, marked by the move away from nationalism towards a more global outlook through the ratification of GATT and NAFTA, made Mexico the second largest FDI recipient after China in a matter of a few years.[33] These increased FDI inflows in Latin America, in turn, appear to have stimulated outward FDI and the development of MNEs in the region.[34] Latin American multinationals, principally from Brazil and Mexico, took up a strategy of globalization, possibly prompted by the entry into their domestic markets of foreign multinationals.[35] Consequently, although recent economic recessions in 2008–2009 and 2015–2016 have reversed inward FDI in the region to 1997 levels in terms of weight in the economy,[36] in 2017, the Latin American outward FDI stock (the region's cumulative FDI assets) was almost twelve times larger than it was in 1995.[37]

Private MNEs from Brazil, Mexico, Argentina, and Chile are leading the way in outward FDI stock, but publicly owned multinational corporations like Petróleos de Venezuela are also relevant actors.[38] In fact, many large corporations in Latin America were born through the privatization of formerly

---

31 Javier Santiso, "The Emergence of Latin Multinationals" (2007) OECD Emerging Markets Network Working Paper 04/2007, 2.

32 Daniels, Krug and Trevino (n 30) 28–29.

33 Claus von Wobeser, "El régimen legal de la inversión extranjera en el TLCAN y sus efectos en los flujos de capital hacia México" in Beatriz Leycegui and Rafael Fernández de Castro (eds) ¿Socios Naturales? Cinco Años del Tratado de Libre Comercio de América del Norte (Instituto Tecnológico Autónomo de México 2000) 225–79.

34 Daniels, Krug, and Trevino (n 30) 29.

35 Santiso (n 31) 5–7; Pablo Toral, *Multinational Enterprises in Latin America Since the 1990s* (Palgrave Macmillan 2011), 1–13.

36 United Nations Economic Commission for Latin America and the Caribbean (ECLAC), "Foreign Direct Investment in Latin America and the Caribbean" (2018) 40.

37 UNCTAD, "World Investment Report 2018, Regional Fact Sheet, Latin America and the Caribbean" (2018).

38 Santiso (n 31) 2.

state-owned enterprises and continue to combine private and public capital, while carrying out activities practically indistinguishable from privately owned enterprises. The continued participation of Latin American governments in enterprises that function like private companies blurs the distinction between the government and corporations as stakeholders in the regime and constitutes another possible point of convergence of interests.

Second, the rise of South–South FDI inflows has altered the investment landscape in Latin America. On the one hand, a significant portion of the growing outward FDI from Latin American states flows to other Latin American states instead of developed economies.[39] Indeed, foreign investment by Latin American MNEs is mainly carried out through acquisitions in other Latin American states, usually in neighboring states, rather than greenfield investment or operation of subsidiaries outside the region.[40] Although economies like Mexico and Chile have several multinationals with truly global operations, many multinationals from other Latin American states, such as Colombia and Peru, have instead chosen to extend their presence regionally.[41] Notably, few Brazilian multinationals operate foreign affiliates.[42]

On the other hand, Latin America has become an important recipient of FDI from Asian developing economies, notably Chinese and Indian multinationals.[43] Between 2003 and 2016, Chinese companies invested over $110 billion in Latin America.[44] The recent isolationist agenda of the United States, including its withdrawal from the Trans-Pacific Partnership, could mean increased importance for Latin America as a target for FDI from other Asian investors.

These developments mean that the corporate stakeholder in the Latin American foreign investment landscape has changed and diversified dramatically over the past few decades. New corporate stakeholders have entered the game and gained relevance vis-à-vis MNEs from traditional capital exporting states. The fact that increased inward FDI appears to have stimulated the growth of local MNEs and outward FDI, although the merits of FDI in the development of economies is disputed, also means that the tenets of the traditional dependency theory correspond less and less with the

---

39 Jose Ramon Perea and Matthew Stephenson, "Outward FDI from Developing Countries" in World Bank Group, *Global Investment Competitiveness Report 2017/ 2018: Foreign Investor Perspectives and Policy Implications* (World Bank 2018) 111.

40 Daniels, Krug, and Trevino (n 30) 27, 45.

41 Daniels, Krug, and Trevino (n 30) 37–38.

42 Daniels, Krug, and Trevino (n 30) 32.

43 Santiso (n 31) 24–25.

44 Rolando Avendano, Angel Melguizo, and Sean Miner, *Chinese FDI in Latin America: New Trends with Global Implications* (Atlantic Council 2017) 1–2.

economic realities of today. Although a Latin American multinational corporation will, of course, function on the same basic premises as any other multinational, including the fundamental necessity to generate profit to shareholders, their emergence on the stage of international trade and foreign investment decreases the appearance of North–South dependence in the regime.

As Latin American economies grow, develop, and start to export capital, the perspective of the Latin American corporation gains more relevance among the myriad of actors that contribute to the shaping of the IIL regime in the region. Importantly, increased capital exports from the region will allow investors from Latin American states to benefit from the reciprocity of investment protections in their foreign investments outside the region. Moreover, today, a total of 34 BITs and 37 other treaties with investment provisions are in force between Latin American states, with key capital exporting states like Argentina and Chile leading in the number of intra-LATAM BITs in force.[45]

However, few ISDS cases have been brought by these new corporate stakeholders to date. Out of a total of 845 concluded and pending ISDS cases, only 23 were brought by investors claiming nationality of a Latin American state, with Chilean investors leading the count with seven cases, all brought against other Latin American states.[46] Notably, most Latin American states, as the state of claimed nationality of the investor, still have no ISDS cases. Indeed, the investors whose claims have so far been adjudicated in ISDS are predominantly medium-large corporations from developed countries.[47]

Nonetheless, the increased presence of new corporate stakeholders in the regional investment landscape means that the composition of potential participants in the system has changed in recent years. How these new participants will contribute to the making of international investment law in the region remains to be seen, but their emergence is a relevant structural change in the regime that has the potential to shape the regime away from the traditional appearance of North–South dependency.

FDI, international investment law and ISDS

Having mapped some of the salient characteristics of the corporate stakeholder in the IIL regime in Latin America, and how those characteristics

---

45 UNCTAD (n 26). This data excludes the Caribbean.
46 UNCTAD (n 5). This data excludes the Caribbean.
47 Susan D. Franck, "Empirically Evaluating Claims About Investment Treaty Arbitration" (2007) 86 *North Carolina Law Review* 29.

have changed over the past few years, this section discusses the existing evidence on how corporations view IIL and what role, if any, it plays in corporate FDI decisions. These considerations are highly relevant to the extent that the existence of IIL is justified by its purported positive impact on FDI flows.

A corporate FDI decision is based on the identification of a business concept and a suitable legal structure, combined with a comprehensive business risk analysis.[48] The law (domestic and international) is a tool that can be used to tailor a suitable structure and to reduce inherent risks.

The FDI literature discussing the determinants of foreign investment is largely focused on the impact of macroeconomic considerations, economic and political reforms, and democratic institutions on FDI. The role played by IIL and investor–state dispute resolution has not been widely studied. One of the reasons is undoubtedly the methodological difficulty of controlling variables and pinpointing causalities where correlations are observed. Where the impact of international investment treaties on FDI has been studied empirically, the results appear to be conflicting.[49] Many legal scholars have argued that the available evidence does not allow for the conclusion that BITs increase FDI inflow. Brazil and its success in attracting FDI despite not having any BITs in force is frequently cited as an anecdotal case to prove the point. However, the fact that Brazil managed to attract high FDI inflows without BITs does not exclude the possibility that those inflows would have been higher with BITs in force.

A significant body of quantitative and qualitative research in other disciplines, notably political science, supports the conclusion that the protection of property rights and investment safety are the driving considerations for corporations when deciding to invest in a foreign country and weigh more heavily in the decision-making process than economic conditions, regime type, taxation, political rights, proximity, or any other determinant.[50] From the corporate perspective, IIL and ISDS can be seen as forming part of the judicial institutions that uphold property rights and safeguard investment safety. After all, investor–state arbitral tribunals exist because states

---

48 Rudolf Dolzer and Christoph Schreuer, *Principles of International Investment Law* (Oxford University Press 2008) 4.
49 Gus van Harten, "A Critique of Investment Treaties" in Kavaljit Singh and Burghard Ilge (eds), *Rethinking Bilateral Investment Treaties: Critical Issues and Policy Choices* (Both Ends, Madhyam and Somo 2016) 42; Dolzer and Christoph Schreuer (n 48) 8.
50 Jensen and others (n 18) 54–56, 65; Joseph L. Staats and Glen Biglaiser, "Foreign Direct Investment in Latin America: The Importance of Judicial Strength and Rule of Law" (2012) 56 *International Studies Quarterly* 193, 194. These studies incorporate qualitative elements in the research, which increases the value of their conclusions vis-à-vis data-based studies.

delegated a part of their judicial power to the institution of investment arbitration. Effective and fair judicial institutions are assurances to corporate investors that their property titles and other property rights will be upheld.[51] The available evidence suggests that corporations care mostly about these assurances when deciding to invest in a foreign country. Notably, these corporate considerations converge with the narratives promoted by other systemic actors, including governments and NGOs: the rule of law and respect for fundamental rights, including property rights, is on the agenda of all systemic actors.

International investment treaties boost the credibility of the host state's commitment not to interfere with property rights and, as such, increase the level of assurances.[52] ISDS, in turn, increases the credibility of the substantive investment commitments by providing direct procedural rights to the investor.[53] The risk of being sued before an international tribunal, combined with the related reputational cost of being judged in the court of public opinion through the media, constrains and disciplines governments planning to implement measures that could violate investment protections. In this sense, the role of independent media as another institution is key.

Nevertheless, this is not to say that credible assurances cannot be obtained without concluding BITs and providing access to ISDS. For example, many states provide for investment protection and stability through domestic investment laws. However, while bilateral investment treaties are certainly not the only way towards credible commitments, they may be helpful where the host state is otherwise facing difficulties in backing up its commitments with credible institutions.

Whichever instrument provides the credibility of commitments, one of the key considerations for a corporate investor, about to inject important sums of money in a foreign operation, is the possibility to reduce the risk of a change in the position of the host government. Even where international investment treaties and other assurances are in place, political change may alter the assumptions on which the investment was made, thereby changing the risk landscape drastically. In this sense, clauses common in BITs that provide for the extended protection of investments made when the treaty was in force, protect corporations against political change even if the treaty

---

51 Jensen and others (n 18) 73; Staats and Biglaiser (n 50).
52 Todd Allee and Clint Peinhardt, "Contingent Credibility: The Impact of Investment Treaty Violations on Foreign Direct Investment" (2011) 65 *International Organization* 401, 404; Peter Kusek and Andrea Silva, "What Matters to Investors in Developing Countries: Findings from the Global Investment Competitiveness Survey" in World Bank Group, *Global Investment Competitiveness Report 2017/2018: Foreign Investor Perspectives and Policy Implications* (World Bank 2018) 20.
53 Allee and Peinhardt (n 52) 404.

is later terminated by a new host government.[54] For international investment treaties to provide meaningful assurances to corporate investors they should contain similar safeguards that provide for a reasonable period of protection from political change.

There is also no evidence for a universal corporate preference for arbitration over litigation, particularly where host state courts are perceived to be independent. Rather, it is reasonable to believe that the weight assigned to the availability of arbitration as an FDI decision factor depends on the relative weight of the other factors in each case. If the host state has a relatively effective local court system, the availability of ISDS alone is unlikely to tip the scale in a corporate FDI decision, but it may still provide additional assurances.

Moreover, even if investment treaties and ISDS are available, the corporate investor should still care about the strength of domestic institutions. First, strong and effective domestic courts safeguard the rule of law in case of future policy change thereby guarding against the reversal of investment policy and laws by future governments.[55] This would include unconstitutional attempts to denounce or withdraw from international treaties, including BITs, without following the applicable constitutional procedures. Second, strong domestic legislatures impose checks and balances on the executive branch and ensure that implementing legislation cannot be modified without congressional approval, even if the executive branch alone can cause withdrawal from a treaty.

Another important aspect in the impact of IIL and ISDS on corporate FDI decisions is state compliance with investment commitments. Indeed, some studies suggest that, while BITs do in fact increase FDI into countries that sign them, their ability to increase FDI inflow is contingent on the subsequent compliance of the states with the assumed commitments.[56] This may explain to some extent why states receive varying levels of FDI after the conclusion of BITs. Being sued in investment arbitration, and particularly losing a case, causes a reputational loss to the respondent state and diminishes the credibility of its commitment to respect investors' property rights.[57] Investors, including corporations, will re-evaluate the risk landscape accordingly and may be more reluctant to invest in a state with a "questionable track record."[58] Thus, even if the state may have obtained an FDI boost from concluding an investment treaty, this boost is lost if

54 Dolzer and Schreuer (n 48) 4–5.
55 Jensen and others (n 18) 75; Staats and Biglaiser (n 49) 194.
56 Allee and Peinhardt (n 52) 402.
57 Allee and Peinhardt (n 52) 404–405 and studies cited therein.
58 Allee and Peinhardt (n 52) 402.

the state fails, or is perceived to potentially be failing, to live up to the commitment.[59]

Interestingly, the negative effect of being sued in investment arbitration alone may be sufficient to cause substantial losses of FDI on states even if they eventually win the dispute.[60] Out of all investment arbitrations concluded against Latin American states where a decision was rendered, over 40 percent of the cases were decided in favor of the state.[61] However, the evidence cited above suggests that investors do not care whether a treaty violation is, in fact, upheld. In their eyes, the reputational loss has been sustained.[62]

Although these conclusions are not limited to corporations but cover investors in general, it is plausible that MNEs feature prominently among the investors that pay attention to ISDS developments, because they have the resources to do so and because large multinationals are key actors in foreign investment. Therefore, the conclusions of the cited study provide valuable insights to the corporate stakeholder's perspective towards IIL. First, they suggest that corporations not only consider international investment protections as additional assurances that increase the credibility of the host state's commitments, but they also monitor ISDS developments and may even reevaluate investment decisions in light of new ISDS cases.[63] Second, they suggest that transparency in ISDS is beneficial to corporations and other investors, because it allows them access to information about state compliance with previously assumed commitments.[64] Although corporations are often assumed to be opposed to transparency in ISDS, this is another aspect where corporate interests may actually converge with the narratives promoted by other actors like NGOs.

On the other hand, it should be noted that the existing empirical studies that suggest that there is a positive correlation between the conclusion of BITs and increased FDI inflows, have not been able to explain precisely how the mechanism of causality is supposed to work. Indeed, correlation is not causality. Thus, caution is advisable when observing correlations between FDI flows and international investment instruments.

To summarize, the available evidence suggests that corporations do care about IIL and ISDS, which can help states increase the credibility of their

---

59 Allee and Peinhardt (n 52) 406–407.
60 Allee and Peinhardt (n 52) 402–403.
61 UNCTAD (n 4). According to UNCTAD, in cases brought against Latin American states (excluding the Caribbean), a decision was rendered in 106 cases. 43 of those decisions were in favour of the state.
62 Allee and Peinhardt (n 52) 415.
63 Allee and Peinhardt (n 52) 402.
64 Allee and Peinhardt (n 52) 408–12.

commitment to respect investors' property rights and investment safety, where other institutions are lacking.

Concluding remarks

Historically, the attitude of the corporate stakeholder towards the traditional conception of the IIL regime as a colonial system,[65] designed to promote the interests of capital exporting states at the expense of non-investment interests, has been accommodating. However, in recent years, corporations have had to respond to criticisms raised by the other participants in the system, including corporate shareholders and NGOs. As a consequence, many corporations and investment funds have voluntarily adopted corporate social responsibility programs and policies setting forth standards of corporate conduct in environmental and social matters.[66] Multinationals in Latin America have embraced practices of social corporate responsibility through initiatives such as Cemex's *Patrimonio Hoy* that provides micro-credit to low-income families to improve housing. ESG (environmental, social and governance) investing, in turn, has exploded in popularity.[67]

These developments speak of the willingness of many corporations to accommodate the other systemic narratives. As a consequence, non-investment interests are becoming more mainstream within the corporate narrative. Over 4,500 companies worldwide have joined the UN Global Compact, an initiative designed to encourage companies to align business interests with core principles on human rights, labor, environment, and anti-corruption. Latin America and the Caribbean has been one of the most active regions in the compact, with the second largest number of participants after Europe and more than 15 networks that support corporations in implementing sustainability objectives within the country-specific context.[68]

As more and more corporations adopt voluntary corporate social responsibility programs and codes of conduct, they set an expected standard of conduct for other corporations. In terms of norm creation, soft law

---

65 Miles (n 19) 19–42.
66 See e.g. Neil Gunningham and Darren Sinclair, "Voluntary Approaches to Environmental Protection: Lessons from the Mining and Forestry Sectors" (OECD Global Forum on International Investment, Conference on Foreign Direct Investment and the Environment, Paris, 7–8 February 2002); Miles (n 19) 241–70.
67 See James Kynge, "The Ethical Investment Boom" *Financial Times* (September 2017) www.ft.com/content/9254dfd2–8e4e–11e7–a352–e46f43c5825d accessed 10 August 2018.
68 United Nations Global Compact, Latin America & Caribbean www.unglobalcompact.org/engage-locally/latin-america accessed 10 August 2018.

instruments like the OECD Guidelines on Multinational Enterprises and the draft UN Norms on the Responsibility of Transnational Corporations and Other Business Enterprises with Regard to Human Rights, combined with voluntary initiatives by MNEs, create "pre-normative noise" that has the potential to affect state behavior.[69] This, in turn, sets the stage for the future creation of customary international law and, possibly, multilateral treaties, on corporate social responsibility and other non-investment concerns.

In fact, many BITs and other investment treaties already contain provisions related to environmental and other non-investment concerns.[70] Recent, so-called new generation BITs involving Latin American states have further prompted this trend.[71] For instance, the new EU–Mexico trade agreement contains provisions aimed at promoting corporate social responsibility practices[72] and ensuring the states' right to regulate in matters of legitimate policy objectives, including public health and the environment.[73] However, substantive *investor* responsibilities in international investment agreements are still largely absent.[74] Ultimately these developments and the direction they will take depend on the contracting states and their policy priorities when negotiating and re-negotiating investment treaties, but corporations can influence these developments through voluntary initiatives.

In addition, the "pre-normative noise" could potentially affect the interpretation of existing treaties through the evolutionary method of interpretation, adopted by some international courts and tribunals, which views treaty terms as capable of evolving over time without being amended by the parties.[75] Although investor–state tribunals are tasked with resolving disputes, not creating jurisprudence, their reasoning contributes to the

---

69 Miles (n 19) 226–30.
70 See e.g. the Agreement between the Swiss Confederation and the United Mexican States on the Promotion and Reciprocal Protection of Investments (signed 10 July 1995, entered into force 14 March 1996) 1965 UNTS 2836, ad art 3.
71 See e.g. Treaty between the United States of America and the Oriental Republic of Uruguay concerning the Encouragement and Reciprocal Protection of Investment (signed 4 November 2005, entered into force 31 October 2006) arts 12–13; Agreement Between Canada and the Republic of Peru for the Promotion and Protection of Investments (signed 29 May 2008, entered into force 1 August 2009, art 11.
72 EU–Mexico Global Agreement (agreement on principle 23 April 2018), Draft Chapter on Trade and Sustainable Development, arts 1, 9, 13.
73 Ibid., Draft Chapter on Investment, art 1.
74 Miles (n 19) 230–231. For model BITs providing for investor obligations, see e.g. Southern African Development Community, "SADC Model Bilateral Investment Treaty Template with Commentary" (2012) 31–41.
75 For the evolutionary method generally, see Eirik Bjorge, *The Evolutionary Interpretation of Treaties* (Oxford University Press 2014).

accumulation of ideas on the meaning of investment treaty terms.[76] To the extent that tribunals are willing to interpret treaties and their objectives in light of contemporary concerns about the protection and conservation of the environment and other non-investment concerns, like the WTO Appellate Body did in its *U.S. – Shrimp* decision, these concerns may find a place in the case law even where not specifically provided for in the terms of the agreement.[77]

Some of these issues have already been addressed by investor–state arbitral tribunals in Latin America. For instance, in *Urbaser v Argentina*, the respondent raised a counterclaim alleging that the claimants were liable under international human rights law. The respondent argued for the existence of investor obligations and a conception of international human rights as being capable of binding non-state actors, including corporations.[78] The claimant, in turn, maintained that international human rights obligations are binding on states, but not on private parties.[79] While the tribunal appeared to reject the proposition that obligations to guarantee human rights may only be borne by states and not private parties,[80] it concluded that the obligation to enforce the human right to water, incumbent on the investor, could only derive from a contract or similar legal relationship of domestic civil and commercial law. Conversely, the tribunal considered that an obligation to abstain could be incumbent on individuals and other private parties.[81]

The discussion in *Urbaser* is illustrative of the difficulties inherent in bringing new, non-state actors on the plane of international law. ISDS tribunals are tasked with applying international law, however, they must simultaneously deal with a participant that does not seem to fit any of the traditional

---

76 Kathryn Gordon and Joachim Pohl, "Investment Treaties over Time: Treaty Practice and Interpretation in a Changing World" (2015) OECD Working Papers on International Investment 2015/02, www.oecd.org/investment/investment-policy/WP-2015–02.pdf accessed 15 August 2018, 12–13; Ole Kristian Fauchald, "The Legal Reasoning of ICSID Tribunals: An Empirical Analysis" (2008) 19 *The European Journal of International Law* 301–364, finding that decisions of other arbitral tribunals were the most cited external reference in the surveyed awards.

77 *United States – Import Prohibition of Certain Shrimp and Shrimp Products* (Report of the Appellate Body, 12 October 1998) WT/DS58/AB/R [129]. See Chapters 10 by Rodrigo Polanco Lazo and Felipe Ferreira Catalán, and 11 by Farouk El-Hosseny, Patrick Devine, and Ilan Brun-Vargas in this volume.

78 *Urbaser S.A. and Consorcio de Aguas Bilbao Biskaia, Bilbao Biskaia Ur Partzuergoa v. Argentine Republic*, ICSID Case No. ARB/07/26 (Award, 8 December 2016) 1156, 1162–1163.

79 Ibid. 1157.

80 Ibid. 1193.

81 Ibid. 1210. For an in-depth discussion on this case, see Chapter 12 by Javier Echaide in this volume.

conceptions of international personality or obligations. Tribunals should be cautious of drawing misplaced analogies just because the IIL regime permits the participation of the investor as a non-state actor. Indeed, corporations, other non-state actors, and even international organizations that do have international personality, do not bear human rights duties unless they exercise jurisdiction over the rights holders.[82] For duties to be feasible, they must be borne by institutions with a sustainable capacity to uphold them.[83] While corporations are, of course, subjects of domestic law and must abide by it, attempting to impose human rights duties on corporations only confuses the supply-side of human rights and undermines their effective realization.

In light of these considerations, IIL could be headed towards greater synergies among the stakeholders through the voluntary accommodation by corporations and the shifting approaches of governments towards increased incorporation of non-investment interests in the substantive law on international investment, which has traditionally been focused on the protection of investments.[84] However, in order to balance the interests at stake in the IIL regime in an effective way, the stakeholders need to talk to each other. Otherwise, the regime will be shaped towards unfeasible solutions, dictated by prevalent policy narratives.

---

82 Henry Shue, *Basic Rights: Subsistence, Affluence, and US Foreign Policy* (Princeton University Press 1996) 9, 167, 169; Samantha Besson, "The Allocation of Anti-Poverty Rights Duties: Our Rights but Whose Duties?" in Krista Nadakavukaren Schefer (ed) *Poverty and the International Economic Legal System: Duties to the World's Poor* (Cambridge University Press 2013) 408–31. Regarding international organizations and human rights duties, see Katarina Lundahl, "The Remedy Gap: A Remedial Perspective to Third-Party Claims in United Nations Peacekeeping Operations from Srebrenica to Haiti" (LLM thesis, University of Helsinki 2014) 48–55.

83 Besson (n 82) 420.

84 Miles (n 19) 213.

8

Sociedad Civil Transnacional y Derecho Internacional Comercial y de Inversiones

Adoración Guamán

Introducción

El papel de la sociedad civil en la vida de los acuerdos de comercio e inversión ha crecido tanto cuantitativa como cualitativamente en los últimos años. La ampliación del número de materias cubiertas por los llamados "acuerdos de nueva generación"[1] ha estimulado el rechazo popular, promovido en gran medida por grupos o movimientos sociales, que ha provocado una reacción de las partes negociadoras en el sentido de acercarse a los distintos actores

---

1 La expresión "acuerdos de nueva generación" va a utilizarse para hacer referencia a aquellos impulsados por la Unión Europea desde el año 2009, caracterizados por incluir, además de objetivos de liberalización más amplios que los anteriores, nuevas esferas de actuación entre las que destacan las cuestiones de cooperación reguladora y, también, las cláusulas de "comercio y desarrollo". Dentro de estos tratados de nueva generación y siguiendo la clasificación de la Unión Europea, vamos a considerar a efectos de este análisis, los siguientes: UE–Corea (Free Trade Agreement Between the European Union and its Member States, of the one part, and the Republic of Korea, of the other part (signed 6 October 2010, entered into force 12 December 2015)); UE–Perú, Colombia, Ecuador (Trade Agreement between the European Union and its Member States, of the one part, and Peru and Colombia, of the other part, as amended by the Protocol of Accession of Ecuador (signed June 2012, entered into force (provisionally) March 2013 (Peru), August 2013 (Colombia), January 2017(Ecuador)); UE– América Central (Agreement Establishing an Association between the European Union and its Member States, on the one hand, and Central America on the other (signed 29 June 2012, entered into force (provisionally) 1 August 2013 (Honduras, Nicaragua and Panama), 1 October 2013 (Costa Rica and El Salvador, and 1 December 2013 (Guatemala)); UE-Canadá (Comprehensive Economic and Trade Agreement between Canada and the European Union (signed 30 October 2016, entered into force (provisionally) 21 September 2017)); UE–Singapur (European Union–Singapore Free Trade Agreement and Investment Protection Agreement (signed 19 October 2018, entered into force (provisionally) 21 November 2019)); UE–Vietnam (EU-Vietnam Free Trade Agreement and Investment Protection Agreement (signed 30 June 2019)) y UE-Japón (Agreement Between the European Union and Japan for an Economic Partnership (signed 17 July 2018, entered into force 1 February 2019)). Para una remisión

de la sociedad civil para intentar incorporar sus demandas, de manera real o retórica, en el seno de las normas de comercio e inversión.

Un rápido vistazo a las negociaciones de los acuerdos de comercio e inversión, desde el NAFTA (North American Free Trade Agreement) al TTIP (Transatlantic Trade and Investment Parnertship) o al CETA (EU-Canada Comprenhensive Economic and Trade Agreement), nos señala que el rol más notable de la sociedad civil respecto de esos acuerdos ha sido la organización de amplias estrategias de movilización en oposición a los mismos. Sin embargo, un análisis de carácter más amplio que atienda al contenido y funcionamiento de los tratados permite apreciar la existencia de otro tipo de interacciones, desde las consultas en la negociación a la participación en la vida del acuerdo, e incluso a la utilización de los mecanismos de resolución de controversias establecidos en los tratados.

De hecho, los "tratados de nueva generación" negociados por la Unión Europea (EU), desde el firmado con Corea en 2009, han introducido los llamados "capítulos de comercio y desarrollo" donde se ubican determinadas cláusulas (como las ambientales, las sociales o las de género) con cuya introducción se ha intentado acallar las críticas y contentar parcialmente determinadas reivindicaciones de los movimientos sociales. Por añadidura, son ya abundantes los tratados que integran mecanismos de participación con la voluntad de incluir, cuanto menos de manera formal, el parecer de los agentes sociales en el desarrollo concreto del contenido de las obligaciones establecidas en el tratado. Además, las dinámicas de funcionamiento de los mecanismos de protección de los derechos de los inversores extranjeros, demuestran cómo el rol de los movimientos sociales a lo largo de los casos dirimidos en los procesos de arbitraje de inversiones es cada vez más activo.[2]

Los siguientes apartados se dedican a la reflexión sobre las distintas interacciones enumeradas tomando para ello como elemento de análisis central el periodo transcurrido entre los años ochenta y la actualidad, con casos

---

bibliográfica sobre la justificación de la caracterización de estos tratados dentro de la categoría de "nueva generación" se remite a: Adoración Guamán, *TTIP: el asalto de las multinacionales a la democracia* (Akal 2015); Adoración Guamán, "La política comercial de la UE y su impacto en los derechos laborales: una aproximación a los posibles efectos de la firma del TTIP y del CETA" (2016) 6 (2) *Lex Social: Revista de Derechos Sociales*. La clasificación de la UE puede encontrarse en *Report from the Commission to the European Parliament, the Council, the European Economic and Social Committee and the Committee of the Regions on Implementation of Free Trade Agreements* (2018) Disponible en https://op.europa.eu/es/publication-detail/-/publication/1bbb43a4-f540–11e9–8c1f-01aa75ed71a1/language-es.

2 Sobre esta cuestión, que no va a abordarse por motivos de espacio, se remite en extenso a: Farouk El-Hosseny, *Civil Society in Investment Treaty Arbitration: Status and Prospects* (Brill 2018).

relativos a América Latina y también a las más recientes experiencias de interacción entre los movimientos sociales europeos y los acuerdos de comercio e inversión impulsados desde la Unión Europea.

Antes de desgranar las ideas anteriores, es necesario abordar una primera, y escueta, reflexión de carácter general para delimitar algunas cuestiones esenciales respecto del sujeto que estudiamos, atendiendo a los conceptos de "sociedad civil", "movimientos sociales" y "stakeholders".

Como es evidente, el concepto de "sociedad civil" es una de las grandes categorías de debate en las ciencias sociales y no es posible abarcar aquí un mínimo reflejo de los análisis respecto de su contenido y evolución. Es posible definir como "sociedad civil" el completo conjunto de asociaciones y movimientos voluntarios que operan tanto fuera del mercado como fuera del aparato estatal primario y que se orientan específicamente a influir en la esfera pública.[3] En este conjunto se incluirían los movimientos sociales, sindicatos, organizaciones no gubernamentales (NGO), organizaciones de base o el llamado "tercer sector".[4] Aun cuando esta definición nos parece acertada, es fundamental para este estudio señalar que la definición utilizada por la Unión Europea, y por los textos orientados al análisis de las dinámicas de participación de la sociedad civil impulsadas por esta organización, es más amplia e incluye tanto los actores mencionados como las empresas o los grupos de negocios.[5]

Dejando momentáneamente a parte la cuestión de la inserción o no de las empresas dentro del concepto de la sociedad civil, es necesario prestar una atención especial a uno de sus actores, los movimientos sociales,[6] dada

---

3 Patrick Heller, "Challenges and Opportunities: Civil Society in a Globalizing World" (2013) 2013/06 UNDP Human Development Report Office Occasional Papers.

4 A modo de muestra del debate, se remite a: Benjamín Arditi, "Trayectoria y potencial político de la idea de sociedad civil" (2004) 66 (1) *Revista Mexicana de Sociología*; Manès Weisskircher, *Civil society* (Routledge 2020); Beate Kohler-Koch and Christine Quittkat, "What is civil society and who represents civil society in the EU? – Results of an online survey among civil society experts" (2009) 28 (1) *Policy and Society*.

5 En este sentido, por ejemplo, el Banco Europeo de Inversiones señala que "Civil society includes a broad range of entities such as non-governmental organisations (NGOs), policy think tanks, research institutions, trade unions, social movements, community-based organisations, business associations and other socio-economic and labour market players." (www.eib.org/en/about/partners/cso/index.htm). Los estudios especializados en la implicación de la Sociedad civil en los acuerdos de comercio e inversión acogen esta acepción amplia, vid. Deborah Martens, Lore Van Den Putte, Myriam Oehri, Jan Orbie, "Mapping variation of civil society involvement in EU Trade Agreements: A CSI Index" (2018) 23 (1) *European Foreign Affairs Review*.

6 Para una definición genérica de "movimiento social" es útil acudir a la clásica que los define como un "tipo de acción colectiva orientada hacia el cambio por una masa

la especial interacción entre el llamado movimiento "antiglobalización" y los tratados históricamente fundamentales (como el NAFTA y el Área de Libre Comercio de las Américas (FTAA). Esta vinculación se reavivó en torno a la propuesta del TTIP (y posteriormente del CETA) contra los cuales se organizaron campañas, hoy vivas, con líneas de semejanza y vínculos claros con los antiguos movimientos altermundistas. En este sentido, es útil recordar, como indica Pleyers, que aquel movimiento marcó el retorno de las reivindicaciones de carácter económico y social, manteniendo a la vez las relativas al reconocimiento, las identidades y la diversidad.[7]

Esta amplitud del movimiento antiglobalización le permitió entroncar y en englobar distintos movimientos sociales, de carácter local, en grandes redes, regionales que se reformularon décadas más tarde. De hecho, el carácter global ha continuado reflejándose en las dinámicas de interacción e influencia transcontinental entre los movimientos que se gestaron y que se organizan en América Latina y los europeos.

Así, es importante señalar, por un lado, las coincidencias en el discurso y en las estrategias de cabildeo o movilización que existen en la actualidad en las campañas contra los tratados de comercio e inversión a ambos lados del Atlántico y, por otro lado, la intensa participación cruzada de actores en los movimientos, que permite un trasiego de saberes y un aprendizaje transcontinental permanente. En este sentido, es posible hablar de una latinoamericanización del discurso crítico con los tratados comerciales y el fomento de la inversión impulsado en Europa especialmente a partir del TTIP y, al mismo tiempo, una aportación del aprendizaje y la experiencia técnica de los movimientos europeos en las más recientes movilizaciones contra los tratados de nueva generación en América Latina. De igual manera, las grandes

descentralizada encabezada de manera no jerárquica" Gerardo Munck, "Algunos problemas conceptuales en el estudio de los movimientos sociales" (1995) 3 *Revista Mexicana de Sociología*. En un sentido similar, se han definido como "colectivos vagamente organizados que actúan de forma conjunta y de manera no institucionalizada con el fin de producir un cambio en la sociedad." Piotr Sztompka, *Sociología del cambio social* (Alianza Editorial 2012). También se han definido como «el proceso de (re) constitución de una identidad colectiva, fuera del ámbito de la política institucional, por el cual se dota de sentido a la acción individual y colectiva». Marisa Revilla, "El concepto de movimiento social: acción, identidad y sentido" (1994) 69 Zona Abierta.

7 Geoffrey Pleyers, *Movimientos sociales en el siglo XXI: perspectivas y herramientas analíticas* (CLACSO 2018). El autor, analizando los "campos de batalla" de los movimientos sociales en América Latina señala que hay cuatro tipos de actores, los movimientos indígenas y campesinos; los movimientos por la democratización; las luchas por la educación; y los movimientos por la paz y la justicia. También indica la existencia de "las luchas por un modelo económico distinto, menos dominado por las corporaciones trasnacionales y los tratados de libre comercio, y una distribución más justa de la riqueza".

campañas globales contra la impunidad de las empresas transnacionales (la *Global Campaign to Dismantle Corporate Power and Stop Impunity*) han integrado ambas visiones, cohonestando la denuncia de los efectos de los mecanismos de solución de controversias inversor Estado (ISDS) y la exigencia de colocar los derechos humanos por encima de los acuerdos de comercio e inversión entre sus exigencias fundamentales.

Estos nuevos actores, en forma de grandes campañas en red, estructuran pléyades de movimientos locales (entroncando en muchas ocasiones con sindicatos y NGO) y conviven, entroncan, nutren y se alimentan del fenómeno de la protesta. En este sentido, es necesario recordar que desde el inicio de la década del 2010 y hasta la fecha cada mes ha estallado una protesta ciudadana en un país, alimentada por muy diversos sujetos y movimientos sociales. Esta nueva ola de acción, estos nuevos sujetos, "han vinculado inseparablemente las dimensiones socioeconómicas y culturales en cada una de sus reivindicaciones y en sus prácticas, mezclando los aspectos subjetivos y socioeconómicos".[8] De hecho, y como se desarrollará a lo largo de los próximos apartados, es perfectamente posible encontrar una línea de continuidad entre las protestas populares más recientes (y los actores/actrices que han sido sujeto de las mismas) y el rechazo a los Tratados Bilaterales de Inversión (BIT) y los ISDS.

Junto con los actores citados (movimientos sociales, NGO y sindicatos) el análisis de la interacción entre la sociedad civil y las normas de comercio e inversión debe enfocarse en otro tipo de actores que, atendiendo al contenido de los acuerdos llamados de "nueva generación" parecen haber eclipsado totalmente, al menos a los ojos de las partes firmantes, a los anteriores: los llamados "stakeholders".

Dentro de esta categoría, utilizada por la Unión Europea y otras organizaciones financieras internacionales para desarrollar sus dinámicas de "apertura" a la "sociedad civil", se integran todos aquellos grupos que están impactados o que pueden verse impactados por una iniciativa de la Unión Europea o son relevantes para un interés o aspecto cubierto por una iniciativa de la Unión, para la cual se requiere su participación en alguna medida.[9]

---

8 Ibid.
9 Según la definición del Eurofound "A stakeholder is an individual, group of persons or organization that can affect or is affected by the decisions of another organization. This definition also includes interest groups related to the organization. A stakeholder's relationship with the focal organization is generally determined by three main attributes: the power to influence the organization; a legitimate relationship with the organization; and an urgent claim on the organization. Ver: www.eurofound.europa. eu/observatories/eurwork/industrial-relations-dictionary/stakeholder. C.f. el capítulo 7 de Claus von Wobeser en este volumen.

La propia EU ha ofrecido un listado de las categorías de "stakeholders" entre los que ha mencionado:[10] ciudadanía y público en general; industria, empresas o trabajadores autónomos y sus organizaciones; trabajadores o "personas en nuevas formas de trabajo" incluyendo autónomos dependientes; agentes sociales (tanto sindicatos como patronales que cumplan con el criterio de representatividad); autoridades públicas; organizaciones no gubernamentales y otros actores relevantes para cada concreta iniciativa.[11]

El papel de los movimientos sociales en la gestación de los acuerdos de comercio e inversión: campañas de rechazo y experiencias de cabildeo

Una perspectiva histórica de la negociación de este tipo de tratados, fundamentalmente aquellos que han afectado a América Latina, es posible afirmar que la interacción crítica (las campañas y movilizaciones contra estos tratados) y los intentos de cabildeo a lo largo de la negociación, fundamentalmente impulsados por el movimiento sindical, han acompañado estos procesos desde hace décadas.[12] Debe recordarse que en América Latina los acuerdos comerciales comenzaron a proliferar a partir de los años noventa (de los 498 acuerdos bilaterales de inversión que hoy se encuentran en vigor en los países de América Latina y el Caribe, 312 fueron firmados en aquella década) y ya en aquella década fueron contestados, tanto por el movimiento sindical como por distintos movimientos sociales que actualizaron sus dinámicas hasta conseguir transnacionalizar sus repertorios y redes.

Como indica Pleyers, el paulatino aumento de estos tratados fue calificado por los actores sociales como un "modelo de democracia vacía" (idea que resuena hoy en las campañas) y que frente a la tecnificación y cierre del modelo de decisión pública se alzaron movilizaciones icónicas que impulsaron movimientos de carácter global. En este sentido, es obligatorio referirse al alzamiento del Ejército Zapatista de Liberación Nacional de 1 de enero de 1994, que coincidió con la entrada en vigor del Tratado y que fue un claro

10 Se acoge como ejemplo el listado de categorías que utilizó la Comisión Europea en el documento "Stakeholder Consultation Strategy. Access to social protection" de 2017. Disponible en https://ec.europa.eu/social/main.jsp?catId=1312&langId=es

11 Tomando como referencia el CETA se aprecia una confusa utilización de ambas categorías. El tratado menciona 19 veces a la "sociedad civil" en ocasiones incluyendo las organizaciones empresariales, en ocasiones como concepto contrario al "sector privado" y con la referencia a "otros stakeholders", expresión que aparece hasta en 13 ocasiones. Esta confusión, que se repite en otros tratados.

12 Mercedes Botto, "Los movimientos sociales y el libre comercio en América Latina: ¿qué hay después del ALCA?" (2014) Revista CIDOB d'Afers Internacionals 105.

preludio del carácter extensivo y transversal del rechazo a la globalización económica basada en la liberalización del comercio.[13]

No obstante esta icónica figura, las posturas de los movimientos sociales respecto de los acuerdos comerciales han sido diversas desde el principio. Así, por ejemplo, la negociación del NAFTA evidenció, siguiendo el análisis de Botto,[14] un conjunto amplio de estrategias desde los movimientos sociales que fueron de la confrontación hasta la negociación a efectos de incluir determinadas cláusulas en el texto final del tratado. Por su parte, el MERCOSUR fue sobre todo un ejemplo de cabildeo sindical y de otras organizaciones con fuerte base nacional.

La reacción al NAFTA tuvo, como es bien sabido, una amplitud mayor. La oposición al tratado se construyó a partir de redes nacionales de carácter multisectorial con escasa articulación entre los tres países y con objetivos diversos, que iban desde la confrontación total a la aceptación de la inevitabilidad del acuerdo y la apuesta por la integración de mínimos sociales y ambientales. La presión sindical y de los movimientos ecologistas conllevó a la adopción de dos acuerdos "paralelos" al tratado,[15] en materia laboral

13 En este sentido ver, Robert W Cox, "Civil society at the turn of the millennium: prospects for an alternative world order" (1999) *Review of International Studies* 25. Pleyers por su parte señala que "Los zapatistas llevaron reivindicaciones a tres niveles: la autonomía de las comunidades indígenas a nivel local, la democratización del sistema político mexicano a nivel nacional y el rechazo de las políticas neoliberales a nivel internacional. Se levantaron en contra de la negación de su propia existencia, ya que los pueblos indígenas eran invisibles en el México que festejaba su "integración al primer mundo", Pleyers (n 7). Para una discusión sobre los pueblos indígenas, ver el capítulo 9 de Sufyan Droubi, Cecilia Juliana Flores Elizondo y Raphael Heffron en este volumen.

14 Como señala Botto "En México se institucionalizó como Red Mexicana de Acción frente al Libre Comercio (RMALC); en Estados Unidos, en cambio, se crearon dos redes con objetivos distintos y de aparición consecutiva: la primera, llamada Citizens Trade Campaign estaba destinada a desarrollar una estrategia de cabildeo con los legisladores con el objetivo de evitar el fast track; la segunda, la Alliance for Responsible Trade (ART), se propuso elaborar una propuesta alternativa y generar lazos con coaliciones semejantes en otros contextos. Lo mismo ocurrió en Canadá, donde en un comienzo se crearon dos redes –una francófona, Coalition Québécoise sur les Négociations Trilatérales, y otra anglófona, Action Canada Network– que más tarde se unieron en la llamada Common Frontiers o Réseau Québécois sur l'Intégration Continentale (RQIC), para trabajar de manera coordinada tras el duro embate que recibieron con el triunfo electoral del Partido Conservador". Botto (n 12)

15 La integración de cláusulas sociales no era una novedad. Estados Unidos ha incluido unilateralmente cláusulas de "desarrollo de los derechos de los trabajadores" en diversos programas comerciales con países en vías de desarrollo desde 1975 (como el Sistema de Preferencias Generalizadas, la iniciativa respecto del Caribe, la zona Andina, África o Haiti), a modo de requisito exigido para obtener los beneficios comerciales. Los primeros tratados bilaterales de comercio con países no considerados en

y ambiental.[16] Más allá de los objetivos incluidos en estos acuerdos, el verdadero problema, tanto del NAFTA como de los subsiguientes acuerdos ha sido precisamente la cuestión de los mecanismos de garantía y sanción, que trataremos en la sección siguiente.

La negociación del FTAA es sin duda el proceso más ambicioso del siglo pasado en términos de libre comercio pero también el máximo exponente de articulación de resistencias. El aprendizaje de la lucha contra el NAFTA así como las redes y los espacios generados en los levantamientos contra el pago de la deuda y los ajustes estructurales fondomonetariastas de los años ochenta fueron insumos que permitieron la articulación de numerosas organizaciones sociales hasta la construcción de una alianza social de carácter continental, un movimiento que sumó a la generalidad de la organización social (campesinos, indígenas, sindicatos, organizaciones ambientalistas, feministas, movimientos territoriales urbanos, piqueteros, entre tantos otros) y que señaló a los Tratados de Comercio como un claro enemigo de los intereses de las mayorías sociales.[17]

---

vías de desarrollo, como Israel en 1985 o Canadá en 1988 no incluyeron una mención a los derechos laborales. El cambio de tendencia se produjo, por la gran presión político-sindical existente, con la aprobación del NAFTA.

16 En concreto, el tema laboral fue ampliamente debatido por cuanto también fue utilizado como punta de lanza de la defensa y "necesidad" de la adopción del tratado, en particular por el gobierno de Estados Unidos pero en general por el conjunto de defensores del tratado. Debido a la presión social y coincidiendo con el inicio del mandato del Presidente Clinton, en 1992 se firmaron los llamados «Tratados Paralelos» en materia laboral y ambiental para responder a la preocupación por los posibles efectos negativos sobre el empleo en los Estados Unidos. El Acuerdo norteamericano en cooperación laboral (North American Agreement on Labor Cooperation between the Government of Canada, the Government of the United Mexican States and the Government of the United States of America (signed 14 September 1993, entered into force 1 January 1994) (1993) 32 ILM 1499 (NAALC)) fue una segunda mejor opción adoptada ante la imposibilidad de conseguir la introducción de las cuestiones laborales en el tratado. Posteriormente la *Trade Act* de 2002 exigió la introducción de cláusulas laborales en todos los tratados de libre comercio bilaterales y regionales que firme EEUU, así como en tratados específicos por sectores y ya en 2007 se aprobó el "Bipartisan Trade Deal" donde se desarrollaron los compromisos laborales. Sobre el NAALC y las consecuencias de la adopción del NAFTA en materia laboral se remite a: Ana Piquer, '*NAALC: An Effective Compromise?*' (2005) Global Law Working Paper 01/05, Simposium Transnational Corporations and Human Rights; Mark Weisbrot, Stephan Lefebvre, and Joseph Sammut, 'Did NAFTA Help Mexico? An Assessment After 20 Years' (2014) 2014–03, Centre for Economic and Policy Research (CEPR).

17 Luciana Ghiotto, "Veinte años de lucha contra el libre comercio en América Latina: algunas reflexiones para las nuevas campañas" (2016) www.alainet.org/es/articulo/179422 Consultado el 15 de marzo de 2020.

La experiencia y las redes consiguieron crear un contrapeso social con capacidad para frenar, con el apoyo político pertinente, el FTAA. En la conformación de este contrapeso destacaron organizaciones más allá de los sindicatos, como la Vía Campesina, creada en 1990 (reflejo del carácter nuclear de las reivindicaciones campesinas dentro de la lucha contra los tratados de libre comercio), los movimientos estudiantiles, ecologistas, anti-deuda, feministas, etc. La creación de redes (o red de redes)[18] como la Alianza Social Continental se conjugó con multitud de encuentros, foros, cumbres y movilizaciones, conformando la lucha hemisférica contra el tratado, que fue creciendo hasta que ya en 2005 se convirtió en un espacio de referencia continental y global de lucha contra el libre comercio.[19] Además, como recuerdan Bringel y Stronzake, "la agenda contra el ALCA no sólo generó nuevas redes, sino que también tuvo una gran centralidad para los movimientos sociales latinoamericanos ya consolidados".[20]

Aunque en la memoria del episodio del FTAA prima la imagen del rechazo, Botto señalaba que, en realidad, también se dieron dos posicionamientos, sucesivos o evolutivos, dentro de la movilización social. En un primer momento, con un mayor protagonismo de las organizaciones del norte con experiencia en la negociación del NAFTA, se primaron las exigencias en pos de una mayor democratización y transparencia del proceso, así como más amplios espacios de participación. En el segundo momento, la estrategia transitó hasta la oposición frontal al tratado y la identificación de un enemigo común actuó como potente elemento aglutinador,[21] que entroncó con otras luchas contemporáneas.[22]

---

18 Ibid.
19 Ver también Héctor De la Cueva, 'Mar del Plata: El ALCA no pasó. Una victoria de la Cumbre de los Pueblos' (2016) 18 OSAL.
20 Breno Bringel and Janaina Stronzake, "La lucha contra el ALCA: aprendizajes, resistencias y construcciones colectivas," en Luis Miguel Uharte and Unai Vázquez (eds) *La década ganada en América Latina: una mirada analítica a las luchas populares* (Universidad del País Vasco 2015)
21 Botto (n 12)
22 Como se recordará en 2005 el proyecto del ALCA se frenó en la Cumbre de Mar del Plata. Por otro lado, uno de los casos más destacables de las resistencias expresadas desde las experiencias normativo-constitucionales desde los gobiernos posneoliberales del Sur es el protagonizado por la República del Ecuador. En el año 2008, durante la realización del proceso constituyente, el Estado ecuatoriano denunció 9 Tratados Bilaterales de Inversión (la mayoría firmados con otros países latinoamericanos). Posteriormente, una vez aprobada la nueva Constitución, el gobierno ecuatoriano inició un proceso de denuncia de otros 13 tratados bilaterales. Además, se procedió a bloquear la firma de nuevos BIT. Por último, el Estado ecuatoriano salió del sistema del ICSID en el año 2009 (Bolivia se había retirado en el año 2006). Es importante señalar que esta voluntad de cambio en la política comercial y de inversión se plasmó

En este sentido, es necesario mencionar que la lucha contra el FTAA se vio rodeada, y reforzada, por una constante de movilización contra las políticas de la WTO. En concreto, la multitudinaria protesta contra la liberalización del comercio mundial de 1999 organizada con ocasión de la reunión de la WTO que paralizó la ciudad de Seattle, delineó con claridad una «geopolítica de resistencias» frente a la construcción de la *Lex Mercatoria*[23] y dificultó las negociaciones de los siguientes pasos para profundizar en los diferentes espacios de impulso de tratados de comercio e inversión.

El colapso de Seattle no fue el primer gran obstáculo en el camino de las negociaciones multilaterales para la liberalización del comercio. Un año antes, en 1998, habían fracasado las negociaciones del Acuerdo Multilateral de Inversiones, esta vez en el seno de la Organización para la Cooperación y el Desarrollo Económico (OECD).[24] Posteriormente, ya en octubre de 2007, Estados Unidos anunció una iniciativa para fortalecer los derechos de propiedad intelectual a través de un acuerdo pluriestatal –no multilateral– acordado fuera del foro de la WTO. Se trataba del Acuerdo Antipiratería (*Anti-Counterfeiting Trade Agreement*). La importante movilización ciudadana prendió la mecha de la oposición en distintos parlamentos nacionales

con claridad en la Constitución de 2009, en particular en el rotundo artículo 422 de la Constitución de 2008, que no puede ser más claro: «No se podrá celebrar tratados o instrumentos internacionales en los que el Estado ecuatoriano ceda jurisdicción soberana a instancias de arbitraje internacional, en controversias contractuales o de índole comercial, entre el Estado y personas naturales o jurídicas privadas». Cabe indicar que Ecuador ratificó el Convenio del ICSID el 4 de agosto de 2021, entrando nuevamente al sistema ICSID.

23 Sobre este término ver, Adoración Guamán 'The corporate architecture of impunity: Lex Mercatoria, market authoritarianism and popular resistance' (2020) State of Power 2020.

24 Debe tenerse en cuenta, por los paralelismos con distintas propuestas actuales, que el AMI se basó en el contenido relativo a inversiones del anterior NAFTA y tenía como objetivo la consecución de un marco multilateral para la inversión internacional que permitiera la máxima liberalización de los regímenes de inversión y la protección de los inversores extranjeros, incluyendo procedimientos de resolución de conflictos específicos. La conclusión de la negociación del acuerdo estaba prevista para 1997. Las rondas de negociación no se publicitaron y los textos fueron conocidos a través de filtraciones hasta que el Parlamento Europeo exigió mayor transparencia. La publicación de los textos en los últimos 12 meses de la negociación no sirvió para acallar las protestas. Cuando en 1998 se presentó ante la opinión pública el texto base que había resultado de las negociaciones, el rechazo fue generalizado. La campaña lanzada por ONG americanas y europeas arrojó luz sobre el texto y explicó el contenido del tratado con el propósito de exponer los graves riesgos que eventualmente supondría su adopción. El esfuerzo de los movimientos sociales en contra del tratado consiguió la propagación del conjunto de críticas señaladas y, con ella, la generación de un rechazo social tan potente que en 1998 el gobierno socialista de Francia decidió retirar a su país de las negociaciones del AMI.

y en el Parlamento Europeo, que rechazó el tratado en el 4 de julio de 2012. Solo 39 eurodiputados votaron a favor.[25]

A partir de aquel momento, las movilizaciones sociales contra los tratados no han sido tan efectivas en términos de evitar su aprobación pero han sido capaces de poner los mismos en el centro de las agendas de los movimientos sociales y políticos nacionales así como de construir redes transnacionales que han trascendido los tratados concretos para orientarse a un rechazo del conjunto de la política comercial, en concreto, de la impulsada desde la EU. En concreto, la campaña más significativa creció al calor de la negociación del TTIP, evolucionó abarcando el rechazo al CETA y mutó en forma de crítica al ISDS, a la impunidad de las empresas transnacionales y al conjunto de la política comercial de la EU. La campaña Stop TTIP consiguió articular una vigorosa resistencia de ámbito nacional e internacional que se multiplicó rápidamente desde el año 2013.[26]

Una de las primeras estrategias de oposición fue la presentación de una Iniciativa Ciudadana Europea exigiendo la paralización de las negociaciones del TTIP y CETA.[27] Más allá de esta campaña, los actos contra el TTIP se

---

25 Ver European Parliament, Press Service, Directorate for the Media, en www.europarl.europa.eu/sides/getDoc.do?type=IM-PRESS&reference= 20120220FCS38611&format=XML&language=EN

26 La movilización empezó fundamentalmente en Alemania, donde un conjunto de movimientos sociales, fundamentalmente ecologista, y la izquierda política se alzaron contra el TTIP en el inicio de las negociaciones formales. Sobre estos inicios, ver Guamán (n 1); Matthias Bauer, "The political power of evoking fear: the shining example of Germany's anti-TTIP campaign movement" (2016) 15 (2) European View.

27 El 15 de julio 2014 cientos de organizaciones políticas, sindicales y sociales, ligadas a las distintas campañas nacionales Stop TTIP, presentaron una propuesta de Iniciativa Ciudadana Europea (titulada Stop TTIP). El texto venía respaldado por más de un millón de firmas procedentes de más de un cuarto de los Estados miembros. Los promotores de la iniciativa solicitaban a la Comisión que recomendase al Consejo de la EU, formado por los jefes de Estado y de Gobierno de los 28 Estados miembro, la revocación del mandato de negociación del TTIP y la no firma del CETA. En septiembre de 2014, la Comisión hizo uso de su facultad de veto y decidió no autorizar el registro de la Iniciativa afirmando que estaba «manifiestamente fuera del ámbito de competencias de la Comisión». La justificación de la Comisión puede encontrarse en: Commission Decision C(2014) 6501 of 10 September 2014 on the refusal to register the European Citizens' Initiative "STOP TTIP" https://curia.europa.eu/juris/ liste.jsf?num=T-754/14. Las siete personas que promovieron la iniciativa elevaron el 10 de noviembre de 2014 un recurso ante el Tribunal General (Asunto T-754/14) solicitando que se anulara esta decisión y que se condenara a la Comisión a pagar las costas del proceso. El 10 de mayo de 2017 la Sala primera del Tribunal General estimó el recurso y señaló que la ICE no puede interpretarse de manera restrictiva, sino que requiere ser entendida de manera amplia al tratarse de un instrumento para mejorar el funcionamiento democrático de la Unión y que confiere a todo ciudadano un derecho general a participar en la vida democrática. Ver: Case T-754/14 – Efler

multiplicaron por diversos países de la Unión Europea y centenares de movimientos sociales, ecologistas, NGO, sindicatos, organizaciones de consumidores, organizaciones de pequeñas y medianas empresas, observatorios de derechos, *Think-Tanks*, institutos de investigación, y un amplio número de intelectuales y académicos se organizaron e involucraron en diversas campañas sectoriales e intersectoriales para denunciar el contenido y las consecuencias del tratado. En un corto plazo se consiguió organizar una campaña a nivel europeo bajo el nombre de Stop TTIP.[28]

Una de las virtualidades de la campaña fue la combinación de la incidencia social, mediante actos, seminarios y uso de redes, y el lobby político. La presión de los movimientos sociales pronto consiguió sumar a numerosos partidos de izquierda y verdes, con distintos niveles de representatividad, a las convocatorias de las campañas. Además, en el ámbito europeo, fue fundamental la coordinación entre los núcleos nacionales, lo que permitió acciones transnacionales y una incidencia especial en el nivel de las instituciones de la EU. Es indudable que la movilización social consiguió un objetivo fundamental como es situar en el centro del debate político la política comercial, habitualmente opacada bajo un manto tecnificado, así, se publicaron centenares de artículos, libros, manuales, panfletos y dípticos sobre los tratados,[29] se hizo una enorme labor de pedagogía entre la ciudadanía pero también entre los propios parlamentarios, de todos los niveles. Una de las repercusiones más claras fue la introducción de cambios en el texto del CETA, como la transformación del ISDS en el Investment Court System (ICS), en un intento de asegurar el apoyo del Parlamento Europeo y aplacar la movilización en contra del tratado. Aunque los movimientos sociales reaccionaron críticamente a esta modificación que fue tildada de "cosmética", la motivación reactiva fue clara.

Las campañas contra el TTIP y el CETA evolucionaron hasta la actual campaña Stop ISDS que aglutina en la actualidad a más de 200 organizaciones europeas, sindicatos y movimientos sociales. En el camino, el rechazo al ISDS se ha plasmado igualmente en el ámbito de la campaña ciudadana

and Others v Commission [2017] Electronic Reports of Cases https://eur-lex.europa.eu/legal-content/EN/TXT/?uri=CELEX%3A62014TJ0754

28 Entre 2014 y 2016 se identificaron un total de 784 acciones relacionadas con TTIP, promovidas por movimientos sociales, fundamentalmente en el ámbito nacional pero también a nivel europeo, gracias a la construcción de redes transnacionales. Ver Manuela Caiani and Paolo Graziano, 'Europeanisation and social movements: The case of the Stop TTIP campaign' (2018) 57 (4) *European Journal of Political Research*.

29 Ver por ejemplo la "Guía práctica para entender los tratados de comercio e inversión: cómo las multinacionales planean apropiarse de tu futuro" lanzada por la Campaña española No al TTIP. Disponible en www.noalttip.org/wp-content/uploads/2018/10/tlc-con-portada-baja.pdf

contra el Tratado sobre la Carta de la Energía y las negociaciones respecto de su reforma. En concreto, en diciembre de 2019, un amplio conjunto de organizaciones envió una carta abierta, dirigida en particular a los ministros de los Estados miembros del tratado, a los comisarios y a los miembros del europarlamento.[30]

En el ámbito latinoamericano, destaca en la actualidad la Campaña América Latina Mejor sin TLC, conformada el 11 de noviembre de 2018, que aglutina a una red de organizaciones, plataformas nacionales y redes regionales[31]. La plataforma ha estado especialmente activa en la denuncia mediática de las consecuencias negativas del Tratado Transpacífico, del Tratado de Libre Comercio entre Chile y Argentina y del acuerdo entre la EU y el MERCOSUR. También fue importante el papel de la campaña en la contracumbre de la reunión del G-20 en noviembre de 2018 en la ciudad de Buenos Aires.

Las clausulas "comercio y desarrollo" como respuesta a las presiones de los movimientos sociales

Más allá de las campañas de rechazo, la acción social y en particular la presión de los sindicatos y de diversos movimientos como los ecologistas o feministas, ha impulsado la inserción en los tratados de un conjunto de cláusulas que incorporan objetivos sociales, de carácter laboral fundamentalmente, ambientales o relativos a la igualdad de género.

El debate sobre la oportunidad, la eficacia y conveniencia de estas cláusulas para alcanzar las diversas exigencias de las organizaciones sociales es enorme. A favor de este tipo de cláusulas es posible afirmar que las mismas son una vía indirecta para asegurar el cumplimiento o la incentivación de objetivos como la mejora de las condiciones laborales establecidas en las distintas partes del acuerdo o la inserción de objetivos como la igualdad de género o la promoción del respeto del ambiente.[32] Sin embargo una

---

30 Open Letter on the Energy Charter Treaty (ECT) 9 December 2019, http://foeeurope. org/sites/default/files/eu-us_trade_deal/2019/en-ect-open-letter1.pdf

31 Ver Argentina Mejor sin TLC en https://mejorsintlc.org/

32 Sobre estas cláusulas la ILO ha afirmado que las mismas: "have been a useful tool for: raising awareness on the employment and social dimensions of globalization; involving social partners during trade negotiation and implementation; and developing cooperative activities with the aim of strengthening the capacity of domestic institutions to better promote labour standards," ver ILO, *Labour-related provisions in trade agreements: Recent trends and relevance to the ILO* (2016) Governing Body, 328th Session. Para una muestra del debate entorno a estas cláusulas se remite a Guamán (n 1)

apreciación del contenido y la utilización efectiva de estas pone en duda su capacidad para el cumplimiento de estos objetivos, al tiempo que evidencia un conjunto de posibles consecuencias negativas que podrían derivarse de este tipo de cláusulas. En este sentido, la falta de eficacia y de mecanismos coactivos para garantizar su cumplimiento se conjuga con el riesgo de que, mediante su utilización se acabe permitiendo que el alcance de los derechos laborales sea establecido o interpretado por normas y mecanismos creados por normas comerciales y protagonizados por expertos en comercio o que su inclusión opere como un elemento para legitimar, per se y sin ahondar en su utilidad real, el conjunto de estos tratados. A efectos de ahondar en esta cuestión, el presente apartado contiene un somero análisis de un subconjunto de las cláusulas citadas, las estrictamente laborales, incluidas en los "acuerdos de nueva generación".

En el ámbito laboral la utilización de estas cláusulas ha proliferado en las últimas dos décadas con contenido muy diverso.[33] Como señala el informe de la Organización Internacional del Trabajo (ILO) de 2017,[34] en 1995 únicamente 4 tratados de libre comercio incluían cláusulas relativas a los derechos laborales, esta cifra aumentó hasta los 21 tratados en el año 2005, alcanzando los 58 en 2013 y los 77 en 2016. Entre las 136 economías que han incluido estas cláusulas, Canadá, Chile, la EU y USA son particularmente activos. Desde entonces ha seguido aumentando, ya no sólo en los acuerdos norte-sur sino también en los norte-norte y sur-sur,[35] lo que demuestra un claro cambio de tendencia cuyos exponentes principales son sin duda el CETA y el TPP, aun así, el 70.1 % de las cláusulas se incluyen en los tratados norte-sur. Es necesario tener en cuenta también que decisiones comerciales unilaterales (como los sistemas de preferencias generalizadas de USA y la EU) han incluido modelos de condicionalidad laboral y que los tratados bilaterales de inversión también han integrado estas cláusulas. En concreto, según datos de 2014, el 80% de los BIT negociados habían incluido ya previsiones laborales.[36]

En relación a los acuerdos impulsados por la EU, la Comisión Europea ha identificado 3 pilares: compromisos de las partes con diversos tratados

---

33 Dentro del concepto "cláusula laboral" la ILO incluye tres tipos de previsiones: "any reference to standards that address labour relations or minimum working terms or conditions; any mechanism to promote compliance with the standard, such as consultative bodies to facilitate dialogue, which can be permanent or temporary; a framework for cooperative activities, such as technical assistance, exchange of best practice, training, and others." ILO *Handbook on assessment of labour provisions in trade and investment arrangements* (2019), International Labour Office.)

34 ILO (n 32)

35 Ibid.

36 Ibid.

multilaterales y convenios de la ILO, estructuras para incluir a las organizaciones de la sociedad civil en la implementación de estos compromisos y una serie de mecanismos para la resolución de controversias en los cuales "árbitros independientes hacen públicas sus resoluciones en relación al grado del cumplimiento de las partes".[37] Dejando la cuestión de la participación en el monitoreo para el apartado siguiente, vamos a repasar someramente los mecanismos de resolución de controversias, directamente conectados con la imperatividad (o la falta de imperatividad) de las cláusulas sociales.

Para ello y a modo de ejemplo vamos a revisar dos modelos, el del Tratado EU-Corea y el del CETA.[38] El artículo 13 del acuerdo EU-Corea, crea un mecanismo propio en dos fases, prohibiendo de manera clara la utilización del resto de los mecanismos de arbitraje del acuerdo para solventar las disputas en materia laboral. Así, el artículo 13.4 y 13.5 establecen en primer lugar la fase de consulta entre las partes como vía de resolución de controversias. Si estas consultas intergubernamentales (sobre incumplimientos laborales que normalmente suelen ser cometidos por entidades privadas) fracasan, se prevé la posibilidad de elevar la cuestión ante un grupo de expertos que presentará un informe. El grado de obligatoriedad de ese informe es nulo, pues el apartado tercero del art. 13.5 dispone que "las Partes *harán todo lo posible* para tener en cuenta el asesoramiento o las recomendaciones del Grupo de Expertos en la implementación del presente capítulo".

---

37 European Commission, "Feedback and Way Forward on Improving the Implementation and Enforcement of Trade and Sustainable Development Chapters in EU Free Trade Agreements" (2018) Non-Paper of the Commission Services http://trade.ec.europa.eu/doclib/docs/2018/february/tradoc_156618

38 Es interesante también atender al modelo del TPP. El capítulo 19 del TPP, bajo el título "labor," incluye un procedimiento de consultas entre las partes para resolver cualquier disputa surgida respecto de su contenido. Solo en el caso de que no sea posible la solución de las disputas mediante el procedimiento de consultas se permite a las partes acudir al procedimiento general de resolución de controversias establecido en el capítulo 28 del TPP para el conjunto del acuerdo, con la excepción de las cuestiones relativas a la inversión para las que el capítulo 9 prevé un mecanismo particular de arbitraje para la solución de controversias entre inversor y Estado (el polémico ISDS). Los sindicatos norteamericanos han criticado duramente este procedimiento de solución de controversias. En su opinión, el mecanismo previsto permite una total discrecionalidad a los Estados y acaba, en el caso de que se llegue al final, en un intercambio de sanciones económicas entre Estados que no son efectivas a la hora de eliminar determinados comportamientos contrarios a los derechos laborales incluidos en el acuerdo y que en numerosas ocasiones derivan de agentes privados frente a los cuales no hay vía alguna de sanción. Los sindicatos consideran que una suspensión de los beneficios del acuerdo podría ser más efectiva que la compensación económica, de difícil cálculo en determinados conflictos. ITUC, CSI, IBG, "Trans Pacific Partnership Labour Chapter Scorecard. Fundamental issues remain unaddressed." Disponible en: www.ituc-csi.org/IMG/pdf/trans_pacific.pdf

Por su parte, el capítulo 23 del CETA, titulado "comercio y trabajo" incluye una serie de medidas dirigidas al establecimiento de mecanismos institucionales para la aplicación del capítulo[39] y a la regulación de los métodos de solución de conflictos, que de nuevo son exclusivos y distintos a los previstos para el resto de las materias del tratado. El art. 23.11 establece con claridad que los compromisos adoptados en el capítulo son obligatorios y ejecutables, pero únicamente mediante los procedimientos de consultas, el acceso al panel de expertos o, por mutuo acuerdo, el recurso a mecanismos de conciliación o de mediación. Es interesante remarcar que durante el procedimiento de consultas, y con el consentimiento de ambas Partes es posible, según el art. 23.9.4, solicitar la opinión de otros organismos, incluyendo los de la ILO o la del propio Comité de desarrollo sostenible. Cualquier decisión adoptada en este procedimiento debe ser publicada. En el caso de que no se llegue a un acuerdo transcurridos 90 días del comienzo de las consultas el art. 23.10 prevé la creación de un Panel de Expertos. El panel está compuesto por tres personas expertas, nombradas por las partes de mutuo acuerdo, cuya tarea es elevar a las Partes una recomendación para la resolución de la controversia. Para la adopción de la resolución, el Panel puede utilizar las guías, resoluciones o decisiones de la ILO, avisando de ello a ambas Partes. Si la resolución concluye confirmando la existencia de un incumplimiento de los compromisos por una de las Partes, esta debe dialogar con la otra y presentar en menos de tres meses un plan con medidas apropiadas para remediar la situación, informando a la otra parte de las acciones o medidas implementadas. El Comité de comercio y desarrollo sostenible tendrá como misión la monitorización del cumplimiento de las recomendaciones del Panel. No hay ningún tipo de previsión de sanciones u otro tipo de responsabilidades por el incumplimiento.

Como puede observarse, los sistemas establecidos para asegurar su cumplimiento son distintos de los establecidos respecto del conjunto de las previsiones consideradas "hard" en los tratados de comercio e inversión. Es evidente que las cláusulas integradas en estos capítulos tienen un carácter de compromiso político sin que su contenido señale una verdadera voluntad de obligar a la contraparte de manera efectiva en la protección o implementación de los estándares laborales internacionales.

---

39 Las Partes deben designar una oficina, a modo de punto de contacto y se prevé la creación del "Comité sobre comercio y desarrollo sostenible," que es un comité especializado en las materias de medio ambiente y trabajo, con una conformación similar a la prevista en el acuerdo con Corea. No se prevé un "Foro de la Sociedad Civil"" como tal, pero sí los comités de expertos donde se mencionan expresamente los sindicatos. Además, cada Parte se obliga a recibir y considerar iniciativas de la sociedad e informar a esos comités.

Esta cuestión, englobada en la crítica por la falta de efectividad que ha sido elevada por sindicatos, NGO y por el Parlamento Europeo,[40] ha llevado a la EU a lanzar un procedimiento de consulta que confirmó la percepción de la falta de efectividad de los mecanismos para garantizar la aplicación de estas cláusulas. En su informe de 2018 titulado "Feedback and way forward on improving the implementation and enforcement of Trade and Sustainable Development chapters in EU Free Trade Agreements",[41] la Comisión consideró impracticable la opción de establecer sanciones económicas por el incumplimiento. En cambio, estableció un "15-point action plan" con el objetivo de "garantizar una implementación y aplicación más efectiva y asertiva de los capítulos sobre comercio y desarrollo sostenible". Este plan incluye una serie de actuaciones englobadas en tres grandes áreas: trabajo conjunto (con los Estados, el Parlamento Europeo y las Organizaciones Internacionales); aumentar el rol de la sociedad civil, incluidos los agentes sociales, en los procesos de implementación; y mejorar la transparencia y la comunicación en relación a la concreta realización de los objetivos de estos tratados. Como señala Harrison, los agentes sociales han considerado estos lineamientos insuficientes, señalando además el amplio escepticismo respecto de la voluntad de la DG Trade de incluir de manera efectiva la priorización de cuestiones laborales, ambientales o de género.[42]

El 17 de diciembre de 2018, la Comisión utilizó el artículo 13.14 del tratado con Corea para abrir consultas con el Estado respecto de la adecuación de la ley sindical coreana (Korean Trade Union Act 1997) y otras leyes laborales con las obligaciones derivadas del acuerdo comercial. Además de listar las medidas internas que se consideran incompatibles el texto de la Comisión indica que los esfuerzos de Corea para ratificar cuatro convenios fundamentales de la ILO (87, 98, 29 y 105) son insuficientes. Posteriormente, el 19 de diciembre, se constituyó un panel de expertos compuesto por dos profesores expertos en derecho internacional y arbitraje (seleccionados por la EU y Corea). El presidente del panel es un abogado especialista en disputas de arbitraje internacional. El panel, que puede consultar a los grupos de consulta previstos en el Tratado y a las organizaciones internacionales que considere necesario, debe presentar su informe a las partes al final de mes de marzo de 2020.

---

40 Sobre la cuestión ver, James Harrison, "The Labour Rights Agenda in Free Trade Agreements" (2019) 20 (5) *Journal of World Investment & Trade*.

41 European Commission, "Feedback and Way Forward on Improving the Implementation and Enforcement of Trade and Sustainable Development Chapters in EU Free Trade Agreements" (2018) Non-Paper of the Commission Services http:// trade.ec.europa.eu/doclib/docs/2018/february/tradoc_156618.

42 Harrison (n 40).

Para finalizar este recorrido cabe apuntar que junto a las cláusulas de carácter netamente laboral encontramos las ubicadas bajo el título de "comercio y ambiente" o rúbricas similares así como las llamadas "cláusulas de género", ambas surgidas igualmente como respuesta a las presiones y denuncias de distintos movimientos sociales y políticos con una creciente repercusión académica. La introducción de una serie de capítulos de "Género y Comercio" se evidencia en los tratados más recientes.[43] La valoración de estas cláusulas desde los movimientos sociales y desde el campo académico ha sido muy crítica, denunciando una estrategia de *pink washing* o intento de legitimación de los tratados con la extensión de la idea de haber introducido una suficiente protección específica al impacto de género, aun cuando las cláusulas presentan graves carencias. Así, autoras como Partenio, Laterra y Ghiotto señalan que estos capítulos sólo comprenden a las mujeres desde dos aristas: como "mujer emprendedora" y como sujetos de endeudamiento, ninguna de las dos visiones es deseable o adecuada para fomentar la igualdad de género.[44]

La utilización de los marcos de "participación establecidos" en los acuerdos de comercio e inversión por los movimientos sociales

Como se ha venido señalando, los tratados de nueva generación han incluido una serie de previsiones que atribuyen un papel a la "sociedad civil" respecto del funcionamiento y monitoreo de los capítulos rubricados como "comercio y desarrollo sostenible", entre otras cuestiones. Los estudios relativos a esta inclusión, como se indicó en la introducción,[45] han adoptado un

---

43 Canadá comenzó a incorporarlos en los años recientes, por ejemplo en la renegociación de su TLC con Chile. También la Unión Europea los está incorporando, por ejemplo en la renegociación de su acuerdo con Chile. A partir de allí, el gobierno de Chile comenzó a sumar este capítulo a TLC intrarregionales con Argentina, Uruguay y Brasil.

44 Por ejemplo, en el capítulo sobre Género y Comercio (capítulo 15) del TLC Argentina-Chile, el eje está puesto sobre el "empoderamiento económico de las mujeres", pero no se toma en cuenta los impactos que la liberalización comercial tiene en todos los ámbitos de la vida de las mujeres. Asimismo, este capítulo empuja la inclusión financiera de las mujeres como llave para el desarrollo del espíritu empresario, lo cual es impulsado por los organismos internacionales financieros cuando lideran las propuestas de empoderamiento económico a través del acceso a préstamos y microcréditos. Vid. Flora Partenio, Patricia Laterra y Luciana Ghiotto, "Análisis del capítulo de Género y Comercio del TLC entre Argentina y Chile" (2019). DAWN y Asamblea Argentina mejor sin TLC. Disponible: http://dawnnet.org/publication/analisis-del-capitulo-de-genero-y-comercio-del-tlc-entre-argentina-y-chile/. Consultado el 15 de marzo de 2019.

45 Martens, Van Den Putte Oehri and Orbie (n 5)

concepto amplio de "sociedad civil", incluyendo especialmente las empresas o, de manera más amplia todavía, el conjunto de "stakeholders". A modo de muestra, es conveniente recordar que, tomando como ejemplo el CETA se aprecia una confusa utilización de ambas categorías. El tratado menciona 19 veces a la "sociedad civil" en ocasiones incluyendo las organizaciones empresariales, en ocasiones como concepto contrario al "sector privado" y con la referencia a "otros stakeholders", expresión que aparece hasta en 13 ocasiones. Esta confusión, que se repite en otros tratados, apunta una tendencia que se ha constatado en la realidad de las negociaciones y funcionamiento de los mecanismos de participación, en los que de facto prima la intervención de los actores económicos.

En todo caso, la inclusión de los actores sociales (y empresariales) en los tratados de nueva generación no ha seguido un patrón homogéneo. De hecho, siguiendo el "índice de participación de la sociedad civil" diseñado por Martens et al.,[46] puede verse claramente cómo el tipo de actores llamados y/o autorizados a la participación, los organismos creados para vehicular la misma, la interacción entre estos mecanismos y las partes firmantes del tratado, los distintos niveles en los que se estructura la negociación y, especialmente, su posibilidad de participación en los mecanismos de control, monitoreo o resolución de controversias entre las partes, varía notablemente.

Siguiendo este índice, puede apreciarse cómo el CETA se encuentra en el lugar más alto, con un resultado de 27 puntos frente a los 9 del acuerdo multipartes entre la EU, Colombia y Perú. Paradójicamente, los movimientos sociales peruanos y recientemente ecuatorianos, apoyados por diversas organizaciones europeas, han utilizado las cláusulas sociales de este tratado para exigir la adecuación de los estándares nacionales a los establecidos en el Tratado.

Cabe recordar que el acuerdo entre la EU y Colombia, Perú y Ecuador,[47] incluye en su título IX (titulado "Comercio y desarrollo sostenible") una

---

46 ibid. El índice establece una serie de 21 indicadores para determinar el grado de participación de la sociedad civil, divididos en las categorías mencionadas.

47 Tras un largo proceso de negociación, el 26 de junio de 2012 la EU firmó un Acuerdo Comercial con Colombia y Perú que se ha venido aplicando provisionalmente desde el 1 de marzo de 2013 para el Perú y el 1 de agosto de 2013 para Colombia. See: Trade Agreement between the European Union and its Member States, of the One Part, and Colombia and Peru, of the Other Part (signed 26 June 2012, entered into force 1 March 2013 (Peru) and 1 August 2013 (Colombia)). Ecuador se adhirió más tarde, tras un tortuoso proceso de desavenencias políticas que culminó con la ratificación del acuerdo el 20 de diciembre de 2016. See: Protocol of Accession of Ecuador to the EU-Colombia/Peru Trade Agreement (signed 12 December 2014, provisionally applied since 1 January 2017).

parte laboral muy limitada, dedicándole sólo un artículo, según el cual cada Parte se compromete con la promoción y aplicación efectiva en sus leyes y prácticas en todo su territorio de las normas fundamentales de trabajo reconocidas a nivel internacional (ILO) y un mecanismo institucional y de monitoreo. Según este mecanismo, establecido en el artículo 280, cada Parte debe designar una oficina dentro de su administración (un "punto de contacto") para implementar aspectos de desarrollo sostenible relacionados con el comercio y canalizar todos los asuntos y comunicaciones que surjan en relación con título IX.

Además, según los artículos 281 y 282 las partes deben crear "comités o grupos nacionales en materia laboral y ambiental o de desarrollo sostenible" (denominados "Domestic Advisory Groups") que tendrán una representación equilibrada de organizaciones representativas en estas áreas. Los comités están autorizados a presentar opiniones y hacer recomendaciones sobre la aplicación del Título, inclusive por iniciativa propia, a través de los respectivos canales internos (los puntos de contacto). Además, el Subcomité de Comercio y Desarrollo Sostenible (creado en el artículo 280) deberá convocar una vez al año, a menos que las Partes acuerden algo distinto, una sesión con organizaciones de la sociedad civil y el público en general, a fin de llevar a cabo un diálogo sobre asuntos relacionados con la aplicación de este Título.

El 19 de octubre de 2017, un total de 24 organizaciones sociales presentaron una documentada petición ante el punto de contacto de la EU, detallando las actuaciones del gobierno peruano en materia laboral y ambiental que consideraban un incumplimiento de las normas contenidas en el acuerdo comercial con la EU.[48] En particular, la queja se enfocó en la realidad laboral y ambiental de sectores como la agricultura, la minería, el petróleo, el gas, los textiles y las confecciones, por su vinculación con el comercio entre las dos partes.[49]

Como señalaron las organizaciones sociales que elevaron la queja, Perú optó por los mecanismos internos y no por el Grupo Consultivo Interno

---

48 Esta queja está disponible en: https://redge.org.pe/sites/default/files/Publicacio%CC%81n%20QUEJA%20TLC%20UE-Peru%CC%81%202017.pdf

49 No era la primera vez que las organizaciones peruanas habían ensayado la vía de las cláusulas sociales en acuerdos de comercio para intentar forzar al estado a evitar la precarización continua de los derechos laborales. En el año 2015 las organizaciones peruanas utilizaron la cláusula del acuerdo entre Estados Unidos y Perú para elevar una queja similar, que dio lugar a tres comunicaciones públicas remitidas por Departamento del Trabajo de los Estados Unidos al Estado peruano. En las comunicaciones se señalaban las limitaciones y falta de eficacia del sistema de inspección de trabajo, la jurisdicción social así como las quiebras en el reconocimiento de las libertades de sindicación y negociación colectiva. Estas comunicaciones fueron utilizadas por los sindicatos peruanos en recomendaciones al gobierno.

como lo tienen todos los países parte del acuerdo, lo cual provocó una serie de críticas relativas a la imposibilidad de participación efectiva, la negación del derecho al voto que tienen algunas organizaciones, la falta de diálogo real, el control gubernamental, la falta de institucionalidad, etc. Tras la presentación de la queja, diversas organizaciones de la sociedad civil peruana, centrales sindicales y organizaciones vinculadas a pueblos indígenas y temas ambientales se constituyen en el Grupo Consultivo Interno (GCI-Perú), sin contar con el reconocimiento del Gobierno peruano.

En respuesta a una pregunta sobre el estado de la queja presentada por la Eurodiputada socialista Rodríguez Piñero, la Comisaria Malmström en nombre de la Comisión Europea, emitió una respuesta en febrero de 2019 señalando que la cuestión se planteó entre las partes por primera vez en la reunión del Subcomité de Comercio y Desarrollo Sostenible de noviembre de 2017. Posteriormente, según la respuesta de Malmström, "la Comisión debatió regularmente el escrito con todas las partes interesadas (autoridades, organizaciones de la sociedad civil, representantes de empresas y medios académicos de Perú) para comprender mejor las cuestiones complejas y de amplio alcance que plantea". La EU llegó incluso a enviar una misión de información a Lima e informar regularmente el grupo consultivo interno creado por el acuerdo.[50]

En octubre de 2018, el Gobierno peruano presentó su respuesta, junto con la situación de los otros dos países miembros del acuerdo en la reunión del Subcomité de Comercio y Desarrollo Sostenible (Quito, diciembre de 2018). El acta publicada de esa reunión[51] revela que, en la misma, los gobiernos se limitaron a exponer informes propios sobre sus avances, con afirmaciones más que cuestionables. A las organizaciones sociales se les reservó únicamente un foro específico de tres horas. Respecto de los "avances" señalados por el gobierno de Perú, las organizaciones sociales han señalado que, pese a los informes del gobierno, los mecanismos de participación no están funcionando.[52] Por su parte, el gobierno de Ecuador presentó como elemento de evidencia de su cumplimiento con los compromisos laborales, una serie de reformas en la contratación realizadas en el año 2018. Una aproximación a estas reformas evidencia como las mismas son en realidad el prototipo de la precarización contractual, promocionando en sectores clave

---

50 La pregunta y la respuesta pueden encontrarse en: www.europarl.europa.eu/doceo/document/E-8–2018–006261-ASW_ES.html

51 Disponible en http://trade.ec.europa.eu/doclib/docs/2019/february/tradoc_157701.pdf

52 Ver RedGE, '*Sociedad civil: una participación que no espera*', 2019. Disponible en: https://redge.org.pe/sites/default/files/8%20%20Info%20sociedad%20civil%20%20GMI%20%282%29.pdf

como el banano o la floricultura, contratos temporales, a tiempo parcial y discontinuos. De hecho, poco tiempo después de aquella reunión, el sindicato de bananeros de Ecuador (ASTAC) presentó con apoyo de un conjunto de organizaciones una queja contra el gobierno de Ecuador por su, más que evidente, incumplimiento de las obligaciones laborales y ambientales reconocidas en el título IX.

Sin atender a esta realidad, ni a la falta de apertura real a la participación que se evidencia en las reuniones del Subcomité de Comercio y Desarrollo Sostenible del acuerdo, en el informe sobre la implementación de los Acuerdos de Libre Comercio de la EU de 2019, la Comisión realizó una valoración positiva de los "esfuerzos" de los países andinos en el desarrollo de las previsiones de las cláusulas señaladas.[53] Además, ha afirmado su completo "compromiso" con el impulso de participación de la sociedad civil, mediante, entre otras cosas, un instrumento financiado con 3 millones de euros.

Observaciones finales

El rápido repaso de los diferentes escenarios que existen en la compleja relación entre sociedad civil y tratados de comercio e inversión evidencia una relación resistencia y acomodación. La protesta continuada contra las distintas negociaciones se ha combinado con la utilización por parte de organizaciones de la sociedad civil de mecanismos establecidos por las partes negociadoras en el seno de los tratados. La introducción de estos mecanismos ha derivado en buena medida de la voluntad de apaciguar la protesta social a través de mecanismos que, dada su escaso nivel de obligatoriedad o de mecanismos de efectiva garantía, no están permitiendo una adecuada resolución o gestión de las demandas de la organizaciones sociales.

El reducido alcance de las posibilidades para la participación de la sociedad civil en la implementación de los tratados evidencia la visión de la misma como funcional al objetivo de rebajar el nivel de objeción ciudadana sin que exista una verdadera voluntad de abrir el espacio del comercio y la inversión al debate con las organizaciones sociales. Ni los débiles mecanismos de efectividad de las cláusulas de comercio y desarrollo ni las limitadas vías de participación ciudadana han provocado hasta el momento una respuesta de la Unión Europea orientada a promover un cambio real en las políticas contrarias a los derechos laborales, o ambientales, desarrolladas en los terceros estados que tiene como contraparte.

53 *Report from the Commission to the European Parliament, the Council, the European Economic and Social Committee and the Committee of the Regions on Implementation of Free Trade Agreements* (n 1)

El débil marco es, además, aprovechado por las partes negociadoras para mantener una apariencia de apertura que les permite sostener la estrategia de búsqueda de la legitimación que perdieron durante la fuerte campaña contra el ALCA, el TTIP o el CETA. Mientras, las campañas se mantienen organizadas y las redes entre movimientos sociales, academia, personas expertas y NGO sostienen una crítica constante a los procesos de negociación y ratificación de los tratados. Por añadidura, la experiencia de Perú y Ecuador demuestra que, aun cuando no es la vía adecuada para la defensa de los derechos asociados al trabajo ni para exigir la eficacia de las normas ILO, la actuación de los mecanismos coadyuva a la generación de vínculos transnacionales y a la expansión de la denuncia de las vulneraciones de derechos, no solo sociales sino del conjunto de derechos humanos en general.

9

Latin America, indigenous peoples, and investments: Resistance and accommodation

Sufyan Droubi, Cecilia Flores Elizondo, and Raphael Heffron

Introduction

Latin America is home to a 44 million-strong indigenous population,[1] distributed in 650 recognized and many non-recognized peoples.[2] These are the peoples who survived the massacres inflicted upon the natives of Latin America since the early days of European "colonization."[3] Millions of individuals have been decimated, and the surviving peoples have suffered the loss of lives, lands, cultures, and languages – much on account of the exploitation of minerals in their territories by domestic and foreign actors, including

---

1 See Joji Carino, "Global Report on the Situation of Lands, Territories and Resources of Indigenous Peoples" (Indigenous Peoples Major Group for Sustainable Development 2019) www.iwgia.org/en/resources/publications/3335-global-report-on-the-situation-of-lands-territories-and-resources-of-indigenous-peoples.html.

2 We adopt the concept of indigenous people enshrined in the Convention Concerning Indigenous and Tribal Peoples in Independent Countries (signed, adopted 27 June 1989, entered into force 5 September 1991) 1650 UNTS 383 (ILO Convention 169), which is centred on the self-identification as indigenous peoples. Also, United Nations, "United Nations Declaration on the Rights of Indigenous Peoples, Adopted by the General Assembly on 13 September 2007 UN Doc A/61/L.67 and Add.1," article 33; Organization of American States, "American Declaration on the Rights of Indigenous Peoples, Adopted at the Third Plenary Session Held on 15 June 2016, OAS Doc AG/RES.2888 (XLVI-O/16)," article I (2).

3 Nadia M. Rubaii, Lippez-De Castro and Susan Appe, "Pueblos Indígenas Como Víctimas de Los Genocidios Pasados y Actuales: Un Tema Esencial Para El Currículo de Administración Pública En América Latina" (2019) 25 *Opera*; Diana Isabel Lenton, "De Genocidio En Genocidio. Notas Sobre El Registro de La Represión a La Militancia Indígena" (2018) 13 *Revista de Estudios sobre genocidio* 47; Richard Gott, "América Latina Como Una Sociedad de Colonización Blanca" (2007) 5 *Estudios Avanzados* 7; Giulio Girardi, "Capitalismo, Ecocidio, Genocidio: El Clamor de Los Pueblos Indígenas" [1994] *Realidad: Revista de Ciencias Sociales y Humanidades* 669; Mónica L Espinosa Arango, "Memoria Cultural y El Continuo Del Genocidio: Lo Indígena En Colombia" [2007] *Antípoda. Revista de antropología y arqueología* 53; Marcia Esparza, "Algunos Factores a Considerar En El Análisis de Un Genocidio Latinoamericano: El Papel de Los Estados Unidos, Colonialismo Interno, Legados de Silencios Sociales" 1 *Revista Contenciosa*; Ignacio Aguilera

foreign investors.[4] Local governments, first as agents of the metropoles and later as organs of the newly independently states,[5] either inflicted the losses directly on these indigenous peoples or legitimized, through law and policies, the infliction of losses by private actors.

Throughout the history of Latin America, indigenous peoples have been invisible to governments and societies, notably in terms of participation in the decision-making respecting the economic exploitation of natural resources in their lands. Indigenous people have also suffered from high levels of inequality, bearing the full costs of the too often unsustainable exploitation of such resources and governments often justified these costs as necessary for the development of the "nation."[6] As resistance erupts,[7] governments argue it is put up by some individuals who either "are stupid, do not know what they say, or are liars";[8] or who are simply manipulated by some hidden forces interested in jeopardizing the development of indigenous peoples.[9] Yet, resistance, either civil or violent, has been the last resort mechanism to counter what indigenous peoples see as illegitimate incursions into their lands and illegitimate attacks on their ways of life.[10] Here, as in other parts of the world, resistance becomes a mechanism for the affirmation, not only of rights, but of identities.[11] Often, governments have responded with accommodation in the form of empty promises and affirmation of rights in law but not in practice. Even the recent achievements in terms of civil and political rights, which are crucial in terms of gaining

Encina and Daniela Torres Araya, "El Estado-Nación Paraguayo En La Dictadura de Alfredo Stroessner y Su Relación Con El Genocidio Aché"; Miguel Alberto Bartolomé, "Los Pobladores Del 'Desierto'. Genocidio, Etnocidio y Etnogénesis En La Argentina" [2004] *Amérique Latine Histoire et Mémoire. Les Cahiers ALHIM.* Les Cahiers ALHIM; Fernando Báez, "El Saqueo Cultural de América Latina" [2008] De la conquista a la globalización. Serie Debates. Venezuela: Melvin.

4 Eduardo Galeano, *Las Venas Abiertas de América Latina* (Siglo xxi 2004) http://adizesca.com/site/assets/e-las_venas_abiertas_de_al-eg.pdf.

5 For instance, Esparza (n 3) (on internal colonialism); Gott (n 3) (proposing that there is a white colonization of Latin America).

6 For a recent telling example, Barbora Valiková, "Análisis de La Posición Ideológica Del Gobierno Ecuatoriano En El Contexto de La Movilización Indígena Antiextractiva" (2016) 33 *Cuadernos del Cendes* 65, 74–5.

7 Ana Cecilia Betancur J (ed), *Movimientos Indígenas En América Latina. Resistencia y Nuevos Modelos de Integración* (IWGIA 2011).

8 Reportedly, this is how Rafael Correa explained the resistance put up by indigenous people against the mining project that his government adopted for Ecuador ("o son tontos, o no saben, o están mintiendo") (cited in Valiková (n 6) 78.)

9 Presidente da República do Brasil, "Speech at the Opening of the 74th United Nations General Assembly, New York" http://funag.gov.br/index.php/en/component/content/article?id=3004 accessed 26 May 2020.

10 Betancur J (n 7); Campaña continental 500 años de resistencia indígena y popular, "Quinientos Años de Resistencia Indígena y Popular En América Latina".

11 Girardi (n 3).

visibility, are not accompanied by effective procedures and institutions.[12] Enjoyment of economic, cultural, and social rights, fundamental in addressing both invisibility and inequality, lags further behind.[13]

In the late twentieth century a new globalization dynamic emerges. Many Latin American governments break with the Calvo tradition,[14] and they embrace with arms open, a wonderful new world – and one of the wonders that this new world offers are (for the most part, bilateral) investment treaties. For indigenous people, investment treaties perpetuate invisibility because these agreements are strongly attached to the traditional concept of statehood, to the principle that the government is the legitimate representative of all the peoples in the territory of the state. Consequently, the government, who has enabled and legitimized the losses inflicted on indigenous peoples by foreign investors, becomes the actor responsible for defending the interests of indigenous peoples in the negotiations of these treaties, and in disputes involving foreign investors. The regime that emerges from investment treaties also aggravates inequality because it fiercely protects the rights of investors.[15] Because indigenous peoples have finally managed to gain some political presence in several countries in the region, in countries which had entered into bilateral investment treaties, the straight-jacket and regulatory chill, which these treaties create,[16] acquire a more sinister contour: they jeopardize the indigenous peoples' fight for equality in political, civil, economic, social, and cultural terms.

From this perspective, two questions arise for the international investment lawyer: what to do when the facts of a situation, for instance mounting resistance towards a project, a policy, or a treaty,[17] make it clear that the local government does not legitimately represent indigenous peoples; and

12 Deborah J. Yashar, "Indigenous Politics and Democracy: Contesting Citizenship in Latin America" (Kellogg Institute 1997) Working Paper 238; Deborah J Yashar, "Resistance and Identity Politics in an Age of Globalization" (2007) 610 The ANNALS of the American Academy of Political and Social Science 160. (Describing very complex social developments that enabled the organization of indigenous movements, but jeopardized political participation.)

13 For instance, The World Bank, "Indigenous Latin America in the Twenty-First Century" (The World Bank 2015) 13 https://documents.worldbank.org/en/publicat ion/documents-reports/documentdetail/145891467991974540/indigenous-latin-america-in-the-twenty-first-century-the-first-decade.

14 Carlos Calvo, *Derecho Internacional Teórico y Práctico de Europa y América. Tomo Primero* (D'Amyot, Durant et Pedone-Lauriel 1868) para 91 (intervention), 191 (jurisdiction) and 294 (full doctrine). See the excellent Chapter 1 by Phillip Burton in this volume.

15 For a definition of the international investment regime, see Chapter 2 by Magdalena Bas in this volume.

16 See Chapters 5 Luciana Ghiotto, 8 by Adoración Guamán, and 12 by Javier Echaide in this volume.

17 For instance, *Copper Mesa Mining Corporation v. Republic of Ecuador*, PCA No. 2012–2 (Award, 15 March 2016) (*Copper Mesa v Ecuador* (Award 2016)); *Chevron*

what to do when the promotion of sustainable development for indigenous peoples clashes with the protection of investors.[18] This chapter addresses these questions through the deconstruction of the mainstream concept of statehood and of the neoliberal belief that the protection of investors reverts to continuous development for all. This chapter draws on critical statehood scholarship,[19] on critical development theories,[20] and on energy justice studies[21] to bring visibility and justice to indigenous peoples and to affirm them

Corporation and Texaco Petroleum Company v. The Republic of Ecuador (II), PCA Case No. 2009–23 (Second Partial Award on Track II, 30 August 2018) (*Chevron v Ecuador (II)* (Second Partial Award 2018)); *Bear Creek Mining Corporation v. Republic of Peru*, ICSID Case No. ARB/14/21 (Award, 30 November 2017) (*Bear Creek v Peru* (Award 2017)).

18 We understand sustainable development as a framework that enables communities to participate in decision-making relating to the intersection of developmental, social, and environmental concerns. Sustainable development has considerations about ecological integrity at the centre of decision-making processes. The Inter-American Court of Human Rights affirms the right to the environment as an autonomous right of universal interest that protects the components of the environment as a juridical interest in itself. This interest exists despite the absence of risk for individuals and thus, the right to the environment entails the protection of nature due to its significance for other organisms with which humans share the planet, as opposed to considerations merely about the utility of the environment for humans. Corte Interamericana de Derechos Humanos, "Medio Ambiente y Derechos Humanos (Obligaciones Estatales En Relación Con El Medio Ambiente En El Marco de La Protección y Garantía de Los Derechos a La Vida y a La Integridad Personal – Interpretación y Alcance de Los Artículos 4.1 y 5.1, En Relación Con Los Artículos 1.1 y 2 de La Convención Americana Sobre Derechos Humanos). Opinión Consultiva OC-23/17." See John C. Dernbach and Federico Cheever, "Sustainable Development and Its Discontents" (2015) 4 *Transnational Environmental Law* 247.

19 Jean d'Aspremont, "The International Law of Statehood: Craftsmanship for the Elucidation and Regulation of Births and Deaths in the International Society" (2013) 29 *Connecticut Journal of International Law* 201.

20 We draw on Latin American scholars, such as Luiz Carlos Bresser-Pereira, "Do ISEB e Da CEPAL à Teoria Da Dependendencia" [2005] Intelectuais e Política no Brasil: A Experiência do ISEB. Rio de Janeiro: Editor a Revan 201; Fernando Henrique Cardoso and Enzo Faletto, *Dependency and Development in Latin America* (University of California Press 1979). We also draw on recent inequality studies, Thomas Piketty, *Capital and Ideology* (Arthur Goldhammer tr, Harvard University Press 2020); Joseph Stiglitz, *Globalization and Its Discontents Revisited: Anti-Globalization in the Era of Trump* (1st edition, Penguin 2017).

21 Kirsten Jenkins and others, "Energy Justice: A Conceptual Review" (2016) 11 *Energy Research & Social Science* 174; Darren A McCauley and others, "Advancing Energy Justice: The Triumvirate of Tenets" (2013) 32 *International Energy Law Review* 107; Raphael J. Heffron and Darren McCauley, "The Concept of Energy Justice across the Disciplines" (2017) 105 *Energy Policy* 658; Raphael J. Heffron, "The Role of Justice in Developing Critical Minerals" (2020) In Press *The Extractive Industries and Society* https://doi.org/10.1016/j.exis.2020.06.018; Sufyan Droubi and Raphael Heffron, "Politics' Continued Erosion of Sustainable Development for Brazil's Indigenous Peoples" (2020) 5 *Peripheries Journal* www.revistaperiferias.org.

as full participants, on their own terms, in international investment law.[22] On a theoretical level, this is a conceptual chapter that falls within socially informed critiques to international law.[23] In the following two sections, we describe the problem of invisibility, and *then*, the problem of inequality. We offer a conceptual framework which tackles these problems in a systematic manner: *first*, we return to invisibility, when we call for the affirmation of the indigenous peoples' right to be consulted and to participate in the decision-making leading to, implementing and enforcing investment treaties; and *then*, we turn to inequality, when we draw on the energy justice literature, to call for the respect and enforcement of certain international law principles and rules as necessary for ensuring justice for indigenous peoples. In the ensuing section, we draw on our theory to articulate a critical reflection of international investment law practice, when we discuss the EU-Mercosur Trade Agreement which also provides for investment regulation, and investor-state arbitration procedures with focus placed on third party intervention and *ius standi*, before concluding with some final remarks.

Indigenous peoples: invisible in bilateral investment treaties

Already has the invisibility of indigenous peoples been affirmed as a problem in international investment law, having the imposition of obligations on investors been proposed as a manner to increase their visibility.[24] Tackling the same problem, without however framing it in terms of visibility,[25] some

22 We draw on the concept of "participants" articulated by Rosalyn Higgins, *Problems and Process: International Law and How We Use It* (Oxford University Press 1995).
23 For instance, Balakrishnan Rajagopal, *International Law from below: Development, Social Movements, and Third World Resistance* (Cambridge University Press 2003).
24 Nicolás M. Perrone, "The 'Invisible' Local Communities: Foreign Investor Obligations, Inclusiveness, and the International Investment Regime" (2019) 113 AJIL Unbound 16. Too often, state policies aimed at the protection of indigenous peoples depend on the prior recognition of their status as indigenous peoples, which evidently increases invisibility of non-recognized indigenous peoples. The present chapter refers to indigenous peoples irrespectively of the formal recognition of their status by local governments. See Ravi de Costa, "Descent, Culture, and Self-Determination: States and the Definition of Indigenous Peoples" (2014) 3 *Aboriginal Policy Studies*.
25 Invisibility is a widespread problem that affects different populations – indigenous, sexual minorities, drug addicts among others – which is usually caused by discrimination, stigma and fear, and which works in two manners, by rendering authorities blind to the specific characteristics of the population, and by preventing individuals from these populations from identifying themselves; it emerges as *absence* in census and data collection and in decision-making processes. See Sara L. M. Davis, "The Uncounted: Politics of Data and Visibility in Global Health" (2017) 21 *The*

authors propose changes to the procedure of investor–state arbitration, to enhance the participation of local communities.[26] We argue that it is the attachment of international investment law to a nineteenth-century concept of statehood embedded in exclusionary development ideologies which perpetuates invisibility. The procedural shortcomings of investor–state arbitration surely reinforce invisibility, but it is not the main culprit. Investors' lack of obligations aggravate inequality between these two participants in the international processes – investors and indigenous communities. In this section, we address invisibility and, in the next, inequality.

Only by attending to the history and current dynamics of the relationship between indigenous people and their governments in Latin American, and the actual standing of indigenous peoples as participants in the international investment processes, can we understand the problem of invisibility in the investment treaty regime. This problem emerges domestically and is perpetuated in international legal processes. Often, it emerges as *demographic* invisibility in data collection and censuses,[27] but the real cause is *identity* invisibility, that is, the invisibility of indigenous people's social, cultural, and economic conditions, which distinguish them from the rest of society.[28] While the causes of *identity* invisibility are complex, discrimination is certainly a major triggering factor. Systemic, ingrained, widespread discrimination causes the government and other actors to deny to indigenous peoples, and fear of discrimination may cause individuals within these peoples not to affirm, their identities.[29] It has been observed that the very idea of

International Journal of Human Rights 1144; Adrian Little and Mark McMillan, "Invisibility and the Politics of Reconciliation in Australia: Keeping Conflict in View" (2017) 16 *Ethnopolitics* 519; Michal Pitoňák, "Mental Health in Non-Heterosexuals: Minority Stress Theory and Related Explanation Frameworks Review" (2017) 5 *Mental Health & Prevention* 63; Genevieve Howse and Judith Dwyer, "Legally Invisible: Stewardship for Aboriginal and Torres Strait Islander Health" (2016) 40 *Australian and New Zealand Journal of Public Health* S14; Evelyn Peters, "Still Invisible: Enumeration of Indigenous Peoples in Census Questionnaires Internationally" (2011) 1 *Aboriginal Policy Studies*.

26 For instance, Lorenzo Cotula and Mika Schöder, "Community Perspectives in Investor-State Arbitration" (International Institute for Environment and Development 2017) https://pubs.iied.org/pdfs/12603IIED.pdf; Jesse Coleman and others, "Third Party Rights in Investor-State Dispute Settlement: Options for Reform" https://uncitral.un.org/en/library/online_resources/investor-state_dispute; Farouk El-Hosseny, *Civil Society in Investment Treaty Arbitration: Status and Prospects* (Brill | Nijhoff 2018).

27 Permanent Forum on Indigenous Peoples, "State of the World's Indigenous Peoples" (United Nations 2009) ST/ESA/328 165.

28 The World Bank (n 13) 18. ("In most cases, however, the main challenge to determine the precise number and distribution of indigenous people is political, related to the legal or implicit definitions of indigeneity that prevail in the region.")

29 Peters (n 25).

"indigenous" arises out of discrimination: a Eurocentrism impregnates the ideas of modernity and progress since the early days of the Latin American nations, leading to the construction of an ideal type of "national," against which the image of "indigenous" is built – as someone who is primitive and who has to be integrated into the national society. Hence, the definition of "indigenous" owes to the colonial period and is reproduced thereafter.[30]

Another triggering factor is ideologies that define development in exclusionary terms. Throughout the history of Latin America, the main development models have been supported by such ideologies. The early liberal-conservatism of the nineteenth and early twentieth centuries emerged from the regional incapacity of the Latin American governments to affirm themselves against Europe, and was content in seeking development for an elite formed by land owners and those in power.[31] Later, the "import substitution industrialization" policies of the 1950s–1980s emerged in a new post-war world of a diminished Europe, and sought uniform development for the nation, bringing development but in very unequal terms.[32] Finally, the neoliberal project of the 1990s and 2000s emerged from the collapse of the Latin American economies, who had to accede to the Washington Consensus to access international funds, and a certain belief that economic openness would lead to economic growth, again leading to an increase in inequality.[33] These models are exclusionary because they seek uniform development for the national society,[34] from which indigenous peoples have historically been excluded.[35] Although more recently indigenous peoples

30 Aníbal Quijano, "El 'Movimiento Indígena' Y Las Cuestiones Pendientes En America Latina" (2005) 119 *Tareas* 31.

31 Amado Luiz Cervo, "Política exterior e relações internacionais do Brasil: enfoque paradigmático" (2003) 46 *Revista Brasileira de Política Internacional* 5, 11.

32 Werner Baer, "Import Substitution and Industrialization in Latin America: Experiences and Interpretations" (1972) 7 *Latin American Research Review* 95.

33 Luiz Alberto Moniz Bandeira, "As políticas neoliberais e a crise na América do Sul" (2002) 45 *Revista Brasileira de Política Internacional* 135. On the Washington Consensus, see Chapter 2 by Magdalena Bas in this volume.

34 For the centrality of the "national" in CEPAL's approach, see Bresser-Pereira (n 20). For the centrality of the "citizen" in the neoliberal approach, see Patricia Richards, *Race and the Chilean Miracle: Neoliberalism, Democracy, and Indigenous Rights* (University of Pittsburgh Press 2013).

35 For instance, indigenous people were considered "categories in transition" for most of the Brazilian history, and all the six first constitutions sought to "integrate" them into society. Danielle Bastos Lopes, "O Direito dos Índios no Brasil: A Trajetória dos Grupos Indígenas nas Constituições do País" (2014) 8 *Espaço Ameríndio* 83; Luana Soncini, "Nem Cidadãos, Nem Brasileiros: Indígenas Na Formação Do Estado Nacional Brasileiro e Conflitos Na Província de São Paulo (1822–1845)" (2013) 9 *Perseu: História, Memória e Política*. Note how this emerges in contrast with the ideas of a "Creole legal conscience" and "Mestizo International Law" as explained in Chapters 1 by Philip Burton, and Chapter 14 by Fabian Cardenas and Jean d'Aspremont in this volume.

acquire civil and political rights, notably with the wave of the 1990s–2000s Latin America constitutions, in practice, they remain absent in decision-making processes.[36] Invisibility continues to be a problem because of the lack of proper procedures and institutions.

Likewise, indigenous peoples' standing as participants in international investment processes is extremely weak – notably when contrasted with investors. The regime of investment treaties creates another level of decision-making processes (governance) that can and does affect the lives of indigenous peoples without providing the latter with effective mechanisms of participation. On itself, this is a serious shortcoming of the regime. But the real problem lies deeper: because of its design, i.e., bilateral or multilateral relationships between states, and bilateral relationships between investors and states, with the government representing the state and all its peoples; and because of the ideology that sustains them, the investment treaty regime is unable to see beyond the veil of the state, to see the indigenous peoples as a legitimate participant in international investment processes.

Actually, that a government represents all the peoples in its territory is a crucial element in the traditional concept of statehood.[37] This principle is the necessary implication of the requirement that a government has "control" and "administration" over the territory,[38] and capacity to enter into relations with other states;[39] in other words, as a corollary of both internal and external effectiveness. Context is fundamental: Latin American countries have embraced the principle that effectiveness is crucial for statehood from the early days of their independence, back in the nineteenth century.[40]

---

36 Bruna Muriel, "Os Povos Indígenas Na América Do Sul: Entre a IIRSA e o Buen Vivir" [2017] Cadernos do CEAS: Revista crítica de humanidades 327, 330.

37 United Nations General Assembly, "Resolution 2625 (XXV). Declaration on Principles of International Law Concerning Friendly Relations and Cooperation among States in Accordance with the Charter of the United Nations. 1883rd Pl Mtg. 24 October 1970." ("...*a government representing the whole people belonging to the territory without distinction as to race, creed or colour*").

38 "Report of the International Committee of Jurists Entrusted by the Council of the League of Nations with the Task of Giving an Advisory Opinion upon the Legal Aspects of the Aaland Islands Question Report" (1920) 3 LNOJ SS [vi], 9 (a sovereign State does not emerge "until a stable political organisation had been created, and until the public authorities had become strong enough to assert themselves throughout the territories of the State without the assistance of foreign troops").

39 "Convention on Rights and Duties of States Adopted by the Seventh International Conference of American States" (1936) 165 United Nations Treaty Series 19, article 1; "Vienna Convention on the Law of Treaties" (signed 23 May 1969, entered into force 27 January 1980) 1155 UNTS 331, articles 7, 8, 46, and 47.

40 Calvo (n 14) para 44 (definition of state). Thomas D. Grant, "Defining Statehood: The Montevideo Convention and Its Discontents" (1998) 37 *Columbia Journal of Transnational Law* 403 (explaining that effectiveness is one of the cruxes of the Montevideo Convention).

Both external (vis-à-vis other countries) and internal (vis-à-vis indigenous peoples, communities formed by run-away slaves, secessionists, and others) effectiveness has historical pedigree, being fundamental in the consolidation and development of the Latin American state.[41] Effectiveness has a clear role in the consolidation and development of Latin American countries within and outside their borders: governments would promote homogeneity internally so as to build and strengthen a nation-state;[42] and externally, so as to become an equal among equals in the international sphere.[43]

Investment treaties would hardly match the Latin American typical government's impetus to self-affirmation as the builder of the national state, because these treaties seriously constrain the government's "regulatory space," if it were not for two factors. First, in the 1980s–90s, there is the dramatic context of the financial crises that affected the region, and also the pull felt by many Latin American governments to emulate the more developed nations, which led these governments to embrace a neoliberal vision of the state.[44] This vision de-emphasizes the role of the government as a direct promoter of development at the same time as it emphasizes its role as an enabler of free movements of capital, products, and investments. For many Latin American decision-makers, demonstrating to their peers in advanced economies that they have established an environment that is favorable to receiving businesses, that they were as "normal" as their

---

41 In fact, Latin American governments have relied *both* on the principle of effectiveness, notably among themselves in the consolidation of the South American borders (Fábio Aristimunho Vargas, *Formação Da Fronteiras Latino-Americanas* (Fundação Alexandre Gusmão 2017) 100) *and* on the formal recognition of their independence by the former metropoles.

42 Calvo draws on Wheaton to clearly distinguish between nation and state, and to affirm the possibility of existence of different nations within the same state. Calvo (n 14) 82 ff. But the point here is different. Exactly because even a quick look at any Latin American country would confirm the existence of multiple and complex nations (indigenous and otherwise), that the building of a "national" state became so important. This intent is clear in educational policies, affirming the European language (Spanish, Portuguese, French, English) as mandatory – see María Odette Canivell, "Nation Building, Utopia, and the Latin American Writer/Intellectual" (2008) 10 *CLCWeb: Comparative Literature and Culture* 4; Michiel Baud, "State-Building and Borderlands" (2000) 87 *Latin American Studies-Centre for Latin American Research and Documentation* 41. On the importance of the promotion of homogeneity for the development model that prevailed in the region in the 1940s–80s, Luiz Carlos Bresser-Pereira, "O Conceito Histórico de Desenvolvimento Econômico"; Bresser-Pereira (n 20).

43 Again, Calvo provides an important example, as his doctrine is articulated within the framework of the principle of equality of states. See Calvo (n 14) para 294.

44 Bandeira (n 33).

"developed" peers,[45] becomes critical. Evidently, this new vision of the role of the state was not uniformly adopted across the region or across individual countries – or even across the same government.[46] But this vision became strong enough to justify the adoption of bilateral investment treaties in countries that have done so.

Second, the governments of these countries do not see the treaties as a threat to their statehood (but some will come to see the treaties as an issue for their sovereignty). The historical need to affirm their statehood had long gone. In fact, the regime of bilateral investment treaties reinforces the principle of effectiveness because governments continue to be the promoters of what is now a neoliberal model of development by imposing this model to diverse actors who oppose it.[47] Often, dissenters were side-lined, marginalized, and silenced.[48] Ensuring internal homogeneity remains as important as seeking external homogeneity. Thus, it could be said that bilateral investment treaties rest on the concept of the state as a homogeneous unit that should be represented by a government – which perpetuates the invisibility of minorities such as indigenous peoples.

There have always been situations in which the interests of the government clash with those of other national actors,[49] notably in respect to economic activities. Generally, in international law practice, the clashes between the interests of a government and those of other national actors do not create a serious challenge to the principle of the state as a unit represented by a government. Moreover, in democracies at least, and most of Latin American states are democracies,[50] processes should exist at the national level to enable

45 Cervo (n 31) 16.
46 The history of the failed attempt carried out by the 1990s' Brazilian government to have the country ratifying bilateral investment treaties illustrates the point. See Fábio Costa Morosini and Ely Caetano Xavier Junior, "Regulação do investimento estrangeiro direto no Brasi: da resistência aos tratados bilaterais de investimento à emergência de um novo modelo regulatório" (2015) 12 *Revista de Direito Internacional* (UNICEUB) 421. See Chapter 4 by Leonardo V P de Oliveira and Marcus Spangenberger in this volume.
47 The complexity of this move can be illustrated with the establishment of the Ministry for De-bureaucratisation in Brazil. Helio Beltrão, "Desburocratização, Descentralização e Liberdade: A Aterrissagem No Brasil Real" (2016) 273 *Revista de Direito Administrativo* 491.
48 C.f. note 8 and accompanying text.
49 For an interesting and provoking analysis, Guillermo J. Garcia Sanchez, "To Speak with One Voice: The Political Effects of Centralizing the International Legal Defense of the State" (2017) 34 *Arizona Journal of International and Comparative Law* 557.
50 Organization of American States, "Inter-American Democratic Charter, Adopted by the General Assembly at Its Special Session Held in Lima, Peru, on September 11, 2001" www.oas.org/OASpage/eng/Documents/Democractic_Charter.htm accessed 7 August 2020.

national actors to weigh in on their governments, for instance, through parliaments and courts. Only in rare situations, clashes between the government and the population or parts of it rebound on the international sphere, leading to the disqualification of a government.[51] These are situations in which the clash of interests is so intense, its implications to the affected national actors are so severe, and domestic procedures are so deficient that the government in question has its legitimacy denounced and is ultimately disqualified as a representative of the state.[52]

Within the regime of investment treaties, a situation that is so critical as to justify the disqualification of a government as a legitimate partner by another state, or to disqualify it as a legitimate representative of the state-party in a dispute before an investor–state tribunal, has rarely, if ever, emerged.[53] Nevertheless, for the reasons described above, the government fails to properly represent indigenous peoples, while the regime of bilateral investment treaties fails to see the indigenous peoples in question. This failure of the regime arises clearly in investor–state arbitration awards settling disputes in which the impact of investments on indigenous peoples has been raised. No attention whatsoever is paid to the special conditions that make the indigenous populations in question what they are, and which explain their resistance to mining and other projects that are inside or close to their lands.

In Copper Mesa, for instance, a complex population formed by mestizos, Afro-descendants, and indigenous people,[54] is defined as "anti-miners."[55] In other words, the definition is investor-centered, is articulated with the reference placed on the investor: exactly the opposite of what should have been done, i.e., the definition of the peoples on their own terms, to properly explain their behavior. The attempts of the investor to create division

---

51 For instance, Organization of American States, "OAS Permanent Council Agrees 'to Not Recognize the Legitimacy of Nicolas Maduro's New Term'" www.oas.org/en/media_center/press_release.asp?sCodigo=E-001/19 accessed 7 August 2020.

52 For all, see Jean D'Aspremont, "Legitimacy of Governments in the Age of Democracy Note" (2005) 38 *New York University Journal of International Law and Politics* 877; Jean d'Aspremont and Eric De Brabandere, "The Complementary Faces of Legitimacy in International Law: The Legitimacy of Origin and the Legitimacy of Exercise" (2010) 34 *Fordham International Law Journal* 190.

53 But there are situations in which an investment or trade agreement comes under fire because one of its parties' behavior, as the Mercosur–EU trade agreement. "France Threatens to Block Trade over Amazon Fires" *BBC News* (23 August 2019) www.bbc.com/news/world-latin-america-49450495 accessed 12 July 2020.

54 Duygu Avcı and Consuelo Fernández-Salvador, "Territorial Dynamics and Local Resistance: Two Mining Conflicts in Ecuador Compared" (2016) 3 *The Extractive Industries and Society* 912, 915.

55 *Copper Mesa v Ecuador* (Award 2016) (n 17) para 4.45.

in the populations,[56] and its behavior that at times is criminal,[57] are narrowly defined in terms of contributory fault.[58] With this, the true meaning of the investor's behavior for the indigenous (and in this case, local) populations,[59] is ignored; as is the true meaning of the government behavior; in other words, the roots of the discontentment, grievance, resistance are lost. Emblematically, the tribunal "notes a regrettable feature of this controversy: a fear and mistrust by anti-miners of all mining, based in part on, the World Bank Inspection Panel's phrase, 'misinformation.' "[60] In other words, relying on a third party report, rather than on the account of the communities themselves, the tribunal laments the communities' resistance, and attributes such resistance to "misinformation," without ever asking whether the communities had legitimate reasons, based not on misinformation, but on their own experience, to justify their stance.

The role that the government of Ecuador played in all this, and the role the tribunal ascribes to it, deserves some thoughts. As the award acknowledges, the powers of the Ecuadorean government in the region had always been weak;[61] and local resistance to the investor has built up forcing the government to change its position towards the investor, from supportive to unsupportive up to a moment when, finally, the government terminates the licenses.[62] But none of this is enough for the tribunal to fully understand the real meaning of the resistance that was put up against the investor and the government, and to acknowledge that mining should never occur while the local population opposed it. Instead, the tribunal has its eyes on the state of Ecuador, and on the government:

> [S]hould the Respondent have *imposed* its will on the anti-miners, acting with all the powers and forces available to a sovereign State, so as to ensure that the Claimant, as the concessionaire under concessions granted by the Respondent, could gain access to the Junín concessions in order to carry out the required consultations and other activities required for its EIS?[63]

56 Ibid. 4.292. On the tactics that the investor used, see *Under Rich Earth* (2017) www.youtube.com/watch?v=QRinnhejBIw accessed 7 July 2020.

57 *Copper Mesa v Ecuador* (Award 2016) (n 17) para 6.100.

58 For further discussions on this case, see Chapters 11 by Farouk El-Hosseny, Patrick Devine, and Ilan Brun-Vargas and 13 by Sebastián Preller-Bórquez in this volume.

59 See, for instance, Movimiento Regional por la Tierra, "Intag, historia de una luz" https://porlatierra.org/casos/127/georeferencial accessed 16 July 2020.

60 *Copper Mesa v Ecuador* (Award 2016) (n 17) para 4.45.

61 Ibid. *4.97, 6.83.*

62 Ibid. 6.101, 6.124.

63 Ibid. 6.82. (Emphasis added)

To what the tribunal answers:

> [R]ather than giving legal force to the factual effect of the *anti-miners'* phys-
> ical blockade of the Junín concessions, the Respondent should have attempted
> *something* to *assist* the Claimant in completing its consultations and other
> requirements for the EIS. It is of course difficult to say now what it should have
> done to resolve all the Claimant' difficulties and, still more so, whether what
> anything it could have done would have changed the Claimant's position for
> the better. Plainly, the Government in Quito could hardly have declared war
> on its own people. Yet, in the Tribunal's view, *it could not do nothing.*[64]

In other words, the wishes of the local populations are a matter for the government, not for the tribunal, to address. What is more, the tribunal expects
the government to reign in the situation, to be effective in the region – even
after acknowledging that the government had always been weak. In fact,
given the design of the regime of bilateral investment treaties, it is difficult
to entertain how the tribunal could have done differently.[65] In strict legal
terms, the total reliance of the regime of bilateral investment treaties on
the traditional definition of statehood, i.e. the state as a unit which is represented by its government, is what makes the regime blind to indigenous
people, perpetuating the invisibility at the domestic level.

Indigenous peoples: inequality in investment treaties

Besides, it is safe to affirm that the regime of investment treaties also perpetuates inequality – not only between countries, which is of a lesser concern here, but between the two non-state participants which this chapter
addresses (investors and indigenous people). Although legal research
looking at the impact of the design and implementation of these treaties

---

64 Ibid. 6.83. (Emphasis added)
65 An interesting aspect is that one of the members of the tribunal, Bruno Simma, when
   serving as *ad hoc* judge in Kosovo, saw it fit to distance himself from the "nineteenth-
   century positivism" to make his now famous distinction between "degrees of non-
   prohibition, ranging from 'tolerated' to 'permissible' to 'desirable.'" *Accordance
   with International Law of the Unilateral Declaration of Independence in Respect
   of Kosovo* (Advisory Opinion) [2010] ICJ 141, 2010 ICJ Reports 403 Declaration
   of Judge Simma [8]. However, no such distinction is made in the present case, with
   the right of the investor being defined in absolute terms. One would be excused to
   ask whether the mining project, while not prohibited in international law, was, in
   the circumstances, desirable, permissible or merely tolerated – and to ask about the
   implications arising therefrom. In any case, on the further developments of the mining
   activities in the Intag area, and for some important insights into the changing, and
   increasingly strong role that the central government is playing in promoting these
   activities. See Avcı and Fernández-Salvador (n 54).

on the levels of inequality that affect indigenous peoples is lacking, it is possible to draw some conclusions from the inequality studies,[66] and on topical studies.[67] Many legal scholars have denounced the regime of investment agreements for promoting a misconception – that the protection of investors attracts investments.[68] But the real misconception lies deeper in the regime: it consists in the again neo-liberal belief that an increase in the inflows of investments into a country automatically rebounds in development for the country. With varying language, the texts of bilateral investment treaties suggest this misconception.[69] There is clear evidence that the individuals negotiating treaties on behalf of states share this belief.[70]

The idea that higher inflows of investments result in more development is based on what Stiglitz calls trickle-down economics: the belief that economic growth results in development for all.[71] Yet, as Stiglitz demonstrates, factors such as corruption involving investors and authorities; cheating by investors; imbalance in the governments' and investors' powers of negotiation; high rents for investors; inappropriate privatization projects that do not remunerate the state for the real value of the lands and resources – all these promote inequality, with investors and local elites capturing most of

66 Joseph E. Stiglitz, *The Price of Inequality: How Today's Divided Society Endangers Our Future* (Penguin Books 2013); Stiglitz, *Globalization and Its Discontents Revisited* (n 20); Thomas Piketty, *Capital in the Twenty-First Century* (Reprint edition, Harvard UP 2017); Piketty (n 20).

67 For instance, Henry Veltmeyer, "Extractive Capital, the State and the Resistance in Latin America" (2016) 4 *Sociology and Anthropology* 774; Matthew Fry and Elvin Delgado, "Petro-Geographies and Hydrocarbon Realities in Latin America" (2018) 17 *Journal of Latin American Geography* 10; Saturnino M. Borras Jr, Jennifer C. Franco, Cristobal Kay, and Max Spoor, "Chapter II: Land Grabbing in Latin America and the Caribbean, Viewed from a Broader International Perspective" (2014) *The land market in Latin America and the Caribbean: concentration and foreignization* 21.

68 For all, Muthucumaraswamy Sornarajah (ed), "Bilateral Investment Treaties," *The International Law on Foreign Investment* (4th edn, Cambridge University Press 2017).

69 To illustrate, the 1996 Canada–Ecuador BIT opens affirming "the purpose of creating favourable conditions for the investments of an investor of one Contracting Party in the territory of the other Contracting Party" before "acknowledging that the promotion and protection of such investments on the basis of a convention will be conducive to stimulating private economic initiatives and will *increase the prosperity of both states.*"

70 Guillermo Aguilar Alvarez and William W. Park, "The New Face of Investment Arbitration: NAFTA Chapter 11" (2003) 28 *Yale Journal of International Law* 365; Lauge N. Skovgaard Poulsen, *Bounded Rationality and Economic Diplomacy: The Politics of Investment Treaties in Developing Countries* (Cambridge University Press 2015) 118 ff.

71 Stiglitz, *The Price of Inequality* (n 66) 8–9.

the riches from the extraction of minerals and other resources, while the majority of the population bears the burdens of environmental degradation, social, and economic losses.[72] It is only by looking at who benefits from such hypothetical growth that one realizes that economic growth does not necessarily rebound into development, notably, into development for the most vulnerable. As many economists argue, the disaggregation of data is important for understanding the specific dynamics of development in different parts of the population.[73] The fact that indigenous people have remained invisible in data collection carried out by both national and international authorities aggravates the misunderstanding about growth leading to development for all.[74] Figure 9.1 illustrates this.

The "elephant curve" clearly suggests that inequality increased globally in the period 1980–2018, with the top centile of the global population capturing 27 percent of the total growth. But we should attend to the situation of the bottom centile and decile, who have not captured the same growth as the second and third bottom deciles. The question that arises is where in the curve Latin American indigenous should be placed? Studies suggest that they occupy the bottom edge of the curve.[75] To be sure, indigenous peoples

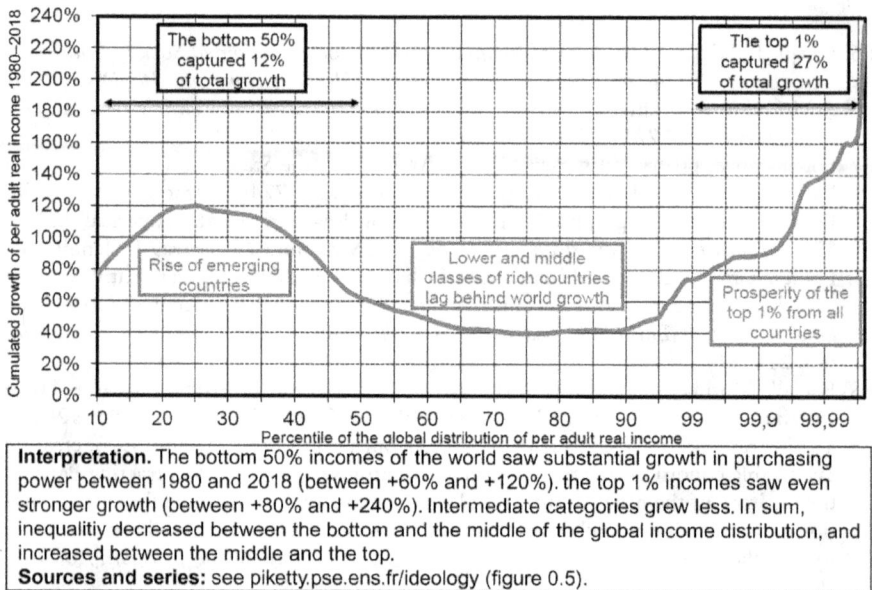

Interpretation. The bottom 50% incomes of the world saw substantial growth in purchasing power between 1980 and 2018 (between +60% and +120%). the top 1% incomes saw even stronger growth (between +80% and +240%). Intermediate categories grew less. In sum, inequalitiy decreased between the bottom and the middle of the global income distribution, and increased between the middle and the top.
Sources and series: see piketty.pse.ens.fr/ideology (figure 0.5).

Figure 9.1 The "elephant curve"

72 Joseph Stiglitz, *Making Globalization Work: The Next Steps to Global Justice* (Allen Lane 2006) ch 5 Lifting the Resource Curse.
73 Piketty (n 20) 670–679.
74 The World Bank (n 13) 14, 15.
75 For all, The World Bank (n 13).

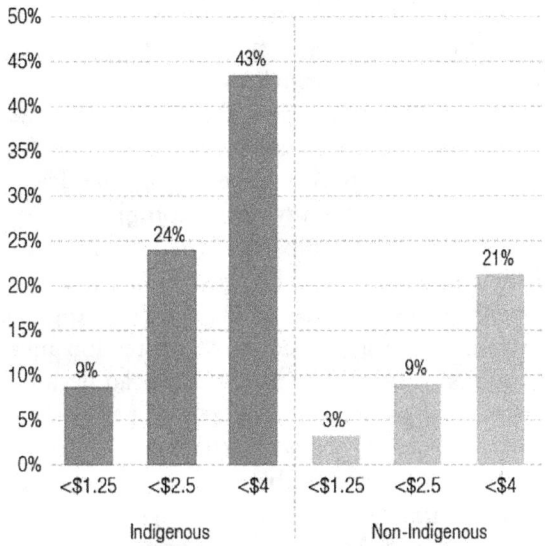

Percentage of people living on less than
US$1.25, US$2.50, and US$4 per Day
Late-2000s weighted average for Bolivia, Brazil,
Ecuador, Guatemala, Mexico, and Peru

Figure 9.2 Poverty inequality

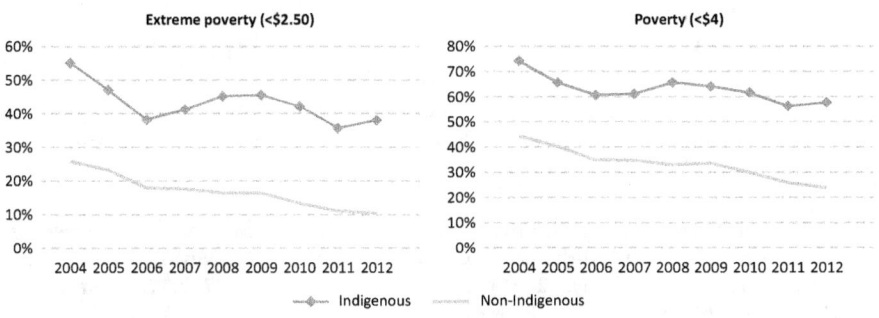

Figure 9.3 Indigenous people and inequality in Ecuador

have been disproportionately affected by poverty and extreme poverty, in contrast with other segments of Latin American societies.

To remain in the example of Ecuador, the growth of inequality, notably to the prejudice of indigenous people, is particularly concerning. Figures 9.2 and 9.3 illustrate this.

The regime of investment treaties perpetuates inequality in two manners. First, the treaties and the manner they are enforced cement the rights of investors – who occupy the top echelons of the "elephant curve" – so as to protect these rights against changes that local parliaments may introduce. In many decisions, the enforcement of the standards of protection is "automatic," with arbitrators rejecting the reasons that lead governments to adopt the decisions subject of the investors' complaints. For instance, with much difficulty arbitrators recognize that the resistance to an investment project, put up by indigenous peoples, is reason enough for the decision that the government makes to cancel licenses.[76] For indigenous peoples, the automatic enforcement of the standards of protection means that, ultimately, the status quo is frozen. This insight is crucial because in many Latin American countries, such as Ecuador, indigenous peoples succeeded in gaining participation in political processes in the late 1990s and in the 2000s.[77] So it becomes clear that this is a problem of inequality – even if invisibility is addressed, there remains the problem of the type of development that can be delivered by the state when designing investment policies. Second, the regime may be fostering inequality domestically; for instance, foreign investments in mining activities in indigenous lands often benefit national (non-indigenous) elites, who are at top tiers of the wealth and income pyramid.[78] Again, the regime offers an immediate, formal solution to the dispute, but it leaves the real problem – perpetuation of inequality – untouched.

It is in this sense – cementing ideologies about growth and investments and establishing rules and procedures that further these ideologies – that the regime of bilateral investment treaties perpetuate inequality. The regime plays a not insignificant role in the maintenance of what Piketty defines as neo-proprietarianism, an ideology that "relies on grand narratives and solid

---

76 See the different manners that the *Copper Mesa, Bear Creek* and *South American Silver* tribunals addressed the point. *Copper Mesa v Ecuador* (Award 2016) (n 17); *Bear Creek v Peru* (Award 2017) (n 17); *South American Silver Limited v. The Plurinational State of Bolivia*, PCA Case No. 2013–15 (Award, 30 August 2018).

77 The World Bank (n 13) 8.

78 Sometimes, this leads to very questionable outcomes, with the elites employing violence to repress indigenous peoples' resistance against mining and other projects. In Copper Mesa, the question arose, being quickly disposed of, as to the propriety of making Ecuador pay for costs that the investor incurred when some of these costs were salaries paid for individuals that behaved criminally towards the local populations. *Copper Mesa v Ecuador (Award 2016)* (n 17) para 7.30.

institutions."[79] In analyzing the European Union, Piketty offers insights that may be applied to the regime of bilateral investment treaties. Piketty recalls that ordoliberalism requires the state to "guarantee free and undistorted competition" and that, in the hands of von Hayek, ordoliberalism calls for "automatic rules" so as to circumvent democratic decision-making.[80] The regime of bilateral investment treaties establishes "automatic rules" in the form of legal entitlements to a class of actors that already occupy the high echelons of the world and regional wealth and income pyramid – not only with treaty provisions on indirect expropriation, full security, fair and equitable treatment etc. but also with decisions adopting approaches to the payment of compensation that are entirely favorable to investors.[81] These entitlements have the potential to aggravate inequality. While the impact of the regime on the government is well-known ("regulatory straight-jacket," "regulatory chill" etc.), the impact on indigenous peoples has not received proper attention. This problem cannot be addressed solely with the affirmation of self-determination and the indigenous peoples' right to participate in the decision-making respecting their lives. The role of participation is much reduced within an environment of automatic rules. Addressing this problem requires a renewed concept of justice and, in this chapter, we show that the concept of energy justice has much to offer in rethinking the type of development that investments should promote.

Insofar as the definition of international investment law remains grounded on the rigid and formalist regime of bilateral investment treaties, the chances for substantial gains in terms of participation and justice are insignificant. But as Piketty clearly demonstrates, inequality regimes are never completely stable and consistent, and they often carry the elements for their own transformation. Once freed of the bounds that narrow it down to the regime of investment treaties, international investment law may offer the conditions for its own renewal. The next sections places sustainable development and justice at the heart of international investment law, to articulate a theory of participation grounded on the self-determination of indigenous peoples, before drawing some conclusions.

Ensuring visibility for indigenous peoples

In the previous section, we argued that the invisibility of indigenous peoples emerges at the domestic level of Latin American countries, only to be perpetuated by the regime of bilateral investment treaties. We identified this regime's attachment to a strong concept of statehood (state as a

79 Piketty (n 20) 705. On narratives, see Chapter 1 by Philip Burton in this volume.
80 Ibid. 706.
81 Heffron (n 21).

unit, represented by a government) which is embedded in ideologies that are exclusionary (state as a homogenous unit, with the government expected to impose itself on dissidents, to promote free movement of capital and ensure the rights of investors) as a problem.

We start by noting that indigenous peoples have become participants in the international sphere,[82] participating in UN procedures,[83] and bringing claims before the Inter-American Court of Human Rights.[84] Only the practice of international investment law, because it is centered on the regime of investment treaties, lags behind. In international investment law, the problem of invisibility can be addressed by reformulating the concept of statehood, if only to attenuate the role that government plays in it and to acknowledge that, today, this concept must reflect a more complex reality of the state than the one that prevailed at the time the concept was fully articulated.[85] Indigenous peoples have been increasingly more present in international processes and progressively better equipped to influence decision-making, as the literature clearly confirms.[86] As mentioned above, indigenous peoples have actively participated in the UN procedures; have brought claims before the Inter-American and African systems of human rights, and US tribes have entered into international agreements.[87]

Progressively, the understanding that indigenous peoples enjoy a higher status than other non-state actors including corporations,[88] has emerged,[89]

---

82 Russel Lawrence Barsh, "Indigenous Peoples in the 1990s: From Object to Subject of International Law" (1994) 7 *Harvard Human Rights Journal* 33. Ibid; Anna Meijknecht, *Towards International Personality: The Position of Minorities and Indigenous Peoples in International Law* (Intersentia nv 2001); Lillian Aponte Miranda, "Indigenous People as International Lawmakers" (2010) 32 *University of Pennsylvania Journal of International Law* 203.

83 S. James Anaya, "Indian Givers: What Indigenous Peoples Have Contributed to International Human Rights Law Access to Justice: The Social Responsibility of Lawyers" (2006) 22 *Washington University Journal of Law & Policy* 107, 118–119.

84 For instance, *Sawhoyamaxa Indigenous Community v Paraguay*, Merits, reparations and costs, Inter-American Court of Human Rights Series C No 146 (29 March 2006); *Saramaka People v Suriname*, Interpretation of the judgment on preliminary objections, merits, reparations and costs, Inter-American Court of Human Rights Series C No 185 (12 August 2008); *Kichwa Indigenous People of Sarayaku v. Ecuador*, Merits and reparations, Inter-American Court of Human Rights Series C No 245 (27 June 2012).

85 "Convention on Rights and Duties of States Adopted by the Seventh International Conference of American States" (n 39).

86 Barsh (n 82) 58–59; Clare Boronow, "Closing the Accountability Gap for Indian Tribes: Balancing the Right to Self-Determination with the Right to a Remedy" [2012] *Virginia Law Review* 1373, 1413–1414.

87 Boronow (n 86) 1414.

88 Ibid. 1377.

89 Anaya, "Indian Givers" (n 83) 119. Barsh (n 82) 58 ff.

which makes international investment law even more idiosyncratic. While one of the early reasons that led indigenous people to seek participation in international processes was to enhance visibility at the national level,[90] today it is clear that they seek the affirmation and recognition of rights both at the international and at the national levels.[91] Thus, their participation in international processes, and their enjoyment of a special status, are facts – the issue is whether there is a right to participation in international processes that could be extended to international investment law.

The right to participation can be defined as a corollary of different rights. In the first place, it can be affirmed as an expression of the right to self-determination.[92] Indigenous peoples' right to self-determination has an interesting history. Technically, their right to self-determination is not a new reality in international law: already in the late nineteenth century, Calvo provides a lengthy explanation of the reasons why self-governance (in fact, he speaks of "semi-sovereignty") of North American indigenous peoples does not jeopardize US statehood.[93] An important aspect that Calvo underlines is

90 Alison Brysk, "Turning Weakness into Strength: The Internationalization of Indian Rights" (1996) 23 *Latin American Perspectives* 38. (Arguing that indigenous peoples resorted to the international system because of domestic powerlessness.) Affirming this to be the case also for US indigenous peoples, Curtis G. Berkey, "International Law and Domestic Courts: Enhancing Self-Determination for Indigenous Peoples" (1992) 5 *Harvard Human Rights Journal* 65, 75. For a more cautious approach, which argues that, in some cases, internationalization strengthened Latin American indigenous movements' struggle for the affirmation of their identities, see Yashar, "Resistance and Identity Politics in an Age of Globalization" (n 12).

91 Boronow goes much further to argue that indigenous peoples may be held internationally responsible for violations of human rights. Boronow (n 86).

92 United Nations (n 2), articles 3 and 4. Organization of American States, "American Declaration on the Rights of Indigenous Peoples, Adopted at the Third Plenary Session Held on June 15, 2016, OAS Doc AG/RES.2888 (XLVI-O/16)" (n 2), article III. Both the UNDRIP and the ADRIP are soft law instruments, but enjoy relatively strong support by states. The preparatory works that led to the adoption of the UNDRIP suggest that consensus began to emerge that the right to self-determination applied to indigenous peoples; see Alexandra Xanthaki, "Indigenous Rights in International Law over the Last 10 Years and Future Developments Feature: Reflections on a Decade of International Law" (2009) 10 *Melbourne Journal of International Law* 27. Indigenous peoples participating in the works that preceded and led to the adoption of the UNDRIP argued that the customary international law right to self-determination applied to them – see Megan Davis, "The United Nations Declaration on the Rights of Indigenous Peoples Commentary" (2007) 11 *Australian Indigenous Law Review* 55. Affirming the customary law character of the right to self-determination, Berkey (n 90) 81.

93 Calvo (n 14) 104–105 para 59. Note that the term "quasi-sovereignty" resonates with the term "quasi-state actors" that appears in Boronow (n 86) 1382 (claiming that indigenous peoples are "not non-state actors" and that they "are more accurately quasi-state actors in that they exercise inherent governmental powers").

that England and, later the US, would not interfere with indigenous people's affairs except to prevent their entering into agreements with enemy or rival nations.[94] Calvo's account is reinforced by Berkey, who offers a solid description of the historical development of the manner that US indigenous peoples' right to self-determination has been reduced to internal self-determination, that is, self-governance.[95]

Nevertheless, much more recently, when indigenous peoples made the case for being recognized as enjoying the right to self-determination at the UN debates that preceded the adoption of the UNDRIP, the right to self-determination became a thorny issue.[96] The interpretations of the nature and extension of the right, as affirmed by the UNDRIP and later by the ADRIP, vary.[97] In our view, the best interpretation is that both instruments acknowledge that the right to self-determination that exists in international law applies also to indigenous peoples, as indigenous peoples have defended.[98]

As to the scope, the right should not be formally divided into internal and external self-determination,[99] but it should be defined as a continuum

---

94   Calvo (n 14) 104–105.

95   Berkey (n 90).

96   Robert T. Coulter, "The Law of Self-Determination and the United Nations Declaration on the Rights of Indigenous Peoples" (2010) 15 *UCLA Journal of International Law and Foreign Affairs* 1.

97   Benedict Kingsbury and William S. Grodinsky, "Self-Determination and 'Indigenous Peoples'" (1992) 86 Proceedings of the Annual Meeting (American Society of International Law) 383; Berkey (n 90); Bartolome Clavero, "The Indigenous Rights of Participation and International Development Policies" (2005) 22 *Arizona Journal of International and Comparative Law* 41; Davis (n 92); James Anaya, "Indigenous Peoples' Participatory Rights in Relation to Decisions about Natural Resource Extraction: The More Fundamental Issue of What Rights Indigenous Peoples Have in Lands and Resources" (2005) 22 *Arizona Journal of International and Comparative Law* 7; Xanthaki (n 92); Sarah Nykolaishen, "Customary International Law and the Declaration on the Rights of Indigenous Peoples" (2012) 17 *Appeal: Review of Current Law and Law Reform* 111; Ricardo Pereira and Orla Gough, "Permanent Sovereignty over Natural Resources in the 21st Century: Natural Resource Governance and the Right to Self-Determination of Indigenous Peoples under International Law" (2013) 14 *Melbourne Journal of International Law* 451; Coulter (n 96); Siegfried Wiessner, "Indigenous Sovereignty: A Reassessment in Light of the UN Declaration on the Rights of Indigenous People" (2008) 41 *Vanderbilt Journal of Transnational Law* 1141.

98   Against this view, differentiating between the right to self-determination acknowledged in the preamble of the UNDRIP and the right to self-determination affirmed in articles 3 and 4 of the same UNDRIP, see Coulter (n 96).

99   Indeed, the US attempt to qualify the right to self-determination as internal self-determination in the UNDRIP had not been successful, and the US has come to support the UNDRIP. See ibid. 21–22.

or plexus of rights,[100] which ultimately would include the right to secession had this not been expressly rejected.[101] Indigenous peoples' right to participate in international processes can be read into this plexus or continuum of rights,[102] but it is also important to note that the right to self-determination has always encompassed participation in decision-making.[103] Moreover, and in second place, whenever participation in international processes is crucial for the protection of other rights, such as the right to property, to cultural heritage or to development,[104] it seems unavoidable that the right to participation must be affirmed in the international sphere.[105]

But the problem of invisibility should also be addressed at the political level. As seen, international investment law rests on an exclusionary development model (trickle-down economics). For indigenous peoples, development has a more nuanced meaning when contrasted with the models that have prevailed in the region, and the model that permeates the regime of

---

100 Jan Klabbers, "The Right to Be Taken Seriously: Self-Determination in International Law" (2006) 28 *Human Rights Quarterly* 186; Coulter (n 96) 15–16.

101 United Nations (n 2), article 46 (1); Organization of American States, "American Declaration on the Rights of Indigenous Peoples, Adopted at the Third Plenary Session Held on June 15, 2016, OAS Doc AG/RES.2888 (XLVI-O/16)" (n 2), article IV. ("Nothing in this Declaration may be interpreted as implying for any State, people, group or person any right to engage in any activity or to perform any act contrary to the Charter of the United Nations or construed as authorizing or encouraging any action which would dismember or impair, totally or in part, the territorial integrity or political unity of sovereign and independent States"). On this point, S. James Anaya, "The Capacity of International Law to Advance Ethnic or Nationality Rights Claims Essays" (1989) 75 *Iowa Law Review* 837. Some authors argue that the right to self-determination continues to include the right to secession as a last resort mechanism; however, this is beyond the scope of the present work. See Coulter (n 96); Pereira and Gough (n 97) 470.

102 Coulter (n 96) 16.

103 Klabbers (n 100) 203. ("Here the importance of political participation comes in. A right to participate enables everyone to take part in political decision making, however small the part may be. It is no coincidence that Hannah Arendt referred to the right to participate (in the context of citizenship) as 'the right to have rights,' indicating that all other possible rights presuppose membership in a political community").

104 Respectively, article 31 UNDRIP and article XXVIII ADRIP; and article 23 UNDRIP and article XXIX ADRIP. United Nations (n 2); Organization of American States, "American Declaration on the Rights of Indigenous Peoples, Adopted at the Third Plenary Session Held on June 15, 2016, OAS Doc AG/RES.2888 (XLVI-O/16)" (n 2).

105 Indeed, UNDRIP Article 40 states that "Indigenous peoples have the right to access to and prompt decision through just and fair procedures for the resolution of conflicts and disputes with States or other parties, as well as to effective remedies for all infringements of their individual and collective rights." United Nations (n 2). Similarly, Boronow (n 86) 1414.

investment agreements. For indigenous peoples, development must occur with the preservation of their identities.[106] The communities themselves are responsible for setting the goals for their development.[107] Because of the role indigenous people play in, for instance, the protection of the environment,[108] because of the importance of their traditional knowledge for the preservation of ecosystems and for addressing the effects of climate change, the lack of sustainable development for indigenous peoples rebounds in the lack of sustainable development for other members of the society.[109]

The discussions about international investment law and sustainable development are not new.[110] However, these discussions do not go far enough in terms of the inclusion of indigenous peoples, essentially because the discussions tend to reinforce – rather than question – the role of the government vis-à-vis investors, calling for the strengthening on the regulatory powers of the government and the restricting of the rights of investors. This approach (strengthening of government; weakening of investors) is understandable – also Stiglitz calls for the reaffirmation of the regulatory powers of the government.[111] While this approach tackles inequality in important ways, it fails to address the problem of invisibility that affects indigenous peoples. Consequently, it is necessary to reformulate the concept of sustainable development in international investment law, to affirm the need for indigenous peoples to actively participate in defining the matters affecting their development.

The participation of indigenous people in decision-making ought to be embedded in meaningful consultation procedures in certain treaty

---

106 Organization of American States, "American Declaration on the Rights of Indigenous Peoples, Adopted at the Third Plenary Session Held on June 15, 2016, OAS Doc AG/RES.2888 (XLVI-O/16)" (n 2), article XXIX.

107 The World Bank (n 13) 14. ("…this report acknowledges that these indicators offer only a partial view of the obstacles preventing many indigenous peoples from achieving their chosen paths of development").

108 Intergovernmental Science-Policy Platform on Biodiversity and Ecosystem Services, "Summary for Policymakers of the Global Assessment Report on Biodiversity and Ecosystem Services" (Zenodo 2019) https://zenodo.org/record/3553579 accessed 14 May 2020.

109 Droubi and Heffron (n 21).

110 Andrew Newcombe, "Sustainable Development and Investment Treaty Law" (2007) 8 *The Journal of World Investment & Trade* 357; Howard Mann, "Reconceptualizing International Investment Law: Its Role in Sustainable Development Business Law Forum: Balancing Investor Protections, the Environment, and Human Rights" (2013) 17 *Lewis & Clark Law Review* 521; Kathryn Gordon, Joachim Pohl, and Marie Bouchard, "Investment Treaty Law, Sustainable Development and Responsible Business Conduct: A Fact Finding Survey" (OECD 2014) 2014/01 https://papers.ssrn.com/sol3/papers.cfm?abstract_id=2469662 accessed 10 June 2020.

111 Stiglitz, *Making Globalization Work* (n 72).

negotiations that, if ratified, would affect their lives. The right to participation emanates from indigenous peoples' rights to self-determination, as
well as from other rights such as the right to property, acting as a limitation to state sovereignty.[112] In this regard, a meaningful consultation
process requires states to obtain the "free, prior and informed consent" of
indigenous peoples; further, states ought to ensure that indigenous peoples
participate in determining the direction of the proposed development, considering the social and environmental implications to those communities.[113]
Thus, meaningful consultations should not be overridden by an "after the
fact" reparation or compensation, a point to which we come back later
when addressing justice.

In this vein, the interpretation of human rights provisions have given rise
to procedural obligations that are indispensable for respecting and protecting substantive human rights, notably, access to information, consultation,
and public participation.[114] Thus, human rights are pivotal for resisting
unsustainable development,[115] and the involvement of indigenous peoples is
key in such endeavor. However, these procedural rights emerge from human
rights instruments as well as from international environmental agreements,
as opposed to international investment law and agreements themselves,
thus limiting the visibility (and affecting the equality) of indigenous peoples

112 Lorenzo Cotula, "Land, Property and Sovereignty in International Law" (2017)
   25 *Cardozo Journal of International and Comparative Law* 219. (In relation to
   property rights, Cotula argues that there is a reconfiguration of the material dimension of the relationships between land, property, and sovereignty, which have been
   transformed by human rights, international investment law, and environmental law.
   This reconfiguration has limited the spaces in which the states can lawfully exercise
   their sovereignty in relation to property rights in their jurisdiction. Cotula recognises
   that property rights need to be taken into consideration along with the right to self-
   determination of indigenous peoples; otherwise, investors and indigenous peoples
   would be at the same level); John Agnew and Ulrich Ostender, "Territorialidades
   Superpuestas, Soberanía En Disputa: Lecciones Empíricas Desde América Latina"
   (2009) 13 *Tabula Rasa*. (Recognizing in debates in political geography the existence
   of "overlapping territorialities," in which the territorialities of the state and indigenous peoples overlap, creating spaces for the impugnation of sovereignty. This
   plurality of territories, where diverse sources of authority emanate, do not necessarily exclude each other).
113 Cotula (n 112); Organization of American States, "American Declaration on the
   Rights of Indigenous Peoples, Adopted at the Third Plenary Session Held on June
   15, 2016, OAS Doc AG/RES.2888 (XLVI-O/16)."
114 Francesco Francioni, "Natural Resources and Human Rights," *International
   Law and Natural Resources* (Elisa Morgera and Kati Kulovesi (eds.), Research
   Handbook on International Law and Natural Resources, Edward Elgar Publishing
   Limited 2016).
115 Ibid.

vis-à-vis foreign investors.[116] Indeed, some authors argue for the reformation of substantive standards to embed human rights obligations into norms for the protection of foreign investment, and ultimately, into investment treaty clauses.[117] Moreover, indigenous peoples' right to participation should also be extended to dispute settlement, specifically, investor–state arbitral tribunals. Amicus curiae is insufficient to guarantee the right to be heard because the acceptance and consideration of amici depends on the discretion of the arbitral tribunals.[118] Thus, there are increasing calls to give indigenous peoples the right to intervene as third parties in cases in which their interest have been affected.[119]

Nevertheless, increasing the visibility and equality of indigenous peoples entails much more than the right to participation in decision-making processes and arbitral tribunals. There is a need to revisit the concept of justice in order to address the systemic issues of international investment law, and in this chapter, we propose energy justice as a framework to rethink the development and the processes promoted by the regime of foreign investments.

Fostering equality for indigenous peoples

Investor–state disputes, in which issues of inequality emerge, constitute a challenge also to arbitrators. For instance, even if (and this is a big if)

116 Jorge E. Viñuales, "Foreign Direct Investment: International Investment Law and Natural Resource Governance," in Elisa Morgera and Kati Kulovesi (eds) *Research Handbook on International Law and Natural Resources* (Edward Elgar Publishing 2016) (in relation to the tensions between what he has called the "State-Investor-Population" Triangle, i.e. the misalignment of the interest between foreign investors, the host sate and its population in the context of the use of natural resources); Julio Faundez, "The Governance of Natural Resources in Latin America: The Commodities Consensus and the Policy Space Conundrum," *Natural Resources and Sustainable Development* (Celine Tan and Julio Faundez, Edward Elgar Publishing Limited 2017)(arguing that developing countries face difficulties in the reconciliation and management of the clashes between the rules for the protection of foreign investment and conventions for the protection of human rights and the environment. Faundez attributes the efficiency of the former to the distinction between hard and soft law, in which international human rights and international environmental instruments are considered soft law due to their imprecision or lack of enforceability. However, Faundez recognises that human rights and environmental obligations are hard law in the context of some Latin American countries as these obligations have been incorporated into their domestic legislations.

117 Cotula (n 112). C.f. Chapter 10 by Rodrigo Polanco Lazo and Felipe Ferreira Catalán (arguing that "the human rights dimension can be recognised in international investment law," the latter evolving to introduce protections in human rights instruments into some international investment agreements).

118 See for example: *Bear Creek v Peru* (Award 2017) (n 17).

119 El-Hosseny (n 26). See below the case study on the right to participation in arbitral proceedings.

arbitrators may see that, in a case at hand, the enforcement of certain standards of protection (fair and equitable treatment, full security) clearly perpetuates inequality on the ground – arbitrators may see no other way but by enforcing the standards, which leads to the automatic enforcement of these standards – unless very high threshold exceptions and defenses (for instance, necessity, contributory fault) are present. The reasons for their seeing no alternative are beyond the present scope – but their background, their overall highly fragmentary approach to law, and the fact that investor lawyers constitute a somewhat insulated epistemic community are certainly some of the reasons. But it could be argued that the clearer the inequalities are, the more reasons the arbitrators may have to change their approach. This is evidenced by decisions which have to deal with strong resistance put up by indigenous peoples and local communities, and which resort to certain concepts (such as contributory fault) in an attempt to address the linkages between the investor's behavior, the resistance, and the government's actions.[120]

At this moment, two facts are important. On the one hand, mounting resistance by indigenous and local populations becomes a factor that cannot be ignored by the arbitrator insofar as the defendant government invokes it to justify the actions of which the investor complains. So, resistance constitutes a reason for both the government to change its policy and the arbitrators to seek new approaches in deciding the case. On the other hand, it is possible to see that the regime of investment treaties contains certain elements that are leading to its own transformation from inside – elements that offer to arbitrators, for instance, solid grounds for new approaches to cases involving issues of inequality. Examples are the change in the language of certain treaties so as to ensure the promotion of sustainable development;[121] the attempt that arbitrators make to bring rules and principles from other fields (for instance, human rights) to weigh in on their decisions;[122] as well as the attempt of investment law scholars to propose theories accommodating these moves into a renewed notion of investment law.

The literature on energy justice falls into a fourth category – the attempt by scholars and practitioners dedicated to the sectors of energy and extractive industries, to reform the field so as to promote equality. Because the concept of energy justice is truly interdisciplinary (drawing on different legal and

---

120 See Chapters 11 by Farouk El-Hosseny, Patrick Devine, and Ilan Brun-Vargas and Chapter 13 by Sebastián Preller-Bórquez in this volume.
121 See Chapter 11 by Farouk El-Hosseny, Patrick Devine, and Ilan Brun-Vargas in this volume.
122 See Chapters 10 by Rodrigo Polanco Lazo and Felipe Ferreira Catalán and 11 by Farouk El-Hosseny, Patrick Devine, and Ilan Brun-Vargas in this volume.

non-legal fields),[123] it helps overcoming the fragmentation of international law and the insulation of investment lawyers from other fields. Because it defines inequality as a problem in terms of justice and argues that respect to certain principles and rules (access to justice, due process, meaningful participation, respect to human rights) is a corollary of justice, it provides solid grounds for the application of such principles and rules within international investment law, and even by investment tribunals. But the concept is also important because it originated in the energy (and energy law) literature. This is a characteristic of the concept that makes it relevant for the present analysis. It is not by chance that the cases before international arbitration tribunals, which affect Latin American indigenous peoples, are in extractive and energy sectors. First, the sectors are very important for the Latin American economy. Second, the nature of the energy sector is one that is centered around risk, and a poor record of environmental, social, and governance issues. Third, because of the geography of the region, the impact of the sector on indigenous peoples has been significant – which is transparent in the pollution of lands and waters.[124] In this manner, proposals for the reform of the energy sector, to foster equality, have the potential to reverberate in international investment law, as they call for the application of principles of international law, and as the call is embedded in a narrative that directly targets, among others, lawyers dedicated to investment law. The epistemic community of investment lawyers cannot ignore this, and formal fragmentation can be overcome with the emphasis on principles of law and on justice.

At its simplest, energy justice is about ensuring respect to fundamental human rights across the so-called energy life cycle, from extraction to production to operation (and supply) to consumption to waste management (including decommissioning). Energy justice provides a comprehensive framework for action as it moves us towards five dimensions of justice.[125] Procedural justice affirms the principles of equality and non-discrimination, due process and the need to comply with legal procedures at local, national, and international levels. Recognition justice is concerned with the

---

123 Jenkins and others (n 21); Heffron and McCauley (n 21); Heffron (n 21); Raphael J Heffron and Darren McCauley, "What Is the 'Just Transition'?" (2018) 88 *Geoforum* 74; Raphael J Heffron, 'The Role of Justice in Developing Critical Minerals' (2020) In Press *The Extractive Industries and Society* https://doi.org/10.1016/j.exis.2020.06.018.

124 Several cases show the impact of foreign investments into the oil and gas sector on indigenous peoples (mostly in the form of pollution). *Copper Mesa v Ecuador* (Award 2016) (n 17); *Chevron v Ecuador (II)* (Second Partial Award 2018) (n 17); *Bear Creek v Peru* (Award 2017) (n 17).

125 Raphael J. Heffron and Darren McCauley, "The Concept of Energy Justice across the Disciplines" (2017) 105 *Energy Policy* 658

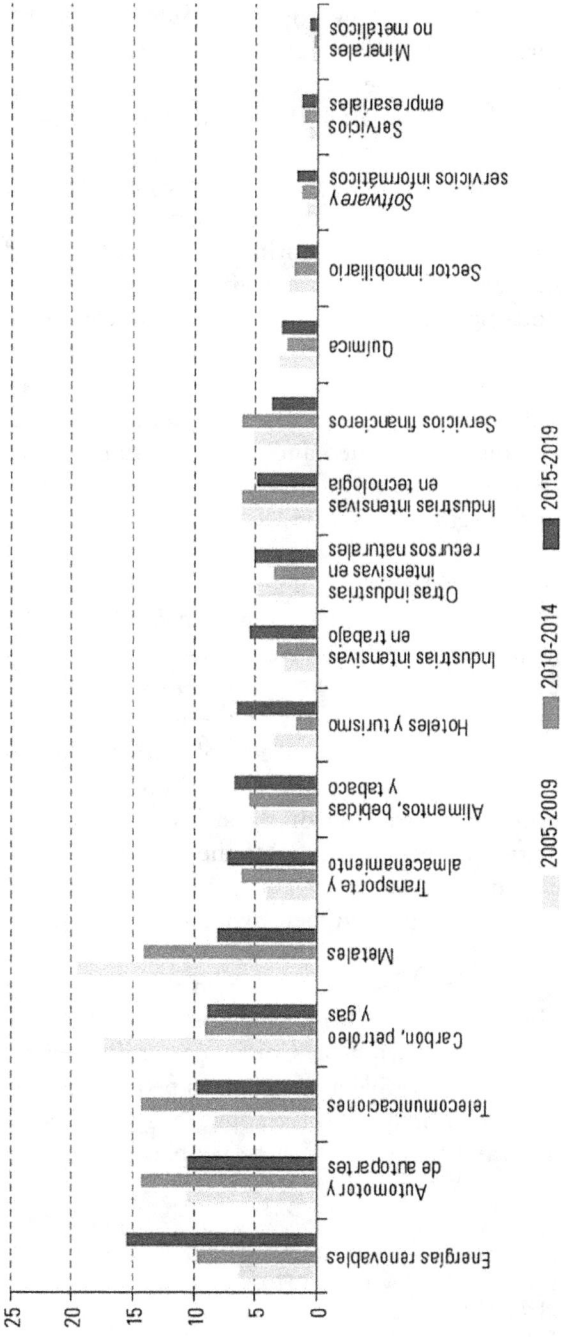

Figure 9.4 Announcements of new projects by sector

Legend:
2005-2009 2010-2014 2015-2019

Sectors (axis categories):
- Energías renovables
- Automotor y de autopartes
- Telecomunicaciones
- Carbón, petróleo y gas
- Metales
- Transporte y almacenamiento
- Alimentos, bebidas y tabaco
- Hoteles y turismo
- Industrias intensivas en trabajo
- Otras industrias intensivas en recursos naturales
- Industrias intensivas en tecnología
- Servicios financieros
- Química
- Sector inmobiliario
- Software y servicios informáticos
- Servicios empresariales
- Minerales no metálicos

recognition of rights of different groups as a (mineral, oil, and gas etc.) project development happens. The concern is whether the rights of indigenous peoples are properly recognized. Distributive justice concerns the distribution of benefits from the energy sector and also the negatives. The main questions that arise are whether (for instance, oil and gas) revenues are shared sufficiently and who bears the costs of the environmental and social damages. Cosmopolitanism justice stems from the belief that we are all citizens of the world. The question is whether transborder and global effects of a project have been considered: the world is defined as one global industry and therefore there will be cross-border effects from energy activities. In terms of indigenous peoples, cosmopolitanism concerns, for instance, the role of indigenous peoples, and the significance of their traditional knowledge, for the preservation of eco-regimes, which affect whole regions or the whole world. Finally, restorative justice requires that any injustice caused by the energy sector should be rectified and it focuses on the need for enforcement of particular laws (i.e., energy sites should be returned to former use, hence waste management policy and decommissioning should be properly done).

As we noted, the language that some of the literature adopts is clearly directed to practitioners in the sectors. For instance, a key practitioner guide written on energy justice identifies a framework for applying energy justice theory to practice (see Figure 9.5).[126]

There is not space to go into details of the five dimensions here, but it is worth calling the attention to the aspects of recognition and procedural justice, since we have been dealing with these aspects in this piece. Energy justice calls for proper recognition of the different social actors that are affected by an energy project. It highlights the need to attend "arguments, feelings and values" of these actors.[127] Further, energy justice calls for recognition of the indigenous peoples on their own terms rather than in the terms of the majority of the population.[128] So, it is not only a question of recognizing those indigenous peoples, who are often ignored in decision-making processes, but it is equally a question of understanding how they should be recognized.[129] Crucially, drawing on Convention 169, energy justice reaffirms that recognition of a people as indigenous people is based on the self-identification of the people in question; second, the social, cultural, religious, and spiritual values and practices of these peoples must be protected and

---

126 Initiative for Energy Justice, *The Energy Justice Workbook* (2019) Available at: https://iejusa.org/wp-content/uploads/2019/12/The-Energy-Justice-Workbook-2019-web.pdf accessed 29 November 2020.
127 McCauley et al. (n 21).
128 Droubi and Heffron (n 21).
129 Jenkins et al. (n 21).

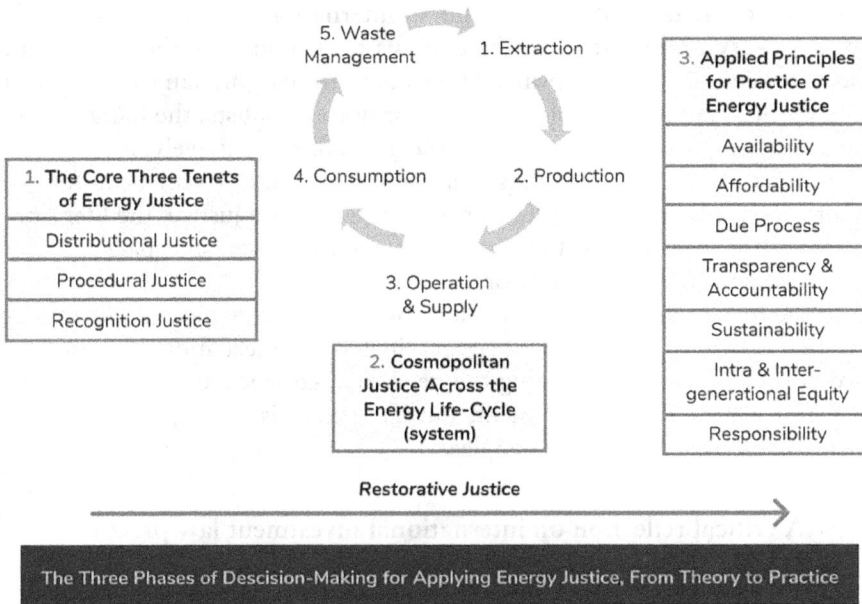

5. Waste
Management

1. Extraction

1. The Core Three Tenets of Energy Justice
Distributional Justice
Procedural Justice
Recognition Justice

4. Consumption

2. Production

3. Operation
& Supply

2. Cosmopolitan Justice Across the Energy Life-Cycle (system)

3. Applied Principles for Practice of Energy Justice
Availability
Affordability
Due Process
Transparency & Accountability
Sustainability
Intra & Inter-generational Equity
Responsibility

Restorative Justice

The Three Phases of Descision-Making for Applying Energy Justice, From Theory to Practice

Figure 9.5 Energy justice from theory to practice

the integrity of their values, practices, and institutions must be respected in national development and individual projects. Note how principles of international human rights law become standards of conduct for the industry (for instance, they are grounds for a strong defense of the social license to operate)[130] – but also become principles that must be observed to ensure justice for indigenous peoples.

Procedural justice calls for compliance with legal processes from start to finish of a project, but emphasizes equality and non-discrimination, making certain links that are valuable for the discussion.[131] Heffron argues that "community engagement in decision-making touches upon the democratic ideal of procedural due process,"[132] recalls that scholars affirm that public participation may have the character of customary international law,[133] and

130 Heffron (n 21). Also see Chapter 13 by Sebastián Preller-Bórquez in this volume.
131 Jenkins and others (n 21).
132 Raphael J. Heffron, Lauren Downes, Oscar M. Ramirez Rodriguez, and Darren McCauley, "The Emergence of the 'Social Licence to Operate' in the Extractive Industries?" (2018) Resources Policy.
133 Ibid.; Chilenye Nwapi, "Can the Concept of Social Licence to Operate Find Its Way into the Formal Legal System Special Issue: Based on Papers from the 2015 Law and Society Association of Australia and New Zealand (LSAANZ) Conference" (2016) 18 *Flinders Law Journal* 349.

notes the affirmation of the principle in international conventions.[134] It is not necessary to go further in the analysis to demonstrate the point: with the reframing of rules and principles of international (human rights) law in terms of justice, in accessible language for non-specialists, the literature on energy justice promotes a change on the ground, progressively, it promotes diffusion and acceptance of these rules and principles. With its call for the enforcement of these principles as necessary to ensure justice, the literature strengthens the principles. In this manner, energy justice helps pave the way for their application by arbitrators.

In the following section, we explore two situations which elucidate that practice in international economic law, including international investment law, is progressively recognizing the need to acknowledge indigenous peoples and sustainable development, but that there is a long way to go to ensure justice for indigenous peoples.

A critical reflection on international investment law practice

Based on the above, a new concept of international investment law could be articulated. On the one hand, the flexibilization of statehood allows for the affirmation of the right of indigenous peoples to participate in all levels of the decision-making affecting their lives, from treaty negotiation to the decision about specific investment projects to the settling of disputes. On the other hand, the emphasis on sustainable development, human rights, and justice, allows the affirmation of their right to participate in the riches derived from the exploitation and exploration of natural resources in their lands. In this manner, international investment law is "freed" from the current practice under investment treaties and redefined as the law regulating the relationships arising from the international flows of investment, the relationship among investors, states, indigenous peoples – and potentially other participants in the international sphere. One should note that this renewed concept only indirectly leads to the imposition of responsibilities and obligations on investors because, as the focus is placed on indigenous people as an international actor, the main concern is that of reaffirming indigenous peoples' rights. In any case, the topic of corporate social responsibility is outside the scope of the present chapter. In this section, we draw on this renewed concept to provide a reflection on the current practice, in the form of negotiation of treaties and investor–state arbitration.

As the negotiation of the EU–MERCOSUR Trade Agreement, which also regulates investments, illustrates, the participation of indigenous peoples in international investment agreements, and ultimately, in defining sustainable

---

134 Heffron et al. (n 132).

development in their territories remains very limited. After 20 years of negotiations, the EU and the MERCOSUR bloc (Brazil, Argentina, Paraguay, and
Uruguay) agreed on the trade pillar of the EU–MERCOSUR Association –
the EU–MERCOSUR Trade Agreement.[135] The EU–MERCOSUR Trade
Agreement states that the Parties should "facilitate the movement of goods
and services from and within the regions." Notably, the Trade Agreement
includes a chapter on "Trade and Sustainable Development" for the integration of sustainable development into trade and investment relationships
(article 1 of the chapter), specifically concerning labor and environmental
issues, recognizing its economic, social, and environmental elements.
Subjecting the enhancement of trade and investment to sustainable development is a step forward in the negotiation of trade agreements. This also
reflects a growing investment treaty practice of incorporating sustainable
development- an important example being the Brazilian cooperation and
facilitation investment agreement, as discussed at length in the first part of
this volume.

The Trade Agreement states that the Parties will integrate sustainable
development by "developing trade and economic relations with the view
of achieving the Sustainable Development Goals," particularly in relation
to labor standards and the environment, by respecting multilateral commitments on labor and the environment, and by increasing cooperation
amongst the Parties.[136] However, the agreement promotes provisions on
trade that seem at odds with the objective of sustainable development, given
the emphasis on increasing the export of commodities linked to deforestation in the region such as sugar, palm oil, beef, and soy.[137] Furthermore,
indigenous peoples remain significantly invisible in the development of the
conception of sustainable development. Indeed, the "Trade and Sustainable
Development" chapter only "promotes", when appropriate and with their

135 EU–Mercosur Trade Agreement: The Agreement in Principle and its Texts (2019)
    (*EU–Mercosur Agreement in Principle*). The Trade Agreement has been agreed only
    in principle and its final text would have to be subjected to a process of ratification
    as part of the association agreement. Also, the text of the association agreement
    has not yet made public by the parties, although a non-governmental organiza-
    tion – Greenpeace Germany – has published in its website a leaked version of the
    text. Greenpeace European Unit, "EU-Mercosur: Leaked Treaty Has No Climate
    Protection, Undermines Democracy" (9 October 2020) www.greenpeace.org/eu-
    unit/issues/democracy-europe/45133/eu-mercosur-leaked-treaty-has-no-climate-
    protection-undermines-democracy/ accessed 17 December 2020.
136 *EU–Mercosur Agreement in Principle* (n 135).
137 Julian Burger, "Challenges for Environmental and Indigenous Peoples' Rights in
    the Amazon Region" (European Parliament 2020) Policy Department for External
    Relations, Directorate General for External Policies of the Union PE 603.488;
    "What's behind the EU-MERCOSUR Trade Agreement" (*Climate Alliance*) www.
    climatealliance.org/activities/european-policy/eu-mercosur.html.

prior informed consent, the involvement of indigenous peoples in relation to the sustainable management of forest for the supply chains of timber and non-timber products.[138] Even more so, the hallmark for trade in products from sustainable managed forests is the law of the country of harvest.[139] At a time when members of MERCOSUR, specifically Brazil, are weakening protections to explore and exploit indigenous peoples' territories,[140] these provisions fall short of ensuring the participation of indigenous peoples in meaningful consultations and in defining sustainable development. Without a meaningful participation, the provision of cosmopolitanism justice is at risk, despite the recognition of indigenous peoples' role in the management of forests. Only when a meaningful participation is ensured, as opposed to merely promoted, the benefits of indigenous peoples' traditional knowledge on the protection of ecosystems can further expand to the whole world.

The EU–MERCOSUR Trade Agreement includes a dispute resolution mechanism in the "Trade and Sustainable Development" chapter, but separate from the general dispute settlement mechanism, and limited in scope. As such, one of the Parties can request the establishment of a Panel of Experts to examine the issue at stake and draft a report with the view of exerting pressure through the publication of the report, thus reducing the enforceability of the measures.[141] However, these dispute resolution mechanisms would not alleviate the invisibility and inequality of indigenous peoples because this would necessitate the state Party, whose interests and understanding of sustainable development may differ from those of indigenous peoples, to lodge a complaint. To ensure justice, in all its dimensions, there needs to be an effective and enforceable system to rectify any injustices concerning the labor and environmental issues that the treaty aims to protect. Burger recommends the establishment of "an effective, affordable and culturally accessible grievance mechanism" at the EU for indigenous peoples to raise allegations of violations by EU corporations relating to the right to participation in decision-making in development projects.[142] This mechanism would certainly increase the visibility of indigenous people if

---

138 *EU–Mercosur Agreement in Principle* (n 135).

139 Ibid.

140 "What's behind the EU-MERCOSUR Trade Agreement" (n 137). Sufyan Droubi, Letícia M Osório and Luiz Eloy Terena, 'The Brazilian Federal Supreme Court Comes to the Protection of Indigenous People's Right to Health in the Face of Covid-19' (*EJIL: Talk!*, 23 December 2020) <https://www.ejiltalk.org/the-brazilian-federal-supreme-court-comes-to-the-protection-of-indigenous-peoples-right-to-health-in-the-face-of-covid-19/> accessed 23 December 2020.

141 *EU-Mercosur Agreement in Principle* (n 135). See also, Chapter 8 by Adoración Guamán in this volume.

142 Burger (n 137).

established. However, we argue that steps should be taken not only to "promote" or "encourage" consultations with indigenous peoples in limited cases, but to "ensure" their participation in decision-making through meaningful consultations in the negotiation of treaties that impact their livelihoods, as well as during the lifespan of any project that is agreed with the participation of indigenous peoples. Only then, international investment law would enable the provision of procedural justice. Participating in defining the kind of development that is warranted from foreign investments (and the distribution of burdens and benefits therefrom) will enable indigenous people to share the benefits from investments, a requisite for distributive justice.

Indeed, the EU Commission has established "Civil Society Dialogues" in order to consult all parts of EU civil society;[143] thus, the negotiation of the EU–MERCOSUR Trade Agreement included dialogues with EU civil society. Furthermore, the Sustainability Impact Assessment Report for the EU–MERCOSUR Trade Agreement included a consultation process with stakeholders and civil society.[144] However, the participation of indigenous peoples either directly or through civil society organizations seemed mostly absent. The Sustainability Impact Assessment Report recommends MERCOSUR members to strengthen their institutional frameworks to protect indigenous rights, and the EU, to encourage European corporations to engage in consultations with indigenous peoples prior to investing in MERCOSUR states.[145] Noticeably, the recommendation focuses on preventing land disputes after planning investment in the area, rather than on the protection of indigenous peoples' rights. Moreover, the recommendations center on strengthening the participation of indigenous peoples at the domestic level, as opposed to increasing their right to participation at the

143 European Commission, "EU Trade Meetings with Civil Society" (*Dialogues*) https://trade.ec.europa.eu/civilsoc/. See Chapter 8 by Adoracin Guamán (explaining that the term civil society is used broadly in the EU context and thus, civil society encompasses corporations, as well as discussing the synergies and cross-fertilizations between social movements in LA and Europe).

144 "Sustainability Impact Assessment in Support of the Association Agreement Negotiations between the European Union and MERCOSUR" (London School of Economics and Political Science 2020); London School of Economics and Political Science, "Sustainability Impact Assessment in Support of the Association between the European Union and MERCOSUR" (2019) Draft Interim Report. The interim report was published after the EU–MERCOSUR Trade Agreement had been agreed in principle and therefore, the recommendations were not incorporated into the agreement.

145 "Sustainability Impact Assessment in Support of the Association Agreement Negotiations between the European Union and MERCOSUR" (n 144).

international level. Hence, these dialogues, and the recommendations there-from, fail to meaningfully increase the visibility of indigenous peoples and to promote fairness by ensuring their meaningful consultation in the negoti-ation of the EU–MERCOSUR Trade Agreement.

Besides the participation of indigenous peoples in certain treaty negoti-ation, debates about the right to participation extend to dispute settlement, in particular, investor–state arbitral tribunals. Currently, the only means of participation for civil society in investment arbitral tribunals lies on the submission of amicus curiae.[146] But, as for instance the cases of *Chevron v Ecuador* and *Bear Creek v Peru* suggest, and as evidenced in case law, there is no consistency among tribunals when dealing with non-parties applica-tions to file written submissions.[147] Moreover, as the literature clearly dem-onstrates, requests to participate more significantly in the proceedings are rejected.[148] In this regards, recent proposals to affirm the participation of civil society in investor–state disputes as third parties gain more substance.[149] Access to arbitral tribunal proceedings is even more relevant in those cases in which foreign investments affects indigenous peoples, without partici-pating in meaningful consultations, where their "free, prior and informed" consent is not obtained during the initial stages of the foreign investment.[150]

However, the implementation of third-party intervention in investor–state disputes face procedural and substantive challenges – from the absence of rules on third-party intervention, to the lack of recognition of third-party intervention in treaties, to the restriction of initiating proceedings to for-eign investors.[151] El-Hosseny makes the case for the implementation of 'non-party' third party intervention on the discretion of arbitral tribunals, in which civil society would be able to "raise, assert and defend" the direct interests of affected communities.[152] As allowing civil society to intervene as a non-disputing party would depend on the arbitral tribunal's discretion, the intervention could be adapted to the circumstances of the case to pre-vent causing prejudice to the disputing parties. Furthermore, non-disputing third-party interveners would have to establish a "direct and substantial

146 El-Hosseny (n 26); Cotula (n 112).
147 *Bear Creek v. Peru (n 17)* (Procedural Order No 5, 21 July 2016) (granting the request for leave); *Chevron v. Ecuador (II) (n 17)* (Procedural Order No 8, 18 April 2011) (rejecting the request for leave).
148 Lucas Bastin, "Amici Curiae in Investor-State Arbitrations: Two Recent Decisions" (2013) 20 *Austl. Int'l LJ* 95; Lucas Bastin, "Amici Curiae in Investor-State Arbitration: Eight Recent Trends" (2014) 30 *Arbitration International* 125.
149 El-Hosseny (n 26).
150 Ibid, 273.
151 Ibid.
152 Ibid, 281.

interest in the outcome of the arbitration," one that has a compelling connection to human rights or the environment.[153] Some authors argue that third-party intervention, even when granted as a 'non-party', will enable civil society to make written and oral submissions to the investor–state arbitral tribunal, i.e. third-party intervention would allow them the right to be heard.[154] However, seemingly, arbitral tribunals would only accept requests for third-party intervention insofar as there are "explicit treaty or arbitration rules" that enable the addition of parties to investor–state disputes, or where both parties to a dispute give their consent.[155] Hence proposals to grant third-party intervention to civil society, even as a 'non-party', would require amending current international investment agreements, or including such provision in new agreements.

The granting of third-party intervention ('non-party') is grounded on the rationale that the only disputing parties in investor–state disputes are the state and the foreign investor, with the foreign investor being the only one with the standing to initiate proceedings. In this regard, third-party intervention concerns "interests" affected, not rights per se. Thus, securing third-party intervention for indigenous people is not the same as having standing.[156] To understand the significance of this point, one only needs to place it in a broader perspective: despite the gains in visibility in Latin America, indigenous peoples continue to face numerous, sometimes insurmountable challenges in access to justice (from language barriers to legal institutional constraints on their ability to come before courts).[157] The granting of a right to intervene to bring their interests before a tribunal, without ensuring proper standing to defend their rights, only perpetuates inequality.

We have previously argued that indigenous peoples cannot be equated to other non-state actors because they have acquired rights in international law. Hence, third-party intervention, especially when granted as a non-party, is arguably insufficient to address the inequality of indigenous peoples *vis-à-vis* foreign investors. This inequality derives from the lack of recognition of indigenous peoples' right to be heard (and arguably to have standing)

153 Ibid.
154 El-Hosseny (n 26). But see: Osgoode Hall Law School, "Public Statement on the International Investment Regime" www.osgoode.yorku.ca/public-statement-international-investment-regime-31-august-2010/ accessed 5 November 2020 (arguing that civil society organizations and local communities shall be full and equal participants in investor–state disputes along with foreign investors when their interests are affected; otherwise, procedural fairness would not be satisfied.)
155 El-Hosseny (n 26).
156 Ibid.
157 Droubi et al (140).

in arbitral tribunals (recognition justice), the absence of a fair distribution of the benefits from the regime (distributive justice), and the inadequacy of procedural rights for indigenous peoples (procedural justice). Possibly third-party intervention could increase, at least to some extent, the visibility of indigenous peoples as their claims concerning the direct and substantial interest affected by the arbitration could be heard. However, as securing third-party intervention will depend on the discretion of arbitral tribunals in a case-by-case basis, there is limited scope for intervention to account for a meaningful participation in arbitral processes. Indeed, El-Hosseny concedes that securing intervention would depend on civil society making a coherent and robust argument in the same level of sophistication and complexity as the arbitral tribunal and the disputing parties – usually represented by highly technical and qualified arbitrators and lawyers.[158]

As previously discussed, indigenous peoples have been advancing their rights in international law – from lodging cases in Human Rights courts to signing international treaties. Despite this, indigenous peoples are likely to face many challenges when it comes to effectively participating in negotiations of treaties and in procedures before arbitration tribunals. Indigenous peoples may see their options reduced by a diversity of obstacles such as the lack of funds for legal representation, language barriers, institutions that are not equipped to deal with intercultural factors.[159] Hence, even if indigenous peoples increase their visibility through their participation in certain treaty negotiations and in defining sustainable development, as well as on arbitral tribunals, inequality can persist due to the asymmetry inherent to the regime. Therefore, the right to participation should be accompanied with supporting systems that enable indigenous peoples to exercise their rights. In this chapter, we argue that this is an issue with the type of justice that investment law delivers, and we argue that the energy justice framework has much scope to address some of the systemic issues that perpetuate the invisibility and inequality of indigenous peoples in international investment law.

Conclusion

We began calling the attention to the importance of indigenous peoples in Latin America and the Caribbean, to the history of invisibility and inequality which these peoples experience. We noted how resistance became a last resort mechanism for indigenous people to fight for recognition and

---

158 El-Hosseny (n 26).
159 Burger (n 137).

for equality. Nevertheless, we argued that much of the systemic failures persist at the state level and that they reproduce the same conditions that lead to invisibility and inequality. We also argued that international investment law should not be reduced to the investment treaty regime. In so doing, we argued that the extant investment treaty regime, because it emphasizes both statehood and the automatic enforcement of the standards of protection of investors, perpetuates both the invisibility and the inequality that affect Latin American indigenous peoples.

Our analysis, which drew from social and economic critiques of the law, developed to demonstrate the argument, explaining how invisibility at the local level becomes invisibility at the international level. Domestically, discrimination and exclusionary development projects lead to the non-recognition of indigenous peoples and, as the investment treaty regime emphasizes a strong principle of statehood, with the government formally representing all of the peoples in its territory, non-recognition is perpetuated at the international level. Then, we moved to the manner that inequality is reproduced at the international level. We came back to national development projects but to emphasize the neoliberal model that took hold of Latin America and the Caribbean as from 1980s – and which called for and justified the entering by the governments into investment agreements. We explained how trickle-down economics, combined with the notion of uniform development, exacerbate inequality of indigenous and vulnerable populations at the local level; and how the automatic enforcement of standards of protection, without proper appreciation to the underlying social factors, cement these inequalities.

To ensure visibility for indigenous peoples, we argued that international law must change its approach to statehood only to fully acknowledge the status of indigenous peoples as actors in the international sphere. We noted how the investment treaty regime exercised such a hold on international investment law that the latter lagged behind other fields in properly recognizing the status of indigenous peoples. We argued for their recognition based on their right to self-determination, but also as a corollary of their role in the protection of the environment and the maintenance of the carrying capacity of ecosystems. Sustainable development – rather than a development model based on trickle-down economics – is a better model that provides the socio, economic, and legal framework for the recognition of indigenous peoples as actors in investment law. As to the scope of the right to participation, we emphasize the need to secure the free, prior, and informed consent of indigenous peoples. Although this analysis also addressed equality, we decided to take on the topic more openly. We first recalled that arbitrators are challenged when they face inequalities, that arbitrators continue to have a propensity to enforce standards of protection automatically, but that resistance put up by indigenous and local communities can create pressure enough for arbitrators to seek changing their approach. At this moment, we noted that the regime of investment treaties shows elements of transformation, which may offer the grounds for new approaches to be adopted. We emphasised energy justice because it is a truly interdisciplinary concept that originates from within the practice of investments – in the sector that has traditionally created injustices and inequalities for indigenous and vulnerable peoples. We showed how energy justice draws on different fields to reframe rights and obligations as requirements of justice, promoting a change on the ground; and to affirm such rights and obligations as general international law, helping pave the way for their application and enforcement.

We closed with a critique to the practice within the investment treaties regime based on our prior analysis – showing some of the shortcomings of the negotiation of investment treaties, when we discussed the EU-MERCOSUR Trade Agreement, and of the investor–state dispute settlement, when we discussed 'non-party' third party intervention and the issue of effective standing. We drew on our analysis to suggest a way forward. We believe that our analysis, though not exhaustive, offers a holistic contribution, by showing how invisibility and inequality leads resistance and how resistance may eventually accomplish visibility and equality. But we emphasized the need for changes to be implemented in treaty negotiation and implementation as well as in the investor-state arbitration procedures. What transpires from the pages above is a tragic history of invisibility and inequality, but it is also an account of how indigenous peoples won a place as actors in international law and how they may help promote deep changes in the investment treaties regime.

Part III

The mosaic of narratives

10

International investment and human rights in Latin America: A quest for balance

Rodrigo Polanco Lazo and Felipe Ferreira Catalán

Introduction: investment law and human rights law

The relationship between foreign investment and human rights is usually examined through the differences between both disciplines. For Dupuy, a fundamental distinction between both systems is that human rights are *per essence* focused on individual human beings while foreign investments deal with investors acting, most of the time, as private companies.[1] This difference has led some scholars and commentators to depict the relationship between the two disciplines as contradictory and with competing interests on its way to address conflicts. Central to this representation is the way in which arbitral tribunals, in the context of investor–state dispute settlement, settle the disputes between investors' rights and human rights.

The antagonism between the two systems is characterized by arbitral decisions which allegedly always favor investors' rights over human rights or any other public interest. In the words of Suda, investor–state arbitration procedures "present a danger of creating a legal regime lacking safeguards of transparency or accountability: a regime skewed towards investors, but one that nevertheless passes judgement on important public interest issues."[2] The perception that investor–state dispute settlement is structurally biased towards the foreign investor[3] has led other commentators to affirm that it is a tool to "remove local populations from any meaningful role in the analysis

---

1 Pierre-Marie Dupuy, "Unification Rather Than Fragmentation of International Law? The Case of International Investment Law and Human Rights Law" in Pierre-Marie Dupuy, Francesco Francioni, and Ernst-Ulrich Petersmann (eds), *Human rights in international investment law and arbitration* (Oxford University Press 2009) 45.
2 Ryan Suda, "The Effect of Bilateral Investment Treaties on Human Rights Enforcement and Realization" in Olivier De Schutter (ed), *Transnational Corporations and Human Rights* (Bloomsbury Publishing 2006) 77.
3 José E Alvarez, "Critical Theory and the North American Free Trade Agreement's Chapter Eleven" (1996) 28 *The University of Miami Inter-American Law Review* 303.

both before and after the establishment of the foreign investment,"[4] and with an opaque system for the appointment of judges who then will biasedly decide on public concerns issues.[5]

In this chapter we will analyze how this debate between foreign investment and human rights has evolved in Latin America through an assessment of jurisprudence and treaty-making involving countries from the region and its own regional system for the protection of human rights. We argue that through the litigation of investor–state disputes Latin American countries have, maybe inadvertently, developed different approaches to introduce human rights arguments as a way to balance their international commitments. Through this exercise, Latin American countries have been able to promote consistency between investor–state dispute mechanisms and the protection of human rights looking for ways to adapt to the challenges of the system. One unexpected outcome has been the degree of involvement paid by some tribunals to human rights arguments whose discussion is, to some extent, limited by the Inter-American Regime of Protection of Human Rights. As we see throughout this book, the region has at the same time absorbed, resisted, and adapted the mainstream approaches to international investment law, as well as developed new ones.

Human rights in the Inter-American system

Latin America is a pioneer region in the adoption of international human rights documents. On 2 May 1948, the American States signed the world's first major international document on the topic: the American Declaration of the Rights and Duties of Man (or the "American Declaration") which preceded by seven months the Universal Declaration of Human Rights.[6] The document was conceived within the framework of the Charter of the Organization of the American States (OAS Charter) but was designed as a non-binding document without any enforcement mechanism. Only in 1960, with the adoption of the statutes of the Inter-American Commission on Human Rights, a truly institutional support was created to oversee the rights enshrined in the American Declaration. The Commission was envisaged as

---

4 Nicolás M Perrone, "The International Investment Regime and Local Populations: Are the Weakest Voices Unheard?" (2016) 7 *Transnational Legal Theory* 383, 2.

5 Gus van Harten, "Perceived Bias in Investment Treaty Arbitration" in Michael Waibel and others (eds), *The Backlash Against Investment Arbitration: Perceptions and Reality* (Wolters Kluwer Law & Business 2010) 433–454.

6 Robert K. Goldman, "History and Action: The Inter-American Human Rights System and the Role of the Inter-American Commission on Human Rights" (2009) 31 *Human Rights Quarterly* 856, 859.

an autonomous entity with the mission of promoting respect for human rights as set forth in the American Declaration.[7]

In November 1969, the Organization of American States adopted the American Convention of Human Rights (hereinafter "American Convention"), also known as the Pact of San José of Costa Rica, which entered into force in 1978 after being ratified by eleven states. The American Convention set forth an ambitious system of enforcement, composed by the Inter-American Commission on Human Rights, whose role is to promote the protection and observance of human rights, and the Inter-American Court of Human Rights (the "Inter-American Court"), an autonomous judicial institution established with the purpose of applying and interpreting the American Convention of Human Rights.[8]

The system of protection created by the American Declaration remains in place although it overlaps in several ways with the system created by the Pact of San José.[9] The Commission can receive petitions from States that are members of both the American Convention and the American Declaration but can only refer cases to the Inter-American Court directed to states that have ratified the American Convention and have recognized the jurisdiction of the Inter-American Court of Human Rights.[10]

Until recently, all the countries in the region were part of these systems and had accepted the jurisdiction of the Inter-American Court.[11] However, in 2012 Venezuela notified its denunciation of the American Convention, which has been in effect since 2013.

Interpretation and enforceability of human rights in the American Convention

The Inter-American Court's mandate is to interpret the American Convention. This instrument is composed by eleven chapters. Chapter II is entitled Civil and Political Rights and encompasses Article 3 to 25, while Chapter III is only composed by Article 26 which deals with the protection of Economic, Social and Cultural Rights.

---

7 Ibid. 862.
8 American Convention on Human Rights (signed 22 November 1969, entered into force 18 July 1978) 1144 UNTS 123, art 1.
9 Pedro Nikken, "Balancing of Human Rights and Investment Law in the Inter-American System of Human Rights" in Pierre-Marie Dupuy, Ernst-Ulrich Petersmann and Francesco Francioni (eds), *Human Rights in International Investment Law and Arbitration* (1st edition, Oxford University Press 2009) 249.
10 Goldman (n 6) 866.
11 Nikken (n 9) 249.

Goldman argues that at the time of its drafting the American Convention "guaranteed many civil and political rights which, although enshrined in domestic law, were largely ignored by the governments of many hemispheric countries. In this sense, the American Convention essentially prescribed maximum, not minimum, human rights."[12] This may explain why the drafters of the Convention were more concerned with creating an extensive catalog of civil and political rights rather than with the inclusion of specific Economic, Social and Cultural Rights.

In 1986, the Inter-American Commission on Human Rights concluded the drafting of the Additional Protocol to the American Convention of Human Rights in the Area of Economic, Social and Cultural Rights, known as "Protocol of San Salvador."[13] However, the Protocol only entered into force in 1999 after being ratified by eleven states. It includes thirteen rights, but individual claims can only be presented regarding the right to freely unionize (Article 8 a) and the right to education (Article 13).

The conceptual distinction between civil and political rights (first generation rights) vis-à-vis economic, social and cultural rights (second generation rights) supposes on the one hand, that civil and political rights require minimal or no intervention by the states, hence are characterized as "negative rights." On the other hand, economic, social and cultural rights require time and resources from the state to be fulfilled, demanding a positive action by the state ("positive rights"), thus subject to states' budgetary constraints and are sometimes referred as "aspirational goals."[14]

However, for an important sector of scholars the distinction is rather artificial than real and human rights must be considered "universal, indivisible, interdependent and interrelated."[15] This integral approach seems to have been recognized in the Preamble of the Protocol of San Salvador which states "the ideal of free human beings enjoying freedom from fear and want

---

12 Goldman (n 6) 866.
13 The Protocol of San Salvador has been ratified by Argentina, Bolivia, Brazil, Colombia, Costa Rica, Ecuador, El Salvador, Guatemala, Honduras, Mexico, Nicaragua, Panama, Paraguay, Peru, Suriname, and Uruguay. "Additional Protocol to the American Convention on Human Rights in the Area of Economic, Social and Cultural Rights 'Protocol of San Salvador'" (adopted, signed 17 November 1988, entered into force 16 November 1999) OASTS No 69 www.cidh.oas.org/Basicos/English/Basic6.Prot.Sn%20Salv%20Ratif.htm accessed 28 February 2019.
14 Jo M Pasqualucci, "The Right to a Dignified Life (Vida Digna): The Integration of Economic and Social Rights with Civil and Political Rights in the Inter-American Human Rights System" (2008) 31 *Hastings International and Comparative Law Review* 1, 9–10.
15 Office of the United Nations High Commissioner for Human Rights ("OHCHR | Vienna Declaration and Programme of Action" para 5 www.ohchr.org/en/professionalinterest/pages/vienna.aspx accessed 28 February 2019.

can only be achieved if conditions are created whereby everyone may enjoy his *economic, social and cultural rights as well as his civil and political rights.*"[16]

Notwithstanding this integral approach, the mechanism to present claims before the Inter-American Court based on economic, social, and cultural rights is severely limited when compared with the civil and political rights.

The inter-American systems of human rights and its challenges

For the countries of the region, the inter-American system of human rights, as described earlier, is a compulsory and integral regional system for the protection of human rights. However, this system is undergoing its own process of criticism and "backlash."

The Inter-American Court adopted in the early 2000s the doctrine of "conventionality control" creating "the international obligation on all state parties to the [Inter-American Court of Human Rights] to interpret any national legal instruments (the constitution, law, decrees, regulations, jurisprudence etc.) in accordance with the [American Convention of Human Rights], with the Inter-American corpus juris more generally (also called the 'block of conventionality')."[17] This started to shift traditional State's perceptions about the Inter-American Court as a complement of national judicial systems, towards one of a supranational court with the capacity of declaring any national law inconsistent with the "block of conventionality."

The Economist, in an article entitled, not without sarcasm, "The Mouse that Ruled," refers to some of the problems faced by the Inter-American Court following the adoption of the block of conventionality doctrine and recent decisions on issues such as same-sex marriage and the beginning of life. At the outset, some countries have suspended their financial contribution to the system and/or called for a reform on the process of selection and nomination of the judges.[18] Budget constraints are one of the biggest threats to the efficiency of the system and have for a long time been identified as an aspect of the system which would benefit from reform.

According to Dulitzky, there is consensus on the important lag existing at the level of the Inter-American Commission on Human Rights, which

---

16 "Protocol of San Salvador" (n 13) [emphasis added].
17 Eduardo Ferrer Mac-Gregor, "Symposium: The Constitutionalization of International Law In Latin America Conventionality Control The New Doctrine of The Inter-American Court Of Human Rights" (2015) 109 *AJIL UNBOUND* 7.
18 "Latin America's Human-Rights Court Moves into Touchy Territory" [2018] *The Economist* www.economist.com/the-americas/2018/02/01/latin-americas-human-rights-court-moves-into-touchy-territory accessed 28 February 2019.

on average takes 5.14 years (with some other stats increasing the average to 7.2 years) to issue a decision.[19] Admissibility by the Inter-American Commission on Human Rights is a pre-requisite to follow a contentious procedure in the Inter-American Court. This process could last, according to stats from the year 2015, an average of 22.2 months.[20]

The relationship of foreign investment disputes and human rights in Latin America

Most of the negative perception regarding the relationship between foreign investment and human rights in Latin America can be traced back to cases where countries of the region acted as respondent states.

The region represents 33 percent of the total number of cases of the International Centre for Settlement of Investment Disputes (ICSID) – the investor–state dispute settlement forum most frequently used – with Argentina being the most frequent respondent followed by Venezuela, and with Mexico and Ecuador also ranked within the top ten respondent states.[21] This has given rise to an important bulk of jurisprudence frequently noted as highlighting the conflicts between the two systems.

For Suda, *Técnicas Medioambientales v United Mexican States* stands as one of the key examples of the threat posed by expansive interpretations of bilateral investment treaties (BITs), after the tribunal held that non-renewal of a landfill operating permit, based on environmental and health related violations and the local community opposition, violated the Spain–Mexico BIT.[22] Perrone has discussed, using as a reference *Aguas del Tunari v Bolivia* (on water privatization) and *Chevron v Ecuador* (on oil exploitation), how BITs can override the right of local communities to participate in the decision of projects that affects them.[23] Burke-White concluded that the decisions issued by ICSID tribunals in the context of Argentina's financial crisis have "raise[d] serious questions as to the

19 Ariel E. Dulitzky, "Muy Poco, Muy Tarde: La Morosidad Procesal de La Comisión Interamericana de Derechos Humanos." www.corteidh.or.cr/tablas/r33492.pdf accessed 28 February 2019.
20 Corte Interamericana de Derechos Humanos, "ABC de la Corte Interamericana de Derechos Humanos" 24, 16. www.corteidh.or.cr/sitios/libros/todos/docs/ABCCorteIDH.pdf accessed 28 February 2019.
21 ICSID, "The ICSID-Case Load Statistics (Issue 2018–1)."
22 Suda (n 2) 73.
23 Perrone (n 4).

legitimacy and viability of the ICSID system."[24] Wells, also analyzing decisions related to Argentina's financial crisis, concluded that one of the reasons to understand the backlash against investment arbitration rely on the conflicting decisions issued by different tribunals on fundamentally the same issues.[25]

The thorny relationship of Latin America with foreign investment is extensively documented and it has several episodes of absorption, resistance, and adjustment. Starting with the regional defense of the Calvo Doctrine, opposing the recognition of an international minimum standard for aliens as invoked by developed countries, followed by its support for a New International Economic Order in the seventies, to the later conclusion of several BITs in the 1990s, which was then followed by a majority ratification of the ICSID Convention, to the most recent decisions of Bolivia (2007), Ecuador (2009), and Venezuela (2012), to denounce the ICSID Convention (and the surprising re-sign of Ecuador in 2021), in an overall context of backlash against investment treaties and international investment agreements.[26]

Despite this latest trend, most countries of the Latin American region remain active participants to the investment treaty system and investor–state dispute settlement but have called for adjustments needed to safeguard state's policy space from "vague standards of protection," which endanger the legitimacy of decisions adopted by democratically elected governments,[27] and to tackle the threat of a "regulatory chill,"[28] which would challenge

24 William W. Burke-White, "The Argentine Financial Crisis: State Liability Under BITs and the Legitimacy of the ICSID System" in Michael Waibel and others (eds), *The Backlash Against Investment Arbitration: Perceptions and Reality* (Wolters Kluwer Law & Business 2010) 407–432.

25 Louis T. Wells, "Backlash to Investment Arbitration: Three Causes" in Michael Waibel and others (eds), *The Backlash Against Investment Arbitration: Perceptions and Reality* (Wolters Kluwer Law & Business 2010) 341–352.

26 Rodrigo Polanco Lazo, "The No of Tokyo Revisited: Or How Developed Countries Learned to Start Worrying and Love the Calvo Doctrine" (2015) 30 *ICSID Review* 172. International Investment Agreements include both bilateral investment treaties and other agreements with investment provisions, usually preferential trade agreements with investment chapters. See the chapters in Part I – The Mosaic of States in this volume.

27 Stephan W. Schill, "International Investment Law and Public Comparatove Law in a Latin American Perspective" in Attila Tanzi and others (eds), *International Investment Law in Latin America / Derecho Internacional de las Inversiones en América Latina*, vol 5 (Brill /Martinus Nijhoff 2016) 29.

28 Kyla Tienhaara, "Regulatory Chill and the Threat of Arbitration: A View from Political Science" in Chester Brown and Kate Miles (eds), *Evolution in Investment Treaty Law and Arbitration* (Cambridge University Press 2011) 606–628.

the capacity of states to develop policies intended to fulfil commitments acquired in international human rights instruments.[29]

A working group from the United Nations Commission on International Trade Law (UNCITRAL) on investor–state settlement reform has been working since the end of 2017 on possible reforms to the system, addressing matters such as the appointment of arbitrators and ways to ensure their independence and impartiality.[30] Latin American countries are actively participating in this exercise; although it might be too soon to assess any regional position it seems that the "appetite" for reform is still present.

But countries of the region have also developed novel approaches to traditional investor–state dispute settlement. The Union of Latin American Countries (UNASUR) championed a reform effort to come with a system with the capacity to replace the ICSID with a regional Centre for the Settlement of the Disputes (Centro de Solución de Controversias en materia de Inversiones).[31] Although countries were able to agree on several dispositions of what would have been the Centre Constitutive Agreement, they needed to achieve consensus in order to adopt an agreement, something that has not happened yet.[32] Furthermore, six countries (Argentina, Brazil, Chile, Colombia, Paraguay, and Peru) have suspended or withdrawn their participation from UNASUR.[33]

Brazil, a traditional outlier of the traditional international investment regime, has developed its own model of cooperation and facilitation investment agreements (CFIAs), and since 2015 has concluded such treaties with Mozambique, Angola, Mexico, Malawi, Colombia, Chile, Ethiopia, Suriname, Guyana, United Arab Emirates, Morocco, Ecuador and India. This model that was also included in the investment chapter of the Economic

---

29 Juan Pablo Bohoslavsky and Juan Bautista Justo, "Combining the Rights of Foreign Investors and Human Rights: Why? How? Who? When?" in Attila Tanzi and others (eds), *International Investment Law in Latin America / Derecho Internacional de las Inversiones en América Latina*, vol 5 (Brill /Martinus Nijhoff 2016) 677.

30 "Working Group III: Investor-State Dispute Settlement Reform | United Nations Commission On International Trade Law" https://uncitral.un.org/en/working_gro ups/3/investor-state accessed 27 February 2019.

31 Rodrigo Polanco Lazo, "Beyond ICSID Arbitration – The Centre for Settlement of Investment Disputes of UNASUR" in Andrea K. Bjorklund (ed), *Yearbook on International Investment Law and Policy 2014–2015* (Oxford University Press 2016) 375–404.

32 Katia Fach Gómez and Catharine Titi, "International Investment Law and ISDS: Mapping Contemporary Latin America" (2016) 17 *The Journal of World Investment & Trade* 515, 515–535.

33 "¿El principio del fin de Unasur? 6 países suspenden su participación" (*CNN*, 21 April 2018) https://cnnespanol.cnn.com/2018/04/21/el-principio-del-fin-de-unasur-6-paises-suspenden-su-participacion/ accessed 28 February 2019.

and Trade Expansion Agreement (ETEA) concluded between Brazil and Peru in 2016, in the 2017 Intra–MERCOSUR Investment Facilitation Protocol, and in in the 2018 Brazil–Chile Free Trade Agreement. CFIAs are notable because they do not include investor–state arbitration.[34] Brazil made a conscious decision not to include investor-state dispute settlement (ISDS) provisions in these agreements, opting instead for creating mechanisms of risk mitigation and dispute prevention, which actively involve both home and host states.[35]

The commonalities between both systems

International human rights and investment tribunals share important commonalities, which could be used as ways of mutual support between both systems. In the words of Simma, "[a]fter all the ultimate concern at the basis of both areas of international law is one and the same: the protection of the individual against the power of the State."[36]

Both disciplines already share this asymmetrical nature, granting individuals rights and protection from the state on which virtually all obligations are imposed. Moreover, in both systems private individuals can present claims against a state, but with some important differences. While in the Inter-American System of Human Rights those claims are by the Inter-American Commission on Human Rights after exhaustion of local remedies, in the large majority of international investment agreements concluded by the Latin American countries the investor often has immediate access to investor–state dispute settlement, usually in the form of arbitration.[37]

Although citations of investor–state dispute settlement awards are still reduced in human rights litigation, scholars have analyzed the way in which investor–state arbitration tribunals have relied on human rights

34 Rodrigo Polanco, *The Return of the Home State to Investor-State Disputes: Bringing Back Diplomatic Protection?* (Cambridge University Press 2019) 59.

35 Fabio Morosini and Michelle Ratton Sánchez-Badin, "The New Brazilian Agreements on Cooperation and Facilitation of Investments (ACFIS): Navigating between Resistance and Conformity with the Global Investment Regime" (2015) 25 www.law.nyu.edu/sites/default/files/upload_documents/Morosini%20-%20Global%20 Fellows%20Forum.pdf accessed 28 February 2019. See Chapter 4 by Leonardo V P de Oliveira, and Marcus Spangenberger in this volume.

36 Bruno Simma, "Foreign Investment Arbitration: A Place for Human Rights?" (2011) 60 *The International and Comparative Law Quarterly* 573, 576.

37 Rodrigo Polanco Lazo and Rodrigo Mella, "Investment Arbitration and Human Rights Cases in Latin America" in Radi, Yannick (ed), *Research Handbook on Human Rights and Investment* (Edward Elgar 2018) 41–92 www.elgaronline.com/view/edcoll/9781782549116/9781782549116.00010.xml accessed 29 January 2019.

jurisprudence to build their decisions[38] and recent awards, such as *Urbaser v Argentina*, seem to have taken this practice even further, drawing particular attention from commentators which have highlighted its "novel analysis of the relationship between human rights and investment law."[39]

The history of Latin America with human rights violation adds a further element to the analysis on how to balance both set of obligations. Pedro Nikken, former President of the Inter-American Court of Human Rights, declared that

> the protection of human rights in the Americas is the struggle against the bloody repression carried out by the military dictatorship that ruled most of Latin American countries until the 1990s. Given that context, the protection of property rights or other mainly economic topic appears to many in the human right community as something too sophisticated, even frivolous.[40]

But this relationship could be different, as both systems share important commonalities and seemingly the role of human rights in investor–state dispute settlement is starting to be recognized in recent case law and investment treaties, as we will examine in the following sections.

The introduction human rights arguments in investor–state dispute settlement

The first step to assess whether it is possible or not to find a mutual support between human rights and investor–state dispute settlement decisions is to identify how and when human rights argumentation can be introduced in the context of investor–state dispute settlement. One key aspect of this debate relies on establishing whether arbitral tribunals have the jurisdiction to know about human rights and whether or not human rights are part of the applicable law.

Regarding the issue of jurisdiction in investor–state dispute settlement litigation, unlike in human rights, international investment agreements usually do not include a distinction based on the type of investors' rights being affected to trigger an investor–state dispute settlement. Under the framework

---

38 James D. Fry, "International Human Rights Law in Investment Arbitration: Evidence of International Law's Unity" (2007) 18 *Duke Journal of Comparative & International Law* 77.

39 David Attanasio and Tatiana Sainati, "Urbaser S.A. and Consorcio de Aguas Bilbao Bizkaia, Bilbao Biskaia Ur Partzuergoa v. The Argentine Republic ICSID" (2017) 111 *The American Journal of International Law*; Washington 744, 747. See Chapter 11 by Farouk El-Hosseny, Patrick Devine, and Ilan Brun-Vargas in this volume.

40 Nikken (n 9) 247.

of ICSID, it is possible to bring a claim if both the home and host are members of the ICSID Convention and it is a legal dispute arising directly out of an investment between the host state and a national of the home state.[41]

The lack of limitations based on the category of the allegedly affected rights does not mean that arbitral tribunals have the jurisdiction to directly know about a violation to human rights. The jurisdiction of the tribunal is still defined by consent in conjunction with Article 25 (1) of the ICSID Convention.[42] This requirement will prevent a tribunal from knowing of a claim against a violation of human rights which is not sufficiently connected with an investment.

The issue of applicable law "refers primarily to the relevant rules governing substantive issues in dispute."[43] In the words of Gazzini,

> [t]he provisions on applicable law included in multilateral treaties [...] and in several BITs pave the way to the application of international law. The application of international law is envisaged – assuming the parties have not agreed otherwise – in disputes brought before ICSID tribunals (Article 42) or left to the discretion of the tribunal (Article 35 (1) UNCITRAL Rules of Article 21 (1) ICC Rules).[44]

The applicability of general international law has been referred to by Simma and Pulkowski, who have indicated that "while different tribunals have occasionally endorsed divergent interpretations of the general international law, there appears to be broad consensus that general international law forms part of the applicable law."[45] If human rights law is part of the applicable law, the arbitral tribunal must interpret those provisions in accordance with the principle of systemic integration contained in Article 31 (3) (c) of the Vienna Convention, which dictates that the interpretation of a treaty "shall take into account, together with the context, any relevant rule of international law applicable in the relations between the parties." As concluded by Simma,

> whether international human rights law is a proper point from which to draw meaning for international investment agreements, depends on whether or not

---

41 Krista Nadakavukaren Schefer, *International Investment Law: Text, Cases and Materials, Second Edition* (Edward Elgar Publishing 2016) 441.
42 Michael Waibel, "Investment Arbitration: Jurisdiction and Admissibility" in Marc Bungenberg and others (eds), *International Investment Law* (CH BECK 2015) 1220.
43 Tarcisio Gazzini, *Interpretation of International Investment Treaties* (Bloomsbury Publishing 2016) 221.
44 Ibid.
45 Bruno Simma and Dirk Pulkowski, "Two Worlds, but Not Apart: International Investment Law and General International Law" in Marc Bungenberg and others (eds), *International Investment Law* (CH BECK 2015) 371.

human rights constitute relevant rules of international law applicable between the parties to such treaties.[46]

Under this general framework, Kube and Petersmann have identified different entry points for human rights argumentations in investor–state dispute settlement: human rights as investor's claims, human rights as a defense of the host state and human rights introduced by third party interveners (e.g. amicus curiae).[47]

Having concluded that it is possible to introduce human rights argumentation in the investor–state dispute settlement context we move on to analyze whether the decisions issued in the context of the Inter-American Human Rights System and investor–state dispute settlement litigation demonstrate or not evidence for support and/or enforceability of human rights guaranteed in the Inter-American system.

Interaction between foreign investment and human rights in the inter-American human rights system

In general terms, the interaction between international economic instruments and human rights was addressed by the Inter-American Court in *Sawhoyamaxa v Paraguay* – as mentioned by Bohoslavsky and Justo[48] – where the Court considered that "the enforcement of bilateral commercial treaties negates vindication of non-compliance with state obligations under the American Convention; on the contrary, their enforcement should always be compatible with the American Convention."[49] This call for compatibility between both types of instruments stresses the relevance of finding a proper balancing of obligations between the two systems.

For Nikken, both systems benefit from each other since the general framework of the Inter-American system promotes an environment which is favorable for guaranteeing investments as the "[r]ule of law and the existence of an independent judiciary are essentials conditions for stability,

---

46 Simma (n 36) 584.

47 Vivian Kube and EU Petersmann, "Human Rights Law in International Investment Arbitration" (2016) 11 *Asian Journal of WTO and International Health Law and Policy* 65.

48 Juan Pablo Bohoslavsky and Juan Bautista Justo, "Combining the Rights of Foreign Investors and Human Rights: Why? How? Who? When?" in Attila Tanzi and others (eds), *International Investment Law in Latin America / Derecho Internacional de las Inversiones en América Latina*, vol 5 (Brill /Martinus Nijhoff 2016) 687.

49 *Sawhoyamaxa Indigenous Community v Paraguay*, Merits, reparations and costs, Inter-American Court of Human Rights Series C No 146 (29 March 2006) [140].

predictability, and security that are generally acknowledged as standards for international protection of the investments."[50]

Furthermore, from a policy perspective, foreign direct investment (FDI) is also a tool for development. Governments rely on FDI to develop projects which can directly impact on people's lives and help the realization of their human rights. While addressing the issue of alleviation of poverty, which is consistent with the integral approach to human rights, Dimsey has argued that FDI

> has a role to play in poverty alleviation to the extent that such investment has the potential to impact on a basic human right concern. Indeed, FDI is relied on by many states precisely for this purpose: to fulfil a basic need of its people that the state is not capable –for whatever reason – of achieving on its own.[51]

The capacity of FDI to contribute to the realization of development and foster human rights is not an uncontested one. For some authors, FDI is used, particularly by autocratic governments in developing countries, to attract investment flows from multinational corporations through a process of erosion of human rights.[52]

Considering the central role of the American Convention for Latin American countries we analyze whether it is possible to find evidence of a reciprocal beneficial relationship between investor–state dispute settlement awards and the jurisprudence of the court. In our analysis we abide to the distinction between civil and political rights and economic, social and cultural rights since, as it has been explained, the American Convention itself provides for different treatments to these categories of rights.

Civil and political rights

A simple reading of the catalogue of rights included in Chapter II of the American Convention, entitled "civil and political rights," seems to suggest that this is the chapter more naturally connected with foreign investment since issues such as the right to property, expropriation, and procedural guaranties are included here. The interest protected behind these rights seems to match

---

50 Nikken (n 9) 248.
51 Mariel Dimsey, "Foreign Direct Investment and the Alleviation of Poverty: Is Investment Arbitration Falling Short of Its Goals?" in Krista Nadakavukaren Schefer (ed), *Poverty and the International Economic Legal System: Duties to the World's Poor* (Cambridge University Press 2013) 161.
52 Olivier De Schutter, Johan Swinnen, and Jan Wouters, *Foreign Direct Investment and Human Development: The Law and Economics of International Investment Agreements* (Routledge 2012) 112. C.f. the analysis in Chapter 9 by Sufyan Droubi, Cecilia Juliana Flores Elizondo, and Raphael Heffron in this volume.

with the interests of foreign investors, and the decisions issued by arbitral-tribunals can be considered a concrete application of those rights. However, an assessment of mutual influence should also consider whether the decisions include elements for the balancing of obligations.

We first address the right to property. As pointed out by Dupuy and Viñuales, "the legal concept and economic reality of property is at the core of any foreign investment scheme, and this concept was recognised as a fundamental right as far back as the 1789 French Declaration of human rights."[53] The American Convention recognizes this right in the following terms:

> Article 21. Right to Property:
>
> 1. Everyone has the right to the use and enjoyment of his property. The law may subordinate such use and enjoyment to the interest of society.
>
> 2. No one shall be deprived of his property except upon payment of just compensation, for reasons of public utility or social interest, and in the cases and according to the forms established by law.
>
> 3. Usury and any other form of exploitation of man by man shall be prohibited by law.

For Nikken,

> [t]he wording of Article 21 and the placement of property among civil and political rights, as well as its exclusion in the Protocol of San Salvador (1988), reveal that in the Inter-American System the concept of property prevails as an individual right, which may be perceived prima facie as favouring the idea of protection of investment as property.[54]

In the case *Ivcher-Bronstein v Perú*, the Inter-American Court held a broad interpretation of the concept of property including participation as a shareholder within it.[55] This identification of property with an economic interest[56] is compatible with the definition of investment as contemplated in several BITs under which investment is usually defined as a broad general concept followed by illustrative examples.[57]

An infraction to the right to property under the American Convention may be followed by reparations. This issue is addressed in Article 63 of the American Convention:

---

53 Pierre-Marie Dupuy and Jorge E. Viñuales, "Human Rights and Investment Disciplines: Integration in Progress" in Marc Bungenberg, Jörn Griebel, Stephan Hobe, and August Reinisch (eds) *International Investment Law: A Handbook* (Nomos Verlagsgesellschaft 2015) 1740–1741.

54 Nikken (n 9) 249.

55 *Ivcher Bronstein v Peru*, Merits, reparations and costs, Inter-American Court of Human Rights Series C No 74 (Judgment, 6 February 2001) (*Ivcher Bronstein v Peru* (Judgment 2001)) [122–123].

56 Nikken (n 9) 250.

57 Nadakavukaren Schefer (n 41) 70.

Article 63.1. If the Court finds that there has been a violation of a right or freedom protected by this Convention, the Court shall rule that the injured party be ensured the enjoyment of his right or freedom that was violated. It shall also rule, if appropriate, that the consequences of the measure or situation that constituted the breach of such right or freedom be remedied and that fair compensation be paid to the injured party.

Since its decisions in *Velásquez-Rodríguez v Honduras*, the Inter-American Court has affirmed that the provision of Article 63.1 is a manifestation of the general international rule of *restitutio in integrum* as described by the Permanent Court of Justice in *Factory At Chorzów*.[58] However, on several occasions the Court has decided that the reparation should be decided by national institutions in accordance with national domestic law.[59] For Nikken, this practice is a departure from the *restitutio in integrum* rule since the issue will be decided by domestic authorities relying on national law instead of applying international law standards. Nikken concluded that the "Court's practice is not to grant large economic compensations for violations of human rights even in cases of expropriation or other interferences with the right to property."[60]

In the context of investor–state dispute settlement, remedies are at the core of the claim brought by affected investors and arbitral tribunals deciding whether or not there is a breach in a state's commitment in a BIT are at the same time addressing the issue of the possible international responsibility of a state.

As explained by Marboe,

The primary obligations of States derive from treaties, customary international law and general principles of law, the sources of international law as enumerated in Article 38 of the Statute of the International Court of Justice, this including bilateral and multilateral investment protection treaties. [...] In the case of an alleged breach of such a primary norm, it is the task of the tribunal to decide if the breach was attributable to the State and what consequences derive from it according to the secondary norms of international law.[61]

Since BITs do not usually contain any secondary rule, the consequences of breaching a BIT's obligation are to be determined in accordance with

---

58 *Velásquez-Rodríguez v Honduras*, Merits, Inter-American Court of Human Rights, Series C No 4 (Judgment, 29 July 1988) [26]; Nikken (n 9) 251.

59 *Cesti Hurtado v Peru*, Merits, Inter-American Court of Human Rights Series C No 56 (Judgment, 29 September 1999); *Ivcher Bronstein v Peru* (Judgment 2001) (n 55); *Five Pensioners v Peru*, Merits, reparations and costs, Inter-American Court of Human Rights Series C No 98 (Judgment, 28 February 2003).

60 Nikken (n 9) 253.

61 Ingrid Marboe, "The System of Reparation and Questions of Terminology" in Marc Bungenberg and others (eds), *International Investment Law* (CH BECK 2015) 1035.

customary international law. Under customary international law, as reflected in Article 31 of the work of the International Law Commission (ILC) on the Responsibility of States for Internationally Wrongful Acts, states are obliged to make full reparation of the damage. In this regard, arbitral tribunals' awards help promote the application of the *restitutio in integrum* in accordance with international customary law thus upholding the rights of the affected part in consistency with the American Convention.

Naturally, Article 21 of the American Convention is also connected with the issue of expropriation. For Fry, this is an area in which it is possible to appreciate synergies between human rights and foreign investment.[62] In *Tecmed v Mexico* the arbitral tribunal referred to the jurisprudence of the Inter-American Court of Human Rights in *Ivcher Bronstein v Perú* to find a violation to the standard of protection, concluding that it should not limit itself to "evaluating whether a formal dispossession or expropriation took place, but should look beyond mere appearances and establish the real situation behind the situation was denounced."[63] It is worth mentioning that in *Tecmed*, the tribunal also quoted jurisprudence of the European Court of Human Rights to address the issue of proportionality between the measure at issue and the public interest behind the measure.[64] The inclusion of an analysis of proportionality has been successfully applied to re-affirm the capacity of states to introduce legitimate measures which do not constitute an illegal expropriation,[65] hence upheaving states' capacity to introduce regulation and avoid the "regulatory chill" effect.

The reference to a decision of the European Court of Human Rights seems consistent with the universalist approach used by the Inter-American Court to interpret the American Convention under which the Court relies on a series of different international instruments thus giving application to an evolutive interpretation of the rights contained in the Convention.[66] The

62 Fry (n 38) 83.
63 *Ivcher Bronstein v Peru* (Judgment 2001) (n 55) para 124.
64 *Matos e Silva, LDA., and Other v. Portugal*, Judgment, ECHR No. 15777/89 (Judgment, 16 September 1996) [92].
65 Jeff Waincymer, "Balancing Property Rights in Expropriation" in Pierre-Marie Dupuy, Ernst-Ulrich Petersmann, and Francesco Francioni (eds), *Human Rights in International Investment Law and Arbitration* (1st edition, Oxford University Press 2009) 301.
66 Marijke de Pauw, "The Inter-American Court of Human Rights and the Interpretive Method of External Referencing: Regional Consensus v. Universality" (Social Science Research Network 2016) SSRN Scholarly Paper ID 2827292 https://papers.ssrn.com/abstract=2827292 accessed 28 February 2019.

Inter-American Court has usually referred in one way or another to the jurisprudence from the European Court of Human Rights. In its jurisdictional decisions between 1987 and 2012, the Court issued 246 decisions and 59.8 percent of them included a reference to European Court of Human Rights decisions.[67]

We now turn to the right to personal liberty. In the American Convention, it is understood that this right is enshrined in a general provision (Article 7.1) which is then followed up by specific clauses:[68]

Article 7. Right to Personal Liberty
1. Every person has the right to personal liberty and security

This general right is then followed by: the right not to be deprived of liberty illegally (Article 7.2), or arbitrarily (Article 7.3), to know the reasons for the arrest and charges made against the detainee (Article 7.4), to judicial control of the deprivation of liberty and reasonableness of the term of preventive detention (Article 7.5), to challenge the legality of detention (Article 7.6), and not to be arrested for debts (Article 7.7).

The Inter-American Court has addressed the scope of personal liberty in Article 7.1 as including the notion of physical liberty. In *Street Children v. Guatemala* the Court stated that "[t]he protection of both the *physical liberty* of the individual and his *personal safety* are in play, in a context where the absence of guarantees may result in the subversion of the rule of law and deprive those arrested of the minimum legal protection."[69] The idea of physical liberty is examined in *Yvon Neptune v. Haiti* where the Court concluded "regarding personal liberty, Article 7 of the Convention protects exclusively the right to physical liberty and encompasses physical conducts that presuppose the physical presence of the holder of the right and that are normally expressed by physical movement."[70] In *Chaparro Álvarez v. Ecuador* the Inter-American Court of Human Rights addresses

---

67 Tania Groppi and Anna Maria Leccis Cocco-Ortu, "Las referencias recíprocas entre la Corte Europea y la Corte Interamericana de Derechos Humanos: ¿de la influencia al diálogo?" (2014) 0 Revista de Derecho Público 837 www.revistaderechopublico. uchile.cl/index.php/RDPU/article/view/33321 accessed 28 February 2019.
68 Inter-American Court of Human Rights, *Análisis de la jurisprudencia de la Corte Interamericana de Derechos Humanos en materia de integridad personal y privación de libertad artículos 7 y 5 de la Convención Americana sobre Derechos Humanos* (Corte Interamericana de Derechos Humanos 2010) 4.
69 *Case of the "Street Children" (Villagrán-Morales et al.) v. Guatemala*, Merits, Inter-American Court of Human Rights, Series C No 63 (Judgment, 19 November 1999) [135] [emphasis added].
70 *Yvon Neptune v Haiti*, Merits, reparations and costs, Inter-American Court of Human Rights Series C No 180 (Judgment, 6 May 2008) [90].

the concept of security by stating that it "should also be understood as protection against all unlawful or arbitrary interference with physical liberty."[71] Based on this decision we conclude that for the Inter-American Court the right to personal liberty is linked with the protection of physical indemnity.

In the context of investor–state dispute settlement, full protection and security (FPS) "is a standard that protects the foreign investor against third party interference in an investment"[72] and is nowadays a common provision in several international investment agreements. Despite the evolution in its scope of protection, the standard is rooted in the protection on the physical indemnity of the investor and its assets. Presenting an historic evolution of the standard, Schreuer affirms: "in a number of cases tribunals seem to have assumed that this standard applies exclusively or preponderantly to physical security and to the host State's duty to protect the investors against violence directed at the person and property stemming from State organs or private parties."[73] In this regard, the FPS Standard can be understood as a concrete application of the standard embodied in Article 7.1 of the American Convention.

The American Convention also recognizes the procedural human right to a fair trial, describing its basic content in Article 8:

Article 8 Right to a Fair Trial

Every person has the right to a hearing, with due guarantees and within a reasonable time, by a competent, independent, and impartial tribunal, previously established by law, in the substantiation of any accusation of a criminal nature made against him or for the determination of his rights and obligations of a civil, labor, fiscal, or any other nature.

Under the large majority of investment treaties, investors are entitled to receive a "fair and equitable treatment" (FET) by the state, a notion that in principle is not directly connected to fair trial. However, the subsequent interpretation of FET clauses in investor–state dispute settlement and more recent investment treaty-making have explicitly included this right as part of the fair and equitable treatment standard.

---

71 *Chaparro Álvarez and Lapo Íñiguez v Ecuador*, Preliminary objections, merits, reparations and costs, Inter-American Court of Human Rights Series C No 170 (Judgment, 21 November 2007) [53].
72 Nadakavukaren Schefer (n 41) 360.
73 Christoph Schreuer, "Full Protection and Security" (2010) 1 *Journal of International Dispute Settlement* 353, 2.

Several investor–state dispute settlement tribunals have hold that a state must afford a fair trial in a case to which an investor is a party. In *Loewen v. United States*, the award found that it is the responsibility of the courts of a state to ensure that litigation is free from discrimination against a foreign litigant and that a person does not become the victim of sectional or local prejudice.[74] Without explicitly mentioning the right to a fair trial, in *Saipem v. Bangladesh*, on the issue of judicial revocation of the authority of an arbitral tribunal without consulting or hearing the arbitrators, the tribunal held that international law requires state courts to abide by generally accepted standards of the administration of justice.[75] In the same line, the decision on jurisdiction in *Toto Costruzioni v. Lebanon* holds that the failure to render justice within a reasonable period of time may constitute a breach of international customary law.[76]

At the same time, a number of international investment agreements include the right to fair trial elements as part of their definition of the FET standard. Under those treaties "fair and equitable treatment" includes the obligation not to deny justice in criminal, civil, or administrative adjudicatory proceedings in accordance with the principle of due process.[77]

Therefore, procedural undue delays or the absence of due process by the states has been considered to be an infraction to the FET standard regularly included in international investment agreements, hence re-enforcing the human right to a fair trial.

---

74 *Loewen Group, Inc. and Raymond L. Loewen v. United States of America*, ICSID Case No. ARB(AF)/98/3 (Award, 26 June 2003) para 123.

75 *Saipem S.p.A. v. People's Republic of Bangladesh*, ICSID Case No. ARB/05/7 (Award, 30 June 2009) para 149–159.

76 *Toto Costruzioni Generali S.p.A. v. Republic of Lebanon*, ICSID Case No. ARB/07/12 (Decision on Jurisdiction, 11 September 2009) para 156–163.

77 Free Trade Agreement between the Government of the Republic of Costa Rica, the Government of the Dominican Republic, the Government of the Republic of El Salvador, the Government of the Republic of Guatemala, the Government of the Republic of Honduras, the Government of the Republic of Nicaragua and the Government of the United States of America (signed 5 August 2004, entered into force 1 March 2006, 1 April 2006, 1 July 2006, 1 March 2007, 1 January 2009) ("DR-CAFTA 2004"), Art. 10.5.2(a); Comprehensive Economic and Trade Agreement between Canada, of the One Part, and the European Union and its Member States, of the Other Part (signed 30 October 2016, entered into force (provisionally) 21 September 2017) [2017] OJ L11/23 ("CETA") Art 8.10.2(a)(b); Comprehensive and Progressive Agreement for Trans-Pacific Partnership (signed 8 March 2018, entered into force 30 December 2018) ("CPTPP"), Art. 9.6.2(a).

Economic, social, and cultural rights

The key provision in the American Convention regarding the protection of economic, social and cultural rights is Article 26, which states:

> Article 26 Progressive Development
> 1. The States Parties undertake to adopt measures, both internally and through international cooperation, especially those of an economic and technical nature, with a view to achieving progressively, by legislation or other appropriate means, the full realization of the rights implicit in the economic, social, educational, scientific, and cultural standards set forth in the Charter of the Organization of American States as amended by the Protocol of Buenos Aires.

The language of the provision has resulted in claimants usually avoiding relying on Article 26. Both the Inter-American Commission on Human Rights and the Court have behaved cautiously to allegations under this article.[78] The reference to the OAS Charter demands an exercise of interpretation by the Inter-American Court since the terms used on it are very broad and even if it is possible to infer a right from the Charter it is "in most cases insufficient to determine what the [Economic, Social and Cultural Rights] right provision commands, permit, or prohibit, or the specific obligations that must been fulfilled by the States."[79]

Given the above, the Court needs to consider different legal instruments when defining the content of economic, social and cultural rights. In providing content to these rights, the Court has confirmed the applicability of the American Declaration in its Advisory Opinion N° 10/89 in which the Court included the American Declaration as "a source of international obligations related to the Charter of the Organization."[80] However, the reference to the American Declaration cannot be interpreted as broadly as to avoid any inference from the OAS Charter.

The Protocol of San Salvador has more properly provided content to the economic, social, and cultural rights in the Inter-American Human Rights

---

78 Elizabeth Salmón, "Los Derechos Económicos, Sociales y Culturales en el Sistema Interamericano: El Artículo 26 de la Convención Americana sobre Derechos Humanos y el Camino hacia una Lectura Social de los Derechos Civiles y Políticos." 51, 37.

79 Oswaldo R Ruiz-Chiriboga, "The American Convention and the Protocol of San Salvador: Two Intertwined Treaties: Non-Enforceability of Economic, Social and Cultural Rights in the Inter-American System" (2013) 31 *Netherlands Quarterly of Human Rights* 159, 171.

80 *Interpretation of the American Declaration of the Rights and Duties of Man within the framework of Article 64 of the American Convention on Human Rights,* Advisory Opinion OC-10/89, Inter-American Court of Human Rights Series A No 10 (Judgment, 14 July 1989) [45].

System, but its application calls for a distinction between states which have ratified the protocol and those who have not. Likewise, as it has already been discussed, the protocol limits the presentation of claims to certain rights which can limit the scope of the claims for which the Inter-American Court has competence.

The Inter-American Court has usually relied on decisions issued by the United Nations Committee on Economic, Social and Cultural Rights.[81] However, these decisions by the Inter-American Court can only clarify the content of rights effectively included in the OAS Charter since its purpose is the interpretation of rights and not the introduction of new rights.

Despite these limitations, Salmón has argued that in practice the Inter-American Court has generated a jurisprudential line with a social interpretation of the economic, social, and cultural rights, and has relied on them when addressing individuals' claims thus providing them with content.[82] This seems to be confirmed by the jurisprudence of the Court which has derived from civil and political rights (such as the right to life, personal liberty, and fair trial, among others) concrete guarantees for individuals.[83]

This practice by the Inter-American Court has allowed the issue of the scope of the rights covered to be tackled but without addressing the limitations in terms of enforceability of such rights, which can have an enormous impact for society. If we take the example of the right to water and the right to health which, as we will see later, has also been invoked in an investor–state framework, the jurisprudence of the Inter-American Court has addressed the right to water through its relevance to satisfy other human rights, particularly in cases related to the conditions of detention and of specific groups of people in special vulnerable situations.[84] This somehow narrower approach to the human right to water shall be understood in light of the cases submitted to the Inter-American Court of Human Rights which probably have not provided the opportunity to asses this right without a necessary link with civil and political rights.

Although investor–state dispute settlement is not a perfect substitute, it does provide states with the opportunity to bring economic, social and cultural rights into disputes as balancing instruments which must be considered by the tribunal when outlining the limitations of the investor' rights.

---

81 de Pauw (n 66) 8.
82 Salmón (n 78) 66.
83 Salmón (n 78).
84 Jimena Murillo Chávarro, "The Right to Water in the Case-Law of the Inter-American Court of Human Rights" (2014) 7 *ACDI – Anuario Colombiano de Derecho Internacional* 39, 47–48.

Investor–state dispute settlement cases and human rights[85]

Increasingly, respondent states have relied on human rights argumentation in their submissions. Particularly relevant has been the invocation of economic, social, and cultural rights such as the human right to health and the right to water. This could be explained by the nature of the disputes which commonly refer to the provision of public services, which after processes of privatization, are being operated by private companies. While many of the defenses can be linked with civil and political rights, the absence of limitation in the category of rights in the context of investor–state dispute settlement has allowed arbitral tribunals to commonly make their decision directly addressing economic, social and cultural rights. In this context, respondent states have brought defenses, and even counter-claims, to justify the measures aimed at safeguarding human rights and/or with the aim of ensuring the provision of a public service. The majority of the cases are related to measures, tariff freezes mostly, taken by Argentina after the financial crisis, with the alleged aim of ensuring the continual provision of gas and water services to the population.[86]

CMS Gas Transmission v. Argentina (2005)

In *CMS Gas Transmission v. Argentina*, the respondent argued that the measures set in place by Argentina, a freezing in the adjustment price mechanism, was adopted with the objective of protecting constitutional rights. Among them, there were some basic treaties on human rights which were recognized as to have a constitutional standing and as such were to be recognized as above other international agreements such as the BIT.[87] The tribunal did not consider that the measure at issue involved a collision between Argentina's Constitution and international treaties since both the Constitution and international treaties recognized the right to property and that the measure at issue did not involve any fundament right.[88] As commented by Meshel, this decision has been criticized for its shallow approach to human rights based on the syllogism "that property is a human right: investments treaties protect property; therefore, investment treaties are treaties which protect rather than harm human rights."[89]

---

85 Unless otherwise mentioned, all investment cases and related documents cited hereinafter are available at www.italaw.com accessed 28 February 2019.

86 On the right to water, see Chapter 12 by Javier Echaide in this volume.

87 *CMS Gas Transmission Company v. The Argentine Republic*, ICSID Case No. ARB/01/8 (Award, 12 May 2005) [114].

88 Ibid. 121.

89 Tamar Meshel, "Human Rights in Investor-State Arbitration: The Human Right to Water and Beyond" (2015) 6 *Journal of International Dispute Settlement* 277, 281.

Azurix v. Argentina (2006)

In *Azurix v. Argentina* authorities of the Province of Buenos Aires ordered Azurix, the operator of water services, not to charge consumers for a few weeks and to pay for its failure to maintain certain water quality standards. The respondent argued the existence of conflict between a BIT and human rights treaties which "must be resolved in favor of human rights because the consumers public interest must prevail over the private interest of the provider,"[90] while the investor argued that the interest of the consumers was protected by the concession agreement.[91] The tribunal concluded that the issue of compatibly "has not been fully argued and the tribunal fails to understand the incompatibility in the specifics of the instant case" since the services to consumers continued to be provided without interruption.[92] In its analysis, the tribunal did not address Argentina's argument based on human rights. According to Thielbörger, this is "regrettable with regard to the human right to water: it would have been exactly in this weighing – whether the underlying intentions of the state could justify the state's actions affecting the investor – where the right could have played a decisive role."[93]

Compañía de Aguas del Aconquija and Vivendi v. Argentina (2006)

In *Compañía de Aguas del Aconquija and Vivendi v. Argentina*, the measure at issue was a unilateral tariff reduction decision and the alleged encouragement by the authorities to the population not to pay their bills as a way to press the investor to renegotiate tariffs. The initial award dismissed all the claims against Argentina, but that decision was later annulled. A second award concluded that Argentina was in breach of both fair and equitable treatment and full protection and security. In its request for annulment Argentina argued that the tribunal had disregarded fundamental issues relating to the disputes between the parties, including that the dispute between the parties related to the right to water as an essential human right.[94] As observed by

---

90 *Azurix Corp. v. Argentine Republic (I)*, ICSID Case No. ARB/01/12 (Award 14 July 2006) [254].
91 Ibid.
92 Ibid. 261.
93 Pierre Thielbörger, "The Human Right to Water Versus Investor Rights: Double-Dilemma or Pseudo-Conflict?" in Pierre-Marie Dupuy, Ernst-Ulrich Petersmann and Francesco Francioni (eds), *Human Rights in International Investment Law and Arbitration* (1st edition, Oxford University Press 2009) 497.
94 *Compañía de Aguas del Aconquija S.A. and Vivendi Universal S.A. (formerly Compañía de Aguas del Aconquija, S.A. and Compagnie Générale des Eaux) v. Argentine Republic (I)*, ICSID Case No. ARB/97/3 (Decision on Annulment, 3 July 2002) [57].

Meshel, "[n]either of the decisions discussed Argentina's human right to water defence."[95] The annulment committee did not explicitly refer to this allegation and concluded that there was not relevant omission.

Sempra v. Argentina (2007)

In *Sempra v. Argentina* the measure at issue was a freezing in the rates of gas distribution services. In this case the issue of human rights was directly addressed in the context of the American Convention. An expert witness was presented with the question on whether the American Convention compelled Argentina to adopt the measure as a way to maintain its constitutional order.[96] Although the witness declared that Argentina was in fact compelled to adopt these measures, the tribunal held that the constitutional order – or the survival of the state – was not imperiled by the crisis and that Argentina has other tools to address the challenges derived from the financial crisis.[97] Since the tribunal analyzed the issue in the context of the maintenance of the constitutional order and survival of the state, Argentina was "precluded from relying on a human right-based defence of necessity in relation to the emergency measures taken during that crisis."[98]

Suez, Sociedad General de Aguas de Barcelona S.A., and Vivendi Universal S.A. v. Argentina (2010)

In *Suez, Sociedad General de Aguas de Barcelona S.A., and Vivendi Universal S.A. v. Argentina*, the freezing of water tariffs for water distribution and waste-water services in the region of Buenos Aires were challenged by the investors. Argentina argued that "[b]ecause of the fundamental role of water in sustaining life and health and the consequent human right to water, it maintains that in judging the conformity of governmental actions with treaty obligations this tribunal must grant Argentina a broader margin of discretion in the present cases than in cases involving other commodities and services."[99]

---

95 Meshel (n 89) 289.
96 *Sempra Energy International v. Argentine Republic*, ICSID Case No. ARB/02/16 (Award, 28 September 2007) [331].
97 Ibid. 332.
98 Meshel (n 89) 282.
99 *Suez, Sociedad General de Aguas de Barcelona, S.A. and Vivendi Universal, S.A. (formerly Aguas Argentinas, S.A., Suez, Sociedad General de Aguas de Barcelona, S.A. and Vivendi Universal, S.A.) v. Argentine Republic (II)*, ICSID Case No. ARB/03/19 (Decision on Liability, 30 Jul 2010) [252].

The tribunal acknowledged that "[t]he provision of water and sewage services to the metropolitan area of Buenos Aires certainly was vital to the health and well-being of nearly ten million people and was therefore an essential interest of the Argentine State."[100] The tribunal analyzed Argentina's defense in the context of a plea of necessity to relieve Argentina of fulfilling its commitments under international treaties and in such context the tribunal did not consider the necessity requirement was fulfilled. Likewise, the tribunal concluded that it was not possible for Argentina to adopt measures, based on its human rights obligations, that went against its commitments under the BITs.[101] For Meshel, despite the acknowledgment of human rights obligations with respect to the right to water, the tribunal analysis is superficial and does not allow the tribunal to engage in a balancing exercise between different obligations.[102]

Impregilo v. Argentina (2011)

The freezing of tariffs and the introduction of a new regulatory framework for water distribution services was the measure at issue in *Impregilo v. Argentina*. The respondent state argued that the measure did not amount to an expropriation since the measure was lawful and proportionate. Argentina further added that, "the regulatory powers of the State were particularly important in order to guarantee its inhabitants the human right to water."[103] The respondent also claimed that its commitments under a BIT should not prevail over human rights instruments and that especial attention should be given to international instruments which provide for the human right to water.[104] In its decision, the tribunal did not consider that the measures were constitutive of an expropriation but concluded that the measures were a violation of the fair and equitable treatment standard. In its conclusion the tribunal did not address Argentina's claims on human rights.[105]

SAUR v. Argentina (2012)

In *SAUR v. Argentina* the tribunal acknowledged the relevance of human rights, and the right to water particularly, as part of the sources of

---

100 Ibid. 260.
101 Ibid.
102 Meshel (n 89) 293.
103 *Impregilo S.p.A. v. Argentine Republic (I)*, ICSID Case No. ARB/07/17 (Award, 21 June 2011) [228].
104 Ibid. 230.
105 Ibid. 330–331.

international law to be observed by the tribunal and concluded that they are part of the general principles of law. The tribunal added that, from the standpoint of the state, the access to clean water is a public service and, from the perspective of the citizen, a fundamental right.[106] However, it concluded that the human right to water and the investor's rights to be protected under the BIT operated at different levels and the respect of both rights must be combined with the rights granted to the investor in the BIT.[107] According to Mashel, although the tribunal noted the task of balancing and supported the human right to water it did not "recognize its potential impact on Argentina's investment protection, thereby largely applying the same restrictive and limited approach of the *Suez* tribunal."[108]

EDF v. Argentina (2012)

In *EDF v. Argentina* the measure at issue included the introduction of the emergency tariff measure to freeze the rate of electricity transmission. Argentina argued that "this measure was in order to guarantee the free enjoyment of certain basic human rights —such as, *inter alia*, the right to life, health, personal integrity, education, the rights of children and political rights which were directly threatened by the socio-economic institutional collapse suffered by the Argentine Republic, where tens of people lost their lives, the right to health, to personal integrity, to work and safety."[109] The tribunal acknowledged its need to be "sensitive to international jus cogens norms, including basic principles of human rights;"[110] it then added that

> [t]he Tribunal does not call into question the potential significance or relevance of human rights in connection with international investment law. However, regardless of any political wisdom in a temporary "pesification" (conversion of foreign currency debt contracts to Argentinean pesos) or provisional freeze of tariffs during the period of crisis, no showing has been made that Argentina was not able to comply with the relevant treaty provisions later, through a rectification of the economic equilibrium which had been disrupted by the emergency measures.[111]

---

106 *SAUR International v. Argentine Republic*, ICSID Case No. ARB/04/4 (Award, 22 May 2014) [330].
107 Ibid. 331.
108 Meshel (n 89) 294.
109 *EDF International S.A., SAUR International S.A. and León Participaciones Argentinas S.A. v. Argentine Republic*, ICSID Case No. ARB/03/23 (Award, 11 June 2012) [192].
110 Ibid. 909.
111 Ibid. 912.

Following this reasoning, the tribunal issued its award based on the *necessity* test to then conclude that Argentina measures were not necessary to protect human rights.[112] For Meshel, this case is similar to *CMS Gas Transmission Company v Argentina* where the tribunal did not analyze Argentina's human rights arguments on their merits to arrive at its conclusion.[113]

Philip Morris Brand Sàrl, Philip Morris Products S.A. and Abel Hermanos S.A. v. Oriental Republic of Uruguay (2016)

One of the cases not related with the Argentina financial crisis is *Philip Morris v. Uruguay*. In this case the challenged measures were the Single Presentation Requirement (SPR), which precluded tobacco manufacturers from marketing more than one variant of cigarette per brand family and the increase in the size of graphic health warnings appearing on cigarette packages (the 80/80 Regulation).[114] In its decision on jurisdiction, the tribunal noted that the BIT "does not prevent Uruguay, in the exercise of its sovereign power, from regulating harmful products in order to protect public after investment in the field have been admitted."[115] The tribunal also stated that "[p]rotecting public health has since long been recognized as an essential manifestation of the State's police power."[116] When assessing the scope of the police power doctrine the tribunal concluded that after the year 2000 a

> range of investment decisions have contributed to develop the scope, content and conditions of the State's police power doctrine, anchoring it in international law. According to a principle recognized by these decisions, whether a measure may be characterized as expropriatory depends on the nature and purpose of the State's actions. Some decisions have relied on the jurisprudence of the European Court of Human Rights, based on Article 1 of Protocol 1 of the Convention.[117]

The tribunal also considered Uruguay's measures as been adopted in "fulfilment of Uruguay's national and international legal obligations for the protection of public health."[118] It particularly addressed the Framework

---

112 Ibid. 914.
113 Meshel (n 89) 282.
114 *Philip Morris Brand Sàrl (Switzerland), Philip Morris Products S.A. (Switzerland) and Abal Hermanos S.A. (Uruguay) v. Oriental Republic of Uruguay*, ICSID Case No. ARB/10/7 ("Philip Morris v Uruguay") (Decision on Jurisdiction, 2 July 2013) (Award, 8 July 2016) [9].
115 *Philip Morris v Uruguay* (2013) 174.
116 *Philip Morris v Uruguay* (2016) 291.
117 Ibid. 295.
118 Ibid. 302.

Convention on Tobacco Control stating that "the FCTC is one of the international conventions to which Uruguay is a party guaranteeing the human right to health."[119]

As already noted by Feria-Tinto:

> a particular slip in the award, however, would be found in footnote 403 where the tribunal referred to Uruguay as a party to the European Convention for the Protection of Human Right [...] It would have been interesting to find reference at this point to other human rights treaties which enshrined the right to health, to which Uruguay is an actual party, including the American Convention on Human Rights, which contains a provision on the right to life whose scope has been interpreted to include positive duties to foster life.[120]

The same author highlighted the relevance of the decision due to its acknowledgement of the Framework Convention on Tobacco Control as one international convention which guarantees the human right to health and by positioning the human right to health in a central place to resolve the dispute.[121]

Urbaser v. Argentina (2016)

A renewed approach to the discussion in human rights as a defense was developed in *Urbaser S.A. and Consorcio de Aguas Bilbao Bizkaia, Bilbao Bizkaia Ur Partzuergoa v. Argentina*. According to the investor, the concession granted by Argentina for the operation of water and sewage services for the province of Greater Buenos Aires faced several constraints put in place by Argentina including the "pesification" of tariffs which destroyed "any chance of obtaining the reasonably expected results,"[122] and in its view this amounted to a violation of fair and equitable treatment, expropriation, discriminatory, and unjustified treatment provisions. Argentina introduced a counterclaim stating that Urbaser did not "provide the necessary investment into the Concession, thus violating its commitments and its obligation under international law based on the human right to water."[123]

Addressing the claim by the investor, the tribunal included a human rights perspective in shaping its expectations, concluding "[t]he protection

---

119 Ibid. 304.
120 Monica Feria-Tinta, "Like Oil and Water? Human Rights in Investment Arbitration in the *Wake of Philip Morris v. Uruguay*" (2017) 34 *Journal of International Arbitration* 601, 618.
121 Ibid. 623–624.
122 *Urbaser S.A. and Consorcio de Aguas Bilbao Biskaia, Bilbao Biskaia Ur Partzuergoa v. Argentine Republic*, ICSID Case No. ARB/07/26 (Award, 8 December 2016) (*Urbaser v Argentina* (Award 2016)) [563].
123 Ibid. 36.

of this universal basic human right constitutes the framework within which Claimants should frame their expectations."[124] However, the tribunal also concluded that "[i]nvoking the human right to water will not aid Respondent in its attempt to exempt itself from any obligations towards the Concessionaire and the investors, as it is Respondent itself who must fulfil the burdens the right to water entails, as stated by the Committee on Economic, Social and Cultural Rights."[125]

Then, the tribunal departed from previous decisions in which human rights and investment obligations were considered to operate at different levels and concluded that Argentina "can and should fulfil both kinds of obligations simultaneously. In so doing, the obligations resulting from the human right to water do not operate as an obstacle to the fulfilment of its obligations towards the Claimants."[126] As noted by Attanasio and Sainati, the *Urbaser* tribunal, "instead of dismissing human right concerns as operating on a different plane from investment law, attempted to integrate human rights obligations with investment protection and generate a consistent set of state obligations."[127]

Regarding Argentina's counterclaim, the tribunal acknowledged that the claimants affirmed that any claim brought on the basis of a violation of human rights is outside of the tribunal's competence. However, the tribunal concluded that said argument is "not sufficient to go so far as excluding on a simple *prima facie* basis any such claim as if it could not imply a dispute relating to an investment"[128] and concluded that it is within its jurisdiction to deal with the counterclaim.[129] This is the "first case in which a tribunal has addressed the merits of a counter-claim (relating to human rights) brought by the state in the context of investment arbitration."[130] The decision to accept a counterclaim by a host state is ground-breaking and certainly will impact the debate of asymmetry in investor–state dispute settlement disputes which have questioned whether host states were always limited to act just as a respondent in these disputes.[131]

Then the tribunal turned its analysis into the issue of whether the human rights treaty posed any obligations to the foreign investor. In its

124 Ibid. 624.
125 Ibid. 693.
126 Ibid. 720.
127 Attanasio and Sainati (n 39) 747.
128 *Urbaser v Argentina* (Award 2016) (n 122) para 1154.
129 Ibid. 1155.
130 Feria-Tinta (n 120) 625.
131 Ibid. 626; Kevin Crow and Lina Lorenzoni Escobar, "International Corporate Obligations, Human Rights, and the Urbaser Standard: Breaking New Ground" (2018) 36 *Boston University International Law Journal* 87, 90.

reasoning the tribunal stated its reluctance "to share Claimant's principled position that guaranteeing the human right to water is duty that may be born solely by the State, and never borne also by private companies like the Claimants."[132] The tribunal argument mentioned that "international law accepts corporate social responsibility as a standard of crucial importance for companies operating in the field of international commerce."[133] With this decision the *Urbaser* tribunal recognizes the existence of corporate human rights obligations.[134] This goes against a backdrop of previous decisions in which human rights obligations have traditionally been understood as obligation only for states. In the words of Attanasio and Sainati: "[i]t mays seem surprising that an investment tribunal, rather than a human rights body, was the first to do so. After all, investment law and investment tribunals are often thought to ignore non-economic social considerations like individual rights."[135]

The award then proceeded to examine the status of the right to water. In its reasoning the tribunal included several human rights instruments, such as the Universal Declaration of Human Rights,[136] the International Covenant on Economic, Social and Cultural Rights and the decision by the UN Committee on Economic, Social and Cultural Rights regarding the right to water and a resolution by the UN General Assembly addressing the same issue.[137] Finally the tribunal concluded that "[i]t is not disputed that the human right to water and sanitation is recognized today as part of human rights and that this right as its corresponding obligation the duty of States to provide all persons living under their jurisdiction with safe and clean drinking water and sewage services."[138] The extension of the acknowledgement of the human right to water is another outstanding feature in *Urbaser*.

Despite its strong endorsement to the acknowledgement of human right to water, the tribunal concluded that there is no provision in the applicable BIT which "has the effect of extending or transferring to the Concessionaire an obligation to perform services complying with the residents' human right to access to water and sewage services."[139] Crow and Lorenzini have analyzed the concept of corporate social responsibility (CSR) in *Urbaser* and have affirmed

132 *Urbaser v Argentina* (Award 2016) (n 122) para 1193.
133 Ibid. 1195.
134 Attanasio and Sainati (n 39) 749.
135 Ibid.
136 *Urbaser v Argentina* (Award 2016) (n 122) para 1196.
137 Ibid. 1197.
138 Ibid. 1205.
139 *Urbaser v Argentina* (Award 2016) (n 122) para 1207.

[t]he Tribunal considered that CSR, on its own, is insufficient to obligate corporations to harmonize internal policies with human rights law and that the focus must therefore be on contextualizing a corporation's specific activities as they relate to the human right at issue in order to determine whether any international law obligations attach to non-State individual.[140]

From the above-mentioned jurisprudence, it is possible to infer an evolution in the way the respondents invoke human rights arguments and how tribunals address these arguments.

Firstly, the respondent invoked human rights arguments to demonstrate the existence of a conflict between the international investment agreement and its human rights obligations. However, arbitral tribunals did not perceive the existence of a conflict between them.

Secondly, human rights commitments are not used to trigger a dispute under the BIT but as defenses for the measures adopted. In this regard, tribunals consider the issue of human rights together with the requirement to configure a state of necessity which can allow the state to depart from the fulfilment of international obligations. At this stage, the tribunals acknowledge the relevance of international human rights commitments but considered that the requirements of necessity did not take place.

Thirdly, tribunals analyze human rights commitments as part of the obligations that must be observed by the state but concluded that they do not triumph over BIT commitments and as such the respondent must abide to both instruments which made the tribunals analyze whether the measures adopted by the respondent are proper to fulfil such objective.

The *Philip Morris v Uruguay* and *Urbaser v. Argentina* cases certainly constitute a new way to address this relationship by placing human rights at the core of the decisions, introducing an exercise of balancing different obligations and in *Urbaser* as a tool to shape the expectations of the foreign investor. In this regard, it is worth mentioning that some of the elements applied in this decision seem to be consistent with suggestion previously put in place by scholars such as Simma who have argued that "foreign investment contracts represent a separate entry point for mediating compliance with internationally guaranteed economic and social rights"[141] and that the introduction of a human rights audit as way for the investor to shape its expectations in accordance with economic, social, and cultural rights.[142]

---

140 Crow and Escobar (n 131) 112.
141 Simma (n 36) 593.
142 Ibid. 595.

Introduction of human rights arguments by third parties

Allegations of human rights by third parties in investor–state dispute settlements have the potential to reinforce the human rights scope in the investment conflict but there is no consistent decision on this matter. In fact, one element against the evidence of possible reinforcement between investor–state dispute settlement and human rights is the lack of a consistent practice in accepting submission by third parties in investor–state dispute settlements.

On the one hand, in *Aguas del Tunari v. Bolivia*, and *Chevron v. Ecuador* the amicus submissions were rejected despite the cases clearly impacting on the public interest and human rights. On the other hand, *amicus curiae* were accepted in the case *Methanex v. USA* although no disposition in the procedural rules (UNCITRAL Arbitration Rules) had a mention to it but the tribunal decided to accept the third-party submission in view of the public interested involved.[143] *Suez v. Argentina* was the first time that an arbitration tribunal under the ICSID rules accepted the participation of civil society despite the opposition by the complainants.[144] In all these cases participation has been requested from several different actors ranging from NGOs (both local and international), civil society organizations (e.g. foundations, institutes), and academia.[145]

---

143 Kube and Petersmann (n 47) 15.
144 *Suez, Sociedad General de Aguas de Barcelona, S.A. and Vivendi Universal, S.A. (formerly Aguas Argentinas, S.A., Suez, Sociedad General de Aguas de Barcelona, S.A. and Vivendi Universal, S.A.) v. Argentine Republic (II)*, ICSID Case No. ARB/03/19 (Order in response to a Petition for Participation as Amicus Curiae, 19 May 2005) ("*Suez v Argentina*").
145 For example, in *Aguas del Tunari v Bolivia* the amici were submitted by the American environmental NGO Earthjustice, Friends of the Earth-Netherlands, as well as by the local grassroots organizations: Coordinadora para la Defensa del Agua y Vida, La Federación Departamental Cochabambina de Organizaciones Regantes, SEMAPA Sur, and the natural persons Oscar Olivera, Omar Fernández, Father Luis Sánchez, and Congressman Jorge Alvarado. In *Chevron v Ecuador*, the amici were submitted by the International Institute for Sustainable Development (IISD) and the local Fundación Pachamama. IISD and Earthjustice also submitted an amici briefs in *Methanex v USA*, as well as the NGOs Communities for a Better Environment, the Blue Water Network of Earth Island Institute and the Center for International Environmental Law (CIEL). CIEL, together with four other local NGOs (Asociación Civil por la Igualdad y la Justicia (ACIJ), Centro de Estudios Legales y Sociales (CELS), Consumidores Libres Cooperativa Ltda. de Provisión de Servicios de Acción Comunitaria, and Unión de Usuarios y Consumidores), submitted amici curiae in *Suez v Argentina*. See *Aguas del Tunari S.A. v. Republic of Bolivia*, ICSID Case No. ARB/02/3 (Letter by NGO to Petition to Participate as amici curiae, 29 January 2003); *Chevron Corporation and Texaco Petroleum Company v. The Republic of*

The importance of these submissions shall not be underestimated since in *Suez v. Argentina*, as noted by Dupuy and Viñuales,[146] the *amicus* included a call for an assessment on the decision impact on human rights and a call for systemic integration of human rights and investment disciplines. Yet, Kube and Petersmann have highlighted that "[t]here is no consistent practice and no clear guidance as to what role *amici* arguments should play in the judicial decision-making. Acceptance and impact of human rights arguments remains subject to the discretion of arbitrators, which have so far failed to develop a consistent and transparent methodology."[147]

Concluding remarks

Investor–state arbitration could be consistent with human rights, instead of undermining them.[148] As we have seen in *Urbaser v. Argentina*, the arbitral tribunal developed an exhaustive analysis of the relationship between the human right to water and the protection of foreign investment, as a result of a counterclaim brought by Argentina against the investor. Although the counterclaim was ultimately rejected, the tribunal ruled that the investment treaty "has to be construed in harmony with other international law of which it forms part, including those relating to human rights."[149] Therefore, compliance with the obligations derived from human rights instruments may well serve as a context for the interpretation of the obligations of states with respect to foreign investors contained in international investment agreements.

The relationship between human rights and foreign investment and protection in Latin America entails a complex scenario for states that have to be respondent in two different forums defending interests that in most of the cases could be described as irreconcilable. The lack of a comprehensive interpretation that integrates both human rights and investment commitments could give more space to states to be inconsistent in complying with its international commitments. For example, the use of human rights as a defense in investor–state dispute settlement in cases that involve social and

Ecuador (II), PCA Case No. 2009–23 (Submission of Amici, 5 November 2010); *Methanex Corporation v. United States of America*, UNCITRAL (IISD's Application for Amicus Standing, 25 August 2000) and (IISD's Supplemental Application for Amicus Standing, 31 August 2000 and 6 September 2000) and *Suez v Argentina* (n 144).

146 Dupuy and Viñuales (n 53) 1758.
147 Kube and Petersmann (n 47) 250
148 Fry (n 38) 82, 148.
149 *Urbaser v Argentina* (Award 2016) (n 122) [1200].

environmental damage does not guarantee that injured victims will obtain remedies or reparations, or that the role of the host state in those human rights violations will be taken into account.

Reconciling the diverse principles of justice underlying human rights and investment tribunals remains a challenging task and unfinished business, but that does not mean that this is impossible or that inconsistent approaches should take into consideration only some human rights and disregard others.[150] We should not see both systems as irreconcilable. A state should not promise investment protection without respect for human rights. The protection of human rights should not be done disregarding commitments made by the state with respect to investments. Human rights could be brought into investor–state dispute settlement to interpret state's investment commitments in a comprehensive way, at the same time that investor–state dispute settlement could also be used to reinforce human rights, particularly civil and political rights, as some of them have been included as standards of protection in investment treaties. Besides the evolution of ISDS case law, the process could be helped with treaty-making that clarifies standards like FET, FPS and expropriation, and their relation with human rights. As we have seen throughout this chapter, Latin American countries have been important (although perhaps unconscious) promoters of the consistency between both systems.

150 Kube and Petersmann (n 47) 27–28.

11

ISDS and human rights: A Latin American dialectic

Farouk El-Hosseny, Patrick Devine, and Ilan Brun-Vargas

Introduction

In 2019, the world watched in consternation fires raging in the Amazon, not only putting at risk one of the most crucial ecosystems on the planet, but also threatening the very existence of the indigenous peoples who inhabit it.[1] The fingers were immediately pointed at logging and farming. At the end of the same year, consumers in the UK were shocked to learn that Christmas cards by the country's leading supermarket chain were alleged to have been made by prison laborers in China.[2] Labor rights and conditions have also taken center stage in football, with FIFA – under unprecedented pressure – creating a Human Rights Advisory Body in 2017 to "ensure respect for human rights," including particularly with regards to the preparations for the next FIFA 2022 World Cup in Qatar.[3] Instances where business and human rights collide now seem to occur constantly – it increasingly appears that the two will continue to be entangled in a complex dialectic.

The broadening emphasis on human rights has trickled its way into investment-treaty arbitration. Yet, a decade ago, it was suggested that "the present role of human rights in the context of investment arbitration is peripheral at best."[4] This statement was rooted in a conception of international law that considers international human rights instruments to impose legal obligations on states only and not on investors.[5] Indeed, under

---

1 Herton Escobar, "Amazon fires clearly linked to deforestation, scientists say" (2019) 365 (6456) *Science* 853.

2 BBC, "Tesco halts production at Chinese factory over alleged 'forced' labour," 22 December 2019 www.bbc.co.uk/news/uk-50883161 accessed 13 January 2020.

3 FIFA, "Third Report by the FIFA Human Rights Advisory Board" (May 2019) https://resources.fifa.com/image/upload/third-report-by-the-fifa-human-rights-advisory-board.pdf?cloudid=sxdtbmx6wczrmwlk9rcr accessed 13 January 2020.

4 Clara Reiner and Christoph Schreuer, "Human Rights and International Investment Arbitration" in Pierre-Marie Dupuy and others (eds), *Human Rights in International Investment Law and Arbitration* (OUP 2010) 83.

5 The primary responsibility of states to protect human rights has arguably since been reaffirmed by the United Nations Guiding Principles on Business and Human Rights

a Westphalian conception of international law, states are after all the *sole* subjects of the international legal order, thus only states carry rights and obligations therein.[6] This conception has come under increasing attack in recent years, including by arbitral tribunals.[7]

Beyond the taxonomies of international law, there is now a generalized expectation that investors must act responsibly, including by not violating human rights, irrespective of the academic debate as to their status as objects or subjects of international law. This expectation has been increasingly raised in investor–state disputes. Academics and practitioners have often adopted polarizing positions on this question, ranging from the expression of indifference to human rights issues in the context of investment law to proposals for developing international arbitration into a system for the routine adjudication of human rights disputes.[8]

Given that the structures of international investment law have historically given scant treatment to human rights, under so-called "First Generation" bilateral investment treaties (BITs),[9] human rights issues have traditionally

---

(*UNGPs*) which impose no direct legal obligations on corporations but instead merely call on corporate actors to "respect" human rights. States obligations to protect, respect, and fulfil socio-economic and cultural human rights was first articulated by the UN Special Rapporteur, Asbjørn Eide, in his 1987 report (see UNCHR (subcommission) Report by Special Rapporteur Asbjørn Eide, "The Right to Adequate Food as a Human Right" (1987) UN Doc E/CN.4/Sub.2/1987/23).

6 Patrick Daillier, Alain Pellet, Mathias Forteau, and Daniel Müller, *Droit International Public* (LGDJ 2009), para 20.

7 Ari MacKinnon, "Why Haven't We Seen More International Human Rights Law Issues in International Investment Arbitration?" in Carlos González-Bueno (ed), *40 under 40 International Arbitration* (Dykinson S L 2018), 323–336. Of particular significance for the erosion of this orthodoxy are the obiter comments of the tribunal in *Urbaser S.A. and Consorcio de Aguas Bilbao Biskaia, Bilbao Biskaia Ur Partzuergoa v. Argentine Republic*, ICSID Case No. ARB/07/26 (Award, 8 December 2016) (*Urbaser v Argentina*, or *Urbaser*) paras 1194–1195 ("… international law accepts corporate social responsibility as a standard of crucial importance for companies operating in the field of international commerce. This standard includes commitments to comply with human rights in the framework of those entities' operations conducted in countries other than the country of their seat or incorporation. In light of this more recent development, it can no longer be admitted that companies operating internationally are immune from becoming subjects of international law.").

8 See footnote 9 below.

9 "First Generation" BITs generally refers to those BITs that were negotiated in the 1980s and 1990s; see more generally John Beechey and Antony Crockett, "New Generation Of Bilateral Investment Treaties: Consensus or Divergence?" in Arthur Rovine (ed), *Contemporary Issues in International Arbitration and Mediation: The Fordham Papers* (Brill 2009).

had limited bearing on the outcome of investment law disputes.[10] However, as issues relating to human rights have progressively permeated the world of international investment law as mentioned above, tribunals have had to wrestle with the question of how to appropriately acknowledge and take into account human rights concerns, as will be closely examined in this chapter.

It is in the Latin American context that much of this debate has played out. Issues relating to human rights have been especially prevalent in Latin American investment-treaty jurisprudence of recent years. This is most notably due to the difficult line Latin American states tread between protecting and promoting multinational activity, in the extractive sectors particularly, and their duties to regulate in the public interest, preserve their natural resources, and protect indigenous communities within their borders. Latin American states are indeed often faced with a difficult balancing act between these competing obligations.[11]

This chapter will first set out a brief overview of those "First Generation" BITs and other agreements that have been relied upon in the jurisprudence of interest. It will then touch upon some of the recently negotiated BITs and other international instruments which seek to establish a more accommodating framework for human rights concerns not only in the context of the protection and promotion of foreign investment, but also in the broader discussion on business and human rights. The chapter then closely examines

---

10 Patrick Dumberry and Gabrielle Dumas-Aubin, "How to impose human rights obligations on corporations under investment treaties? Pragmatic guidelines for the amendment of BITs" in Karl P. Sauvant (ed), *Yearbook on International Investment Law and Policy* (Barnes and Noble 2011–2012) 569; Silvia Steininger, "What's human rights got to do with it? An empirical analysis of human rights references in investment arbitration" (2018) 1 *Leiden Journal of International Law* 2. This is not helped by the fact that very few BITs or multilateral investment treaties overtly impose human rights obligations on corporate actors (an OECD study found that in 2014 only 0.5 percent of 2,107 investment treaties feature human rights considerations www.oecd.org/investment/investment-policy/WP-2014_01.pdf accessed 13 January 2020, or that investment law and human rights law have often been conceptualized as self-contained regimes at international law, although this view is arguably waning (see Anne Peters, "The Refinement of International Law: From Fragmentation to Regime Interaction and Politicization" (2016) Max Planck Institute for Comparative Public Law & International Law (MPIL), Research Paper No 2016–19 https://ssrn.com/abstract=2823512 or http://dx.doi.org/10.2139/ssrn.2823512 accessed 13 January 2020).

11 The overwhelming majority of Latin American states are party to international law instruments recognizing rights of indigenous communities to be consulted and participate in decisions concerning their lands – see Convention concerning Indigenous and Tribal Peoples in Independent Countries (signed and adopted 27 June 1989, entered into force 5 September 1991) 1650 UNTS 383. Also see Chapters 10 by Rodrigo Polanco Lazo and Felipe Ferreira Catalán (in relation to balancing human rights and international investment law) and 9 by Sufyan Droubi, Cecilia Juliana Flores Elizondo and Raphael Heffron (in relation to indigenous peoples' rights and international investments) in this volume.

the latest jurisprudence touching on human rights in investment-treaty arbitration and outlines the various approaches that have been adopted by tribunals confronted by human rights concerns. This is followed by concluding remarks as to whether investment-treaty tribunals are proving responsive to the pressures arising from the exponential emphasis on human rights.

Historical absence of human rights from investment treaties

"First Generation" BITs focus exclusively on investment protection and promotion. Unlike more recently negotiated BITs, with the exception of legality in the making and conduct of investments, "First Generation" BITs do not impose obligations on investors, nor do they deal with human rights or, more generally, the state's prerogative to regulate in the public interest.[12]

It is axiomatic, however, that states may expropriate or nationalize foreign assets for a public purpose, so long as compensation is paid. This is reflected in the UK–Bolivia BIT (1988) relied upon in *South American Silver*:[13]

---

12 The same cannot be said in respect of all free trade agreements, some of which included references to human rights in preambles; see for example the preambles of the cooperation agreements concluded by the European Communities during the 1990s–2000s: Free Trade Agreement between the European Free Trade Association (*EFTA*) and the Kingdom of Morocco (signed 19 June 1997, entered into force 1 March 2000) ("Reaffirming their commitment to pluralistic democracy based on the rule of law, human rights and fundamental freedoms, and recalling the principles of the United Nations Charter"); Free Trade Agreement between the EFTA States and the Republic of Macedonia (signed 19 June 2000, entered into force 1 May 2002) ("Reaffirming their commitment to pluralistic democracy based on the rule of law, human rights, including rights of persons belonging to minorities, and fundamental freedoms, and recalling the principles of the United Nations Charter"); Free Trade Agreement between the EFTA States and the Hashemite Kingdom of Jordan (signed 21 June 2001, entered into force 1 September 2002) ("Reaffirming their commitment to the principles of the United Nations Charter, in particular pluralistic democracy based on the rule of law and political and economic freedoms and observance of human rights, including rights of persons belonging to minorities"); Free Trade Agreement between the European Free Trade Association and the Republic of Singapore (signed 26 June 2002, entered into force 1 January 2003) ("REAFFIRMING their commitment to the principles set out in the United Nations Charter and the Universal Declaration of Human Rights"); Free Trade Agreement between the EFTA States and the Republic of Chile (signed 26 June 2003, entered into force 1 December 2004) ("REAFFIRMING their commitment to democracy, the rule of law, human rights and fundamental freedoms in accordance with their obligations under international law, including principles and objectives set out in the United Nations Charter and the Universal Declaration of Human Rights").

13 *South American Silver Limited v. The Plurinational State of Bolivia*, PCA Case No. 2013–15 (Award, 30 August 2018) (*South American Silver*).

Investments of nationals or companies of either Contracting Party shall not be nationalised, expropriated or subjected to measures having effect equivalent to nationalisation or expropriation (hereinafter referred to as "expropriation") in the territory of the other Contracting Party except for a public purpose and for a social benefit related to the internal needs of that Party and against just and effective compensation.[14]

Similarly, BITs typically provide investors guarantees to "fair and equitable treatment" (FET) and "full protection and security" (FPS), with the breach of such standards giving rise to an action for compensatory damages. This is reflected in the Canada–Venezuela BIT (1996) relied upon in *Crystallex*:[15]

Each Contracting Party shall, in accordance with the principles of international law, accord investments or returns of investors of the other Contracting Party fair and equitable treatment and full protection and security.[16]

In contrast to later generations of BITs, "First Generation" BITs do refer to the state's police powers to enact *bona fide* measures in the public interest as an exception to investment protection and promotion guarantees. Indeed, tribunals applying "First Generation" treaties, such as the North American Free Trade Agreement (NAFTA),[17] resorted to general principles of international law (as opposed to the text of the treaty *strictu sensu*) to uphold said powers. For example, in *Methanex*, the tribunal found that:

… an intentionally discriminatory regulation against a foreign investor fulfils a key requirement for establishing expropriation. But as a matter of general international law, a non-discriminatory regulation for a public purpose, which is enacted in accordance with due process and, which affects, *inter alios*, a foreign investor or investment is not deemed expropriatory and compensable unless specific commitments had been given by the regulating government to

14 Agreement between the Government of the United Kingdom of Great Britain and Northern Ireland and the Government of the Republic of Bolivia for the Promotion and Protection of Investments (signed 24 May 1988, entered into force 16 February 1990, terminated 14 May 2014), art 5.

15 *Crystallex International Corporation v. Bolivarian Republic of Venezuela*, ICSID Case No ARB(AF)/11/2 (Award, 4 April 2016) (*Crystallex*).

16 Agreement between the Government of Canada and the Government of Venezuela for the Promotion and Protection of Investments (signed 1 July 1996, entered into force 28 January 1998) (*Canada-Venezuela BIT*), art 2(2).

17 Compare with the new Agreement between the United States of America, the United Mexican States, and Canada (signed 30 November 2018, entered into force 1 July 2020) (*USMCA (2018)*) art 14.16 ("Nothing in this Chapter shall be construed to prevent a Party from adopting, maintaining, or enforcing any measure otherwise consistent with this Chapter that it considers appropriate to ensure that investment activity in its territory is undertaken in a manner sensitive to environmental, health, safety, or other regulatory objectives").

the then putative foreign investor contemplating investment that the government would refrain from such regulation.[18]

That said, a requirement of legality in the making of the investment is found in numerous "First Generation" BITs. The contemporaneous model BITs of various European states, as well as others such as that between India and Mauritius, are notable examples.[19] States have often invoked the legality requirement as a defense vis-à-vis investors in investment-treaty arbitrations, including in combination with the principle of "unclean hands."[20] The Argentina–Spain BIT (1991), invoked in *Urbaser*, provides an illustration:[21]

Each Party shall protect in its territory the investments made in accordance with its laws ... [22]

18 *Methanex Corporation v. United States of America*, UNCITRAL (Final Award of the Tribunal on Jurisdiction and Merits, 3 August 2005) (*Methanex*), p. 278. See also the tribunal in *Chemtura v Canada* stating that "[it] considers in any event that the measures challenged by the Claimant constituted a valid exercise of the Respondent's police powers. As discussed in detail in connection with article 1105 of NAFTA, the [Pest Management Regulatory Agency of Canada] took measures within its mandate, in a non-discriminatory manner, motivated by the increasing awareness of the dangers presented by lindane for human health and the environment. A measure adopted under such circumstances is a valid exercise of the State's police powers and, as a result, does not constitute an expropriation," *Chemtura Corporation v. Government of Canada*, UNCITRAL (formerly *Crompton Corporation v. Government of Canada*) (*Award, 2 August 2010*) (*Chemtura*), para 266.

19 OECD, *International Investment Perspectives* (2004) 125. See e.g. Draft Agreement between the Government of the Republic of France and the Government of the Republic of [...] on the Reciprocal Promotion and Protection of Investments (adopted 2006) (France Model BIT) art 3 ("Each Contracting Party shall promote and admit on its territory and in its maritime area, in accordance with its legislation and with the provisions of this Agreement, investments made by investors of the other Contracting Party."); Treaty between the Federal Republic of Germany and [...] concerning the Encouragement and Reciprocal Protection of Investments (adopted 2008) (Germany Model BIT) art 2(1) ("Each Contracting State shall in its territory promote as far as possible investments by investors of the other Contracting State and admit such investments in accordance with its legislation."). Agreement between the Government of the Republic of Mauritius and the Government of the Republic of India for the Promotion and Protection of Investments (signed 4 September 1998, entered into force 20 June 2000, terminated 22 March 2017) art 2 ("This Agreement shall apply to all investments made by investors of either Contracting Party in the territory of the other Contracting Party, accepted as such in accordance with the laws and regulations, whether made before or after the coming into force of this Agreement.").

20 See Zachary Douglas, "The Plea of Illegality in Investment Treaty Arbitration" (2014) 29 (1) *ICSID Review* 155, 186; see also the *Hulley* tribunal's analysis of the principle of "unclean hands" in *Hulley Enterprises Ltd. v. Russian Federation*, PCA Case No. 2005–03/AA226 (Final Award, 18 July 2014), paras 1343–74.

21 *Urbaser v Argentina* (Award 2016) (n 7).

22 Agreement between the Argentina Republic and the Kingdom of Spain on the Reciprocal Promotion and Protection of Investments (signed 3 October 1991, entered

As will be discussed directly below, a new generation of treaties and instruments is now going further, not only in terms of clarifying the state's right to regulate in the public interest, but also referring explicitly to human rights.

Incorporation of human rights in new international instruments

Recent years have seen unambiguous efforts by several states, academics, practitioners, and civil society stakeholders to elaborate mechanisms to account for human rights violations in the context of international business more generally, including international investment. These efforts are divided into two categories: substantive and procedural.

Substantive innovations

Beyond soft law instruments,[23] international trade and investment treaties are increasingly referring to human rights.[24] Human rights norms may already be taken into account through (i) a systemic interpretation of international law, if the relevant norm is enshrined in an international treaty, in accordance with article 31(3)(c) of the Vienna Convention on

---

into force 28 September 1992) Agreement between the Argentina Republic and the Kingdom of Spain on the Reciprocal Promotion and Protection of Investments (signed 3 October 1991, entered into force 28 September 1992) (*Argentina-Spain BIT (1991)*) art 3(1).

23 Soft law is composed of those responsibilities stemming from non-binding guidelines, codes and voluntary principles. For a fuller discussion of soft law "scepticism," see Melaku Geboye Desta, "Soft law in international law: an overview" in Andrea Bjorkland and August Reinisch (eds), *International Investment Law and Soft Law* (Edward Elgar Publishing 2012) 45–47. The Equator Principles is a notable example of a soft law instrument. The principles, in their fourth iteration since 2003, were initially based on the IFC Standards and World Bank guidelines on social and environmental sustainability. They provide a framework for risk management in relation to social and environmental concerns by requiring the implementation of impact assessments, monitoring and reporting mechanisms. The latest iteration of 18 November 2019 contains additional human rights and environmental commitments in recognition of the Paris Agreement; *see* International Finance Corporation (IFC), "IFC Performance Standards on Environmental and Social Sustainability" (2013); and World Bank Group, "Environmental, Health, and Safety Guidelines," now part of the "Environmental and Social Framework" (ESF) (2018).

24 The amalgamation between international trade or business treaties and international investment treaties may seem, at first, incongruent for obvious reasons. However, the increasing emphasis on the regulatory plane on human rights correlates with the increasing invocation of human rights in investment treaty arbitration and is therefore worth mentioning.

the Law of Treaties (**VCLT**);[25] or (ii) domestic law, if the relevant norm is enshrined in municipal law.[26] Their contents may not necessarily overlap. For example, while there is still debate as to whether a right to water has crystallized under international law, a number of states have unequivocally recognized that right in domestic legislation, including in their constitutions.[27]

The novelty, however, is for international trade and investment treaties to effectively legislate for human rights by expressly referring to them. Such references fall along a broad spectrum, ranging from quasi-hortatory statements to the imposition of hard obligations on businesses and investors.

At the softer end of this spectrum, for example, the Ecuador–EFTA Comprehensive Economic Partnership Agreement (2018) provides in its

25 Vienna Convention on the Law of Treaties (signed 23 May 1969, entered into force 27 January 1980) 1155 UNTS 331, art 31(3)(c) ("There shall be taken into account, together with the context: ... Any relevant rules of international law applicable in the relations between the parties."); on the systemic interpretation of international investment law in order to take into account human rights, see Bruno Simma, "Foreign Investment Arbitration: A Place for Human Rights?" (2011) 60 *International and Comparative Law Quarterly* 573.

26 Municipal law may be the applicable law in ICSID proceedings in the scenario contemplated under article 42(1) of the ICSID Convention, which provides that: "The Tribunal shall decide a dispute in accordance with such rules of law as may be agreed by the parties. In the absence of such agreement, the Tribunal shall apply the law of the Contracting State party to the dispute (including its rules on the conflict of laws) and such rules of international law as may be applicable." See Convention on the Settlement of Investment Disputes Between States and Nationals of Other States (signed 18 March 1965, entered into force 14 October 1966) 575 UNTS 159, 4 ILM 532. In the alternative, tribunals treat municipal law as a question of fact. On the relevance of human rights norms under municipal law, see Francesco Francioni, "Access to Justice, Denial of Justice and International Investment Law" (2009) 20 *European Journal of International Law* 729.

27 Uruguay and Ecuador have unconstitutionalized the privatization of water services. Other states' constitutions that have referred to the right to water include – *inter alia* – Bolivia, Laos, Ethiopia, Gambia, Guatemala, Panama, Uganda, South African, Venezuela, and Zambia. For instance, the article 27 of the South African Constitution states that: "(1) Everyone has the right to have access to... (b) sufficient food and water... (2) The state must take reasonable legislative and other measures, within its available resources, to achieve the progressive realization of each of these rights." See the Constitution of the Republic of South Africa (No. 108 of 1996) www.gov. za/documents/constitution/1996/a108-96.pdf accessed 13 January 2020. Tunisia's recently promulgated constitution provides under article 44 that: "*Le droit à l'eau est garanti. La préservation de l'eau et son utilisation rationnelle sont un devoir pour l'Etat et la société.*" See *Constitution de La République Tunisienne*, dated 26 January 2014 www.marsad.tn/fr/constitution# accessed 13 January 2020. For a detailed analysis, see Farouk El-Hosseny, *Civil Society in Investment Treaty Arbitration: Status and Prospects* (Brill Nijhoff, 2019), 149–155.

first article that it is "based on ... the respect for democratic principles and human rights."[28] Similarly, the Armenia–EU Comprehensive and Enhanced Partnership Agreement (2017) provides that "[r]espect for ... human rights ... as enshrined in ... relevant human rights instruments ... constitute an essential element of [the treaty]."[29]

Slightly further along the spectrum comes the reaffirmation of the state's right to regulate, discussed above. For example, the Norway Model BIT (2015) states as follows:

> Nothing in this Agreement shall be construed to prevent a Party from adopting, maintaining or enforcing any measure otherwise consistent with this Agreement that it considers appropriate to ensure that investment activity is undertaken in a manner sensitive to health, safety, human rights, labour rights, resource management or environmental concerns.[30]

The commentary to the model indicates that this is a "headline provision" whose "main significance ... is as an additional interpretive factor in determining the scope of the agreement's protection provisions."[31] Similarly, the Canada–EU Comprehensive Economic and Trade Agreement (2016) illustrates the types of objectives that are likely to fall under the state's right to regulate, recalling the parties' right to regulate "to achieve legitimate policy objectives, such as the protection of public health, safety, the environment or public morals, social or consumer protection or the promotion and protection of cultural diversity."[32] The Argentina–Chile Trade Agreement (2017) contains a similar provision.[33]

---

28 Comprehensive Economic Partnership Agreement between the EFTA States and the Republic of Ecuador (signed 25 June 2018, entered into force 1 November 2020) art 1.1.

29 Comprehensive and Enhanced Partnership Agreement between the European Union and the European Atomic Energy Community and their Member States, of the one part and the Republic of Armenia, of the other (signed 24 November 2017) art 2.

30 Agreement between the Kingdom of Norway and [...] for the Promotion and Protection of Investments (published 15 May 2015) (Norway Model BIT) art 12.

31 See Government of Norway, "Comments on the Individual Provisions of the Model Agreement" (2015) para 2.10.

32 Comprehensive Economic and Trade Agreement between Canada and the European Union (signed 30 October 2016, entered into force (provisionally) 21 September 2017) ch Eight, sect D, art 8.9.

33 Free Trade Agreement between the Republic of Argentina and the Republic of Chile (signed 2 November 2017, entered into force 1 May 2019) (*Argentina-Chile FTA (2017)*) art 8.4 ("For purposes of this Chapter, the Parties reaffirm the right of each Party to regulate in its territory to achieve legitimate public policy objectives, such as the protection of health, safety, the environment, public morals, social or consumer protection, or the promotion and protection of cultural diversity") (free translation from Spanish). Commentators note that the enumeration of legitimate public

Furthermore, some treaties incorporate references to principles of corporate social responsibility (CSR), and other standards of investor conduct. An early attempt to account for investor conduct in a treaty by reference to CSR can be found in Canada's free trade agreements (FTAs) concluded with Colombia and Peru in 2008.[34] At the time, the agreements were coined "FTAs with a heart,"[35] particularly in light of their advancement of CSR in the following terms:

> Each Party should encourage enterprises operating within its territory or subject to its jurisdiction to voluntarily incorporate internationally recognized standards of corporate social responsibility in their internal policies, such as statements of principle that have been endorsed or are supported by the Parties. These principles address issues such as labour, the environment, human rights, community relations and anti-corruption. The Parties remind those enterprises of the importance of incorporating such corporate social responsibility standards in their internal policies.[36]

Brazil's practice in relation to its Comprehensive Investment Facilitation Agreements (CIFAs) provides a good example of two variations of the CSR clause. Brazil's earlier treaties contain a reference to CSR principles followed by an itemized list of such principles – without reference to a specific instrument. For example, the Brazil–Peru Economic and Trade Expansion Agreement (2016) contains a "best efforts" obligation for investors to comply with "the following voluntary principles and standards for responsible business conduct."[37]

policy objectives in the treaty is likely to facilitate and generalize the resort to a proportionality analysis for violations. See Carmen Martinez Lopez, Lucy Martinez, "Proportionality in Investment Treaty Arbitration and Beyond: An 'Irresistible Attraction'?" (2015) 2 *BCDR International Arbitration Review* 261.

34 Free Trade Agreement between Canada and Colombia (signed 21 November 2008, entered into force 15 August 2011); Free Trade Agreement between Canada and the Republic of Peru (signed 29 May 2008, entered into force 1 August 2009) (Canada–Peru FTA (2008)).

35 See video of the Canadian Department of Foreign Affairs, Trade and Development, "Sommaire: libre-échange avec la Colombie et le Pérou" www.youtube.com/watch?v=rS5QOtQOSM8 accessed 13 January 2020.

36 Canada–Peru FTA (2008) (n 34) art 810.

37 Economic and Trade Expansion Agreement between the Federative Republic of Brazil and the Republic of Peru (signed 29 April 2016) art 2.13(2). This is also the case of the Cooperation and Investment Facilitation Agreement between the Federative Republic of Brazil and the Republic of Colombia (signed 9 October 2015) art 13; Cooperation and Investment Facilitation Agreement between the Federative Republic of Brazil and the United Mexican States (signed 26 May 2015) art 13; Cooperation and Investment Facilitation Agreement between the Federative Republic of Brazil and the Co-Operative Republic of Guyana (signed 13 December 2018) art 15;

In a clear attempt to ossify soft law principles, more recent treaties make direct references to CSR instruments, such as the OECD Guidelines for Multinational Enterprises (2011),[38] the United Nations Guiding Principles on Business and Human Rights (UNGPs) (2011),[39] or Recommendation

Cooperation and Investment Facilitation Agreement between the Federative Republic of Brazil and the Republic of Suriname (signed 2 May 2018) art 15; Cooperation and Investment Facilitation Agreement between the Federative Republic of Brazil and the Republic of Ecuador (signed 25 September 2019) art 14; Cooperation and Investment Facilitation Agreement between the Federative Republic of Brazil and the Kingdom of Morocco (signed 13 June 2019) art 13; and the Intra-MERCOSUR Cooperation and Facilitation Investment Protocol (signed 7 April 2017, entered into force 30 July 2019).

38 *Argentina–Chile FTA (2017)* (n 33) art 8.17 ("The Parties reaffirm their commitment to the internationally recognized standards, guidelines and principles of corporate social responsibility that have been adopted or are supported by the Parties, including the OECD Guidelines for Multinational Enterprises, and each Party shall seek to encourage persons operating in its territory or subject to its jurisdiction to voluntarily incorporate these standards, guidelines and principles into their business practices and internal policies") (free translation from Spanish); Free Trade Agreement between Brazil and Chile (signed 21 November 2018) (*Brazil-Chile FTA (2018)*) art 8.15 ("Investors and their investments should make their best efforts to comply with the OECD Guidelines for Multinational Enterprises of the Organisation for Economic Cooperation and Development") (free translation from Spanish); Cooperation and Facilitation Investment Agreement between the Federative Republic of Brazil and the United Arab Emirates (signed 15 March 2019) art 15 ("Investors and their investment shall strive to achieve the highest possible level of contribution to the sustainable development of the Host State and the local community, through the adoption of a high degree of socially responsible practices, based on the voluntary principles, and standards set out in the OECD Guidelines for Multinational Enterprises"); Agreement between the Federative Republic of Brazil and the Federal Democratic Republic of Ethiopia on Investment Cooperation and Facilitation (signed 11 April 2018) art 14 ("Investors and their investment shall strive to achieve the highest possible level of contribution to the sustainable development of the host State and the local community, through the adoption of a high degree of socially responsible practices, based on the principles and standards set out in this Article and the OECD Guidelines for Multinational Enterprises (MNEs) as may be applicable on the State Parties"); *USMCA (2018)* (n 17) art 14.17 ("The Parties reaffirm the importance of each Party encouraging enterprises operating within its territory or subject to its jurisdiction to voluntarily incorporate into their internal policies those internationally recognized standards, guidelines, and principles of corporate social responsibility that have been endorsed or are supported by that Party, which may include the OECD Guidelines for Multinational Enterprises. These standards, guidelines, and principles may address areas such as labor, environment, gender equality, human rights, indigenous and aboriginal peoples' rights, and corruption").

39 *Brazil–Chile FTA (2018)* (n 38) art 16.3(3) ("The Parties shall promote the implementation of the 2011 United Nations Guiding Principles on Business and Human Rights") (free translation from Spanish).

CM/REC (2016) of the Committee of Ministers to Member States on human rights and business.[40]

At the harder end of the spectrum, certain treaties attempt to impose binding obligations on investors or reinforce the state's powers to pursue investors for human rights breaches.

With respect to international trade generally, Ecuador has spearheaded efforts for the conclusion of the Draft Legally Binding Instrument to Regulate in International Human Rights Law, the Activities of Transnational Corporations and Other Business Enterprises (Draft Instrument), which seeks to regulate the activities of transnational corporations and other business enterprises.[41] The scope of the instrument is ambitious as it seeks to apply to all business activities – not only those of a transnational character – and to "all international human rights and those recognized under domestic law."[42] The Draft Instrument does not seek to impose legally binding international law obligations on businesses *per se*. Instead, the Draft Instrument focuses on the rights of victims under domestic law and creates binding obligations for states to prevent and offer effective remedies in their national order for human rights violations committed by business activities. The Draft Instrument contains a conflict of jurisdiction rule providing that victims may bring their claims, "independently of their nationality" either before (i) the victim's home courts; (ii) the courts of the place where the violations occurred; or (iii) the business operator's home courts.[43] The variety

---

40 Agreement on reciprocal promotion and protection of investments between … and the Kingdom of the Netherlands (adopted 22 March 2019) (*Netherlands Model BIT (2019)*) art 7 ("The Contracting Parties reaffirm the importance of each Contracting Party to encourage investors operating within its territory or subject to its jurisdiction to voluntarily incorporate into their internal policies those internationally recognized standards, guidelines and principles of corporate social responsibility that have been endorsed or are supported by that Party, such as the OECD Guidelines for Multinational Enterprises, the United Nations Guiding Principles on Business and Human Rights, and the Recommendation CM/REC(2016) of the Committee of Ministers to Member States on human rights and business").

41 UN Open-Ended Intergovernmental Working Group on Transnational Corporations and other Business Enterprises with Respect to Human Rights Chairmanship, "Zero Draft of a Legally Binding Instrument to Regulate, in International Human Rights Law, the Activities of Transnational Corporations and other Business Enterprises" (2018) (*Zero Draft*), and UN OEIGWG Chairmanship, "Revised Draft of a Legally Binding Instrument to Regulate, in International Human Rights Law, the Activities of Transnational Corporations and other Business Enterprises" (2019) (*Revised Draft*) (both, indifferently, *Draft Instrument*).

42 United Nations Human Rights Council, "Draft report on the fifth session of the open-ended intergovernmental working group on transnational corporations and other business enterprises with respect to human rights" (2020) UN Doc A/HRC/43/XX para 15.

43 *Draft Instrument* (n 41) art 7.

of available *fora* is complemented by the power accorded to the chosen forum to apply the law of any of the three places.[44] However, so far, the Draft Instrument has received a mixed reception due to its perceived vilification of business.[45]

As concerns international investment treaties, the Morocco–Nigeria BIT (2016) provides that "[i]nvestors and investments shall uphold human rights in the host state."[46] The BIT adds that "[i]nvestors and investments shall not manage or operate the investments in a manner that circumvents international environmental, labour and human rights obligations to which the host state and/or home state are Parties."[47]

Furthermore, more recently, the Netherlands adopted a model BIT (2019) that explicitly mentions "human rights, environmental protection and labor laws."[48] The treaty requires that effective remedies be available in cases of "business-related human rights abuse."[49] Moreover, the treaty allows arbitral tribunals to "take into account an investor's non-compliance with the UN Guiding Principles on Business and Human Rights" when assessing damages.[50] The practical implication of providing investor obligations in the treaty is that it opens the possibility of a reduction of damages under the doctrine of contributory fault.[51] This general principle is codified at article 39 of the International Law Commission's Articles on

---

44 *Draft Instrument* (n 41) art 9.

45 Alluding to precedents of human rights violations by other parties, see generally the *Chevron v Ecuador* saga where the representatives of indigenous communities were found to have bribed judges and ghost-written court decisions, United States District Court, S.D. New York, *Chevron Corp. v Donziger*, 974 F. Supp. 2d 362 (S.D.N.Y. 2014) (4 March 2014).

46 Reciprocal Investment Promotion and Protection Agreement between the Government of the Kingdom of Morocco and the Government of the Federal Republic of Nigeria (signed 3 December 2016) (*Morocco–Nigeria BIT*) art 18(2).

47 Ibid. art 18(4). Similarly, the Southern African Model BIT on Sustainable Development (2012) provides that investors and their investments "have a duty to respect human rights in the workplace ... community ... and State in which they are located." See Southern African Development Community Model Bilateral Investment Treaty Template (2012) (*SADC Model*) art 15.

48 *Netherlands Model BIT (2019)* (n 40) art 7.

49 Ibid. art 5.

50 Ibid. art 23.

51 Contributory fault (also known as *faute contributive, faute de la victime, culpa de la víctima* or *culpa concurrente*) is an axiomatic legal concept of tort and civil liability, enshrined in a plethora of national laws, that most notably allows the reduction of damages owed to victims in light of their conduct, including as a result of the exacerbation of the damage suffered by way of their own fault. See Farouk El-Hosseny, Patrick Devine, "Contributory Fault under International Law: A Gateway for Human Rights in ISDS?", (2020) 35 ICSID Review 105.

State Responsibility for Internationally Wrongful Acts (the ILC Articles), which provides as follows:

> In the determination of reparation, account shall be taken of the contribution to the injury by wilful or negligent action or omission of the injured State or any person or entity in relation to whom reparation is sought.[52]

Accordingly, an investor's failure to comply with human rights or environmental protection could result in a reduction of damages if a tribunal considers that said failure contributed to the damage incurred as a result of a host state's breach of the treaty. As will be discussed further below, article 39 has provided the basis for such reductions of damages in a number of investment treaty arbitrations.

Procedural innovations

A number of procedural innovations have, in recent years, had a marked impact on the relationship between human rights and international investment law. For example, and as made clear in *Burlington* and *Urbaser*, states have an interest in agreeing the availability of counterclaims in advance with investors.[53] In this regard, it is significant that the Colombia–UAE BIT (2017) establishes as a jurisdictional requirement that the investor provide a form annexed to the treaty when filing arbitral proceedings against a contracting state. The annexed form provides that the investor consents to the possibility of facing adverse claims made by the respondent (i.e. counterclaims) "including alleged breaches of applicable international law or the respondent Party's law."[54]

The second innovation worthy of comment is found in the Netherlands Model BIT (2019) and aims at ensuring that the tribunal is composed of arbitrators qualified in the field of international human rights. In the event of a dispute, the appointing authority "shall make every effort to ensure" that the members of the tribunal possess expertise in public international law "which includes environmental and human rights law."[55]

---

52 Draft Articles on Responsibility of States for Internationally Wrongful Acts, adopted by the Commission at its fifty-third session in 2001 (Final Outcome) (adopted 3 August 2001) UN Doc A/56/10, 43, UN Doc A/RES/56/83, Annex, UN Doc A/CN.4/L.602/Rev.1, GAOR 56th Session Supp 10, 43 (*Draft Articles on State Responsibility (2001)*) art 39.

53 *Burlington Resources, Inc. v. Republic of Ecuador*, ICSID Case No. ARB/08/5 (Decision on Ecuador's Counterclaims, 7 February 2017) (*Burlington*).

54 Bilateral Agreement for the Promotion and Protection of Investment between the Republic of Colombia and the United Arab Emirates (signed 12 November 2017) (*Colombia-United Arab Emirates BIT (2017)*) art 13.3.

55 *Netherlands Model BIT (2019)* (n 40) art 20.5.

A further development still permeating through the international arbitration community is the Hague Rules on Business and Human Rights Arbitration (the Hague Rules).[56] The Hague Rules were adopted in 2019 with the aim of offering a one-stop contractually-selected forum for investors to have business and human rights disputes solved in a fair, transparent, and unbiased manner by practitioners who are familiar with both international investment/commercial law and human rights.[57] Here again, the Hague Rules have been met with a mixed reception. Some observers are concerned about how the rules might stand in the way of the UN business and human rights process by minimizing the primary responsibility of states in respect of human rights and hindering the development of other accountability mechanisms against corporations before domestic courts or against states before international human rights courts.[58] In turn, corporations seek clarifications to ensure that claimants cannot initiate multiple proceedings either in arbitration or before national courts, or both.[59]

In summary, there are multiple international trade and investment instruments now seeking to take into account human rights issues, going far further than the formerly limited non-binding hortatory statements and general appeals to soft law. However, the fruits of the increasing normatization of human rights within the international trade and investment arena are yet to be fully seized by international tribunals and many of the developments cited above remain embryonic and in a state of flux. However,

---

56 The Hague Rules were developed by a working group headed by Bruno Simma and under the auspices of the Centre for International Legal Cooperation (*CILC*) in the Hague. They are inspired in part by, and build on, the so-called "Bangladesh Accord" (the Accord on Fire and Building Safety in Bangladesh), which provides for the arbitration of labor condition disputes in the garment sector. See https://bangl adeshaccord.org/resources accessed 13 January 2020. For a summary, see Jaaklo Salminen, "The Accord on Fire and Building Safety in Bangladesh: A New Paradigm for Limiting Buyers' Liability in Global Supply Chains?" (2018) 66 (2) *The American Journal of Comparative Law.*

57 CILC, "Elements for Consideration in Draft Arbitration Rules, Model Clauses and Other Aspects of the Arbitral Process" (2018) 5 www.cilc.nl/cms/wp-content/uploads/2019/01/Elements-Paper_INTERNATIONAL-ARBITRATION-OF-BUSINESS-AND-HUMAN-RIGHTS-DISPUTE.font12.pdf accessed 13 January 2020.

58 CILC, "Summary of Sounding Board Consultation Round 1 – Results Elements Paper on the Hague Rules on Business and Human Rights Arbitration" (2019) 4–5 www.cilc.nl/cms/wp-content/uploads/2019/06/Summary-Paper-Sounding-Board-Consultation-Round-1-%E2%80%93-Results.pdf accessed 13 January 2020.

59 CILC, "Summary of Sounding Board Consultation Round 1 – Results Elements Paper on the Hague Rules on Business and Human Rights Arbitration" (2019) 4–5 www.cilc.nl/cms/wp-content/uploads/2019/06/Summary-Paper-Sounding-Board-Consultation-Round-1-%E2%80%93-Results.pdf accessed 13 January 2020.

investment-treaty jurisprudence has tentatively begun to test and experiment with some of these developments, as discussed directly below.

Assessment of human rights arguments by investment-treaty tribunals

The invocation of human rights in investment treaty arbitration cannot be treated monolithically. Issues relating to human rights are raised in distinct circumstances giving rise to different dynamics and issues for consideration by tribunals. For the purposes of structuring our analysis, human rights concerns can generally be considered to come before investment tribunals in three principal scenarios.

In the first scenario (Scenario 1), a human rights objective (e.g., public health or environmental protection) is advanced by a state as the justification for a measure adversely affecting investors. This usually arises where a state is under two conflicting obligations – human rights and investor protection – and acts in favor of the former so allegedly breaching the latter.[60] Here it is the *state's measure* that is under scrutiny and it is for the tribunal to determine whether the human rights objective pursued by the state renders the measure lawful under the treaty.

In the second scenario (Scenario 2), a state adopts measures in response to alleged human rights violations by an investor. Here it is the *investor's conduct* and its respect for human rights norms which is under scrutiny. In such situations, it is the investor, through its behaviour, that may have precipitated the measure that it is now claiming against.[61]

In the third scenario (Scenario 3), closely related to the second, states may bring *counterclaims* against investors for human rights abuses. Here human rights arguments are deployed as a sword, rather than a shield, by the state.[62]

These three scenarios are discussed in turn below.

State measures protecting human rights and/or the public interest

There are numerous examples in Scenario 1, where states have adopted measures to further human rights and/or public interest objectives, which

---

60 See Mehmet Toral and Thomas Schultz, "The State, a Perpetual Respondent in Investment Arbitration? Some Unorthodox Considerations" in Michael Waibel and others (eds), *The Backlash against Investment Arbitration* (Kluwer 2010) pt 5, ch 25, 577, 581–582.

61 See Ioana Knoll-Tudor, "The Fair and Equitable treatment Standard and Human Rights Norms" in Pierre-Marie Dupuy and others (eds), *Human Rights in International Investment Law and Arbitration* (OUP 2010) 339.

62 See Ina C. Popova and Fiona Poon, "From Perpetual Respondent to Aspiring Counterclaimant? State Counterclaims in the New Wave of Investment Treaties" (2015) 2 *BCDR International Arbitration Review* 223.

were subsequently challenged before investor–state tribunals.[63] Two recent Latin American cases are paradigmatic of this scenario.

In *Crystallex*, the investor acquired rights to develop gold deposits. However, despite assurances from various ministries, the environmental permit required for the development of the deposits was denied and the relevant contract terminated, with Venezuela citing concerns as to possible environmental degradation in the region.[64] In response, Crystallex brought a claim under the Canada–Venezuela BIT (1996), arguing that the permit had been denied in an arbitrary manner and so procedural guarantees accorded to it under the treaty had been violated. In this regard, Crystallex made three principal submissions: firstly, that the environmental concerns advanced for the denial of the permit had never been raised in the four-year approval process; secondly, that the denial was unsupported by any study demonstrating the impact the project would have on the region; and finally, that there were similar and existing projects in the region that had already been authorized.[65]

Although the tribunal recognized that Venezuela "had the right (and the responsibility) to raise concerns relating to global warming, environmental issues [and] ... biodiversity" and regulate for public purposes,[66] it concurred with Crystallex, finding that "the way [the environmental concerns] were

---

63 See e.g. *Metalclad Corporation v. The United Mexican States*, ICSID Case No. ARB(AF)/97/1 (Award, 30 August 2000) paras 92–93 (ecological concerns over hazardous waste); *International Thunderbird Gaming Corporation v. The United Mexican States*, UNCITRAL (Arbitral Award, 26 January 2006) para 127 (regulation on gambling for the protection of public morals.); *Glamis Gold Ltd. v. United States of America*, UNCITRAL (Award, 8 June 2009) para 127 (human rights of indigenous people); *Chemtura v Canada* (Award 2010) (n 18) para 131 (protection of public health and the environment); *Apotex Holdings Inc. and Apotex Inc. v. United States of America (III)*, ICSID Case No. ARB(AF)/12/1 (Award, 25 August 2014) para 2.15 (protection of public health). See also, Catharine Titi, *The Right to Regulate in International Investment Law* (Hart 2014) 276 ("recent arbitral jurisprudence has tentatively started to reference the state's regulatory interest even when the latter are not encapsulated in black and white treaty language or in confirmed general international law") and Ivar Alvik, *Contracting with Sovereignty: State Contracts and International Arbitration* (Hart 2011) 261 ("'[The] right to regulate' has increasingly been conceptualized in investment jurisprudence as an inherent power of the state (police powers), which is defined through a distinction between legitimate non-compensable regulation and deprivatory regulation equivalent in effect of expropriation or a breach of, for example, fair and equitable treatment standard in an investment treaty.") and Yulia Levashova, *The Right of States to Regulate in International Investment Law: The Search for Balance Between Public Interest and Fair and Equitable Treatment* (Kluwer 2019)ch 7.
64 *Crystallex v Venezuela* (Award 2016) (n 15) para 44.
65 Ibid. para 277.
66 Ibid. para 591.

put forward by Venezuela ... present[ed] significant elements of arbitrariness" and concluded that Venezuela had violated a number of treaty protections (fair and equitable treatment, minimum standard of treatment, and the right against indirect expropriation).[67] The *Crystallex* tribunal therefore found that legitimate public policy interests should not be pursued to the detriment of protections afforded to foreign investments under the BIT.

On the other hand, in *Philip Morris*,[68] a much-publicized case concerned the plain packaging of cigarettes, the majority reached a markedly different conclusion, stating that "the responsibility for public health measures rests with the government and investment tribunals should pay great deference to governmental judgments of national needs in matters such as the protection of public health."[69] The majority further noted that "[c]ontrary to the Claimants' contention, the Challenged Measures were not 'arbitrary and unnecessary' but rather were potentially 'effective means to protect public health.'"[70] The majority also referred to the principle of police powers in the following terms: "the Challenged Measures were a valid exercise by Uruguay of its police powers for the protection of public health. As such, they cannot constitute an expropriation of the Claimants' investment."[71]

The above jurisprudence confirms a generally accepted principle – states do not have *carte blanche* to further human rights and/or public interest objectives, they may only do so in harmony with their obligations under international investment law. To take the *Crystallex* example, states cannot further environmental protection arbitrarily – that protection has to be pursued within the limits of the fair and equitable treatment that states have committed to afford investors.

Investor breaches of human rights

Cases reflecting Scenario 2 are equally on the rise and are particularly relevant to arbitrations in the extractive sector, as evidenced by the following cases.

In *Copper Mesa*,[72] the investor's mining concessions were terminated by Ecuador for lack of prior consultations with local communities. These

---

67 Ibid. para 591.
68 *Philip Morris Brand Sàrl (Switzerland), Philip Morris Products S.A. (Switzerland) and Abal Hermanos S.A. (Uruguay) v. Oriental Republic of Uruguay*, ICSID Case No. ARB/10/7 (Award, 8 July 2016) (*Philip Morris*). It is worth noting that the claimants' appointed arbitrator, Gary Born, dissented.
69 Ibid. (n 68) para 399.
70 Ibid. (n 68) para 306.
71 Ibid. (n 68) paras 286, 307.
72 *Copper Mesa Mining Corporation v. Republic of Ecuador*, PCA No. 2012–2 (Award, 15 March 2016) (*Copper Mesa*).

consultations were meant to take place as part of the Environmental Impact Study (EIS) required under Ecuadorian law as a condition precedent to the project's development. The Ministry of Mines subsequently rejected the mining company's EIS because it found no evidence that some of the communities – those who most fiercely opposed the project – had been consulted. The concessions were terminated in November 2008, without compensation to the investor.

The human rights concerns (specifically, the right to prior consultation of local stakeholder communities) raised by Ecuador were first analyzed at the jurisdictional stage of proceedings under the doctrine of unclean hands. Ecuador submitted that the claimant's claims were inadmissible *ratione materiae* because the claimant approached the tribunal with "unclean hands," having failed to comply with applicable Ecuadorian and international laws.[73]

However, the tribunal considered it was "too late" for Ecuador to bring this argument because "[a]ll, or almost all, of such alleged conduct took place in Ecuador, openly and in view of the Respondent's governmental authorities ... Yet, ... not a single complaint was made by the Respondent" during that period.[74] The tribunal preferred "to take into account the Claimant's case not in the form of the doctrine of unclean hands as such, but rather under analogous doctrines of causation and contributory fault"[75] applying to the merits of the claimant's claims.[76]

In this regard, the tribunal concluded that Copper Mesa had "ma[de] the situation far worse" by "recruiting and using armed men, firing guns and spraying mace at civilians, not as an accidental or isolated incident but as part of premeditated, disguised and well-funded plans to take the law into its own hands."[77] Accordingly, the tribunal found that the claimant had contributory fault for the expropriation of its investment and that its conduct had contributed to 30 percent of its injury.[78]

The *Bear Creek*[79] arbitration arose out of strikingly similar facts to *Copper Mesa*. In *Bear Creek*, the investor's mining project failed to gain stakeholder consent from local communities so giving rise to months of

---

73 Ibid. (n 72) para 5.4.
74 Ibid. (n 72) para 5.63.
75 Under article 39 of the *Draft Articles on State Responsibility (2001)* (n 52).
76 *Copper Mesa* (n 72) para 5.65.
77 Ibid. para 6.99.
78 Ibid. paras 6.98–6.102. Also see Chapters 13 by Sebastián Preller-Bórquez (on social license and contributory faul) and 9 by Sufyan Droubi, Cecilia Juliana Flores Elizondo and Raphael Heffron (in relation to indigenous peoples' rights) in this volume.
79 *Bear Creek Mining Corporation v. Republic of Peru*, ICSID Case No. ARB/14/21 (Award, 30 November 2017) (*Bear Creek*).

violent protests from local communities, culminating with the intervention of the army. Following the protests, Peru decided to revoke the decree granting mining rights to Bear Creek and the company filed for arbitration under the Canada–Peru FTA (2009).

Peru presented two objections, alleging first that the investment was unlawfully obtained and secondly, that Bear Creek had failed to acquire a "social licence" from local communities.[80] The tribunal dismissed both arguments as bars to jurisdiction and admissibility because it found that the treaty did not contain a legality requirement. Instead, the tribunal considered that these points were better addressed "in the examination of the merits."[81]

On the merits, the tribunal found Peru to have indirectly expropriated Bear Creek's investment but disagreed on the degree to which potential human rights breaches by the investor were relevant to contributory fault.[82] Peru submitted that the amount of damages should be reduced, or eliminated altogether, because the social unrest was a direct consequence of Bear Creek's conduct.[83] According to Peru, Bear Creek's conduct towards local communities was insufficient or violated the ILO Convention 169 provisions on the communities' right to the respect of their relationship with their land, their right to be consulted, and their right to participate in the management of natural resources on their land.[84]

On analysis, a majority of the tribunal rejected Peru's argument, not as a matter of principle but rather because it found that Peru had not met its burden of proving that its breaches of the FTA were to some extent caused by Bear Creek. Indeed, the tribunal concluded that because Peru approved Bear Creek's efforts to obtain a social license, it "cannot in hindsight claim that this conduct ... was insufficient, and caused or contributed to the social unrest in the region."[85]

However, in a dissenting opinion, Philippe Sands considered that Bear Creek's acts and omissions "contributed in material ways to the events that unfolded and led to the Project's collapse."[86] In his view, the evidence

---

80 Jean-Michel Marcoux and Andrew Newcombe, "Bear Creek Mining Corporation v Republic of Peru: Two Sides of a 'Social License' to Operate" (2018) 33 *ICSID Review* 653.

81 *Bear Creek* (n 79) para 335.

82 Ibid. para 663; and *Bear Creek Mining Corporation v. Republic of Peru*, ICSID Case No. ARB/14/21(Partial Dissenting Opinion of Professor Philippe Sands, 30 November 2017) *(Sands Opinion)* para 4.

83 *Bear Creek* (n 79) para 560.

84 Ibid. para 567.

85 Ibid. para 412.

86 *Sands Opinion* (n 82) para 6.

adduced by Peru "clearly established the claimant's contributory responsibility," and in particular that the collapse was due to Bear Creek's inability to obtain a "social licence."[87] Therefore, he concluded that a 50 percent reduction in the damages awarded should have been applied.[88]

Lastly, in *South American Silver*, Bolivia revoked the mining rights held by the claimant's subsidiary alleging that the subsidiary had "committed several abuses that led to an unsustainable escalation of violence that endangered the life and rights of the Local Communities and the public officials and forced the State [...] to decree Reversion as an ultima ratio."[89]

In response, South American Silver brought a claim under the Bolivia–UK BIT (1988). Bolivia raised the issue of human rights violations (the claimant's subsidiary's various abuses) in the context of jurisdiction (as did Ecuador in *Copper Mesa*), arguing that the claimant's claim was inadmissible given it did not have clean hands. However, the tribunal noted that the clean hands doctrine was not referred to in the text of the BIT nor was it part of the general principles of international law and so dismissed this argument and proceeded to consider the issues on the merits.[90]

At the merits stage the tribunal found that "despite having implemented a community relations program, the Company had serious shortcomings in its relationship with the community from the outset which were not corrected, despite the recommendations of the consultants hired to assess such programs."[91] The tribunal considered that the claimant's legitimate expectations should have been colored by the knowledge that it was operating in an area inhabited by the indigenous communities and that it should have adjusted its behavior accordingly.[92]

Nonetheless, applying a test of proportionality, the tribunal found that the investment had been expropriated for the public purpose of protecting life and that this expropriation was unlawful given Bolivia had failed to provide the compensation promised by the Reversion decree.[93] Bolivia then requested a reduction of the amount of damages owed asserting that the investor had contributory fault for the expropriation in light of its failures to gain stakeholder consent. However, the tribunal considered the claim inapposite, stating that the obligation to compensate arose from Bolivia's *failure to provide compensation* (and not from the fact of the expropriation) and that the tribunal "may not reduce the amount of compensation owed to the investor for a Treaty

87 Ibid. para 4.
88 Ibid. para 40. Also see Chapter 13 by Sebastián Preller-Bórquez in this volume.
89 *South American Silver* (n 13) para 381.
90 Ibid. para 453.
91 Ibid. para 490.
92 Ibid. para 648.
93 Ibid. para 610.

violation unrelated to its conduct," i.e. the failure to pay compensation which was distinct from the act of expropriation itself.[94]

In light of the above cases, it would appear that tribunals prefer to assess allegations of human rights abuses holistically at the merits stage eschewing attempts to deal with them in the context of admissibility under the doctrine of clean hands. Secondly, tribunals have principally dealt with such breaches at the merits stage via the mechanism of contributory fault resulting in a reduction of damages where investors are found to have committed human rights abuses.

However, applying the mechanism of contributory fault in a human rights context is far from a given. In *South American Silver*, the tribunal recognized that the investor had committed abuses culminating in an escalation of violence which led to expropriation by Bolivia.[95] Nevertheless, Bolivia's argument of contributory fault was rejected because the state's violation of the BIT – lack of compensation for the expropriation – was found to be unrelated to the investor's abuses, therefore not leading to a reduction in damages.[96] On similar facts, in *Bear Creek*, the majority determined that, although the investor failed to garner stakeholder support, it should not be considered to have contributory fault for the breaches of Peru given it had discharged all its responsibilities at international law in good faith.[97] Conversely, in *Copper Mesa*, the argument of contributory fault was successful in a context where the tribunal alluded to the fact that the state had turned a blind eye to the investor's human rights violations.[98]

Human rights counterclaims

As regards Scenario 3, the use of counterclaims by respondent states, while relatively common in interstate litigation,[99] has slowly but gradually emerged in recent years in investment treaty arbitration. Counterclaims provide a means for states to bring investor violations of human rights within the jurisdiction of arbitral tribunals. This has been apparent in both investment treaty jurisprudence and in certain investment treaties which now explicitly provide for the possibility of states bringing counterclaims, such as the

---

94 Ibid. para 875.
95 Ibid. paras 505, 507.
96 Ibid. para 875.
97 *Bear Creek* (n 79) para 664.
98 *Copper Mesa* (n 72) para 5.63.
99 See e.g. International Court of Justice (*ICJ*), "Rules of the Court," art 80 ("The Court may entertain a counter-claim only if it comes within the jurisdiction of the Court and is directly connected with the subject-matter of the claim of the other party").

previously mentioned Colombia–UAE BIT.[100] The use of counterclaims to address alleged human rights breaches by investors is arguably derivative of *Urbaser* which can be considered as clearing a route for human rights counterclaims that had traditionally been thwarted by jurisdictional concerns.[101]

The dispute in *Urbaser* arose as a result of Argentina's financial crisis in 2001–2002. The claimant was a shareholder in a concessionaire that supplied water and sewerage services to the city of Buenos Aires. Argentina's emergency economic measures during the crisis caused the concession financial loss and it eventually became insolvent. The claimant commenced arbitral proceedings against Argentina for violations of the Spain–Argentina BIT (1991).

In response, Argentina submitted a counterclaim on the basis that by failing to make the required investments in water and sewage, Urbaser had compromised the basic human right to water of the inhabitants of the city affected by this under-investment.[102]

Argentina had to overcome the conventional hurdles facing counterclaims relating to questions of consent, applicable law, and jurisdiction.[103] The tribunal found that, under the BIT, claims by states were not excluded by the language of the dispute resolution provision and that Urbaser had consented to the use of counterclaims.[104] The tribunal further confirmed

---

100 Eric De Brabandere, "Human Rights Counterclaims in Investment Treaty Arbitration" (2018) Grotius Centre Working Paper No 2018/078-IEL 1. See e.g. *Colombia – UAE BIT (2017)* (n 54) art 13 ("the Investor's acceptance of the possibility of facing claims by the Respondent against them"); Agreement on Promotion, Protection and Guarantee of Investments among Member States of the Organization of the Islamic Conference (signed 5 June 1981, entered into force February 1988) (*OIC Agreement*) art 17 ("each party has the right to resort to the Arbitration Tribunal for a final decision on the dispute"); Investment Agreement for the COMESA Common Investment Area (signed 23 May 2007) art 28(9) ("A Member State against whom a claim is brought by a COMESA investor under this Article may assert as a defence, counterclaim, right of set off or other similar claim, that the COMESA investor bringing the claim has not fulfilled its obligations under this Agreement, including the obligations to comply with all applicable domestic measures or that it has not taken all reasonable steps to mitigate possible damages").

101 Edward Guntrip, "Urbaser v Argentina: The origins of a host State human rights counterclaim in ICSID arbitration?" www.ejiltalk.org/urbaser-v-argentina-the-origins-of-a-host-state-human-rights-counterclaim-in-icsid-arbitration/ accessed 13 January 2020.

102 *Urbaser* (n 7) para 36.

103 See more generally Dafina Atanasova and Josef Ostransky, "The Legal Framework for Counterclaims in Investment Treaty Arbitration" (2014) 31 *Journal of International Arbitration* 391.

104 The terms of article X of the Spain–Argentina BIT permitted either party to the dispute to commence claims (para 1143), thus including the possibility of a counterclaim (para 1144) and the terms in which the claimant accepted the offer to arbitrate did not exclude counterclaims (paras 1146–48) (*Argentina–Spain BIT (1991)*) (n 22).

that the counterclaim fell within its competence and had a sufficient connection to Urbaser's principal claim given both claims were "based on the same investment, or the alleged lack of sufficient investment, in relation to the same Concession."[105]

Having established jurisdiction over the counterclaim, the tribunal turned to its merits. As a starting point, the tribunal noted that although corporate social responsibility is a standard of crucial importance for companies operating in the field of international commerce, "[CSR obligations] are not, on their own, sufficient to oblige corporations."[106] The tribunal then analyzed the counterclaim of Argentina through two distinct lenses: (i) as constituting part of the general legal framework of international law in which the investment was integrated; and (ii) on the basis of the applicable law as set out in the BIT.[107]

Firstly, the tribunal determined that corporations operating internationally can no longer be considered to be immune from becoming subjects of international law.[108] Rather, the tribunal highlighted the importance of "contextualising a corporation's specific activities" in order to determine whether international law obligations attach to it.[109] The tribunal therefore moved to characterize the context of the investor's activities as they related to human rights.[110] Following a review of human rights materials – including the Universal Declaration of Human Rights (1948), the International Covenant on Economic, Social and Cultural Rights (1966), and the United Nations Guiding Principles on Business and Human Rights (2011) – the tribunal identified that there was only a negative obligation on private parties not to engage in activities undermining human rights and not a positive obligation to actually provide for them.[111]

Secondly, the tribunal considered the applicable law to the counterclaim given the BIT did not itself establish any human rights standards.[112] On this point, the tribunal recalled that a "BIT cannot be interpreted and applied in a vacuum" and referred to Article 31(3)(c) of the VCLT providing for the consideration of "any relevant rules of international law applicable in the relation between the parties."[113] The tribunal also noted the BIT's provision

---

105 *Urbaser* (n 7) para 1151.
106 Ibid. para 1195.
107 Ibid. paras 1195–1221.
108 Ibid. para 1195.
109 Ibid. para 1195.
110 Ibid. paras 1196–1199.
111 Ibid. paras 1196–1199.
112 Ibid. para 1194.
113 Ibid. para 1200.

on applicable law which provided for the application of the BIT concurrently with other treaties and "general principles of international law" and thus the BIT was not a "closed system," therefore allowing the tribunal to make reference to certain legal sources outside of the BIT when identifying obligations which may bind the claimant.[114]

Nonetheless, although the tribunal established jurisdiction over the counterclaim it ultimately dismissed it on the merits.[115] The tribunal concluded that "the human right to water entails an obligation of compliance on the part of the state, but it does not contain an obligation for performance on part of any company providing the contractually required service" because "the investor's obligation to ensure the population's access to water is not based on international law."[116]

Following the precedent set by *Urbaser*, the tribunal in *Aven*[117] was also called upon to consider a counterclaim by Costa Rica under the DR–CAFTA Treaty. In *Aven*, local stakeholders discovered that the claimants' beach resort project had only been granted the relevant permissions pursuant to a forged environmental impact report. Following this revelation, Costa Rica's environmental protection administration inspected the investors' premises and revoked the investment's environmental permit. The tribunal found that the "wetlands was [*sic*] indeed impacted by works undertaken by Claimants … Forests were also impacted"[118] and accordingly determined that the revocation was lawful so dismissing all alleged treaty breaches.

However, during proceedings, Costa Rica submitted an environmental counterclaim for the damage caused to the wetlands and forest. Considering its jurisdiction over the counterclaim, the tribunal distinguished between two separate questions: first, whether host states could sue investors before a treaty-based tribunal – despite the dispute settlement chapter only conferring *locus standi* on investors by defining "claimant" as an investor and "respondent" as a state; and secondly, whether the treaty not only accorded rights to investors but also imposed obligations upon them for which they could then be found in violation.[119]

With respect to the first question regarding the possibility of state-initiated claims, the tribunal determined that "the Treaty Parties [...] contemplated the possibility of counterclaims"[120] and reviewed the treaty's

114 Ibid. para 1191.
115 Ibid. para 1221.
116 Ibid. para 1202. On the right to water, see Chapter 12 Javier Echaide in this volume.
117 *David R. Aven, Samuel D. Aven, Giacomo A. Buscemi and others v. Republic of Costa Rica*, ICSID Case No. UNCT/15/3 (Final Award, 18 September 2018) *(Aven)*.
118 Ibid. (n 117) paras 585–586.
119 Ibid. paras 731–742.
120 Ibid. para 731.

provisions describing types of arbitrable disputes to conclude that they covered disputes giving rise to counterclaims.[121]

As concerns the second question regarding investor obligations, the tribunal concurred with the finding in *Urbaser* that it can no longer be admitted that investors operating internationally are immune from becoming subjects of international law, "particularly in the field of environmental law."[122] It concluded however that the treaty provisions on environmental measures did not, in and of themselves, impose positive obligations upon investors.[123] This was not, however, the principal reason for dismissing the counterclaim. Rather, the tribunal noted that under the 2010 UNCITRAL Arbitration Rules, counterclaims are to satisfy certain procedural requirements such as containing a statement of facts, indication of relief sought, amongst others.[124] The tribunal found that these were lacking.[125] Costa Rica attempted to cure the defects of its counterclaim in post-hearing briefs, but the tribunal found it to be too late because the post-hearing phase did not afford the claimants a possibility of replying.[126]

In summary, it can be seen from the above cases that human rights arguments are becoming increasingly prevalent in the investment treaty arena. While states have long invoked them as a defense, counterclaims to account for alleged human rights violations by investors and arguments relating to contributory fault constitute relatively new innovations in this sphere. The nascent jurisprudence with respect to both aspects will doubtless continue to evolve in the coming years.

Concluding remarks

It is axiomatic that the primary responsibility of securing human rights rests on the state. It is for the state to "respect, protect, and fulfil" human rights.[127] This principle is increasingly being tested and developed on both the regulatory and adjudicatory levels.

On the regulatory level, the limited binding obligations set out in new treaties constitute a significant step forward. However, exhortatory

---

121 Ibid. para 735.
122 Ibid. para 739.
123 Ibid. para 742.
124 Ibid. para 744.
125 Ibid. para 745.
126 Ibid. para 746.
127 States' obligation to protect, respect, and fulfill socio-economic and cultural human rights was first articulated by the UN Special Rapporteur, Asbjørn Eide, in his 1987 report. See Report prepared by Asbjørn Eide, "The Right to Adequate Food as a Human Right" (1987) UN Doc E/CN.4/Sub.2/1987/23.

statements and reaffirmations of the state's right to regulate are unlikely to spark a sea change. That said, treaty drafters have undoubtedly entered a phase of exploration and experimentation with new provisions and mechanisms seeking to be more inclusive of human rights concerns. Although some of the proposed instruments and initiatives may have a limited immediate impact, they constitute a strong statement of intent on behalf of certain quarters of the legal community and some states.

On the adjudicatory level, the tribunals in *Urbaser* and *Aven* agreed that it can no longer be admitted that investors operating internationally are immune from becoming subjects of international law. Both tribunals were, however, dismissive of soft law CSR standards being enough "on their own"[128] or "in and of themselves"[129] to impose positive human rights obligations for corporations. Beyond soft law, it is uncontroversial that negative obligations, in the form of obligations to abstain from abuses, apply to investors.[130] Exploring the distinction, the *Urbaser* tribunal noted that prohibitions of committing acts in violation of human rights were of immediate application to individuals and private parties.[131] Moreover, the *Urbaser* tribunal considered that the *context of an investor's activities*, as it relates to human rights, is important in determining whether international law obligations attach to it.[132] Following this approach, the tribunal found that in the context of the human right to water investors are only subject to a negative obligation to abstain from engaging in activity aimed at frustrating that right.[133] This approach was also followed by *South American Silver* finding that the nature of the investor's mining activities implied that it had to seek the assent of local indigenous communities.[134]

That said, tribunals appear to be confined to the toolset made available to them by states in the relevant investment treaties and by the general principles of international law. In this regard, the most significant development in the jurisprudence stems from the increasing adoption of the mechanism of contributory fault to address alleged human rights violations by investors.

128 *Urbaser* (n 7) para 1195.
129 *Aven* (n 117) para 743.
130 Mehmet Toral and Thomas Schultz, "The State, a Perpetual Respondent in Investment Arbitration? Some Unorthodox Considerations" in Michael Waibel and others (eds), *The Backlash against Investment Arbitration* (Kluwer 2010)pt 5, ch 25, 577; Lahra Liberti, "Investissements et droits de l'homme" in Phillipe Kahn and Thomas Wälde (eds), *New Aspects of International Investment Law/Les aspects nouveaux du droit des investissements internationaux* (Brill 2004) 790, 834.
131 *Urbaser* (n 7) para 1210.
132 Ibid. para 1195.
133 Ibid. para 1199.
134 *South American Silver* (n 13) para 477.

Although the jurisprudence is in a protean form, and in the absence of the imposition of direct human rights obligations on investors in BITs, contributory fault has the potential to act as a conduit for the importation and review of human rights concerns which formerly may have been considered to lie beyond the ken of arbitral tribunals. Notwithstanding the regulatory flux, investment treaty arbitration is indeed proving responsive to the increased pressures and prevalence of human rights concerns but appears to be incorporating and accommodating such changes by flexing its traditional structures as opposed to any radical revolution.

12

Inversiones internacionales y el derecho humano al agua: análisis desde una nueva perspectiva interdisciplinaria

Javier Echaide

Introducción

El derecho humano al agua potable está reconocido internacionalmente como un derecho humano independiente y positivo desde el año 2010, cuando fue sancionada la Resolución 64/292 de la Asamblea General de las Naciones Unidas (AG-ONU). Es un claro ejemplo de lo que es el desarrollo progresivo del derecho internacional, que no necesariamente se relaciona con nuevas tecnologías, sino que muchas veces trata sobre temas muy antiguos pero no por ello reconocidos o regulados por el derecho internacional. Sin embargo, el reconocimiento de nuevos derechos, y sobre todo de nuevos derechos humanos como es el caso del acceso al agua potable y al saneamiento, dentro de un derecho internacional con características de alta fragmentación, no necesariamente implica un avance sin tensiones e incluso contradicciones.

El fenómeno de la fragmentación en el derecho internacional no es para nada nuevo y no todos los autores lo entienden como algo problemático. Sin embargo, el crecimiento de áreas distintas dentro del derecho internacional, con objetos de estudio disímiles, a distintas velocidades y con mecanismos sancionatorios de distinta eficacia, sí puede significar, ante normas y derechos contrapuestos, problemas teóricos para los estudiosos del derecho con consecuencias prácticas en cuanto a su aplicación.

El área del derecho internacional de las inversiones es un área de reciente estudio a raíz de la gran cantidad de tratados bilaterales de inversión (TBI) celebrados desde la década de 1990. Asimismo, desde la crisis económica conocida como la "Gripe Asiática" (1997) se evidencia un fuerte crecimiento en la cantidad de demandas dentro de instituciones como el Centro Internacional de Arreglo de Diferencias relativas a Inversiones (CIADI), de un promedio de 1.48 demandas por año durante los primeros 25 años (1972–1996) a un promedio de 12.66 demandas por año tan solo en los siguientes 6 años. Tal crecimiento no puede en nada compararse con el actual nivel de demandas: un promedio de 46.8 nuevas demandas por año a partir del 2012.[1]

El discurso dominante sostiene que el flujo de inversiones goza de buena salud y que el régimen internacional que lo protege (el conjunto de TBI y el sistema de arbitraje internacional al que cualquier empresa inversionista puede acudir) son un mecanismo barato, rápido y eficaz para garantizar dicha protección. Pero, ¿por qué se dan entonces estos incrementos tan sorprendentes en la cantidad de reclamos por parte de las empresas transnacionales? ¿Acaso más reclamos por protección no deberían significar que las inversiones internacionales se encuentran en un mayor riesgo? Mostrar que el mecanismo de solución de diferencias inversor-Estado (ISDS, por sus siglas en inglés) está más activo que nunca, da un mensaje positivo para el propio mecanismo en cuanto a que resulta ser muy utilizado, pero al mismo tiempo puede evidenciar una crisis en cuanto a la estabilidad del sistema internacional de inversiones. Al mismo tiempo, estos indicadores no acaban de responder una pregunta pendiente sobre una de las promesas de origen del sistema: ¿es este sistema un promotor para la atracción de las inversiones extranjeras? ¿Una mayor fragmentación del sistema jurídico internacional es acaso algo beneficioso para el mismo y los actores que intervienen en él? ¿Qué implica que el desarrollo fragmentado de áreas del derecho internacional como el de los derechos humanos y los tratados de protección de inversiones no logren tener una interconexión eficaz?

La perspectiva de nuestro estudio es y debe ser multidisciplinaria. El estudio de fenómenos de las inversiones internacionales debe encararse desde las relaciones internacionales, la economía política internacional, el derecho y la sociología jurídica. Este acercamiento enriquece el estudio de los fenómenos que acarrea el régimen de protección de inversiones a nivel internacional.

Gracias a este desarrollo fragmentado y a diferentes velocidades, así como al contexto posterior a la Guerra Fría, el auge del neoliberalismo y la apertura de mercados a nivel internacional, se desarrolló un marco legal de derecho público internacional para favorecer estrictamente al capital privado transnacional, y con un sistema de resolución de disputas disponible para corporaciones multinacionales a través del arbitraje internacional de instituciones como el CIADI. Los laudos arbitrales son vinculantes y operan con una fuerza mucho mayor que otras instancias porque aplican condicionamientos económicos a los Estados para crear nuevos marcos regulatorios.

---

1 Fuente, Elaboración propia en base a ICSID Cases, 2020–1. Ver https://icsid.worldb ank.org/en/Documents/resources/The%20ICSID%20Caseload%20Statistics%202 020–1%20Edition-ENG.pdf consultado en Junio 2020.

Ello se observa en el denominado "enfriamiento regulatorio" (*chilling effect*) en el desarrollo de políticas públicas: los Estados, al momento de decidir si aplicar o no políticas públicas que puedan afectar los intereses de inversionistas extranjeros, suelen evitar implementarlas para evadir el riesgo de demandas arbitrales en el CIADI u otros foros por parte de empresas multinacionales. Este efecto de enfriamiento resulta en una externalidad negativa de la protección de las inversiones extranjeras que no es considerada por el sistema. A su vez, la seguridad jurídica que los inversionistas a menudo demandan en sus reclamos termina ganando un mayor peso con respecto a la seguridad jurídica que también merecen las comunidades afectadas por las acciones de las empresas de inversión, lo que provoca una asimetría legal en diferentes niveles: entre intereses públicos y privados; entre el capital nacional y el transnacional; entre los mercados interno y externo; entre países en desarrollo -generalmente importadores de capital- y países desarrollados; así como, entre el derecho y las obligaciones de las empresas transnacionales. La no regulación también puede implicar una violación de derechos, y este efecto de enfriamiento, también marcado por una asimetría legal en diferentes niveles, puede violar los derechos humanos que son la base de la coexistencia de la comunidad internacional desde 1945: es por eso que tienen un carácter *erga omnes* en el derecho internacional.

El caso del agua potable y el saneamiento, y en particular en el caso de Argentina, son un ejemplo. A partir de la Resolución 64/292 AG-ONU no hay dudas respecto al reconocimiento de que el acceso al agua potable en cantidad y calidad suficientes es un derecho humano básico y universal. Sin embargo, los efectos antes mencionados amenazan una regulación que haga que este reconocimiento sea efectivo. Si bien el derecho humano al agua se ve comprometido por el sistema que protege las inversiones extranjeras, esto provoca una seria contradicción de las normas dispositivas contra las normas indisponibles en el derecho internacional como es el caso de violaciones a los derechos humanos. Y, sin embargo, tal contradicción no genera responsabilidades ni para los Estados ni para las empresas que se benefician de este sistema. Son los costos sociales los que, hasta el momento, pagan por el *status quo* vigente que genera amplias mayorías perjudicadas y lucrativos beneficios para unos pocos.

Problemas con el régimen internacional de protección de inversiones

Nos focalizaremos en los diversos problemas que hemos podido detectar del régimen de protección de inversiones a nivel internacional. Existen diferentes aspectos que resultan interesantes al momento de hacer análisis en cuanto a la situación de las inversiones internacionales en América Latina. La recepción de inversión extranjera directa (IED) en América Latina registró un alza a partir del año 2000, en un contexto de crisis a partir de fines de 2001 con la crisis argentina que se propagó a casi toda la región, pero con precios altos en el mercado de materias primas a nivel internacional que justificó que las inversiones extranjeras se centrasen especialmente en el sector de extracción de recursos naturales, profundizándose así la primarización de las economías locales.[2]

Pero a raíz de la crisis regional e internacional vivida desde 2008, merecen que sean introducidos nuevos debates en torno a las IED y su papel sobre el desarrollo y el crecimiento económico. En la región se han venido elaborando algunas perspectivas críticas novedosas[3] acerca del papel que juegan las inversiones en la región, más aun cuando su impacto en materia ambiental, de los derechos humanos y de las políticas públicas se reciente sin que por ello se evidencie un despegue de la región en cuanto a los indicadores de desarrollo, empleo y reducción de la pobreza.[4] Todo lo contrario: la región

---

2 Igal Kejsefman, 'La economía argentina en la postconvertibilidad (2002–2015). Un debate en torno a la tesis primario-extractivista' (2019) 33 Trabajo y sociedad: Indagaciones sobre el empleo, la cultura y las prácticas políticas en sociedades segmentadas www.redalyc.org/jatsRepo/3873/387361141021/html/index.html consultado en Junio 2020.

3 Distintas redes y plataformas ciudadanas nacionales se organizaron en una red latinoamericana llamada 'América Latina Mejor sin TLC' y que sigue los avances de los TLC y los TBI en la región. Ver https://americalatinasintlc.org/ (consultado en Junio 2020). Allí se nuclean desde organizaciones sindicales regionales hasta asambleas de vecinos afectados por los impactos ambientales de los tratados de libre comercio y de inversión en toda la región. Para profundizar más, ver 'Megaminería y zonas de sacrificio' (América Latina Mejor sin TLC, 22 Junio 2020) https://americalatinasintlc. org/2020/06/22/megamineria-y-zonas-de-sacrificio/ (casos de megaminería en Perú, México, Argentina y El Salvador); 'TLC y Derecho Humano al Agua' (América Latina Mejor sin TLC, 22 Junio 2020) https://americalatinasintlc.org/2020/06/22/tlc-y-derecho-humano-al-agua/ (casos de afectación del derecho humano al agua en Argentina, Bolivia y Chile); Pablo Castro, 'Lorena DiGiano: 'Hay que parar los monopolios de medicamentos y vacunas" (América Latina Mejor sin TLC, 17 mayo 2020) https:// americalatinasintlc.org/2020/05/17/lorena-di-giano-hay-que-parar-los-monopolios-de-medicamentos-y-vacunas/ (casos contra el monopolio de medicamentos y vacunas), para citar ejemplos.

4 La relación entre inversiones, empleo y pobreza fue trabajado por la Comisión de Auditoría Integral sobre Tratados de Inversión y el Sistema de Arbitraje (CAITISA) que fuera conformada en 2013 a instancias del gobierno de la Rep. de Ecuador para realizar una auditoría ciudadana independiente y que finalizó su trabajo en 2015 y en 2017 presentó su informe final al presidente Rafael Correa. Para acceder al mismo, ver CAITISA, Informe Ejecutivo: Auditoría integral ciudadana de los tratados de protección recíproca de inversión y del sistema de arbitraje en materia de inversiones en Ecuador (Quito, Ecuador, Mayo 2017). https://caitisa.org/boletines/ consultado en Junio 2020.

experimenta un fuerte incremento de los niveles de pobreza e indigencia pero, sobre todo, un incremento notable en los indicadores de desigualdad social.[5] Si es que se ha vivido un "auge de las inversiones en la región", ¿por qué ello no se ha traducido en un cumplimiento de las promesas que tanto economistas como decisores políticos manifiestan en forma constante en favor de la atracción de inversiones como motores del bienestar social?

A dos décadas de funcionamiento del sistema, existen preguntas que son necesarias de realizar hoy respecto del régimen de protección de inversiones a nivel internacional. Estas son algunas posibles:

- ¿Qué está ocurriendo actualmente con las inversiones a nivel internacional?
- ¿Por qué es necesario hacer este tipo de estudios hoy?
- ¿Está todo bien con el sistema internacional de protección de inversiones?
- ¿Por qué está ocurriendo esto?
- ¿Qué tipo de reglas están implicadas en el ISDS?
- ¿Hay beneficios, y en tal caso, para quién?
- ¿Hay quien pueda ser perjudicado por estas reglas?
- ¿Dónde se encuentran los impactos? ¿En qué sectores y con quiénes?
- ¿Qué se necesita hacer?

Entendemos que estos cuestionamientos son pertinentes, pues se suman a voces cada vez más repetidas respecto de un llamado de reforma del sistema o mismo de su disolución y reemplazo por otro tipo de mecanismos.[6]

Invertir en el mundo de los negocios siempre implica un riesgo. Y cuando la inversión se realiza fuera del país, es entendible que el riesgo aumente. Ahora, así como los beneficios son apropiados en forma privada, también debe hacerse lo mismo con el riesgo. ¿Cómo podría entenderse como razonable que, si el riesgo se socializa en manos de exigirle al Estado huésped de la inversión garantías de lucro, los beneficios sean aprovechados en forma

---

5 Ver CEPAL, 'La matriz de la desigualdad social en América Latina', Reunión de la Mesa Directiva de la Conferencia Regional sobre Desigualdad Social (Santo Domingo, 1 Noviembre 2016) https://repositorio.cepal.org/bitstream/handle/11362/40668/4/S1600946_es.pdf consultado en Junio 2020.

6 Ver ISDS Platform, 'Ante la reciente avalancha de demandas contra corporaciones en tribunales arbitrales contra nuestros países, decimos basta!', Declaración ante el Foro Mundial de Inversiones de UNCTAD (Nairobi, Kenia, Junio 2016) http://isds.bilaterals.org/?ante-la-reciente-avalancha-de&lang=es; Public Services International, 'Carta Global sobre el Proceso de Reforma de ISDS en la CNUDMI' (Public Services Internationa, 31 Octubre 2018) http://www.world-psi.org/es/carta-global-sobre-el-proceso-de-reforma-de-isds-en-la-cnudmi; Seattle to Brussels Network, 'El ISDS en una peligrosa encrucijada' https://foeeurope.org/sites/default/files/eu-us_trade_deal/2017/el_isds_en_una_peligrosa_encrucijada.pdf; ISDS Impactos, 'Los Impactos del Sistema de Protección de Inversiones en América Latina' http://isds-americalatina.org/, consultado en Marzo 2019.

privada? La privatización de los beneficios a costa de la socialización de los riesgos es un *modus operandi* en el cual las corporaciones pretenden externalizar los riesgos de su propia inversión. Y quienes asumen ese riesgo son los Estados anfitriones de la inversión extranjera asumiendo el otorgamiento de privilegios por encima de los derechos de los inversionistas locales o del resto de la ciudadanía dentro de su territorio y como compromisos legales. Estas obligaciones, al ser asumidas legalmente, pueden ser ejecutadas y los foros para hacerlo son a elección del interesado, es decir de la empresa, quien claramente optará por un ámbito internacional que sea lo más favorable posible a sus intereses de cobro.

Aquí no impera el criterio de justicia sino el criterio de resarcir de la forma más eficientemente posible los reclamos del inversionista por una obligación legal en principio incumplida y que lo afecta económicamente. No son pocos los tribunales arbitrales en el CIADI que aplican el método de expectativas legítimas del inversionista como forma de calcular el monto indemnizatorio en un caso por incumplimiento contractual, sea por un contrato de concesión pactado entre la empresa y el Estado que fue violentado, o por alguna obligación que figura en un TBI. El método de expectativas legítimas es un ejemplo de cómo los parámetros de eficiencia reemplazan a los parámetros de justicia en un tribunal, pues toma lo alegado por el demandante, es decir de tan solo una de las voces en el litigio, como punto de análisis para el cálculo indemnizatorio. La justificación para ello se basa en un análisis económico del derecho que sostiene que no hay nadie mejor que el supuesto perjudicado como para medir la dimensión de su perjuicio.[7] Sin embargo esta postura evita contrastar los dichos e información alegada como criterio de la indemnización con los dichos e información de la contraparte: el Estado. Se toma como supuesto que el Estado es sobre quien se posa el foco de análisis para saber en qué medida violó o no los compromisos asumidos. No se repara en buscar un criterio *justo* de indemnización, sino uno *eficiente*. Y por "eficiente" se entiende que es en términos de lo establecido por la parte demandante, es decir el inversionista.

En términos históricos, el primer tratado bilateral de protección de inversiones (TBI) fue firmado entre Alemania y Pakistán el 25 de noviembre de 1959. Este tipo de tratados poseen un estrecho vínculo con los tratados de libre comercio (TLC),[8] pues muchas de sus cláusulas poseen a los TLC como fuente, tales como la cláusula de trato nacional o la cláusula de la nación

---

7 Eduardo Sordeur, *Análisis Económico del Derecho. Una introducción* (Abeledo Perrot 2011).

8 'Acuerdos sobre inversion en el hemisferio Occidental: un compendio'. Disponible en http://www.ftaa-alca.org/ngroups/ngin/publications/spanish99/intro99.asp consultado en Diciembre 2018.

más favorecida, por ejemplo. Pero también porque los TLC suelen contener capítulos de inversiones en su interior y que no son más que un TBI adentro de un TLC.[9] Estos acuerdos alcanzaron salto cuantitativo hacia la década de 1990.

Desde la década de 1990 los países latinoamericanos han celebrado TBIs y tratados de libre comercio (TLC). Su justificación se basa en otorgar un marco jurídico favorable a los inversionistas para fomentar la captación de IED, brindándole garantías en pos de una "seguridad jurídica" que incentivara la atracción de los flujos de inversión hacia América Latina.

El problema radica en que dicho marco legal trae aparejado un sistema en materia de solución de controversias que prorrogan la jurisdicción doméstica en favor de tribunales arbitrales internacionales o extranjeros que laudan según *lex specialis* sin contemplar otras obligaciones que el Estado ha celebrado tanto en el marco internacional como local. Retomaremos esta idea más adelante. Valga mencionar por ahora que la mayor parte de la literatura especializada no reconoce problema alguno con este punto: el Estado decide sobre su propia soberanía y, en virtud de previas negociaciones libres entre pares con los otros Estados partes de los TBI y los TLC, cede su jurisdicción como garantía de confianza de que las obligaciones legales plasmadas en dichos tratados han de ser cumplidos. Así, el inversionista privado extranjero debería encontrar incentivos suficientes para invertir, y si algo sale mal, el sistema funciona como garantía de la inversión realizada.

Sin embargo, bajo esta lógica general aparente, se presentan problemas jurídicos de diversa índole:

Compromisos públicos que protegen intereses privados

El régimen protege a los inversionistas privados extranjeros que no son parte en los tratados celebrados. Por ende, se trata de acuerdos internacionales que no benefician directamente a los firmantes sino a terceros, desplazando el interés público por el interés individual. Ello contradice uno de los principios generales de derecho que entiende que en una situación de

---

9 Actualmente esta tendencia generalizada es posible que se encuentre cediendo. En todo caso, debe analizarse en cada TLC de manera individual. Por ejemplo, no aparece un capítulo de inversiones en el TLC entre el Mercosur y la UE (ver www. cancilleria.gob.ar/es/acuerdo-mercosur-ue). Habiendo más de 3.000 TBI en todo el mundo según UNCTAD (ver UNCTAD, 'Investment Policy Hub' https://investmentpo licyhub.unctad.org/IIA, consultado en Diciembre 2018), es posible que los aspectos de inversión ya estén regulados por tratados bilaterales específicos, por lo que un TLC solamente podría modificar un TBI anterior o no tocar esta área regulada, adoptando una posición conservadora en la materia.

conflicto entre derechos, el interés público y general debe primar sobre el interés privado particular.

Los TBI no atraen la inversión extranjera

La empiria de los últimos 25 años demuestra que los TBI y el ISDS no atraen la inversión extranjera, ni promueven el empleo o el desarrollo.[10] La tendencia general de las IED –al menos en América Latina- oscila a los largo de las últimas dos décadas sin relación con la firma de este tipo de acuerdos, por lo que no puede aseverarse que haya existido un "boom" en materia de inversión extranjera causado luego de que un país haya celebrado sus TBI. No obstante, es precisamente tal justificación el motivo central para la firma de estos tratados, sosteniendo que brindarían seguridad jurídica al inversor para brindarle importantes incentivos para atraer y captar los flujos de inversión global. Dicha justificación no posee comprobación en los hechos, por lo que se trata de una mera presunción sin un respaldo empírico que sea concluyente. Sí se ha visto cómo en algún caso particular un inversionista puede estar interesado en la firma de un TBI, pero se trata de un proyecto de inversión individual que no puede compararse con las justificaciones que se esgrimen a nivel general, ocultándose así lo que en realidad es: la firma de un acuerdo que comprometerá a toda la sociedad para beneficiar a una sola empresa extranjera y por encima del resto. En cambio, se buscan excusas aludiendo al bienestar social, el crecimiento económico, la "lluvia de inversiones" y el desarrollo, que no tienen un correlato con los datos. Lo que se observa es la aplicación de más de dos décadas de este tipo de tratados sin que América Latina haya alcanzado un nivel de desarrollo o haya aumentado la prosperidad de sus poblaciones; por el contrario América Latina es el continente más desigual del planeta.[11] A más de 20 años de funcionamiento de la mayoría de los TBI, todavía no existe una sola fuente concluyente que asegure que los TBI hayan servido para la atracción de las inversiones extranjeras,[12] siendo

10 CAITISA, 2017, *Informe Ejecutivo*. Disponible en https://caitisa.org/boletines/ consultado en Junio 2020; CAITISA, 'Introducción' http://caitisa.org/index.php/home/ enlaces-de-interes consultado en Diciembre 2018.
11 Ver CEPAL, 'CEPAL: Pese a avances recientes, América Latina sigue siendo la Región más desigual del mundo' (comunicado de prensa, 8 Junio 2017) www.cepal.org/es/ comunicados/cepal-pese-avances-recientes-america-latina-sigue-siendo-la-region-mas-desigual-mundo consultado en Febrero 2019.
12 Ver Omar E García-Bolívar, 'La crisis del derecho internacional de inversiones extranjeras: propuestas de reforma' (2015) 3 (5) Revista de la Secretaría del Tribunal Permanente de Revisión. Cecilia Olivet (CAITISA 2017). Disponible en https://caitisa.org/index.php/noticias/boletines/informetbi consultado en Febrero 2019.

este además el principal argumento por el cual se firmaban. Por consiguiente se incumplen los postulados establecidos en numerosos preámbulos y objetivos de los TBI, así como los argumentos que han justificado la celebración de estos acuerdos y el establecimiento del sistema.

Faltan análisis interdisciplinarios y estudios de impacto

Paradójicamente, tras dos décadas de implementación de este régimen, siguen faltando los estudios de impacto de las inversiones extranjeras en materia de empleo, desarrollo y reducción de la pobreza. Por lo general, los estudios existentes demuestran lo contrario: que la mayor parte de IED arriba a un país para comprar una empresa o un sector que ya está en funcionamiento, generando muy poca cantidad de empleos nuevos.[13] Es más, suele ocurrir lo contrario: luego de la adquisición suele entrarse en un período de reducción de costos y achicamiento de la planta de empleados, lo que se traduce en despidos de trabajadores. Por otro lado, el análisis en la materia en estudio no puede ser abordado desde un punto de vista estrictamente legal o económico, pues afecta cuestiones sociales, ambientales, sobre las relaciones internacionales, las políticas públicas, etc. Por ende, el análisis debe realizarse desde un ámbito multidisciplinario que contemple –al menos- los campos del derecho, la sociología, la economía, la ciencia política, las relaciones internacionales y las ciencias ambientales.

Un sistema desbalanceado

Los TBI otorgan derechos a los inversionistas pero no obligaciones, en tanto éstas recaen solamente en los Estados, por lo que un "derecho" al que no se le apareja una obligación o un control que le contrapese y que favorece a ciertos entes (los inversionistas extranjeros sobre los inversionistas nacionales) más bien constituye un privilegio que no se encuentra debidamente fundado ni en derecho ni en los hechos. También es un sistema que favorece los intereses privados respecto de los públicos en pos de una seguridad jurídica para las empresas transnacionales, lo cual marca un sistema parcializado. Para obtener un sistema balanceado se debe equiparar una seguridad jurídica que no sea exclusiva de los actores económicos sino

---

13 Ver CAITISA, Informe Ejecutivo: Auditoría integral ciudadana de los tratados de protección recíproca de inversión y del sistema de arbitraje en materia de inversiones en Ecuador (Quito, Ecuador, Mayo 2017). https://caitisa.org/boletines/ consultado en Junio 2020.

de toda la comunidad sopesando derechos y obligaciones de los sectores involucrados y afectados.[14]

Inseguridad jurídica

La seguridad jurídica es una motivación recurrente en la celebración de los TBI. Suele alegarse que el establecimiento de estas reglas favorece un clima de inversiones extranjeras, lo cual es un argumento para garantizar su atracción. Por ende, sería lógico suponer que un país que haya firmado medio centenar de estos acuerdos seguramente haya visto multiplicar sus inversiones extranjeras de forma abrumadora. Pues este argumento es empíricamente falso. No hay datos que sostengan que la firma de 30, 40, 50, 70 TBI haya sido el causante de una "lluvia de inversiones" provenientes del extranjero en ningún país del mundo. Al contrario, estos acuerdos abren frentes para que empresas provenientes del país contraparte en estos tratados puedan demandar a los Estados ante tribunales internacionales de arbitraje por cualquier violación que ellas consideren.

Asimismo, hemos visto que este régimen afecta el interés público y el interés general, lo que contrariamente a lo que se sostiene, genera un entorno de inseguridad jurídica para la población en general en tanto no puede decidir sobre sus propios recursos o sobre las políticas públicas, lo cual torna al sistema de un grado de ilegitimidad importante. Casos como el presentado por la empresa Vattenfall contra Alemania ante el CIADI (Caso CIADI Nro. ARB/09/6) en donde la empresa sueca demandó internacionalmente al Estado por la decisión política tomada por el nuevo gobierno de la ciudad-Estado de Hamburgo, el cual había sido electo en elecciones libres con una plataforma en la que establecía que impondría restricciones ambientales a la explotación de una de las centrales eléctricas de carbón en la ciudad. El nuevo gobierno cumplió con su promesa electoral, para lo cual la empresa alegó que la medida era "similar a una expropiación" y violaba el trato justo y equitativo.[15] La seguridad jurídica que Alemania debió otorgarle a Vattenfall significó la inseguridad jurídica de los ciudadanos alemanes que debieron afrontar los costos de esta demanda a la vez que vieron afectados su capacidad de elegir soberanamente sobre las políticas públicas.

---

14 En relación con los derechos de pueblos indígenas, ver el capítulo 9 de Sufyan Droubi, Cecilia Juliana Flores Elizondo y Raphael Heffron en este volumen.

15 Javier Echaide, 'El derecho internacional de las inversiones, los derechos humanos y la gobernabilidad democrática', en Armin Von Bogdandy, Pedro Salazar Ugarte, Mariela Morales Antoniazzi, and Franz Christian Ebert., *El constitucionalismo transformador en América Latina y el derecho económico internacional. De la tensión al diálogo* (Universidad Nacional Autónoma de Mexico, Instituto Max Planck Institute de Derecho Público Comparado y Derecho Internacional Público 2018) 148.

Déficit democrático

El marco legal y el arbitraje en inversiones (ISDS, por sus siglas en inglés[16]) no es un régimen democrático en el sentido de que adolece de todo escrutinio público (*accountability*) por sus altos niveles de tecnicismos y su secretismo amparado en un alto desconocimiento general de la población sobre cómo puede afectar a las políticas públicas, a las cuentas públicas y al presupuesto general del Estado, y a sus decisiones soberanas. La crítica a los TBI, que originalmente provino de movimientos sociales y ONGs, hoy hace eco dentro de círculos académicos y de funcionarios internacionales. Estas observaciones han detectado que el funcionamiento de este régimen de protección de inversiones dificulta seriamente la promoción de un orden internacional democrático y equitativo. Diagnostican un déficit democrático creciente, no solamente en los mecanismos de transparencia y participación de estos acuerdos, sino también en sus efectos. El relator especial de Naciones Unidas, Alfred-Maurice Zayas advirtió que:

"la solución de controversias entre inversores y Estados plantea un desafío particular para el orden democrático, en particular cuando los Gobiernos que han sido elegidos democráticamente para llevar a cabo determinadas políticas sociales son demandados por los inversores precisamente en razón de esas políticas democráticamente escogidas. (…)

Si bien los tribunales internacionales pueden y deben declarar inadmisibles los casos improcedentes de abuso del derecho a presentar comunicaciones (…) o de abuso de procedimiento, los tribunales de solución de controversias entre inversores y Estados rara vez lo hacen y aceptan los litigios improcedentes y vejatorios que ocasionan enormes gastos a las partes, lo cual es especialmente perjudicial para los países en desarrollo."[17]

Falta de transparencia

El sistema es poco transparente en términos de evitar secuencias frecuentes de intercambio de roles entre jueces y partes (las llamadas "puertas giratorias"

16 Siglas en inglés de *Investor State Dispute Settlement*. Bajo estas siglas es como se conoce al sistema internacional de solución de controversias inversor-Estado, que en términos genéricos agrupa a diversos tribunales o centros de arbitraje internacional tales como el Centro Internacional de Arreglos de Diferencias relativas a Inversiones (CIADI) del Banco Mundial, la Corte Permanente de Arbitraje (CPA) internacional, la Cámara de Comercio Internacional (CCI), la Cámara de Comercio de Estocolmo, o las reglas de la *United Nations Commission on International Trade Law* (UNCITRAL) o la Comisión de Naciones Unidas de Derecho Comercial Internacional, en español.
17 ONU, Asamblea General, Promoción de un orden internacional democrático y equitativo, Nota del Secretario General [Informe del Experto Independiente Alfred-Maurice de Zayas] [UN Doc A/70/285] (5 Agosto 2015).

o "cambios de sombrero"), en donde hoy una persona puede ser árbitro y al día de mañana la misma puede representar los intereses de una empresa inversionista, y pasado volver a ser árbitro, al tiempo que es formador de opinión y doctrina que se citarán en los casos que se discutan en el sistema.

Los árbitros no son decisores políticos pero actúan como tales

Los árbitros laudan desde un punto de vista jurídico, pero con fuertes análisis económicos y no legales. Sistemas de cálculo de evaluación de daños como los "daños en expectativa" provienen de un análisis económico del derecho y no del derecho en sí mismo. Ello favorece la situación de laudar desde el punto de vista del inversor, cuando éste no es un decisor público. Sin embargo, el efecto de los laudos arbitrales en materia de inversiones genera gastos en indemnizaciones y efectos posteriores que tuercen la voluntad del decisor público en materia de políticas públicas que ha de poder aplicar, desplazando así la voluntad de la ciudadanía aun cuando ella se exprese en elecciones libres.

Club de árbitros

Más de la mitad de los casos en el mundo en materia de arbitraje sobre inversiones se ha concentrado en apenas un puñado de quince árbitros, marcando un círculo muy cerrado de árbitros altamente influyentes dentro del sistema con un sesgo pro-inversor que desbalancea una relación ecuánime al momento de decidir.[18]

Abusos en cuanto a la manipulación de las reglas

Se incrementa el grado de abusos que se observan en cuanto a la manipulación de las reglas y argumentos para favorecer a los inversionistas dentro del ISDS. Situaciones como los pedidos de recusación de árbitros rara vez son concedidos incluso en situaciones en donde se han detectado relación entre el ingreso económico de un árbitro vinculado a una empresa demandante y a los laudos que él mismo dicta. El caso del pedido de recusación de Gabrielle Kaufmann-Kohler en el caso Suez y otros v. Argentina[19] por

---

18 Cecilia Olivet and Pia Eberhardt, *Cuando la injusticia es negocio. Cómo las firmas de abogados, árbitros y financiadores alimentan el auge del arbitraje de inversiones* (CEO and TNI 2012). Disponible en: www.tni.org/files/download/cuando_la_injusticia_es_negocio-web.pdf consultado en Diciembre de 2018.
19 *Suez, Sociedad General de Aguas de Barcelona, S.A. and Interagua Servicios Integrales de Agua, S.A. v. Argentine Republic (formerly Aguas Provinciales de Santa Fe, Suez,*

la nacionalización de la empresa Aguas Argentinas S.A. fue notorio. La árbitro suiza participaba del board de UPS, una empresa controlante del Grupo Suez, y sus ingresos personales por dicho cargo dependían de los beneficios que la empresa generaba. Ella no sólo podía influir en un laudo favorable a la empresa Suez, lo cual le dotaba de falta de imparcialidad, sino que además podía ser beneficiada económicamente por el resultado del laudo que ella misma podía ayudar a generar. Argentina solicitó en dos oportunidades un pedido de recusación –el primero al momento de detectar la participación en la empresa controlante y el segundo al saber que podía ser económicamente beneficiada- pero sus pares no consideraron que fueran motivos suficientes como para que ello alterase su buen juicio y su imparcialidad. Ella continuó como árbitro y el laudo resultó favorable a la empresa demandante.

Rompe la equidad al favorecer a sectores de poder

Las reglas han sido especialmente diseñadas para favorecer a sectores con poder que, a partir de su implementación, han visto incrementado dicho poder al cabo de las últimas dos décadas. México iba a volver a tener un crecimiento acelerado, con capacidad de generar empleo, con estabilidad de precios, sin devaluaciones, etc., lo más elemental de cualquier proyecto económico. El hecho es que la economía mexicana ha crecido 0,98% como tasa media anual durante 20 años, o sea prácticamente está estancada, menos del 1% del PIB por habitante, que es la tasa más baja de cualquier estrategia económica que México ha tenido después de la revolución mexicana y en toda la historia. Si se compara con el resto de América Latina -según información de la CEPAL-, es de los que menos ha crecido, y no estamos hablando de un año bueno o un año malo, estamos hablando de la media durante 20 años.[20] En Perú la política de apertura comercial y los TBI han sido anteriores a los acuerdos comerciales y definieron la política de apertura comercial, blindándola de posibles cambios de política pública y modificando la configuración del comercio hacia una matriz

---

Sociedad General de Aguas de Barcelona y Interagua Servicios Integrales de Agua v Argentina), ICSID Case No. ARB/03/17 (*Suez I*); *Suez, Sociedad General de Aguas de Barcelona, S.A. and Vivendi Universal, S.A. (formerly Aguas Argentinas, S.A., Suez, Sociedad General de Aguas de Barcelona, S.A. and Vivendi Universal, S.A.) v. Argentine Republic (II)*, ICSID Case No. ARB/03/19 (*Suez II*).

20 Entrevista a Alberto Arroyo Picard. Ver Fernando Andrade C, 'Arroyo Picard analiza el Impacto del TLC en México 20 años después' www.uasb.edu.ec/web/spondylus/contenido-uasb?arroyo-picard-analiza-el-impacto-del-tlc-en-mexico-20-anos-despues (consultado en Junio 2020).

agroexportadora.[21] Centroamérica es la subregión más pobre de América Latina, con los indicadores sociales más deteriorados de nuestra región y de los mayores niveles de concentración de la riqueza a pesar de contar a la fecha con más de 70 TLC vigentes y más de 80 TBI. Allí viven 30 millones de personas de un total de 42 millones en condición de pobreza, un 60% de la población centroamericana vive en la pobreza. Casos como los de Guatemala con un 59.3% o de Honduras con un 65.7% de pobreza evidencian que esta estrategia económica no es para nada la salida que mejora las condiciones de vida de las personas. En materia de concentración de la riqueza, para el año 2014 el PIB Nominal de la región fue aproximadamente de unos $140.000 millones de dólares, y el 91% de esa riqueza fue concentrada en manos de tan sólo 965 personas.[22] Chile es uno de los países más liberalizados de América Latina y del mundo. Sin embargo, el estallido social vivido a fines de 2019 expuso la contracara del modelo económico implementados desde 1973 por la dictadura militar: que también es uno de los países más desiguales del planeta. De acuerdo con el índice de Gini (que mide la distribución de los ingresos con un coeficiente que va de 0 —igualdad absoluta— a 1 —desigualdad absoluta—), la inequidad en Chile es de 0,454, según datos de la Cepal.[23]

El *chilling effect*

El ISDS y las reglas de protección de inversiones de los TBI y los TLC generan un efecto de "enfriamiento regulatorio"[24] (*chilling effect*) o una auto-inhibición en los Estados de aplicar políticas públicas que, aun cuando sean favorables a la población en general o a las comunidades afectadas por la explotación de la inversión, prefieren dejar de lado más y mejores políticas

21 Ana Romero Cano, 'Tratados de Libre Comercio, blindando la inversión extranjera'. Ver www.nodal.am/2018/11/tratados-de-libre-comercio-blindando-la-inversion-extranjera-por-ana-romero-cano/ consultado en Junio 2020.

22 Jorge Coronado, 'Nuevas y viejas amenazas de los Tratados de Libre Comercio (TLCs) para Centroamérica'. Ver www.nodal.am/2018/11/nuevas-y-viejas-amenazas-de-los-tratados-de-libre-comercio-tlcs-para-centroamerica-por-jorge-coronado/ consultado en Junio 2020.

23 Darío Mizrahi, 'Mitos y verdades de la desigualdad en Chile: hasta qué punto explica el estallido que sacude al país'. Ver www.infobae.com/america/america-latina/2019/11/09/mitos-y-verdades-de-la-desigualdad-en-chile-hasta-que-punto-explica-el-estallido-que-sacude-al-pais/ consultado en Junio 2020.

24 Juan Pablo Bohoslavsky, *Tratados de protección de las inversiones e implicaciones para la formulación de políticas públicas (especial referencia a los servicios de agua potable y saneamiento)* (CEPAL Julio 2010). Disponible en: www.cepal.org/es/publicaciones/3769-tratados-proteccion-inversiones-implicaciones-la-formulacion-politicas-publicas consultado en Enero 2019.

regulatorias en pos de evitar demandas de arbitraje internacional de parte de las empresas transnacionales.

Resabio legal colonial

En gran parte de los países en vías de desarrollo –y esto se ve especialmente en los países del África y muchos de Asia, no así en América Latina-, esta arquitectura legal ha sido implantada como un mecanismo post-colonial que ha perpetuado las relaciones de dependencia económica y restricción de la soberanía.[25] Si bien la reducción del espacio para las políticas públicas (*policy space*) es producto del *chilling effect* y esto aplica tanto a todos los países del mundo, la situación latinoamericana es particular en este sentido, pues por los procesos de independencia latinoamericanos han sido anteriores a los africanos o los asiáticos. En este sentido, las razones que motivaron que este régimen de protección de inversiones haya sido adoptado por los países de América Latina tiene más que ver con una estrategia de inserción de las empresas multinacionales en las cadenas globales de valor, así como en la presión que los organismos multilaterales de crédito han tenido en la región en momentos de crisis y reestructuración de sus deudas externas, por ejemplo. No se trata simplemente de un andamiaje post-colonial que la metrópoli dejó al abandonar su presencia en la colonia, sino un mecanismo mucho más complejo que tiene que ver con la relación de las clases dominantes locales con su estrategia de inserción económica en los mercados internacionales para favorecer sus exportaciones, aunque desde un lugar dependiente y no de control autónomo de dichos mercados.

Aumento de la conflictividad social

Que ese chilling effect implica una dicotomía entre la amenaza de demandas o la falta de inversión extranjera versus un aumento de la conflictividad social. Los Estados suelen optar por proteger el derecho de la inversión frente a los derechos humanos, ambientales o sociales, lo cual agrava el escenario de conflictividad social. El caso de la "Guerra del Agua" en Bolivia en 2000 fue muestra de ello: la empresa privada Aguas del Tunari –subsidiaria en última instancia de la transnacional norteamericana Bechtel- asumió la concesión de distribución de agua de Chochabamba. Inmediatamente aumentó las tarifas hasta llegar a un 300%. El aumento de las tarifas motivó una

---

25 Muthucumaraswamy Sornarajah, *The International Law of Foreign Investment* (Cambridge University Press 2010).

verdadera sublevación popular[26] que acabó con la concesión de la empresa, la cual demandó a Bolivia ante el CIADI por $40 millones de dólares. A raíz de la movilización social y a pesar de tener un laudo de jurisdicción favorable, el caso fue desistido por la empresa que acordó una indemnización simbólica de 0,50 centavos de dólar (2 bolivianos). La actividad minera a cielo abierto y a gran escala ("megaminería") en provincias como San Juan, Catamarca o Mendoza en Argentina y las graves consecuencias sociales[27] – como la pérdida irrecuperable de afluentes en San Juan a raíz de repetidas contaminaciones por la transnacional canadiense Barrick, por ejemplo-[28] y sin embargo cualquier cambio en la legislación ambiental sobre este tipo de proyectos queda seriamente arriesgado de recibir demandas internacionales en el CIADI, siendo que el sector minero (junto al del gas y el petróleo) es el que más demandas atrae ante dicho organismo a nivel mundial.[29]

Profundiza las asimetrías

Estos modelos y reglas de arbitraje, lejos de minimizarlas, profundizan las asimetrías que favorecen a las empresas transnacionales como entes ganadores de la globalización frente al debilitamiento de los Estados-nacionales como centros monopólicos de generación normativa. Virtualmente se crea un sistema paralelo de generación de normas en donde los Estados pierden la capacidad de controlar el proceso de generación de las mismas, recayendo en un sistema en donde las relaciones de poder en materia económica condicionan la base material de las reglas que se crean. El escrutinio de la ciudadanía se encuentra ausente en todo este proceso.

Se trata de un canal unidireccional de la responsabilidad y a la medida de su pretensión

Aunque técnicamente no lo prohíbe, resulta abrumadora la distancia existente entre la cantidad de demandas interpuestas por las empresas

26 Thomas Kruse, 'La Guerra del Agua en Cochabamba, Bolivia: terrenos complejos, convergencias nuevas' (2005). Ver http://biblioteca.clacso.edu.ar/clacso/gt/2010110 9025721/5kruse.pdf consultado en Junio 2020.

27 Horacio Machaado, Maristella Svampa, Enrique Viale, *15 mitos y realidades de la minería transnacional en Argentina: guía para desmontarel imaginario prominero* (Colectivo Voces de Alerta 2011.). Ver http://biblioteca.clacso.edu.ar/Argentina/iigg-uba/20161025033400/15mitos.pdf consultado en Junio 2020.

28 Ver 'Un nuevo derrame en la mina Veladero' (Página 12, 30 Marzo 2017) www.pagina12. com.ar/28713-un-nuevo-derrame-en-la-mina-veladero consultado en Junio 2020.

29 Fuente, ICSID Cases, 2020–1. Ver https://icsid.worldbank.org/en/Documents/resour ces/The%20ICSID%20Caseload%20Statistics%202020–1%20Edition-ENG.pdf consultado en Junio 2020.

transnacionales contra los Estados que la que los Estados han realizado contra las empresas. En tanto el sistema está diseñado para proteger la inversión –y por definición la disciplina económica entiende a la inversión como la participación del capital privado dentro de la economía-, se encuentra previamente inclinado a considerar más los reclamos de los particulares que los de los Estados. Esto hace que el Estado sea el que más asiduamente se siente en el banquillo al ser la responsabilidad del Estado la que esencialmente se analiza respecto a si ha violentado o no el derecho de los inversionistas a ver protegida su inversión.

Esto resulta un régimen sesgado de la responsabilidad internacional. El sistema no contempla otros grados de responsabilidad del Estado en el sentido de generar contextos adversos al cumplimiento de los derechos de las comunidades o de los derechos humanos. Tampoco observa la responsabilidad de las empresas en cuanto a los posibles daños que su inversión ha generado y que ellas puedan ser halladas responsables en cuanto se han beneficiados por tales actos lesivos. Menos observa el sistema sobre la presión política que ejercen las empresas para que tales derechos se vean violados en pos de su beneficio económico.

Por ende, el sistema se encuentra diseñado a la medida del interés de las empresas transnacionales y no en base a una visión ecuánime en donde puedan ponerse en la misma balanza beneficios y perjuicios de los actores involucrados en los casos a tratar.

Favorece la fragmentación del derecho internacional

La dispersión jurisdiccional en el derecho internacional es amplia. El ISDS y los TBI sólo analizan una forma específica de la responsabilidad del Estado por violaciones al derecho de propiedad de la inversión. En torno a esta cuestión se ha montado no sólo un régimen legal específico para esa protección, sino además una diversidad de foros sobre los que el inversionista puede elegir libremente de acuerdo a las probabilidades de éxito de su reclamo. Esta especie de *forum shopping* distorsiona la imparcialidad del sistema por cuanto los foros deben competir entre sí por recursos económicos (costas y honorarios), convirtiéndolo en un verdadero "mercado de la justicia".

La aplicación de este marco normativo dentro de un sentido fragmentado del derecho internacional provoca que se vea alterado el orden de prelación o la prioridad en el cumplimiento de las obligaciones en el derecho internacional. Los derechos humanos se ven desplazados frente al cumplimiento del derecho de las inversiones, haciendo que normas de carácter dispositivo adquieran en los hechos una prioridad frente a obligaciones con efecto *erga omnes* o normas del *jus cogens* internacional.

La asimetría entre el derecho de inversiones y los derechos humanos

Si bien hemos observado que el régimen de protección de inversiones acarrea una serie de problemas teóricos y prácticos con las reglas legales que constituyen dicho régimen, por una cuestión de extensión sólo me concentraré en la relación entre el régimen de protección de inversiones y su afectación a los derechos humanos, en especial con los casos vinculados al agua potable y saneamiento.

Los derechos humanos son un cuerpo legal producto de la terrible experiencia que significó para la humanidad la II Guerra Mundial. Se trata de un conjunto de derecho que establece los parámetros de la convivencia social global a partir de la segunda mitad del siglo XX: una especia de "nuevo contrato social" para la comunidad internacional que fija derechos y obligaciones esencialmente para los Estados. No se trata – como muchos abogados de empresas especializados en el arbitraje de inversión podrían interpretar – de "argumentos pro-Estado" sino precisamente de todo lo contrario: cualquier litigante en materia de derechos humanos sabe que el primer ente a quien se le reclama legalmente el cumplimiento de este conjunto de derechos es precisamente al Estado, lo que lo convierte en el primer centro de imputaciones en cualquier acción judicial. Sostener que la defensa de los derechos humanos es una "defensa estatista" es no realmente comprender el alcance del problema o pretender negarlo, lo cual radica en uno de los principales inconvenientes para hallar una solución: la negación. Lo que los derechos humanos implican es un conjunto de directrices con el objeto de *evitar los abusos*, situaciones como las que se vivieron durante la II Guerra Mundial así como otras.

Uno de los problemas hoy radica en la cuestión de la subjetividad. Las normas en materia de derechos humanos principalmente se enfocan en un centro de imputación esencial, que es la figura del Estado, aunque no es la única. Pero sí sabemos que, ante un caso de violación de un derecho humano, el Estado es directa o indirectamente responsable. Quien comete los abusos que acarrean una violación legal a los derechos humanos son entes con poder. Y en definitiva es de lo que el Derecho siempre trató: de limitar el poder. Por ende, el estudio y la aplicación del Derecho siempre se ha encontrado con este mismo problema: se trata de una puja entre centros de poder con el resto de la comunidad.

El rasgo diferencial de nuestro momento histórico se caracteriza por el hecho de que los principales centros de poder no son ya los Estados sino actores privados. Este fenómeno se inició a partir de la década de 1970 pero se profundizó en 1990 mediante la flexibilización del trabajo asalariado y la relocalización de las filiales de grandes empresas generando que la cadena de montaje y la producción de valor se globalizaran. El proceso de acumulación de estas empresas se extendió a distintos Estados que comenzaron a competir por atraer sus inversiones. Pronto el escenario cambió, se buscaron normas internacionales para proteger esas inversiones (los TBI), pero las normas que protegían a los ciudadanos y sus comunidades de los abusos de los agentes poderosos siguieron siendo las mismas. Con ello se demuestra no sólo la fragmentación del derecho internacional, sino también que su progresivo desarrollo no se da de manera simultánea sino en distintas velocidades y de acuerdo a intereses: la década de 1990 marcó un salto cuantitativo sorprendente en cuanto a los TBI firmados, pero ello no fue algo casual, pues el sujeto interesado para el establecimiento de esas reglas ya existía y pedía su expansión. Ese sujeto eran las empresas transnacionales; las vías materiales para su expansión eran las cadenas globales de valor; y el marco jurídico que lo garantizaba y las protegía eran los tratados de inversión y los capítulos de inversiones de los tratados de libre comercio.

El área del derecho internacional de las inversiones es un área de reciente estudio a raíz de la gran cantidad de TBI celebrados desde la década de 1990. Asimismo, desde la crisis económica conocida como la "Gripe Asiática" (1997) se evidencia un fuerte crecimiento en la cantidad de demandas dentro de instituciones como el Centro Internacional de Arreglo de Diferencias relativas a Inversiones (CIADI), de un promedio de 1.48 demandas por año durante los primeros 25 años (1972–1996) a un promedio de 12.66 demandas por año tan solo en los siguientes 6 años. Tal crecimiento no puede en nada compararse con el actual nivel de demandas: un promedio de 46 nuevas demandas por año a partir del 2012.[30]

El discurso dominante sostiene que el flujo de inversiones goza de buena salud y que el régimen internacional que lo protege (el conjunto de TBI bilaterales y el sistema de arbitraje internacional al que cualquier empresa inversionista puede acudir) son un mecanismo barato, rápido y eficaz para garantizar dicha protección. Pero, ¿por qué se dan entonces estos incrementos tan sorprendentes en la cantidad de reclamos por parte de las empresas transnacionales? ¿Acaso más reclamos por protección no deberían significar que las inversiones internacionales se encuentran en un mayor riesgo? Mostrar que el mecanismo de solución de diferencias inversor-Estado (ISDS, por sus siglas en inglés) está más activo que nunca, da un mensaje positivo para el propio mecanismo en cuanto a que resulta ser muy utilizado, pero al mismo tiempo puede evidenciar una crisis en cuanto a la estabilidad del sistema internacional de inversiones. Al mismo tiempo, estos indicadores no acaban de responder una pregunta pendiente sobre una de las promesas

---

30 Fuente, Elaboración propia en base a ICSID Cases, 2020–1. Ver https://icsid.worldb
ank.org/en/Documents/resources/The%20ICSID%20Caseload%20Statistics%202
020–1%20Edition-ENG.pdf consultado en Junio 2020.

de origen del sistema: ¿es este sistema un promotor para la atracción de las inversiones extranjeras? ¿Una mayor fragmentación del sistema jurídico internacional es acaso algo beneficioso para el mismo y los actores que intervienen en él? ¿Qué implica que el desarrollo fragmentado de áreas del derecho internacional como el de los derechos humanos y los tratados de protección de inversiones no logren tener una interconexión eficaz?

La falta de sincronía normativa en el derecho internacional, sumada a su previa fragmentación, resulta crítica en tanto el conflicto de normas internacionales de protección de inversiones y de derechos humanos se torna cada vez más evidente. El derecho humano al agua potable está reconocido internacionalmente como un derecho humano independiente y positivo desde el año 2010, cuando fue sancionada la Resolución 64/292 de la Asamblea General de las Naciones Unidas (AG-ONU). Es un claro ejemplo de lo que es el desarrollo progresivo del derecho internacional, que no necesariamente se relaciona con nuevas tecnologías, sino que muchas veces trata sobre temas muy antiguos pero no por ello reconocidos o regulados por el derecho internacional.

La perspectiva de nuestro estudio es y debe ser multidisciplinaria. El estudio de fenómenos de las inversiones internacionales debe encararse desde las relaciones internacionales, la economía política internacional, el derecho y la sociología jurídica. Este acercamiento enriquece el estudio de los fenómenos que acarrea el régimen de protección de inversiones a nivel internacional.

Gracias a este desarrollo fragmentado y a diferentes velocidades, así como al contexto posterior a la Guerra Fría, el auge del neoliberalismo y la apertura de mercados a nivel internacional, se desarrolló un marco legal de derecho público internacional para favorecer estrictamente al capital privado transnacional, y con un sistema de resolución de disputas disponible para corporaciones multinacionales a través del arbitraje internacional de instituciones como el CIADI. Los laudos arbitrales son vinculantes y operan con una fuerza mucho mayor que otras instancias porque aplican condicionamientos económicos a los Estados para crear nuevos marcos regulatorios. Ello se observa en el denominado "enfriamiento regulatorio" (*chilling effect*) en el desarrollo de políticas públicas: los Estados, al momento de decidir si aplicar o no políticas públicas que puedan afectar los intereses de inversionistas extranjeros, suelen evitar implementarlas para evadir el riesgo de demandas arbitrales en el CIADI u otros foros por parte de empresas multinacionales. Este efecto de enfriamiento resulta en una externalidad negativa de la protección de las inversiones extranjeras que no es considerada por el sistema. A su vez, la seguridad jurídica que los inversionistas a menudo demandan en sus reclamos termina ganando un mayor peso con respecto a la seguridad jurídica que también merece las comunidades afectadas por las acciones de las empresas de inversión, lo que provoca una asimetría legal en diferentes niveles: entre intereses públicos y privados; entre el capital nacional y el transnacional; entre los mercados interno y externo; entre países en desarrollo -generalmente importadores de capital- y países desarrollados; así como entre el derecho y las obligaciones de las empresas transnacionales. La no regulación también puede implicar una violación de derechos, y este efecto de enfriamiento, también marcado por una asimetría legal en diferentes niveles, puede violar los derechos humanos que son la base de la coexistencia de la comunidad internacional desde 1945: es por eso que tienen un carácter *erga omnes* en el derecho internacional.

El caso del agua potable y el saneamiento, y en particular en el caso de Argentina, son un ejemplo. A partir de la Resolución 64/292 AG-ONU no hay dudas respecto al reconocimiento de que el acceso al agua potable en cantidad y calidad suficientes es un derecho humano básico y universal. Sin embargo, los efectos antes mencionados amenazan una regulación que haga que este reconocimiento sea efectivo. Si bien el derecho humano al agua se ve comprometido por el sistema que protege las inversiones extranjeras, esto provoca una seria contradicción de las normas dispositivas contra las normas indisponibles en el derecho internacional como es el caso de las obligaciones sobre derechos humanos. Y, sin embargo, tal contradicción no genera responsabilidades ni para los Estados ni para las empresas que se benefician de este sistema. Son los costos sociales los que, hasta el momento, pagan por el *status quo* vigente que genera amplias mayorías perjudicadas y lucrativos beneficios para unos pocos.

En su reporte del año 2015 sobre fragmentación del derecho internacional, la Comisión de Derecho Internacional (CDI) de Naciones Unidas trabajó sobre las posibles contradicciones entre normas internacionales dispositivas y normas de efecto *erga omnes*.[31] En dicho informe concluyó que, si bien las normas er*ga omnes* no constituyen un rango jerárquicamente superior en el derecho internacional general respecto de otras normas, poseen una prioridad en el cumplimiento frente a las demás obligaciones internacionales que los estados partes de un tratado han decidido libremente incluirlas en sus relaciones jurídicas. Esto significa que, entre una norma de

---

31 CDI, Informe de la Comisión de Derecho Internacional sobre trabajo en su quincuagésima séptima sesión, 2 Mayo-3 Junio y 11 Julio-5 Agosto [UN Doc A/60/10, GAOR 60th Session Supp 10]; CDI, Fragmentación del derecho internacional: dificultades de la diversificación y expansión del derecho internacional. Informe del Grupo de Estudio de la Comisión de Derecho Internacional: finalizado por Martti Koskkenniemi (2006) [UN Doc A/CN.4/L.682]; Javier Echaide, 'Sobre el derecho humano al agua y la fragmentación del derecho internacional: el regimen internacional de protección de inversions vis-á-vis las obligaciones erga omnes en materia de derecho humanos' (2014) 12 *Revista Electrónica del Instituto de Investigaciones Jurídicas y Sociales Ambrosio Gioja*.

carácter *erga omnes* y una norma dispositiva como un TBI, la primera debe ser cumplida con prioridad sobre la segunda.

La doctrina es pacífica en cuanto a que los tratados de derechos humanos poseen obligaciones que provienen de toda la comunidad internacional para toda la comunidad internacional, y que sus disposiciones no pueden ser dejadas de lado por los Estados en situaciones de reciprocidad. Se trata de un conjunto de obligaciones que forman parte del nuevo pacto de convivencia entre las naciones del mundo tras el Holocausto, por lo que ningún Estado puede, libremente, desentenderse. Ello es lo que significa un efecto *erga omnes* en el derecho internacional: la indisponibilidad de las obligaciones que surgen de esos tratados.

Sin embargo existe todavía un debate acerca de la jerarquía de las normas de derechos humanos. El derecho internacional general solamente reconoce dos jerarquías: las normas imperativas sobre las dispositivas. Las imperativas –o *jus cogens* internacional- no sólo priman sobre las otras sino que cualquiera que les sea incompatible causa su nulidad absoluta. La característica de causar la nulidad de cualquier otra norma incompatible, es propia del *jus cogens*, no así de las obligaciones erga omnes que no poseen tal jerarquización y, en consecuencia, no provoca tales efectos. El debate se da en cuanto a definir si los tratados de derechos humanos –además de tener un efecto *erga omnes*- son de *jus cogens* o no.

Actualmente este desarrollo a múltiples velocidades del derecho internacional está provocando una asimetría normativa que relega los derechos de las comunidades frente a la explotación de los recursos y el ánimo de lucro de las grandes empresas. Ello constituye un problema desde una variedad de ópticas y disciplinas. Económicamente, no parece ser sostenible un modelo basado en el agotamiento intensivo y extensivo de los recursos. Eso lleva a una escasez que elevará los precios hasta hacerlos impagables, llevando a los consumidores a un callejón sin salida. Ecológicamente, queda a la vista que la rapiña no es sustentable por su propio agotamiento. Pero además, el tipo de explotación utilizado no presta la atención necesaria sobre los efectos contaminantes nocivos que las empresas no suelen evitar o enmendar (incluso a veces resulta imposible hacerlo).[32] Legalmente, las empresas transnacionales no suelen responsabilizarse por tales actos. Su explotación –que les genera beneficios importantes- provoca daños que ellas no asumen

---

32 En Argentina, la mina a cielo abierto Alumbrera, de la empresa transnacional canadiense Barrick Gold en la zona de Valadero, provincial de San Juan, sobre la Cordillera de los Andes, ha provocado la contaminación de dos ríos en forma irrecuperable debido a derrames de agua contaminada con arsénico, material necesario para la separación de la roca de los minerales buscados. No existe cuantificación posible de este daño y, sin embargo, no se ha responsabilizado a la empresa por ello hasta el momento.

o que, incluso, resultan irreparables. Pero además, se ha avalado el desarrollo de un cuerpo normativo que conduce a un cuello de botella en cuanto a asistir a posibles afectados: si se las castiga con recisiones contractuales por mala prestación de servicios- por ejemplo-, la empresa inversionista puede demandar al Estado ante tribunales arbitrales por violación del trato justo y equitativo amparado en los TBI y ganar su reclamo.[33] Ello hace que cualquier medida, sea una regulación general o una medida particular, deba afrontar su "contramedida" dentro de los tribunales arbitrales, incurriendo en gastos de defensa para el Estado que son absolutamente injustificados. En términos políticos, se observa una transferencia de recursos de manos públicas a privadas, ya que las indemnizaciones por las demandas presentadas por los inversionistas deben ser aportadas por los contribuyentes al Estado. Socialmente, las comunidades se encuentran desprotegidas en tanto se enfrentan a una realidad legal desequilibrada y en la que, para hacer valer sus derechos, requieren de recursos económicos que usualmente no poseen, mientras que para las empresas se trata de parte de su giro de negocio.

Las asimetrías son evidentes y reflejan un problema que no recae en cuestiones formales solamente (como ser en la capacidad de seleccionar buenos árbitros, por ejemplo), sino en algo que es de fondo: *el problema son las reglas*, es el régimen mismo y las contradicciones que provoca.

El derecho humano al agua

Como dijimos, el reconocimiento del derecho humano al agua como un derecho humano autónomo se dio a partir de la sanción de la Resolución 64/292 de la Asamblea General de la ONU en el año 2010. Sin embargo, ese derecho ya se lo venía reconociendo aunque no autónomamente sino como un derecho implícito dentro de otros derechos humanos.

Los tratados internacionales se rigen en las condiciones de su vigencia. Ello significa que el texto plano de los tratados es insuficiente para entender el alcance de las obligaciones legales que dichas normas jurídicas imponen: a ello deben sumársele las reservas y los alcances de la letra del tratado. Si bien los tratados son redactados y firmados por voluntad de los Estados, las interpretaciones así como la observancia del cumplimiento de tales textos suelen corresponder a organismos internacionales creados por los Estados a tal efecto o, si así no fuera, a órganos judiciales internacionales. En consecuencia, esta área de estudio suele recaer en los doctrinarios y en los juristas del derecho más que en los políticos que alternan los poderes públicos de cada Estado. Se da así una compleja relación entre la voluntad creadora del

---

33 *Suez II* (n 19).

Estado como ente soberano y cuya representación cae –generalmente- en políticos electos por sus pueblos y los juristas expertos que trabajan en las comisiones de los organismos internacionales, pero cuya generación normativa suele ser no vinculante (*soft law*). La voluntad creadora de normas vinculantes la tienen los primeros, mientras que los últimos son quienes acuden a la interpretación y alcance de las normas sin alterar su espíritu.

El Comité de Derechos Económicos, Sociales y Culturales (CDESC) es el órgano creado por el Pacto Internacional de Derechos Económicos, Sociales y Culturales (PIDESC) de 1966, y que congrega a 169 Estados parte a la fecha:[34] es decir, prácticamente toda la comunidad internacional. Fue creado por voluntad de los Estados signatarios en virtud de la resolución 17 del Consejo Económico y Social de la ONU (ECOSOC) del 28 de mayo de 1985 para verificar el cumplimiento del Pacto.

En el año 2000 el CDESC, dependiente del Consejo Económico y Social (ECOSOC) de la ONU, publicó su Observación General Nro. 14 a fin de interpretar el alcance de "el derecho al disfrute del más alto nivel posible de salud" (art. 12 del PIDESC).[35] En dicha Observación el CDESC estableció que:

> "(…) la redacción expresa del párrafo 2 del artículo 12 reconoce que el derecho a la salud abarca una amplia gama de factores socioeconómicos que promueven las condiciones merced a las cuales las personas pueden llevar una vida sana, y hace ese derecho extensivo a los factores determinantes básicos de la salud, como la alimentación y la nutrición, la vivienda, el acceso a agua limpia potable y a condiciones sanitarias adecuadas, condiciones de trabajo seguras y sanas y un medio ambiente sano."[36]

La Observación General 14 introdujo la cuestión del derecho al agua como condición indispensable para el cumplimiento de otros derechos, como el derecho al disfrute de salud del más alto nivel posible, y dejó en claro que para ello el acceso a una fuente de agua potable segura era condición básica esencial.

Posteriormente, en el año 2002, el mismo organismo emitió su Observación General Nro. 15 sobre "el derecho humano al agua" (arts. 11 y 12 del PIDESC),[37] profundizando así uno de los puntos que se vislumbró

---

34 UN, International Covenant on Economic, Social and Cultural Rights (adopted 16 December 1966, entered into force 3 January 1976) 993 UNTS 3.

35 Ver CESCR, 'El derecho al disfrute del más alto nivel posible de salud:. 11/08/2000, E/C.12/2000/4, CESCR Observación General 14 (General Comments)" www.acnur. org/fileadmin/Documentos/BDL/2001/1451.pdf consultado en Marzo 2019.

36 Ídem, párr 4.

37 Ver Red-DESC, 'Observación General No 15: El derecho al agua' (artículos 11 y 12 del Pacto Internacional de Derechos Económicos, Sociales y Culturales) www. escr-net.org/es/recursos/observacion-general-no-15-derecho-al-agua-articulos-11-y-12-del-pacto-internacional consultado en Marzo 2019.

con la Observación General anterior. En esta nueva Observación se sostuvo que:

"2. El derecho humano al agua es el derecho de todos a disponer de agua suficiente, salubre, aceptable, accesible y asequible para el uso personal y doméstico. Un abastecimiento adecuado de agua salubre es necesario para evitar la muerte por deshidratación, para reducir el riesgo de las enfermedades relacionadas con el agua y para satisfacer las necesidades de consumo y cocina y las necesidades de higiene personal y doméstica.

3. En el párrafo 1 del artículo 11 del Pacto se enumeran una serie de derechos que dimanan del derecho a un nivel de vida adecuado, "incluso alimentación, vestido y vivienda adecuados", y son indispensables para su realización. El uso de la palabra "incluso" indica que esta enumeración de derechos no pretendía ser exhaustiva. El derecho al agua se encuadra claramente en la categoría de las garantías indispensables para asegurar un nivel de vida adecuado, en particular porque es una de las condiciones fundamentales para la supervivencia. Además, el Comité ha reconocido anteriormente que el agua es un derecho humano amparado por el párrafo 1 del artículo 11 (véase la Observación general Nº 6 (1995)). El derecho al agua también está indisolublemente asociado al derecho al más alto nivel posible de salud (párrafo 1 del artículo 12) y al derecho a una vivienda y una alimentación adecuadas (párrafo 1 del artículo 11). Este derecho también debe considerarse conjuntamente con otros derechos consagrados en la Carta Internacional de Derechos Humanos, en primer lugar el derecho a la vida y a la dignidad humana."

Al mismo tiempo la observación reconoció que el derecho al agua figuraba ya incluido en un gran número de documentos internacionales, tales como tratados, declaraciones y otras normas, como por ejemplo en la Convención sobre la Eliminación de Todas las Formas de Discriminación contra la Mujer,[38] en donde se dispone que los Estados Partes asegurarán a las mujeres el derecho a *"gozar de condiciones de vida adecuadas, particularmente en las esferas de [...] el abastecimiento de agua"*. También en la Convención sobre los Derechos del Niño[39] se exige a los Estados Partes que luchen contra las enfermedades y la malnutrición mediante *"el suministro de alimentos nutritivos adecuados y agua potable salubre"*.

Los tratados internacionales de derechos humanos que entrañan obligaciones específicas en relación con el acceso al agua potable y el saneamiento son: la Convención sobre la eliminación de todas las formas de

---

38 Convención sobre la Eliminación de Todas las Formas de Discriminación contra la Mujer (UNGA Res 34/180 adoptada 18 de diciembre 1979, entrada en vigor 3 de septiembre 1981) 1249 UNTS 13, Art. 14, párr 2.

39 Convención sobre los Derechos del Niño (adoptada 20 de noviembre 1989, entrada en vigor 2 de september 1990) 1577 UNTS 3, CTS 1992/3, UN Doc A/RES/44/25, UN Reg No I-27531, Art. 24, párr 2.

discriminación contra la mujer, aprobada en 1979 (art. 14.2)); el Convenio N° 161 de la Organización Internacional del Trabajo (OIT) sobre los servicios de salud en el trabajo, aprobado en 1985 (art. 5); la Convención sobre los Derechos del Niño, aprobada en 1989 (arts. 24 y 27.3)); y la Convención sobre los derechos de las personas con discapacidad, aprobada en 2006 (art. 28). Todas estas obligaciones fueron creadas por voluntad de los Estados, pues se trataban de convenciones internacionales, por lo que el CDESC estaba observando el alcance de la existencia del derecho humano al agua bajo las obligaciones del Pacto y en relación con el cumplimiento de los derechos humanos allí elaborados.

Al año siguiente, en 2003, la Comisión de Derechos Humanos de Naciones Unidas (CDH) publicó el Informe del Alto Comisionado para los Derechos Humanos sobre "Los derechos humanos, el comercio y las inversiones".[40] Dicho informe rescata el hecho que los Estados se han comprometido a respetar, proteger y realizar los derechos humanos dentro de cada país, en cualquier contexto, como el de la liberalización de las inversiones. Es más, los derechos humanos son parte indispensable de un orden social e internacional que los Estados se han comprometido a sostener desde la Segunda Guerra Mundial y que es el pilar en el que se basa todo el andamiaje legal del derecho internacional en el que incluso se encuentran los tratados bilaterales de protección de inversiones (TBI). El mismo informe admite que, la liberalización reduce en cierta medida el campo de acción y el alcance de las políticas de los Estados con respecto a los inversionistas y las inversiones, e insta a los Estados a que con la liberalización no se debe comprometer la acción y las políticas estatales de promoción y protección de los derechos humanos, y en la medida en que los acuerdos de inversión se refieran a cuestiones de derechos humanos, los Estados tienen el deber de reglamentar (el deber de realizar los derechos humanos). Para que la liberalización de las inversiones tenga eficacia también habrá que adoptar medidas complementarias de promoción y protección de los derechos humanos como: a) Equilibrar los derechos y las obligaciones de los inversionistas y realizar esfuerzos constantes para promover la responsabilidad social de las empresas –tanto por voluntad propia (no vinculante) como mediante el reconocimiento de la responsabilidad directa de los inversionistas por las actividades que realicen por lo que respecta a los derechos humanos (vinculante)-. b) Proteger los mecanismos nacionales, regionales e internacionales

---

40 ONU, Comisión de Derechos Humanos, Derechos Humanos, el Comercio y las Inversiones, Informe del Alto Comisionado para los Derechos Humanos, *Alto Comisionado de Las Naciones Unidas para los Derechos Humanos*, [UN Doc E/CN.4/Sub.2/2003/9] (2 Junio 2003) https://undcs.org/es/E/CN.4/Sub.2/2003/9con sultado en Marzo 2019.

de vigilancia de las violaciones de los derechos humanos. c) Promover medidas en el propio país de origen vinculando la liberalización de las inversiones con que los países ricos cumplan su compromiso de proporcionar el 0,7% de su producto nacional bruto (PNB) como asistencia oficial para el desarrollo y con especial hincapié en atender las necesidades de inversión y desarrollo de los países pobres.

La vinculación de inversiones y derechos humanos está dada por el contexto del proceso de privatizaciones: la llegada de empresas de capitales privados –generalmente empresas transnacionales- al sector público para administrar e incluso adquirir empresas estatales activó el sistema de protección de inversiones que se encontraba vigente pero de forma embrionaria. Con las privatizaciones se incentivó la firma de nuevos TBI y el sistema creció exponencialmente en la década de 1990. Por ello es que el Alto Comisionado estudió en su informe las consecuencias de la privatización para los derechos humanos debido a la participación del sector privado en el abastecimiento de agua y el saneamiento y recomendó: a) Incluir explícitamente la promoción y protección de los derechos humanos en los objetivos de los acuerdos de inversión. b) Garantizar el derecho y el deber de los Estados de regular. c) Promover las obligaciones y los derechos de los inversionistas. d) Promover la cooperación internacional como parte de la liberalización de las inversiones. e) Promover los derechos humanos en el contexto de la privatización y destacar la necesidad de promover el imperio de la ley por medio de la participación popular, la transparencia, la legitimidad, la igualdad y la rendición de cuentas, al igual que en la implementación y vigilancia de los acuerdos de concesión del sector privado. f) Incrementar el diálogo sobre los derechos humanos y el comercio sumando a los delegados de los países ante la Organización Mundial de Comercio (OMC) en calidad de miembros u observadores en la CDH. g) Actividades futuras. Como un posible campo de futuras investigaciones, el Alto Comisionado interino sugiere que se tomen en consideración la elaboración de metodólogas de evaluación de las consecuencias que tienen en los derechos humanos los reglamentos o políticas comerciales y de inversión y la asistencia apropiada que se necesita para ponerlas en efecto.[41]

En 2005, el Relator Especial de la CDH emitió su informe sobre el Derecho al Agua Potable y Saneamiento, y en 2006 el Consejo de Derechos Humanos de la ONU adoptó su Decisión 2/104 "Los derechos humanos y el acceso al agua", en donde "decide pedir a la Oficina del Alto Comisionado de las Naciones Unidas para los Derechos Humanos que, teniendo en cuenta las opiniones de los Estados y otros interesados,

---

41 Javier Echaide, *El derecho humano al agua potable y los tratados de protección recíproca de inversiones* (Thompson Reuters – La Ley 2018).

efectúe, dentro de los límites de los recursos existentes, un estudio detallado sobre el alcance y el contenido de las obligaciones pertinentes en materia de derechos humanos relacionadas con el acceso equitativo al agua potable y el saneamiento que imponen los instrumentos internacionales de derechos humanos, que incluya conclusiones y recomendaciones pertinentes al respecto, para su presentación al Consejo antes de su sexto período de sesiones".[42] El mismo será producido y entregado al año siguiente y establece que "ha llegado el momento de considerar el acceso al agua potable y el saneamiento como un derecho humano, definido como el derecho a un acceso, en igualdad de condiciones y sin discriminación, a una cantidad suficiente de agua potable para usos personales y doméstico, [...] y adoptar medidas para garantizar que esta cantidad suficiente sea de buena calidad, asequible para todos y pueda recogerse a una distancia razonable del hogar de la persona.".[43]

En el año 2010, la Asamblea General de Naciones Unidas (AG-ONU) sancionó la Resolución 64/292 "El Derecho Humano al Agua Potable y Saneamiento",[44] reconociendo tal derecho humano en forma autónoma. En tal declaración la Asamblea General:

"1. Reconoce que el derecho al agua potable y el saneamiento es un derecho humano esencial para el pleno disfrute de la vida y de todos los derechos humanos;

2. Exhorta a los Estados y las organizaciones internacionales a que proporcionen recursos financieros y propicien el aumento de la capacidad y la transferencia de tecnología por medio de la asistencia y la cooperación internacionales, en particular a los países en desarrollo, a fin de intensificar los esfuerzos por proporcionar a toda la población un acceso económico al agua potable y el saneamiento;"

En consecuencia, al menos a partir de 2010 no cabe duda alguna acerca de la consideración del derecho al agua potable y saneamiento como un derecho humano básico y universal.

Ese mismo año, la CDH de Naciones Unidas, haciéndose eco de la Resolución 64/292 de la AG-ONU y de los instrumentos anteriores, emitió su Resolución 15/9 "Los Derechos Humanos y el Acceso al Agua Potable y

---

42 Ver Consejo de Derechos Humanos, Decisión 2/104, 'Los derechos humanos y el acceso al agua' www2.ohchr.org/english/issues/water/docs/HRC_decision2–104_sp.pdf consultado en Marzo 2019.

43 Ver Consejo de Derechos Humanos, Informe Anual del Alto Comisionado de las Naciones Unidas para los Derechos Humanos E Informes de la Oficina del Alto Comisionado y Del Secretario General, A/HRC/6/3 (16 Agosto 2007) https://undocs.org/pdf?symbol=es/A/HRC/6/3 consultado 18 Marzo 2021.

44 Ver ONU, Asamblea General, Resolución 64/192. El derecho humano al agua y el saneamiento, [UN Doc A/RES/64//292] (3 Agosto 2010).

el Saneamiento".[45] Dicha resolución "*Afirma* que el derecho humano al agua potable y el saneamiento se deriva del derecho a un nivel de vida adecuado y está indisolublemente asociado al derecho al más alto nivel posible de salud física y mental, así como al derecho a la vida y la dignidad humana", así como "*Reafirma* que los Estados tienen la responsabilidad primordial de garantizar la plena realización de todos los derechos humanos y que el hecho de haber delegado en terceros el suministro de agua potable segura y/o servicios de saneamiento no exime al Estado de sus obligaciones en materia de derechos humanos", y exhorta a los Estados a que, entre otras medidas, "Garanticen la existencia de remedios eficaces para las violaciones de derechos humanos estableciendo mecanismos de rendición de cuentas accesibles al nivel adecuado".

Asimismo, resulta interesante que dicha resolución recuerde a los Estados que éstos:

"(...) deben asegurarse de que los proveedores de servicios no estatales: a) Cumplan con sus responsabilidades en materia de derechos humanos en todos sus procesos de trabajo, en especial dedicándose activamente, junto con el Estado y otros interesados, a detectar posibles abusos contra los derechos humanos y encontrar soluciones para paliarlos; b) Contribuyan a proveer un suministro constante de agua potable segura, aceptable, accesible y asequible y servicios de saneamiento de buena calidad y en cantidad suficiente; c) Integren los derechos humanos en las evaluaciones de impacto cuando sea pertinente, a fin de determinar los desafíos en materia de derechos humanos y contribuir a superarlos; d) Elaboren mecanismos eficaces de reclamación para los usuarios y se abstengan de obstaculizar el acceso a los mecanismos de rendición de cuentas de base estatal".

Al año siguiente, en 2011, ese mismo órgano dictó su Resolución 16/2 "El Derecho Humanos al Agua Potable y el Saneamiento"[46] con similares directrices a las antedichas.

Al margen de todos los instrumentos internacionales citados, vale recordar lo que la Carta de las Naciones Unidas establece:

"Artículo 1.- Los propósitos de Naciones Unidas son: (...) 3. Realizar la cooperación internacional en la solución de problemas internacionales de carácter económico, social, cultural o humanitario, y en el desarrollo y estímulo del respeto a los derechos humanos y a las libertades fundamentales de todos, sin hacer distinción por motivos de raza, sexo, idioma o religión."

---

45 Ver ONU, 'Resolución aprobada por el Consejo de Derechos Humanos, 15/9. Los Derechos Humanos y el acceso al agua potable y el saneamiento', A/HRC/RES/15/9 (6 Octubre 2010) https://documents-dds-ny.un.org/doc/UNDOC/GEN/G10/166/36/PDF/G1016636.pdf?OpenElement consultado en Marzo 2019.
46 Ver ONU, 'Resolución aprobada por el Consejo de Derechos Humanos, 16/2. El derecho humano al agua potable y el saneamiento', A/HRC/RES/16/2 (8 Abril 2011) https://documents-dds-ny.un.org/doc/RESOLUTION/GEN/G11/124/88/PDF/G1112488.pdf?OpenElement consultado en Marzo 2019.

"Artículo 2.- Para la realización de los Propósitos consignados en el art. 1, las Organización y sus miembros procederán de acuerdo con los siguientes Principios: (…) 2. Los miembros de la Organización, a fin de asegurarse los derechos y beneficios inherentes a su condición de tales, cumplirán de buena fe las obligaciones contraídas por ellos de conformidad con esta Carta."

El establecimiento y observancia de los derechos humanos no es una simple retórica o una aspiración a conseguir, sino que conforma la base del nuevo "contrato social" sobre la cual la comunidad internacional decidió establecer sus reglas y parámetros de comportamiento luego de la Segunda Guerra Mundial. El derecho humano al agua, así como los demás derechos humanos, forman parte de esa base fundamental. En particular con este derecho, se trata de la condición *sine quanon* para que sea posible la vida de todo organismo en el planeta Tierra: imposible es, por ende, el poder garantizar una protección de inversión alguna si no existen seres humanos vivos que puedan generarla.

En el mismo sentido, la Declaración Universal de los Derechos Humanos afirma:

"Artículo 25.- 1. Toda persona tiene derecho a un nivel de vida adecuado que le asegure, así como a su familia, la salud y el bienestar, y en especial la alimentación, el vestido, la vivienda, la asistencia médica y los servicios sociales necesarios; (…)"

"Artículo 28.- Toda persona tiene derecho a que se establezca un orden social e internacional en el que los derechos y libertades proclamados en esta Declaración se hagan plenamente efectivos."

Esa especie de "nuevo pacto social" de la comunidad internacional también se verifica en los arts. 55 y 56 de la Carta de las Naciones Unidas:

"Artículo 55.- Con el propósito de crear las condiciones de estabilidad y bienestar necesarias para las relaciones pacíficas y amistosas entre las naciones basadas en el respeto al principio de igualdad de derechos y al de la libre determinación de los pueblos, las Organización promoverá:

a. niveles de vida más elevados, trabajo permanente para todos, y condiciones de progreso y desarrollo económico y social;
b. la solución de los problemas internacionales de carácter económico, social y sanitario, y de otros problemas conexos; y la cooperación internacional en el orden cultural y educativo; y
c. el respeto universal a los derechos humanos y a las libertades fundamentales de todos, sin hacer distinción por motivos de raza, sexo, idioma o religión, y la efectividad de tales derechos y libertades."

"Artículo 56.- Todos los miembros se comprometen a tomar medidas conjunta o separadamente, en cooperación con la Organización, para la realización de los propósitos consagrados en el Artículo 55."

Por su parte, el art. 103 del mismo texto deja claro que:

"Artículo 103.- En caso de conflicto entre las obligaciones contraídas por los miembros de las Naciones Unidas en virtud de la presente Carta y sus obligaciones contraídas en virtud de cualquier otro convenio internacional, prevalecerán las obligaciones de esta Carta."

Este último artículo establece como obligaciones con efecto erga omnes todos aquellos emanados de la Carta de las Naciones Unidas. También es de pleno consenso que las obligaciones de derechos humanos poseen efectos *erga omnes* para la comunidad internacional. Ello implica, cuanto menos, una prioridad en el cumplimiento respecto del resto de obligaciones dispositivas en el derecho internacional general y particular, incluyendo los tratados de inversión y comercio.[47] Existe incluso un debate abierto respecto de si los derechos humanos constituyen o no normas de derecho imperativo (*jus cogens*) en el sistema internacional, aunque no hay consenso aun respecto de ello.[48]

Contradicciones entre los tratados de inversión y los derechos humanos

El debate crítico sobre los AII no surge ya de grupos marginales sino de un número creciente de académicos, ONG y funcionarios internacionales. Estas observaciones han detectado que el funcionamiento de este régimen de protección de inversiones dificulta seriamente la promoción de un orden internacional democrático y equitativo. Diagnostican un déficit democrático creciente, no solamente en los mecanismos de transparencia y participación de estos acuerdos, sino también en sus efectos. El relator especial de Naciones Unidas, Alfred-Maurice de Zayas advirtió[49] que:

"(...) la solución de controversias entre inversores y Estados plantea un desafío particular para el orden democrático, en particular cuando los Gobiernos que han sido elegidos democráticamente para llevar a cabo determinadas políticas sociales son demandados por los inversores precisamente en razón de esas

---

47 Javier Echaide, 'Demandas en el CIADI y el derecho humano al agua' (2017) 15 (31) *International Law Revista Colombiana de Derecho Internacional* 99.

48 Carlos Zelda, 'Ius Cogens y Derechos Humanos: Luces y sombras para una adecuada delimitación de conceptos' (2002) 8(17) *Agenda Internacional* 129–56. Juana Inés Acosta-López y Ana María Duque-Vallejo, 'Declaración Universal de Derechos Humanos, ¿norma de ius cogens?' (2008) 12 *International law: revista colombiana de derecho internacional*. Disponible en http://www.scielo.org.co/scielo.php?script=sci_arttext&pid=S1692–81562008000100002 consultado en Febrero 2019.

49 ONU, Asamblea General, Promoción de un orden internacional democrático y equitativo, Nota del Secretario General [Informe del Experto Independiente Alfred-Maurice de Zayas] [UN Doc A/70/285] (5 Agosto 2015)

políticas democráticamente escogidas. (…) Si bien los tribunales internacionales pueden y deben declarar inadmisibles los casos improcedentes de abuso
del derecho a presentar comunicaciones (…) o de abuso de procedimiento, los
tribunales de solución de controversias entre inversores y Estados rara vez lo
hacen y aceptan los litigios improcedentes y vejatorios que ocasionan enormes gastos a las partes, lo cual es especialmente perjudicial para los países en
desarrollo."

En su Informe del Experto Independiente sobre la promoción de un orden
internacional democrático y equitativo de 2015,[50] de Zayas sostuvo:

"17. El árbitro español Fernández-Armesto señala que: "Cuando me despierto
por la noche y pienso en el arbitraje, no deja de asombrarme que los Estados
soberanos hayan aceptado en absoluto un procedimiento de arbitraje sobre
inversiones (…) Se otorga a tres ciudadanos particulares el poder de examinar,
sin restricción alguna y sin procedimiento de apelación, todas las acciones del
gobierno, todas las decisiones de los tribunales y todas las leyes y reglamentos
dimanantes del parlamento".[51] Efectivamente, es inquietante que los árbitros
puedan desatender principios básicos como el respeto por el "margen de discre-
ción" de los Estados, la legislación estatal e incluso las decisiones judiciales de
los tribunales superiores del país. La unidireccionalidad de la protección de los
inversores no ha contribuido a una cultura de cooperación entre los inversores
y los Estados sino que ha estimulado una agresiva tendencia a los litigios y ha
demostrado generar una "congelación de la regulación". El arbitraje puede
tener lugar en Washington, con los auspicios del CIADI del Banco Mundial,
pero existe una variedad preocupante de opciones de foros, y pueden constitu-
irse tribunales en el marco de la Corte de Arbitraje Internacional de Londres, la
Cámara de Comercio Internacional, la Cámara de Comercio de Estocolmo, el
Centro de Arbitraje Internacional de Hong Kong o la Comisión de las Naciones
Unidas para el Derecho Mercantil Internacional (CNUDMI). Hay un número
creciente de procesos de arbitraje que priman los beneficios por encima de los
derechos humanos[52]. Según la UNCTAD, muchos procesos de arbitraje para la
solución de controversias entre inversores y Estados son completamente confi-
denciales y solo se dispone de información en relación con aproximadamente

50 ONU, Consejo de Derechos Humanos, 'Informe del Experto Independiente sobre la
promoción de un orden internacional democrático y equitativo, Alfred-Maurice de
Zayas', [UN Doc A/HRC/30/44] (14 de Julio de 2015).
51 George Monbiot, 'This trasatlantic trade deal is a full-frontal assault on democracy'
(The Guardian, 4 November 2013) www.theguardian.com/commentisfree/2013/nov/
04/us-trade-deal-full-frontal-assault-on-democracy accessed 12 March 2021(citado
en el original).
52 Centro Europeo de Derechos Constitucionales y Humanos, 'Human rights inapplic-
able in international investment arbitration?'; puede consultarse en www.ecchr.de/
worldbank/articles/human-rights-inapplicable-in-international-investment-arbitra-
tion.html (citado en el original).

608 sentencias[53]. El Experto Independiente se refiere a su próximo informe a la Asamblea General y señala unos pocos casos como ejemplos de prácticas contenciosas y sus consecuencias para los derechos humanos".[54]

Incluso cita un conocido caso sobre agua potable y saneamiento ante el Centro Internacional de Arreglo de Diferencias relativas a Inversiones (CIADI), del Banco Mundial.

"22. El caso Aguas del Tunari S.A. c. la República de Bolivia se refería a un contrato de privatización del abastecimiento de agua de Cochabamba, que incluía concesiones por un período de 40 años con un flujo de efectivo anual garantizado. El acuerdo recibió el apoyo del Banco Mundial, que impuso la privatización como condición para el crédito. Los accionistas mayoritarios de Aguas eran la empresa estadounidense Bechtel y la multinacional española Abengoa. Después de que el contrato entrara en vigor en 1999, los precios del agua aumentaron considerablemente. Se produjeron manifestaciones populares en favor del derecho a un abastecimiento de agua asequible, y el Gobierno de la época declaró la ley marcial e intentó sofocar las protestas utilizando la fuerza militar. Tras el fallecimiento de un adolescente de 17 años, el Estado Plurinacional de Bolivia canceló el contrato de privatización, lo que dio lugar a una demanda por valor de 50 millones de dólares por parte de Aguas".[55]

Y en sus recomendaciones instó que los Estados dejen "sin efecto las decisiones de los procedimientos de solución de controversias entre inversores y Estados y del CIADI que violen los derechos humanos," así como también "mostrarse solidarios con los Estados que deseen modificar o dar por terminados sus [TBI] [o sus] acuerdos de libre comercio [...] o que busquen dejar sin efecto sentencias arbitrales," agregando además "tomar medidas ante los inversores y las empresas transnacionales que violen el derecho internacional de los derechos humanos."[56]

De hecho, han sido repetidos los casos en donde los Estados fueron directamente demandados por diferencias en materia de inversión dentro del sector de agua potable y saneamiento. Hasta el momento se contabilizan once casos, dentro de los cuales se halla el mencionado arbitraje "Aguas del

---

53 UNCTAD, IIA Issues Note, núm 1 (Febrero de 2015); puede consultarse en unctad. org/en/PublicationsLibrary/webdiaepcb2015d1_en.pdf (citado en el original).

54 Ver ONU, Consejo de Derechos Humanos, 'Informe del Experto Independiente sobre la promoción de un orden internacional democrático y equitativo, Alfred-Maurice de Zayas', [UN Doc A/HRC/30/44] (14 de Julio de 2015).

55 ibid párr 22.

56 Ver ONU, Consejo de Derechos Humanos, 'Informe del Experto Independiente sobre la promoción de un orden internacional democrático y equitativo, Alfred-Maurice de Zayas', [UN Doc A/HRC/30/44] (14 de Julio de 2015).

Tunari c. Bolivia" y "Biwater Gauff c. Tanzania", siendo los nueve restantes contra Argentina. Argentina no es solamente el país que más demandas en el mundo ha acumulado ante el CIADI, sino que además es, por lejos, el más demandado en el sector de agua potable y saneamiento.[57] Y sin embargo, con toda la normativa vigente desde tantas décadas atrás, solamente dos casos mencionan el concepto "derechos humanos" no solamente en sus laudos, sino también en todas sus actuaciones: los casos de "Suez, y otros c. Argentina" –por el caso "Aguas Argentinas"[58]- y "Urbaser c. Argentina"[59].

En abril de 2015 se emitió el laudo "Suez y otros v. Argentina" por el caso de Aguas Argentinas S.A.[60] Se trató del contrato de privatización de

---

57 La totalidad de casos registrados en el CIADI sobre agua potable y saneamiento hasta el momento son: Aguas del Tunari v Bolivia (*Aguas del Tunari S.A. v. Republic of Bolivia*, ICSID Case No. ARB/02/3) y Biwater Gauff v Tanzania (*Biwater Gauff (Tanzania) Limited v. United Republic of Tanzania*, ICSID Case No. ARB/05/22) fueron los dos casos ajenos a la Argentina. Los demás fueron Compañía Aguas del Aconquija y Vivendi Universal v Argentina (*Compañía de Aguas del Aconquija S.A. and Vivendi Universal S.A. (formerly Compañía de Aguas del Aconquija, S.A. and Compagnie Générale des Eaux) v. Argentine Republic (I)*, ICSID Case No. ARB/97/3); Aguas Provinciales de Santa Fe, Suez, Sociedad General de Aguas de Barcelona y Interagua Servicios Integrales de Agua v Argentina (*Suez, Sociedad General de Aguas de Barcelona, S.A. and Interagua Servicios Integrales de Agua, S.A. v. Argentine Republic (formerly Aguas Provinciales de Santa Fe, Suez, Sociedad General de Aguas de Barcelona y Interagua Servicios Integrales de Agua v Argentina)*, ICSID Case No. ARB/03/17); Aguas Cordobesas, Suez, Sociedad General de Aguas de Barcelona v Argentina (*Aguas Cordobesas, S.A., Suez, and Sociedad General de Aguas de Barcelona, S.A. v. Argentine Republic*, ICSID Case No. ARB/03/18); Suez, Sociedad General de Aguas de Barcelona, S.A. and Vivendi Universal, S.A. v Argentina (*Suez, Sociedad General de Aguas de Barcelona, S.A. and Vivendi Universal, S.A. (formerly Aguas Argentinas, S.A., Suez, Sociedad General de Aguas de Barcelona, S.A. and Vivendi Universal, S.A.) v. Argentine Republic (II)*, ICSID Case No. ARB/03/19); Azurix v Argentina (*Azurix Corp. v. Argentine Republic (I)*, ICSID Case No. ARB/01/12); Azurix (Azurix Mendoza) v Argentina (*Azurix Corp. v. Argentine Republic (II)*, ICSID Case No. ARB/03/30); SAUR International v Argentina (*SAUR International v. Argentine Republic*, ICSID Case No. ARB/04/4); Impregilo v Argentina (*Impregilo S.p.A. v. Argentine Republic (I)*, ICSID Case No. ARB/07/17); Urbaser y Consorcio de Aguas Bilbao Biskaia, Bilbao Biskaia Ur Partzuergoa v Argentina (*Urbaser S.A. and Consorcio de Aguas Bilbao Biskaia, Bilbao Biskaia Ur Partzuergoa v. Argentine Republic*, ICSID Case No. ARB/07/26). Javier Echaide, 'Demandas en el CIADI y el derecho humano al agua' (2017) 15 (31) *International Law Revista Colombiana de Derecho Internacional*. Javier Echaide, *El derecho humano al agua potable y los tratados de protección recíproca de inversiones* (Universidad de Buenos Aires and Thompson Reuters / Ed. La Ley 2018).

58 Suez, y otros c. Argentina por el caso "Aguas Argentinas", *Suez v. Argentine Republic (II)* (n 57).

59 Urbaser c. Argentina *Urbaser v. Argentine Republic* (n 57).

60 Suez y otros c. Argentina por el caso de Aguas Argentinas S.A., *Suez v. Argentine Republic (II)* (n 57).

agua más grande del mundo que cubría la ciudad de Buenos Aires y la zona metropolitana circundante y que actualmente agrupa a cerca de 16 millones de habitantes. Las corporaciones francesas Suez y Vivendi Universal y la española Aguas de Barcelona conformaron un consorcio llamado "Aguas Argentinas S.A." que sería la empresa encargada del suministro por 30 años. En 1999 comenzó un contexto de crisis económica que eclosionaría a fines de 2001 y durante el año 2002 en la crisis más grave de la historia argentina. En ese contexto, la empresa decide demandar a la Argentina ante el CIADI ante la negativa por parte del gobierno de permitir un aumento tarifario para soportar las pérdidas económicos, aún en un contexto en donde el 57.8% de la población se encontraba bajo la línea de pobreza.[61] Recién en marzo de 2006, el gobierno argentino rescindió el contrato con Aguas Argentinas S.A. por incumplimiento de inversiones acordadas en el contrato, baja calidad en el servicio prestado, 11 multas incumplidas por un total de 10 millones de pesos, y altos niveles de nitratos superiores a los permitidos en el suministro de agua comprobado en la zona sur de las afueras de las ciudad de Buenos Aires (Temperley, Lomas de Zamora y Lanús) poniendo en riesgo la salud de unas 300,000 personas.[62]

Previamente a la emisión del laudo de fondo, la empresa había sostenido que "«*la importancia pública e institucional*» *del caso no existe*"[63] (sic), aun cuando se trataba del servicio de agua potable de los tres distritos de mayor población del país con un total aproximado de 17 millones de personas afectadas (casi la mitad de la población argentina en ese momento). El tribunal del CIADI debió admitir que el caso involucraba "*potencialmente cuestiones de interés público*", y que era un servicio público básico para millones de personas que "*podrían plantear una amplia gama de cuestiones complejas en materia de derecho público e internacional, incluidas consideraciones relativas a los derechos humanos*".[64] No obstante ello, el

61 La situación social, cifras del índice para octubre 2002, El nivel de pobreza es cada vez más alto: 57.8% de la población (Diario Clarín, 1 Febrero 2003), ver www.clarin.com/economia/nivel-pobreza-vez-alto-578-poblacion_0_S1ifc5GlCte.html consultado en Marzo 2019.

62 Argentina, *Decreto 303/2006 P.E.N.* (2006).

63 Citado en párr 18, pág 6 de la Resolución en Respuesta a la Petición de Transparencia y Participación en Calidad de *Amicus Curiae* del Tribunal del CIADI, de fecha 19/05/2005, *Suez v. Argentina (II)* (n 57) (Order in response to a Petition for Participation as Amicus Curiae, 19 May 2005). Ver Javier Echaide, 'Demandas en el CIADI y el derecho humano al agua' (2017) 15 (31) *International Law Revista Colombiana de Derecho Internacional*. Javier Echaide, *El derecho humano al agua potable y los tratados de protección recíproca de inversiones* (Universidad de Buenos Aires and Thompson Reuters / Ed. La Ley 2018) 213.

64 Párr 19, pág 7 de la Resolución en Respuesta a la Petición de Transparencia y Participación en Calidad de *Amicus Curiae* del Tribunal del CIADI, de fecha 19/05/

tribunal no manifestó una sola palabra respecto de los derechos humanos como consideración al momento de resolver, ni en el laudo sobre responsabilidad emitido en 2010 ni en el laudo indemnizatorio dictado nada menos que cinco años después por la suma de US$ 405 millones.

El valor promedio del agua en Argentina en 2004 era de US$ 0.48 por m3, lo que lleva a un monto total de US$ 5.76 al año por m3 de agua. Si nuestros cálculos son correctos, para el tribunal la tarifa anual proyectada por tasa de inflación en 21 años debería haber sido de US$ 7,834.73 (casi US$ 653 mensuales). A esto se le suma la condición que el tribunal fijó, de que debía haberse realizado un ajuste tarifario del 18.2% nominal (13.2% anual), además de un préstamo a la empresa sin intereses y por un año a fin de sanear sus cuentas, afectadas por la crisis.

Basándose en su decisión sobre responsabilidad en contra de la Argentina, el tribunal decidió establecer su cálculo indemnizatorio no sobre la inversión efectivamente realizada sino sobre el flujo de caja que Aguas Argentinas S.A. tenía y *"el que esperaban las partes en la Concesión para compensar a las Demandantes por las sustanciales inversiones que habían realizado en los sistemas de agua y alcantarillado de Buenos Aires... para otorgarles una rentabilidad razonable"*. Así, el tribunal proyectó lo que consideró un "escenario probable" del porvenir de la empresa en la Argentina desde el 2015 al 2023 (incluso aventurándose a fijar la inflación argentina, el crecimiento poblacional y las condiciones macroeconómicas no durante el próximo semestre sino durante los próximos 8 años) para fijar los criterios que el Estado debería haber seguido para no violar los TBI.

Si trasladamos el criterio del tribunal del CIADI a la aplicación tarifaria en dólares por litro (al año del laudo), el agua en Buenos Aires debería costar US$ 2 por litro aproximadamente, lo cual significa unas 6,300 veces más de lo que la población pagaba en ese momento. Para ponerlo en una perspectiva tangible: el tribunal del CIADI entendió que en Argentina una ducha de agua de 10 minutos debería costar unos US$ 163.50 aproximadamente.[65] El costo de las tarifas es un tema delicado, pues es la puerta de acceso económico al pleno goce del derecho humano al agua. Los informes de Naciones Unidas al respecto reconocen que dicho goce no debe ser gratuito

2005, Caso ARB/03/19. Ver Javier Echaide, 'Demandas en el CIADI y el derecho humano al agua' (2017) 15 (31) *International Law Revista Colombiana de Derecho Internacional*; Javier Echaide, *El derecho humano al agua potable y los tratados de protección recíproca de inversiones* (Universidad de Buenos Aires and Thompson Reuters / Ed. La Ley 2018) 213.

65 Javier Echaide, 'Demandas en el CIADI y el derecho humano al agua' (2017) 15 (31) *International Law Revista Colombiana de Derecho Internacional*. Javier Echaide, *El derecho humano al agua potable y los tratados de protección recíproca de inversiones* (Universidad de Buenos Aires and Thompson Reuters / Ed. La Ley 2018).

(pues resulta razonable recurrir a cierta recaudación de ingresos para el mantenimiento y mejoras del servicio) pero tampoco tarifado a valor de mercado (resolviendo así los posibles problemas de sectores de población con ingresos modestos o nulos que no podrían acceder a una fuente que garantice su supervivencia). Resulta evidente que los criterios utilizados por el CIADI para este tipo de casos se encuentran absolutamente alejados de lo que el concepto de "asequible" puede significar para el goce del derecho humano al agua, poniéndolo en riesgo.

El caso de "Urbaser y otro c. Argentina",[66] laudado posteriormente en 2016, trató de forma mucho más profunda la relación entre el régimen internacional de protección de inversiones y el derecho humano al agua potable y al saneamiento. El contexto fue similar al caso "Suez y otros c. Argentina": los mismos antecedentes de privatización del servicio de agua potable en la década de 1990, la misma crisis económica del año 2001–2002, el mismo pedido de las empresas privatizadas de aumentar las tarifas para minimizar pérdidas, la misma negativa del gobierno. Sólo que la demanda de Urbaser fue iniciada en 2007 y la concesión con la que había sido beneficiada había sido por una zona del Gran Buenos Aires no incluida en la concesión de Aguas Argentinas S.A.

Este tribunal del CIADI se distanció en varios criterios respecto del que laudó el caso "Suez" un año antes, definiendo al trato justo y equitativo en forma menos exigente que su predecesor, que lo equiparó a las expectativas legítimas del inversionista. Definió que el daño producido por el gobierno argentino por pérdidas a la empresa al negar el aumento tarifario se encuadraba en un caso de estado de necesidad parcial, dado que la crisis incluía un origen de factores internos y externos. En ese sentido, el tribunal aclaró:

> "720. Las Demandantes aceptan que Argentina tenía dos tipos de obligaciones: sus obligaciones referentes al derecho de la población al agua y sus obligaciones hacia inversores internacionales. La República Argentina puede y debe cumplir con ambos tipos de obligaciones de forma simultánea. Así, las obligaciones resultantes del derecho humano al agua no constituyen un obstáculo al cumplimiento de las obligaciones hacia las Demandantes. (...)" [los destacados nos pertenecen].

Queda claro que el criterio de prioridad en el concepto de obligaciones con efecto *erga omnes* no formó parte del utilizado por el tribunal del CIADI para laudar en el caso. Si hubiera sido así, el tribunal hubiera entendido que el derecho humano al agua debe cumplirse prioritariamente y no de manera simultánea respecto de las obligaciones emanadas de los TBI. Los tribunales

---

66 Urbaser y otro c. Argentina *(Urbaser v Argentina (n 57))*. Ver capítulos 10 de Rodrigo Polanco Lazo y Felipe Ferreira Catalán y 11 de Farouk El-Hosseny, Patrick Devine y Ilan Brun-Vargas en este volumen.

del CIADI llamativamente no observan la contradicción en materia de obligaciones que alertan todos los informes internacionales de organizaciones de derechos humanos y de Naciones Unidas, lo cual evidencia la flagrante fragmentación del derecho internacional en secciones que pierden total contacto entre sí y hacen oídos sordos a estos efectos perniciosos para el cumplimiento del *rule of law* en el ámbito internacional.

Incluso el tribunal reconoció que el gobierno de Argentina aplicó las medidas de emergencia (la devaluación del peso) y su impacto sobre las tarifas ya que se encontraba obligado en función de su derecho constitucional y una política elemental de la salud de la población con el objeto de preservar el acceso al agua potable.[67] Sin embargo, deja su análisis allí sin tomar en cuenta, por ejemplo, conocidas obligaciones en materia de tratados dadas por el derecho internacional. La Convención de Viena sobre Derecho de los Tratados de 1969, en su art. 46, establece:

> "46. Disposiciones de derecho interno concernientes a la competencia para celebrar tratados.
>
> 1. El hecho de que el consentimiento de un Estado en obligarse por un tratado haya sido manifiesto en violación de una disposición de su derecho interno concerniente a la competencia para celebrar tratados no podrá ser alegado por dicho Estado como vicio de su consentimiento, a menos que esa violación sea manifiesta y afecte a una norma de importancia fundamental de su derecho interno.
>
> 2. Una violación es manifiesta si resulta objetivamente evidente para cualquier Estado que proceda en la materia conforme a la práctica usual y de buena fe." [los destacados nos pertenecen].

El gobierno argentino alegó que la empresa Urbaser había incumplido con sus inversiones, las que habían sido acordadas en el contrato de concesión, lo cual podía dar lugar a incumplimientos mutuos, y que tal violación contractual afectó derechos humanos básicos, la salud de los usuarios, así como el medio ambiente de miles de personas que vivían en extrema pobreza. A pesar de que la parte demandante sostuvo que *"la decisión sobre violaciones de derechos humanos se [encontraba] fuera de su jurisdicción."*,[68] el tribunal se halló competente para entender una contrademanda sobre derechos humanos e inversiones,[69] ya que Argentina reconvino la demanda contra la empresa ante el tribunal por esos mismos argumentos, lo cual abrió una posibilidad de que los tribunales del CIADI puedan sentar posiciones sobre el tema. El tribunal desestimó la reconvención, no sin antes reconocer que *"Realmente, son pocos los casos en los que se han presentado demandas reconvencionales en arbitrajes de inversiones y son igualmente*

---

67 *Urbaser v Argentina (n 57)*), párr 723.
68 ibid párr 1129
69 ibid párr 1154

muy escasos los supuestos en los que los estados receptores fueron los que instaron el arbitraje."[70]

Evidentemente el tribunal no deseó indagar sobre la importancia fundamental que puede significar para un Estado su propia Constitución Nacional y las obligaciones constitucionales que, tal como reconoce, justificaron las medidas tomadas por el gobierno.

Finalmente el tribunal halló responsable a Argentina por violación al trato justo y equitativo, rechazando las demás argumentaciones demandadas por las empresas. Condenó a Argentina a pagar una indemnización –cuyo cálculo postergó para otro momento- sumando US$ 1 millón que el Estado deberá pagar en concepto de costas del arbitraje. En su laudo, el tribunal entendió –con buen criterio- que las empresas transnacionales no son sujeto de derecho internacional pero que no obstante ello, no quita que puedan ser titulares de derechos y obligaciones. De hecho los TBI son fuente de estos derechos, mas no agregan ninguna obligación que las empresas deban contraer, lo que desbalancea la situación jurídica como hemos sostenido previamente. Pero el tribunal desestimó la contrademanda de Argentina por violación del derecho humano al agua por parte de las empresas concesionarias debido a que los tratados de derechos humanos establecen obligaciones de hacer para los Estados y obligaciones de no hacer (es decir, el no interferir o el respetar) para las empresas:

> "(…) garantizar el derecho humano al agua representa una obligación de hacer. Esta obligación recae en los Estados y no es posible imponerla a una empresa conocedora del ámbito de suministro de servicios de agua y saneamiento. Para que esa obligación de hacer sea aplicable a un inversor particular, es necesario un contrato o una relación jurídica similar de derecho civil y comercial. En ese caso, la fuente de la obligación de hacer del inversor es el derecho local y no el derecho internacional general. La situación es diferente si lo que está en juego es una obligación de no hacer, como la prohibición de realizar actos que violan los derechos humanos. Dicha obligación puede ser de aplicación inmediata no sólo respecto de los Estados sino también respecto de las personas físicas y otros particulares. Sin embargo, en lo que respecta al presente caso, no es eso lo que está en discusión."

Conclusión

La fragmentación del derecho internacional es un problema que actualmente hace peligrar la unicidad de dicha área como un cuerpo normativo único,

---

70 ibid párr 1131

coherente y estable. En pos de brindar seguridad jurídica a un grupo –los grandes capitales transnacionalizados- y con el fin de atraerlos, los Estados han celebrado tratados internacionales para brindarles derechos de protección sin contraprestaciones, quebrando de ese modo premisas básicas como las de igualdad jurídica (con los inversionistas locales, por ejemplo) o el de balancear derechos con obligaciones. Pero también se pierde una visión totalizadora del Derecho como disciplina reguladora de las conductas sociales, en tanto los TBI se configuran como un área hermética, autorregulada, que va adquiriendo ajenidad del derecho internacional general.

El siglo XX procuró un avance significativo en virtud de ir dejando paulatinamente atrás el carácter incompleto del derecho internacional: más de 60 millones de muertos en la Segunda Guerra Mundial y el exterminio de más de 6 millones en campos de concentración, bajo tortura y tratos inhumanos y degradantes, fue el límite para que la comunidad internacional sentara las bases de nuevas reglas de convivencia, progresivas, que aseguraran derechos fundamentales para todos. En ello reside el carácter de "orden público internacional" de los derechos humanos y las normas de *jus cogens* internacional: en el hecho de que nadie puede prescindir de ellos para sus relaciones jurídicas.

Pues el derecho internacional de las inversiones, basados en los TBI y en los laudos de tribunales arbitrales como el CIADI y otros, ponen en duda esa verdad. El derecho humano al agua resulta innegable tanto de manera directa –esto es, en su condición como derecho humano autónomo-, como indirecta –en relación respecto de condición básica para el cumplimiento de otros derechos humanos-. Se ha citado aquí una cantidad importante de normas internacionales, tanto emanadas por voluntad de los Estados como dictadas por organismos internacionales, que establecen que el acceso a una fuente de agua potable, segura y asequible para uso individual y familiar es un derecho humano básico y universal. Pues la asequibilidad y la seguridad de dicho derecho han sido cuestionados en ocasiones reiteradas. Casos como los de "Aguas del Tunari c. Bolivia", "Suez y otros c. Argentina" y "Urbaser y otro c. Argentina" aportan distintas pruebas de cómo los tribunales del CIADI, amparándose estrictamente en el marco de los TBI, condenan las políticas públicas llevadas a cabo por los Estados para garantizar el derecho humano al agua en momento de crisis. Los tres tribunales hallaron responsables a los Estados de violaciones a los TBI sin ir más allá sobre las posibles responsabilidades compartidas ante este tipo de casos. Entendemos que debería resultar claro que el pretender que el costo de una ducha a US$ 163.50.- no es lo que debería comprenderse por "asequible" en cuanto a la accesibilidad del agua potable como derecho humano. Más aún en el caso de poblaciones en situación de pobreza o indigencia.

Los tribunales del CIADI mantienen este tipo de criterios, así como el de desentender que la empresa concesionaria por el suministro de agua potable y, por ende, de su accesibilidad no tiene responsabilidad alguna bajo su competencia. Si bien tribunales como el del caso "Urbaser" reconocieron que podían atender casos sobre derechos humanos e inversiones (algo que debería ser considerado al menos debatible, puesto que ya existen tribunales de derechos humanos en los ámbitos regional e internacional), no han avanzado en el sentido de explorar lo que puede hallarse como principio general de derecho reconocido por cualquier nación civilizada[71] como ser la responsabilidad concurrente, es decir por causas diferentes. Es claro que existe responsabilidad internacional del Estado por violación al derecho humano al agua en estos casos, y también debe dejarse en claro que los derechos humanos no son un argumento "pro-Estado" para exculparlos de tal responsabilidad en los arbitrajes y procesos judiciales en la materia, pero desentender las responsabilidades de quien tiene en sus manos directamente la posibilidad de llevar agua a las casas de la gente es ver una "seguridad jurídica" que no guarda la imparcialidad que el sistema pretende o dice sostener, o mismo que la comunidad internacional necesita para poder estructurar y hacer observar el *rule of law*.

La responsabilidad concurrente es aquella que precisamente define que dos o más agentes deban responder ante la misma violación pero por causas distintas: el Estado por su violación al deber de garantizar los derechos humanos (el derecho humano al agua, en el caso particular de estudio) y la empresa transnacional concesionaria por su violación a interrumpir u obstaculizar que el mismo sea asequible y de calidad. Esto es algo que no ha sido explorado por los tribunales del CIADI y hace peligrar, junto con un conjunto de críticas antedichas, un orden democrático más allá de los formalismos: un orden en el que la rendición de cuentas (*accountability*) sea algo palpable en favor de las comunidades, que son las que en definitiva sufren los perjuicios de afrontar el pago de las indemnizaciones a las empresas vía impuestos y, al mismo tiempo, el beber agua cara y de mala calidad.

En Argentina, las comunidades afectadas por la disminución y/o contaminación del agua se han agrupados en asambleas ciudadanas. Los casos más paradigmáticos hasta el momento son las existentes en Andalgalá[72] (provincia de Catamarca), Jáchal[73] (provincia de San Juan)

---

71 El art. 38 del Estatuto de la Corte Internacional de Justicia enumera parcialmente las fuentes del derecho internacional público.

72 Ver Laura Borse, 'Andalgalá cumplió sus 500 caminatas por la vida y contra la megaminería' (La izquierda, 25 Junio 2019) http://www.laizquierdadiario.com/Andalg ala-cumplio-sus-500-caminatas-por-la-vida-y-contra-la-megamineria consultado en Junio 2020.

73 Ver 'Jáchal y San Juan reclaman la prohibición de la minería a cielo abierto tras el derrame de cianuro en la mina de Barrick Gold' (La Vaca, 18 Octubre 2015) www.lavaca. org/notas/jachal-y-san-juan-reclaman-la-prohibicion-de-la-mineria-a-cielo-abierto-tras-el-derrame-de-cianuro-en-la-mina-de-barrick-gold/ consultado en Junio 2020.

y Mendoza[74] (provincia de Mendoza). En las tres provincias argentinas la actividad minera ha causado casos de contaminación de los afluentes hídricos de manera importante, y sin embargo ello no ha motivado aún el cierre de dichas concesiones. En estos casos vemos cómo los casos de resistencia social por la conservación del agua no necesariamente se refleja en casos sobre agua potable y saneamiento ante el CIADI: los tres casos son situaciones con empresas mineras. Distinto puede ser en Osorno,[75] Chile, donde Suez ya ha amenazado en demandar el Estado chileno[76] debido a la finalización del contrato de concesión de la empresa de distribución de agua potable ESSAL, situación que quizás se asemeje a la experiencia de Aguas Argentinas (también liderada por Suez y Aguas de Barcelona) en la ciudad de Buenos Aires, pero con un diferencial de resistencia social mayor en un país como Chile, donde la designación del agua como bien privado se encuentra garantizado a nivel constitucional,[77] y en donde la eclosión social ha puesto en jaque un modelo económico que

---

74 Ver Camila Giacchino, 'La provincia de Mendoza, en Argentina, restringe la actividad minera' (Lexlatin, 10 Enero 2020) https://lexlatin.com/reportajes/provincia-mendoza-argentina-restringe-actividad-minera consultado en Junio 2020.

75 Ver José Luis Vargas, 'La crisis por el agua en Osorno versus la valiosa defensa de los ríos por parte de comunidades mapuche' (El Desconcierto, 19 Julio 2019) www.eldesconcierto.cl/2019/07/18/la-crisis-por-el-agua-en-osorno-versus-la-valiosa-defensa-de-los-rios-por-parte-de-comunidades-mapuche/ consultado en Julio 2020.

76 Ver 'Española Suez amenaza con acudir a arbitraje de inversión contra Chile' (CiarGlobal, 16 Junio 2020) https://ciarglobal.com/espanola-suez-amenaza-con-acudir-a-arbitraje-de-inversion-contra-chile/; Gustavo Orellana, 'Suez exige "la inmediata suspensión" del proceso de caducidad del Essal y amenaza con acudir a intancias internacionales' (La Tercera, 15 Junio 2020) www.latercera.com/pulso/noticia/suez-exige-la-inmediata-suspension-del-proceso-de-caducidad-de-essal-y-amenaza-con-acudir-a-instancias-internacionales/CHFEDBHXBFF4RGRE6WLCGTNCSM/; y Chile Mejor sin TLC, 'Amenaza Suez de arbitraje internacional: ejemplo claro de por qué el TPP-11 sea rechazado en el senado' (bilaterals.org, 18 Junio 2020) www.bilaterals.org/?amenaza-de-suez-de-arbitraje&lang=en consultado en Julio 2020.

77 Art. 19, inc. 24, último párrafo de la Constitución Política de Chile establece: "Los derechos de los particulares sobre las aguas, reconocidos o constituidos en conformidad a la ley, otorgarán a sus titulares la propiedad sobre ellos." Con este inciso constitucional se establece el régimen privado sobre derecho de aguas que incluso pueden cotizarse por sitios web de las empresas proveedoras que realizan la solicitud de dichos derechos ante la ante la Dirección General de Aguas del Gobierno de Chile. Ver https://ghesstion.cl/landing/landing-derechos-de-agua/?gclid=Cj0KCQjw3ZX4BRDmARIsAFYh7ZIBRb7EWMw84Z5oA2bD3z_kHLEGn91d1laf3ezhYFqkQNacqRy951QaApvKEALw_wcB consultado en Julio 2020.

históricamente se lo ha tenido como "modelo" y que ahora entró en una profunda crisis.

Sólo una verdadera interpretación hermenéutica del derecho puede romper con los compartimentos estancos en donde el conservadurismo jurídico se ha instalado, pues las contradicciones de este régimen con otras áreas del derecho internacional resultan cada vez más evidentes, por lo que deben ser atendidas. Y estar a la altura de tales desafíos es un llamado del que ya no podemos hacernos los desentendidos.

13

Investors' need to obtain social license:
A sustainable development argument
in investor–state dispute settlement

Sebastián Preller-Bórquez

Introduction

Sustainable development has raised great interest in many fields of know-ledge since it was put forward by the *Brundtland Commission* in 1987.[1] Since then, sustainable development has been further elaborated in the field of international policy and law, mostly under the auspices of the United Nations.[2] This chapter will start from the premise that sustainable development implies the need to strike a balance between economic growth, social development, and the protection of the environment, the inherently cross-cutting dimension of which aims to permeate all activities performed both by governments and private entities.[3] Indeed, as an objective broadly shared by the international community, it is argued that this narrative of balance

---

1 World Commission on Environment and Development, "Our Common Future" (1987).
2 See, among other milestones on this topic: United Nations Conference on Development and Environment, Rio de Janeiro, Brazil, 1992; the *Rio Declaration*, Report of the United Nations Conference on Environment and Development, Annex I, A/CONF.151/26 (Vol I), Rio de Janeiro, 3–14 June 1992; *Agenda 21*, Report of the United Nations Conference on Environment and Development, Annex II, A/CONF.151/26 (Vol I), Rio de Janeiro, 3–14 June 1992; the *Earth Summit+5*, United Nations General Assembly Resolution S-19/2, A/S-19/29, 19th Special Session Agenda Item 8, 11th Plenary Meeting, 28 June 1997; the *Johannesburg Declaration on Sustainable Development*, United Nations, *Report of the World Summit on Sustainable Development* (2002), p. 1; the *Johannesburg Plan of Implementation*, United Nations, *Report of the World Summit on Sustainable Development* (2002), p. 7; *The Future We Want*, UN General Assembly Resolution A/RES/66/288, 11 September 2012; the *2030 Agenda for Sustainable Development*, UN General Assembly Resolution A/RES/70/1, 25 September 2015; the *2018 Nelson Mandela Peace Summit*, UN General Assembly Resolution A/RES/73/1, 3 October 2018.
3 For authors referring to the concept and evolution of sustainable development, see: Philippe Sands, "International Law in the Field of Sustainable Development"

subjacent to sustainable development is able to permeate down through the different layers of transnational activities as, in the words of Birnie, Boyle, and Redgewell, sustainable development may not always entail "a preservationist approach but a value judgment that may be development-oriented."[4] As such, sustainable development has added elements to assess the behavior of all different kinds of participants when engaging in transnational activities, joining, therefore, the efforts made internationally through other mechanisms, towards the same end.[5]

In the field of international investment law, the literature has been prone to suggest that investment protection and sustainable development may seem

(1994) *LXV British Yearbook of International Law* 303; Yoshiro Matsui, "The Road to Sustainable Development: Evolution of the Concept of Development in the UN" Paul J I M de Waart and Konrad Ginther Erik Denters (eds), *Sustainable Development and Good Governance* (Martinus Nihjoff 1995); Ulrich Beyerlin, "The Concept of Sustainable Development" in Rudiger Wolfrum (ed), *Enforcing Environmental Standards: Economic Mechanisms as Viable Means?* (Springer 1996); Duncan French, *International Law and Policy of Sustainable Development* (Manchester University Press 2005); David G Victor, "Recovering Sustainable Development" (2006) 85 *Foreign Affairs* 91; Nico J Schrijver, *The Evolution of Sustainable Development in International Law: Inception, Meaning, and Status* (Brill 2008) 329 Récueil des Cours 217; Ángel J. Rodrigo, "El Desarrollo Sostenible Como Uno de Los Propósitos de Las Naciones Unidas" in Xavier Pons (ed), *Las Naciones Unidas desde España. 70 Aniversario de las Naciones Unidas. 60 Aniversario del ingreso de España a las Naciones Unidas* (ANVE 2015); Ángel J. Rodrigo, *El Desafío Del Desarrollo Sostenible* (CEI – Marcial Pons Ediciones Jurídicas y Sociales SA 2015). For authors holding a critical stand on the way sustainable development came up to life as a formula to soften North–South relations in light of stronger international environmental-based restrictions on the exploitation of natural resources, see: Xavier Pons, "Desarrollo Sostenible y Financiación Del Desarrollo" [2002] Agenda ONU 109; Karen Morrow, "Rio+20, the Green Economy and Re-Orienting Sustainable Development" (2012) 14 *Environmental Law Review* 279; Ruth Gordon, "Unsustainable Development" in Shawkat Alam, Sumudu Atapattu, Carmen G. Gonzalez, and Jona Razzaque (eds), *International Environmental Law and the Global South* (Cambridge University Press 2015).

4 Patricia Birnie, Alan Boyle, and Catherine Redgwell, *International Law and the Environment* (3rd edn, Oxford University Press 2009) at 385.

5 See, for instance: the United Nations Global Compact, available at www.unglobalcompact.org/what-is-gc/mission/principles accessed 5 January 2020; the OECD Guidelines for Multinational Enterprises, available at http://dx.doi.org/10.1787/9789264115 415-en accessed 5 January 2020; the World Bank Group International Finance Corporation Performance Standards on Environmental and Social Sustainability, available at https://unctad.org/en/PublicationsLibrary/diaepcb2015d5_en.pdf accessed 5 January 2020; the UNCTAD Investment Policy Framework for Sustainable Development, available at https://unctad.org/en/PublicationsLibrary/diaepcb2015d5 _en.pdf accessed 5 January 2020.

contradictory goals, having to waive one in the benefit of the other.[6] In this sense, the well-known race-to-the-bottom argument warns ourselves on the implicit peril when regulatory endeavors for protecting the environment or observing social rights are carried out by the same entity that has to attract foreign investment in order to achieve its own goals regarding economic growth.[7] The way in which the parties strike a balance between multiple interests is the Achilles heel of the international foreign investment system;[8] whereas its strength lies on the ever-increasing need of investment to contribute to the state's economic growth. However, on the other side of the coin, diverse environmental and social concerns are left aside if all concurrent interests are balanced exclusively under the light of economic growth. Preventing potential social and environmental risks posed by investment developments falls within the competence of the states who must deal with this through the adoption, in their national legislation, of different mechanisms intended to curve the adverse effects of foreign investment upon local communities or the environment.

6 Makane Moïse Mbengue and Deepak Raju, "Energy, Environment and Foreign Investment" in Eric De Brabandere and Tarcisio Gazzini (eds), *Foreign Investment in the Energy Sector: Balancing Private and Public Interests* (Brill and Nijhoff 2014) at 176.

7 As described by Affolder, "governments are key environmental overseers [...] but they are also tasked with attracting mining investment and participating in mining projects as tax collectors, equity participants, and dividend receivers. These multiple (and conflicting) roles can undermine government's ability to operate as an effective regulator" (Natasha A Affolder, "Rethinking Environmental Contracting" (2010) 21 *Journal of Environmental Law and Practice* 155 at 160). Such understanding is quite well depicted by the race-to-the-bottom argument which in simple words, as explained by Viñuales is no more than "States wishing to attract foreign investment to further their development will have an incentive to lower their environmental protection standards. In such situation, other States may be led to do the same in order to avoid a competitive disadvantage, with a resulting overall decline of environmental protection" (Jorge E. Viñuales, "Foreign Investment and the Environment in International Law: An Ambiguous Relationship" (2010) 80 *British Yearbook of International Law* 244 at 249. See also: UNCTAD and Sustainable Business Institute at the European Business School, "Making FDI Work for Sustainable Development" (2004) at 55. Also see Chapter 9 by Sufyan Droubi, Cecilia Juliana Flores Elizondo, and Raphael Heffron in this volume.

8 As Dimsey states, "Foreign investors are usually involved because of the promise of certain financial return, while host states, themselves lacking the necessary technology and other resources, need the investment but cannot ignore the concerns, and in particular the purchasing power, of their population. This divergence of interests can lead to tension in which the potential for disputes is rife" (Mariel Dimsey, "Arbitration and Natural Resource Protection" in Shawkat Alam, Jahid Hossain Bhuiyan, and Jona Razzaque (eds), *International Natural Resources Law, Investment and Sustainability* (Routledge 2018) at 132.

One of these mechanisms is to establish the obligation for investors to attain social license before the commencement of the investment development. Social license refers to the strategies adopted by a host state to avoid both foreseen and unforeseen potential social impacts and the consequent risks of development projects.[9] Mechanisms to attain social license may range from social planning and social impact assessments to stakeholder consultations, or agreements with the host community, all of which are closely oriented to sustainable development.

This chapter aims to show the performance of sustainable development narrative of balance in order to assist the construction of successful arguments when defending the measures taken based on the investor's failure to attain social license. The analysis will show that in the narrative of balance subjacent to sustainable development, host states may find a way to resist the mainstream rules of international investment law mostly established for the protection of foreign investors rather than for the protection of local communities and the environment. Thus, the sustainable development narrative of balance may provide a tool for host states to accommodate social and environmental concerns in a regime that appears to be mostly designed to protect investors engaging in transnational businesses.

This chapter is divided into four sections. The first section aims to describe the expected role of host states and the paradigm of the protection of the investment identified in current foreign investment regimes. The second section addresses the legal basis found in international law for the creation of obligations relating to the attainment of social license and their relationship with sustainable development. The third section analyses the *Pac Rim Cayman LLC v. The Republic of El Salvador*[10] and the *Bear Creek Mining Corporation v. Republic of Peru*[11] ICSID awards in which the measures taken by the host state based on the alleged failure of the investor to comply with its obligation to attain social license are reviewed in order to determine the responsibility of the former. This section also explores the place where the reasoning of both ICSID tribunals intersects with the function contended by the sustainable development narrative of balance. Finally, the

---

9 Abdullah Al Faruque, "Sustainable Mining, Human Rights and Foreign Investment: Nexus and Challenges" in Shawkat Alam, Jahid Hossain Bhuiyan, and Jona Razzaque (eds), *International Natural Resources Law, Investment and Sustainability* (Routledge 2018) at 298.

10 *Pac Rim Cayman LLC v. Republic of El Salvador*, ICSID Case No. ARB/09/12 (Award, 14 October 2016) (*Pac Rim v El Salvador* (Award 2016)).

11 *Bear Creek Mining Corporation v. Republic of Peru*, ICSID Case No. ARB/14/21 (Award, 30 November 2017) (*Bear Creek v Peru* (Award 2017)). See Chapter 11 by Farouk El-Hosseny, Patrick Devine, and Ilan Brun-Vargas in this volume.

fourth section, elaborating on the award to the *Bear Creek* case, discusses the application of the contributory fault standard and the potential use that the sustainable development narrative of balance may have to this end by providing a comprehensive assessment of the investor's obligation to attain social license.

Before developing this argument further, a preliminary caveat is warranted. Different attempts have been conducted both in international law doctrine[12] and in international courts and tribunals[13] to endorse sustainable development with a normative character able to constrain states and international organizations' behavior. However, as it could be inferred so far, this chapter does not elaborate on any of these theories; rather, the objective is to integrate the sustainable development narrative of balance within the adjudicatory process as an argumentative resource.[14] This effort is sought to promote the development of an adjudicatory process in ISDS that addresses the economic, social, and environmental dimensions converging in these disputes adequately.

12 See: Philippe Sands, "International Law in the Field of Sustainable Development: Emerging Legal Principles" in Winfried Lang (ed), *Sustainable Development and International Law* (Graham and Trotman/Martinus Nijhoff 1995); Philippe Sands, "Environmental Protection in the Twentieth Century: Sustainable Development and International Law" in N. J. Vig and R. S. Axelrold (eds), *The Global Environment. Institutions, Law and Policy* (1999); Philippe Sands, "International Courts and the Application of the Concept of 'Sustainable Development'" (1999) 3 *Max Planck UNYEB* 389; Vaughan Lowe, "Sustainable Development and Unsustainable Arguments" in Alan Boyle and David Freestone (eds), *International Law and Sustainable Development: Past Achievements and Future Challenges* (Oxford University Press 1999); Marie-Claire Cordonier Segger and Ashfaq Khalfan, *Sustainable Development Law Principles, Practice, and Prospects* (Oxford University Press 2004); N. Schrijver and F. Weiss, *International Law and Sustainable Development. Principles and Practice* (Martinus Nihjoff 2004); Birnie, Boyle, and Redgwell (n 4); Klaus Bosselmann, *The Principle of Sustainability: Transforming Law and Governance* (Routledge 2008); Elisabeth Bonanomi Burgi, *Sustainable Development in International Law Making and Trade: International Food Governance and Trade in Agriculture* (Edward Elgar Publishing Inc 2015); Virginie Barral, *Le Développement Durable En Droit International: Essai Sur Les Incidences Juridiquez d'une Norme Évolutive* (Bruylant 2016).
13 See: *Gabčíkovo-Nagymaros Project (Hungary/Slovakia)* (Judgment) [1997] ICJ Rep 7; *United States – Import Prohibition of Certain Shrimp and Shrimp Products* (Report of the Appellate Body, 12 October 1998) WT/DS58/AB/R; *Award in the Arbitration regarding the Iron Rhine ("Ijzenen Rijn") Railqay between the Kingdom of Belgium and the Kingdom of the Netherlands* (2005) 27 RIAA 35 ("Iron Rhine"); *Pulp Mills on the River Uruguay (Argentina v Uruguay)* (Judgment) [2010] ICJ Rep 14.
14 In this line of thoughts, see: Lowe (n 12) for whom sustainable development could be better understood as an interstitial norm, i.e. an element of the process of judicial reasoning aimed at aiding judges to perform their adjudicatory task.

The role of the host state and the paradigm of the protection of the investment

There is a growing need to reconcile all conflicting interests stemming from the activities of both private and state-owned companies operating transnationally and those interests that host states must preserve.[15] On the one hand, foreign investment regimes are clearly aimed at making the globe a space suitable for the business sector to develop economic activities not just within their national borders but also abroad, allowing investments in foreign economies and carrying out high-capital projects. On the other hand, states face the need to adopt competitive legislation efficiently, promoting social development and the protection of the environment, whilst providing foreign investors with a steady and attractive environment for developing their investments.[16]

Certainly, host states are in a troublesome position both regarding foreign investors, on the one side, and the community they must look after and the environment they are entrusted to protect, on the other. As such, the role of host states could be addressed at least from a twofold perspective. Firstly, it could relate to the active role that states must perform in their path for development by attracting foreign investment, granting investors with a secure legal framework and competitive market conditions to put inflows of foreign investments serving economic and social development. Secondly, host states are also expected to perform an active role of surveillance

15 On the one hand, the structural deficiencies of the current foreign investment regime are not related exclusively to the private sector's role, but also to state-owned companies. On the other hand, these structural differences go beyond traditional understandings related to the Global North and the Global South. As Morrow argues: "It is also increasingly apparent that, while development does indeed breed environmental degradation and the oppression of marginalised groups, notably indigenous peoples, this too is not limited to the activities (colonial, neo-colonial or otherwise) of the developed world – developing countries are just as capable of such behaviour in their own pursuit of development" (Morrow (n 3) at 282). See also: Elena Merino Blanco, "State Owned Oil Companies, North-South and South-South Perspectives on Investment" in Shawkat Alam, Jahid Hossain Bhuiyan, and Jona Razzaque (eds), *International Natural Resources Law, Investment and Sustainability* (Routledge 2018).

16 Shawkat Alam, "Natural Resource Protection in Regional and Bilateral Investment Agreements: In Search of an Equitable Balance for Promoting Sustainable Development" in Shawkat Alam, Jahid Hossain Bhuiyan, and Jona Razzaque (eds), *International Natural Resources Law, Investment and Sustainability* (Routledge 2018) at 108. According to this author, "IIAs have primarily been concerned with creating a stable regulatory environment to enable or encourage FDI in a host state. IIAs have achieved this through two primary mechanisms supported by 'umbrella' clauses: the development of 'standard' protection standards and the incorporation of stabilisation clauses" (ibid. at 115).

vis-à-vis the investment/investor, observing both national and international legal frameworks, the needs of their community, and the protection of the environment. In this latter role, states are expected to exercise their right to intervene, taking action on behalf of their economic interests and the protection of both the community and the environment.[17] The right to intervene materializes through the right of the host state to regulate investment activities *ex ante* as well as *ex post* through the adoption of measures whenever risks of an adverse impact to the community or the environment are envisaged. The exercise of this sovereign power may be the consequence of the investor's failure to comply with the law in force or a behavior that cannot be tolerated by the host state under international law.[18]

In exercising its surveillance role, a state is expected to prevent any disruption caused by an investment project upon the surrounding community or the environment by taking the adequate measures for halting or lessening the negative impacts of the investment; but such reaction will not always be cost-free. The reaction of host states to a perceived social or environmental threat will certainly induce a change in the existing relationship between the host state and the investor. The counteracting measure will, as such, be based on the host state's sovereign power and justified according to domestic law and regulations and/or international law.[19] In this sense, once a risk to the environment or a given community is perceived, the host state should interfere by modifying its legal relationship with the investor, by renegotiating the investment contract or amending the legal framework in order to neutralize the perceived adverse effects.

Certainly, the constraints to exercise these police powers have been an issue in Latin America, particularly under old generation BITs, being difficult to contest that the protection of the investment has been the paradigm underpinning the whole structure of foreign investment regimes since its beginnings. As pointed out by Sornarajah, "historically, the paradigms *[on which arguments in ISDS are built]* were developed in the context of the

---

17 Notably, host states "are keen to preserve sufficient policy space for the regulation and possible control of *[the]* industry, including the right to intervene whenever they consider this necessary" (Joachim Karl, "FDI in the Energy Sector: Recent Trends and Policy Issues" in Eric De Brabandere and Tarcisio Gazzini (eds), *Foreign Investment in the Energy Sector: Balancing Private and Public Interests* (Brill and Nijhoff 2014) at 21.

18 Although the investor is not expected to comply with the latter.

19 Referring to the energy sector, Karl considered that "countries need to safeguard the public interest by appropriate regulation of investments in the energy sector to minimize potential negative effects. Labour, social, safety and environmental laws in particular are essential to ensure that such FDI contributes to sustainable development and inclusive growth" (Karl (n 17) at 23).

disputes between the United States and Latin American states,"[20] therefore, the aim and purpose of investment agreements has been to grant foreign investments with a broader scope of protection, working as counterbalance to host states' sovereign powers. Such paradigm finds corollary in many provisions of international investment agreements. As Alam argues:

> the challenge for developing countries wishing to improve their equitable natural resources management is in implementing an adequate process which allows foreign investors to exercise their right to due process, and where necessary, adequate compensation in instances of expropriation, but which also preserves the capacity of states to legislate domestically for the protection of natural resources where these are impacted by investment.[21]

Host states most certainly face many difficulties in balancing the several convergent and conflicting interests both of their own and of the investor. Linked to this is the unavoidable reality for host states who find themselves taking part in ISDS procedures where disputes regarding such competing interests are sought to be settled. Moreover, taking into account that predictability is not one of the attributes of international investment arbitration[22] and that both ISDS procedures and IIAs law are based on the strong paradigm of protecting the rights of the investors *vis-à-vis* host states' interferences,[23] a paramount concern for host states should be to avoid ISDS procedures particularly because of the potential cost these may entail.[24]

However, host states still must comply with their duty to safeguard the community and the environment from the adverse effects the economic activity carried out by foreign investors may cause or is actually producing.

---

20 Muthucumaraswamy Sornarajah, *The Settlement of Foreign Investment Disputes* (Kluwer Law International 2000) at 77.

21 Alam (n 16) at 117.

22 See: Muthucumaraswamy Sornarajah, *The International Law on Foreign Investment* (3rd edn, Cambridge University Press 2010).

23 It has been argued that the high standards of protection of the investment set in IIAs are in great part due to the power that transnational companies have in the realm of international relations as their ability "to subscribe a set of principles which are protective of its interests and promote this set of principles as constituting the law that should be applied in the event of a dispute" is widely recognised, but also because of the role played by lawyers defending TNCs interests inasmuch as they "contribute to the growth of a set of international principles which are aimed at the protection of foreign investors and their home states" (Sornarajah (n 22) at 78–79).

24 As commented by Kulick, "international investment law *[...]* exerts such control *[upon the exercise of public authority]* by handing trump cards to non-State actors that can pursue their rights, originating in an international law source, before an international Tribunal" (Andreas Kulick, *Global Public Interest in International Investment Law* (Cambridge University Press 2012 at 148).

Indeed, investment regimes place the host state in a position of guardian of the public interest vested with powers to exercise public authority upon the investor's rights.

In their role of surveillance, host states always have, at least theoretically, the right to counteract against perceived disturbances caused to the environment or a community by a given foreign investment project, through the measures they deemed adequate.[25] Arguably, states enjoy sufficient scope of maneuver to regulate – *ex ante* and *ex post* – the way the investment should be carried out. However, what also holds true is that in exercising this power, host states may still have to bear the consequences of the measures adopted if these are found to infringe the rights set forth for protecting the investment. In other words, if the state wants to halt or mitigate the environmental or social impacts caused by an investment project, it will have to pay the price for doing so – unless host states' measures reach the high threshold set to rule out the infringement in each of the standards the claimant presumably considered breached. As Sornarajah has found, the emergence of the state's obligation to compensate for the negative effects on the investment that the exercise of its regulatory powers may cause finds support in ISDS since, from the perspective of the business sector and home states, "dispute settlement mechanisms committed to giving protection to the foreign investment is beneficial to economic development [...] dispute settlement must be guided by principles which will promote the free flow of foreign investment by assuring it of protection against capricious behaviour by states."[26]

As will be shown below, a measure considered to be in breach of a given standard of protection or to amount to the expropriation of the investment will oblige the host state to remedy the investor's economic loss. This holds true unless the respondent state succeeds in persuading the tribunal that the measure meets the threshold set for considering it lawful, excluding, therefore, the state's responsibility. Were the conduct of the state deemed to be unlawful, the following would be to argue for the application of the contributory fault standard and ascertain the extent to which the acts or omissions of the investor contributed to its own injury, having to bear the weight of its own negligence. Consequently, the amount of compensation would be adjusted accordingly, reducing the amount otherwise payable by the host state.

25 As the tribunal to the *S.D. Myers v Canada* case acknowledged, tribunals "do not have an open-ended mandate to second-guess government decision-making" which will suggest that there could be a margin, although limited, for the tribunal to assess state's motivation and the suitability of the measures taken to tackle the issue they were intended to address (*S.D. Myers, Inc. v. Government of Canada*, UNCITRAL (Partial Award, 13 November 2000), paragraph 261).

26 Sornarajah (n 22) at 79.

Social license in international law and sustainable development

Investment projects do not occur in a vacuum and it is undeniable that many of them produce considerable impacts upon host states' local communities. These impacts may be of different degrees and connotation, and there could even be some investments that will not have any impact whatsoever.

However, for those investments that may entail potential adverse effects upon local communities, and in order to create a space for cooperation between the investor and these communities, in their relevant domestic regulations, host states can establish the obligation for the investor to conduct different actions to attain social license in order to avoid the potential, adverse social impacts of development projects, through mechanisms such as social planning, social impact assessments, stakeholder consultations, or agreements with the host community. All these mechanisms are closely oriented to sustainable development as they aim to balance the converging economic interests of the investor with the social and environmental concerns borne by local communities, by securing agreements that satisfy both parties.

From declarations in strong legal wording to its creation as a proper due diligence obligation, several international law instruments have referred to the relevance of attaining social license to evaluate and address the potential social impact that different activities may have upon indigenous and local communities.

Although timidly, Principle 22 of the 1992 Rio Declaration on Environment and Development[27] is clear in linking the relevant role of indigenous and local communities to the achievement of sustainable development, recognizing that:

> Indigenous people and their communities, and other local communities, have a vital role in environmental management and development because of their knowledge and traditional practices. States should recognize and duly support their identity, culture and interests and enable their effective participation in the achievement of sustainable development.

Related to the above Principle 22 is Principle 1 of the 2002 New Delhi Declaration of Principles of International Law Relating to Sustainable Development, which declares that the duty of states to ensure a sustainable use of natural resources would entail the duty to manage natural resources "in a rational, sustainable and safe way so as to contribute to the development of their peoples, with particular regard for the rights of indigenous

---

27 UN Doc. A/CONF.151/26 (vol. I); 31 ILM 874 (1992). See Chapter 9 by Sufyan Droubi, Cecilia Juliana Flores Elizondo, and Raphael Heffron in this volume (in relation to indigenous peoples' right in determining sustainable development).

peoples, and to the conservation and sustainable use of natural resources and the protection of the environment, including ecosystems."[28]

In the same vein, Article 32 of the United Nations Declaration on the Rights of Indigenous Peoples[29] reads as follow:

> 1. Indigenous peoples have the right to determine and develop priorities and strategies for the development or use of their lands or territories and other resources.

> 2. States shall consult and cooperate in good faith with the indigenous peoples concerned through their own representative institutions in order to obtain their free and informed consent prior to the approval of any project affecting their lands or territories and other resources, particularly in connection with the development, utilization or exploitation of mineral, water or other resources.

> 3. States shall provide effective mechanisms for just and fair redress for any such activities, and appropriate measures shall be taken to mitigate adverse environmental, economic, social, cultural or spiritual impact.

Additionally, Article 15 of the International Labour Organization Convention No. 169 Concerning Indigenous and Tribal Peoples in Independent Countries provides:

> 1. The rights of the peoples concerned to the natural resources pertaining to their lands shall be specially safeguarded. These rights include the right of these peoples to participate in the use, management and conservation of these resources.

> 2. In cases in which the State retains the ownership of mineral or sub-surface resources or rights to other resources pertaining to lands, governments shall establish or maintain procedures through which they shall consult these peoples, with a view to ascertaining whether and to what degree their interests would be prejudiced, before undertaking or permitting any programmes for the exploration or exploitation of such resources pertaining to their lands. The peoples concerned shall wherever possible participate in the benefits of such activities, and shall receive fair compensation for any damages which they may sustain as a result of such activities.[30]

Furthermore, within the realm of the Convention on Biological Diversity, the Nagoya Protocol on Access to Genetic Resources and the Fair and Equitable Sharing of Benefits Arising from their Utilization is conclusive in determining the great relevance of the proceedings aiming at achieving

28 UN Doc. A/CONF.199/8, 9 August 2002.
29 Annex to the General Assembly Resolution 61/295 on the Rights of Indigenous Peoples, 13 September 2007.
30 Convention concerning Indigenous and Tribal Peoples in Independent Countries (signed, adopted 27 June 1989, entered into force 5 September 1991) 1650 UNTS 383.

consent or approval from indigenous and local communities when accessing their traditional knowledge associated with genetic resources. In its Article 7, the Protocol establishes that:

> In accordance with domestic law, each Party shall take measures, as appropriate, with the aim of ensuring that traditional knowledge associated with genetic resources that is held by indigenous and local communities is accessed with the prior and informed consent or approval and involvement of these indigenous and local communities, and that mutually agreed terms have been established.[31]

Following these developments in international law, host states have adopted legislation imposing the requirement for investors to obtain social license as a condition to be met before the commencement of their investment development. Although there have not been many cases dealing with this topic, two controversies have emerged between investors and host states where the attainment of social license has been the center of the debate. This, in turn, has given arbitral tribunals the opportunity to engage with the analysis of the concept, its scope, and extent within the realm of international investment law.

Evaluation of the host state's responsibility for measures adopted after the investor's breach of the obligation to attain social license

The following section examines two awards rendered by ICSID arbitral tribunals in cases where the measures challenged by the investor were taken by the host state based on the alleged failure of the former to comply with the obligation to attain social license. This study will explore the extent to which the adjudication process accommodated the sustainable development narrative of balance to assess in each case the state's responsibility for the eventual breach of the investment standards of protection.

The first of these cases is *Pac Rim Cayman LLC v. The Republic of El Salvador*.[32] In this case, according to the host state's domestic law, the investor was required to obtain consent from landlords of a property located on the area of a subsoil mining project. The conflict emerged after the refusal of the host state to grant the exploitation concession to the investor based on its failure to comply with the submission of the "property title for the

---

31 Nagoya Protocol on Access to Genetic Resources and the Fair and Equitable Sharing of Benefits Arising from their Utilization, UNEP/CBD/COP/DEC/X/1, Annex I, 29 October 2010, p 5.

32 *Pac Rim v El Salvador* (Award 2016) (n 10).

real estate or authorised permissions, in legal form, from the landowner"[33] as required by domestic mining law. The ICSID tribunal was called among other issues to interpret a domestic law provision in order to determine the extent of the investor's obligation to find such social license as part of the conditions established to turn an exploration concession into an exploitation one. The parties to the case had different understandings on the actual extent of the required consent, being the investor's belief that the condition was met by attaining the consent only of those landowners likely to be directly affected, whereas, for the host state, such understanding fell short by not considering the entire surface area of the requested concession.[34]

The tribunal rejected the investor's understanding based on three criteria: a) the behavior and decisions taken by the investor; b) the recognition of a fair degree of deference to that interpretation of domestic law issued by the host state's authorities before the emergence of the dispute; and, c) a teleological argument was deployed by the tribunal.[35] This third argument – as reproduced below – embraces sustainable development in its core inasmuch as it stresses the relevance of achieving an exhaustive consent of those landowners that are considered to be directly affected by the concession, as well as of those that could be indirectly affected. Although not expressly mentioning sustainable development, the tribunal declared, referring to the wording and scope of the domestic provision subject to interpretation, that:

> Read literally, it can be stretched to describe the full surface area of the requested concession. However, applied to underground mining conducted under modern mining practices [...], that literal interpretation does not seem to make much practical sense, whether viewed from the perspective of the proposed concessionaire, the Respondent (as the owner of the sub-soil) or the individual owners and occupiers of the full surface area. Equally, also a matter of practical sense, it would unduly truncate the wording to limit its application to only that part of the surface area directly impacted by the proposed mining infrastructure at the surface. What matters, in practice, are the potential risks posed to surface owners or occupiers; and, inevitably, those risks may not be the same over the full surface area of the requested concession, particularly over the full 30-year period of the requested concession.[36]

In the reasoning of the tribunal, it is observed that, in order to adequately interpret the domestic provision, there is a need to strike a balance between the economic aim of developing the mining project *vis-á-vis* the need to protect the land-owners and occupiers from the risks that such projects may

33 El Salvador's Mining Law Article 37(2)(b).
34 *Pac Rim v El Salvador* (Award 2016) (n 10) at paragraph 8.12.
35 Ibid. at paragraphs 8.29–32.
36 Ibid. at paragraphs 8.32.

cause, i.e. between an economic interest and a legitimate social concern. On the one hand, based on the merits, the tribunal determined that consent must reach owners and occupiers in the whole surface area of the concession. On the other hand, a time perspective is also taken into account, which is aimed at integrating a future perspective approach within the wording of the regulation subject to interpretation. This long-term approach led the tribunal to include the need to consider even those owners or occupiers that could be indirectly affected by the project within the investor's obligation. In other words, the tribunal articulated the obligation of the investor to attain social license from a sustainable development perspective. This is so, inasmuch as it determined which was or could be the local community actually affected and then call for the achievement of a balance between the interests of the investor to move on with its project and the concern for lowering the potential social risks that may be generated by it. The investor, not having satisfied such balance or, what is the same, not having completely and adequately fulfilled its obligation to attain social license from a sustainable development perspective, made the arbitral tribunal to dismiss its claim regarding the determination of the responsibility of the host state.

The second case, also substantiated before an ICSID arbitral tribunal, concerns *Bear Creek Mining Corporation v. Republic of Peru*.[37] In this case, the host state – Peru – argued that the measure challenged by the investor, i.e. the revoking of a permit previously granted to the investor to carry out its investment project, was an exercise of its police powers aiming at the prevention of border blockades and social unrest in the area. Such measure was taken according to the respondent, in light of the investor's failure to achieve an adequate degree of social license – which was claimed to be the cause of the social unrest of the communities living nearby the project implementation area. As stressed by the ICSID arbitral tribunal to the *Bear Creek* case, although social license is not a concept "clearly defined in international law, all relevant international instruments are clear that consultations with indigenous communities are to be made with the purpose of obtaining consent from all the relevant communities."[38] Out of these lines, it is possible to infer that social license refers to the process of consultation that has to be conducted by the interested investor in order to obtain consent from all relevant, indigenous, and local communities. If one thinks on sustainable development as related to the need to halt or lessen all significant adverse social or environmental impacts caused by economic development through the achievement of a balance among the different, convergent

---

37 *Bear Creek v Peru* (Award 2017) (n 11). See Chapter 11 by Farouk El-Hosseny, Patrick Devine, and Ilan Brun-Vargasin in this volume.
38 Ibid. paragraph 406.

interests, attaining social license is clearly heading, in this case, to such an end in a preventive way.

Differently from the *Pac Rim* case, here the tribunal did not find that the investor was in breach of its obligation to attain social license; rather it reached the conviction that the host state's appreciation of the investor's compliance was wrong. Therefore, the measure taken on the assumption that the investor failed to attain social license was regarded as a violation of the investment protection standards. Thus, the responsibility of Peru was established.

The ensuing section will discuss the application of the contributory fault standard and the potential use that the sustainable development narrative of balance may have to this end by providing a comprehensive assessment of the investor's obligation to attain social license. The evaluation of this thesis will be performed by elaborating further on the reasoning conveyed by the tribunal to the *Bear Creek* case.

Evaluation of the outreach made to attain social license for the purposes of the application of the contributory fault standard

The framing principle for reparation of damages to the victim of a wrongful act or omission is that "reparation must, as far as possible, wipe out all the consequences of the illegal act and re-establish the situation which would, in all probability, have existed if that act had not been committed."[39] Article 39 on the contribution to the injury of the Articles on Responsibility of States for Internationally Wrongful Acts,[40] however, establishes that "[i]n the determination of reparation, account shall be taken of the contribution to the injury by wilful or negligent action or omission of the injured State or any person or entity in relation to whom reparation is sought." Interestingly, there is not much literature on the application of the contributory fault standard.[41] The following paragraphs will deal with the

---

39 *Factory At Chorzów (Germany v Poland)* (Judgment, Claim for Indemnity, Merits, Judgment No 13) [1928] PCIJ Series A No 17, paragraph 47.

40 Annex to the General Assembly Resolution 56/83, A/56/49(Vol.I)/Corr.4, 12 December 2001.

41 Some authors, as Hober, stated that contributory fault of the investor could be taken into account at the stage of damages of the arbitration and that it is the tribunal who has the discretionary faculty to determine the compensation amount (Kaj Hober, "Compensation: A Closer Look at Cases Awarding Compensation for Violation of the Fair and Equitable Treatment Standard" in Katia Yannaca-Small (ed), *Arbitration Under International Investment Agreements: A Guide to the Key Issues* (Oxford University Press 2010) at 576). Mostly all handbooks on international investment law

assessment of the investor's contributory fault when measures taken by host states are grounded on preventing or minimizing the adverse effects of the investment development on the community and/or the environment.

The idea of looking for the investor's contributory fault to the injuries on grounds of both social and environmental concerns[42] was raised firstly in the *Copper Mesa Mining Corporation v. The Republic of Ecuador* case[43] brought before an arbitral tribunal constituted according to the rules of the Permanent Court of Arbitration (PCA). Ecuador, the host state, was sued by the investor for unlawfully expropriating the investment, as well as for breaching the FET and FPS clauses, which, according to the investment agreement, governed the relationship between the parties. Particularly, the claimant raised a domestic law passed by Ecuador as the source of the infringements. However, Ecuador argued that such domestic law "was adopted for the legitimate public policy purposes of protecting public health and the environment where the requirement to consult the local population on the basis of an EIS was specifically intended to protect the residents and local communities and to reduce the environmental impacts of mining activities."[44] Therefore, the measure adopted was within the margin allowed for exercising its police powers legitimately. Interestingly, the tribunal was of the belief that its function was not to pass judgment upon the motivation that led the host state to declare the termination of the mining concessions, but to check whether the procedural aspects of its implementation were consistent with due process and whether they were not discriminatory nor arbitrary. However, after finding the host state responsible, when the liability and the amount of compensation owed by the respondent were determined, the tribunal examined each of the parties' contribution to the prior facts

---

devote just a few lines to refer a few cases where tribunals have applied the contributory fault standard to reduce the damages otherwise payable to the investor: Christopher F. Dugan and others, *Investor-State Arbitration* (Oxford University Press 2008) at 602–603; Rudolf Dolzer and Christoph H Schreuer, *Principles of International Investment Law* (Oxford University Press 2008) at 273; Meg Kinnear, "Damages in Investment Treaty Arbitration" in Katia Yannaca-Small (ed), *Arbitration Under International Investment Agreements: A Guide to the Key Issues* (Oxford University Press 2010) at 565–566. However, a monograph on the topic was published recently: Martin Jarret, *Contributory Fault and the Investor Misconduct in Investment Arbitration* (Cambridge University Press 2019). Also see Chapter 11 by Farouk El-Hosseny, Patrick Devine, and Ilan Brun-Vargas in this volume.

42 Contributory fault to the injury assessed on different grounds see: *MTD Equity Sdn. Bhd. and MTD Chile S.A. v. Chile*, ICSID Case No. ARB/01/7 (Award, 25 May 2004), paragraphs 242–246.

43 *Copper Mesa Mining Corporation v. Republic of Ecuador*, PCA No. 2012–2 (Award, 15 March 2016).

44 Ibid. at paragraph 1.16.

that led to the termination of the concessions and asserted that the investor had to bear part of the outcome on its own, thus reducing the amount to be paid by the respondent by 30 percent.[45]

Similarly, in the *Bear Creek* case, the application of the contributory fault standard was put forward by the respondent state for the Tribunal's assessment. However, recalling the findings achieved in a previous ICSID case,[46] the arbitral tribunal asserted that in order for a host state's international responsibility to be excluded based on the investor's omission or fault, two conditions had to be met: firstly, the host state had to prove that there was an omission or fault attributable to the investor; and, secondly, it had to prove the existence of a causal link between such omission or fault and the alleged harm suffered,[47] placing the burden of proof, therefore, upon the host state. In the tribunal's words, "[w]hile Claimant could have gone further in its outreach activities, the relevant question for the Tribunal is whether Respondent can claim that such further outreach was legally required and its absence caused or contributed to the social unrest, so as to justify Supreme Decree 032."[48] Although the parameter for assessing the Claimant's outreach was found in a national document regulating citizen participation in the mining subsector, reference to some articles of the International Labour Organization Convention No. 169 Concerning Indigenous and Tribal Peoples in Independent Countries were also brought to the analysis. Special regard was put on Article 15 about the inclusion of peoples in the use, management, and conservation of natural resources and the procedures to consult them in order to accurately measure the degree up to which their interests would be prejudiced. Clearly, the tribunal in this case did not make a difference between responsibility and liability.

Although the examination of the claimant's contributory fault to the injuries suffered "appears to be relatively rare in investment arbitration,"[49] in his partially dissenting opinion,[50] Philippe Sands, respondent's appointee to the arbitral tribunal, argued for reducing the amount of damages awarded to the investor in light of its own contribution to the social unrest and protests that led the host state to take the decision to revoke the investor's rights to operate the mine.[51] The state of rebellious dissatisfaction of

45 Ibid. at paragraph 6.64.
46 *Abengoa, S.A. y COFIDES, S.A. v. United Mexican States*, ICSID Case No. ARB(AF)/09/2 (Award, 18 April 2013).
47 *Bear Creek v Peru* (Award 2017) (n 11) at paragraph 410.
48 Ibid. paragraph 408.
49 Dugan and others (n 41) at 603.
50 *Bear Creek Mining Corporation v. Republic of Peru*, ICSID Case No. ARB/14/21 (Partial Dissenting Opinion of Professor Philippe Sands, 30 November 2017).
51 Ibid. at paragraph 4.

the communities inhabiting the area where the mine was settled was supposed to be a reaction to the contamination of the local land and the nearby Lake Titicaca. For Sands, massive and growing social unrest was caused in part by the investment project, leaving the host state "with no option but to act in some way to protect the well-being of its citizens."[52] According to Sands, "the evidence before the Tribunal is that the Respondent has clearly established the Claimant's contributory responsibility, by reason of its acts and omissions, to the social unrest that left the Peruvian government in the predicament it faced, and the need to do something reasonable and lawful to protect public well-being." In his arguments on the claimant's contributory responsibility to the local community unrest, Sands went on explaining that:

> In particular, the Project collapsed because of the investor's inability to obtain a "social license", the necessary understanding between the Project's proponents and those living in the communities most likely to be affected by it, whether directly or indirectly. It is blindingly obvious that the viability and success of a project such as this, located in the community of the Aymara peoples, a group of interconnected communities, was necessarily dependent on local support. In this regard, the Project can hardly be said to have got off to a good start, with the Claimant making use of a degree of subterfuge, by obtaining permits in the name of one of its own lowly employees – Ms Villavicencio, a Peruvian national – which it, as a foreign corporation, was not at the time authorised or lawfully entitled to obtain. If nothing else, the absence of transparency at that early stage of the Project can only have contributed to an undermining of the conditions necessary to build trust over the longer term. The discontent that followed, expressed by many members of the affected local communities, was foreseeable.[53]

Accordingly, for Sands, obtaining social license would be in some cases "blindingly obvious" if one takes into account the external factors surrounding the investment. Whereas for the majority of the tribunal the critical issue was if the outreach shall constitute a legal requirement to authorize the investment, the gravitating question was to address whether the scope of the implemented outreach plan was an adequate one or not. For Sands, instead, the gravitating question is that "[a]s issues become more inter-related it will be incumbent upon those involved in arbitrating disputes with an environmental element to strive for balance, balance between potentially competing objectives of environmental protection on one hand, and the protection of rights of foreign investors on the other hand. Neither of these important societal interests should trump the other, they should be

---

52 Ibid. at paragraph 2 and 4.
53 Ibid. at paragraph 6.

treated in an integrated manner."[54] Sadly, the piece from where this quote is taken dates back to the year 2007 and in its conclusion reads: "It may be that the cases reflect a 'generational issue': that environmental issues remain novel with the consequence that it will take time to fully integrate environmental concerns into the better established norms of foreign investment protection."[55] Ten years later, when the award to the *Bear Creek* case was released, the same generational issue appears to be still on top, oppressing both social and environmental concerns.

The perspective conveyed by Sands is aptly expressed in the narrative of balance that is subjacent to sustainable development, where the three dimensions are not perceived as alternatives but as mutually reinforcing elements.[56] The articulation of this narrative would have provided a comprehensive understanding of the elements that had to be weighed in order to determine the contributory fault of the investor, even though the obligation to attain social license was considered fulfilled.

Conclusion

This chapter discussed the strong tension existing between the need of states to introduce themselves to foreign investors as keepers of highly attractive environments in which to develop investments, whilst at the same time comply with their duty to adopt efficient legislation and other mechanisms to protect their local communities and the environment from the adverse effects of developmental projects. Furthermore, the study acknowledged the existence of constraints for states wanting to curve these adverse effects in an international legal framework that considers the protection of the investment as its core paradigm. Indeed, the exercise of sovereign powers, altering either foreign investors' expectations on the benefits of the investment or affecting their right of property over the investment, always risks a claim before international arbitral tribunals where non-investment-related interests are often demoted.

To counteract this situation, the study showed the role that the narrative of balance subjacent to sustainable development may have to aid host states

---

54 Philippe Sands, "Litigating Environmental Disputes: Courts, Tribunals and the Progressive Development of International Environmental Law" in Tafsir Malick Ndiaye and Rudiger Wolfrum (eds), *Law of the Sea, Environmental Law and Settlement of Disputes: Liber Amicorum Judge Thomas A. Mensah* (Martinus Nijhoff 2007) at 313.

55 Ibid. at 325.

56 In this line, see *Iron Rhine* (n 13) at 59.

in advancing their social and environmental concerns to ISDS, and to make this forum more comprehensive of the different dimensions integrating foreign investment disputes. To this end, the study focused on the performance that such narrative had in disputes concerning the breach of the investment standards of protection by measures taken by host states based in the presumed failure of the investor to attain social license. The analysis went on exploring the role that sustainable development narrative of balance had to exclude the host state responsibility and the application of the contributory fault standard. In both stages of ISDS proceedings, the field seemed to be open to articulate the law applicable to the dispute according to sustainable development grounds.

Finally, it is worth mentioning that the strategic use of the sustainable development narrative of balance in ISDS may contribute to the creation of progressive jurisprudence by setting legal precedents while also contributing to clarify international standards and making them comprehensive of the different interests converging in foreign investment disputes. However, it must be acknowledged that judges and arbitrators play a crucial role in promoting the integration of this narrative of balance in international adjudication.

14

International investment law in Latin America: universalizing resistance

Fabian Cardenas and Jean d'Aspremont

Introduction

It is argued in this chapter that international investment law does what it does by virtue of its ambivalent relationship towards universality. With a specific emphasis on Latin American legal thought and practice, it is particularly shown in the following sections how international investment law come to simultaneously accommodate claims of universality as well as resistance thereto. This chapter first shows the extent to which, at an abstract level, the sources metaphoric discourse enables the simultaneous vindication of both universality and resistance to universality. It then elaborates on how the enabling of an ambiguous engagement with universality came to inform the systematic use and espousal of the sources of international law in international legal thought and practice in Latin America. Afterwards, the attention turns to how this ambivalence manifests itself in the way in which the content is allocated to the concepts of international investment law like the international minimum standard and the standard of compensation. The chapter ends with a few concluding remarks on how such ambivalence towards universality is not accidental and makes the claim that resistance to universality is a form of cynicism at the service of universality itself.

The sources of international law as a metaphoric discourse

The language of international law is deeply metaphoric. Many of its key paradigms or rules are verbalized through a metaphor.[1] It suffices to think of "self-determination," "immunity," "reparation," "personality," "organizations," "competence," etc. Even the idea that law is "international" or that of the "state" has a metaphoric dimension. This chapter zeroes in on what

---

1 See gen. Harlan Cohen, "Metaphors of International Law" in Andrea Bianchi and Moshe Hirsch (eds), *International Law's Invisible Frames* (Oxford University Press 2021).

is probably international law's most famous metaphor, namely the sources of international law.[2]

Needless to say that speaking in metaphoric terms is far from being innocent. In particular, the "sources" of international law can be construed as evoking the fountainhead of a stream, that stream being international law. The metaphor of the "sources" accordingly expresses a *strength*, which is that of water that springs out of the earth and that comes to constitute an unstoppable stream of water. Still following this metaphor, international law is supposed to spring out of the social, coalescing into an unstoppable stream. The metaphor of the sources can also refer to some natural *necessity*. Like the water that springs out of the earth, international law is meant to be a natural phenomenon, one that necessarily happens.[3] From that perspective, there necessarily is international law that springs out of the social. In the same vein, the metaphor of the sources also manifests a certain idea of *purity*, that of the pristine water earthly pollutants have not yet marred. It thus projects the idea of international law that is pure when it is rolled out of the institutions or processes that have generated it, having not yet been abused or misinterpreted by its addressees or the law-appliers. The metaphor of the sources also plays a convenient ontological role for it comes to provide international law with a beginning.[4] Indeed, from the perspective of the source, it suffices one to trace the water stream and one will find its beginning. The metaphor of the sources of international law thus postulates that international law always has an identifiable and traceable origin. The metaphor of the sources eventually puts the monopoly of international law-making in the hands of a selected and reduced group of people with particular interests, those that manage the soil, the pump or the fountainhead.

---

2 See the cover of the *Oxford Handbook of the Sources of International Law* which illustrates the metaphor of the sources. See Samantha Besson and Jean d'Aspremont, the *Oxford Handbook of the Sources of International Law* (OUP, 2017). On the metaphor of sources, see more generally François Ost, "Conclusions générales" in Isabelle Hachez Yves Cartuyvels, Philippe Gérard, François Ost and Michel Van de Kerchove (eds) *Les sources du droit revisitées* (vol 4, Presses de l'Université Saint-Louis 2019) 865–997, esp. 868–869, 870–876.

3 On the ideas of naturalistic necessities and naturalized knowledge, see Judith Butler, *Gender Trouble. Feminism and the Subversion of Identify* (Routledge, 2d edition, 1990), 45. See also Judith Butler, *Notes Toward a Performative Theory of Assembly* (Harvard University Press 2018), 5 and 40–41.

4 Traditional manuals tend to equate international law with the sources and its very beginning. See e.g. *Hersch* Lauterpacht, "Règles Générales du Droit de la Paix," *Collected Courses of The Hague Academy of International Law* (Vol 62, The Hague Academy of International Law, The Hague 1937), 150. "And the source evidences the very existence of the field"; as Oppenheim said back in 1902 "where we find that such [international legal] rules rise into existence, there is the source of them."

Strength, necessity, purity, traceability, and inclusivity. These are at least five images which, by virtue of the very metaphor of the sources, come to be associated with the idea of international law.[5] This is metaphoric discourse at its peak.

It is important to highlight that metaphors are never true or false, for they are modes of representation and thus modes of meaning.[6] They are rather either efficacious or inefficacious in creating particular necessities. Precisely because they are modes of representation and of meaning, metaphors can be turned on their heads and made to represent the exact opposite of the image they were initially supposed to project or support. Said differently, metaphoric discourse can be appropriated with a view to reversing the meaning being produced through metaphoric structure.[7] In that sense, the resort to metaphoric discourse always makes one vulnerable to the versatility of meaning.[8]

The versatility of metaphoric discourse can be illustrated as follows. For instance, as far as the sources of international law are concerned, the metaphor can be turned around to project the image of a source that dries up, referring to a situation where the flow of water comes to lack pressure to spring out of the soil. The image of source can also come to represent a source where the springing water, despite being steady, falls short of constituting a stream but is spread around, is scattered, and simply absorbed back by the soil. The source can likewise come to refer to the dependence of a water on the aquifer it originates in and thus to the

---

5 Given the images of international law that such metaphors projects, it should be no surprise that the metaphor of the sources of international law has proved very popular in the consolidation of international law in the modern era. For some remarks on the modern character of sources doctrine, see Thomas Skouteris, "The Sources of International Law: Tales of Progress" (2000) 13 *Hague Yearbook of International Law* 11, 11–17; David Kennedy, "The Sources of International Law" (1987) 2 *American University International Law Review* 1. See also Jean d'Aspremont, "Bindingness" in Jean d'Aspremont and Sahib Singh (eds), *Concepts for International Law: Contributions to Disciplinary Thought* (Edward Elgar 2019) 67; Rose Parfitt, "The Spectre of Sources" (2014) 25 *European Journal of International Law* 297.

6 Steven L. Winter. *A Clearing in the Forest. Law, Life and Mind* (The University of Chicago Press 2001), 65–66. See also more generally Jacques Derrida, "La mythologie blanche. La métaphore dans le texte philosophique" in Jacques Derrida *Marges de la Philosophie* (Editions de Minuit 1972), at 247–324.

7 This phenomenon has been theorized by Jean-Jacques Lecercle as a move of counter-interpellation. See Jean-Jacques Lecercle, *De l'interpellation: sujet, langue, idéologie* (Editions Amsterdam 2019). On the idea of interpellation, Louis Althusser, "Ideology and ideological state apparatuses (Notes towards an investigation)," in *Lenin and Philosophy and Other Essays* (Monthly Review Press 1971), 142–147, 166–176.

8 Steven L. Winter, *A Clearing in the Forest. Law, Life and Mind* (The University of Chicago Press 2001), 66.

constant risk of water being contaminated when it springs out. Finally, the source can also project an image of water being squandered, spilling constantly without being captured or preserved. Far from expressing strength, necessity, purity, and traceability, the metaphor of sources can thus come to refer to drought, sprinkle, contamination, and waste. In other words, because of the versatility of metaphors, those who are confidently mobilizing the metaphor of the sources of international law to express strength, necessity, purity, traceability, and inclusivity may end up associating international law with drought, sprinkle, contamination, waste, and exclusion.

The following discussion on international investment law will show that the versatility of the sources metaphoric discourse simultaneously enables processes of inclusion geared towards claims of universality and processes of exclusion geared towards claims of autonomy and independence. It will be demonstrated that it is this very ambivalence of the sources metaphoric discourse that contributed to the success of the sources discourse in Latin America.

The success of the sources metaphoric discourse in Latin America

It is commonly assumed that international investment law primarily originates in bilateral investment treaties and investment chapters contained in free trade agreements that are supplemented by general standards found in customary international law.[9]

The sources metaphoric discourse has had a resounding success in Latin America. In fact, the metaphor of the sources as systematized in Europe has been later deployed in Latin America,[10] to support claims of the universality of international law. This meant, for those outside the European centre, to

9 On the sources of international investment law, see gen. Eric De Brabandere and Tarcisio Gazzini (eds), *International Investment Law: The Sources of Rights and Obligations* (Brill 2012). See also the chapters of Jorge E. Viñuales "Sources of International Law: Conceptual Foundations of Unruly Practices" and Stephan W. Schill "Sources of International Investment Law: Multilateralization, Arbitral Precedent, Comparativism, Soft Law" in Samantha Besson and Jean d'Aspremont (eds), *The Oxford Handbook of the Sources of International Law* (Oxford University Press 2017).

10 See Samantha Besson and Jean d'Aspremont, "The Sources of International Law: An Introduction" in Samantha Besson and Jean d'Aspremont (eds), *The Oxford Handbook of the Sources of International Law* (Oxford University Press 2017), at 8–14; See also the references mentioned by Jean d'Aspremont, *Formalism and the Sources of International Law* (Oxford University Press 2011), 38–82. Comp. with the work of Han Fei Zi on legalism in Ancient China. See Han Fei Tzu, Basic Writings (transl. by Burton Watson) (Columbia University Press 1964).

qualify for this universal international law – and thus to be part of the clubs of civilized[11] – one had to espouse the sources of international law discourse.[12] Against this backdrop, it should not be surprising that some of the most known modern Latin American international scholars like Andres Bello,[13] Carlos Calvo,[14] and Alejandro Alvarez[15] resolutely adopted the sources of international law discourse with a view to making the Americas part of the universal international law.[16] In this respect, it is fair to say that, as *criollos*, or Latin American nationals with a Spanish or Portuguese descent,[17]

11 The idea of civilization was yet another of these metaphors, one that particularly thrived in the nineteenth century and which provided the idea of evolution, advancement and superiority, constituting the perfect argument to achieve the universalization of international law. See gen. Liliana Obregón, "Identity formation, theorization and decline of a Latin American international law" in Paula Wojcikiewicz Almeida and Jean-Marc Sorel (eds), *Latin America and the International Court of Justice: Contributions to International Law* (Routledge Research in International Law 2017) 8.

12 See Alejandro Alvarez, *International Law and Related Subjects from the Point of View of the American Continent* (The Endowment 1922) ch III. Alejandro Alvarez, The Necessity of unifying The Anglo-American and Latin-American Schools of International Law and of Creating a Pan-American School.

13 Andrés Bello was a significant and influential political and intellectual figure in the nineteenth century in Latin America and he was born in Venezuela, "In the aftermath of independence, Bello provided the most successful blueprint for nation building by emphasizing legal, social, and cultural elements in addition to the requisite political stability and economic viability." Iván Jaksič (ed), *The Selected Writings of Andrés Bello* (Oxford University Press 1997), 16.

14 Carlos Calvo was an Argentine jurist author of the well-known "Calvo Doctrine" which in simple terms means that "who had taken the position that under international law aliens had no rights greater than citizens of the host country" in Andreas F Lowenfeld, *International Economic Law Series* (2nd edn, Oxford University Press 2008) 475.

15 Alejandro Alvarez was a Chilean jurist and "the most renowned Latin American international legal scholar of the twentieth century, was dedicated to the persistent promotion of projects of a continental (American), regional (Latin American), and universal international law (...) He also co-founded or participated in the major academic and political institutions of international law of the first half of the twentieth century, including the International Court of Justice (ICJ), where he was a judge from 1946 to 1955" in Liliana Obregon, "Noted for Dissent: The International Life of Alejandro Alvarez" (2006) 19 *Leiden Journal of International Law*, 983.

16 "America has had, and still possesses, in international matters, a uniform doctrine on a great many subjects pertaining to the interests of civilization in general or that of our continent, a logical consequence of the fact that all the countries of the New World have passed through the same struggle for independence and have had practically the same interests and the same problems." See Alejandro Alvarez, *International Law and Related Subjects from the Point of View of the American Continent.* (The Endowment 1922), ch. III. Alejandro Alvarez, The Necessity of unifying The Anglo-American and Latin-American Schools of International Law and of Creating a Pan-American School.

17 "The term criollo (from the Latin creare – to create) was first used in the sixteenth century to designate black slaves born in the Americas (as opposed to bozales or African-born slaves). By the seventeenth century it had become a pejorative term that was

they fought for a two-fold agenda that somehow reflected their "criollo conscience."[18] On the one hand they aimed at earning a seat for Latin American States in the club of civilized in order to ensure equality with their European counterparts.[19] This was the universalizing side of their project.[20] On the other hand, they sought to shield their battered independence in the new continent in ways that acknowledge their particular needs and particularity.[21] That

applied by the Spanish conquerors to a person born in America of European heritage but suspected of being the product of miscegenation. Nonetheless, Creoles shared a hierarchical superiority and legal equality with the Spaniards as part of the 'Republic of the Spanish', a jurisdiction which also included the castas (mixed peoples) and free blacks at a lower level. All these categories were constituted in legal terms through separate jurisdictions, privileges, and restrictions. Despite their status as a local elite, their continuous claims to whiteness, and their legal superiority over Indians, castas, free blacks, and slaves, Creoles were perceived by the Spanish as impure Europeans and were seldom allowed to hold the most important administrative posts or have access to privileges reserved for the Spanish-born" in Liliana Obregon, "Noted for Dissent: The International Life of Alejandro Alvarez" (2006) 19 Leiden Journal of International Law, 983. The term "crioulos" also applies to Brazilians with Portuguese descent. See Mafra, Adriano, and Christiane Stallaert. "Orientalismo Crioulo: Dom Pedro II e o Brasil do Segundo Império/Creole Orientalism. D. Pedro II and Brazil in the Second Empire." *IBEROAMERICANA* (2016): 149–168. http://journals.iai.spk-berlin.de/index.php/iberoamericana/article/download/2117/1914. Regarding the "criollos" in Latin American international law see also Chapters 1 by Philip Burton and 9 by Sufyan Droubi, Cecilia Juliana Flores Elizondo, and Raphael Heffron in this volume.

18 Liliana Obregon has defined Creole legal consciousness as a "broad set of problems, strategies, uses, and ideas about the law that were shared among a group of Latin American lawyers in the post-independence era." See Liliana Obregon, "Noted for Dissent: The International Life of Alejandro Alvarez" (2006) 19 *Leiden Journal of International Law*, 983.

19 "Through exceptionalist discourses Latin Americans have had a long history of thinking about difference and identity as a response to European domination, as an almost immediate result of the Spanish colonial project. However, within these forms of exceptionalism the Latin American intellectual continues to desire inclusion in the Eurocentric discourse because Eurocentrism is presented 'as the final proof of legitimate knowledge' and 'a real and important concern of Latin American intellectuals is participation in the construction and/or deconstruction of that knowledge: to participate in the "universal" conversation, interdependently as it were'." in Liliana Obregon, "Noted for Dissent: The International Life of Alejandro Alvarez" (2006) 19 *Leiden Journal of International Law*, 983.

20 For more on Latin American International Law and how important Latin America was to the field see Ricardo Abello-Galvis and Walter Arévalo-Ramírez, "Contribuciones del Derecho Internacional Latinoamericano al Derecho internacional Público a través de los primeros cursos de la Academia de Derecho Internacional," Ricardo Abello-Galvis and Walter Arévalo-Ramírez (eds), *Derecho Internacional Público, Derecho Internacional de la Inversión Extranjera. Reflexiones y diálogos* (1st edition, Editorial Universidad del Rosario 2019) 3–17.

21 Alejandro Alvarez, *International Law and Related Subjects from the Point of View of the American Continent* (The Endowment 1922) ch III. Alejandro Alvarez, *The Necessity of unifying The Anglo-American and Latin-American Schools of International Law and of*

was how they presented resistance. For either objective, the sources of international law was the discourse to be resorted to. Indeed, the abovementioned
versatility of the sources discourse enables sources to be either inclusive and
work for a universalization of international law or exclusive and preserve the
autonomy as well as the independence from international law. It is by virtue
of this fundamental ambivalence of the sources discourse that the criollos generalized the sources discourse and became those through which the sources
metaphoric discourse was introduced into Latin America.

It must be emphasized that the introduction of metaphoric sources discourse
in Latin America by Andres Bello, Carlos Calvo, and Alejandro Alvarez and
other criollo lawyers is possibly no coincidence. They experienced a lack of
belonging, as they were considered neither Americans nor Europeans, however
they wanted to overcome this situation by adopting the European standards
of civilization within the new continent, with the particular twist that could
accommodate their own circumstances. Latin American international law has
experienced this very same fluctuation between universalization and particu-
larization, inclusion and exclusion, and such dynamism has been possible precisely thanks to the sources being volatile metaphors.[22]

That Latin American elite and policy-makers proved receptive to the criollos's metaphoric discourses is probably no accident either.[23] This part of
the world had been buffeted by the colonialism they experienced through
physical, economical, and political interventions.[24] By the nineteenth century, and with their recently independent states, Latin American elite and
policy-makers felt neither tied up nor free from their former colonizers.
Hence, by adopting and adapting the European-made international law,
they deemed it would be possible to offset the lack of identity as they
would be considered civilized and therefore equals, but with the assurance
of a legal regime that would protect them from further intervention.[25] So,
whereas, on the one hand, Latin American elite and policy-makers claimed
to be part and important contributors of this new international law, which

Creating a Pan-American School. Also see Alfredo Cock Arango, *Derecho Internacional
Americano* (Imprenta Nacional, Universidad Nacional de Colombia 1948).

22 On their multifaceted identity, see the remarks of Liliana Obregon, "Noted for
Dissent: The International Life of Alejandro Alvarez" (2006) 19 *Leiden Journal of
International Law*, 983.

23 Arnulf Becker Lorca, "Universal International Law: Nineteenth-Century Histories of
Imposition and Appropriation" (2010) 51 *Harv Int'l LJ* 475.

24 Juan Pablo Scarfi, *The Hidden History of International Law in the Americas, Empire
and Legal Networks* (Oxford University Press 2017), Vicente Marotta Rangel,
"International Law, Regional Developments: Latin America" (2008) Oxford Public
International Law http://opil.ouplaw.com accessed 29 September 2020.

25 Liliana Obregón, "Identity formation, theorization and decline of a Latin American
international law" in Paula Wojcikiewicz Almeida and Jean-Marc Sorel (eds) *Latin
America and the International Court of Justice: Contributions to International Law*
(Routledge 2017) 8.

envisaged a universalistic perspective of international law, on the other, they were eager to defend their own approach particularly concerning sensible issues of autonomy and independence.[26] The sources metaphoric discourse simultaneously enabled them to fight these two battles. Indeed, while the universalistic approach is well evident in the way they adopted the inclusive sources discourse as has been designed by the most renowned European international legal scholars,[27] the sources discourse also allowed them to vindicate and shield Latin American states' autonomy and independence.

This ambivalence is well-illustrated by the use of the sources discourse in the well-known and so-called Monroe,[28] Drago[29] and the Calvo

26 "Contribuciones del Derecho Internacional Latinoamericano al Derecho internacional Público a través de los primeros cursos de la Academia de Derecho Internacional," Ricardo Abello-Galvis and Walter Arévalo-Ramírez (eds), *Derecho Internacional Público, Derecho Internacional de la Inversión Extranjera. Reflexiones y diálogos* (1st edn, Editorial Universidad del Rosario 2019) 3–17.

27 Arnulf Becker Lorca, "Universal International Law: Nineteenth-Century Histories of Imposition and Appropriation" (2010) 51 *Harv Int'l LJ* 475. Liliana Obregón also explains how Andrés Bello endorses a speech produced in Europe, and makes it part of his founding project for independent nations and for the region. See Liliana Obregón, "Construyendo la región americana: Andrés Bello y el derecho internacional" in González-Stephan y Juan Poblete (eds), *Andrés Bello y los estudios latinoamericanos* (Serie Criticas, Universidad de Pittsburgh: Instituto Internacional de Literatura Iberoamericana 2009).

28 Alejandro Álvarez explained the Monroe Doctrine in the following terms: "First, it is necessary not to confound the Monroe Doctrine with the policy of supremacy or imperialism, as ordinarily viewed, especially in this country. Secondly, in the Monroe Doctrine as contained in the message of 1823 it is necessary to distinguish two parts entirely different: the declaration of President Monroe concerning the non-intervention of the United States in European affairs, and the declarations concerning the political independence of the New World. The first part only is a personal policy of the United States and was enunciated before Monroe by Washington in his farewell address to the American people. This policy the United States can abandon if it wishes. The second part of the Doctrine is not a personal policy of the United States but a Doctrine professed by all states of the New World. Consequently the opinion of different statesmen and publicists of Europe that the United States will abandon the Monroe Doctrine because of her actual intervention in European affairs, is unacceptable. Thirdly, in regard to the second part of the Monroe Doctrine or continental doctrine it is necessary to limit the Monroe Doctrine to the three principles contained in the message of 1823 and complete it by two other declarations of presidents of the United States, accepted also by the countries of Latin America. These two developments of the Monroe Doctrine are: An American state cannot cede on any ground a portion of its territory to a European state; and the European states can not occupy permanently any portion of American territory" in Alejandro Alvarez, *International Law and Related Subjects from the Point of View of the American Continent* (Washington, The Endowment, 1922) ch IV. Alejandro Alvarez, Monroe Doctrine: Its Importance in the International Life of the States of the New World.

29 Luis M. Drago was an Argentine jurist, he played a significant role in the history of diplomacy, author of the Drago doctrine: "it is impossible to read Dr. Drago's

doctrines,[30] that were aimed at both anchoring Latin American States in the universality of international law and sheltering their autonomy and independence.[31] While the Monroe and the Drago doctrines were meant to avoid further European military interventions in their former colonies or to assure the payment of their debts, the Calvo doctrine aimed at safeguarding investment law disputes within the boundaries of domestic jurisdiction and on the basis of domestic law.[32] This oscillation between the universalistic acquisition of international law and the claim for one's autonomous and independent take on international law is a possibility that is offered by

correspondence on this matter without perceiving that he was a friend of American cooperation, and a convinced believer in the principles of the Monroe Doctrine" in Dexter Perkins, "Discursos y escritos by Luis M Drago" (1942) 22 (1) *The Hispanic American Historical Review* www.jstor.org/stable/2507015 accessed: 4 September 2020, 108–110. "Luís María Drago in 1902 instructed the Argentinian ambassador in Washington to seek United States ('US') support for a principle which later became known as the Drago Doctrine: 'that the public debt can not occasion armed intervention nor even the actual occupation of the territory of American nations by a European power' His argument was twofold: that the creditors involved in the State debts were aware of the risks involved, which were taken account of by the conditions of the loans, and that the sovereignty of the debtor State prohibited execution of the entitlements either by forcible intervention or any territorial occupation (c.f. the Monroe Doctrine of 1823)" Wolfgang Benedek, "Drago-Porter Convention (1907)" (2007) Oxford Public International Law http://opil.ouplaw.com accessed 29 September 2020.

30 "The Calvo Doctrine, which he originally expressed in his 1863 treatise on international law (...) More precisely, the doctrine was born out of a sense of imbalance in the exercise of diplomatic protection, which Calvo perceived as an infringement by stronger States over the sovereign rights of weaker States. The Calvo Clause, which was later developed, was a corollary of the Calvo Doctrine, which came to be incorporated in concession agreements between States and aliens. The Calvo Clause was in essence a waiver of diplomatic protection running from the concessionary company to the conceding State. (...) The Calvo Doctrine rests upon one core proposition: aliens should not be entitled to any rights or privileges not accorded to nationals" Patrick Juillard, "Calvo Doctrine/Calvo Clause 2007" (2007) *Oxford Public International Law* http://opil.ouplaw.com accessed 29 September 2020.

31 The importance of autonomy and independence in Latin America is related to its historical background. Alejandro Alvarez has addressed this by explaining that: "After their liberation, the states of Latin America feared that not only the mother country, but any one of the powerful European states, might make attempts against their independence or at least against their political life." See Alejandro Alvarez, *International Law and Related Subjects from the Point of View of the American Continent* (The Endowment 1922) ch IV. Alejandro Alvarez *Monroe Doctrine: Its Importance in the International Life of the States of the New World* (Oxford University Press 1924).

32 About the existence of Latin-American International Law see Arnulf Becker Lorca, "International Law in Latin America or Latin American International Law? Rise, Fall, and Retrieval of a Tradition of Legal Thinking and Political Imagination" (2006) 47 *Harv Int'l LJ* 283.

the sources metaphoric discourse and which was fully exploited by Latin American elite and policy-makers.[33]

The diverging projects pursued by international investment law in Latin American

The previous section has shown that the ambivalence of the sources meta-phoric discourse *vis-à-vis* universality has ensured its rapid introduction and success in Latin America. This section will seek to demonstrate that the contemporary legal thought and practice regarding the determination of the content of international investment law in Latin America has perpetuated such ambivalent relationship with universality.[34] This section provides a few remarks on the diverging virtues assigned to international investment law in the Latin American context. In the ensuing sections, specific attention will be paid to the debate on the content of the international minimum standard and the standard of compensation.

Divergent and even opposing necessities have been construed through international investment law in Latin America. Indeed, the idea according to which international investment law is sourced from bilateral invest-ment treaties, investment clauses contained in free trade agreements and

33 Regarding the tensions between universalism and autonomy see further in this volume, Philip Burton, "Constructing the Calvo Doctrine: Claims to universality and charges of particularism". According to Burton, through the Calvo Doctrine "partici-pants sought to clothe their preferences in the language of universalism, while seeking to expose the particularist predilections of their rivals."

34 Alejandro Alvarez stated that the principles of International American Law were: "Absolute independence of the States without any limitation in their autonomy and independence except by legally consented treaties, political and legal equality of the American States, freedom of each one of the American States to conduct their internal and international affairs in the best way that the States themselves deem con-venient, sincere and duly manifested solidarity among the States of the American con-tinent, equality of individual guarantees, as well as of civil rights between nationals of the American States and foreigners, proscription of the means of physical coercion, that is, of the use of violence as a system of sanction of the norms of International Law, right of the new governments to be recognized by other governments, preva-lence of the law of neutral States over that of States at war, interest in maintaining international relations with the different States of the other continents and of the American States with each other" in Alfredo Cock Arango, *Derecho Internacional Americano* (Imprenta Nacional, Universidad Nacional de Colombia 1948. The new wave of treaties (bit's) has changed "old" customary principles on investment like the permanent sovereignty on natural resources see Rudolf Dolzer and Christoph Schreuer, *Principles of International Investment Law* (2nd edn, Oxford University Press 2012) 5.

customary standards[35] can be used to sustain different necessities. The project of the longed-for image of common prosperity as well as the perception of a continued domination and inequality can be equally sustained.[36] This amplitude allows that both universalistic approaches that present international investment as geared towards to the common good and resistance approaches that vindicate an understanding of investment regimes as individualistic and autonomous can coexist. The ambivalence of the images associated with international investment law is produced through the same discursive device. None of such diverging images are either right or wrong, but, rather, efficacious or inefficacious in how they are experienced. In this regard it could be pointed out that while the autonomy or independent perspective cannot be underestimated, the universalistic approach claiming the shared good of international investment has often been more effective. The former would, for instance, built on the idea that aliens' benefits should never surpass the boundaries and interests of states,[37] whereas the latter perspective would conceal that treatment given to aliens should attain the best and most beneficial practices that the

35 On customary international investment law, see Jean d'Aspremont, "International Customary Investment Law: Story of a Paradox" in Eric de Brabandere and Tarcisio Gazzini, eds., *International Investment Law: The Sources of Rights and Obligations* (Brill 2012) at 5–47; Rudolf Dolzer and Christoph Schreuer, *Principles of International Investment Law* (2nd edn, Oxford University Press 2012) 12; Jorge E. Viñuales, "The source of international investment law" in Samantha Besson and Jean d'Aspremont (eds), The *Oxford Handbook on the Sources of International Law* (Oxford University Press 2018).

36 Rodrigo Polanco Lazo and Anqi Wang "Intra-Latin America Investor-State Dispute Settlement. (2020)" in Julien Chaisse, Leila Choukroune, and Sufian Jusoh (eds), *Handbook of International Investment Law and Policy* (Springer Singapore 2020) Jorge E. Viñuales, "International Investment Law and Natural Resource Governance" (2015) E15 Initiative. Geneva: International Centre for Trade and Sustainable Development (ICTSD) and World Economic Forum, www.e15initiative.org/ accessed 28 September 2020. UNCTAC, "World Investment Report 2015 Reforming International Investment Governance" (2015) E.15.II.D.5, https://unctad.org/en/PublicationsLibrary/wir2015_en.pdf accessed 28 September 2020. For a critical perspective of investment law see Antony Anghie, *Imperialism, sovereignty and the making of International Law* (Cambridge University Press 2004).

37 Xavier Fernández Pons and Claudia Manrique Carpio, "La retirada de algunos países latinoamericanos del ciadi: ¿cuáles son sus consecuencias jurídicas?" in José Manuel Alvarez Zarate (ed), *¿Hacia dónde va América Latina respecto del Derecho internacional de las inversiones?* (Universidad Externado de Colombia 2015). For the implications of international investment law for the governance of natural resources, particularly as regards access, autonomy and independence as well as distribution see Jorge E. Viñuales, "International Investment Law and Natural Resource Governance" (2015) E15 Initiative. Geneva: International Centre for Trade and Sustainable Development (ICTSD) and World Economic Forum, www.e15initiative.org/ accessed 28 September 2020.

same aliens receive elsewhere, even if it goes beyond the edges of national jurisdiction.[38]

The enabling of such diverging necessities particularly resonates in the Latin American context. It is submitted here that a broad comparative reading of bilateral investment treaties' texts makes it possible to identify roughly three kinds of clauses found in conventional investment law that aim at creating a universalistic necessity of international investment in Latin America as a root of common prosperity.

The clause used during the 1980s by the United States in their bilateral investment treaties with Latin American countries openly argues that the regime will "increase prosperity in the two signatory states."[39] Prosperity has been included in some versions of bilateral investment treaties signed between European and Latin American states too, which assert that investment protection regimes are adopted "with the view to promoting individual initiatives of business and favouring economic prosperity of both parties."[40] Yet, most bilateral investment treaties concluded between continental European and Latin American states explicitly affirm that: "such investments will stimulate the flow of capital and technology and the economic development of the Contracting Parties."[41] So, instead of choosing the nebulous concept of prosperity they decided to focus on a term which does not seem to be less vague but that has been more commonly referred

---

38 Roland Kläger, *Fair and Equitable Treatment in International Investment Law* (1st edn, Cambridge University Press 2011) 21 and Rudolf Dolzer and Christoph Schreuer, *Principles of International Investment Law* (2nd edn, Oxford University Press 2012) 5.

39 Treaty between the United States of America and the Republic of Panama Concerning the Treatment and Protection of Investments (signed 27 October 1982, entered into force 30 May 1991) S Treaty Doc No 99–14.

40 Bilateral Agreement for the Promotion and Protection of Investments between the Government of the United Kingdom of Great Britain and Northern Ireland and Republic of Colombia (signed 17 March 2010, entered into force 10 October 2014).

41 Agreement on encouragement and reciprocal protection of investments between the Kingdom of the Netherlands and the Republic of Bolivia (signed 10 March 1992, entered into force 1 November 1994, terminated 1 November 2009); Agreement between the Government of the French Republic and the Government of the Republic of Ecuador on the reciprocal encouragement and protection of investments (signed 7 September 1994, entered into 10 June 1996, terminated 23 May 2018); Agreement Between the Government of The Republic of France and The Government of the United Mexican States on The Reciprocal Promotion and Protection of Investments (signed 12 November 1998, entered into 12 October 2000); Agreement between the Republic of Peru and the Federal Republic of Germany on the Promotion and Reciprocal Protection of Investments (signed 30 January 1995, entered into force 1 May 1997).

to within the UN system such as that of development.[42] Additionally, most recent formulas, like the one included in the widely used US BIT Model, state that investment protection regimes "will stimulate the flow of private capital and economic development of the parties" and that it "will maximize effective utilization of economic resources and improve living standards."[43] The latter not only sets up economic development as the necessity but also says that it will be achieved through the maximum use of resources that will ultimately increase living standards.

This intended necessity sustaining that international investment regimes bring prosperity, economic development or even the improvement of living standards is not only presented as a justificatory scheme for most investment treaties but it is a common trope[44] in mainstream international investment law literature which usually assumes the said benefits as a matter of fact. Indeed, the idea that prosperity, well-being or better living standards follows international investment can be considered one of those beliefs on which international law rests.[45] As beliefs, they are a set of construed and commonly accepted ideas which do not originate from objective criteria – just as mainstream scholarship tend to claim – but which are the product of conceptual manufactures created through discourses that evolve by the interaction of the members comprising the international law epistemic community.[46]

---

42 See critical literature on the very concept of development, Kevin Crow, "The Concept of Development in International Economic Law: Three Definitions and an Inquiry into Origin" (2017) 14 (2) *Manchester J Int'l Econ L* 169; Arturo Escobar, *Encountering Development: The Making and Unmaking of the Third World* (Princeton 1995). Ricardo Contreras, "How the Concept of Development Got Started" (1999) 9 *Transnat'l L & Contemp Probs* 47

43 Treaty between the Government of the United States of America and the Government of [...] concerning the Encouragement and Reciprocal Protection of Investment 2012 (2012) (*United States Model BIT (2012)*). Examples in Latin America include the Treaty between the United States of America and the Oriental Republic of Uruguay concerning the Encouragement and Reciprocal Protection of Investment (signed 4 November 2005, entered into force 31 October 2006) S Treaty Doc No 109–9 (2006), as well as the Treaty between the United States of America and the Argentine Republic Concerning the Reciprocal Encouragement and Protection of Investment (signed 14 November 1991, 20 October 1994) S Treaty Doc No 103–2 (1993), 2 UST 103).

44 Jean d'Aspremont "Unlearning Some Common Tropes" Sufyan Droubi and Jean d'Aspremont (eds), *International Organisations, Non-State Actors and the Formation of Customary International Law* (Manchester University Press 2020).

45 Jean d'Aspremont, *International Law as a Belief System* (University of Manchester 2017).

46 Fabian Cardenas and Jean d'Aspremont 'Epistemic Communities in International Adjudication' (2020) Oxford Public International Law, http://opil.ouplaw.com accessed 29 September 2020.

Although it cannot be denied that Western literature usually led the shaping of such beliefs, it is also certain that its malleable nature allows the presence of opposing perspectives too.[47] Those beliefs are posited through concepts which are later filled by further complementary or even contradictory developments.[48]

Hence, concomitantly with an image of international investment distributing prosperity among participants, there have been also well-known opposing resistance perspectives. TWAILers for instance, with increasing popularity in Latin America, go further to affirm that international investment law provokes the upsurge of imperialism.[49] And although mainstreamers tend to present former contrasting approaches just as old fashioned or odd non mainstream viewpoints which are simply informed as anecdotic elements of the history of development of international investment law,[50] we deem that they exist because they are all feasible discursive outcomes that could be formed thanks to the inherent ambivalence of the regime and its pursued projects. This is possible because of the versatility of the discourses, which turn out being efficacious as they provide the desired meaning that is added to them. The consolidation of an image of common prosperity that originates in universalistic approaches has therefore been seriously contested in Latin America both by scholars as well as by the practice of social movements that continue to gain acceptance within the region.[51] Those not sufficiently estimated critical views emerge also as a result of the two-folded way in which they have experienced international investment in Latin America.[52]

47 Harlan Grant Cohen, "Metaphors of International Law" in Andrea Bianchi and Moshe Hirsch (eds), *International Law's Invisible Frames – Social Cognition and Knowledge Production in International Legal Processes* (Oxford University Press 2020).

48 Harlan Grant Cohen, "Metaphors of International Law" in Andrea Bianchi and Moshe Hirsch (eds), *International Law's Invisible Frames – Social Cognition and Knowledge Production in International Legal Processes* (Oxford University Press 2020).

49 See Antony Anghie, *Imperialism, sovereignty and the making of International Law* (Cambridge University Press 2004).

50 "While early international investment stories often had a post-colonial plot, the emergence of multinational corporations, post-Cold War economic liberalisation, the proliferation of international investment agreements and the establishment of a relatively privatised system of investment dispute settlement procedures have injected the system with new dynamics." in Roland Kläger, *Fair and Equitable Treatment in International Investment Law* (1st edition, Cambridge University Press 2011).

51 On this regard see further in this book Chapter 8 by Adoración Guamán.

52 Xavier Fernández Pons y Claudia Manrique Carpio, 'La retirada de algunos países latinoamericanos del CIADI: ¿cuáles son sus consecuencias jurídicas?' in José Manuel Álvarez Zarate (ed), ¿Hacia dónde va América Latina respecto del Derecho internacional de las inversiones? (Universidad Externado de Colombia 2015); Rodrigo

Henceforth Latin American elite and policy-makers can see international investment not as a prosperity booster but as an obstacle to autonomy and independence too, a vehicle of domination, a one-way mechanism of economic acceleration, or a very expensive regime that is only providing a great economic burden for developing countries.[53]

The extent to which Latin American states tend to perceive international investment nowadays, which is usually aligned with the view of capital-importing states as a whole, can be explained as follows: firstly, they envisage the regime as an apparatus of domination. Although some discourses on international investment law brag on the abundant adoption of bilateral investment treaties by Latin American states which, according to them, supports the customary nature of the standards contained within them, this opposite discourse explains that the adoption of bilateral investment treaties are usually the result of economic, diplomatic, and political pressure which is evident among others in the fact that such capital-importing states do not even have a say in the negotiation of the texts as their only option is to accept the terms, conditions, and wording of the treaty models

Polanco Lazo, Anqi Wang "Intra-Latin America Investor-State Dispute Settlement." (2020) in Julien Chaisse, Leila Choukroune and Sufian Jusoh (eds) *Handbook of International Investment Law and Policy* (Springer Singapore 2020); Jorge E Viñuales, "International Investment Law and Natural Resource Governance" (2015) E15 Initiative. Geneva, International Centre for Trade and Sustainable Development (ICTSD) and World Economic Forum, www.e15initiative.org/ accessed 28 September 2020. UNCTAC, "World Investment Report 2015 Reforming International Investment Governance" (2015) E.15.II.D.5, https://unctad.org/en/PublicationsLibrary/wir2015_en.pdf accessed 28 September 2020; Howard Mann, "Reconceptualizing international investment law: its role in sustainable development" (2013) 17 (2) *Lewis & Clark Law Review*; Sonia Rodríguez Jiménez, "El CIADI frente a Argentina, México, Ecuador y Bolivia. Una actualización," Biblioteca Jurídica Virtual del Instituto de Investigaciones Jurídicas de la Universidad Nacional Autónoma de México (UNAM), 191. https://archivos.juridicas.unam.mx/www/bjv/libros/6/2815/13.pdf accessed 28 September 2020. See Chapter 9 by Sufyan Droubi, Cecilia Juliana Flores Elizondo and Raphael Heffron in this volume.

53 María Teresa Gutiérrez Haces and Adelina Quintero Sánchez, "Hacia la construcción de un régimen internacional de protección a la inversión extranjera," Biblioteca Jurídica Virtual del Instituto de Investigaciones Jurídicas de la Universidad Nacional Autónoma de México (UNAM) (2016); Karen Remmer, "Investment Treaty Arbitration in Latin America" (2019) 54(4) *Latin American Research Review* 795; Natasha Suñé, "Arbitraje en América Latina. Consideraciones en materia de inversiones" (2015) 3 (5) *Rev. Secr. Trib. Perm. Revis* 191; Attila Tanzi, Alessandra Asteriti, Rodrigo Polanco Lazo and Paolo Turrini (eds), *International Investment Law in Latin America: problems and prospects* (Nijhoff International Investment Law Series Vol 5, Brill 2016).

unilaterally drafted by capital-exporting states.[54] Secondly, they also sustain that a treaty that purports equality between unequal parties only aggravates inequality. So although investment treaties are supposedly beneficial for both parties, which implies the possibility for investors of the two states to invest in the other, it happens that investment only occurs in one direction and only investors from the developed state actually come to do business in the developing state.[55] It rarely happens the other way around with recently emerged exceptions like Brazil becoming a capital-exporting state vis-á-vis other Latin American states.[56]

Moreover, many Latin American elite and policy-makers want to make visible the economic burden that international investment jurisdiction has meant for them. And although international investment was brought as an attractive mechanism for prosperity and better living, Latin American states are nowadays involved in international investment disputes in which investors pursue the payment of big compensations that have a considerable negative impact on the economies of the respondents.

Twenty-nine percent of the cases registered with the ICSID place Latin America as the region with more investment arbitration cases against it.[57] The increase in claims seems to be directly proportional to the ratification of investment protection treaties by Latin American countries. In the 1990s international investment policies encouraged the liberalization of the economies, opening up to foreign investment in Latin American states through the signing of treaties[58] that are currently the subject of cases pending worth $40 billion (USD $40,000,000,000) and that in concluded cases have meant the payment of over thirty one billion dollars.[59] In 69 percent of the cases in which a Latin

---

54 Rodrigo Polanco Lazo and Anqi Wang, "Intra-Latin America Investor-State Dispute Settlement" in Julien Chaisse, Leila Choukroune and Sufian Jusoh (eds), *Handbook of International Investment Law and Policy* (Springer Singapore 2020); Rumana Islam, *The Fair and Equitable Treatment (FET) Standard un International Investment Arbitration: Developing countries in context* (1st edn, Springer 2018).

55 With regards to the reasons why Latin American states entered into the first BITs generation despite such economic inequality see Lauge N. Skovgaard Poulsen, *Bounded rationality and economic diplomacy: The politics of investment treaties in developing countries* (Cambridge University Press 2015).

56 In this regard see Chapter 4 by Leonardo V P de Oliveira and Marcus Spangenberger within this volume.

57 ICSID Caseload – Statistics.

58 Wilson A. Mamani Prieto, "La dinámica de los acuerdos internacionales de inversión en los andinos" (2013) 13 *Anuario Mexicano de Derecho Internacional* 549, 582.

59 Cecilia Olivet and Bettina Müller, "Juggling crises, Latin America's battle with COVID-19 hampered by investment arbitration cases" (Transnational Institute 25 August 2020). Recovered from https://longreads.tni.org/jugglingcrises

American country has been involved, investors have succeeded.[60] Likewise, at the ICSID, 31 percent of the claims against a Latin American State end with an arbitration award that grants the applicant's claims in whole or in part.[61] Within the region Argentina ranks first with 61 open cases and two more recent applications against,[62] followed by Venezuela, Mexico, Ecuador, Bolivia, and Peru, which together accumulate 73 percent of the claims.[63]

All those heavy burdens generated by investment jurisdictions have enabled the experience of distinct necessities in Latin America. They have nurtured discourses that inevitably lead to exclusive agendas of autonomy and independence, which have been reinforced after the wave of withdrawals from investment jurisdictions by Latin American states.[64] So while they have been caused in part thanks to the economic burden that investment regimes have signified, they have also made possible the departure from universalistic discourses supported on the allegedly common prosperity of all.

Opposing necessities of international investment law in Latin America are possible due to the ambivalence of the discourses that sustain them. They can take the twist that international lawyers want them to take, no matter if they work for either capital-exporting or capital-importing states, private companies, civil society, indigenous communities or academic institutions affiliated either with the mainstream or critical thinking.[65]

The international minimum standard

The ambivalent relationship towards universality that has allowed discourses of resistance and independence in international investment law as a whole has

60 ISDS En Números, Impactos de las Demandas de Arbitraje de Inversores contra Estados de América Latina y El Caribe. Recovered from: https://isds-americalatina. org/en-numeros/
61 ICSID Caseload – Statistics.
62 "Los reclamos recientes se suman a un historial extenso de juicios perdidos que exigieron al país el pago de sumas millonarias y en dólares." Alan Soria Guadalupe, "La Argentina es el país más demandado del mundo ante el Ciadi" (La Nación 3 Febrero 2020) Recovered from https://isds.bilaterals.org/?la-argentina-es-el-pais-mas&lang=en
63 ISDS En Números, Impactos de las Demandas de Arbitraje de Inversores contra Estados de América Latina y El Caribe. Recuperado de: https://isds-americalatina. org/en-numeros/
64 It has been argued that the recent withdrawal of Bolivia, Ecuador and Venezuela have boosted a backlash against investment law in Latin America. See David Ma, "A BIT Unfair? An Illustration of the Backlash Against International Arbitration in Latin America" (2012) 2 *Journal of Dispute Resolution* 571.
65 On this regard see Part II – The Mosaic of Non-State Actors in this volume.

made also possible the allocation of various signified that can be loaded in the signifiers of the regime itself. Such ambivalence has had effects in the way that the most fundamental principles of international investment law are expressed or projected. They can be also oriented in furtherance of divergent agendas, either of inclusion or exclusion, universalistic or autonomic. One of the core principles of international investment law, such as the minimum standard, has not been immune to this phenomenon provided the discordant meaning that is usually attached to it. Those opposing discourses are manifested either in the idea that aliens should only receive the treatment that nationals get within a domestic jurisdiction or in the belief that aliens have rights that go beyond what national legislations provides.

A view that has proved efficacious on giving meaning to the international minimum standard sustains that international investment is somehow safeguarded by a set of rules developed through "general international law."[66] According to it, investors are granted a standard of treatment that should be respected in a foreign country even if domestic laws provide a smaller range

---

66 Sometimes the use of the term "general international law" is used to argue that a certain customary rule needs no demonstration just because it is "obvious" or undisputed. For uses of the "general international law" in ICJ jurisprudence see *Elettronica Sicula SpA (ELSI) (United States v Italy)* (Judgment, Merits) [1989] ICJ Rep 15, para 111; "... the international standard is nothing else than a set of rules, correlated to each other and deriving from one particular norm of general international law, namely that the treatment of alien is regulated by the law of nations." Andreas H. Roth, *The Minimum Standard of International Law Applied to Aliens* (Leiden, Sijthoff 1949). In Bilateral investment treaties reference has been made to a set of rules of international law to refer to compensation for loses "in respect of restitution, indemnification, compensation or other settlement, treatment consistent with international law and no less favourable than that it accords to its own investors or to investors of any third State" Agreement Between the Government of Canada and the Government of the Republic of Argentina for the promotion and protection of investment (signed 5 November 1991, entered into force 29 April 1992). In the event of disputes between the Contracting Parties "The provisions of this Treaty shall remain in force even in the event of disputes between the Contracting Parties, without prejudice to the right to take such interim measures as are permitted under the general rules of international law" Treaty between the Federal Republic of Germany and the Republic of Haiti Concerning the Promotion and Reciprocal Protection of Capital Investment (signed 14 August 1973, entered into force 1 December 1975) 1016 UNTS 83. Also, some treaties have alluded to a set of international customary norms which protect investment as "Article 10.5: Minimum Standard of Treatment: 1. Each Party shall accord to covered investments treatment in accordance with customary international law, including fair and equitable treatment and full protection and security. 2. For greater certainty, paragraph 1 prescribes the customary international law minimum standard of treatment of aliens as the minimum standard of treatment to be afforded to covered investments. (...)" Colombia – United States Trade Promotion Agreement (signed 22 November 2006; entered into force 15 May 2012) 22 November 2006.

of protection.[67] It is claimed to be an international legal rule that accompanies investors wherever they go in spite of the mandates of domestic legal orders. So, in case of incongruity between national legislation regulating foreign investors and such standard, the latter should always prevail.[68]

The allocation of meaning has not only been an issue on the minimum standard itself but in what it specifically entails as well. In this respect, it is common to refer to the US BIT Model in which Article 5.1 provides the following: "Each party shall accord to covered investments treatment in accordance with customary international law, including fair and equitable treatment and full protection and security."[69] This model incarnates the dominant perspective – often associated with capital-exporting states' view– suggesting that the minimum standard consists of fair and equitable treatment together with protection and security.[70] However there have been also views that perceive fair and equitable treatment and protection and security as conventional additions to the minimum standard just as it is suggested by the UNCTAD Secretary study which stresses the lack of uniformity contained in investment treaties as well as in the disagreeing perspectives of capital-importing states.[71]

67 Some definitions found in doctrine are: This notion "provides that international law requires States to afford a common standard of treatment to aliens in their territory, and that international law does not obligate States to treat aliens and its nationals equally" in Hollin Dickerson, "Minimum Standards" (2010) Oxford Public International Law http://opil.ouplaw.com accessed 9 September 2020; "(...) the international minimum standard sets a number of basic rights established by international law that States must grant to aliens, independent of the treatment accorded to their own citizens" in Organisation for Economic Co-operation and Development (OECD) "Fair and Equitable Treatment Standard in International Investment Law" (2004) Working Papers on International Investment, http://dx.doi.org/10.1787/675702255 435 accessed 11 September 2020.

68 Regarding the prevalence of international law over national or domestic law, e.g. *Accordance with International Law of the Unilateral Declaration of Independence in Respect of Kosovo* (Advisory Opinion) [2010] ICJ 141, 2010 ICJ Reports 403 and *Applicability of the Obligation to Arbitrate Under Section 21 of the United Nations Headquarters Agreement of 26 June 1947* (Advisory Opinion) [1988] ICJ Rep 12; Eileen Denza, "The relationship between international and national law" in Malcolm D. Evans (ed), *International Law* (1st edition Oxford University Press 2003) and Tim Hillier, *Sourcebook on Public International Law* (Routledge-Cavendish 1998).

69 *United States Model BIT (2012)* (n 43).

70 Giorgio Sacerdoti, "Bilateral Treaties and Multilateral Instruments on Investment Protection (Volume 269)" in Collected Courses of the Hague Academy of International Law http://dx.doi.org/10.1163/1875–8096_pplrdc_A9789041111111_02 accessed 9 September 2020. "OECD Draft Convention on the Protection of Foreign Property" (1968) 7 ILM 117 art 1.

71 UNCTAC, "Fair and Equitable Treatment" (1999) UNCTAD/ITE/IIT/11 (Vol III) https://unctad.org/en/Docs/psiteiitd11v3.en.pdf accessed 28 September 2020.

Yet, it is this lack of a unified or commonly accorded meaning that has allowed the resilience of the standard. According to Kläger "this vagueness is both a blessing and a curse for international investment law. While it ensures the adaptability and flexibility of the investment protection standards, it also entails a certain degree of indeterminacy and even vacuity."[72] However, the ambivalence of the minimum standard has not come into existence without precedent as it has been positioned in international law gradually in a history distinguished by the clashes of experienced necessities between capital-exporting and capital-importing states.[73] The immediate historical roots of the minimum standard will demonstrate why it is a flexible concept whose meaning has been inconsistently assigned by elites and policy-makers to promote different kinds of agendas.

It is commonly argued in the literature that the investment protection regime finds its roots in the international protection of aliens abroad,[74] the application of which gave rise to international litigation which – as is well-known – proved instrumental in the elaboration of a mechanism of state responsibility,[75] first seen in the form of diplomatic protection. The protection of aliens found in international law allegedly took the form of an "international minimum standard"[76] to which aliens abroad were purportedly entitled. It will not come as a surprise that, at that time, aliens falling under such protection were first and foremost investors.[77] It is true that these rules on the protection of aliens were not limited to the protection of their property against unlawful expropriation but also enshrined standards

72 Roland Kläger, *Fair and Equitable Treatment in International Investment Law* (1st edn, Cambridge University Press 2011) 3.

73 Kate Miles, *The origins of International Investment Law, Empire, Environment and the safeguarding of capital* (Cambridge Studies in International and Comparative Law 2013). Antony Anghie, *Imperialism, sovereignty and the making of International Law* (Cambridge University Press 2004).

74 Andreas H. Roth, *The Minimum Standard of International Law Applied to Aliens* (Leiden, Sijthoff, 1949); Edwin Montefiore Borchard, *The Diplomatic Protection of Citizens Abroad, or, the law of international claims* (Banks Law Pub 1915).

75 See gen. the first report Report on International Responsibility by Mr F V Garcia-Amador, Special Rapporteur, A/CN.4/96, *Yearbook of the International Law Commission,* 1956, vol II.

76 See also Edwin Borchard, "The Minimum Standard of Treatment of Aliens" (1940) 3 (4) *Michigan Law Review* 445; see also Andrew Paul Newcombe and Lluís Paradell, *Law and Practice of Investment Law – Standards of Treatment* (Kluwer Law International 2009) 11–13.

77 Charles Leben, "La Théorie du contrat d'Etat et l'évolution du droit international des investissements" (2003) 302 *Collected Courses of the Hague Academy of International Law* (2003) 126.

for the treatment of aliens regarding their life and security as well.[78] Yet, they also benefited investors and provided some elementary protection to the international flux of capitals.

Whilst it is commonly argued that the international minimum standard came to constitute, in the late nineteenth and early twentieth century, a customary international rule also benefiting foreign investment, the content of the protection so offered to aliens remained in limbo and the object of incommensurable controversy, thereby putting into question the customary status commonly attributed to that rule.[79] Indeed, capital-importing states opposed any international standard that would depart from the treatment reserved to nationals. The opposition of capital-importing states to the idea of an international minimum standard found its expression in the *Calvo Doctrine* according to which no state should be required to offer more protection to foreign investors than that offered to its own nationals: as long as there was no discrimination against foreign-investor, or infringement of any international legal rule.[80] Proponents of this national treatment were bolstered by the Russian revolution and the decrees of nationalization adopted by the Bolchevik governments which drew no distinction between Russian nationals and foreign-owned property. Although that instrument never entered into force, an expression of that position is also found in the famous 1933 Convention on the Rights and Duties of States signed at the Seventh Pan-American Conference (the so-called Montevideo Convention).[81] At the other end of the spectrum, capital-exporting states contended national treatment was deemed insufficient. To them, the treatment that a State would reserve to its own citizens could be far lower than that generally expected by capital-exporting states.[82] This controversy as to the content of the

---

78 Stephan W Schill, *The Multilateralization of International Investment Law* (Cambridge Univeristy Press 2009) 25; Andreas H Roth, *The Minimum Standard of International Law Applied to Aliens* (Leiden, Sijthoff 1949) 127; Edwin Borchard, *Diplomatic Protection of Citizens Abroad* (Banks Law Pub 1915).

79 On the debate on the customary status of the international minimum standard, see Jean d'Aspremont, "International Customary Investment Law: Story of a Paradox" in Eric de Brabandere and Tarcisio Gazzini (eds), *International Investment Law: The Sources of Rights and Obligations* (Brill 2012) at 5–47.

80 See Alwyn V Freeman, "Recent Aspects of the Calvo Doctrine and the Challenge to International Law" (1946) 40 *AJIL* 131; see also Wil D. Verwey and Nico J. Schrijver, "The Taking of Foreign Property Under International Law: A New Legal Perspective" (1984) 15 *Netherlands Yearbook of International Law* 3, 96; Andrew Paul Newcombe and Lluís Paradell, *Law and Practice of Investment Law – Standards of Treatment* (Kluwer Law International 2009) 13–14.

81 See article 9 of the Convention on the Rights and Duties of States signed at the Seventh Pan-American Conference (Montevideo Convention, 1933) 70 *AJIL* 445 (1970).

82 Surya P. Subedi, *International Investment Law: Reconciling Policy and Principle* (Hart Publishing 2008) 7–11. On the reasons for offering a better treatment to

international minimum standard came to a head in the framework of the League of Nations' codification enterprise, which in 1930, failed in codifying the law on responsibility for treatment of aliens.

The grave divergences as to the content of the protection to which aliens abroad were entitled did not seem sufficient to thwart the belief of a customary protection of aliens abroad, including of foreign investors. In fact, notwithstanding the profound disagreements between capital-exporting states and capital-importing states international investment lawyers never balked at affirming the customary character of the international minimum standards which foreign investors were entitled to as all aliens abroad. The unchartered waters in which the elementary protection of foreign capital through the international minimum standard was left never constituted, in the eyes of investment lawyers, an obstacle to the affirmation of a customary international minimum standard. In the absence of any prospect to regulate foreign investment through conventions between capital-exporting and capital-importing states, customary international law was elevated into the natural medium by virtue of which protection of capital would be elaborated. Customary international law was not only considered the natural source of the law of investment protection. It was also seen as being able to withstand the wide-ranging dissonance echoed in the world stage as to which protection foreign investors ought to be offered.

The history of development of investment protection is thus also the story of the development of a *divergence-proof customary regime* resting on an extremely minimalistic threshold of convergence in terms of practice and *opinio juris*. But, in the pre-1945 history of investment law, there is more than a conception of custom that falls short of a converging general practice and *opinio juris*.[83] The reconstructions of the investment protection of that time under the banner of customary international law also betrays a conception of *indeterminacy-proof customary law*, the idea that some indeterminate standards can grow into customary rule. The best illustration thereof probably lies in the finding of the famous 1926 *Neer* case, which is deemed to constitute the expression of customary international law.[84] Just as it has been suggested that its original formula did not freeze

---

non-nationals, see ECHR, *James and others v. The United Kingdom*, Judgment, ECHR No 8793/79 (Judgment, 21 February 1986), para 63.

83 See gen. Jean d'Aspremont, "International Customary Investment Law: Story of a Paradox," in Eric de Brabandere and Tarcisio Gazzini (eds), *International Investment Law: The Sources of Rights and Obligations* (Brill 2012) at 5–47.

84 "The treatment of an alien, in order to constitute, in order to constitute an international delinquency, should amount to an outrage, to bad faith, to wilful neglect of duty, or to an insufficiency of governmental action so far short of international standards that every reasonable and impartial man would readily recognize its

in time but keeps evolving as "both the substantive and procedural rights of the individual in international law have undergone considerable development' since the 1920s."[85] It is accordingly fair to say that the conception of sources of international investment law that emerges from the pre-1945 era of investment protection thus bespeaks a very permissive and loose concept of customary law.

This is so precisely because in spite of the aforementioned substantive ambiguity it is commonly asserted that the minimum standard of treatment is customary international law.[86] On this regard it should be noted that it is not rare in international law to find rules whose customary nature is strongly "campaigned"[87] even before knowing (or letting know) what they mean or entail.[88] The minimum standard is one of such cases. So the allegedly customary rule ends up existing after mainstream perspectives assure it does.

---

insufficiency." *L. F. H. Neer and Pauline Neer (U.S.A.) v. United Mexican States*, Mexico/USA General Claims Commission (Decision, 15 October 1926) 4 RIAA 60, 61–62.

85 *Mondev International Ltd. v. United States of America*, ICSID Case No. ARB(AF)/99/ 2 (Award, 11 October 2002) (*Mondev v USA* (Award 2002)).

86 See in this sense "Once it has admitted a foreign investment, a host state is subject to a minimum standard of customary international law" (Rudolf Dolzer and Christoph Schreuer, *Principles of International Investment Law* (2nd edn, Oxford University Press 2012)). "Abundant precedents have determined the existence of a minimum standard of treatment in favour of aliens as part of customary international law" Raúl Emilio Vinuesa, "National Treatment, Principle" (2011) Oxford Public International Law http://opil.ouplaw.com accessed 9 September 2020. "The international minimum standard is a principle found in customary international law that governs the treatment of aliens. It is based on the principle that State[s] have obligations to aliens independent of any obligations they have more generally under international human rights law" Hollin Dickerson, "Minimum Standards" (2010) Oxford Public International Law http://opil.ouplaw.com accessed 9 September 2020. "32. The international minimum standard is a norm of customary international law which governs the treatment of aliens, by providing for a minimum set of principles which States, regardless of their domestic legislation and practices, must respect when dealing with foreign nationals and their property" (Organisation for Economic Co-operation and Development (OECD), "Fair and Equitable Treatment Standard in International Investment Law" (2004) Working Papers on International Investment http://dx.doi.org/10.1787/675702255435 accessed 11 September 2020).

87 Fabian Cardenas, "Custom as the Product of Successful Argumentative Campaigns" Sufyan Droubi and Jean d'Aspremont (eds), *Non-State Actors and the Formation of Customary International* (Manchester University Press 2020).

88 Some notions of international law have been classified by the legal literature as international custom, but there is still debate about what they are or what they exactly mean. For instance, the crime of aggression, the crime of genocide and the precautionary principle. For a comprehensive analysis, see Sergey Sayapin, *Aggression in*

Ultimately, the debate on whether the standard is or is not custom does not depend on the demonstration of state practice and *opinio juris* supporting it but on the documentary display of opposing perspectives.[89] Mainstream doctrine usually asserts as a matter of fact the standard's customary nature,[90] which is naturally reaffirmed – though not demonstrated – by some arbitral awards[91] while critical third world perspectives, like those consistently claimed in Latin America, tend to deny it.[92] The former's reasons are limited

International Criminal Law, Historical development, comparative analysis and present state (Springer 2014), William A. Schabas, *Genocide in International Law. The Crime of Crimes* (2nd edition, Cambridge University Press 2009) and Caroline E. Foster, *Science and the Precautionary Principle in International Courts and Tribunals, Expert Evidence, Burden of Proof and Finality* (Cambridge University Press 2011).

89 Fabian Cardenas, "¿Un caso de "volver al 'futuro"?: Las Conclusiones sobre la Identificación del Derecho Internacional Consuetudinario de la Comisión de Derecho Internacional de la ONU" (2020) *Vniversitas* 69 https://ssrn.com/abstract=3635736 accessed 29 September 2020.

90 Organisation for Economic Co-operation and Development (OECD) "Fair and Equitable Treatment Standard in International Investment Law" (2004) Working Papers on International Investment http://dx.doi.org/10.1787/675702255435 accessed 11 September 2020; Rudolf Dolzer and Christoph Schreuer, *Principles of International Investment Law* (2nd edn, Oxford University Press 2012); Raúl Emilio Vinuesa, "National Treatment, Principle" (2011) Oxford Public International Law http://opil.ouplaw.com accessed 9 September 2020; Hollin Dickerson, "Minimum Standards" (2010) Oxford Public International Law http://opil.ouplaw.com accessed 9 September 2020.

91 In *Glamis Gold, Ltd. v United States* the arbitral tribunal stated "563. There is no disagreement among the State Parties to the NAFTA, nor the Parties to this arbitration, that the requirement of fair and equitable treatment in Article 1105 is to be understood by reference to the customary international law minimum standard of treatment of aliens." Indeed, the Free Trade Commission ("FTC") clearly states, in its binding Notes of Interpretation on July 31, 2001, that "Article 1105(1) prescribes the customary international law minimum standard of treatment of aliens as the minimum standard of treatment to be afforded to investments of investors of another Party. (…) The protection afforded by Article 1105 must be distinguished from that provided for in Article 1102 on National Treatment" (*Glamis Gold Ltd. v. United States of America*, UNCITRAL (Award, 8 June 2009) para 563). See also *Mondev v USA* (Award 2002) (n 85) para 111, 114, 115.

92 Manuel R Garcia-Mora, "The Calvo Clause in Latin American Constitutions and International Law" (1950) 33 *Marq L Rev* 205; Stephan Schill, The Multilateralization of International Investment Law (Cambridge University Press, 2009) 27–28. Rodrigo Polanco Lazo, "Lessons Learned and Lessons to Be Learned: Investment Law & Development for Developed Countries" (2014). SELA (Seminario en Latinoamérica de Teoría Constitucional y Política) Papers 136. https://digitalcommons.law.yale.edu/yls_sela/136 accessed 28 September 2020; "[T]he universal acceptance of the customary concept of the minimum standard is still not certain, even today" in Roland Kläger, *Fair and Equitable Treatment in International Investment Law* (1st edition, Cambridge University Press 2011).

to the existence of investment instruments containing the standard[93] while the latter emphasize their constant and continuing opposition.[94] The various signifiers of the minimum standard are possibly due to the ambivalence of such discourses which can be accommodated to prompt either universalism or particularism.

Although it is not the main purpose of this chapter to take sides on the actual nature of the allegedly "inveterate" standards of international investment law, it is one of its main claims that the sources sustaining the regime does not offer consistency precisely because they are ambivalent discourses that allow the production of different and even opposing necessities which end up being efficacious as long as they result instrumental in the furtherance of dissimilar agendas. In spite of the common reference made by mainstream literature on international investment law to the orthodox catalogue of the sources of international law (namely, treaties, custom, and principles)[95] what we see is a number of investment treaties supposedly operating within the boundaries of a not well recognizable minimum standard claimed to be customary. So what is essentially a conventional regime, which in principle should operate in light of the law of the treaties, ends up being extended to fill all unforeseeable vacuums through professedly customary international law. As for the identification criteria of the latter it should be reiterated that it is reduced to a yes and no confrontation which normally overlooks the explicit manifestation of opposing views like the one presented by critical Latin American perspectives that do not indulge the minimum standard's customary status but preponderate more familiar principles like the permanent sovereignty over natural resources and the validity of the Calvo Doctrine.

93	"Since the beginning of the twentieth century the preponderant doctrine has supported an 'international minimum standard'. A majority of the states represented at the Hague Codification Conference endorsed that standard, and it was affirmed in the Declaration on Permanent Sovereignty over Natural Resources in 1962. The standard is articulated in bilateral investment treaties, and has been applied by many tribunals and claims commissions." James Crawford. *Brownlie's Principles of Public International Law* (8th edn, Oxford 2018).

94	Manuel R. Garcia-Mora, "The Calvo Clause in Latin American Constitutions and International Law" (1950) 33 *Marq L Rev* 205. Stephan Schill, *The Multilateralization of International Investment Law* (Cambridge University Press 2009) 27–28.

95	Rudolf Dolzer and Christoph Schreuer, *Principles of International Investment Law* (2nd edn, Oxford University Press 2012); James R. Crawford, *Brownlie's Principles of Public International Law* (8th Edition, Oxford University Press 2012), Hugh Thirlway, "The sources of international law" in Malcolm D. Evans (ed) *International Law* (1st edition Oxford University Press 2003) and Tim Hillier, *Sourcebook on Public International Law* (Routledge-Cavendish 1998).

In this regard it is worth noting that the process of alleged consolidation of the minimum standard concurs with the changing circumstances experienced through the 90s by Latin America. Thus, while modern Latin American international lawyers were more unbound to actively promote an autonomy-and-independence-oriented perspective that hampered the customary recognition of the minimum standard, end of the century lawyers were somehow tied by new neoliberal agendas that reached the region and that were usually linked with an opening for investment from the north. That scenario was used as an opportunity for capital-exporting states not only to pressurize the increased signing of bilateral investment treaties and free trade agreements but to assure the customary consolidation of the minimum standard as a result of a discourse that turned out to be more efficacious and prevalent for a time. However, it is well evident that the standing of opposing perspectives on the very existence and actual meaning of the minimum standard of treatment is proof of its ambivalent nature and its corresponding efficacy to sustain divergent agendas.

The standard of compensation

Following the foregoing argumentative pattern, various signified have been also allocated to the standard of compensation to promote either universality or agendas of resistance positioned through independence and particularism. Even the alleged customary international nature of the standard of compensation has been proposed thanks to the possibility that those ambivalent discourses have to create alternative necessities. The manufacturing process of this standard has followed the same heuristic pattern both in general international law as well as in international investment law.

Compensation can be claimed either as a consequence of an unlawful or a lawful act of expropriation. On the one hand, the general approach to compensation fundamentally conceived as a modality of reparation when restitution is not possible after the commission of an international wrongful act, is deemed to demand the payment of "any financially assessable damage including loss of profits insofar as it is established."[96] Doctrine and tribunals have appropriated the general concepts of these Articles as customary international law, including the standard of compensation. This perspective has been positioned in spite of the earlier reluctance of states to be involved in an

---

96   Draft Articles on Responsibility of States for Internationally Wrongful Acts, adopted by the Commission at its fifty-third session in 2001 (Final Outcome) (adopted 3 August 2001) UN Doc A/56/10, 43, UN Doc A/RES/56/83, Annex, UN Doc A/ CN.4/L.602/Rev.1, GAOR 56th Session Supp 10, 43.

international treaty on international responsibility and as a result of the documentary support received to the latest work of the ILC.[97]

On the other hand, and with regards to the standard of compensation following a lawful expropriation, it is well-known that investment lawyers were quick to see in the so-called Hull formula an expression of customary international law.[98] This standard of conduct is extracted from a letter written by the US Secretary of State Cordell Hull to Eduardo Hay, the Mexican minister of foreign affairs who stated that "the rules of international law allowed expropriation of foreign property, but required 'prompt, adequate and effective compensation.' "[99] So the payment of financially assessable damage does not necessarily result from the verification of an international wrongful act but just as a consequence of expropriation in spite of it being in accordance with or against international law. Compensation from this standpoint would not necessarily be a consequence of international responsibility.

However, it could be said that the particular approach of the Hull formula coexisted with the Permanent Court of International Justice's general approach taken in the Chorzow Factory Case, which supports the principle of compensation with a view of repairing the consequences of an illegal act, pinpointing the need to proof the necessary wrongfulness of the act of expropriation.[100]

97 Case Concerning *Ahmadou Sadio Diallo (Guinea v Democratic Republic of the Congo)* (Judgment, Preliminary Objections) [2007] ICJ Rep 582, at para 39. See ICSID tribunal decisions as *CMS Gas Transmission Company v. The Argentine Republic*, ICSID Case No. ARB/01/8 (Award, 12 May 2005), *Enron Creditors Recovery Corporation (formerly Enron Corporation) and Ponderosa Assets, L.P. v. Argentine Republic*, ICSID Case No. ARB/01/3 (Award, 22 May 2007), and *Sempra Energy International v. Argentine Republic*, ICSID Case No. ARB/02/16 (Award, 28 September 2007). Stephen Mathias, "The Work of the International Law Commission on Identification of Customary International Law: A View from the Perspective of the Office of Legal Affairs" (2016) 15 *Chinese J Int'l L* 17.

98 See the 1938 exchange of notes between the US Secretary of State, Cordell Hull and the Mexican Minister of Foreign Affairs in connection to the expropriation of agrarian land and oil fields owned by American citizens in Mexico in the 1920s and 1930s, reproduced in Hackworth, *Digest of International Law* (Vol III, et seq 1942) 655. See gen. Jean d'Aspremont, "International Customary Investment Law: Story of a Paradox," in Eric de Brabandere and Tarcisio Gazzini (eds), *International Investment Law: The Sources of Rights and Obligations* (Brill 2012) at 5–47.

99 Andreas F Lowenfeld, *International Economic Law Series* (2nd edn, Oxford University Press 2008) 476–481.

100 *Factory At Chorzów (Germany v Poland)* (Judgment, Claim for Indemnity, Merits, Judgment No 13) [1928] PCIJ Series A No 17 "the essential principle contained in the actual notion of an illegal act – a principle which seems to be established by international practice and in particular by the decisions of arbitral tribunals – is that

Here at this point it is already possible to appreciate the coexistence of different necessities flowing from the same signifier. On the other hand, the counter-balancing Mexican position – reasserting the traditional view of capital-importing states that the only treatment an alien was entitled to, was the treatment reserved to nationals and according to which the aggrieved investor can only claim national treatment before national courts – was not deemed a serious impediment to the existence of such a customary rule. Under the name of customary international law, the views of capital-exporting states were thus said to have prevailed in the pre-1945 world order,[101] irrespective of the absence of any acquiescence by capital-importing states.[102] And once more when international investment law was faced with a clash of opposing perspectives, mainstream scholarship took sides and alleged the existence of such customary rule just out of their own assertion. If the mainstream two-element approach to customary international law would have prevailed in this regard we could not but witness totally opposing practice – if any – and *opinio juris* hindering the emergence of the rule. However, we have instead mainstream scholarship asserting compensation's customary nature that downplays contrary opinions just as curious historical anecdotes. So the prevailing necessity did not appear as a consequence of a static formula but as a product of a particular efficacious discourse, which in this case was aligned with the mainstream view usually defended by capital-exporting states.

reparation must, as far as possible, wipe out all the consequences of the illegal act and re-establish the situation which would, in all probability, have existed if that act had not been committed. Restitution in kind, or, if this is not possible, payment of a sum corresponding to the value which a restitution in kind would bear."

101 See e.g. Steffen Hindelang, "Bilateral Investment Treaties, Custom and a Healthy Investment Climate – the Question of Whether BITS Influence Customary International Law Revisited" (2004) 5 (5) *Journal of World Investment & Trade* 789.

102 For some doubts on the customary character of customary international law before the Second World War, see Patrick Juillard, "L'évolution des sources du droit des investissements" (1994) 250 Collected Courses /VI 76. According to Juillard, the only protection that could have existed in customary international law was the protection of goods and not of capitals. For a similar challenge to the prevailing idea that the pre-1945 practice manifested the existence of customary rules in terms of a standard of compensation, see Stephan W. Schill, *The Multilateralization of International Investment Law* (Cambridge University Press 2009) 28 (S. Schill talks about the "shaky foundations of the standards of customary international law with regard to the protection of aliens and their property"). It is interesting to note that the arbitral tribunal in *CME Czech Republic BV v Czech Republic* also seemed to recognize that the Hull formula never secured consensus until the last decades of the twentieth century. See *CME Czech Republic B.V. v. The Czech Republic*, UNCITRAL (Final Award, 14 March 2003), para 497.

It did not come as a surprise that the distrust in the international community as to the standards of treatment afforded to foreign investment persisted after the second world war. Even though Resolution 1803 on the Permanent Sovereignty over Natural Resources of 14 December 1962[103] can be read as a tentative compromise between the positions of capital-exporting and capital importing countries by not excluding "appropriate compensation,"[104] UN General Assembly Resolution 1301 of 1 May 1974 on the Declaration on the Establishment of the New International Economic Order[105] incontrovertibly backed away from the idea of an obligation to provide compensation for the expropriation of foreigners and did away with the obligation to pay compensation,[106] a position that was later repeated by General Assembly Resolution 3281 of 12 December 1974 on the Charter of Economic Rights and Duties of States.[107] So it was evident that not the

103 See gen. Stephan W Schill, *The Multilateralization of International Investment Law* (Cambridge University Press 2009) 37–38; see Stephen M. Schwebel, "The Story of the UN's Declaration on Permanent Sovereignty over Natural Resources" (1963) 49 *American Bar Association Journal* 463; Karol N. Gess "Permanent Sovereignty over Natural Resources: An analytical review on the United Nations declaration and its genesis" (1964) 13 (2) *International & Comparative Law Quarterly* 398. Surya P. Subedi, *International Investment Law: Reconciling Policy and Principle* (Hart Publishing 2008) 21–23; Rudolf Dolzer, "Permanent Sovereignty over Natural Resources and Economic Decolonization" (1986) 7 *Human Rights Law Journal* 217.

104 See UNGA Resolution 1803 (XVII) 1962. "Nationalization, expropriation or requisitioning shall be based on grounds or reasons of public utility, security or the national interest which are recognized as overriding purely individual or private interests, both domestic and foreign. In such cases the owner shall be paid appropriate compensation, in accordance with the rules in force in the State taking such measures and in accordance with international law. In any case where the question of compensation gives rise to a controversy, the national jurisdiction of the State taking such measures shall be exhausted. However, upon agreement by sovereign States and other parties concerned, settlement of the dispute should be made through arbitration or international adjudication."

105 See Jagdish N. Bhagwati, *The New International Economic Order* (MIT Press 1978); Jeffrey A. Hart, *The New International Economic Order* (Palgrave Macmillan 1983); T. Walde, "A Requiem for the New International Economic Order," in Gerhard Hafner and Ignaz Sidl-Hohenveldem (eds) *Liber Amicorum Professor Ignaz Seidl-Hohenveldern: In Honour of His 80th Birthday* (Kluwer Law International, 1988) 771; Surya P. Subedi, *International Investment Law: Reconciling Policy and Principle* (Hart Publishing 2008) 23–27; Charles N. Brower and John B. Tepe, "The Charter of Economic Rights and Duties of States: A Reflection or Rejection of International Law" (1975) 9 *The International Lawyer* 295.

106 UN. Declaration on the Establishment of a New International Economic Order, A/RES/S-6/3201. www.un-documents.net/s6r3201.htm.

107 See gen. Andrew Paul Newcombe and Lluís Paradell, *Law and Practice of Investment Law – Standards of Treatment* (Kluwer Law International 2009) 31–33.

Hull formula nor the Calvo doctrine were completely reliable in terms of compensation, but the practice was characterized rather by its inconsistency which once more proves the instability of the ambivalent discourse that supports today's customary standard of compensation.

It is not at all unreasonable to claim that there was a very strong opposition that lingered in the 1960s and 1970s to developing (and socialist countries continued to bar) the emergence of a minimal consensus necessary for a customary international regime of protection of investment. And even if there could have been customary international rules back then, the uncompromising 1974 UN General Assembly resolutions must be read as having ditched the little customary international law existing at that time. It is surely not the very evasive and non-normative 1962 Resolution that could be said to contain the seeds of a customary international investment protection regime.[108]

However, despite the very strong anti-customary signals, the pre-1945 story repeated itself after the second world war. Customary international law kept the same luster among international investment lawyers, and particularly among arbitral tribunals which gave very little weight to these UNGA resolutions defiant of the Western capital-protective vision.[109] Only the International Court of Justice in the *Barcelona Traction*[110] case

---

108 Patrick Juillard, "L'évolution des sources du droit des investissements" (1994) 250 *Collected Courses* /VI 78 et seq.; Matthew C. Porterfield, "An International Common Law of Investor Rights?" (2006) 27 *University of Pennsylvania Journal of International Economic Law* 79; Charles H. Brower, "Structure, Legitimacy, and NAFTA's Investment Chapter" (2003) 36 *Vanderbilt Journal of Transnational Law* 37, 66.

109 For an overview of the practice of arbitral tribunal of that time, see Stephan W. Schill, *The Multilateralization of International Investment Law* (Cambridge University Press 2009) 38; Patrick M. Norton, "A Law of the Future or a Law of the Past?" (1991) 85 *Am. J. Int'l L* 474.

110 *Barcelona Traction, Light and Power Company Limited (New Application, 1962) (Belgium v Spain)* (Judgment, Second Phase) [1970] ICJ Reports 3, para 46–47 ("Considering the important developments of the last half-century, the growth of foreign investments and the expansion of the international activities of corporations, in particular of holding companies, which are often multinational, and considering the way in which the economic interests of States have proliferated, it may at first sight appear surprising that the evolution of law has not gone further and that no generally accepted rules in the matter have crystallized on the international plane. Nevertheless, a more thorough examination of the facts shows that the law on the subject has been formed in a period characterized by an intense conflict of systems and interests. It is essentially bilateral relations which have been concerned, relations in which the rights of both the State exercising diplomatic protection and the State in respect of which protection is sought have had to be safeguarded. Here as elsewhere, a body of rules could only have developed with the consent of those concerned.

and the arbitrator in the *Texaco v. Libya*[111] award remained lucid and clear-sighted about the state of the law of investment protection in the post-1945 period.

As for the present and future of the standard of compensation it could be added that its core elements remain as vague as its mere existence. Just to illustrate, see the challenges faced with the definition and establishment of "market value," "fair market value," "genuine value," or even "just compensation" which only provide international investment arbitrators with a wider grade of discretion to keep shaping the standard and its allegedly customary nature at their own image and likeness. This discretional capacity is of course possible thanks to the ambivalent signified and varied necessities that can be construed for the standard of compensation and the adjustable nature that can be instrumentalized to further particular agendas either of universalism or resistance through particularism.

Concluding remarks: universalizing resistance

This chapter has sought to shed light on international investment law's ambivalent relationship with universality, and especially on how such ambivalence plays out in Latin American legal thought and practice. It has been shown that both in terms of law-identification and content-determination, international investment law has constantly been accommodating universalism and resistance thereto.

It is submitted at this final stage that such finding of ambivalence should not be deemed spectacular or out of the ordinary. Indeed, not only is such ambivalent relationship with universality not unheard of,[112] more fundamentally such ambivalence can itself be understood as the manifestation of the resistance to universality being itself absorbed by the latter.[113] According to this reading, enabling resistance could be construed as

The difficulties encountered have been reflected in the evolution of the law on the subject").

111 *Texaco Overseas Petroleum Company/California Asiatic Oil Company v. the Government of the Libyan Arab Republic* (Compensation for Nationalized Property) (Award, 19 January 1977) (1978) 17(1) International Legal Materials para 85–87.

112 See e.g. Maiko Meguro, "Redefining the Role of States in International Law on Environment? Beyond the Antagonism between Universality and Particularity" in Isil Aral and Jean d'Aspremont (eds), *International Law and Universality* (forthcoming 2021).

113 See Sundhya Pahuja, "The Postcoloniality of International Law" (2005) 46 *Harvard International Law Journal* 459.

another universalizing strategy.[114] Actually, it is not unusual for a discourse, let alone for international law, to nurture self-resistance.[115] When this is the case, self-resistance allows the discourse to continuously renew and reinvent itself. International legal thought and practice contain plenty of manifestations of such moves of self-resistance that allow international law to project an image of permanent renewal and reinvention.[116] It is argued here that the same goes with claims of universality and resistance described in this chapter in relation to international investment law in Latin American legal thought and practice. All the attempts to vindicate the autonomy of the particular and resist universality that have been described here are always the reverse expression of the universal they counter-balance, such particulars being only a type of non-universal that continues the universal.

114 On the universalizing project of international comparative law, see Jean d'Aspremont, "Comparativism and Colonizing Thinking in International Law" (2020) 57 *Canadian Yearbook of International Law*.

115 See gen. Peter Sloterdijk, *Critique of Cynical Reason* (University of Minesta 1987). See also "The difficulty of Inquiring the Moderns" in Bruno Latour, *An Inquiry into Modes of Existence* (Harvard University Press 2013) 152–178. See also Noam Chomsky and Michel Foucault, *The Chomsky-Foucault Debate on Human Nature* (The New Press 2006) at 172. Comp. with the notion of autoimmunity of Jacques Derrida. See Jacques Derrida, *The Beast and the Sovereign* (Volume 2 University of Chicago Press 2011) at 84.

116 On this aspect of legal discourses, see gen. Jean d'Aspremont, "International Legal Methods: Working for a Tragic and Cynical Routine" in Rossana Deplano and Nicholas Tsagourias (eds), *Handbook on Research Methods in International Law* (Elgar 2020). See also the remarks of Antonio Gramsci for whom self-criticism is a form of modern fashion. See Antonio Gramsci, *Selections from the Prison Notebooks* (edited and translated by Quentin Hoare and Geoffrey Nowell Smith, Lawrence and Wishart 2003) 254–55. See also the remarks of Terry Eagleton, *The Function of Criticism* (Verso 2005) at 9–12 and 21–22.

Index

EU authorised representative for GPSR:
Easy Access System Europe, Mustamäe tee 50,
10621 Tallinn, Estonia
gpsr.requests@easproject.com

www.ingramcontent.com/pod-product-compliance
Lightning Source LLC
Chambersburg PA
CBHW050623280326
41932CB00015B/2498